INTRODUCTION TO THE SERIES

Econometrics had its principal start at the beginning of the 20th Century, achieved recognition with the founding of the Econometric Society in 1930, and flourished in the second half of the century. As we prepare to enter a new century, the subject is expected to make important gains on the shoulders of two developments: (1) an increasingly plentiful and more frequent supply of quantitative information, bringing many econometric studies into the realm of large sample theory, (2) accessibility of computational facilities to implement statistical treatment of much richer economic specifications, especially those involving nonlinearities and a very wide scope of substantive economic activities. This series aims to build, in these directions, on the 20th Century achievements of econometrics.

The typical examples of new directions are the working of global financial markets, the modeling of economic development, the management of large microeconomic data files for new insights into economic behavior, and the blending of other social statistics with conventional economic data in interdisciplinary models. The series plans to cover textbooks, research monographs, conference proceedings, and econometric software techniques with full documentation, etc.

This, inaugural, volume of selected papers of Nobel Laureate Lawrence R. Klein provides a bridge from the *old* to the *new*. The selection covers economics, econometric theory, modeling and forecasting, macroeconomic analysis and public policy, both nationally and internationally.

The Editors

CONTENTS

PART II. ECONOMETRIC MODELS AND METHODOLOGY   111

International Economics & Finance

Growth

PART IV. POLICY FORMULATION 577

PART V. CLOSING REFLECTIONS 629

Lawrence Klein receiving the Nobel Diploma and Medal from the hand of the King, His Majesty Carl XVI Gustaf, Stockholm, December 10, 1980.

MORE ON "FORTY YEARS OF 'RIGOROUS OBSERVATIONAL POSITIVISM'" AND YEARS BEYOND

KANTA MARWAH

Lawrence Klein has taught us to look at economic issues through the rigorous medium of econometrics. For him, it is not enough that a theoretical argument be logically consistent and self-contained. The question must be asked, does it work? As Paul Samuelson has said,

> "...when schools evolve and paradigms are born and die, it is forced upon you that *what ultimately shapes the verdicts of the scientist juries is an empirical reality out there.*"[1]

Klein's interests extend from the technical side of economic issues to some of the most difficult problems of economic policy, including peace research. His writings blend together methodology, real world relevance and quantitative approach with attention to the philosophical side of each issue. As an innovator in the construction, use and validation of macroeconometric models, he has pioneered a world-wide industry with econometric forecasting which has become a basic planning tool for most corporations and governments. "Few, if any, researchers in the empirical field of economic science have had so many successors and such a large impact as Lawrence Klein," reads his Nobel citation. Indeed, a number of international programs have grown from his work, including Project LINK which consists of interlocking models of some 80 nations and developing areas. Students, research scholars and practitioners find in his writings a stimulus to fresh thought.

Klein's contributions are profound and far reaching across a wide spectrum of topics in both economic and econometric theory, methodology, and applied econometrics. His bibliography spans a half-century, including books,

articles, and chapters in conference proceedings, festschriften, and thematic books. One such volume of solely scientific collections, mainly from his relatively early articles, was edited by Jaime Marquez in 1985.[2] Several of these seminal articles have become classics. This volume continues in similar spirit with more of the

---

[1] Paul A. Samuelson, "My life philosophy: Policy credos and working ways," in *Eminent Economists: Their Life Philosophies*, ed. Michael Szenberg (Cambridge University Press, Cambridge, 1992).

[2] *Economic Theory and Econometrics*, ed. Jaime Marquez (Blackwell Publisher, Oxford, 1985).

same and more.[3] And yet, it is different. For it includes some articles, but largely chapters, or book excerpts that were mostly written since 1980, the approximate cut off date of the first volume, and the year of his Nobel Prize.

Also, it includes things that were published in very limited or obscure editions. Thus it provides a more complete picture of Klein's scholarly career and most importantly, his current reflections on the state of economic science. All these writings are in the vanguard of thinking about economics in a global domain.

The thirty-six plus selections are organized in Five Parts, not necessarily in chronological order, but by major themes or subject proximity.

The five major themes are: Economic theory reconsiderations; econometric models and methodology; applied econometrics; policy formulation; and closing reflections. An editorial commentary introduces each Part individually. In two additional introductory chapters, Klein gives an autobiographical research

commentary and writes about his professional life philosophy.

In his autobiographical research commentary for the 1985 volume, Klein wrote, "applied econometrics has been the theme of my life's professional work, with occasional forays into economic theory or econometric theory." Following in the same spirit, Part III on applied econometrics covers the largest number of selections over a wide range of topics. These are organized into four subsections: *Anticipations & Forecasting; Phillips Curve; International Economics and Finance; and Growth.* The subsection covering international economics and finance specifically fills the gap left in the Marquez 1985 volume.

The papers assembled in this volume are testimony to the impact of Klein's work blending both theory and practice. Several selections include statements relating to his policy positions. As early as 1946, Klein had developed the requisite micro foundations of the macro Keynesian paradigm. He believes, however, that both macro and micro theories stand in their own rights, but measuring of variables endogenously through an appropriate aggregation process ought to ensure consistency between the two. A proper route to aggregation that he now recommends involves the use of distribution functions. To him, the common practice of assuming a representative agent specification is not acceptable. It is basically inappropriate because it assumes away the problem.

Klein's one general message on macroeconomics is that whereas it is important not to forget the micro foundations of macroeconomics, it is equally crucial to recognize the macro reality of microeconomics. He has another message that permeates several papers. He believes that the best way to handle many complex interrelationships in the economy simultaneously is through a system that represents the Keynes–Leontief–neoclassical synthesis. Such a system ought to cover necessarily both the demand and supply side characteristics of the economy.

Indeed, he emphasizes the role of "expectation" variables in the construction

---

[3]The above title of this introductory chapter is an expansion of the title of the introductory chapter in Marquez (1985). Marquez's original title, as he explained on page 1 of his volume, was inspired by Paul Samuelson.

of a real life, and operationally meaningful, model of an economy. But he believes that own-model-generated expectations used by modern theorists are misleadingly called *rational* expectations. In constructing his own models, he prefers to generate expectation variables by alternative techniques such as from surveys of agents' anticipations, and surely considers such "expectations" as not "*irrational*." He had successfully demonstrated the use of expectation variables based on survey data even in the 1950s, decades before the sudden discovery of the new fashion of *rational* expectations.

Klein prefers alternative techniques to own-model-generated expectations on both theoretical and statistical grounds. His main argument is that modern theorists derive results from own-model-generated expectations "by a purely hypothetical intellectual process without even considering whether they have any behavioral meaning." Statistically, "*they require the unknown model to provide estimates of expectations data based on parameter estimates that also depend on the expectation data.*" For a model builder, it amounts to overworking the sample, "*asking it to provide both the extra data needed and the parameters based on those data.*"[4]

Klein's comments on the currently popular modeling techniques are instructive. He puts them in proper historical perspective. We are somewhat surprised to learn from the *master* that Cointegration, Error Correction, Calibration and VAR techniques have all been previously considered but set aside as econometrics developed. Specifically, his concern is that the reliance on time series "leans heavily on statistical theory but is nearly empty in the field of economics." Nor do VAR models render much help from the point of view of policy analysis because they assume that all variables are endogenous. Klein asks a pertinent question as to "[h]ow well this kind of theoretical specification serve us when there is an oil embargo or similar supply side shock? Will it survive an event like the breakdown of Bretton Woods?" Of course, it does not imply "that the mainstream structural model can foresee such momentous events, but once an event occurs, the structural model is readily capable of analyzing its effects." And yes, he accepts that the time series analysis can be used in searching for and describing relationships about the macroeconomy.

Klein expresses an abiding faith in using forecasts for making macroeconomic policy. "I agree that forecasting is difficult, but I feel that it cannot be avoided." Will economic forecasts ever improve? In his judgment, the most promising route is to use high-frequency data, at daily, weekly, and monthly intervals. He recommends that "rolling forecasts should be made for the medium-term horizon" and these should be used to update "a new look-ahead for an extended horizon" frequently. In other words, by combining high-frequency time series analysis with mainstream structural models of customary quarterly frequency, we keep forecasts updated and make the model more useful for relevant policy analysis. Surely the ever improving expanding information flow of this modern age "represents a gain that is virtually

---

[4] *The State of Economic Science, Views of Six Nobel Laureates*, ed. Werner Sichel (W. E. Upjohn Institute for Employment Research, Kalamazoo, Michigan, 1989), p. 48.

asking to be exploited."

Klein summarily dismisses Lucas' policy critique by virtue of the unreality of own-model-generated expectations. For him, this critique is simply a contrived argument "that is known, in advance, to recommend noninterventionism." He also shows that both monetarism and populist type of supply side economics stand fully discredited by the actual economic experience.

Klein looks at pivotal economic issues from a global vantage point. On growth of a developing economy, he suggests a two-gap model paradigm. His Project LINK model has become a major vehicle for him to examine international economic policies, to forecast world trade, to track capital movements, and to study growing regionalism and other issues in the global domain.

Klein's overall reflections on the state of economic science and the role of economists can best be summed up in his own words. "Much of the new work [in economic science] is very good, although I find it hard to perceive a true breakthrough... My problem is with the sterility of those aspects that have become very popular and enthrall young, fertile, productive minds without offering clear advancement of the science."[5] Students and researchers should find this cautionary note particularly noteworthy.

"Philosophically, I do not believe that the market system, in even its purest form, provides adequate self-regulatory responses. The economy definitely needs guidance — even leadership — and it is up to professional economists to provide public policy makers with the right information to deliver such leadership. As for the methods of doing this, I see no alternative to the quantitative approach of econometrics."[6]

Let me conclude these introductory remarks with a personal note. It was over three and a half decades ago, in the fall of 1959, that I first met Lawrence Klein at the University of Pennsylvania. Fresh from my undergraduate studies in India, I had just arrived at the University of Pennsylvania to join the graduate program in economics. In the first term when I took his graduate course in econometrics, Klein asked me to be his research assistant. He has been my inspiration ever since, as my teacher, my mentor, my colleague, and my confidant.

When Yew Kee Chiang of World Scientific Publishing Co. invited me to undertake this project, I felt deeply honored. I am indeed grateful to him for giving me this opportunity. And, in the process of assembling this collection of Lawrence Klein's papers, I have learned a lot more about the man and his work. I feel truly enriched.

---

[5] *The State of Economic Science, ibid.*
[6] See chapter on "My Professional Life Philosophy," in this volume.

AN AUTOBIOGRAPHICAL RESEARCH COMMENTARY, CONTINUED[†]

LAWRENCE R. KLEIN

For the most part, the writings selected by Professor Marwah for this volume date from a later period than those chosen by Jaime Marquez in a previous volume of my collected papers. The present selection includes several papers written after 1980; it also includes more chapters from books, both before and after 1980. The emphasis on 1980 is significant because some social researchers have investigated what Nobel Laureates *do* after they receive their prizes. Naturally, my scholarly interests were different and more aggressively pursued when I was younger, during the 40s, 50s, 60s, and 70s, but I did keep fairly busy during the 80s and 90s. There are social pressures to do some things as obligatory repayments to the world of economic scholarship, from which accumulated knowledge was absorbed. Also, there is an assumption that one has freedom to follow any line of investigation that catches one's fancy after having joined what my former colleague Tjalling Koopmans called the "Nobelity," but life did not work out that way for me; I simply kept my older work habits, but made some concessions to aging and took up some more general kinds of economic issues.

It was a pleasure and honor to be grouped with many eminent friends, colleagues, and acquaintances in Michael Szenberg's collections of autobiographically reported *Life Philosophies*. I found the personal unveiling of philosophical views of many economists, all together, to be interesting and stimulating.

For my own part, I revealed myself as attached to a quantitative bent that found expression in the *trinity* of econometrics — economic analysis, statistical method, and mathematics. I feel comfortable when these three subjects are blended. In "My professional life philosophy," I used the occasion to assert my objection to the rule of parsimony for economics, where I think that the problems are very complicated and can be understood only in the context of large, complicated systems. Fortunately, my professional life has evolved in an environment where hardware, software, and data bases have expanded enormously and have become very congenial.

[†] This is a continuation of "An autobiographical research commentary," *Economic Theory and Econometrics*, ed. Jaime Marquez (Blackwell, Oxford, 1985).

My predilection for theory validation in economics attempts to relate microeconomic and macroeconomic analysis to one another through aggregation theory, use the complexity of nonlinearity, expand horizons to the global economy, use interdisciplinary analysis and make policy studies with the best econometric tools, as stated in my *Philosophy*, are all taken up in more detail in the separate papers of this collection.

This statement of "My professional life philosophy" was written fairly recently, but it summarizes the path that I have taken since the early 1940s.

In this *Commentary*, I plan to follow the sections (Part I, II, etc.) that Professor Marwah has carved out for this book. The selections in Part I deal broadly with macroeconomics, but that subject is closely identified with Keynesian economics. My interests were in econometrics from my undergraduate days, but the first concentrated field of study was, not surprisingly, associated with my dissertation research, on the subject of *The Keynesian Revolution*. I joined the ongoing Keynesian debate about 4 to 6 years after publication of the *General theory*, and my views about the subject evolved over a few decades.

I. Jacob Marschak, my first postdoctoral employer, insisted that I base my econometric modeling on received economic theory and that I justify macroeconomic specifications on the basis of reasoning about individualistic decision making, with proper attention to the problem of aggregation. I had already been introduced to aggregation and index theory as an undergraduate, in the classes of Francis Dresch at Berkeley, and I started to deal with the problem along his lines but reconsidered many thorny issues in debates with my colleagues at the Cowles Commission in Chicago. During my visits to Europe, especially with Ragnar Frisch in Oslo, and to Japan with Michio Morishima and Shinichi Ichimura, I thought about issues of extending the narrow Keynesian model serially to the supply side, the open economy, and the developing economy, seeing some of these aspects of economic life first hand during the late 40s and the 50s. These were the impressions that led me to try to extend the Keynesian model to more general conditions, integrate my conception of this theory with other branches of economics (international trade, economic development, and neoclassical analysis) and, as will be discussed below in connection with econometric model building, to combine input–output models with macroeconometric models.

In my dissertation, *The Keynesian Revolution*, I first tried to formalize the relationships between microeconomic theory of the household and firm, and Keynesian macroeconomic theory, with attention paid to aggregation and, by the mid 60s, was able to polish up the equation systems for the second edition of *The Keynesian Revolution*. At the same time I was able to consider aspects of the open economy and the developing economy. I always felt that it was better to build on the Keynesian framework than to take a destructive and negative approach, claiming that any deficiencies meant a return to the drawing boards to try to develop something entirely different. The latter approach appears to be more attractive to the present generation of macroeconomists, and I feel that their analysis suffers from this negative attitude. What I find lacking in contemporary macroeconomics is a constructive attitude. The theory of the 1980s and 1990s provides little guidance for economic policy, partly because the theory-builders are subjectively opposed to positive policy, and partly because they lack a tested theory of behavior. I doubt that they can make usable predictions from their theoretical models, and they seem not to care, but I take predictive ability seriously, as the most rigorous test of abstract economics. These are the attitudes that shape my remarks on "The Keynesian revolution: Fifty years later," delivered at a symposium at Pennsylvania in 1992.

Some economists of the present generation claim that there is little basis for macroeconomics as a separate subject; it is, in their opinion, simply an adding-up of the propositions of microeconomics. In my paper "What is macroeconomics?" written for Don Patinkin's *Festschrift*, I argue that some concepts, analyses, and economic issues are inherently macroeconomic, while others can be derived from microeconomics only after painstaking attention is paid to the formulas and processes of aggregation.

While my first attempts to deal with the problem of aggregation were inspired by Francis Dresch when I was studying at Berkeley, I later began to appreciate more the use of distribution functions for "weighted" summation, as these issues were discussed at the Cowles Commission in the late 40s. In general, distributional matters deserve more explicit treatment in macroeconomic theory. This refers to income, wealth, employment size, demographic, and other distributions in economics. So much of present economic troubles, whether at home among microeconomic agents or abroad among nations and regions, involve dissatisfaction with prevailing distributions, especially of income and wealth, that macromodeling in terms of unweighted aggregates or, even worse, in terms of the "representative agent," fail to deal with the relevant distribution issues.

Finally, I was interested, when I first came to Pennsylvania, in 1958, in the possibility of constructing complete macroeconomic models by putting together, systematically, many important ratios from economic–statistical annals (savings, labor's share, velocity, capital–output ratios). I was a bit surprised to find a great deal of interest in that simple exercise; so I returned to that theme and extended the analysis to simpler concepts, not only ratios, that appear to stand the test of time in economics. I did not, however, put the diverse concepts together, into a complete model in the later (follow-up) paper for this volume, which was delivered to a broader intellectual audience, beyond professional economists. These concepts, strategic ratios and other balance relationships, are often long-run in nature; therefore they should be used as limiting criteria for validity of dynamic systems; i.e., such systems should converge to established long-run relationships among economic variables. I find this combination of short- and long-run dynamic properties to be of key importance for model building.

My interests in macroeconomic modeling were first inspired by the possibility of sharpening the debate about macroeconomic theory, particularly the Keynesian theory, vs. classical theory, but it carried naturally into the objectives of my first professional job, after leaving MIT in 1944. I joined the staff of the Cowles Commission in order to prepare a new U.S. macromodel that would be useful in assessing the possibilities for postwar economic policy formation. That was the beginning of my long association with the problems of macroeconometrics that were then being tackled afresh at the Cowles Commission.

While still at MIT, I had some joint responsibility for organizing a statistics seminar (extracurricular) and one of our external visitors was Trygve Haavelmo, who gave us an advance peek at his celebrated paper on "The statistical implications of a system of simultaneous equations."[1] It turned out that the central problem being posed for research at Cowles, by Jacob Marschak and Tjalling Koopmans, was a fresh attempt at U.S. model building by using Haavelmo's new ideas about econometric theory. It proved to be an exciting time for me and enabled me to build on the Keynesian lessons that were taught to me at MIT by Paul Samuelson.

II. Should one look first at properties of economic data and then rationalize their interrelationships on a more abstract or theoretical basis, or should one reverse this sequence? The early econometricians considered these issues and the foundations for development of the subject took the second route. First, develop an underlying theory and then prepare a data base with statistical methodology to describe, test, and apply empirical models of the economy. I still believe that the best way to proceed is from a theoretical model to observation and then to statistical inference. There can, of course, be occasional references to observed regularities and reformulations after data reject some aspects of *a priori* theory (*cum* institutional information). This, as remarked above, is of most importance in testing long-run system properties.

In chronicling the history of macroeconometrics with my former students, Ronald Bodkin and Kanta Marwah, we first looked at the early thinkers who had theoretical visions of the economy in the absence of much data. Their approaches were however mathematical or quantitative or capable of being cast into the form of macroeconometric models. Formal macroeconometrics began with the work of early members of the Econometric Society; such as Frisch, Tinbergen, and others; but they drew, in turn, on the imaginative work of earlier thinkers who had even less access to systematic data collections and computational aids.

Our knowledge about the economy, though substantial, is both incomplete and uncertain; therefore we try to learn from actual experience, as well as through the logic of collegial debate. Progress tends to be gradual and cumulative on a step-by-step basis. When I returned to the United States from Oxford in the late 1950s, I set about to build new models at Pennsylvania, having learned from previous attempts at Chicago, Michigan, and Oxford. We model builders generally recognized that

---

[1] T. Haavelmo, "The statistical implications of a system of simultaneous equations," *Econometrica* **11** (January, 1943), pp. 1–12; L. R. Klein, "The statistics seminar, MIT, 1942–43," *Statistical Science* **6** (No. 4), pp. 320–30.

data were scarce, and we long thought about the potential in obtaining regular quarterly data on the national accounts. In fact, preliminary studies with a small model and interpolated quarterly data had already been published by Harold Barger and me, but that effort, though a small step forward, failed to satisfy our business-cycle curiosity. I was, thus, pleased to learn that more extensive quarterly data than ever were available in the early 1960s.

One of my first research activities at Pennsylvania was to put together a new U.S. macromodel in a quarterly time frame. At the same time, I wanted to draw upon explicit surveys of consumer expectations, reflecting my years at the Survey Research Center in Michigan and also starting my quest for a more powerful treatment of expectations in macroeconometrics, in general.

The "Postwar Quarterly Model" that I prepared at Pennsylvania was the forerunner of the Wharton Model, since Pennsylvania's Economics Department was then located in the Wharton School. This model also became a forecasting vehicle, which later supported the activities of the Wharton Econometric Forecasting Unit (Wharton EFU).

In the earlier days of econometrics, our critics were economists who did not want to see the subject move in a formal, mathematical, quantitative direction and also those who favored empiricism without a strong base in economic theorizing. By and large, the critics also had another agenda, namely, one of no intervention by public authorities in the economy, either for macroeconomic guidance, business-cycle stabilization (except monetary policy), or regulation. Mathematical and formal statistical methods were viewed with suspicion as paving the way to socialism.

After the Second World War, it soon became clear that mathematical and statistical methods were growing in economics, eventually to become predominant. The recent critics contributed to the non-interventionist predilections of the earlier critics by challenging macroeconometric model building on the treatment of expectations, the use of *a priori* theory (or information) for the purposes of identification, and the application of models for policy analysis or forecasting.

The specific form of expectations models, by generating expectations that are fully consistent with the models being estimated, i.e., "rational" expectations, has been attractive to the generation of economists of the 1970s and beyond, but I always found this approach to be unrealistic, and singularly unhelpful in guiding economic policy or in forecasting. Either the formulas of adaptive expectations or the more powerful approaches of introducing direct surveys of expectations looked more promising to me. Problems of identification and (lack of) uniqueness would have been enough to steer econometricians away from such methods during the developmental years before the War. Such issues were used to eliminate other unpromising leads in the budding field of econometrics, but the rational expectations theorists could see a way to serve their inherent distaste for stabilization policy through the mechanism of model-generated expectations. Some exponents of "rational" expectations use the concept solely as a way of making expectations endogenous, and they are not necessarily against the positive use of economic policy.

The ideas of "rational" expectations fit well with crude empiricism and also with *monetarism*, the latter being the sole simplistic tool that would be acceptable to extreme monetarists for macroeconomic stabilization. In my approach to model building for the economy as a whole, I begin with the idea that the real world is very complicated and cannot be effectively understood or guided by simple rules, such as those that underlie monetarism or those that can be treated by single equation time series methods or even those that can be treated by vector autoregression methods (VAR). The vector methods are not usable for large scale systems, as only a few variables are simultaneously considered. That is the price paid for not using economic theory to do some of the work and relying only, or mainly, on patterns in manifest data. In my Taiwan lectures (Chung-Hwa Institute) in 1982, I took up some of these issues. It appeared to me that the newer work in macroeconometrics and time series analysis claimed too much, particularly by asserting that large scale macroeconometric models had failed to predict the inflationary indexes of the 1970s. That is simply incorrect. Macromodels in the mainstream have been very good predictors of economic events and have been steadily improving. Among the many forecasts of inflationary trends in the early 1970s, after the first oil shock, the macroeconometric forecasts that I produced were definitely high in comparison with judgmental forecasts.

There is one solid point, however, in support of time series analysis, once one fully recognizes and appreciates its fallibilities. Time series information is significantly expanding — in scope, sample size, availability, and fineness of measurement. In the beginning, there were only annual data points (or less frequent). Now, we have an abundance of monthly economic statistics, and are getting much more information on a weekly, daily, hourly, real-time basis. This enables statisticians to use large sample theory with confidence. Many more branches of the economy are capable of being monitored by time series data, taking us into fresh areas of investigation; whereas, early economists who were making quantitative investigations had to work laboriously to put together a few sparse series. Now from computer memory, many series with long histories are readily available for direct statistical analysis by the methods of econometrics. This is a new situation and has significant bearing on the mode of present econometric research.

In addition to the information and computer developments that influenced the directions of econometric research in the last three or more decades, the opening up of the world economy to trade, capital flows, and to more complete international integration has also been important in shaping econometric research. Macroeconometrics moved from national to world model building. I took up this problem by helping to organize the LINK model, originally to study the international transmission mechanism, but eventually to study total trade flows through large-scale trade matrices, to deal with exchange rate movements, capital flows, and economic development round the world. By the 1980s, LINK had become established as a leading world model, functioning to this day in world forecasting and simulation analysis of economic policy formation. Those are the subjects of my 1983 paper in

Prévision et Analyse économique. It is also prominent in the challenges and pathways for macroeconometrics in the future. I have always felt good about getting sound macroeconometric modeling started in countries that lacked such systems — at first in Western Europe but later in Africa, Asia, Latin America, and the Middle East. China presented an interesting case, and well within a decade after the beginning of reform, modern methods of econometric model building were in place in Chinese institutions. Socialist economy model building was also initiated in the LINK project for the Soviet Union and for the economies of Eastern Europe. These systems served well in trying to interpret short run movements of these economies within the world system, but now have been entirely rebuilt, after the collapse of the USSR and the CMEA trading system.

The careful use of economic theory was one stepping stone for macroeconometric model building, and I remain firmly committed to that approach. A second step is to embed a model's structure in the social accounts. That should be at the heart of macroeconomics. One of the drawbacks of the modern school is that not enough attention is paid to the system of accounts. I was strongly influenced by Ragnar Frisch, Simon Kuznets, Wassily Leontief and Richard Stone in this respect. It is no accident that they were all honored, at an early stage in the history of Nobel Laureates, in economics. Their work was of the utmost importance, and I eventually came to look at model building as an exercise in *explaining* all the entries in a complete social accounting system. That approach came to me after the shortcuts of the *Keynesian Revolution*, but it is to be remarked that Keynes put Stone and James Meade to work in the British Treasury during the War to construct national income accounts for the U.K.

Econometricians have generally under-appreciated the importance of input–output analysis, largely because it is regarded more as a technological and accounting analysis and does not rely heavily on statistical inference based on probability theory. In designing social accounts, however, input–output analysis plays an important role, together with national income and flow-of-funds accounting. For many years, I looked at various ways of combining input–output modeling with more conventional econometric modeling. The relevant procedures started to take shape in the Social-Science-Research-Council–Brookings model project and ultimately flowered at Wharton Econometrics, where a great deal of supply-side, industry, and longer term analysis was found to be important for private sector users.[2] With the enthusiastic contributions of Ross Preston and other dissertation-oriented students at Pennsylvania, we finally worked out standardized procedures for combining input–output with macroeconometric modeling in a feedback mode. These steps show up in the methodological sections of modeling activity in this volume. Not surprisingly, they attracted attention in various presentations to Soviet economists.

---

[2]Franklin M. Fisher, Lawrence R. Klein, and Yoichi Shinkai, "Price and output aggregation in the Brookings econometric model," *The Brookings Quarterly Econometric Model of the United States*, eds. J. S. Duesenberry *et al.* (Rand McNally & Co., Chicago, 1965), pp. 651–79.

After we had refined the techniques for combining input–output systems with macroeconometric models in full feedback mode, I was able to present the structure of such systems to Soviet economists, the first opportunity being a modeling conference held at Novosibirsk in 1970. Before going to the Soviet Union, I had interesting discussions on the structure of these combined systems with economists in Bratislava, Czechoslovakia. From that point forward, contacts with Soviet and East European econometricians flowered on the basis of preliminary interchanges during the late years of the 1960s.

The ultimate combination of flow-of-funds modeling with national income modeling came later and is an area for a great deal of promising research, much of it being done by my Japanese colleague, Mitsuo Saito, and the close-knit group of Kobe students who trained under him.

When I went in 1990 with fellow laureates to Edinburgh, for a service at the graveside of Adam Smith, to mark the bicentennial of his death, I prepared a conference paper on some quantitative aspects of the *Wealth of Nations*. Most commentators on Smith referred to his moral philosophy and general theorizing about the "invisible hand," sometimes on a highly selective basis to promote their own predilections about economic philosophy. Smith was a many-sided person and frequently treated economic problems in a way that is contrary to the thinking of some *laissez-faire* economists.

I tried to be objective and studied such questions as whether business cycles in the 19th and 20th century sense existed in Smith's 18th century. I used Smith's, Harold (later Lord) Wilson's, and William (Lord) Beveridge's data to look at some of the issues from the vantage point of time-series analysis. By and large, I confirmed Wilson's previous conclusions that cyclical regularities that economists would classify as business cycles did not occur in Smith's time.

Finally, let me return to the question of expectations in economics. It was not only Keynes but also G. L. S. Shackle who strongly emphasized the role of expectations long before the modern exponents of "rational" expectations came upon the scene. The early contributions were very good, and certainly none the worse for their ignorance of the modern theory of "rational" expectations. I stand by my convictions that the most important analyses of expectations will come through the in-depth use of the sample survey method, where we try to get at realistic expectations and not some theorist's hypothetical suppositions, and treat some of these matters in the Shackle *Festschrift*. Over a number of years I maintained a dialog with Shackle about Keynesian economics and expectations.

III. On the subject of economic forecasting, as stated above, I still hold by my minority point of view that ability to predict, in a wide sense of the term, is the ultimate test of a model. True, ex-ante prediction is the only rigorous and verifiable criterion for model validity that is not tainted by too much knowledge in the hands of the analytic economist. Of course, forecasting must be replicated over-and-over again so that a decent statistical sample of trials is available. There are few forecasters that keep or publish verifiable records.

This preoccupation on my part with forecasting performance has led me into research on some specific issues:

1. The intensive use of expectations or anticipatory variables.
2. The replicability and reproductibility of forecasts.
3. The use of appropriate error bands for predictions.

III.1. With respect to expectations, I have already stated my overall position in Part II, but my research has led me to try to explain ("endogenize") measured expectations, to try to include several anticipatory variables in macroeconometric models (orders, investment intentions, housing starts, building permits, and survey responses about future spending, income, or price movements). The measured expectations variables are statistically significant, and they do make marginal contributions to improved forecasting precision. Also they can be explained by other simultaneous variables. While they are significant, they do not yet yield to statistical treatment that would lead to orders-of-magnitude improvements in forecast accuracy. There are some fundamental uncertainties in economics, and we shall never be able to forecast economic events with very high scientific precision. In spite of there being an irreducible minimum of error, we should be able to make modest improvements of a few percentage points, step-by-step, as we build better systems, with better data, in more refined applications.

III.2. Over the decades, since my first serious attempt at forecasting from a macroeconometric model, at the end of the Second World War, there have been notable successes at crucial stages (after Korea, after Vietnam, the Nixon Control period, the oil embargoes of the 1970s) and also in terms of the overall historical record, but one stubborn problem remained, namely, how to adjust a model so that it would start on a forecast extrapolation exercise at prevailing initial values, given frequent data revisions and new information flows about exogenous and endogenous variables at the very moment of forecast calculation. There are various ways to deal with these problems, but until recently, we econometricians have used subjective adjustments to initialize the extrapolation process. A criticism of such adjustments is that they are not replicable; i.e., other econometricians could not precisely duplicate the forecasts.

To handle this problem, I have used time series methods to extrapolate the main *high frequency* indicators that official statisticians use in building the national income and product accounts (NIPA) on a quarterly basis. The accounting relationships underlying national expenditure and national income have been used, together with time-series methods, to project the quarterly NIPA reports for six month (two-quarter) periods. Macroeconometric models can then be initialized in each forecast period to duplicate, with high precision, the main NIPA magnitudes. Since the

NIPA are available in both current and constant prices, I implicitly estimate price movements, as well.

In an exercise that started just prior to the Gulf War in 1990, I documented, with J. Y. Park, the weekly forecasts of this high frequency model, and we were able to anticipate the 1990–91 business cycle movements of the U.S. economy far better than many others, specifically those using purely empirical statistical methods without any economic theory guidance. In my system, reported in Part III, the accounting structure of real and nominal NIPA and expectations variables, used according to my preferences for sample survey information, were very helpful in contributing to the success of the particular combination of time series and macroeconometric model forecasts. In this sense, one of the thorny issues in the use of macroeconometric models shows a possibility of being resolved, and some new advances in forecasting can be made, because the present state of this model enhancement procedure has not yet exhausted the stores of information in weekly or daily data, some of the cross correlations among strategic indicators, and entirely new sources of survey data on expectations.

III.3. Econometrics is a statistical subject, based on the laws of probability; therefore results of econometric estimation and application of estimates are subject to error. There is a strong tendency for practitioners to present results in *point* values, but each of these points is but a single value in an entire statistical range or region. If the region is presented rather than the point values, alone, it is immediately apparent that there will be deviations from point values and uncertainty associated with all econometric results. There are many sources of error such as stochastic disturbances to the equations of econometrics, errors of parameter estimates, observation error for sample data, error in measuring exogenous variables, and error in equation specification. Record keeping, measurement of precision in prediction or estimation, and stochastic simulation are all techniques for assessing the degree of uncertainty in econometric results and in using results by policy makers. Ever since I engaged in forecasting applications fifty years ago, I have been trying to judge error, decompose error, reduce error, and school policy makers in decision making under uncertainty — uncertainty of the type encountered in econometrics. These subjects are covered in presentations at conferences such as the Michigan outlook conference and also the paper in the *Festschrift* volume for my former student, Professor Sir James Ball.

Simulation techniques, which are used in evaluating forecast error for large scale models, are also used for contributing to macroeconomic theory, in particular to estimate the overall sensitivity, in a macroeconomic sense, to major changes in the economic environment for a nation, an international region, or the entire world. In the United States, it was observed, after the oil shocks of the 1970s, that both inflation and unemployment rose simultaneously. This economic situation has been called "stagflation," i.e., stagnant or falling output coupled with inflation. This was a point at which anti-Keynesian economists tried to exploit the events by discrediting the typical Keynesian trade-off between unemployment and inflation, which they called the Phillips curve. Their conclusions were entirely wrong, both in macroeconomic analysis and in macroeconometrics.

In the first place, A. W. Phillips, in his famous paper that establishes the "Phillips Curve," studied the (inverse) relationship between *wage change* and *unemployment.* There is very significant difference between wage change and inflation. Naturally they are related, but not in a simple way, especially when productivity was being so disturbed by the oil shocks of the 1970s. When I was in Oxford during the 1950s, I had interesting meetings with Phillips because I had introduced relationships between wage change and unemployment in U.S. macroeconometric models, and we were in complete agreement about the interpretation of such relationships in terms of wage adjustment for clearing of supply–demand imbalances in the labor market, as such — not in the goods market where price adjustments cleared the imbalances.

The second error of the anti-Keynesian theorists was that there is a big difference between a *structural* equation, focusing on labor market clearing, and a *trade-off* relationship in a large scale multivariate system, where the "disturbed" relationship between one pair of endogenous variables in the whole interrelated set is being estimated.

In my paper "The longevity of economic theory" in a *Festschrift* volume for Wilhelm Krelle, I spelled out all these distinctions. The crux of the matter, simply put, is this: When a large variety of supply-side disturbances hit a dynamic economic system, there are many circumstances in which the inflation–unemployment relationship is positively sloped — "stagflation" — as in the decade of massive changes in the world oil market. Actually, other kinds of supply-side disturbances are fully capable of producing the same effects. These are amply illustrated in a book that I edited on comparisons of properties of major U.S. macroeconometric models.[3] On the other hand, when disturbances or exogenous policy changes occur on the demand side, the trade-off relationships between inflation and unemployment are typically negatively sloped. These points are so obvious and so easily demonstrated that it is hard for me to see why they have not yet penetrated the thinking of the anti-Keynesian schools of thought.

The Phillips curve provides a strategic concept for price determination in an expanded model that combines Keynesian macroeconomics and neoclassical economics — the Keynesian–neoclassical synthesis, which is discussed in Part I of this volume.

Some subsequent treatments of the labor market after Phillips, in which sight is lost of the supply–demand clearing property of the Phillips curve, contain what is called the *natural* rate of unemployment and often assert that the Phillips curve is

---

[3] *Comparative Performance of US Econometric Models* (Oxford University Press, New York, 1991).

vertical in the long run. These concepts are, in my opinion, backward steps.[4] At the theoretical level, the substitute for the Phillips curve to achieve price determination is usually some variant of the quantity theory of money (monetarism). Markets have been extremely unfriendly to that concept in the last two decades, prompting U.S. central bank authorities to drop M_1, and then M_2, as primary monetary targets. They apparently realized that to move on to M_3, etc., would be no better.

In contrast, the Phillips curve has, in fact, stood the test of time. This is the subject of my contribution to Raymond Courbis' collection of Phillips curve investigations in *Prévision et Analyse Économique*. Phillips pointed the way, with emphasis on a very simple relationship between wage change and unemployment in the U.K. My earlier investigations for the U.S. were, like those of Phillips, simple first steps. Distributed lags, cost-of-living adjustments, trade-union pressures, demographic changes in the labor force, and statistical information flows in labor markets all contributed to improvement of the estimated structural equations. The extended Phillips curve stands up very well as a multivariate, nonlinear econometric equation.

Some of these same arguments come up again in the study of the international economy, particularly in the conference volume of the Federal Reserve Bank of Boston, but other issues are important for the global economy, some of which I examined in connection with Project LINK and some in independent analyses.

In addition to interpreting and forecasting events in the world economy stemming from the oil embargo and OPEC pricing, the LINK system was used, or showed the need, for explaining endogenous exchange rates after the demise of Bretton Woods parities and for dealing with new tendencies towards protectionism in the late 1970s.

There was a long period of pre-war protectionism, followed by wartime controls and then (semi) fixed parities. When the world turned towards a floating rate system, partially or wholly, econometricians had to develop fresh data bases and new kinds of structural equations in models where exchange rates became endogenous. This led to examinations of purchasing-power-parity, interest parity, capital flows, balance of payment accounts and other variables that might be relevant for estimating exchange rates.

At first, the data base was weak and exchange rate projections were not very good. This was a challenging situation. A paper in the present volume dealt with capital flows and exchange rates as endogenous variables. This was written with Kanta Marwah during a sabbatical year that she spent in Philadelphia. The paper was presented at an international meeting of Project LINK in the autumn of 1982. Basically, the idea was to try to determine exchange rates as values that would bring supply and demand for several countries' currencies into equilibrium. This is the same principle of market clearing that is found in goods markets, labor markets,

---

[4]Exponents of the *natural* rate concept have provided very misleading estimates — far too high — of the degree of unemployment that could be tolerated in the U.S. without inflation, in the first half of the 1990s.

and domestic capital markets. In the international case, however, the supply and demand for each country's currency will depend on trade balances (generated by LINK) and capital flow balances for which we needed to estimate new equations for such things as equity portfolio flows, foreign direct investment, international loans, and official transfers. This is actually in the spirit of combining flow-of-funds accounting with traditional NIPA systems, but it focuses on international flows.

We compiled data on nine items of net capital movements for six countries (Canada, France, Germany, Japan, U.S., U.K.). From a pooled sample of annual time series and cross-section observations, we estimated stochastic equations and accounting identities that enabled us to try to determine equilibrium exchange rates at points where foreign demand for home currency generated by balance on current account is equal to total supply generated by a net outflow of capital. Effects for individual countries were taken into account by using dummy variables, and risk effects were measured by standard deviations of long and short run yield spreads.

We obtained preliminary, but promising, results. With larger, more comprehensive, and more reliable data, accuracy of prediction could be significantly improved, but methodologically, this research indicates the way to estimate exchange rates in the context of a complete international model.

Another aspect of $\overline{\text{LINK}}$ analysis involves barriers to trade flows, in the form of tariffs or other direct blockages to trade, called non-tariff barriers. Free trade is generally accepted among economists as being an optimal mode of operation among countries, based on the arguments of the principle of comparative advantage. These are microeconomic arguments and can be extended to complete general equilibrium systems. I have often wondered how they worked out in macroeconomic analysis. Simulations with the LINK system showed how GDP, inflation, trade balances and other macroeconomic magnitudes are affected, country-by-country, in a statistical sense, if duties or other trade barriers are imposed by individual countries or groups of countries. By and large, the findings agree with what one would expect, on the basis of analogs of microeconomic analysis. This is what Vincent Su and I discussed on the basis of simulating the LINK model. These results open the way for policy analysis of regional trade groupings and various international agreements such as the Uruguay Round, establishment of NAFTA, and future regional configurations, such as an Asia-Pacific trading area.

In connection with the process of making exchange rates endogenous within the LINK system, I looked at the possible contribution to the solution of the problem through the use of purchasing-power-parity (PPP), but with some skepticism because of discussion with my colleague of many years, Irving Kravis, who felt that departures from PPP were very significant and prevalent. I found, however, in research with two Pennsylvania students, Victor Filatov and Sharokh Fardoust, that exchange rate movements of major industrial countries modeled in the LINK system satisfied PPP in the long run, i.e., over decade-long periods in a dynamic, cross-country sample.

A global analysis, outside the confines of the LINK system, dealt with the existence of principles of monetarism. I have long been interested in the monetarist viewpoint, but mainly from a critical angle. The problem for monetarism is that velocity is neither constant, nor easily predictable. Without these properties the monetarist view does not lead to reliable policy decisions in the simplistic form that its proponents would like.

The Keynesian view is that velocity is a function of interest rates, among other things. This is simply another way of specifying the doctrine of liquidity preference. For individual countries, the relation between velocity and interest rates can be readily established, but does such a relationship exist on a global basis? I chose this issue as the central point of interest in a contribution to a *Festschrift* volume for an old friend of my Oxford days, Colin Clark. I thought that an audacious global statistical subject would be fitting in Colin's honor because that was often his style. I found that world monetary and financial data were supportive of the idea that global velocity depends on interest rates.

When I remarked earlier that the world productivity slowdown of the 1970s was pervasive and probably associated with the oil shocks of that decade, I was mainly interested in the effects on the inflation–unemployment trade-off. But there is more to that remarkable change in the time shape of productivity curves. The industrial structure of many countries was also changing. Competitiveness, shifts among leadership industries, changing fortunes for job opportunities and other dynamic events led me to look at international data, across countries and industries, for clues about the changes taking place and to investigate the credibility of such popular ideas as the "hollowing-out" of individual countries, the passing of manufacturing industries in the heartland of America, the appearance of the "rust belt," and similar beliefs. Journalistic appraisals of the economy quickly gravitate to what is happening at the moment of headline preparation. I have learned to be highly skeptical of the quick assessments of trend-like changes on the basis of very short observation spans. Two articles on productivity and restructuring are included in this volume.

It is natural to find new technologies coming to the fore. The modern high-technology sectors in electronics, telecommunications, biomedicine, computing, and similar fields is a true trend development, but it was incorrect to assume that declining or low productivity would prevail on a trend basis in the United States or that manufacturing would decline. I found reason to expect American productivity to recover from the unusual experience of the 1970s; as it has, in fact, done. I also found that the manufacturing share of total output in the U.S. had not declined very much, certainly by much less than the manufacturing employment share. This is an aspect of the productivity recovery. Simulations with the enlarged Wharton Model, including a fairly detailed input–output module had been quite important in studying the effects of industrial restructuring.

In rounding out Part III, there is a section on growth models, with two selections dealing with the subject from an Asian perspective. My association with Asian economics began with a visit to Japan in 1960 to collaborate with colleagues and students on the construction of macroeconometric models of Japan, some of which paid a great deal of attention to the growth process. In 1979, when relations between China and the United States were renormalized, I began a series of visits to China, on which occasions old contacts were renewed and a series of new associations were started. In particular, an econometrics workshop in 1980 brought econometrics and related aspects of model building before the nascent community of Chinese economists. With Youcai Liang, who also spent a great deal of time at Pennsylvania, I estimated a fairly simple two-gap model for China. The work took place during the second half of the 1980s, and, by now, the data base has been considerably expanded and the economic system reformed, enabling much larger and more intricate models to be built, rivaling those of other major economies in the LINK system. The two-gap model was built with some pedagogical aspects in mind, but also because I believe that this kind of system serves as a paradigm for developing countries in the same sense that an IS–LM system is a paradigm for advanced industrial economies.

At the present, China is developing extensive data banks, is fluent in international computer software, appreciates econometric theory, and is now able to generate domestically-conceived econometric models that are sophisticated, up to world standards, and usable for economic policy formation. The next step will be to produce higher frequency models, beyond the annual time unit.

Japan emphasized export-led growth, starting in the 1950s, and continues along these lines today, although the domestic market has been growing in significance for several years. In many respects, other East Asian economies have followed the Japanese route. I first noted this in the late 1960s and early 1970s, on the occasion of visits to Taiwan and South Korea. The concept of export-led growth has spread throughout the Asia Pacific region and is now important for Chinese growth. The key, however, for the growth process is the ability to import strategic materials, capital of world-class technology, modern services, and modern know-how, so that other Asian economies can follow the Japanese economy in its subsequent steps into the realm of high technology.

China needs imports in order to produce for growth but also has the world's largest domestic market potential; so the role of export-led growth is not the sole feature of the so-called East Asian Miracle, and the Chinese subset of this economic phenomenon. Exportation is, of course, important, but mainly as a means for partial payment for the necessary imports, thus relieving the potential burdens that can accompany massive foreign capital inflow. Also, as discussed in the previous section, U.S. productivity is recovering from its setback of the 1970s, and the world's most attractive market is becoming increasingly competitive, making export-led growth by others that much more difficult.

IV. My professional career began in the mid 1940s, during a period of unusual optimism about the future — in economics, politics, social reform, and, above all, in an environment of peace, given what the world had to put up with in pre-war Germany and Japan, not to mention deep economic depression. Policy proposals looked very attractive then, as a result of establishment of

the UN, for peaceful coexistence among nations

the IMF for stability in foreign exchange markets

the World Bank for development

Keynesian economics, together with the Employment Act in the USA, for full employment

the Beveridge Plan for cradle-to-grave social security.

In real life, these dreams about society have turned out imperfectly; but even with the imperfections, things went reasonably well on this course for about 25 years after the end of World War II. In the narrow economic sphere, Keynesian economic policy appeared to be straightforward and working as it was supposed to do.

To deal with the economic issues that arose as we entered the 1970s, the policy line looked clear to me — to elaborate and enhance the Keynesian model by adding a full-blown supply side Keynesian–neoclassical synthesis with a marriage of macroeconometric modeling and input–output modeling. From these expanded models, we would be able to deal with structural defects, technological changes in the industrial make-up, accommodation of new demographic trends, and, above all, supportive economic forecasting for the successful implementation of policy. I even went so far as to slip some of these thoughts into the election campaign of 1976, when I coordinated the successful economic task force of Jimmy Carter. After the campaign, however, I yielded to mainstream political economists from the Democratic side, and returned to academic issues.

Big changes were taking place on the U.S. socio-politico-economic scene as we entered the 1980s, but I did not give up my views on how to model the economy, how to make forecasts, or how to formulate policy. These views show through in two policy oriented papers, one for the *Handbook of Econometrics*, where I emphasized the needs for a solid econometric base to support structural policies that go far beyond conventional demand management in the Keynesian fashion. The macroeconomics community wanted to refute or ignore the Keynesian message, but I wanted to build on it, as a foundation. I still believe that my view is the correct one. Problems of distribution, demographics, and technology are of extreme importance for the macroeconometric tasks of the 1980s and 1990s.

A group of French and U.S. policy makers, who were influential towards the end of the 1970s, planned a joint meeting to be convened in an elegant (remodeled) research institute in Paris during 1981, and I was assigned the task of summarizing U.S. economic policy prior to the 1980s, followed by judgments of near term policy projections. Given the outcome of the 1980 elections, however, it became imperative to invite prominent members of President Reagan's economic team. There were, therefore, two types of presentations from the American side at those Paris meetings. I appraised U.S. policy through the eyes of the Keynesian–neoclassical synthesis in which the energy and raw material problems of the 1970s were significantly taken into account for their role in economic performance. Also, other structural issues were combined with more standard macroeconomic issues. As for the near-term projections, it was possible to foresee the internal contradictions of the Reagan policies from the very start, especially the dangers of unchecked deficit expansion, but as always in economic projections, when massive changes are building up, it is difficult to anticipate the huge imbalances even when one is decidedly on the high side of consensus at the beginning.

After my brief foray into political economy during the latter part of the 1970s, I did some journalistic writing about economic affairs. For the most part the issues discussed in the newspaper columns that I regularly serviced dealt with contemporary topics, i.e., views of "economic news," and are not suitable for reproduction in this volume of more serious scholarly selections, but one item that appeared in my regular columns for the *Los Angeles Times* took up some issues of supply-side economics, as this topic was viewed by the economists of the Reagan Administration. I went into the supply side of macroeconomics in my Presidential Address to the American Economic Association in 1977, which was a summing up of thoughts that had come to me for several prior years, perhaps a decade earlier, but supply-side economics to the members of the Reagan Administration was simply restraint of central government participation or association with the economy. It took the blunt form of tax rate reduction, deregulation, and more complete reliance on the "magic of the market." In the article for the *Los Angeles Times*, I tried to assess their supply-side performance into the fourth year of their first term.

This autobiographical research commentary brings the record essentially up to date. Whether there will be enough substance for a later volume of collected papers remains to be seen. But I do intend to continue working along three main lines:

1) To continue to consume and exploit the fruits of the "Information Age," I hope to be able to take high-frequency forecasting to a higher degree of refinement, using more weekly and daily information, with very little time delay. Also, the high-frequency research warrants extension in an international direction, both linked and unlinked across countries.

2) The LINK model is a system with no end in sight. There are always more countries to consider and more detailed information about countries that are already in the system, not to mention the need for strengthening existing linkages.

3) The end of the Cold War has important economic implications. I have made several attempts to relate military activity to economic performance — after World War II, after the Korean War, after the Vietnam War, during and after the Gulf War, and after the Cold War. It is to be hoped that constructive econometric analysis of the post Cold War environment will be fruitful.

MY PROFESSIONAL LIFE PHILOSOPHY[*]

LAWRENCE R. KLEIN

It is difficult to deal with this subject under a single heading. To contain the discussion and lend form, I shall deal only with *professional* life. The personal biographical details about my entry into the study of economics have been taken up in other publications.[1] Obviously personal, family, social, and other aspects of life interact with professional life, but I shall try to stick as closely as possible with *professional* life and treat it under four main headings: (1) teaching, (2) research, (3) policy, and (4) other professional activities of an economist. Before I get into the life philosophical aspects, let me first clarify and spell out the meaning of the selected categories.

Teaching, of course, means meeting with classes, but teaching goes far beyond that specific activity. We teach members of our research staff or policy makers with whom we consult. We teach when we are called upon to lecture before audiences all over the world, sometimes in classrooms and sometimes in general halls. We teach when we write. This is obviously the case with textbook writing, but it is also the case with popular or semipopular writing too. Teaching, in the present context, is to be understood as general pedagogy.

Research can be theory spinning, working out explanations for users of economic ideas, or delving into the statistics of the real world to describe, discover, or analyze economic hypotheses. Research can be quantitative or qualitative, although it will become clear to the reader of this essay that I have distinct leanings to the quantitative side. Since I work in the mixed field of econometrics — mixing statistics, mathematics, and economics — what might seem like applied research is actually basic research in econometrics if it is trying to do something original and abstract in any or all parts of the mixture. I must state that I have considerable difficulty in making this point clear to some of my colleagues in econometrics, who often imply that pure theoretical research in econometrics can proceed without any economic

---

[*]From *Eminent Economists: Their Life Philosophies*, ed. Michael Szenberg (Cambridge University Press, Cambridge, 1992), pp. 180–189.

[1]See *Les Prix Nobel, 1980* (Stockholm: Almqvist & Wicksell International, 1981), pp. 269–272; Lawrence Klein, "An autobiographical research commentary," in *Economic Theory and Econometrics*, ed. Jaime Marquez (Blackwell Publisher, Oxford, 1985), pp. 5–22; "Lawrence R. Klein," *Lives of the Laureates*, eds. William Breit and Roger W. Spencer (MIT Press, Cambridge, Mass., 1986), pp. 21–41.

content and that, if economic content is brought to bear on the issue, it must involve applied econometric research.

Economic policy, whether reached through the medium of econometrics or otherwise, is usually associated with prescriptions for public officials. This is often, but not always, the case. There are many groups who try to formulate policy even though they do not act in any official capacity. They are merely "friends of society." Also policy decisions may be made by executives in the private sector. Policy means, to me, the formulation of decision making in economic life.

An economist does not solely teach, do research, or work in an office for others. I, and many colleagues, simply use our professional position — for me, my university base — for operating throughout the world, undertaking many activities, as a professional, simply because they are thought to be good for society. They may or may not generate extra income, but often they do. We might be called upon to endorse something, not a commercial product, but an idea, a report, a proposal. We might engage in some enterprise activities that are professionally based. We might try to establish professional contact in areas where there has been a period of isolation, as in the Third World or the socialist world. There are countless activities, committee assignments, or appearances that have no direct bearing on teaching, research, or policy but that are deemed important enough for me or my colleagues to want to be professionally involved.

Teaching

For instruction in general economics, nothing unusual fits into my life style, except possibly the use of the computer as a visual teaching aid. Many, if not most, of our students at both graduate and undergraduate levels are now computer literate. By using the computer in classroom examples, it becomes possible to do more things — to be more exploratory by way of economic conditions and hypotheses — but the most important aspect of the computer approach to teaching is that it enables and encourages the student to work out problems from basic data and other building blocks. In this way, students obtain a better understanding of the subject.

For my main interest, my first love, *quantitative economics* is best taught along the lines of "learning by doing." This is easiest at the advanced graduate level, where students have already acquired a number of quantitative tools, not only the use of the computer, but also statistical methods and an ability to reason in an economic way. Learning by doing consists of working out realistic economic patterns and making quantitative analyses from them. Estimation of elasticities, productivities, reaction effects, and many other general concepts should be made by the students and then used for the analysis of economic issues. If these issues happen to be burning questions of the day, so much the better, because student interests are then heightened.

I grew up searching for data that are relevant to economic inquiry. Since we cannot "create" data in our subject through designed and controlled experiments, we must use whatever data are available through observation of life's economic laboratory. Data are scarce and elusive in economics; therefore, every student needs a solid stint at serious data preparation — searching, transforming, and using data for inferential purposes. I want my students to appreciate the data problem and acquire experience in working with source materials. It is much like assigning great books in the history of economic ideas. Students should read Smith, Ricardo, Marx, Mill, Walras, Marshall, Wicksell, Keynes, Schumpeter, Viner, Knight, and others, *in the original*. Also, they should learn how to use the library, even though they now have the luxury of drawing on large data banks, available at the touch of keys.

Findings in quantitative economics, particularly econometric findings, should be brought to bear on teaching at all levels, from the most elementary to the most advanced. It is a general practice in the teaching of economics to sketch out classroom diagrams in a purely casual way, sometimes for pure aesthetics. The curves are smooth, have many nice properties, and interact or shift in a way that often suits the expositor more than the real world. I believe in the use of realistic diagrams. Careful methods should be used to develop demand, supply, production, expenditure, trade, price formation, and other relationships in such a way that they are calibrated to the world in which we live, or to one that can be documented, historically or geographically. The intensive use of the computer, brought right into the classroom, makes this possible. Computer-generated diagrams that depict actual markets or economies should be at the base of diagrams. For my tastes, teachers do not have poetic license for teaching the subject in a purely personal way. There should be objectivity and, above all, realism in economic teaching, and this should be effective at the level of visual aids.

At all levels of teaching, for both undergraduate and graduate students, there should be close touch with daily news. The stock market crash and its monitoring provide more insight into the workings of financial markets and the economy than ordinary textbook paragraphs. As I write these lines, such things as Soviet restructuring, the depreciation of the U.S. dollar, and commodity price signals for the conduct of monetary policy are contemporary news items that should be followed by all students. Even the most abstract lectures in econometrics can draw interesting material from the data on dynamics of commodity price signals.

Research

Good research needs motivation, and the researcher must be completely wrapped up in the method or substance of his inquiry. Tastes vary a great deal among academic scholars, but, for me, the blends of methodoloy, real-world relevance, and the quantitative approach came together with the philosophical side. They pointed at an early stage to the then-budding field of econometrics. Although some rudimentary thoughts about this subject were germinating in my mind as an undergraduate, once I fould out that there was a formal subject just being established in the field of econometrics, I knew immediately what my calling would be.

Econometrics rests on three legs, and I find it hard to get enthusiastic about research in any limited subset. The research that has always caught my fancy was in all three together. The typical problem should consist of

statement of the issue to be investigated (economics),
specification of the models (mathematics and economics),
preparation of the data base (quantitative economics and method),
estimation of the model (statistical method),
validation of the model (statistics and economics), and
use of the model for policy and other forms of analysis (statistics and economics).

Sometimes, especially for particular audiences or users, research may be concentrated on only parts of this list, but my own econometric investigations have usually tried to encompass all the steps sequentially in order to fashion an entire research project.

It bothers me that people will devote a great deal of attention to general linear models. It may be very much worthwhile for gaining insight by analogy, but the mathematical system representations for the general linear case could be anything — a problem in psychology, engineering, demography, or whatever — and it generally lacks economic specificity. Also, economic life does not follow a linear model. Linear systems yield elegant closed-form results, but not truly economic results, and are but indications of results that we should be seeking. In some sense they provide approximations to reality, but econometrics should, especially in the computer age, seek to deal more directly with the problem of nonlinearity.

Econometric research is necessarily concerned with model specification. Drawing on scientific analogies, many econometricians have followed the rule of *parsimony*. They seek a transparent, easily manageable, and elegant model. The smallest or most compact system that is capable of generating the results that interest them is the preferred system.

I disagree fundamentally with this point of view for our subject. Given that economics is a nonexperimental discipline resting on a sparse data base, we cannot be sure that the parsimonious system that appears to work well in an environment of limited experience will continue to work well when put to extrapolative use. I have watched one simple theory after another break down in predictive applications during the past 45 years of active economic research operations.

In contrast with the parsimonious view of natural simplicity, I believe that economic life is enormously complicated and that the successful model will try to build in as much of the complicated interrelationships as possible. That is why I want to work with large econometric models and a great deal of computer power. Instead of the rule of parsimony, I prefer the following rule: the largest possible system that can be managed and that can explain the main economic magnitudes as well as the parsimonious system is the better system to develop and use.

An aspect of research that has always intrigued me is team research. This fits well with my view that good econometric research should focus on the use of large systems. The lone scholar can, of course, be productive, but my first job, after leaving graduate school, was as a recruited member of a research team at the Cowles Commission, and that was an unforgettable experience. Given that I think that the true economy is large, detailed, and complicated, it is only natural that a team approach be used. In the development of the Brookings Model, the successive generations of the Wharton Model, the organization of Wharton Econometrics, the forming of Project LINK, not to mention work at such research centers as the National Bureau of Economic Research, the Survey Research Center, and the Oxford Institute of Statistics, the team approach worked very well for me, and I do believe that a good part of the world's economic problems can be treated in this manner.

In other fields of inquiry team research appears to work very well, but is not necessarily recommended exclusively. Laboratories group principal investigators, research assistants (many at the postdoctoral level), and laboratory technicians. This mode of research has proved to be very productive. In economics and other social sciences, there is certainly room for lone scholars — many of whom make the best contributions — but there is also an important place for team research, and I personally have always functioned in the latter kind of environment.

In teaching, it makes me feel good to find that students have gone on to make recognized achievements in later professional life. In research, the good feeling comes when things work out the way that received doctrine says that they should. When we find that Marshall–Lerner conditions hold or do not hold, that demand functions satisfy the fundamental equations of value theory, that our macrodynamic models are capable of generating documented characteristics of business cycles, that growth models satisfy von Neumann conditions for an expanding economy, then I get a good feeling that the laborious efforts have paid off. Similarly, when we have learned to harness the computer *now* for problems that seemed to be out of reach *some years ago*, I have a warm feeling inside.

Economic Policy

Whether a professional economist should get involved in policy is a matter of taste and personality. There is much to be said for remaining detached, independent, and purely scholarly or academic. Also, there are degrees of involvement in policy making for an economist; some may be directly and formally involved by virtue of official appointments in both the public and private sectors. Others may be only informally involved through giving advice, if requested, and writing on policy issues. Some have to be actual policy makers; I prefer to have a sense of detachment and serve only informally as a policy person when requested. As far as public policy is concerned, I believe that we have duties and responsibilities to act in *pro bono publico* servicing of the economy.

There is obvious self-satisfaction in seeing one's own efforts being put to use. That, in itself, should be a motivating factor in bringing economists into the policy arena. In addition, some economists want to be involved in a public policy process because they support the general notion of activist, interventionist decision making in order to guide the economy on a good path, i.e., a path of stable equilibrium growth along which economic improvement takes place. Others may want to be involved in order to block activist policy, but that is definitely not to my tastes. I do encounter such activity frequently.

Philosophically, I do not believe that the market system, in even its purest form, provides adequate self-regulatory responses. The economy definitely needs guidance — even leadership — and it is up to professional economists to provide public policy makers with the right information to deliver such leadership. As for the methods of doing this, I see no alternative to the quantitative approach of econometrics, but I do realize that all policy issues are not quantitative and measurable. At times, subjective decisions must also be made.

In the field of macroeconomics, policy decisions, mainly at the public level, are confined to such broad categories as fiscal, monetary, and commercial policy, but decisions in the aggregate are not sufficient to guide the complicated modern economy. Supply-side policies, sometimes called structural policies, are needed. These encompass agriculture, energy, R&D, industry, income distribution, social welfare, naturally regulated sectors, demography, job training, and many other fields. In the present context, supply-side policies mean those that draw on the economic relationship of production, cost, technology, and efficiency of organization. These concepts are not to be confused with the popular notions of supply-side economics that have come to be associated purely with tax cutting and deregulation, to a large extent for their own sake.

Econometric information, to be useful in policy formation, must be detailed. In many instances partial analysis of specific industries, markets, or decision processes will fit the policy need, but in general we need to move in the direction of preparation of large-scale complex systems in order to help policy makers. In this respect, significant advances in computer technology and the provision of detailed information through associated telecommunications processes are making it ever more possible to push econometrics in the direction of serving policy makers.

Other Professional Activities

Organizations of economic or a broader range of scholarly activities need direction from interested members who are willing and able to devote time to such activities. Administration, committee work, and special assignments can be time consuming but rewarding and important. For me, a day spent in committee meetings is not necessarily a day lost, but committee work can be overdone. In many cases, however, I have stumbled upon some of the my best research leads as a result of participation in committee meetings. I have always felt that it was proper to devote a fair amount of time to such activities. Universities and professional organizations depend heavily on committee input. That is effectively how they are run, and at least a large number of persons have to be willing to contribute; otherwise, we shall all be the worse for it. Service of this sort extends beyond the narrowly conceived professional body to community, social, religious, and other organizations that need economic input.

Some Views on Economic Substance

In this essay, I do not want to take up discussion of particular economic issues such as specification of models, or strategic parts of them, the explanatory power of certain relationships (Phillips curve, production functions, demand systems), or matters of doctrine such as classical vs. neoclassical vs. Keynesian vs. Marxian vs. monetarist. I do, however, want to close with some general thoughts about what might be useful or not in organizing thinking about the economy.

Consider first micro- and macroeconomics. Which is more important or more fundamental? In awarding credit for two semesters of economic principles, my departmental colleagues clearly favor microeconomics over macroeconomics in the sense that a term's credit for the former can stand alone, but in order to obtain credit for successful completion of a semester in macroeconomics, the student must also complete a semester's requirements in microeconomics. I have worked at various times on the technical problems of building a bridge between micro- and macroeconomics in terms of index number construction, but I do believe that macroeconomics stands on its own as a separate subject and cannot be entirely derived from microeconomics. The overall business cycle, the overall rate of inflation, and other concepts are peculiarly macroconcepts that are integral parts of macroeconomics with their separate explanations. I strongly disagree with the idea that the beginning student should not get credit for a semester of macroeconomics without a semester's credit in microeconomics. There is much more, in a very deep sense, to macroeconomics than the pure summation of results from microeconomics. Also, there is a misconception, in general, as to what constitutes macroeconomics, because there are two dimensions to aggregation — over commodities and services, and over economic units (firms and households). Specific and narrow market analyses, which involve intricate aggregation over economic units, are important in price determination, yet they are not purely microeconomic since they involve aggregation in at least one of two dimensions.

Where does fundamental understanding about the working of the economic process lie, in the real or in the monetary sector? In a true sense, both are important, and one cannot meaningfully exist without the other. At an earlier stage of my career, I thought that the real sector was, by far, the more important and that a good understanding of the economy could be achieved without careful reference to the monetary sector.

Over the years, particularly in studying the macroeconomy, I have come to appreciate, more and more, the role of money and of the whole monetary sector. I think that *monetarism* is fundamentally flawed, and dangerous when used as a doctrinaire policy approach, but I do believe now that *money matters*; it is not everything, but it does matter. That is perhaps the chief outcome of the debate between the monetarists and the rest of the economics profession.

The sensitivity of housing, consumer expenditures on durables, and business investment to fluctuations in interest rates convinced me of the significance of the monetary sector to the above-mentioned activities of the real sector. Similarly, exchange rate determination is significant for understanding exports, imports, and trade balances.

During the 1960s, I became increasingly interested in international economic issues. That was the time when I shifted many of my interests toward international model building. The planning meetings for the establishment of Project LINK took place in 1968. I was impressed, as were many of my colleagues (not only Pennsylvania colleagues, but associates from around the profession), that the U.S. economy could not be properly analyzed without much more careful attention being paid to the international sector. There was an early recognition that the U.S. economy was no longer *closed.*

Textbooks of economic principles generally treat the United States first as a *closed* system and then introduce, almost as an afterthought, some modifications to deal with international trade and payments. I find this misleading, even to the point of being incorrect. I believe that exporting, importing, determination of currency rates, and capital flows should form an integral part of the teaching from the first day of class and that U.S. economics should be taught as an *open* subject. That is certainly the way that I teach freshman economics.

While I do concede the importance of getting the monetary sector right, I have not lost my confidence in the importance of research, development, innovation, and their roles in the dynamics of the economy. As I have said, both the money and real sectors are important but, for me, science, technology, and production function changes are real processes of extreme interest at the present time. Supply-side economics has a great deal of meaning handed down from successive generations of economists, after 1776, but this interpretation of the supply side is far different from the simplistic and populist approaches through tax cuts.

Since econometrics itself is interdisciplinary, it should not be surprising that I hold interdisciplinary studies in high esteem for developing our ideas about the economy. Very serious collaboration with scientists, engineers, and general technologists can be very important for advancing our understanding of the functioning of the real economy. A full supply- *and* demand-side economics must have a great deal to say about these related disciplinary activities, as well as others in the social sciences.

References

Adelman, F. and I., 1959, "The dynamic properties of the Klein–Goldberger model," *Econometrica* **27**, pp. 596–625.

Arrow, K. J. and Gerard Debreu, 1954, "Existence of an equilibrium for a competitive economy," *Econometrica* **22**, pp. 265–290.

Houthakker, H. S., 1955, "The Pareto distribution and the Cobb–Douglas production function in activity analysis," *The Review of Economic Studies* **XXIII**, pp. 27–31.

Klein, L. R., 1946, "Macroeconomics and the theory of rational behavior," *Econometrica* **14**, pp. 93–108.

——, 1973, "Dynamic analysis of economic systems," *International Journal of Mathematical Education in Science and Technology* **4**, pp. 341–359.

—— and H. Rubin, 1947–48, "A constant-utility index of the cost of living," *The Review of Economic Studies* **XV**, pp. 84–87.

Lerner, A. P., 1962, "Microeconomics and macroeconomics," in *Logic, Methodology and Philosophy of Sciences*, eds. E. Nagel, P. Suppes and A. Tarski (Stanford Univ. Press, Stanford, CA), pp. 474–483.

Theil, H., 1954, *Linear Aggregation of Economic Relations* (North-Holland, Amsterdam)

PART I

ECONOMIC THEORY RECONSIDERATIONS

EDITORIAL *i*

The six papers included in Part I represent Lawrence Klein's reconsiderations of economic theory — especially macroeconomics — from three main perspectives: The economic propositions that have stood the test of time and can be accepted as "laws"; (rational) micro-foundations of macroeconomics; and a generalized model of the Keynesian–classical synthesis with a built-in supply side associated with Leontief's interindustry structure. Klein's reconsiderations are formulated from an empirical vantage point, and he puts them forward in relation to contemporary economic history and analysis.

The first paper is a communication delivered at the House of American Academy of Arts and Sciences on January 12, 1983, in Boston, Massachusetts. In this communication, Klein explains the nature and meaning of economic laws, sifts through a series of economic propositions and underscores some of those which *have* and *have not* stood the test of time. He concludes that indeed, "important non-trivial laws exist" and, with a proper understanding of the noise component and of the degree of uncertainty involved in drawing conclusions from their applications, "they can be used to good advantage."

Specifically, he argues that among time-honored early propositions, Pareto's law of income distribution, albeit in a restricted sense, Engel's law of food expenditure, the Keynesian proposition about consumer expenditure, the doctrine of comparative costs, and the principle of purchasing power parity have stood the test of time. And, similarly, among more recent propositions, the portfolio principle of "spreading risk by diversifying portfolio composition," the Phillips curve relationship between wage changes and unemployment (seemingly refuted by some economists but "is working out just as it should be expected to perform"), and the "law of the sinusoidal limit" ("how iterated averaging (smoothing) of time series transforms it into a sine wave") explaining the existence of business cycles do qualify as laws of economics.

Judging by the same litmus test of empirical validity, Klein shows that five Great Ratios — the savings ratio, the capital–output ratio, the wage share ratio, the velocity ratio and the labor participation ratio — that economists often treat as stable parameters, are generally "not stable enough to qualify as economic laws." Nor do large-scale econometric models qualify as such laws. Likewise, there yet remains to be found strong empirical support for von Neumann's result of long-run equality between real growth rate and real interest rate, Harold Hotelling's principle of use of natural resources, and the Hecksher–Ohlin theorem on the relative availability and use of factors of production in relation to trade flows and specialization. Arthur

3

Okun's law of three-to-one relationship between Gross National Product and unemployment broke down in the 1970s. Finally, the two old laws, Walras' law and Say's law, essentially are not behavioral, but accounting equations which in conjunction with a larger simultaneous equation system show that a freely competitive economy can always generate optimal equilibrium solutions.

"What is macroeconomics?" (1993) is a restatement about rational foundations of macroeconomics — an elegant restatement of the aggregation problem. Klein first dealt with this subject almost 50 years ago at the beginning of his professional life. His two classic papers, "Macroeconomics and the theory of rational behavior," *Econometrica* **14**, April (1946), and "Remarks on the theory of aggregation," *Econometrica* **14**, October (1946) have been reprinted in the 1985 volume edited by Jaime Marquez. The paper reprinted in this volume is a crucial reminder to the late arrivals in economics that macroeconomics does exist in its own right and is not a *simple* aggregation of microeconomic results. It was written for the volume in honor of Don Patinkin.

In the paper, Klein principally discusses three techniques that form the bridge between microeconomics and macroeconomics. (a) Representative agent specification by which "macroeconomic relationships are designed as close analogs of microeconomic specifications." He regards this technique as a cop-out; it may lead to elegant theorems, but they are not useful in making macroeconomic judgments because the assumptions behind it do not hold. (b) Constructing indexes "that transform the simultaneous equation system of microeconomics into analog system of macroeconomics." This technique is powerful and does provide solutions, but these solutions are not easy and may be very cumbersome. (c) Using distribution functions, that is, integrating the microeconomic function over the joint frequency distribution of explanatory variables. The derived (integrated) macroeconomic equation would then be expressed as a function of the mean and other parametric characteristics of respective distributions of the same explanatory variables (across all agents).

Approach (c) is straightforward and practical, and what Klein now recommends. He illustrates it with an example using a micro demand function. (Examples of actual implementation of the joint frequency distributional framework of approach (c), as suggested by Klein, are found in L. Lau, D. Jorgenson, and T. Stoker, "Welfare comparison under exact aggregation," *American Economic Review* **69** (1980); T. Stoker, "Completeness, distribution restrictions and the form of aggregate functions," *Econometrica* **52** (1984).) In conclusion, Klein stresses that in order to produce desirable results, it is highly important for public policy focused on microeconomic principles not to ignore its macroeconomic perspectives and underlying distributions.

The other papers included in Part I relate to evolution of Klein's thinking on the Keynesian system, in theory and practice, and its relevance for a contemporary economy. The "Technical appendix" (1947) contains a mathematical model of Keynes' *A Treatise on Money*; mathematical derivation of the system of the

General Theory, and comparison of mathematical versions of the Keynesian and Classical models. A rigorous mathematical derivation of the Keynesian system is structured on microfoundations of three core macroeconomic functions, namely consumption, investment, and liquidity preference functions. While comparing the Keynesian model with the Classical model, there is also treatment and discussion of the long-run equilibrium as a special case consistent with Pigou's (1943), "The classical stationary state," *Economic Journal* **53**. Indeed, those who believe that micro underpinnings of macroeconomics began to first appear in the late 1960s and 1970s would do well to work through the "Technical appendix."

The models presented in the "Technical appendix" are among the first available mathematical models of the Keynesian and Classical economics. Klein used these models in parts to develop the analytical discussion of another classic paper, "Theories of effective demand and employment," *Journal of Political Economy* **55**, April (1947), reprinted in the Marquez (1985) volume. Associated empirical statements, together with other econometric material, of a mathematically specified Keynesian system were laid out in one of the two new chapters, Chapter IX, of the second edition of *The Keynesian Revolution* (1966). Chapter IX, titled "The econometrics of the general theory," contains a reestimated Klein–Goldberger model of the U.S. economy; statistical equations for consumption, investment and liquidity preference functions for a range of countries (Japan, Israel, Netherlands, United Kingdom, India) that show the universality of the Keynesian revolution; some remarks on the future of Keynesian economics; and suggestions for the future directions of research in macroeconometric modeling.

The other new chapter in the second edition of *The Keynesian Revolution*, Chapter VIII, titled "The Keynesian revolution revisited," represented Klein's reconsiderations of the Keynesian analysis and its underlying theoretical system almost 20 years later. In it, Klein reevaluated the Keynesian theory "in the light of our knowledge of actual functioning of the economy, the knowledge that has been built up by econometric studies." This chapter shows how early, right from the beginning, Klein recognized the general importance of econometric models as guides to policy, importance of larger models, and importance of making a distinction between a pedagogical model and a real life working model.

Klein expressed the view that although the *General Theory* was an intellectual breakthrough, it was too simple for judging the real world. He looked upon the Keynesian theory as essentially a system of equations. But for this system to become a useful tool, it must include a public sector, be disaggregated, and made dynamic. Klein explicitly delineated the directions in which consumption function, investment function, liquidity preference function, production and labor demand functions, labor supply and wage determination equations each needed to be extended. He also believed that a larger system extended along these lines would be capable of treating problems of inflation, faster growth and study of underdeveloped countries. "The Keynesian revolution revisited" was first published, two years earlier, in *The Economic Studies Quarterly* **XV**, November (1964).

In his essay, "The neoclassical traditions of Keynesian economics and the generalized model," a decade and a half later in 1982, Klein gave us another major appraisal of the state of Keynesian thinking in the background of contemporary economic history and public policy. This was a much needed period assessment of the system at a time when mainstream macroeconomics and econometric models had both come under heavy clouds and nonconstructive attacks from the critics.

To start with, he emphasized that two basic principles of neoclassical economics, the use of optimizing behavior and clearance of markets, are rooted in the Keynesian system. This he had already rigorously demonstrated in his work on "microfoundations," as seen above. Second, he underscored an absolute need of a large model containing both demand and supply sides if public policy is to handle the intricacies of contemporary economic problems. "There is no alternative, in my opinion, to the large-scale system that combines the overall thinking of Keynes with the intersectoral thinking of Leontief." He then outlined an accounting and mathematical prototype framework of a synthesized Keynes–Leontief system — that is a framework of "an extended model, built around a Keynesian core and integrated with appropriate supply-side relations." He concluded this essay with succinct observations on the failure of *monetarism*, the contrived nature of the *rational-expectations* critique of public policy, applications of *optimal control theory* and *supply-side economics*.

"The Keynesian revolution: Fifty years later, a last word" reflects Klein's current views on the status of Keynesian thought. It was prepared by way of a response to "constructive critics" who had commented from various perspectives on his conception of *The Keynesian Revolution* at a conference held in Philadelphia on April 10, 1992 to mark the fiftieth anniversary of its first publication. The commentators included Edmund Phelps, on theoretical perspectives; Albert Ando, on policy evaluation; Thomas Cooley, on research perspectives; Alan Blinder, on policy implications; and panellists from a round table discussion. Klein's response illuminates a number of theoretical issues such as the concept of the natural rate of unemployment and efficiency wages as a way of looking at the equilibrium problem, the Phillips curve, the Lucas critique, the bridging of the gap between micro- and macroeconomics, principal agent theory, postwar business cycles, forecasting from econometric models, the role of public policy, and so on.

1

SOME LAWS OF ECONOMICS[†]

Economists, at a time of reflection, often note how little we know about the universe that we are trying to describe. Tonight, I am going in precisely an opposite direction by trying to list some things that we do know, in the form of economic laws.

It is very difficult, and may well not be possible, to find better available statements about the concept of economic laws than is found in Marshall's *Principles*, chapter III, entitled "Economic Generalizations or Laws."[1] Marshall observed that economic science is based on the same considerations and procedures that are used in other sciences, but he contrasted economics with "exact sciences." He also remarked,

> *A science progresses by increasing the number and exactness of its laws, by submitting them to tests of ever increasing severity, and by enlarging their scope till a single broad law contains and supersedes a number of narrower laws, which have been shown to be special instances of it.*

In many respects economic research proceeds in this way, but we economists find it very difficult to come to definitive decisions along the way about which laws to reject or accept and have a hard time establishing a single broad law. It is my opinion that the most important feature of economic science giving rise to its lack of decisiveness is our inability to perform controlled experiments on a comprehensive replicated level. In this respect, we acknowledge unfavorable comparisons between the inexactness of economics and other social sciences, on the one hand, and natural sciences, on the other.

Experimentation is very important but not the whole of the comparison. Marshall makes a comparison between the sciences of the tides (inexact) and the laws of gravitation (exact), and indicates that economics is akin to the former. But a more frequent modern comparison that is relevant for economics is between meteorology or seismology, on the one hand, and astronomy, on the other. Inaccurate predictions are made about weather and earthquakes, while accurate predictions are made about the movements of the heavenly bodies. In all three cases there is no opportunity for controlled experimentation, yet the differences in precision are great.

[†]From *Bulletin of the American Academy of Arts And Sciences,* Vol. **XXXVI** (January, 1983), pp. 23–45.
[1]A. Marshall, *Principles of Economics* (Macmillan, London, 1936), 8th edition.

Economic prediction is, in many respects, similar to weather prediction. The comparisons with seismology are more recent, but I have an intuitive feeling that we make better predictions of economic phenomena than seismologists do of earthquakes. A reason, or a description, of the problem with weather prediction is that a large component in the end result comes from atmospheric turbulence. In the same sense, the residual random disturbance in economic relations accounts for a large part of our inaccuracy of prediction. In economics, as in meteorology, the noise-to-signal ratio is inherently large, while in astronomy it is small; therein lies the reason for the discrepancy in predictive performance.

Marshall spoke of economic laws as *tendencies* rather than as precise causal statements. His frame of reference was insightful, but general and logical. I intend, in this communication, to try to be more specific and empirical in trying to indicate just what it is that economists can assert with the authority of laws. I shall try to cover a variety of cases, but there is no attempt or thought of being completely comprehensive.

Some Great Ratios

A number of years ago, I tried to put together a self-contained macro model (simultaneous equation system) of the economy as a whole by considering only a few ratios that economists use:

the savings ratio (rate)
the capital–output ratio
the wage share
the velocity ratio (quantity equation of money)
the labor participation ratio

Economists often analyze the economic situation as though some or all of these ratios are stable parameters (constants).

The U.S. savings ratio hovered around 10 percent for a long period of time and has more recently been lower, fluctuating near 5 percent. This low value is frequently cited as being responsible in part for our presently high interest rates and poor rate of growth performance in the United States. A more favorable case at higher levels is that of Japan. A high savings rate has been a factor in Japan's amazing success in economic growth. There is wide variation in the size of the rate across countries, and it is hardly a stable ratio in the short run. If the tendency towards constancy of the savings rate is to have any standing as a law of economics, it would have to be as a long-run proposition, say the savings rate averaged over a decade or more. Some economists make this a central point of their analysis, but it is not widely enough accepted or established to be classified as a basic law of economics.

The same may be said of the capital–output ratio (or the crude acceleration principle of investment when it is put in change form). It is not sufficiently stable. But the share of wages in total production does seem to exhibit more empirical regularity. Paul Douglas implied this in his lifetime investigations summed up under the heading "Are There Laws of Production?"[2] Wage–price guideline programs, which may yet see their day in more comprehensive implementations of income policies, are, in a sense, derived from inversions of the constancy of labor's share.

Personally, I have more faith, as an empirical economist, in the constancy of labor's share for the interpretation of inflation than in the quantity theory of money, which relies on the constancy of the velocity of circulation of money. The foundations of monetarism, now popular in the formation of economic policy in many parts of the world, rely on the stability of some form of velocity, and I would side with President Frank Morris of the Federal Reserve Bank of Boston, who argues that the concept of money is undergoing such great change that the monetarist rules do not apply, especially in day-to-day monetary management.[3] His arguments are quite contemporary, but I believe that velocity has not been stable in the past.

Principles of demography and economics together are needed to explain movements of the labor force and participation rate. So many surprises in both the short and long run have occurred in economists' expectations about unemployment as a result of change in labor force growth that we can have little confidence in the stability of the participation rate. First it was the baby boom; now it is the aspirations of working women that are cited as reasons for finding unusually high rates of unemployment.

Generally speaking, the Great Ratios are not stable enough to qualify as economic laws, except possibly the wage share of production, although they are interesting for use in crude speculative analysis with small models of scholarly or pedagogical nature. By averaging or smoothing the ratios they may show more stability, but generalizations into dynamic relations with steady-state properties or as multivariate relations within the context of larger complete systems may lead to more stability. For example, the present controversy about the validity of monetarism does not rest entirely on the stability of velocity ratios but on the stability of generalized equations for the demand for money. It is my assessment, though, that even with these generalizations the status of monetarism does not qualify as an economic law. I would not say either that the large-scale econometric models that I and my associates put together as systems for prediction qualify. Our models contain many components that may qualify as economic laws, and I do believe that our models provide the best means available at this time for charting our economic future, but I would not elevate the status of the Wharton Model to a collective economic law; it is too uncertain and tentative even though it has scored the best forecasting record of any other system or approach that has been documented for systematic testing.

---

[2]Douglas' presidential address to the American Economic Association was more positive than that of others, for he genuinely believed that economists could say something about the laws of production, *American Economic Review* **38** (1948), pp. 1–41.

[3]Related findings of Benjamin Friedman of Harvard and policy arguments of Anthony Solomon of the Federal Reserve Bank of New York add much weight to the inference of instability of the monetarist laws.

Some Economic Laws

What *are* some economic laws that can be accepted as having stood the test of time? In the list that follows there are many laws that play important roles in comprehensive models, although they do not constitute the entire models, by themselves.

Pareto's law of income distribution: Pareto observed that there is a tendency for individual incomes to be distributed so that the logarithm of the number of persons with income in excess of a given level is a negative linear function of the logarithm of that income level. This is an elegant and simple law of income distribution and can be used to good advantage in many analytical studies, but it does not hold on a universal scale — across countries and time periods. It has not been found to hold for the entire range of the income distribution, but it does hold on a broad scale for upper income groups. In a restricted sense, it could qualify as a law of economics. Interesting interpretations have been put forward to show how peoples movements among income classes tend to generate the Pareto law, but these analytical arguments are usually based on controversial assumptions. Taking Marshall's views of economic laws as general tendencies, we can say that Pareto's law of income distribution or various complementary laws (for the lower tail, e.g.) can be considered as economic laws.

Another old law has more substantiation, namely Engel's law of food expenditure — the fraction of income spent on food decreases as the level of income rises. This law is not very specific. It does not say how fast this ratio falls. But the general statement of the law, with varying numerical parameters for different countries, was found to hold uniformly by Hendrick Houthakker on the occasion of the centenary of the formulation of the law. To this very day, if we look at the family expenditure–income data for the U.S., U.K., and other major countries they show clearly a falling tendency for the fraction of income spent on food as we move up the income scale.

Many decades later, after Engel formulated his law of food expenditure, J. M. Keynes stated a fundamental psychological law about total consumer expenditure. He said that consumers, in the aggregate, would spend on consumption only a fraction of an increase in income. In more technical terms he asserted that the marginal propensity to consume is positive but less than unity. The magnitude of the marginal propensity to consume varies from situation to situation, but it is, as far as I know, always less than unity. The general statement holds. A stronger law, that aggregate consumption depends only on aggregate income, either contemporaneously or with a distributed time lag, is not always validated, but the strict Keynesian proposition, like Engel's proposition, can stand as a law.

A stable savings ratio is a more specific law than Keynes'. The early research of Simon Kuznets suggested, from an empirical point of view, that U.S. consumers saved about 10 percent of their income, particularly when smoothed into decade numbers.[4] This empirical regularity prompted Milton Friedman to formulate his

---

[4] A stable national savings ratio, encompassing personal, business, government and net foreign savings, has been called Denison's Law, but it is no more solidly established than is Kuznets' earlier observation on personal incomes.

highly structured permanent income hypothesis that long-run consumer expenditures or savings are proportional to long-run income. The permanent income hypothesis has been provocative and stimulated much research activity but cannot be said to have withstood the test of time to qualify as an economic law. Data of the last two or three decades cast doubt on the stability of the savings–income ratio. In a similar way, Milton Friedman's restatement of the stability of the velocity ratio into long-run money demand functions has not been established as an economic law. In fact, the instability of money demand relationships, as indicated above, brings into question the entire monetarist theory of the macro economy.

The laws of economics that have been discussed so far involve some behavioral principles, and if human beings decide to vary their behavior from average observed practice, the laws may be upset. But other laws hold in economics, by definition. Some are implied accounting balances and in that sense nothing but truisms. They may not be, however, evident, especially to the nonprofessional; therefore, it is meaningful to give them the elevated status of laws. Walras' law, called by that name, is essentially an accounting identity. Put one way, it states that the incomes paid to factors for producing all the goods and services marketed should equal the value of the goods sold, both consumer goods and producer goods (investment). In contemporary social accounting systems, this relationship routinely appears in the tables of correspondence between the national income and the gross national product (or expenditure). After some institutional items of reconciliation, we find that the GNP should equal the national income (paid to the factors of production), but there is a *statistical discrepancy* which arises because all the items of Walras' law are measured independently and imperfectly. In a logical sense, the law should hold exactly, but in an empirical accounting sense it holds inexactly. At the present time, the United States has a GNP value of about $3,000 billion, and the associated statistical discrepancy is estimated within a range of no more than plus or minus $10 billion.

Similarly, on a world scale, total imports should equal total exports, when measured in common (numeraire) units of valuation. In analogy with scientific laws, this accounting identity may be called a *law of conservation*, in the sense that no goods get lost in accounting for the trade that moves from one country to another. Again, measurement is imperfect, and separate accounting for imports and for exports leaves us with a world discrepancy of some $20 billion or more, associated with a world trade total of about $2,000 billion.

A law of roughly the same vintage as Walras' law is Say's law of markets. It says, optimistically, that everything that gets produced will get sold, or that "supply creates its own demand." Philosophically, it could be interpreted as saying that supply motivates economic activity. During the Great Depression, this point of view was strongly challenged by Keynes and his followers, who claimed that demand was the driving force. In the depressed conditions of the interwar period, the Keynesian point of view was undoubtedly more correct, but this position is being challenged today by supply side economics. The adherents of the latter school have not openly claimed that they are advocating the acceptance of Say's law, but occasionally their arguments suggest that they believe in it. It would be stretching imagination to say that Say's law has been verified or validated. While we can accept Walras's law as an accounting identity which holds in practice, to the extent of our powers of observation, we cannot cite empirical support that is widely accepted as validating Say's law. Nor would we, in any sense, claim that "demand creates its own supply."

It is not a case of one view or the other; both supply and demand aspects are simultaneously relevant. Marshall wisely noted that both blades of a scissors do the cutting, and we should not look at the supply side of economic life exclusively for insight into the workings of the system any more than we should look solely to the demand side. But the *law of supply and demand* does have wide acceptance. It is based on the assumption and observation of a tendency of markets to get cleared, by finding a price that brings supply and demand into balance. In a more realistic and dynamic statement of this law, we say that when supply exceeds demand in a given market, price in that market tends to fall in an attempt to bring about a balance between supply and demand. It states, conversely, that when demand exceeds supply, price tends to rise. it is not quantitative in the sense of saying how much or how fast price will change in the face of an imbalance between supply and demand; that will depend on the economic motivations of the particular consumers and producers in the market being examined.

Every day there are literally millions of transactions going on everywhere in playing out this dynamic law. But it can be obstructed. Price controls, freezes, and guidelines halt its working or modify it. To give a contemporary example that all can appreciate, in the present situation in the world oil market, a global oil glut is often referred to. Supply exceeds demand in this market at the present time, and there is correspondingly a tendency of prices to fall. In the past several years, OPEC nations have largely fixed the price of oil, particularly in the period after the embargo of 1973. But sideline observers kept saying that the laws of economics would work, and gradually they have assumed more importance in the world oil market. By now, we are seeing the law of supply and demand at work, with prices falling in order to wipe out a condition of excess supply. Furthermore, if the OPEC nations are successful in restricting output significantly, for a protracted period of time, they will be able to eradicate the present situation of excess supply, and price could resume its upward path again, but this would be a path that is determined by the laws of economics and not governed by religious fervor or political opportunism.

Walras' law and the law of supply and demand (leading to market clearing) are both components of larger systems — mathematical systems of simultaneous equations — which show that in equilibrium a freely competitive economy produces an optimal solution. This solution is optimal in the sense that it produces a state of affairs in which no economic agent can be made better off without causing another agent to be worse off, at the same time. We call this situation one of *Pareto Optimality*. This, of course, is not to be confused in any sense with Pareto's law of distribution but is an analytical and logical proposition about economic behavior.

We cannot easily, perhaps never will, observe an economy in a state of competitive equilibrium and cannot test the existence of a condition of Pareto Optimality. The principles of a competitive economy are useful in guiding our thinking and understanding of the system; they form the intellectual base of "trust busting," but they are not one of the economic laws that I am talking about tonight. The laws of supply and demand can be estimated statistically, and Walras' law is measured rather closely in our social accounting tabulations, but the principles of optimality are not observable or testable in the same sense.

In the field of international economics, a rich assortment of economic propositions has developed, and I shall draw on three of them for some comment. The first to be considered is the doctrine of comparative costs. It is not stated as a law, but as a doctrine that shows the gains from free trade, much as the doctrine of optimality derives from the analysis of the working of a competitive domestic economy. Free competition and free trade are both conditions for the existence of optimality.

"The doctrine of comparative costs maintains that if trade is left free, each country *in the long run* tends to specialize in the production of and to export those commodities in whose production it enjoys a comparative advantage in terms of real costs, and to obtain by importation those commodities which could be produced at home only at a comparative disadvantage in terms of real costs, and that such specialization is to the mutual advantage of the countries participating in it." The statement of the doctrine by J. Viner is clearly in the spirit of Marshall's concept of laws of economics.[5] He speaks of *tendencies* that prevail in the *long run*.

In principle, costs could be measured, together with imports and exports, for a number of countries. Statistical measures of their mutual bilateral trade in association with their comparative costs could validate or refute this proposition. In treating this doctrine as an economic law, it would have to be tested on a broad scale. Cost estimation is difficult, and many bilateral flows are to be considered simultaneously in order to come to a comprehensive conclusion.

A number of country pairs have been investigated for various industry groupings. In a recent dissertation completed at the University of Pennsylvania, Toshiko Tange estimated production relations and costs in a number of manufacturing industries (2-digit groupings) for the U.S. and Japan, respectively. She found a high correlation between export activity and cost efficiency, thus lending support to the doctrine. In looking casually at trading activity around the world, I would say that the long-run tendency predicted by the doctrine does take place.

A related proposition, or theorem, of international economics concerns relative availability and use of factors of production in relation to trade flows and specialization. It is known as the Hecksher–Ohlin theorem. In general terms, it states that a country tends to export the goods that intensively use the factors of production with which it is abundantly endowed and imports those goods that use the factors with which it is poorly endowed. Paul Samuelson extended these propositions with

---

[5] J. Viner, *Studies in the Theory of International* (Harper, New York, 1937), p. 438.

a factor price equalization theory, i.e., factors, move, if at least one is fully mobile, between countries, tending to bring factor prices into mutual equality.[6]

Like the laws of comparative advantage, the theorems about international specialization and price equalization are logical propositions that are hard to describe or verify empirically. They depend on very strict assumptions about competition, free mobility, availability of information, and similarity of tastes and preferences among countries. Also, they are carefully proved for the two good, two country case, which is only indicative of the workings of a multilateral system of general equilibrium. The strict assumptions are not met in practice, yet there is a feeling among many, if not most, economists that actual conditions are close enough to those assumed that an underlying tendency exists to satisfy the conclusions.

In a highly provocative and stimulating statistical study, Wassily Leontief showed that the United States trade patterns did not satisfy intuitive feelings about the workings of the Hecksher–Ohlin theorem.[7] He found that the United States exported products with relatively high labor content and imported those with relatively high capital content. Intuition would supposedly have expected the opposite.

From the point of view of documentation from widely accepted empirical studies, we cannot place the logical propositions about trade into the form of economic laws, but there is an analogous kind of proposition, known as the doctrine of purchasing power parity (PPP), that does come closer to being accepted as a fundamental law of economics in my sense. Purchasing power parity claims that exchange rates between currency pairs move in the same proportion as relative rates of inflation in the two countries (or in one country against a weighted combination of countries — in figuring both exchange valuations and relative inflation rates). This doctrine can be stated in terms of comparative cost changes. When stated in terms of export price changes, it can be interpreted as the law of one price, namely, that an internationally traded good should cost the same, anywhere in the world, when cost is compared in a common currency unit of account. Of course, transport and other institutional differences can exist.

Many careful students of international economics have studied the statistics of exchange rates and price movements between countries, only to conclude that PPP does not hold. In my opinion, these studies are too specialized, looking only at a pair of countries, at one time, and some particular commodities. A few of these studies have been for long historical episodes, but most have concentrated, recently, on the period since 1973, when the present floating system of exchange rates came into being.

Short-run variations in exchange rates are related to many things, such as interest rate differentials, reserve positions, payments balances, capital flows, and international psychological tensions. But also, inflation differentials are important

---

[6]P. A. Samuelson, "International trade and the equalization of factor prices," *Economic Journal* (June 1948).
[7]Wassily Leontief, "Domestic production and foreign trade: The American position re-examined," in *Proceedings of the American Philosophical Society* (September 1953).

and in the long run are the dominant factors that PPP says that they ought to be. In a fresh approach to this issue, I and some of my colleagues on Project Link have found that PPP does hold — with annual statistics, over long stretches of time (about a decade or more), and across countries. Our investigations are for price indexes averaged over many commodities and recognize that some countries may show more sensitivity of exchange rate changes to inflation differentials than PPP indicates, while others may show less sensitivity. Our findings are truly those of a tendency, in the Marshallian sense. As a scatter plot of percentage changes in dollar exchange rates against percentage changes in export prices relative to U.S. export prices shows, there is definitely a relationship. On average, it is close to the strict PPP relationship, which is the negatively sloped line with unit gradient, but there is significant scatter or variance about the line. It does not hold perfectly or nearly perfectly. The deviations are generous. Several countries' results over the period 1971–1980 are plotted in a time series of cross sections. There is good support for a law of economics here, but it is only a tendency, subject to error variance.

To a large extent, the economic laws considered up to this point have been time-honored propositions, mainly developed in the nineteenth century. Let us turn now to some twentieth century research into some laws of economics.

The modern theory of portfolio analysis goes in many intricate directions, some dictated by institutional structures in financial or credit markets and some by developments in the theory of risk. But, at the core, nearly all the results are derived from a single proposition: "Don't put all your eggs in one basket."[8] The proposition of spreading risk by diversifying portfolio composition is a well-known proposition that has been handed down from one generation of investors (scholarly investigators) to another. A theorem concludes that if the variance of a portfolio's net returns is to be minimized subject to achieving a given average rate of return, the best investment policy is to diversify holdings. By the same token, the maximization of average return, subject to a given variance, will lead to the same result. This is a normative rule, and it is generally observed that there is diversification, but individuals may ignore it. The lucky ones will do well, but the unfortunate ones will lose a great deal by guessing wrong on a concentrated portfolio. Investment advice is usually to diversify, so we can find it prevalent in practice, but this is hard to show or substantiate, empirically. It is the perceived widespread acceptance that leads me to classify it as a law of economics.

Harold Hotelling, who contributed fundamentally to several fields, had his successes in economics. He established a law on the exploitation of exhaustible natural resources, and these issues have come to the fore in connection with the analysis of energy problems after 1973. Hotelling's principle is that natural resources should be exploited at rates that tend to equalize the rate of return on all assets together, both exhaustible assets and other assets, mainly those traded regularly in financial and commodity markets. Hotelling's principle should be looked at as long-run ten-

---

[8]G. H. Leavens, "Diversification of investments," *Trusts and Estates* (May 1945).

dency, much as I looked at PPP, above; it should not hold tightly, in every short-run situation. It should hold on average, across assets and markets.

Attempts at statistical verification of Hotelling's principle have not been significantly successful at this time, so we are not able now to cite it as a law of economics, but the chances are good that it will be established as an intermediate to long-term tendency.

Just as Harold Hotelling spanned many disciplines and made highly original contributions to several, so did John von Neumann, during the productive era of the 1920s, 1930s, 1940s, and 1950s. Although we shall remember von Neumann for many insightful contributions to economics, we ought to remember him most for his important contribution to growth theory in his celebrated paper on intersectoral growth and expansion.[9] Given the usual restrictive assumptions about models of general equilibrium, von Neumann found that the real growth rate of a dynamic economy should equal the real interest rate in long-run equilibrium.

A particularly strict and unusual assumption of the von Neumann model was that workers consume all their income and save nothing. Correspondingly, entrepreneurs save all their income and spend nothing on consumption from their current receipts. Michio Morishima and others relaxed this assumption and established that the real rate of interest should equal the real growth rate divided by the entrepreneurs' marginal savings coefficient. The latter coefficient should be near one, if less than one, and this is seen to be only a minor modification.

It may seem like a very abstruse bit of theorizing with results that are useful only in theoretical discussion, yet a topical issue of the day is: How long can real interest rates continue to prevail in the face of slow growth (recession) in the real economy? If we look at the disparity between today's real interest rate of some 7 or 8 percent and a negative or near zero growth rate, it is relevant questioning whether this state of affairs can prevail for long. The von Neumann result, interpreted as a fundamental economic law, suggests that nominal and real interest rates must eventually (soon) come down from their elevated position and fall into line with real growth of the economy. The inflation rate has recently fallen. The prevailing rate is different when computed from different price indexes, but let us say that the underlying inflation rate is about 5 percent. A representative interest rate would be a treasury bill rate of about 13 percent. This would make the real interest rate at 8 percent. When the economy starts to grow, it could sustain a value just below the former trend rate of 4 percent. Let us say that 3 percent would be maintainable. To bring the real interest rate down from 8 percent to about 3 percent would require a reduction in the *nominal* interest rate, assuming that the inflation rate will not be further reduced. This is the way that the laws of economic growth can be applied to the analysis of medium-term prospects for the economy. In the short run, the growth rate and real interest rate can diverge, but not for long, i.e., more than two

---

[9] J. von Neumann, "A model of general economic equilibrium," *Review of Economic Studies* **XIII** (1945–46), pp. 1–9.

three years; so eventually, I look for easier monetary policy. To say that balance between the real interest and growth rates is to be attained does not indicate how it will be done. It may happen through policy changes, behavioral decision, or a combination of both. Many plausible scenarios can be developed.

In the post World War II period, with the implementation of the Keynesian system of thought as the mainstream model of macroeconomic reasoning and policy implementation, there was a companion analysis, known as the Phillips curve, to explain inflationary phenomena. In his original contribution, A. W. Phillips established a relationship between nominal wage changes and unemployment. I do believe that, as properly stated in the spirit of Phillips' original investigation, it is a sound proposition, although it is in need of elaboration to take account of the dynamics of labor market developments, changing demographic structure, and price change. In these added dimensions, a law of economics prevails. It has never, in this sense, broken down in its relatively brief existence. It is my opinion that stagflation of the past decade or so, where we have had simultaneously inflation and high unemployment, did not refute the existence of the Phillips curve, although many economists adopted that point of view. I do not mean to go into all the subtle and technical details of the difference between a Phillips curve relationship (between wage changes and unemployment) and a trade-off relationship (between inflation and unemployment), but they are quite different, according to my analysis, and I would claim that during these very days we are witnessing the workings of the Phillips curve relationship on a very broad scale. At present high levels of unemployment, the bargaining power of labor is weakened to such an extent that wage cuts, wage pauses, or wage moderation are the rule in labor market development. As a law of economics, the Phillips curve is working out just as it should be expected to perform and is a very significant development in contributing to the present lessening of inflationary pressure, through a wage price linkage, namely, productivity.

During the 1950s and early 1960s, when the Phillips curve was just being discussed by economists, Arthur Okun noted that the macroeconomic statistics conformed to a close relationship between unemployment and GNP. An increase of one percentage point in unemployment was associated with a decrease of three percentage points in GNP. His colleagues were so impressed by the strength of this relationship that it came to be called Okun's law. But the three-to-one relationship broke down in the 1970s, when productivity increases came to a halt and when there was a surge in the labor force. Extremely simple relationships, particularly bivariate correlations, often look "impressive" for a relatively brief span of time and then break down, just when the investigator convinces himself that he has found a basic law and starts to apply it in the policy process. Economics is like that, and the tests of time in replication, statistical significance, and relative frequency of correct forecast provide exacting batteries of tests that are difficult to pass. To qualify as an economic law, one must ultimately establish more than a decade or two of high correlation. Okun's law is an interesting item of curiosity, but it is not a fundamental economic law, any more than the two-to-one ratio between black and white unemployment rates which has roughly prevailed in the United States for many years.

Finally, in this review of some important economic laws, I come to the laws of the business cycle. In this field there may be many laws about the duration, amplitude, lead-lag patterns, and other characteristics, but the proposition that I find most fascinating is the "law of the sinusoidal limit." This phenomenon, due independently to R. Frisch, G. Yule, and E. Slutsky, is a mathematical result that shows how iterated averaging (smoothing) of an erratic time series transforms it into a sine wave. Frisch was the most astute in seeing how this probability process relates to dynamic economic life, but the greatest meaning has been given to the business cycle content of this idea by Irma Adelman, who showed how stochastic simulation of macroeconometric models produced regular maintained cycles, where only severely damped oscillations existed in a deterministic mode.[10] Subsequent studies have extended, replicated, and verified Professor Adelman's findings. This line of reasoning provides statistical and analytical evidence about the existence of the business cycle; it makes the cycle system-free and an aspect of the dynamic-stochastic nature of economic life. This line of research provides convincing evidence of the existence and explanation of the business cycle as a fundamental law of economic dynamics, just at a time when some economists thought that they had laid the cycle to rest — the finetuners of the 1960s and others felt that they were about to do so; more recently, the supply siders and other exponents of "Reaganomics."

In the 1960s, the view of the conquering of the cycle prompted the Committee on Economic Stability of the Social Science Research Council to convene an international meeting entitled "Is the Business Cycle Obsolete?" Fortunately, the participants found the cycle very much alive (though weakened in amplitude) just prior to the recurrence of a fresh downturn, in 1969. The absence of a cycle for nine years during the 1960s was a short-run statistical event that prompted the premature feeling of having abolished the cycle.

Two upper turning points in the next decade and two already in the 1980s (U.S.A.) have made us keenly aware of the presence of the business cycle and have even revived discussion of a recurrence of major depression, which we have not seen for about one-half century.

But the importance of the laws of economics is not easily learned. On more than one public occasion, I have pointed out to senior members of the Administration's economic team that they planned a five-year expansion of the economy in 1981 without allowance for the existence of a recession in normal cyclical fashion. To my amazement, they replied that they would, by their policies, obliterate the business cycle. Woe to the political economist who thinks that he can defy the laws of economics, for it is the onset of the 1981 recession that caused their program to unravel. Has not the same thing been happening to our British colleagues, not to mention the Poles?

---

[10]I. and F. Adelman, "The dynamic properties of the Klein–Goldberger model," *Econometrica* **27** (1959), pp. 596–625.

Some Qualitative Laws

For the most part, I have been discussing quantitative or numerical laws of economics: labor's share, the income elasticity of food consumption, the distribution of income, equality of real interest, and growth rates, but I have also mentioned some very general laws such as the law of supply and demand. Some economists would eschew attempts at careful measurement and related policy recommendations based on statistical estimates of the laws of economics. They prefer to state the laws in qualitative or directional terms, relying on the unseen hand of the free market process to give guidance to the economy.

In discussion of the present fashions in supply side economics (SSE), interpreted as responses to large-scale tax cuts, it has been noted that the proponents of SSE could point to logical arguments in support of the directions of effects big enough and fast enough to make their recommendations work as expected? Unfortunately, for the economic health of our nation, I fear that reliance on qualitative laws is inadequate in this case and that the effects are too small and too slow to achieve the desired objectives.

At a conference on supply side economics, Milton Friedman declared that it was not particularly a matter of the specialized concepts of SSE but simply a matter of "good" economics. "Good" economics would tell us that demand curves slope downwards (respond negatively to price) and that supply curves slope upwards (respond positively to price). Armed with these two qualitative laws, economists could recommend sensible policies. There is a great deal of merit to this point of view, even though it did not work out as planned during 1981–82.

High energy prices eventually induced conservation and general restriction of demand so that a significant contribution has been made to the lessening of the overriding importance of energy for the functioning of the economy, especially for the reduction of imports.

When the dollar was depreciated during 1977–79, people were very impatient in wanting to see an improvement in the current account balance of the United States. In the early stages of the currency depreciation we were the victims of the J-curve effect. The relevant international balances moved in a perverse direction because of lags and incomplete pass-throughs of exchange rate changes, but eventually the laws of economics showed through, and the current account responded positively, possibly exaggerating the movement towards surplus and a stronger dollar.

As another example of negatively sloped demand functions, we should consider the response of demand for houses, cars, and capital goods in the face of high interest rates during 1980–82. In an expected way, demand fell markedly and the high rates helped to generate a recession. In these three examples — energy, trade, and durable goods — demand was sensitive to price. As prices rose, demand fell or as prices fell demand rose. The expected effects occurred in all cases.

Consider now the other side of the qualitative proposition: Supply responds positively to price. In this respect, high energy prices induced more drilling and exploration for energy. It also got some projects on synthetics under way. Supplies were significantly increased, as expected.

According to SSE, lower tax rates make after-tax rewards (wages and interest) more attractive. There should be more effort and more savings. We cannot yet see these two things, but they could appear with some time delay.

But Milton Friedman neglected to point out that supply curves do not always slope upwards. In economics, there is a law of the backward bending supply curve of labor. If wage rates are sufficiently high, people may supply less effort because it is easier for them to meet spending targets, and they may enjoy leisure a great deal. If taxes are cut too far, we may find in a qualitative sense a reversal of the shape of the supply curve of effort. This may be one reason why the econometric estimates of labor supply are so pessimistic about the strength of the effect in the interests of SSE.

Summary and Conclusion

There *are* laws of economics. The degree of uncertainty shown by the noise component is not always appreciated by the outsider. If for some reason or another people have been led to expect too much from an economic analysis of a problem they may conclude that there are no laws of economics or that economists are not properly interpreting them. A realistic understanding of what some typical laws of economics are and the degree of uncertainty that must be involved in drawing conclusions from them should indicate that important nontrivial laws exist and that they can be used to good advantage, even if not to the satisfaction of all.

It is not easy to establish laws of economics, and it is especially dangerous to draw strong conclusions or base important decisions on apparent correlations, especially in simple bivariate relationships that are discerned in small samples or other sources of limited evidence. Many of these apparent laws break down on embarrassing occasions.

The laws of economics will rarely be sharp enough to allow us to make correct judgments 95 percent of the time within narrow quantitative limits, say plus or minus 5 percent. Economic assessments must be placed within much wider error bands; otherwise our conclusions will be so general as to be nonoperational or even empty. Realistic targets for the band of validity of economic judgments based on the laws of economics should be perhaps to aim for correctness two-thirds of the time with precision bands of plus or minus 10 percent.

2

WHAT IS MACROECONOMICS?[†]

Some economists are reported to claim that there is no such thing as *macroeconomics* in its own right. There is *microeconomics*, which is correctly reasoned and which can be summed appropriately, in order to derive statements about the macroeconomy. In my own university, there is a tragic state of affairs — by virtue of the democratic principle of majority rule — which sought to permit a beginning student to get credit for one semester of microeconomics without successfully completing a semester of macroeconomics; but not to get credit for a semester of the latter without successfully completing a semester of the former. Students were formerly required to complete both semesters in order to get credit, and there was an attempt to obtain relaxation of this rule in a non-symmetrical fashion. Sometimes, democracy can produce strange results. Eventually the forces of reason were victorious but only after a temporary vote against macroeconomics.

I intend to argue in this lecture that *macroeconomics* is, indeed, a subject by itself, and it goes without saying that students ought to get credit for a semester of either subject, micro or macro, without the other.

There should be microeconomic foundations for macroeconomics, but important parts of macroeconomics have no counterpart in microeconomics, and it is not always possible to obtain satisfactory microeconomic foundations for every aspect of macroeconomics. It may not necessarily be a good research strategy to develop macroeconomics by a summation of microeconomic propositions, but we cannot judge that issue without first understanding what macroeconomics is all about.

Micro- and Macroeconomics Described

The economy is composed of atomistic units. They are households, firms, nonprofit institutions, and public offices or agencies. These units are people or are peopled. Also the economy consists of individual goods and services that are produced and consumed (or held) by these atomistic units. The individual goods and services are exchanged in markets or by the directives of central planners. The working of the microeconomy is described or analyzed at levels. At a partial level, the behavior of atomistic units is analyzed and cast into a theoretical mold. The theory of household behavior, the theory of the firm and the theory of market clearing,

---

[†]From *Monetary Theory and Thought*, eds. H. Barkai, S. Fischer, and N. Liviatan (The Macmillan Press, London, 1993), pp. 35–51.

constitute microeconomic analysis in the 'Western' economy. The corresponding issues are different for the centrally planned economy.

At the general, as opposed to partial, level the analysis of the microeconomy is described by the Walrasian system. This model of *general* equilibrium shows how optimising agents trade goods on markets to establish prices at which markets clear. The partial analyses of microeconomics are used in order to obtain relations that imply optimality, and market clearing is used in order to complete the analysis through the determination of prices. The Walrasian system is conceptually a mathematical system of simultaneous equations, and its solution shows the atomistic levels of consumption, production, asset/liability holding; and prices of all goods and services in the economy.

There are two aspects of this model that should be distinguished in the present discussion, namely the *general* or *simultaneous* nature of the system and the *equilibrium* nature of the system. While the latter aspect is an important property and central to the interpretation of market clearing prices, it is not the main issue in drawing a distinction between micro- and macroeconomics. Simultaneity is important because macroeconomics *must* involve feedback throughout the system being studied. Feedback or indirect effects are so important that they cannot, usefully, be left out of consideration. On the other hand, microeconomics, for a good part, studies behavior of individual units in situations where *other things are assumed to be given*, especially market clearing prices or rates, and feedback is neglected.[1]

The Walrasian system is very large, numbering more equations and variables than one can imagine, but it can be given a very elegant representation as in the celebrated Arrow–Debreu (1954) theorem. It is very restrictive in that all the assumptions of perfect competition are used in order to get meaningful results, and it is clearest as a static analysis. The partial analyses of microeconomics can more readily encompass imperfections and dynamics.[2]

Some powerful conclusions can be drawn from Walrasian microeconomics, the most important being the assertion of Pareto optimality of the economy under the stringent assumptions of market perfection. The system is so complicated and so detailed that other conclusions are hard to draw. It is certainly not a practical system. In partial analysis, many more conclusions can be reached, but they are all incomplete; they depend on unknown and unspecified feedbacks from the total system that are often incorrectly assumed away by holding some variables, like price, constant when they really are not.

In some cases the feedbacks may be small; so very good approximations can be made from partial analysis, but microeconomists are not always good at showing or knowing when the feedbacks do not matter. It is also important to realize that Pareto optimality is a weak proposition. It tells one little or nothing about the income or wealth distribution, and that is a problem that permeates microeconomics,

---

[1] This is the basis for Lerner's (1962) distinction.
[2] Lerner (1962) noted that Joan Robinson and Edward Chamberlin made only limited departures from the restrictive assumptions of competitive microeconomics.

namely, an inadequate treatment of distributional effects. It will also be shown that it is a problem of macroeconomics, but it will be argued that this forms the crucial link between the two branches and makes it inherently difficult but not impossible to derive macroeconomics from microeconomics.

It always seemed to me that the central planners wanted (or should have wanted) to use the power of the computer to emulate the workings of the market from the general equilibrium version of microeconomics. They were never successful in doing this, but possibly they were using the wrong underlying model. They seem to be concluding, at least in the present generation, that it is better to establish the market itself instead of making computer approximations for control planning directives.

Macroeconomics deals essentially with the economy as a whole. Perceptive macroeconomists do try to take feedback effects into account although there is far too much uncareful analysis that takes some key macroeconomic magnitudes as given when they really are not.

In analogy with the Walrasian approach, macroeconomics deals with systems of simultaneous equations in which the variables are interrelated. The difference is that the systems are small. Systems of fewer than ten equations or even as many as 20000 are small in the Walrasian sense, but the ability to deal in a practical sense with systems as large as 100 simultaneous equations actually waited for the introduction of the high-speed electronic computer.

Two key features of macroeconomics are: (a) aggregation over atomistic agents; (b) aggregation over goods and services. In his important book on aggregation, Theil (1954) deals with three kinds of aggregation, including time aggregation with (a) and (b). Aggregation over time poses significant analytical and statistical problems but it is not an inherent feature of macroeconomics. Both microeconomics and macroeconomics should be dynamic and, for some purposes, as finely divided into time units as possible; the focus in this paper will be on aggregation over agents and goods/services. The typical variable of a microeconomic formulation should be written as:

x_{ijt} = Consumption, production, or holding of the ith commodity by the jth agent, at time period t.

Macroeconomic magnitudes are:

$x_{..t}$ = Aggregated consumption, production, or holding of commodities by the community of agents at time t.

$x_{.jt}$ = Aggregated consumption, production, or holding of commodities by the jth agent at time t.

$x_{i.t}$ = Consumption, production or holding of the ith commodity by the community of agents at time t.

In order to aggregate over i, commodities must be reckoned in common units, such as monetary units, energy units, weight units, and so on. This introduces index problems for measuring appropriately a macro price or a macro quantity.

In order to aggregate over j, agents must be reckoned in common units, such as persons, equivalent adults, net worth, acreage. Often, aggregation is made over all households, treating each one as equivalent or weighting by number of persons per household. This is practical and simple but does not always lead to accurate macroeconomic analysis.

Admittedly, variables like $x_{.jt}$ and $x_{i.t}$ lie between atomistic quantities and complete macro quantities, but they do have significant macroeconomic content. Frequently they are treated as though they are microeconomic magnitudes, pure and simple.

There is a received theory of microeconomics exemplified by utility maximisation at the household level or the institutional level, profit maximisation at the firm level, and market clearing involving the interaction of all agents.

Until the onset of the *Keynesian Revolution*, macroeconomics was not considered to be a separate branch of specialization in economics, but what is now called macroeconomics was a definite part of economic literature and application of economic policy. The Keynesian system was formalized into systems of simultaneous equations and macroeconomic analysis developed as a separate subject for studying either the systems or specific aggregate magnitudes. The Keynesian Model was merely a trigger for the development of macroeconomics as a separate subject. Many competing model or competing components of models are in the history of economics.

Some typical macroeconomic relationships that have a time-honored place in the history of thought are:

(a) The acceleration principle

$$I_t = \alpha \delta(GNP)_t .$$

Real net investment (summed over enterprises and types of capital goods) is proportional to the change in GNP. I_t and $(GNP)_t$ are in constant prices, being calculated according to index theory.

(b) The quantity equation of money

$$M_{it}(\$) = k_i[GNP(\$)]_t .$$

The stock of cash balances of type i held by households, institutions, and enterprises is proportional to GNP. Both $M_{it}(\$)$ and $[GNP(\$)]_t$ are measured in current dollar (nominal) units. The factor of proportionality depends on the kind of cash balance being considered.

Other such relationships as the wage share of GNP, the savings income ratio, the Phillips curve relationship connecting wage change to unemployment, and the labor force participation rate are also important macroeconomic relationship. These relationships make sense; they have empirical bases, particularly in extended multi-variate form; they are based on logical *a priori* reasoning. They were not originally derived from some optimization process, but after they were used extensively, they were rationalized by a traditional microeconomic analysis for the *representative* agent.

The Keynesian Model that was constructed in order to interpret the arguments of the *General Theory of Employment, Interest, and Money*, used some of these relationships or others that are quite similar. They assemble into a consistent set of simultaneous equations, whose analysis essentially constitutes macroeconomics. These systems, Keynesian or other, stand by themselves, although they can be rationalized, after the fact, by microeconomics. There may be some relationships that were first derived by microeconomic analysis and then given a macroeconomic interpretation, but they are, at best, rare. The general procedure in the history of economic thinking is to observe empirical regularities, then create an explanatory rationalization. These rationalizations have not typically come from microeconomic theory, but some have, after other rationalizations were first put forward.

Prior to the *Keynesian Revolution*, macroeconomics was not taught in American academic institutions as a subject under that title; the same material was covered in classes on *business cycles*. Now, business cycles are studied from the point of view of their being generated by macroeconomic systems. In macroeconometrics, with appropriate introduction of stochastic components, this procedure has been very productive and illuminating.[3] In a nonstochastic mode, but using critical nonlinearities, cyclical results in macroeconomics were obtained by Hicks, Frisch, Goodwin, Kaldor, Kalecki and Tinbergen.

Let us consider the concept of business cycles. According to the underlying theory, there is a peculiar inherent dynamic rhythm to the macroeconomy. In the leading statistical compendium of U.S. cyclical information, *Business Conditions Digest (BCD)*, there are hundreds of statistical series presented every month, but they are mainly macroeconomic magnitudes.[4] Referring back to the notation $x_{..t}$, $x_{i.t}$, the entries can be interpreted in terms of the types of aggregation implied by the subscripts to these variables. The cyclical content of the analysis provided by *BCD* is in the lead–lag structure of the data with respect to a reference cycle. The reference cycle, itself, is a macroeconomic composite and not microeconomic. The lead–lag relationships are not deduced by optimization theory of microeconomics: they follow from the technical organization of economic activity such as the time required to fill orders, make deliveries, plan structures, etc. Business cycles are the result of the combined action of all atomistic agents, but this result is not apparent in microeconomic theory; it is an aggregative outcome.

---

[3] See Adelman and Adelman (1959) and Klein (1973).

[4] Unfortunately, the U.S. government is planning to suspend publication of *BCD*, as an ill-conceived economy move.

The composition of business cycles can usefully be split into the internal dynamics of the simultaneous equation system (the *propagation* aspect, according to Ragnar Frisch) and the external shocks (the *impulse* aspect). The leads and lags account for part of the make up of the cycle, as explained already, but the stochastic component, the shocks, are random disturbances to the economy which have meaning as the summation of countless individualistic factors. The micro aspects of these factors are tiny and not observable; it is only their aggregate effect that can be estimated. Probability theory can explain their distribution as the sum of many individualistic items. The time patterns, in moving average representation, of random variables tend to be cyclical. There are micro components to this analysis, but all we can deal with through estimation is the macro outcome in the form of limit processes — law of large numbers and sinusoidal limits. These are essentially macroeconomic and unrelated to optimization theory.

The Role of Distribution Theory

There are techniques for deriving macroeconomic propositions from microeconomics. The whole corpus of macroeconomics cannot be so derived, but much of it can. In the process of designing and specifying macroeconomics in this way, many complications are introduced and it may not be the best procedure even though it could be a correct procedure. Three procedures form the bridge between microeconomics and macroeconomics. They are: (a) representative agent specification; (b) index construction; (c) introduction of distribution functions.

By representative agent specification, I mean that macroeconomic relationships are designed as close analogs of microeconomic specifications. A microeconomic specification states that the individual firm produces up to the point that marginal revenue equals marginal cost. Is there a corresponding macroeconomic relationship? Macro marginal revenue and macro marginal cost are not well defined concepts, although they are often used as though they are. It might be assumed, for example, that all firms are similar and have the same kind of technological constraint, face the same kind of demand function for outputs and face the same kind of factor supply function for inputs. The relationships for the representative firm are taken to be those for the macroeconomy. The conditions for the correctness of this procedure are severely restrictive. A sufficient condition is that if all prices facing the agents move in fixed proportion, many micro propositions hold at the aggregate level. Interesting and elegant theorems can be established along these lines, but they are not useful in making correct or perceptive macroeconomic judgments because the assumptions do not hold; they are ridiculous. It is relatively easy to build, from micro principles, a complete macro system based on representative agent reasoning, but it would not be a useful system.

Macroeconomic systems are not unique. There is more than one way to represent a macroeconomy. Each such representation is an approximation of the real world. The representative agent approximation is a poor and weak approximation. The approximations provided by (b) and (c) above are more powerful, but they are also more complicated. The economists who would derive macroeconomics from microeconomics have not faced up to the problems associated with (b) and (c).

In special cases, straightforward indexes can be constructed that transform the simultaneous equation systems of microeconomics into analog systems of macroeconomics but either the special systems that lend themselves to this transformation in a simple, transparent way are too restrictive or they imply such complicated indexes that they defy ordinary interpretation.[5] There are solutions to the problem posed in this way, but they are not easy solutions. The data requirements are overly demanding and the necessarily complicated index constructions do not exist.

A more straightforward approach is provided by (c). The microeconomic relationship

$$y_{ijt} = f_{ij}(x_{ijt}) + e_{ijt}$$

can be given a macroeconomic interpretation as

$$E(y_{it}) = \int_0^\infty f_i(x_{it})p(x_{it})dx_{it} + \int_{-\infty}^\infty e_{it}q(e_{it})de_{it}.$$

E denotes expected value (population mean)

$p(x_{it})$ = probability density of x_{it}; i is a *commodity* indicator.
$q(e_{it})$ = probability density of e_{it}; i is a *commodity* indicator.

The integration ranges over all *agent* values of x_{it} and e_{it}. In this specification, drawn from the microeconomic relation between y_{ijt} and x_{ijt}, the corresponding macroeconomic relationship depends on the distribution of x_{it} across all agents.

To be specific, by way of illustration, the distribution of income across households would affect the expected level of demand for commodity i by the household sector. This can be seen directly and explicitly from a simple Engel curve analysis. Let x_{ijt} be expenditure on the ith commodity by the jth household, and let y_{jt} be the jth household income. In this example, there is only one subscript on y_{jt} because the income variable is the same for different items of demand.

The (linear) Engel curve for the jth household is

$$x_{ijt} = \alpha_{ij} + \beta_{ij}y_{jt} + e_{ijt}.$$

This is the appropriate linear Engel curve for item i, and the parameters are assumed to vary by household. The corresponding macroeconomic equation for N households is:

$$\frac{1}{N}\sum_{j=1}^N x_{ijt} = \frac{1}{N}\sum_{j=1}^N \alpha_{ij} + \frac{1}{N}\sum_{j=1}^N \beta_{ij}y_{jt} + \frac{1}{N}\sum_{j=1}^N e_{ijt}$$

or

$$\bar{x}_{it} = \bar{\alpha}_i + \tilde{\beta}_i\bar{y}_t + \bar{e}_{it}$$

---

[5] See Klein (1946).

where

$$\tilde{\beta}_i \bar{y}_t = \left[\frac{\sum\limits_{j=1}^{N} \beta_{ij} y_{jt}}{\sum\limits_{j=1}^{N} y_{jt}} \right] \left[\frac{\sum\limits_{j=1}^{N} y_{jt}}{N} \right]$$

$\bar{x}_{it}$, $\bar{y}_t$ and $\bar{e}_{it}$ are all simple arithmetic averages, but

$$\tilde{\beta}_i = \frac{\sum\limits_{j=1}^{N} \beta_{ij} y_{jt}}{\sum\limits_{j=1}^{N} y_{jt}}$$

is a weighted arithmetic average and *depends on the distribution of income.* The weights are income shares for the jth household.[6]

If α_{ij} and β_{ij} were identical for all households, then there would be a complete analogy between the *micro* and the *macro* relations. This is, of course, restrictive and is the case that is favorable for the representative agent approximation. If β_{ij} varies across households, the correspondence between micro and macro relationships depends on the distribution of income. If the Engel curve is nonlinear, then the corresponding macro relationship depends, in general, on the distribution of income whether or not the coefficients are the same across households. The prior expression

$$\int_0^\infty f_i(x_{it}) p(x_{it}) dx_{it}$$

gives a general relationship that involves the distribution of income, whether or not the relationship belongs to a particular parametric class.

The linear expenditure system provides an interesting example of a specification that is directly derivable from optimality decisions of individual agents yet which aggregates into tractable macroeconomic relationships with appropriate use of distribution functions. This system was first put forward as a simple linear expression (linear in variables, but not in parameters) that simultaneously satisfied the standard microeconomic postulates of budget constraint, homogeneity (no 'money illusion'), and the Slutsky symmetry conditions.[7] We were quite aware of its aggregation simplicity at the time that this system was first derived. The equations are

$$p_i x_{ij} = p_i \alpha_{ij} + \beta_{ij} \left(y_j - \sum_{k=1}^{n} p_k \alpha_{kj} \right) + e_{ij}$$

$$\sum_{i=1}^{n} \beta_{ij} = 1.$$

---

[6]If the relationship were log linear instead of linear, the corresponding mean values are logarithms of geometric means.

[7]Klein and Rubin (1947–48)

The macroeconomic equation for the ith commodity can be written as

$$\frac{1}{N}\sum_{j=1}^{N} p_i x_{ij} = \frac{p_i}{N}\sum_{j=1}^{N} \alpha_{ij} + \frac{1}{N}\sum_{j=1}^{N} \beta_{ij}\left(y_i - \sum_{k=1}^{N} p_k \alpha_{kj}\right) + \frac{1}{N}\sum_{j=1}^{N} e_{ij}.$$

Since p_i does not vary by agent in this specification, the first term aggregates into a linear function of p_i ('own' price); a weighted sum of income

$$\sum_{j=1}^{N} \beta_{ij} y_i = \tilde{\beta}\bar{y}$$

Where $\tilde{\beta}$ depends on the distribution of income, as above; and a linear function of all the prices ('own' and 'others'). In more compact form, $\tilde{\beta}_i$, could be made to depend on the distribution of supernumerary income.

For this macroeconomic simplicity, it is necessary to pay the price of restrictive assumptions, namely that the agents' utility functions must all be of one restrictive class, the displaced Cobb–Douglas

$$u_j = A_j \prod_{i=1}^{n} (x_{ij} - \alpha_{ij})^{\beta_{ij}}$$

that the population of agents is fixed, that borrowing and lending has not been introduced, that the stochastic (error) term has been introduced as additive to the current price (nominal) specification.

Some of these assumptions can be absorbed into generalized specifications that lack the simplicity of the original linear expenditure system, and some are benign, but the point of this exercise is to show what must be done in order to derive macroeconomics from microeconomics, and it appears to me that the exponents of this approach to macroeconomics fail to face up to these underlying issues.

This example shows the kind of distributional problems that arise in specification of the ith demand function in a macroeconomic system, and the fact that the system is commodity-specific does not get around many of the major problems.

The linear expenditure system is also useful in showing what is involved in deriving the most macro of all demand functions, namely the aggregate consumption function, which is a centerpiece of the Keynesian system. The ith demand function must be aggregated over all commodities. It is

$$\frac{1}{N}\sum_{i=1}^{n}\sum_{j=1}^{N} p_i x_{ij} = \frac{1}{N}\sum_{i=1}^{n} p_i \sum_{j=1}^{N} \alpha_{ij} + \frac{1}{N}\sum_{i=1}^{n}\sum_{j=1}^{N} \beta_{ij}\left(y_j - \sum_{k=1}^{n} p_k \alpha_{kj}\right)$$

$$+ \frac{1}{N}\sum_{i=1}^{n}\sum_{j=1}^{N} e_{ij}.$$

This says that total expenditure is a linear function of price level (a price index, in fact) and a linear function of supernumerary income, dependent on the distribution of that income.

It is important to note that the index of the price level that is suitable for this aggregate consumption function is weighted by demand parameters that reflect the distribution of minimum or committed amounts of consumption that are used in defining supernumerary income. This is based on a very specific form of index construction.

The aggregate Keynesian consumption function depends also on interest rates. This could be introduced in the linear expenditure system if one of the items is future consumption with a price equal to the discounted level of future prices. The interest rate will affect the discounted price.

It is, therefore possible to derive a meaningful Keynesian consumption function from microeconomic behavior, but its underlying assumptions and dependence on distributional changes must be brought appropriately into the macroeconomic analyses that use this function.

The point to be made is that distribution functions, not only of income but of all variables jointly that vary across the index of summation or integration, provide a crucial link between micro- and macroeconomic relationship. Any particular parametric specification of the underlying microeconomic relationship provides only an approximation; therefore all aggregate relationships of macroeconomics are, in s sense, approximations. A macroeconomic system is just an approximation to the true Walrasian model of the microeconomy, but neglect of distributional factors when the system is nonlinear or when parameters vary over the indexes of aggregation can be serious and make for poor approximations.[8] The reasons above show why distribution functions of economic variables play such an important role for the macroeconomic approximation. It means that the macroeconomist cannot simply derive propositions by adding up microeconomic relationships or propositions. If the macroeconomist is to rely on microeconomics and aggregate analysis, then he or she must be prepared to supply the relevant distributional analysis, which can be very complicated in multivariate relationships or in sizable systems, with or without highly multivariate relationships. But much of macroeconomics involves a search for approximate relationships that will stand up robustly for analysis and be more tractable than the system that would follow from careful adding up of microeconomic relationships. It is by no means evident that good and useful macroeconomics can be derived by summation of microeconomics, and it is undoubtedly true that the exponents of this approach have made little or no contribution to the necessary distributional analysis. Representative agent analysis is mostly trivial and often misleading.

Specific useful aggregations involving well known distribution functions can be developed on the side of production as well as consumption. H. Houthakker has shown, in a paper that is all too little appreciated, that if the production possibilities are described by a set of linear, fixed proportion relationships and if the production

---

[8]The similarities between specifications with variable parameters, across agents, and with nonlinearities should become evident from this exposition.

ratios are distributed according to Pareto's law of distribution, the resulting production function is of the Cobb–Douglas type.[9] He thus marries Leontief's system of fixed proportions at the micro level, the Pareto distribution, and the Cobb–Douglas function at the macro level. His proposition can be generalized to produce other types of macro production functions.

The distributions that are relevant for the principle of aggregation for conversion of macro- to microeconomics are summaries, often expressed in terms of a few parameters of microeconomic quantities. Their distribution can be generated by stochastic processes that are guided by empirical observation, microeconomic theory, or institutional economics. They are very important and intricate, but receive all too little attention from microeconomic analysts.

Macroeconomic Policy

A great deal of economic policy is macro oriented although some of the analyses of policy are based on microeconomic theory. The traditional areas of macroeconomic policy are fiscal and monetary policy. Fiscal policy may be implemented on the expenditure side or the revenue (tax) side. For the most part, fiscal and monetary policies are aimed at large groups of people or firms. Macroeconomic impact and reaction are the main features of these policies. Individual people and firms pay taxes, receive benefits, participate in public spending activities, or engage in financial transactions. But policy makers are not, or ought not to be, interested in the individual responses, as long as people are law abiding. They should be interested in the effects on the economy as a whole. Since some policy relationships are nonlinear or otherwise distinguished by individualistic magnitudes, such as children's allowances or age-specific features of tax laws, the evaluation of the aggregate effects of policy changes will depend on underlying distributions. These may be income distributions, age distributions, family size distributions, or other distributions. The same aggregation problems involving distributions are needed in order to understand and appreciate economic policy. Fiscal policy analysis requires the same kind of distributional information that is used in Engel curve analysis for consumer expenditure studies.

When tax reform was studied and later introduced in the United States during the latter part of the 1980s, the reasoning was predominantly microeconomic, to some extent based on representative agent analysis, and to some extent combined with distribution functions, but the working of tax reform involved much more than microeconomics. There needed to be a full investigation of the macroeconomic feedbacks from market interest rates, the general price level, and overall activity.

Inadequate attention to macroeconomic effects on total collections, aggregate investment activity, and aggregate savings activity were not carefully studied. As a result some economists are asking for reconsideration of the treatment of the investment tax credit, accelerated depreciation, and savings incentives. Total activity,

---

[9] At the symposium, Zvi Griliches reminded me of Houthakker's famous paper (Houthakker, 1955).

total capital formation, and overall deficit reduction leave much to be desired as outcomes of tax reform. In this case, microeconomic focus without macroeconomic perspective produced a result that did not do as much economic good as could have been achieved.

In the case of monetary policy, authorities have several objectives. Some deal with interest rate movements, some with exchange rates and some with credit flows, but a central objective is inflation control. Inflation is defined as the upward movement of the general level of prices. That, by itself, is a macroeonomic consideration. The cause sometimes comes from specific prices, such as food and fuel, but at other times many prices move together. As long as they do not all move proportionally, a significant index problem is involved. The general index of prices is, *par excellence*, a macroeconomic magnitude. It does not refer to the prices of any particular good or subset, but to a weighted average of all prices. Money and credit market relations, except for individual portfolios, are genuine macroeconomic relationships. When all sides of the market are brought together, the outcome for final determination of the general price level, exchange rates, and interest rates are macroeconomic phenomena. Money, on the supply side of this market, is not directed at individual agents but to the economy as a whole.

Microeconomic principles have been applied to the Central Bank — the Open Market Committee of the Federal Revenue System — using decision theory to develop policy reaction functions. If we actually know the individual tastes and desires of the members of the FOMC, it would make sense to develop a policy reaction function along microeconomic lines of optimisation according to decision theory. But the composition of the FOMC changes over the years, and we do not have the means to ascertain their objective preferences. Some econometricians would use statistical inference to determine the reaction function, but there is no statistical universe that allows one to use the propositions of probability theory and the law of large numbers. The behavior of 12 people, whose composition is not constant, does not constitute a good statistical population. It is therefore very risky to try to estimate a statistical model of FOMC's reaction to macroeconomy. Conditional statements about macroeconomic effects of alternative decisions by the FOMC are useful, but they are so uncertain that it is not helpful to consider them as optimal in the same sense that behavior of atomistic agents in the total economy are assumed to try to make optimal choices in their own interest.

While fiscal and monetary policies are the main macroeconomic policies, there is considerable interest in commercial policy. By commercial policy, I mean policy that pays close attention to exports and imports with a view of keeping them in good balance. What is a good balance varies with the general economic environment, which is, in fact, a macroeconomic concept.

A simple policy rule could be to promote the interests of free trade, but this could mean the retention of free and open competition with other nations in the exporting and importing of goods and services. For the most part, free trade is commodity-specific. The appropriate policy is to prevent barriers from developing for the importation or exportation of goods and services. Since the rules apply to all exporters and all importers, i.e., to the total market, there is a dimension of aggregation involved, but unfair practices may be traced back to individual producers and consumers. There is, nevertheless, a macro dimension.

At the corresponding theoretical level, the arguments that support the policies of free trade are microeconomic arguments based on the notion of comparative advantage. The advantages concerned refer to individual traders dealing with distinct goods and services. Of course, if all production and consumption relations were identical between trading nations, the micro arguments in support of free trade would be relevant for the totality of agents in the market and for the trading economies, as wholes.

In general, however, the macroeconomic results of commercial policy are not obvious. If free trade, combined with perfect competition (within and between nations) leads to Pareto optimality, does it also lead to the maximization of GNP (nationally or worldwide)? The justification of free trade is sometimes argued on the basis of the assertion that it maximises GNP of countries or gross world product (GWP). This macroeconomic result can be examined in the context of macroeconomic models, and it has some plausibility, but it cannot be derived in any straightforward way by adding up microeconomic results.

Feedback effects from the functioning of the economy as a whole are especially important in connection with commercial policy and the analysis of the trade balance. Associated with the trade balance is the total international payments balance, covering unilateral transfers and capital flows. The total balance of payments has great significance for the determination of interest rates and currency exchange rates, both of which feedback on the payments balances themselves. These are very much macroeconomic phenomena, guided by central bank, exchequer, and total financial market decisions or movements.

One of the most important international economic developments of our time is the buildup of debt in developing countries. This is a decidedly macroeconomic issue, and has had enormous effects on economic performance of entire countries in the third world. Of course, individual borrowers and lenders concluded many of the agreements, although some were negotiated at the macro sovereign level. The issue is that the debts were negotiated, in significant amounts, at market interest rates such as LIBOR or US PRIME (plus risk premia), and the service charges, which count as invisible imports for the borrowing country, were subject to wide swings, particularly increases, as a result of worldwide rises in interest rates. These rate rises, in turn, were associated with the particular macroeconomic monetary policies chosen by leading creditor countries for fighting their own domestic inflation situations.

There is very little guidance — not zero, but small — from microeconomics for dealing with this massive problem. Negotiations among country representatives, central bankers, and supra-national organizations have been required to deal with this problem. It is a macroeconomic policy issue, *par excellence*, and solutions are not to be found in microeconomic analysis.

Other problems in international finance require negotiation and cooperation among nations. The highest form of international economic cooperation is called *policy coordination.*By coordination procedures, countries try at the macroeconomic level to moderate large discrepancies such as payment deficits, abnormal debt, or severely unequal distributions of GWP among country values of GNP. All these coordinating policies can be unraveled back to atomistic decisions, but they cannot be dealt with analytically at such a refined level. Peaceful relations among nations cannot wait upon nor live with the usual microeconomic adjustments through pure market processes. There must be macroeconomic decision making that can grasp the essence of the problem in a reasonable (manageable) number of dimensions, and cut through difficulties to a workable international solution. This is what global policy coordination is meant to achieve.

References

Adelman, F. and I., 1959, "The dynamic properties of the Klein–Goldberger model," *Econometrica* **27**, pp. 596–625.

Arrow, K. J. and Gerard Debreu, 1954, "Existence of an equilibrium for a competitive economy," *Econometrica* **22**, pp. 265–290.

Houthakker, H. S., 1955, "The Pareto distribution and the Cobb–Douglas production function in activity analysis," *The Review of Economic Studies* **XXIII**, pp. 27–31.

Klein, L. R., 1946, "Macroeconomics and the theory of rational behavior," *Econometrica* **14**, pp. 93–108.

———, 1973, "Dynamic analysis of economic systems," *International Journal of Mathematical Education in Science and Technology* **4**, pp. 341–359.

——— and H. Rubin, 1947–48, "A constant-utility index of the cost of living," *The Review of Economic Studies* **XV**, pp. 84–87.

Lerner, A. P., 1962, "Microeconomics and macroeconomics," in *Logic, Methodology and Philosophy of Sciences*, eds. E. Nagel, P. Suppes and A. Tarski (Stanford Univ. Press, Stanford, CA), pp. 474–483.

Theil, H., 1954, *Linear Aggregation of Economic Relations* (North-Holland, Amsterdam).

3

TECHNICAL APPENDIX†

A Mathematical Model of the *Treatise*

In order to get a comprehensive picture of the structure of the *Treatise*, we can best formulate a simple model of the complete system. For easy reference, we define again all the relevant variables:

I	is the market value of investment.
S	is the value of savings.
Q	is the windfall profits.
r	is the interest variable.
$\bar{r}$	is the market rate of interest.
O	is the physical volume of output.
R	is the physical volume of consumption.
C	is the physical volume of investment.
E	is the incomes paid out to the factors of production.
Π	is the price level of output as a whole.
P	is the price level of consumption goods.
P'	is the price level of investment goods.
M_3	is the stock of savings deposits.
M_2	is the stock of business deposits.
M_1	is the stock of income deposits.
V_1	is the income velocity of circulation.

Wicksell defined the natural rate of interest as either that rate which achieves price stability or that which equates savings and investment. Keynes applied this idea to his definitions of savings and investment to get the equation

$$S(r) = I(r)$$

whose solution in r determines the natural rate of interest. Actual or observable savings-investment which occurs in the market may be quite different from that calculated by substituting the natural rate in the savings or the investment function. Observable investment would be

$$S(\bar{r}) + Q(\bar{r}) = I(\bar{r})$$

---

†From *The Keynesian Revolution* (2nd ed., Macmillan, New York, 1966), pp. 255–279. (1st ed., 1947, pp. 189–213)

where $\bar{r}$ is the market rate, of course. Wicksell considered $\bar{r}$ as given by the banking system within limits; i.e., he stated that the banks were free to determine $\bar{r}$ as long as their reserve position enabled them always to supply the proper amount of credit corresponding to the rate set.

Keynes also assumed that the banks could determine the market rate of interest at $\bar{r}$. Furthermore he thought that they could control the volume of savings deposits, $\overline{M}_3$. These controls are certainly questionable, but let us follow the mechanical procedure of going where his assumptions lead us. The interest equation along with the others discussed in Chapter I and certain obvious relations can be written as follows:

$$I(r) = S(r)$$
$$Q = Q(r)$$
$$r = \bar{r}$$
$$\Pi O = E + Q(r)$$
$$PR = E - S(r)$$
$$M_3 = B(P')$$
$$M_3 = \overline{M}_3$$
$$O = \overline{O}$$
$$M_1 V_1 = E$$
$$V_1 = \overline{V}_1$$
$$M_1 = \overline{M}_1$$
$$C + R = O$$
$$P'C = I(\bar{r}).$$

In order, we have the savings-investment equation, the profit function, the autonomously set market rate, the "fundamental equation" for the determination of Π, the definition of savings (or, alternatively, our version of the "fundamental equation" for the determination of P), the bearishness function, the given stock of savings deposits, the given output, the definition of income velocity, the given velocity, the given stock of income deposits, the division of output into consumption goods plus investment goods, and finally a definition of the market value of investment. We now find ourselves with as many equations as variables when we distinguish between the natural and market rates as distinct variables.

The first equation can be solved for the natural rate of interest, say, r_0. Substituting the market rate in $Q(r)$, we next calculate the windfall profits. Adding the observable savings and the windfall profits, we get the actual level of investment, $S(\bar{r}) + Q(\bar{r})$ or $I(\bar{r})$. The equation of bearishness yields a solution $P' = P'_0$; furthermore the ratio $I(\bar{r})/P'_0$ gives C_0, the volume of real investment. From the equation

$$C_0 + R = \overline{O}$$

R_0, the volume of consumption, can be calculated. We are now left with three equations

$$\Pi\overline{O} = E + Q(\bar{r})$$
$$PR_0 = E - S(\bar{r})$$
$$\overline{M}_1\overline{V}_1 = E$$

to get the three variables Π, P, E. The weak point in this system is the most important element of later-Keynesian economics, namely, a theory of effective demand. A quantity equation is Keynes' sole theory of the determination of E, and the validity of this theory depends upon the assumption that the banking system can determine the stock of income deposits $\overline{M}_1$, as well as the total stock of money. Elsewhere, Keynes also put forth the "theory of effective demand" that $E/\overline{O}$ is institutionally given as efficiency earnings.

It is interesting to see that even if the "fundamental equation" for the price level of consumption goods be left as Keynes wrote it in the *Treatise*, the system does not become more or less determinate. This equation can be written, with the unwarranted assumption, as

$$P = \frac{E}{O} + \frac{I' - S}{R}$$

Where $I' = $ the cost of production of investment goods. The assumption

$$I' = E\left(\frac{C}{O}\right)$$

merely adds another equation to determine the one new variable, so that the determinateness of P is, in a sense, unaffected.

Keynes did not recognize $Q \neq 0$ as an equilibrium situation, and for the case $Q = 0$ we do get a more consistent, although strictly classical, theory. For the equilibrium position he did support the quantity theory, as the quotation in Chapter I shows. The model would now become

$$I(\bar{r}) = S(\bar{r}) \qquad\qquad \Pi\overline{O} = RP + S(\bar{r})$$
$$\overline{M}_1 = \left(\frac{1}{\overline{V}_1}\right)\Pi\overline{O} \qquad\qquad C + R = \overline{O}$$
$$\overline{M}_3 = B(P') \qquad\qquad P'C = I(\bar{r}).$$

In this case we have enough equations to determine all the free variables.

If we consider only the following self-determined part of the system,

$$I(\bar{r}) = S(\bar{r})$$
$$\overline{M}_1 = \left(\frac{1}{\overline{V}_1}\right)\Pi\overline{O}$$

we see that Keynes was as classical as he could possibly be. At the going market rate of interest, all savings flow unobstructed into investment, and the amount of money determines the price level. Full-employment output is taken as given because it comes from the background equations of the complete system.

Mathematical Derivation of the System of the *General Theory*

The Consumption Function and Liquidity-Preference Function. Consider an individual household trying to maximize its utility function, which depends on the consumption of present and future commodities, and its structure of assets in the form of money and various types of securities. The maximization process is not unrestricted. We must impose a restraining condition which states that holdings of liquid assets at the beginning of any given period, plus the interest earned on securities held during the period, plus other income not spent on commodities during the period (savings), equal the liquid assets held at the end of the period. In other words, this condition requires that the rate of change of the stock of liquid wealth shall equal savings or that the stock of liquid wealth shall equal historically accumulated savings. We ignore the possibility of holding goods (inventories) on the part of the household, but this type of behavior will be included under the investment activity of business firms.

Let us write

$$u = u(x_{11}, \ldots, x_{n1}, \ldots, x_{1T}, \ldots, x_{nT}, b_{11}, \ldots, b_{s1}, \ldots, b_{1T}, \ldots, b_{sT}, m_1, \ldots, m_T) \tag{1}$$

$$m_{t-1} + \sum_{i=1}^{s}(1 + r_{it})b_{i,t-1} + y_t - \sum_{i=1}^{n} p_{it}x_{it} = m_t + \sum_{i=1}^{s} b_{it} \quad t = 1, 2, \ldots, T \tag{2}$$

where u = utility of a particular household, x_{it} = consumption of the ith commodity in the tth period of the future; b_{it} = the holding of the ith security at the end of the tth period of the future; m_t = the holding of cash balances at the end of the tth period of the future; r_{it} = the interest rate corresponding to the ith security at the end of the $(t-1)$th period of the future; y_t = the noninterest income of the tth period of the future; p_{it} = the price of the ith commodity in the tth period of the future; T = the last period of the time horizon over which utility is maximized.

Our problem now is to maximize (1) subject to (2). First we form the function

$$\phi = u + \sum_{t=1}^{T} \lambda_t \left[m_{t-1} + \sum_{i=1}^{s}(1 + r_{it})b_{i,t-1} + y_t - \sum_{i=1}^{n} p_{it}x_{it} - m_t - \sum_{i=1}^{s} b_{it} \right].$$

Next, we derive the necessary conditions for a maximum:

$$\frac{\partial \phi}{\partial x_{it}} = \frac{\partial u}{\partial x_{it}} - \lambda_t p_{it} = 0 \tag{3}$$

$$i = 1, 2, \ldots, n; \ t = 1, 2, \ldots, T$$

$$\frac{\partial \phi}{\partial b_{it}} = \frac{\partial u}{\partial b_{it}} + \lambda_{t+1}(1 + r_{i,t+1}) - \lambda_t = 0 \tag{4}$$

$$i = 1, 2, \ldots, s; \ t = 1, 2, \ldots, T$$

$$\frac{\partial \phi}{\partial m_t} = \frac{\partial u}{\partial m_t} + \lambda_{t+1} - \lambda_t = 0 \tag{5}$$

$$t = 1, 2, \ldots, T$$

$$\lambda_{T+1} = 0 \text{ by definition}.$$

The set of equations $(3), (4), (5)$ along with the constraints in (2) enable us to solve for all the $x's$, $b's$, and $m's$ in terms of the prices, interest rates, incomes, and the initial conditions. These solutions are the demand equations for the flows of commodities and the stocks of liquid assets. We write them as

$$x_{it} = x_{it}(p_{11}, \ldots, p_{nT}, r_{11}, \ldots, r_{sT}, y_1, \ldots, y_T, m_0, b_{10}, \ldots b_{s0}) \tag{6}$$

$$i = 1, 2, \ldots, n; \ t = 1, 2, \ldots, T$$

$$b_{it} = b_{it}(p_{11}, \ldots, p_{nT}, r_{11}, \ldots, r_{sT}, y_1, \ldots, y_T, m_0, b_{10}, \ldots, b_{s0}) \tag{7}$$

$$i = 1, 2, \ldots, s; \ t = 1, 2, \ldots, T$$

$$m_t = m_t(p_{11}, \ldots, P_{nT}, r_{11}, \ldots, r_{sT}, y_1, \ldots, y_T, m_0, b_{10}, \ldots, b_{s0}) \tag{8}$$

$$t = 1, 2, \ldots, T.$$

The form of the constraints (2) are such that the separate variables $y_1, m_0, b_{10}, \ldots,$ $b_{s0}, r_{11} \ldots r_{sl}$ always occur in the particular form

$$m_0 + \sum_{i=1}^{s}(1 + r_{i1})b_{i0} + y_1 . \tag{9}$$

Our model is dynamic because it represents a maximization over a future time period. The whole complex of future prices, interest rates, income, etc., must be based on the personal anticipations of the individual household. We shall assume that the anticipated future time pattern of any variable is a function of the past and current history of that variable. In a discrete model this historial pattern can be represented by a function of all the lagged values of the particular variable in question. A model with lagged variables will give us a dynamic Keynesian system, but for our purposes of comparative statics we shall assume that all the lags are zero and hence work only with current values of all the variables; hence let us rewrite $(6), (7), (8)$ statically as

$$x_i = x_i(p_1, \ldots, p_n, r_1, \ldots, r_s, y, a) \tag{10}$$

$$i = 1, 2, \ldots, n;$$

$$b_i = b_i(p_1, \ldots, p_n, r_1, \ldots, r_s, y, a) \tag{11}$$

$$i = 1, 2, \ldots, s;$$

$$m = m(p_1, \ldots, p_n, r_1, \ldots, r_s, y, a) \tag{12}$$

where[1]

$$a = m + \sum_{i=1}^{s} b_i.$$

Define consumption as

$$\sum_{i=1}^{n} p_i x_i = c \tag{13}$$

and total security holdings as

$$\sum_{i=1}^{s} b_i = b. \tag{14}$$

If we have a suitable aggregation procedure, we can write

$$c = c(p, r, y, a) \tag{15}$$
$$b = b(p, r, y, a) \tag{16}$$
$$m = m(p, r, y, a) \tag{17}$$

in which r and p are the interest and price aggregates respectively. If we further impose the customary homogeneity conditions on our demand equations, they become

$$c/p = c^*(r, y/p, a/p) \tag{15a}$$
$$b/p = b^*(r, y/p, a/p) \tag{16a}$$
$$m/p = m^*(r, y/p, a/p). \tag{17a}$$

Suppose that these equations are linear, as family-budget data suggest.

$$c/p = d_0 + d_1 r + d_2 y/p + d_3 a/p \tag{15b}$$
$$b/p = e_0 + e_1 r + e_2 y/p + e_3 a/p \tag{16b}$$
$$m/p = f_0 + f_1 r + f_2 y/p + f_3 a/p. \tag{17b}$$

The community[2] demand functions follow by summation over all individuals. Consider (15b), for example, with all variables pertaining specifically to the individual household marked with a subscript i.

$$\sum_i c_i/p = \sum_i d_{0i} + \left(\sum_i d_{1i} \right) r + \frac{\sum_i d_{2i} y_i}{\sum_i y_i} \frac{\sum_i y_i}{p} + \frac{\sum_i d_{3i} a_i}{\sum_i a_i} \frac{\sum_i a_i}{p} \tag{18}$$

$$C/p = d_4 + d_5 r + d_6 Y/p + d_7 A/p$$

---

[1] The appropriate variable is a because the only component of (9) which does not involve anticipated values is $m_0 + \sum_{i=1}^{s} b_{i0}$.

[2] The reader should remember that we have been dealing with the individual household thus far.

where

$$d_4 = \sum_i d_{0i}; d_5 = \sum_i d_{1i}; d_6 = \frac{\sum_i d_{2i}y_i}{\sum_i y_i}; d_7 = \frac{\sum_i d_{3i}a_i}{\sum_i a_i}$$

$$C = \sum_i c_i; Y = \sum_i y_i; A = \sum_i a_i.$$

Similarly we obtain

$$B/p = e_4 + e_5r + e_6Y/P + e_7A/P \tag{19}$$

$$M/p = f_4 + f_5r + f_6Y/p + f_7A/p. \tag{20}$$

The variable A/p is equal to $M/p + B/P$. We can, obviously, eliminate B/p between (18), (19), and (20) to get

$$C/p = d_8 + d_9r + d_{10}Y/p + d_{11}M/p \tag{18a}$$

$$M/p = f_8 + f_9r + f_{10}Y/p. \tag{20a}$$

These are the usual Keynesian consumption function and liquidity preference function respectively. In most cases, we assume, however, $d_{11} = 0$. Some empirical evidence supports this view.[3] Another method of transforming (18) and (20) directly into the Keynesian equations is to consider A/p as representative of the aggregate real wealth of the community. If this real wealth is capable of producing the income stream Y/p, we can write

$$A/p = \frac{Y/p}{r} \tag{21}$$

which is the capitalization, at the going interest rate, of the income which the wealth of the community produces. By substituting (21) into (18) and (20), we can eliminate A/p as a separate variable of the system.

If income and consumption are variables of the system, we have the definition

$$S/p \equiv Y/p - C/p \equiv -d_4 - d_5r + (1 - d_6)Y/p - d_7A/p \tag{22}$$

in which $S =$ savings.

Equation (22) is the savings function. It is redundant to use both the savings function and the consumption function in the system.

It should be noted that in the above derivations the variable y was called non-interest income. However, in the constraining equation (2), interest income and noninterest income always enter additively; hence we can consider (10), (11), (12) as solved in terms of income including interest as well as in terms of noninterest income. Equations (18) and (20) are more convenient if the variable Y includes interest income. It should also be noted that d_6, d_7, e_6, e_7, f_6, and f_7 are weighted averages of individual parameters, the weights being the individual money incomes

---

[3] See L. R. Klein, "A post-mortem on transition predictions of national product," *Journal of Political Economy* **LIV**, (1946), p. 289.

or liquid assets. If the distribution of income and that of wealth do not change radically over short periods, these weighted averages may be regarded as stable parameters of the system rather than as variables.

The *Investment Function, General Case*. The entrepreneur will be assumed to behave, with regard to the purchase of capital assets, according to the principles of profit maximization over the anticipated future life of the asset in question. The anticipated profits which are to be maximized can be written as

$$\pi = \int_0^T (py - wN)e^{-p\theta}\,d\theta - q\left(\frac{I}{q}\right) \tag{23}$$

where p = price level of output, y = volume of output, w = wage rate, N = employment, ρ = discount rate, T = entrepreneurial horizon, q = price of new capital goods, I = money value of investment.[‡]

The last term is not included under the integral sign because it represents an outlay on durable equipment, which will produce goods and services over the whole horizon. The input of labor and the output of goods will be flows coming forth during the entire period $(0, T)$, but the capital outlay will be made once and for all at the beginning of the planning period. Other terms, such as the market value of existing capital, could also appear in the profit function although they have no influence on the maximizing conditions.

The rational entrepreneur will now behave so as to maximize π subject to the production function

$$y = y\left(N, \frac{I}{q}, K\right)^4 \tag{24}$$

where $K = \int_{-\infty}^0 (I/q)\,d\theta$, the accumulated volume of capital at the beginning of the period. The resulting maximization condition will be

$$\frac{\partial \pi}{\partial\left(\frac{I}{q}\right)} = \int_0^T p\left(1 - \frac{1}{\eta}\right)\frac{\partial y}{\partial\left(\frac{I}{q}\right)}e^{-p\theta}\,d\theta - q = 0 \tag{25}$$

when η = elasticity of demand. This equation establishes a relation between p, y, N, K, ρ, q, and I/q, which can be called the investment function or the schedule of the marginal efficiency of capital. The term under the integral is the discounted stream of future returns expected to be realized from the use of the newly purchased capital equipment, I/q. The discount rate, ρ, is that rate which discounts this stream to the current purchase price of new capital, q. This is precisely Keynes' formulation of the marginal efficiency of capital.

---

[4]We write the production function this way in order to show technological distinction between new and old capital. The distinction can be carried much further to show the technological differences between capital goods of all age groups. The function (24) is a convenient compromise between the most general case and the case where no distinction is made.[*]

The demand for labor, as well as new capital, follows in a similar fashion from this model of profit maximization. We can maximize profits with respect to small variations in labor input. This leads to

$$\frac{\partial \pi}{\partial N} = p \left(1 - \frac{1}{\eta}\right) \frac{\partial y}{\partial N} - w = 0 . \tag{26}$$

The marginal value productivity of labor is equated to the wage rate, giving us the demand schedule for labor.[5]

The Investment Function, Special Case. There are two unknown functions which enter into the make-up of the marginal efficiency of capital, the elasticity of demand and the marginal productivity of new capital. We know the elasticity of demand in the case of perfect competition, but if competition is assumed to be imperfect we can simplify the problem by assuming the elasticity coefficient to be constant. In view of much empirical evidence that constant elasticity demand functions fit the observed data well, the latter assumption is not bad. We also have much empirical evidence concerning the production function. A slight variation of the familiar Cobb–Douglas production function to the form

$$y = BN^\alpha \left(\gamma_1 K + \gamma_2 \frac{I}{q}\right)^\beta e^{g(t)} \tag{27}$$

is consistent with the output–input data of many industries and also of the economy as a whole.

By making use of these two empirical facts and substituting in our profit-maximizing equation, we obtain

$$\frac{\partial \pi}{\partial \left(\frac{I}{q}\right)} = \int_0^T p \left(1 - \frac{1}{\eta}\right) \frac{\beta \gamma_2 y}{\gamma_1 K + \gamma_2 \left(\frac{I}{q}\right)} e^{-p\theta} d\theta - q = 0 . \tag{28}$$

Let us assume that the entrepreneur who does not know the value of the integrand over each time period of the horizon anticipates the integrand to take on the same value (current value) for each time point of this horizon. We then have

$$q = \beta \gamma_2 \left(1 - \frac{1}{\eta}\right) \frac{py}{\gamma_1 K + \gamma_2 \left(\frac{I}{q}\right)} \int_0^T e^{-p\theta} d\theta \tag{29}$$

$$\frac{I}{q} = \beta \left(1 - \frac{1}{\eta}\right) \frac{py}{q} \frac{1}{\rho} (1 - e^{-T\rho}) - \frac{\gamma_1}{\gamma_2} K .$$

[5]In this demonstration we have assumed a very simplified type of economy. To say that firms maximize the profit function (23) is not as realistic as it should be; some firms, as well as households, are concerned about the structure of their assets. A more complete theory should assume that firms maximize a utility function which depends on the time patterns of future profits, of the stock of fixed capital, of the stock of liquid assets, of the stock of inventories. The more general theory leads to many more equations in the micro-system — but can also be reduced to macro-systems like that of Keynes'. We have merely attempted to demonstrate simple theories that lead to the Keynesian system. In the case of the theory of the household, we could not have been much less general, because we had to show the foundations of the theory of liquidity preference, which is not possible without introducing the asset structure specifically.

This is our Keynesian investment function. If $p = q$ or $p = vq$, then we get the customary version of the Keynesian function

$$\frac{I}{p} = \beta \left(1 - \frac{1}{\eta} \right) y \frac{1}{\rho} (1 - e^{-T\rho}) - \frac{\gamma_1}{\gamma_2} K \tag{30}$$

or

$$\frac{I}{p} = f(y, \rho, K).$$

We can also write this result in terms of money values instead of real values to get

$$I = f^*(py, \rho, qK). \tag{31}$$

In all the short-run theories, we assume that K or qK is given by the past history of the system and enters only as a parameter in the investment function. We also assume that we can write r, the interest rate, for ρ because the difference between the two can only be accounted for by subjective risk elements which are not to be explained by our theory and must be taken as given.

We can also see clearly why the investment function is likely to be interest-inelastic as the horizon, T, is shortened, which we believe to be the case today.

$$\frac{\partial \left(\frac{I}{p} \right)}{\partial \rho} = -\beta \left(1 - \frac{1}{\eta} \right) \frac{y}{\rho^2} (1 - e^{-T\rho}) + \beta \left(1 - \frac{1}{\eta} \right) \frac{y}{\rho} T e^{-T\rho}$$

$$= \beta \left(1 - \frac{1}{\eta} \right) \frac{y}{\rho} \left[T e^{-T\rho} - \frac{1}{\rho} (1 - e^{-T\rho}) \right] \tag{32}$$

$$\frac{\partial^2 \left(\frac{I}{p} \right)}{\partial \rho \partial T} = \beta \left(1 - \frac{1}{\eta} \right) \frac{y}{\rho} (-T\rho e^{-T\rho}) < 0. \tag{33}$$

Investment is less sensitive to the discount rate as the period $(0, T)$ is contracted, because the *absolute value* of $\partial \left(\frac{I}{p} \right) / \partial \rho$ falls with declining T.

The steps which were completed in order to derive the Keynesian investment function can be considered to apply either to the individual firm or to the community. The justification for their application to the community is based on the theory that the profit maximizing equations of microeconomics hold in analogy for the macro-system if the aggregates of the latter system are properly measured.[6]

Mathematical Models of Keynesian and Classical Economics

In order to compare two different economic theories, it is very helpful to construct mathematical skeletons of the system supported by each theory. The differences in analytical structure between these two skeletons should show clearly the essential differences between the two theories.

---

[6]See L. R. Klein, "Macroeconomics and the theory of rational behavior," *Econometrica* **XIV** (1946), p. 93.

The most general form of the Keynesian system consists of the savings-investment equation, the liquidity-preference equation, and the background relations from the real part of the system. It can be written as follows:

$$S(r, Y) = I(r, Y) \tag{34}$$

$$M = L(r, Y) \tag{35}$$

$$Y = py \tag{36}$$

$$y = y(N) \tag{37}$$

$$w = p \left(1 - \frac{1}{\eta} \right) y'(N) \tag{38}$$

$$N = F(w) \tag{39}$$

where S = money savings, I = money investment, M = the stock of cash balances, r = the interest rate, Y = money income, y = real income, p = the price level, N = employment, w = the wage rate, η = the elasticity of demand.[7] In this short-run model we assume that the stock of capital is given, i.e., $K = \overline{K}$. It is further assumed that these equations have particular shapes. Specifically,

$$\frac{\partial S}{\partial r} \geqq 0 \text{ and small in absolute value}$$

$$\frac{\partial S}{\partial Y} > 0$$

$$\frac{\partial I}{\partial r} \leqq 0 \text{ and small in absolute value}$$

$$\frac{\partial I}{\partial Y} > 0$$

$$\frac{\partial L}{\partial r} < 0 \text{ and large in absolute value}$$

$$\frac{\partial L}{\partial Y} > 0$$

$$\frac{dF}{dw} = \infty \text{ for } N \leqq N_0 \text{ where } N_0 \text{ is full employment}$$

$$0 \leqq \frac{dF}{dw} < \infty \text{ for } N > N_0.$$

It is true, of course, that there are just enough equations to determine all the independent variables except M, which is assumed given by bank policy.

---

[7] We have suppressed the price level as an explicit variable in the savings function.

The classical model can also be written in terms of a few simple equations. It is

$$S(r) = I(r) \tag{40}$$

$$M = kY \tag{41}$$

$$Y = py \tag{42}$$

$$y = y(N) \tag{43}$$

$$w = py'(N) \tag{44}$$

$$N = f\left(\frac{w}{p}\right) \tag{45}$$

with the conditions

$$\frac{\partial S}{\partial r} > 0$$

$$\frac{\partial I}{\partial r} < 0$$

$$K = \overline{K}.$$

Many economists have maintained that the principal difference in these two systems rests in the substitution of $N = F(w)$ for $N = f(w/p)$. This we do not believe to be true, for by inserting the latter supply equation into the Keynesian system in place of the former, we can still get a system which does not automatically obtain full employment. A more significant distinction between the systems occurs in the determination of the variables Y. In the classical system, we can always solve the last three equations uniquely for $\frac{w}{p}$, N, and y. Then the quantity equation serves merely to determine the absolute level of prices, p (or wages, w), while r is obtained from the savings-investment equation. There is no direct theory of the determination of Y, merely one of the determination of p for a given level of full employment. We can call the employment full in this case, because the value calculated for N lies on the supply curve of labor — all who want to work at the going real wage rate are hired.

It has been argued that the classical economists really thought of the savings-investment equation as depending upon Y as well as r, and the money equation as depending upon r as well as Y. If this argument is correct, does it mean that the classical economists had a theory of effective demand? We shall now show that it does not. One method of showing this is to construct a very general system which includes, formally, both classical and Keynesian economics. Then we shall show that one result follows if we use classical reasoning, and another result follows if we become Keynesians.

This system will be one that is homogeneous of order zero in prices in all equations except that dealing with cash balances. If we change all prices and wages by the same proportions, we do not change any of the real magnitudes in the homogeneous equations. Furthermore, there will be perfect competition in all markets.

Our system can be written in terms of any *numéraire*. Following Keynes, we shall use the wage-rate as our *numéraire*; thus the following relations will hold.

$$Y = wY_w, \ S = wS_w, \ I = wI_w, \ M = wM_w, \ L = wL_w \qquad (46)$$

where the subscripts denote variables measured in wage units. The model is

$$S_w(r, Y_w) = I_w(r, Y_w) \qquad (47)$$
$$M_w = L_w(r, Y_w) \qquad (48)$$
$$wY_w = py \qquad (49)$$
$$y = y(N) \qquad (50)$$
$$w = py'(N) \qquad (51)$$
$$N = f\left(\frac{w}{p}\right). \qquad (52)$$

If every equation holds simultaneously, then we have a perfect equilibrium of perfect competition. The classical solution fits this case. From the solution of (49)–(52) we obtain

$$\left(\frac{w}{p}\right) = \left(\frac{w}{p}\right)_0$$
$$N = N_0$$
$$y = y_0$$
$$Y_w = (Y_w)_0.$$

Substitute $(Y_w)_0$ into the savings-investment equation and solve the equation

$$S_w(r, (Y_w)_0) = I_w(r, (Y_w)_0)$$

for $r = r_0$. Substitute r_0 and $(Y_w)_0$ into the money equation and calculate the level of money wages from

$$M_w = \frac{\overline{M}}{w} = L_w(r_0, (Y_w)_0)$$

Since we know $(w/p) = (w/p)_0$ and w_0, we can get p_0. Every variables takes on unique value, and we have full employment because all willing workers are hired at the real wage $(w/p)_0$.

Now, let us proceed as Keynesians. Solve again (49)–(52). Substitute the full-employment income, $(Y_w)_0$, into the savings-investment equation. Is there always a solution for $r > 0$ from the equation

$$S_w(r, (Y_w)_0) = I_w(r, (Y_w)_0)?$$

There is always such a solution within the framework of classical economics because the classicals assumed shapes for these functions so that they would always intersect in the positive quadrant of the $(S_w - I_w, r)$-plane. The classical theory of interest assumes that savings decisions and investment decisions both respond sensitively to changes in the rate of interest. But Keynesian economics assumes that both functions are interest-inelastic. Under these conditions there may be no solution $(r > 0)$ to the above equation when Y_w is at a full-employment level. In order for the equation to hold, something must give way: either r or Y_w. Obviously r cannot give way because it is bounded by the restriction $r > 0$. But (Y_w) can change. If Y_w falls from $(Y_w)_0$ to $(Y_w)_1$, we may be able to get savings equal to investment. In fact, Y_w will fall until the two surfaces $S_w(r, Y_w)$ and $I_w(r, Y_w)$ adjust to an equilibrium. If we have the plausible conditions

$$S_w(0, (Y_w)_0) > I_w(0, (Y_w)_0)$$

and

$$\frac{\partial S_w}{\partial Y_w} > \frac{\partial I_w}{\partial Y_w}$$

then falling income will finally bring savings and investment into equilibrium. But falling incomes bring about decreased employment. In the equation

$$wY_w = py \tag{49}$$

substitute (51) to get

$$Y_w = \frac{P}{w}y = \frac{y(N)}{y'(N)}.$$

This substitution implies that regardless of the shifting adjustments, the demand curve for labor will hold. If there is ever any conflict between the demand and supply of labor in the perfectly competitive case like the one we are considering (e.g., one of no trade-union influence), we can be certain that a short demand will dominate a long supply. Hence in the latter equation, with $y'(N)$ a decreasing function of N, a smaller value of Y_w can be balanced only by a smaller value of N. It is not meaningful to assume that employed workers move downward along their supply schedule of labor,[8] for they would be accepting a smaller real wage than employers would be willing to pay. But it is meaningful to assume that they move upward along the demand curve for labor[9] and get the highest possible real wage offered for the amount of labor corresponding to the reduced level of income. In this position, the demand for labor at the going real wage will be less than the supply, and the difference represents unemployment.

We conclude from this argument that a perfect equilibrium of perfect competition is always possible in classical economics and is incompatible with Keynesian economics. The only type of unemployment that can appear in a classical model is that due to friction and other imperfections or the unwillingness to work at going real wage rates. To explain unemployment in the Keynesian model, it is not

---

[8]See Fig. 5, Ch. III.
[9]See Fig. 5, Ch III.

necessary to introduce any frictions; it is only necessary to substitute a theory of effective demand for a theory of interest.

Will this unemployment which we have explained above be an equilibrium position? It is true within the classical system that money wage cuts always increase the level of employment and income. If wage cuts operate with the same force in the Keynesian system, the unemployment position will quickly be wiped out, since we have assumed perfect competition in every market, including the labor market. Classicists would argue that the excess supply of workers will be wiped out because they will compete with each other for jobs by cutting wages and thus restore full employment. But the two systems have different structures. An employment-creating process in one system may not have the same effects in the other system.

Since we have a completely determined system we can truncate it at any place we choose. Hence we can write

$$S_w(r, Y_w) = I_w(r, Y_w) \tag{47}$$

$$M_w = L_w(r, Y_w) \tag{48}$$

$$w = \bar{w} \tag{53}$$

which is equivalent to the entire system above.[10] The first two equations can be solved for r, and Y_w in terms of M_w, which in turn equals M/w. Assume a bank policy favorable to the orthodox argument, namely, $M = \overline{M}$ is held constant. Then output, Y_w, is a function of $\bar{w}$, the wage rate. Suppose that the unemployed workers cut wages. What is the effect on Y_w? It is easy to calculate a multiplier of the form

$$dY_w = \frac{dY_w}{dM_w} dM_w \tag{54}$$

which will tell us the increment to output as a result of a wage cut.

Differentiating, totally, the first two equations of the truncated system, we get

$$\frac{\partial S_w}{\partial r}\frac{dr}{dM_w} + \frac{\partial S_w}{\partial Y_w}\frac{dY_w}{dM_w} = \frac{\partial I_w}{\partial r}\frac{dr}{dM_w} + \frac{\partial I_w}{\partial Y_w}\frac{dY_w}{dM_w} \tag{55}$$

$$1 = \frac{\partial L_w}{\partial r}\frac{dr}{dM_w} + \frac{\partial L_w}{\partial Y_w}\frac{dY_w}{dM_w} . \tag{56}$$

Treating this system as two equations in the two variables, $\frac{dY_w}{dM_w}$, $\frac{dr}{dM_w}$, we can solve to obtain

$$\frac{dY_w}{dM_w} = \frac{\frac{\partial I_w}{\partial r} - \frac{\partial S_w}{\partial r}}{\frac{\partial L_w}{\partial Y_w}\left(\frac{\partial I_w}{\partial r} - \frac{\partial S_w}{\partial r}\right) - \frac{\partial L_w}{\partial r}\left(\frac{\partial I_w}{\partial Y_w} - \frac{\partial S_w}{\partial Y_w}\right)} . \tag{57}$$

---

[10]The fact that all equations do not hold exactly in the Keynesian system does not prevent us from taking this system as completely determined. Every equation except one holds, but all the variables take on unique values because the demand for labor dominates the supply. From the imperfect relation we get $(\omega/p)_1$, N_1.

Professor Samuelson has shown that if a dynamic model, for which our static system is the stationary solution, is to be stable then the denominator must be negative.[11] It follows that

$$\frac{dY_w}{dM_w} \geqq 0 \, ; \tag{58}$$

there are some positive effects from wage cuts. But the fact that these positive effects are seriously limited in magnitude may have some bearing on the result.

In the limiting case where the investment schedule is completely interest-inelastic and/or the liquidity-preference schedule is infinitely interest-elastic there is zero stimulus as a result of wage cuts.

$$\lim \quad \frac{dY_w}{dM_w} = 0$$

$$\frac{\partial I_w}{\partial r} \to 0$$

$$\frac{\partial L_w}{\partial r} \to -\infty \, . \tag{59}$$

Wages can be cut endlessly, but no increased output and employment will result. After some short period of high-level unemployment in an environment of wage cuts, hyper-deflation will set in. Producers will continuously find it more profitable to wait for wage costs to fall further and will postpone economic activity. If there are no frictions in the system, this process will go on until social revolution explodes the economy.

In the case where we do not go to the limit, the multiplier, dY_w/dM_w, will be a small positive quantity.[12] In this event, a sufficiently large multiplicand will make the product (of multiplier and multiplicand) a sizable quantity. However, the wage-cutting argument must rest upon a small multiplicand. Wage cuts will engender anticipations of further wage cuts unless they are kept small. A large multiplicand and small multiplier will lead to results identical with those of the limiting case — hyper-deflation. A small multiplicand and a small multiplier will do no good; their joint effect will not cure unemployment. We really need a small multiplicand and large multiplier to bring the standard arguments into their own, but this situation is not feasible in a Keynesian system.

The possibility exists (though small) that wage cuts may alter the schedules of decisions to invest and to save. If we write

$$I_w(r, Y_w) - S_w(r, Y_w) = -\alpha \tag{60}$$

$$M_w = L_w(r, Y_w) \tag{48}$$

---

[11] Behind this result, there is the very reasonable assumption that $0 < \frac{\partial I_w}{\partial Y_w} < 1$.

[12] We are assuming $\partial I_w/\partial r = -\epsilon(r, Y_\omega)$ and $\partial L_w/\partial r = -1/\delta(r, Y_\omega)$ where ϵ and δ are small positive quantities.

where α represents a positive shift of the investment schedule relative to the savings schedule, we can also calculate

$$\frac{dY_w}{d\alpha} = \frac{\frac{\partial L_w}{\partial r}}{\frac{\partial L_w}{\partial Y_w}\left(\frac{\partial I_w}{\partial r} - \frac{\partial S_w}{\partial r}\right) - \frac{\partial L_w}{\partial r}\left(\frac{\partial I_w}{\partial Y_w} - \frac{\partial S_w}{\partial Y_w}\right)} . \tag{61}$$

In this multiplier equation, it is not the multiplier which is limited, rather the multiplicand. The multiplier is positive and will stimulate employment if coupled with a large enough multiplicand, $d\alpha$. There will be forces acting to increase savings and thus reduce $d\alpha$, while there will be other forces which will stimulate and also retard investment. Whatever positive forces exist to make $d\alpha$ large will be counteracted by the negative forces so that the final result is uncertain, though probably not large. The reasons for this final judgment are presented more fully in the text above.

The Long-Run Equilibrium

At any point of time the economic system can be regarded as tending toward a long-run stationary state in which there is no net investment and in which all existing capital equipment is exactly replaced. This idea does not mean to imply that the stationary state will necessarily be reached, but any dynamical system can be considered as approaching a stationary norm which changes at different periods of time but always exists as a useful concept. Outside factors will from time to time introduce shocks within the dynamical system which will make it tend toward a different stationary state. The question to be investigated now, in the light of Keynesian economics, is concerned with the level of employment in the long run. Will the stationary state be one of full employment? The classical economists who first talked about the stationary state certainly assumed full employment for their long-run theory. Recently, Professor Hansen[13] has disputed the classical position with the argument that the institutional and psychological makeup behind the determinants of effective demand may be such that the system will settle down to a long-run, under-employment equilibrium. Professor Pigou[14] was not long in coming to the rescue of the classical writers, and attempted to salvage their theory. It will be very useful to consider, in some detail, Professor Pigou's case and to trace its full implications.

Reckoning in terms of wage units we can easily write down a system to represent the long-run equilibrium, which is consistent with that of Pigou.

$$M_w = L_w(r, Y_w) \tag{48}$$

$$S_w(r, Y_w, K_w) = 0 \tag{62}$$

---

[13] *Fiscal Policy and Business Cycles* (Norton, New York, 1941), p. 288.
[14] "The classical stationary state," *Economic Journal* **LIII** (1943), p. 343.

$$I_w(r, K_w) = 0 \tag{63}$$

$$wY_w = py \tag{49}$$

$$wK_w = pK \tag{64}$$

$$y = y(N, K) \tag{65}$$

$$w = p\frac{\partial y}{\partial N} \tag{66}$$

$$N = f\left(\frac{w}{p}\right). \tag{52}$$

The above model for the long-run equilibrium is essentially that of Pigou and not the result that would follow from a dynamical Keynesian model, where the variable representing time is allowed to increase without limit. In the Keynesian version of this model, Y_w would appear in the investment equation and K_w would not appear in the savings equation.

If an economically meaningful solution to these equations should exist, then full employment would follow, and the stationary state would represent perfect equilibrium of perfect competition. But Pigou has agreed that the added condition, $r > 0$ may make the system over-determined. That is to say, there may be no solution for r which has economic meaning when all other variables are at a full-employment level. There must be some least value of $r > 0$, and if this value will not bring savings and investment into equilibrium at their zero levels, then something must give way in the system. In reality employment is the thing that will give way,[15] such that a solution for r exists consistent with less-than-full employment values of the other variables. However, Pigou represented this system of equations as an impasse. He did not object to the conclusions of the classical economists, but he objected to the structure of their model because he refused to admit the existence of an imperfect equilibrium condition. For Keynesians this system represents a situation of unemployment due to the overthrow of the classical interest theory. The market phenomenon of sticky wages will explain why the unemployment position is one of equilibrium.

The ace in the hole for Pigou was a slight modification of the savings schedule to the form

$$S_w(r, Y_w, K_w, M_w) = 0. \tag{67}$$

The substitution of this function for the other savings function (62) in conjunction with the other equations of the system, Pigou thought, enabled him to save the classical doctrine. His argument was the following: since it is reasonable to assume $\partial S_w/\partial M_w < 0$, a flexible-wage policy will always push savings to the required zero level after r has been lowered to its minimum value. It is obvious from the relation, $M_w = \overline{M}/w$, that wage cuts serve to increase the stock of money, M_w. If increases

---

[15]It is employment and not something else which gives way for reasons similar to those given previously in connection with the short-run models.

in M_w diminish the desire to save, then a flexible-wage policy can always insure the zero level of savings at full employment because unemployed workers will always bid w to such a low value that just the correct amount of savings is forthcoming. In this case the added condition on the interest rate does not make the system over-determined.

Pigou's argument, however, is not quite convincing, and the classical point of view has not yet been saved. The assumption of unlimited wage cuts, as has been pointed out above, is a very dangerous tool when we take into account any realistic considerations of anticipations in the economic process. Professsor Pigou *must* rest his argument on the fact that a very small wage cut will immediately restore high levels of employment, so that a deflationary spiral is to be avoided. In particular, he must show that in his system the relation

$$dY_w = \frac{dY_w}{dM_w} dM_w \tag{68}$$

yields a large positive multiplier, dY_w/dM_w, so that a small multiplicand can induce a large increment in income, dY_w. We must consider, then, the conditions which make for large or small values of dY_w/dM_w.

The system

$$M_w = L_w(r, Y_w) \tag{48}$$
$$S(r, Y_w, K_w, M_w) = 0 \tag{67}$$
$$I(r, K_w) = 0 \tag{63}$$
$$w = \overline{w} \tag{53}$$

is equivalent to the larger system with the background equations because with $\overline{M}$, given by the banking system, the first three equations in conjunction with the background equations are sufficient in number to solve for all variables. Thus we can consider the first three equations as solved for r, Y_w, K_w in terms of w (or M_w) and w as determined along with p, N, K from the background equations. Whatever this value of w turns out to be, we shall call it $\overline{w}$. Pigou, in his paper, actually assumed $Y_w = \overline{Y}_w$ instead of $w = \overline{w}$, but the difference is not essential. As a matter of fact, in his *Employment and Equilibrium*, he pointed out that either $w = \overline{w}$ or $Y_w = \overline{Y}_w$ was implicitly assumed by the classical economists.

Suppose now that the solution to the abbreviated system is one of less than full employment with $w = \overline{w}$, in other words, forces are imposed upon the system so that the relations hold only imperfectly. Pigou's process is then to lower w in the equations as a result of the competition for jobs. The stimulus to employment from this lowering of w can be seen from

$$\frac{dY_w}{dM_w} = \frac{\frac{\partial S_w}{\partial K_w} \frac{\partial I_w}{\partial r} - \frac{\partial I_w}{\partial K_w} \left(\frac{\partial S_w}{\partial r} + \frac{\partial S_w}{\partial M_w} \frac{\partial L_w}{\partial r} \right)}{\frac{\partial S_w}{\partial K_w} \frac{\partial I_w}{\partial r} \frac{\partial L_w}{\partial Y_w} - \frac{\partial I_w}{\partial K_w} \left(\frac{\partial S_w}{\partial r} \frac{\partial L_w}{\partial Y_w} - \frac{\partial L_w}{\partial r} \frac{\partial S_w}{\partial Y_w} \right)} . \tag{69}$$

With Pigou's assumptions

$$\frac{\partial S_w}{\partial K_w} \leqq 0, \frac{\partial S_w}{\partial r} \geqq 0, \frac{\partial S_w}{\partial Y_w} > 0, \frac{\partial S_w}{\partial M_w} < 0, \frac{\partial I_w}{\partial r} < 0, \frac{\partial I_w}{\partial K_w} < 0, \frac{\partial L_w}{\partial r} < 0,$$

$$\frac{\partial L_w}{\partial Y_w} > 0 \tag{70}$$

it follows that

$$\frac{dY_w}{dM_w} > 0. \tag{71}$$

But the size of the multiplier will depend, as in the short-run models, on the structure of the entire system.

In the long run, it is reasonable to expect that the rate of interest will be pushed toward its least possible value. If the stationary state is one of such foresight that there are no minimum risks connected with borrowing, the interest rate can fall to the minimum costs of making loans on the part of the banks. This will undoubtedly bring the rate near zero. In the case of the presence of borrowing risks, the bottom to the interest rate may be somewhat higher, but no matter which point of view is adopted, the rate should be in a range in which the liquidity-preference schedule has great interest-elasticity. While the condition of interest-elasticity seems to follow directly from the Keynesian assumptions about the bottom to the interest rate, it can easily be shown that this condition follows also from Pigou's system.

Instead of the liquidity function, as we have written it, he used the relation

$$r = g\left(\frac{M_w}{Y_w}\right) \tag{72}$$

in which M_w/Y_w represents the Marshall "k." He assumed

$$g\left(\frac{M_w}{Y_w}\right) > 0$$

and

$$\frac{dr}{d\left(\frac{M_w}{Y_w}\right)} < 0$$

for all

$$\frac{M_w}{Y_w} > 0.$$

In addition he stated that the function g falls asymptotically towards zero for large values of M_w/Y_w. Thus when the interest rate is small and near zero, as it will be in the stationary state, we get

$$\frac{dr}{d\left(\frac{M_w}{Y_w}\right)} < 0$$

and small in absolute value. From the inverse relation

$$\frac{M_w}{Y_w} = g^{-1}(r)$$

we can calculate

$$\frac{\partial M_w}{\partial r} = Y_w \frac{d[g^{-1}(r)]}{dr} = Y_w \frac{d\left(\frac{M_w}{Y_w}\right)}{dr} < 0. \tag{74}$$

Where r is small, Pigou's assumptions imply that $d(M_w/Y_w)/dr$ is large in absolute value, so that $\partial M_w/\partial r$ will also be numerically large, although negative.

The consequences of an elastic liquidity-preference schedule are that the stimulative effects of wage cuts will be very slight. In the multiplier expression, all terms not involving $\partial L_w/\partial r$ do involve either $\partial S_w/\partial r$ or $\partial S_w/\partial K_w$ as factors. Pigou admitted that the magnitude of both these slopes of the savings function would be extremely small, numerically. In the limiting case where these terms tend to zero and the liquidity preference function tends toward infinite interest-elasticity we get

$$\lim \quad \frac{dY_w}{dM_w} = -\frac{\frac{\partial S_w}{\partial M_w}}{\frac{\partial S_w}{\partial Y_w}}$$

$$\frac{\partial S_w}{\partial r} \to 0$$

$$\frac{\partial S_w}{\partial K_w} \to 0$$

$$\frac{\partial L_w}{\partial r} \to -\infty. \tag{75}$$

The size of the multiplier depends upon the relative sizes of $\partial S_w/\partial M_w$ and $\partial S_w/\partial Y_w$. The only way to determine the multiplier is to obtain quantitative estimates of the parameters of the savings function. Econometric results show that $\partial S_w/\partial Y_w$ is in the neighborhood of 0.2 or 0.3, but the past data have never shown a significant correlation between S_w and M_w when all other variables are taken into account. It is likely that $\partial S_w/\partial M_w$ is numerically small. This is consistent with Pigou's admission of the possibility that $\partial S_w/\partial K_w$ is small. The respective influences of M_w and K_w on S_w would be expected, *a priori*, to be of the same order of magnitude.

The modification of the savings function has really done very little to enable Pigou to abstract from the deflationary aspects of expectations. In this case, even if we admit flexible wages, full employment will not be readily achieved. With the existence of unemployment, workers will continue to cut wages in their competitive struggle for jobs, but there will be little stimulus to increased employment, and expectations of further wage cuts must certainly develop. Producers will postpone action in anticipation of further wage cuts; prices will be depressed; and the economy will travel downward in a hopeless spiral. As before, we introduce the condition of rigid wages to show why the system will stay in the imperfect equilibrium condition and not collapse as a result of the deflationary spiral.

However, there is one case which may be labeled as an extremely classical situation in which Pigou's results can be obtained but which does not follow from his assumptions. One of the important aspects of this situation is contained within the following statement by Keynes:

> "In a static society or in a society in which for any other reason no one feels any uncertainty about the future rates of interest, the Liquidity Function L_2, or the propensity to hoard (as we might term it) will always be zero in equilibrium. ... Thus if it is practicable to measure the quantity, O, and the price, P, of current output, we have $Y = OP$, and therefore, $MV = OP$; which is much the same as the Quantity Theory of Money in its traditional form.[16] "

If we assume, as a characteristic of the stationary state, that there is no uncertainty as to the future rate of interest, then the liquidity-preference equation can be replaced by the quantity equation, and the effects of wage cuts should be favorable to employment. In fact for this case it follows that

$$\frac{dY_w}{dM_w} = \frac{1}{\frac{\partial L_w}{\partial Y_w}} \tag{76}$$

The multiplier is the income velocity of circulation of cash balances (or the reciprocal of the Marshall "k"). This value has been estimated at two or three for the United States; consequently we should expect, in this case, a favorable result from wage cuts which could quickly restore full employment and avoid the disastrous results of hyper-deflation. If this model is what the classical economists had in mind for their stationary state, then perhaps they were correctly following their assumptions.

Notes to the Original Edition

‡ Page 262. A superior accounting treatment of this same problem is given by D. Jorgenson in *The Brookings Quarterly Econometric Model of the U.S. Economy,* eds. J. Duesenberry, G. Fromm, L. R. Klein, and E. Kuh (Rand McNally, Chicago, 1965). The beauty of his approach is that the relevant price concept becomes *user cost* of capital, thus placing Keynes' concept in its proper role.

* Page 262. In recent work the idea of distinguishing between old and new capital has been more formally and completely treated in vintage models of production.

Editorial Notes

1. All chapter references are to the chapters in *The Keynesian Revolution,* unless specified otherwise. For example, footnotes 8 and 9 refer to chapter III of *The Keynesian Revolution.*
2. *Treatise* refers to J. M. Keynes, *Treatise on Money* (Harcourt Brace, New York, 1930, 2 Vols.).

---

[16] *General Theory*, pp. 208–209.

3. *General Theory* refers to J. M. Keynes, *The General Theory of Employment, Interest, and Money* (Harcourt Brace, New York, 1936).

4. In **Notes to the Original Edition**, ‡ Page 262 and * Page 262 are respectively equivalent to ‡ Page 42 and * Page 42 in this Volume.

4

THE KEYNESIAN REVOLUTION REVISITED[†][*]

It is almost twenty years since the preceding chapters were first published. For most of this period, I have concentrated my attention on statistical studies of the consumption, investment, and liquidity-preference functions and on economy-wide models. It is now time to turn this attention, to some extent, at least, toward the interpretation of empirical findings. It is time to reconsider the Keynesian Revolution, and I propose to do so in this chapter. There have been many interpretive articles on Keynes and the *General Theory* — after ten years, after fifteen years, and after twenty years — but I shall approach the matter in a different way, as a summary of years of econometric testing and studying of the accounts of such quantitative work by others in the field.

The Meaning of the Keynesian Revolution

The primary contentions of Keynesian theory as set down in this book can be summarized in a form that gives us scientific agreement on our terms of reference. The Keynesian system is

1. A theory of the determination of total income (output or employment).
2. A theoretical explanation of the possibility of under-employment equilibrium.
3. A group of doctrines in public policy about how to control the economy at desired levels of economic activity.
4. A long-run view on the historical trend of capitalism.

I shall consider all these main contentions of Keynesian theory, but principally, I am concerned with the first and second. I want to re-examine the theory of income determination in the light of our knowledge of the actual functioning of the economy, a knowledge that has been built up by econometric studies.

The Keynesian thinking of the 1930s stimulated national income-accounting and related data gathering activities. These developments might have progressed without the Keynesian influence, but surely not as swiftly. The new developments in statistical annals made available a body of data that is almost ideal for testing the theory. The testing has been done largely by econometricians who build models of

---

[†]From *The Keynesian Revolution*, 2nd ed. (Macmillan, New York, 1966), Chap. VIII, pp. 191–226.
[*]Parts of this essay were presented in lectures given at Osaka University, October 1, 1963; Hitotsubashi University, October 9, 1963; and Nagoya University, November 13, 1963. Reprinted from *The Economic Studies Quarterly* **XV** (Nov., 1964), pp. 1–24.

the Keynesian type, but with numerical parameters, that are carefully determined by accepted statistical methods. Unfortunately, Keynes was not sympathetic with this approach to the study of his ideas, and the task of checking the theory has fallen to outsiders.[1] People from the "inside" group at Cambridge never followed through with a careful statistical check of the theory, although they would have been eminently qualified to do so.

The close followers of Keynes, in England and America (the neo-Keynesians), have often advocated the implementation of his theoretical ideas in the formation of public economic policy. At an early stage, it was recognized that this policy implementation would require accurate predictions of the macroeconomy, and econometric model-building has this goal precisely in mind. After some years of disappointment, Keynesian followers argued that accurate predictions were not needed and that trial-and-error methods would be satisfactory. I feel that this is an extremely dangerous position. There is really no suitable alternative to the econometric approach. Given the slow motions of our democratic legislative processes, which have been amply demonstrated in recent years, we cannot rely on quick decisions for implementing a trial-and-error approach. We need the kind of model-building that the original Keynesians disdained. Built-in stabilizers, such as progressive tax systems and transfer payments, help in the face of slow-moving legislatures, but they are temporary, partial, and inadequate to the whole task of economic stabilization.

The Elements of the Formal Model: The pillars of the model of income determination are widely recognized as the marginal propensity to consume (or save), the marginal efficiency of capital, and liquidity preference. After the interpretations, in consistent mathematical form, by Hicks and Lange, Keynesian thinking settled along these lines,[2]

$$S(r, Y) = I(r, Y)$$
$$M = L(r, Y)$$

where Y is aggregate money income, r is the interest rate, and M is the nominal stock of cash. The three pillars are represented as $S(r, Y)$, the propensity to save; $I(r, Y)$, the marginal efficiency of capital schedule; and $L(r, Y)$, the liquidity-preference function. This is an informative and succinct way of expressing the theory in what I would now like to call a *pedagogical* model. I want to emphasize that this is only a crude framework for thinking and illustrating main ideas. It has teaching attributes but obscures so much of life that it cannot be thought of as a *working* model.

But the very simplicity of this pedagogical model gets us into theoretical difficulty. It is a closed system of two relationships in two unknown variables, r and Y,

---

[1] J. M. Keynes, "Professor Tinbergen's method," *Economic Journal* **XLIX** (1939), pp. 558–568. See also, Professor Tinbergen's reply, "On a method of statistical business-cycle research," *Economic Journal* **L** (1940), pp. 141–154.

[2] Hicks, *op. cit.* Lange, "The rate of interest and the optimum propensity to consume," *op. cit.*

given exogenous control over M by the monetary authorities. This latter assumption will come under scrutiny and be seriously questioned, but for the moment we shall accept it. The trouble with this simple model is that it cannot be extended from a theory of income determination to a theory of employment without making it more complicated. Furthermore, it violates received economic theory in the matter of money illusion or homogeneity, in a mathematical sense. Aggregate income is defined as *money* income, yet neo-classical theory would suggest that the equilibrium system should be stated in terms of *real* income. Employment is directly related to real income, not money income.

If we were to redefine the income variable as y (aggregate real output) and also recognize the homogeneity postulates, our system would be

$$S(r,y) = I(r,y)$$
$$\frac{M}{p} = L(r,y).$$

This may be a more satisfactory version, but it is incomplete because there are three variables to be determined: $r, y,$ and p. We need to close the system by extending it in such a way that the price level is explained. To do this, we shall have to extend the system to include production functions, factor-demand, and factor-supply functions. A proper statement of Keynesian economics must include all these extended relationships. Indeed, Keynes did start out with notions of labor supply and demand in the *General Theory*, but he failed to give a self-contained, explicit, and internally consistent mathematical model of all the relationships. In the many renditions that have been handed down over the past twenty-five years, it has been thought that the three pillars are adequate; but they are not, either theoretically or practically. We cannot escape from thinking in terms of the whole system.

Even the extended system, with production, factor-supply, and factor-demand functions added, is not adequate for serious applications. The system of two equations and the extended versions that include approximately five or six equations have been analyzed over and over again by scholars in the period since 1936, and there is very little that can be added by going over this ground again. It appears to be more fruitful to consider more elaborate and far-reaching extensions of the theory from the realm of pedagogy to that of realism and application.

Extension of the Basic Model

How does the system have to be extended before it becomes a useful working tool?

A public sector must be added. The model as stated in pure pedagogical form makes little provision for public economic action. It permits monetary control over M. Government expenditures are frequently added as exogenous investment, and tax-transfer relationships are incorporated. This gives a framework for a multiplier analysis of public policy.

In reality, the public sector is more endogenous than is commonly recognized. Social and educational expenditures depend on population growth and distribution; highways are needed to meet the traffic generated by consumer purchases of cars; public construction may follow movements in interest rates. There are many ways in which the public sector responds to the economic climate, but, admittedly, national defense and other government expenditures or revenue decisions are exogenous. Nevertheless, it is a gross and misleading over-simplification merely to add some exogenous government variables to the standard models.

The system must be opened with respect to foreign trade. The simplest models depict an isolated, closed economy. They are possibly good approximations for some of the world's large self-sufficient economies, but most nations rely heavily on foreign trade. The available theoretical extensions with foreign-trade multipliers are useful, as steps in the right direction for opening the system, but they are inadequate. They lead to the general overall impression that exports are good (employment-creating) and imports are bad (employment-destroying). This is not generally so. In large industrial nations that import competitive goods, an expansion of imports cuts into domestic activity. In some countries, however, imports of raw materials and capital equipment of a non-competitive type help production markedly. In Japan's economy, for example, imports are absolutely necessary to its functioning at a high level.

A suitably extended open system must allow explicity for the productivity of imports, the terms of trade, and the balance-of-payments position, in addition to the simple income effects of the familiar foreign-trade multiplier. To deal adequately with the open economy and to tackle problems that have recently arisen in the foreign sector of many economies, we would have to make a fairly major extension of the simple models.[3]

The system must be made dynamic. Except for some notes on the trade cycle, the *General Theory* dealt with a static model. The world is dynamic, and no static model will give a widely applicable representation of it. There have been interesting dynamizations of the simple model, but these fail to show the realistic dynamics. A suitable lag structure is important in showing the relationship between the long and short run in this theory. Without benefit of elaborate dynamizations, analysts have misjudged the magnitude of multipliers, especially in the short run. The empirical studies of Goldberger and Suits have shown forcefully that short-run multipliers

---

[3]To emphasize that we need to be reminded of the importance of introducing government and foreign sectors into the basic model, I cite a leading textbook on what might be called the neo-Keynesian theory. See Gardner Ackley, *Macroeconomic Theory* (Macmillan, New York, 1961). Ackley's book is built essentially around a model of a domestic economy with no government activity. However, as a result of his later experience as chief economic counselor to the President of the United States, advocating Keynesian-type policies, I suspect that he might want to extend his model in the way indicated for government activity and foreign trade, as payments problems have been ever present in his tenure of office.

(one year or less) are barely greater than unity.[4] In the long run they build up to preconceived ideas derived from static analysis, but the build-up is slow.

The accounting relationship between capital stock and net investment should automatically introduce trend dynamics into the system. Keynes circumvented this effect by using the artificial assumption that capital stock can be treated as constant in the short run. This is an extremely curious assumption, because investment, which is by definition a change in capital stock, occupies a central role in the theory. It can perhaps be explained by noting that the percentage expansion of capital must be tiny in the short run, while the percentage expansion of investment is not. If the short run is taken to mean one, two, or three years this assumption is quite misleading, for capital formation can make itself felt significantly within one year and decidedly so within three years. The static short-run equilibrium model is, thus, an artifact. At a minimum, the production function must be generalized to take account of the productivity of capital, and the marginal productivity of labor is not a simple demand function because it depends on the level of capital stock. The marginal productivity of capital must be properly linked to the Keynesian notion of marginal efficiency of capital, and in this way the lack of contradiction between classical real theories of interest and the Keynesian monetary theory can be made clear.

The system must be disaggregated. It is useful for teaching purposes to regard the entire producing economy as one huge enterprise and develop the analog theory of the single firm to explain the macroeconomy; but the modern economy is too complex to yield to such simplified treatment. Realistic applications will require an explicit recognition of at least a few sectors. The particular sectors displayed and the degree of disaggregation ultimately chosen will depend on the policy objectives to be considered. My main contention is that some form of macro-model is still workable as a useful tool in applied economics. It is much less aggregative than the usual Keynesian models, but it is not nearly as detailed as the theory of Walras or the empirical schemes of Leontief or Orcutt.[5] The extended Keynesian system that has realism may need to have approximately ten sectors and may be enlarged to have as many as twenty to thirty without going to Leontief's detail of 500 industrial classifications or to Orcutt's family-individual firm level. There is still an important role for macroeconomics, but the order of the magnitude of detail is considerably above that of Keynes and his immediate followers. A ten-sector system that explains sector prices, wages, employment, investment, and similar variables mushrooms in size rapidly.

---

[4] A. S. Goldberger, *Impact Multipliers and Dynamic Properties of the Klein–Goldberger Model*, (North Holland, Amsterdam, 1959). D. B. Suits, "Forecasting and analysis with an econometric model," *American Economic Review*, **LII** (1962), pp. 104–32. Interestingly enough, Keynes first guessed at a multiplier of 1.5 for the United Kingdom. In an open economy this may be high for the short run but not so high as others. See p. 41, Goldberger.

[5] W. W. Leontief, *The Structure of the American Economy*, 1919–1939 (Oxford University Press, New York, 1952). G. H. Orcutt, *et al.*, *Microanalysis of Socioeconomic Systems: A Simulation Study* (Harper and Bros., New York, 1961).

A Reconsideration of The Keynesian Relationships

When the *General Theory* was first being discussed and intellectually digested, there was a feeling on the part of many scholars that profound truths of an amazing sort were contained in the inter-relationships connecting the three pillar functions. I felt at the time I wrote the *Keynesian Revolution* that a full understanding of this simple model had enabled us to interpret economic events of the period since World War I with great insight. My feeling now is that the *General Theory* is an intellectual breakthrough, but that it is too simple for judging the real world. When it was mechanistically and naively applied to events of the period after World War II, for purposes of economic prediction, it was usually found that there were major factors not accounted for in the simple model that had determined the course of the economy. The theory must be regarded as a *core* theory with *kernels* of truth. It needs substantial amplification for reaching the whole truth. Also, it does not rest on a carefully laid and well-documented statistical base. In terms of today's standards, it would be classed as containing "casual empiricism."

It is almost inevitable that the intensive investigation of the consumption, investment, and liquidity-preference functions by an army of econometrician-scholars would turn up numerous points of detail that qualify the simple theory based on 2 or 3-parameter functions. On looking carefully at each of the main functions, from a statistical viewpoint, I feel that the theory must necessarily be expanded by a large measure to take into account some neglected factors.

The propensity to consume or save: The Keynesian idea of the existence of a basic psychological law establishing a relationship between aggregate consumption and aggregate income, with slope less than unity, needs obvious extension to account for taxes, transfer payments, income distribution, lags, relative prices, and possibly wealth. Keynes was well aware of these qualifications to the simple relationship implied by his basic psychological law, but he undoubtedly felt that a function

$$C = C(y), \quad 0 < dC/dy < 1$$

was adequate for most situations.

Modification of the consumption function to take taxes and transfers into account is standard procedure in statistical studies, when *disposable* income has become the relevant explanatory variable. This modification comes about once the system is extended to include the public sector, even if in the most rudimentary form.

Income distribution effects were investigated empirically in the form of Pareto-coefficients as explanatory variables, just after the *General Theory* was first published. These effects were generally dismissed as being of negligible size, although discernible. An argument in support of the neglect of income-distribution effects was the linearity of the Engel curves of total spending or saving estimated from family budget studies.[6] More recent studies of sample surveys of consumer budgets

---

[6] Cf. p. 59 above.

have changed this picture. Modern surveys contain many more high-income recipients than did those of the 1920s or 1930s. For scientific sampling reasons, there is deliberate over-sampling in the upper income groups, and post-war prosperity has changed the distribution of income by placing a larger number of persons in the top groups. Curvature of the Engel curve becomes evident in, roughly, the top decile, compared with the bottom 90 percent; therefore, recent studies reveal a more significant nonlinearity in the Engel curves.[7] The revealed nonlinearities do not necessarily imply a short-run sensitivity of aggregate consumption or savings to changes in the distribution of income, and most time-series studies with aggregative or annual statistics show little effect of changes in the (factorial) distribution of income. Over decades and longer stretches of time, changes in the distribution of income may be more significant. For example, it is customarily felt that one of the reasons why Japan has been a high-saving country over the past 100 years is that a highly unequal distribution of income has been maintained. If there is a future tendency toward more equality, this may promote a higher rate of consumption and a lower rate of saving.

The lag structure of economic relationships has become a very popular problem of econometric analysis in recent years. Stock-adjustment forms of relationships have been proposed for a wide variety of types of behavior. In the case of consumption, the lag structure is usually expressed as

$$C = \alpha_0 + \alpha_1 \sum_{i=0}^{\infty} \lambda^i y_{-i} ,$$

or

$$C = \alpha_0(1 - \lambda) + \alpha_1 y + \lambda C_{-1} .$$

This is also the time-series form of Friedman's *permanent-income hypothesis*, although it was in use by econometricians long before that consumption theory was proposed.[8] It is this lag structure that accounts for large differences between long- and short-run multipliers. This can be seen readily by observing that statistical estimates of α_1 and λ in the preceding relationship give values

$$\text{est. } \alpha_1 \sim 0.65$$
$$\text{est. } \lambda \sim 0.35 .$$

This gives a one-period m.p.c. of only 0.65 but a long-run m.p.c. of est. $\alpha_1/(1 - \lambda) \sim 1.0$.

---

[7]L. R. Klein, "Statistical estimation of economic relations from survey data," *Contributions of Survey Methods in Economics* (Columbia University Press, New York, 1954), pp. 189–240.
[8]M. Friedman, *A Theory of the Consumption Function* (Princeton University Press, Princeton, N. J., 1957).

The stock-adjustment form of lag distribution employed is directly applicable to consumer-spending on durable goods, for it was first developed in detail for investment in fixed capital.[9] This does not mean that the lag distributions do not apply to non-durable consumption, but the parameters of the lag process are probably different for different types of consumer goods. This suggests the fruitfulness of the disaggregation of total consumption into durables and non-durables — possibly even further. Such disaggregation is an essential extension of the original and simple Keynesian model. But disaggregation may have deeper implications than the proliferation of consumption functions with different lag distributions; it may force us to consider the introduction of relative prices.

In the Keynesian system, income effects predominate over relative price effects, and this may be quite plausible as long as a high degree of aggregation is used. The more disaggregation there is into types of goods and services, the more important relative prices become in some equations.

The one relative price considered by Keynes explicitly is the price of future compared with present goods; in other words, the interest rate. Although Keynes considered interest effects in some detail, and seemed to attach great importance to the role of interest, the history of subsequent Keynesian analysis (after the *General Theory*) is one of a minimization of interest effects. The theory of existence of under-employment equilibrium appears to depend on interest inelasticity of spending decisions. As far as consumer-spending is concerned, Keynes was truly doubtful about the magnitude of interest effects, and subsequent statistical studies have justified this doubt. There is no empirical evidence, so far, that shows significant interest effects on total spending or saving by consumers after income effects are taken into consideration. That is not to say that wide movements of interest rates and relative prices, much wider in the short run than have been observed, will have no influence on total spending or saving. However, the evidence indicates that fluctuations of the sort that we have witnessed will not have a marked influence.[10]

The influence of wealth has come into the consumption-function discussion in different ways. Pigou stimulated much interest by his analysis of the effect of real-cash holdings. This was generalized and elaborated by Patinkin to the real-balance effect, including all consumer wealth and not simply cash wealth. The same ideas appear in disguised form in Friedman's permanent-income hypothesis.[11] There is strong evidence for the permanent-income hypothesis, in a *weak* form, as we have shown here in the lag distribution. More direct studies of real liquid assets or total real wealth are somewhat less conclusive. In America, after World War II, there is evidence of a strong liquid-asset effect, but this influence seems to have diminished

[9]L. M. Koyck, *Distributed Lags and Investment Analysis* (North-Holland, Amsterdam, 1954). H. B. Chenery, "Overcapacity and the acceleration principle," *Econometrica* **XX** (1952), pp. 1–28.

[10]In the latter part of the 1950s, interest rates moved to higher levels in many countries than had been observed for two decades. This induced some significant shifts in portfolio composition, but not in the overall choice between saving and spending.

[11]Pigou, "The classical stationary state," *op. cit.* D. Patinkin, *Money, Interest and Prices* (Row, Peterson and Co., Evanston, Ill., 1956). Friedman, *op. cit.*

of late. A combination of circumstances — large consumer accumulations of liquid wealth, low consumer stocks of durables, military victory, and a productive system intact — may have been extremely favorable in bringing out an abnormal effect of liquid-asset holdings.

The wealth effects are unusually important because, following Pigou's line of argument, they insure the reaching of full employment in equilibrium and argue against the Keynesian theoretical concept of under-employment equilibrium, a subject to which we shall return.

Many people are impressed with the rise of consumer credit as an institution fostering high-level consumption. Should consumer debt or the state of the credit market for such debt be a particular aspect of wealth or interest that should be introduced as a variable in the consumer function? *A priori*, there is much plausibility in the arguments about the influence of consumer credit, especially on purchases of durables, but most statistical studies have until now failed to uncover a separate effect that is independent of incomes and lag distributions.[12] Consumer credit is usually restricted to a time duration of only twelve to twenty-four months, and it is not impossible for people to accumulate capital values for purchases of consumer durables in that period of time. Credit, therefore, has appeared to affect the time shape of spending much more than its total amount.

Finally, I want to comment on the more general Keynesian philosophical outlook on consumption. It is an implicit supposition in Keynesian economics, especially the business-cycle aspects, that capital formation is volatile (impulsive, dynamic, variable), while consumption is passive (regular, stable, steady). Consumption is seen as adjusting to the macro-environment that is created by investment. This is not to say that consumption remains constant, but that the consumption function does. Consumption moves along the stable function. Statistically, we ought to find a high-correlation function for consumption and a comparatively low-correlation function for investment. That is precisely what we do find; but we also find that, among consumption types, durables have low-correlation equations, like investment functions. The volatility of consumer durables and spending on luxuries, such as entertainment, some personal services, or vacations, have been large enough to make consumption as a whole volatile. The history of the postwar economy, first in the United States, then in Western Europe, and then in Japan, is grossly misunderstood if one fails to appreciate the autonomous role of consumption. Many American fluctuations have been offset by contrary movements in consumption. Katona and his colleagues in consumer-survey research have strongly emphasized this activist role of the consumer,[13] while oldline Keynesians, such as Mrs. Robinson, have continued to place most of the activating stress on investment. She has argued

---

[12]Some newer results suggest that characteristics of the consumer credit market (downpayment percentages, contract length, and interest charges) affect car purchases and possibly other consumer durables.

[13]G. Katona, *The Powerful Consumer* (McGraw-Hill, New York, 1960).

that investment plays such an activating role that it creates its own profits.[14] The Keynesian role of consumption is, however, outmoded, and it will not be possible to capture the spirit of the next phases of economic development unless one takes a more balanced view of consumer behavior.

The stable, aggregative, static, bivariate consumption function of the simplest Keynesian model will no longer serve our analysis adequately. At a minimum, we must allow for taxes, transfers, lags, and some degree of disaggregation. It is probably true that income distribution, relative prices, or wealth will also be of some significance, and some disaggregated components will have exogenous dynamic impulses that will be propagated throughout the economy as a whole.

The propensity to invest (m.e.c.): Direct statistical testing of the strict form of the Keynesian theory of marginal efficiency of capital (m.e.c.) is very difficult because we cannot find data on *expected marginal profits* associated with an act of investment. It is difficult to measure profits in any case, but expected profits are subjective, and marginal profits are not generally recorded in business accounts. If the production function is of a specific type, such as the Cobb–Douglas function, it is possible to transform the theory into a testable form using observed data, provided that expected market variables can be approximated by lag values. The stock-adjustment forms of investment functions,

$$I = \beta_0 + \beta_1 \frac{p_{-1}y}{q_{-1}} + \beta_2 K_{-1}$$
$$K = K_{-1} + I$$

are the type that would be implied. I = capital formation, y = aggregate output, p = price of output, q = price of capital services, K = stock of capital. This function can be modified by the inclusion of an interest-rate variable, and if only one price-level variable is used, relative price ceases to be part of the first variable.

The original formulations of the static Keynesian model omitted lags, the stock of capital, and relative price. They included an interest variable, however. Subsequent statistical work showed minor or nil effects of interest on investment. The results of aggregative time-series analysis were fortified by the direct questioning of business respondents about their decision-making process. On reconsideration, I am inclined to attach little significance to the sample survey results obtained in the 1930s.[15] The samples were not well designed by modern standards, and the questions about intricate matters outside the realm of actual business experience were much too direct. Modern survey techniques in sample design, questionnaire structure, and interviewing methods are vastly improved, although they have not been intensively applied to the question of the interest elasticity of investment. Conclusions from the time-series results may have been premature, for results obtained since 1952 in samples that contain several observations at widely varying interest

---

[14] J. Robinson, *The Accumulation of Capital* (Richard D. Irwin, Inc., Homewood, Ill, 1956).
[15] Cf. pp. 65–66 above.

levels show that interest is a significant variable in equations of investment behavior. The new results show statistical significance for interest variables; they do not necessarily show high elasticity.

Other variables of significance in statistical investment functions are business cash flow (gross operating profit), business liquidity, or explicit measures of capacity utilization. The last mentioned can be used as a replacement for the capital-stock variable.

There are two kinds of investment that have proved to be of great importance in recent economic fluctuations; but they received little specific attention from Keynes; they are residential construction and inventory investment. Residential construction merits separate treatment in disaggregation, because it is strongly influenced by its own demographic factors and may receive special forms of public support. Inventory investment may follow familiar lines of stock-adjustment theories, but its adjustment parameters imply a very different reaction lag, one that gives rise to short business cycles of less than four years' duration. Speculative variables of price-level change and interest-rate change may also be peculiar to inventory investment. These, then, are compelling reasons for some disaggregation of investment beyond that originally given by Keynes. Followers of Keynes were quick to investigate these specific types of investment, but it must be recognized that the theory needs extension to include these in a consistent and fully determined manner.

Another philosophical view found in Keynesian thinking, similar to the passive role attributed to consumption, as discussed here, is the outlook for a long-run decline in the m.e.c. This pessimistic outlook for investment does not appear to be justified by recent events, either in the industrialized economies of the United States and Western Europe or in the newly developing countries. New inventions inspired by the scientific developments of World War II, such as radar, automated devices, and atomic power, were not foreseen. Prospects are that new discoveries will continue to flow; new investment opportunities will continue to arise; and the long-run m.e.c. need not necessarily decline. Who is to say what the economic prospects of the moon are?

Liquidity preference: The doctrine of liquidity preference is developed for an economy in which people make a choice between only two possible types of assets, money or bonds. Furthermore, the bonds considered are best thought of as perpetuities; then bond price and interest rate are connected in a simple reciprocal relationship. The supply of money is considered to be exogenously controlled by the central banking system (the monetary authorities).

The debate between the loanable-funds theorists and the liquidity-preference theorists has led into many blind alleys. In a truly interdependent system it is generally not possible to establish unique lines of causation; we can, however, construct approximate special cases that give the main flavor of the theory. To do this for the Keynesian model so that we have an unqualified liquidity-preference theory, I think we need to construct an artificial economy in which currency and interest-bearing bank accounts are the only allowable assets. All lending for investment is to be made through the creation of bank loans. In this situation, there is no separate price for marketable assets; there is only an interest cost of bank loans or an interest gain on bank deposits. The bank accounts are non-marketable assets with a fixed money price.

This theory can be used only to explain the kernel of an idea; it is not a realistic analysis of a complicated money market. There are three lines of development that need to be followed to make this theory workable: (1) More assets or debt instruments must be considered — bills, bonds, equities, cash, savings accounts, and goods. (2) More classes of holders must be considered — private households, non-financial companies, private banks, non-bank financial institutions, foreigners, central bank, and public treasury. (3) A supply theory of money must be developed.

The modern theories of portfolio selection in which average return and risk are separately considered have been applied by Tobin to the theory of liquidity preference, and this appears to be a fruitful line of theoretical development for rationalizing the liquidity-preference theory in a multiple asset economy.[16] Intellectually it is a more satisfying explanation than Keynes', and it follows in the tradition of time-honored principles of sound investment counseling — diversification of holdings to minimize risk. In view of Keynes' early work on subjective probability theory, we might have expected the master himself to have worked out this line of analysis in liquidity-preference theory, but the inspiration appears, instead, to have come from the work of von Neumann and Morgenstern.[17]

A new development is coming forth in empirical monetary analysis, namely, accounts for the flows of funds through the economy.[18] These statistical tables promise to do for monetary analysis what national income accounts have done for real-economy analysis. The flow-of-funds accounts are sub-divided by type of asset-debt holders, and future empirical studies will undoubtedly clarify behavioral patterns in the money market. We do not yet have as unambiguous a statistical pattern of this type of behavior as we do of consumption and investment. There are results, however, that suggest that price-level changes influence money holdings, illustrating that the holding of goods or equities ought to be considered in the portfolio. Profit rates influence company holding of cash; therefore, equity investments are relevant to business liquidity decisions. We have seen strong reactions in recent years, on the

---

[16] J. Tobin, "Liquidity preference as behavior towards risk," *Review of Economic Studies* **XXV** (1957–1958), pp. 65–86, and "The theory of portfolio selection," in *The Theory of Interest Rates*, eds. F. H. Hahn and F. P. R. Brechling (Macmillan, London, 1965), pp. 3–51; see also, D. Patinkin, "An indirect-utility approach to the theory of money, assets, and savings," *ibid.*, pp. 52–79.

[17] J. M. Keynes, *A Treatise on Probability* (Macmillan, London, 1921); J. V. Neumann and O. Morgenstern, *The Theory of Games and Economic Behavior* (Princeton University Press, Princeton, N. J., 1946). Curiously enough, this part of the von Neumann–Morgenstern celebrated study has made a greater impact on economic theory than the central theories of bargaining and game-playing.

[18] M. A. Copeland, *A Study of Moneyflows in the United States* (National Bureau of Economic Research, New York, 1952) and Federal Reserve staff, *Flow of Funds in the United States, 1939–1953* (Board of Governors of the Federal Reserve System, Washington, 1955); see also, *Federal Reserve Bulletin* **45**, (August, 1959), pp. 828–859, 1046–1062.

part of households, to changes in rates on savings accounts or to potential capital gains in equities. It is quite apparent that the theory must be extended by type of asset and type of holder.

Most of the empirical econometric works that have followed the Keynesian inspiration have achieved the greatest measures of success in explaining the behavior of the real economy. The link between the real and money economy has been poorly established in a statistical sense, and possibly the link is really weak. In addition, the statistical equations of the money market itself are not firmly established. One of the special Keynesian hypotheses, that of the liquidity trap, as shown by a high-interest elasticity of cash holdings at low rates, has been observed in a few instances. But it is not yet definitely established.

If the monetary sector of the Keynesian model is disaggregated by the type of asset holder, as suggested here, there will almost certainly have to be a theory of money supply, because asset–debt decisions of private banks, central banks, and the public treasury will determine money supply. It is the crudest over-simplification to say that the central authorities control the stock of cash balances exogenously. In America they fix discount rates, reserve requirements (within legislative limits), and engage in open market dealings with government securities; in Japan they principally make advances to private banks or the public treasury, control foreign exchange, and watch over reserve positions; in the United Kingdom they fix the Bank Rate, control overdrafts, and control foreign exchange. These are only some principal control activities. Monetary authorities regulate equity markets, cooperate with treasury officials in managing the public debt, fix entire schedules of bank charges or rates, control terms of consumer credit and home-mortgage markets, regulate the financial activities of insurance companies, and engage in a host of other peripheral financial activities. By these diverse means, they hope to control the money supply. Sometimes bank reserves are plentiful; sometimes they are scarce. This provides ample evidence that in the short run the authorities cannot make the money supply just what they want it to be.

An explicit theory of money supply has been developed by Brunner, and new statistical models of this aspect of behavior are being prepared.[19] The parameters will be the actual control magnitudes that the central bank can regulate. As in the case of the real government sector, some of these supply relationships will involve variables from the private sectors; thus, money supply will become an interdependent (partially) endogenous sector of the whole system.

Production and labor demand functions: The Keynesian theory is not wedded to any particular type of production function. It could be consistent with a linear function, a Cobb–Douglas function, the new version of constant-elasticity of substitution (C.E.S.) functions, or other aggregative relationships. The characterization of a particular output level as full-employment output has been pedagogically

---

[19]K. Brunner, "A schema for the supply theory of money," *International Economic Review* **II**, (1961), pp. 79–109.

attractive and popular in rule-of-thumb policy analysis, but it is not satisfactory in its treatment of capital stock. As noted earlier, the artificiality of the short-run static model with given capital stock is inconsistent with the productivity of current investment. Labor-capital substitution and variable capital stock are two requirements for a suitable production function in the theory. Productivity parameters are so different among major industry groupings (agriculture, manufacturing, tertiary industry) that disaggregation ought to be as rewarding for production as for consumption functions.

Labor demand is usually thought of as a transformation of the marginal productivity functions for labor. If capital is regarded as a variable in the production function, the marginal productivity function for labor will not generally define employment as a function of real wage alone. It would be necessary to combine marginal productivity functions for all factors to derive an explicit labor-demand schedule of the usual type. Also, if the production function is linear, marginal productivity will be constant, and the labor-demand function will have to rest on different foundations for the macro-model.

The Cobb–Douglas function and the implied constancy of labor's share provide an attractive combination in which the share equation is used for labor demand even though it is not written as a function of employment and real wage alone. This gives, however, an interpretation of an observed empirical regularity within the context of the Keynesian model. The arguments made previously about the necessity of including the production, labor-demand, and labor-supply functions in the model place the equation of labor's share on an equal footing with the consumption function and similar equations of macroeconomics. When we take up the question of the applicability of the Keynesian theory to problems of inflation, we shall see more clearly how the equation of labor's share, or other versions of marginal productivity, are used for explaining the absolute price level.

This pair of equations, the production function and the marginal productivity equation for labor, can be given a different interpretation in the Keynesian system. Because aggregate output is basically determined by effective demand through the savings-investment equality, we can look upon the production function as a *labor-requirements* function, given the stock of capital. From the point of view of establishing main lines of causation, this would mean writing the production in an inverted form. Instead of writing

$$y = f(N, K),$$

we would write

$$N = g(y, K).$$

For some, but not the most general, methods of statistical estimation, this choice is of significance, but for the inherent algebra of non-stochastic models it would not be an essential modification. It is, however, instructive.

Similarly, the marginal productivity equation for the Cobb–Douglas form of production can be inverted from its usual form as labor's share into an equation of price mark-up over unit labor costs. This is done explicity in the discussion of inflation that follows. Again in terms of causal interpretation, the equation of marginal productivity can be looked upon as a price-formation equation instead of as a labor-demand equation.

Labor supply and wage determination equations: For a given wage rate (presumably set by trade-union institutions) and labor force, the Keynesian model has proved to be a powerful theory for explaining the determination of total income and employment, in a simplified form as a teaching theory and in an extended form as a working model. For closing the system with respect to wage and price-level determination, however, we need a labor-supply function and a market-adjustment process of wage determination. Also, for investigating the theoretical possibility of underemployment equilibrium, these two relationships are essential.

So far, our main criticism of the Keynesian theory is that it needs extension — disaggregation, more endogenous processes, dynamization, opening with respect to foreign trade, and so forth. On the question of labor supply, however, Keynes was definitely confused and in error. He suggested that labor supply is a function of the money wage and not the real wage. Of course, we can show the possibility of the existence of an underemployment equilibrium if there is an assumed "money illusion" or inhomogeneity in the supply behavior of workers. Schumpeter stressed repeatedly that the challenging theoretical problem was to make all the classical assumptions about behavior under perfect competition and then show the possibility of an underemployment equilibrium. This is the problem that must be faced by Keynesian economics.

The idea of money illusion in labor supply has surely been refuted by behavior during the postwar inflation. No one has been more conscious of the encroachment of rising prices on wage gains than have individual workers and their trade unions. The demand for built-in escalation in labor contracts is a supreme recognition of the fact that the wage-bargain and terms-of-employment offer is in real wages and not money wages. Most contracts are finally written in terms of money wages, but the bargaining process is completely alert to the relationship between prices and wages. There is no illusion in behavior. Empirical equations of labor supply have not been satisfactorily established as functions of real wages, but they are no more firmly established as functions of money wages. The supply of male labor in the able-bodied age ranges is so conventional and standardized that it is difficult to obtain good endogenous explanations of macro-labor supply functions empirically. The real possibilities of determining cyclically sensitive labor-supply functions seems to be in the marginal sectors of the labor force — working wives, students, and semi-retired persons. A strong case for demographic disaggregation can be made in this market.

The statistical studies of wage determination have been found to be more fruitful than those of pure labor supply. These relationships take the form of dynamic change in wage rates as a function of excess supply (unemployment) in the labor market. The money wage is the market adjustment variable, but it has been found to be clearly related, with time lag, to price-level changes too. The equation takes the form

$$\Delta\omega = \delta_0 + \delta_1 U + \delta_2(\Delta p)_{-1}\,.$$

In this linear approximation, the money-wage rate changes are made a joint function of unemployment and previous price change. The contract is struck in terms of money wage; that accounts for the choice of a left-hand variable. The indicator of market conditions is U (unemployment), and the lag of wage change behind price change recognizes the facts that wages change in contractual displacements and lag behind price changes. There is no behavioral money illusion on the part of workers, but they cannot adjust continuously to price change and tend to lag behind. This is an inhomogeneous equation, but if it is imbedded in a system that is otherwise homogeneous, the complete model has the property that inhomogeneity occurs only for the dynamic variant.[20] When the system is held stationary ($\Delta\omega = 0$, $\Delta p = 0$), it is homogeneous in the classical sense. The moving or dynamic system thus contains a theory of absolute wage and price determination that is most closely tied to developments in the labor market. By contrast, the classical view is that the absolute price or wage determination would be most closely tied to developments in the money market. If δ_0 is significantly positive, we have a possible position of underemployment equilibrium.

This is a line of argument that seems essential for the Keynesian theory of underemployment equilibrium. Wage-determination equations of the preceding type have recently become very popular and are known as Phillips curves.[21] The investigations by Phillips have established interesting properties of these equations, especially on a long-run basis, but such equations were repeatedly used in econometric investigations long before the researches of Phillips.

Summing Up the Keynesian Model

Simple multiplier models or three equation models involving the propensity to consume, the marginal efficiency of capital and liquidity preference are useful teaching devices. The Keynesian theory, viewed as a model that can explain the determination of output, employment, wage rate, price level, interest rate, and other variables must be larger. In the first place, it must include production, labor demand, and labor-supply functions. Secondly, it must be extended in a number of directions in order to approach realism and usefulness. These extensions will involve disaggregation, dynamization, and expansion of the scope of endogeneity. The systems that are now built by econometricians to describe economic activity in the United States, Canada, the United Kingdom, Netherlands, India, Japan, and other countries are

---

[20] If we used percentage change in wage rates, percentage change in price level, and percent of the labor force unemployed as variable in the wage-determination equation, we would have a form of homogeneity across time periods, but not for any given period, using lagged values as initial conditions.

[21] A. W. Phillips, "The relation between unemployment and the rate of change of money wage rates in the United Kingdom, 1861–1959," *Economica*, N. S. **XXV** (1958), pp. 283–300.

actually members of the Keynesian family of models, but they do not closely resemble the parent system on the surface. They are much larger and are more complicated. It requires careful examination by consolidation and tracing of main lines of causation to show that they are extensions of the Keynesian system. Most of the extensions are straightforward and can be traced to their Keynesian roots. The effects of real balances on spending and the analysis of wage determination are distinctly different and not simple extensions of the original model.

The main conclusion is that the *General Theory* is all too simple. Knowing what we do now about several aspects of economic behavior, I find it hard to become satisfied with a model couched solely in terms of the three pillars stated in their simplest form; however, it was undoubtedly the simplicity of the final construct that led to such wide acceptance of the theory at an early stage. If it had been stated in terms of a 30-, 50-, or 100-equation model such as what we use in today's econometric analysis, it is doubtful that many students would have paid close attention to it. Most people would have ignored it, leaving it as a problem of analysis for specialists willing to linger over its details.

An Interpretation of the Keynesian Revolution in the Light of some Postwar Economic Developments

For the most part, our appeal to empirical results in the previous sections was technical and specialized. I was motivated in that discussion by detailed statistical matter, using the most powerful techniques with great care, for the analysis of behavior in one part of the economy after another. The kind of research that underlay the studies mentioned is that required for building a large-scale econometric model to be used in forecasting and policy formation. Now, I want to turn to some looser empirical observations on broader aspects of the Keynesian Revolution. I am not inquiring into the existence of each kind of behavior relation in the system. I am taking an overview of the whole economy and looking at points of Keynesian policy and philosophy.

In the first years after World War II, it seemed that the problems that gave rise to the Keynesian Revolution — deep depression and large-scale unemployment — had disappeared and that the economic world would have to deal with inflation, dollar shortage, and other new problems outside the scope of the Keynesian analysis. There was a tendency to discredit the Keynesian theory and argue that it had led to incorrect predictions.

In the United States, economic conditions were strongly influenced by the need to meet the backlog of pent-up wartime demand, by the demographic pressures of an increased birth rate, and by large foreign-assistance programs. The Korean War provided another strong economic stimulus at a time when some of these motivating factors were beginning to weaken. In Western Europe and Japan, the main problem was reconstruction and the re-establishment of foreign trade. These influences were bullish for some time.

There are two issues involved in appraising these developments. First, had the typical Keynesian problems really vanished, and were the bullish stimuli temporary? Second, is the Keynesian system capable of dealing with this new variety of problems? In this section, I shall take up only the first of these issues. I shall consider the second one subsequently.

It is true that Keynesians were caught unaware by the inflationary problems of post World War II and that they failed to appreciate the wage and price pressures that were generated by high levels of employment. Having missed the unexpected turn of economic events, several economists over-reacted in the opposite direction and foresaw a long-run problem of inflation and sought new models to analyze it. The permanence of inflationary pressure proved to be as unreal as the persistence of depression. During the latter part of the 1950s, the United States found itself faced with reasonably steady prices, a substantial hard core of unemployment, and excess capacity.

Now, we are faced again with the typical Keynesian problems, and they might have occurred much sooner in the 1950s were it not for Korea, the emergence of new nations from colonial status, and other events not dependent on domestic activity in the United States and other industrial nations. The prevalence for a number of years in America of an unemployment rate in excess of 5 per cent looks very much like an example of the Keynesian underemployment equilibrium, and it does not seem to be explainable by market imperfections. It is, pure and simple, a case of deficient *effective demand.* The United States remained for much longer than desired at such a low rate of activity because of the unwillingness or inability of the public authorities to apply the requisite heavy dose of Keynesian medicine.

The long-run decline in m.e.c., or the American view expounded in the *stagnation thesis*, is not well founded in recent developments. The cyclical and short-run aspects of Keynesian analysis can be interpreted in the light of postwar developments; the stagnation thesis seems to be less plausible. Our recent difficulties with unemployment and excess capacity may be only cyclical and not secular. Technological change and its influence are too uncertain for us to make a premature judgment about very long-run developments.

Two points of Keynesian policy doctrine that seemed quite acceptable until a few years ago have sadly disappeared with the emergence of political conservatism. Keynes taught us (1) that inflation is better than deflation[22] and (2) that sound domestic economic policy in support of full employment should not be sacrificed to the vagaries of international trade and finance.

The rise of conservative governments in the United States and the United Kingdom in 1952 led to an abandonment of these principles and a return to orthodox monetary policy. The campaigns to save the pound (£) and later the dollar ($) were important steps in the departure from Keynes' views. Both governments were quite

---

[22]Cf. p. 4.

successful in holding prices steady, breaking away from cheap money, and keeping exchange rates constant at the expense of unemployment and low growth rates.

Domestic economic policy in the United States is always constrained nowadays by the balance-of-payments situation. Public authorities have proposed a Keynesian-type remedy that they think will be compatible with our external position and steady prices. They proposed the celebrated tax cut of 1964. This was a massive dose of the Keynesian medicine already mentioned and has generally been considered an unusual triumph of the new approach in economic stabilization. The tax cut of 1964 worked much as Keynesian economic analysis would have led us to believe it should work. It improved the level of economic activity, but it was not large enough to restore full employment. More of such cuts or other stimulative policies would be needed to bring about full employment, but these would probably endanger price stability and worsen the balance of payments; therefore, we find no rush on the part of authorities to extend these policies all the way to full employment.

An examination of the conditions leading to the tax cut of 1964 is revealing, for Keynesian economists argued in 1962 and 1963 that such a stimulus was needed. Timidity, or inability, or lack of insight restrained public authorities from enacting tax reductions while the economy lost potential output and employment for many months. Furthermore, this large-scale experiment gives us a good opportunity to judge the order of magnitude of multiplier effects. In the first year or two of this cut, it appears that real G.N.P. is higher by approximately the real value of the cut. This multiplier is nearly unity (in absolute value). It is smaller than the expenditure multiplier by a factor that equals the marginal propensity to consume in simple models. Generally speaking, these multiplier values are properly modest in size and much in line with econometric studies of Keynesian-type models. As previously mentioned (cf. p. 41) Keynes had good intuitive guidance in working with a conservatively valued expenditure multiplier of 1.5.

Once the tax cut was passed by the United States Congress and its effects became visible, it was accepted by people of widely differing shades of economic opinion. However, the discussion and political process leading to the cut were cumbersome and slow for the efficient working of the new methods of stabilization policies. Some discretionary authority on the part of the executive branch of the tripartite American system is needed. Complete reliance on the slow-moving fiscal powers of the Congress may prove inadequate to the full implementation of Keynesian doctrines.

Extending the Scope of the System — Inflation, Fast Growth, and Underdeveloped Economies

Inflation: Whether the postwar inflation problem is merely a cyclical phase or a secular trend, we want a system of analysis that is capable of dealing with this problem as well as that of deflation. It is my contention that the system is fully capable of dealing with inflation if generalized in the way I have emphasized in this chapter. The price level or wage level is as much an endogenous variable in this generalized system as is national income, aggregate employment, or the interest rate.

The inflation problem has been studied in terms of the quantity theory of money, the inflationary gap, and wage push (more generally cost push or administered prices). The generalized Keynesian model contains all three kinds of inflation analysis simultaneously. I would not like to base my analysis on any one approach alone, least of all on the quantity theory of money. I think that the generalized system takes parts of all three and uses them in an interrelated way without imparting a unique casual influence to any one.

The Keynesian doctrine of liquidity preference can be looked upon as a generalization of the quantity theory of money. In place of writing

$$\frac{M}{p} = ky\,,$$

where

$$k = \frac{1}{v} = \text{constant}\,,$$

we write

$$\frac{M}{p} = k(r, \Delta r, \Delta p)y\,.$$

In these equations M = stock of cash balances (nominal), p = price level, y = aggregate output, k = Cambridge constant, v = velocity, r = interest rate.

The approach here is only symbolic; it does not go into the complications of asset types and different groups of asset holders. It shows that M and p are not strictly proportional as the quantity theory suggests, but that they are closely related depending on how r, Δr, and Δp affect k. In the strict quantity theory, y is fixed at its full-employment level. In the Keynesian system, full-capacity output is not necessarily reached at all times; therefore, the money equation is only a partial system by itself. However, because the Keynesian system includes the quantity equation as a special case, there is no incompatibility involved.

Keynes, in *How to Pay for the War*, initiated the inflationary-gap analysis. The primary variables considered in this approach are savings and investment. If at full-capacity output, investment exceeds savings, there is an inflationary gap, and if savings exceed investment there is a deflationary gap. Graphical analysis of these situations are only first approximations because the price level is not explicitly determined in simple savings-investment models. Full-capacity output, as distinct from the concept of full-employment output, cannot be determined unless the dynamic relationship between capital and investment and capital-labor substitution are brought into the analysis. In spite of these complications, the savings–investment balance is an important criterion for the determination of inflationary pressure. During World War II, this method of analysis was popular, but emphasis gradually shifted to the concept of cost-push, or wage, or administered price inflation.

The analysis is simple enough. Prices are determined as mark-ups over prime costs, especially wages. If trade unions establish abnormally high wage rates, prices will be marked up over these, resulting in an upward inflationary movement. Import prices for the open economy are also prime costs giving rise to the same kind of inflationary push. Administered prices are those of giant cartels or monopolies, whose products might be used as materials and, therefore, prime costs, in other industries — giving rise to inflationary pressure.

The mark-up of prices over wages finds expression in a transformation of the equation of labor's share. From

$$wN = \alpha py$$

we can write

$$p = \frac{1}{\alpha} w \left(\frac{N}{y} \right) .$$

This is Weintraub's formula, which he proposes as a simple substitute for the classical quantity equation in explaining inflation.[23] In place of k or $1/v$, he uses the constant α (labor's share) as the strategic parameter. This equation establishes a proportional relationship between p and w, given the reciprocal of productivity N/y. Productivity is assumed to grow along a smooth trend.

The equation of labor's share, it was noted, enters the Keynesian system as a form of the marginal productivity of labor or the demand-for-labor equation. This treatment of the inflation problem is therefore, already contained in the Keynesian system. The position is not changed if the coefficients are modified by monopoly elements (administered prices) or the inclusion of imports as productive factors and prime costs. The Keynesian theory takes no special stand on the presence or absence of competition; it can deal with monopolistic elements. It can also be extended to encompass foreign trade.

Some of the arguments about administered price inflation have been concerned with key sectors of the economy. In America the bellwether steel industry and other particular oligopolies are singled out, and the macroeconomic Keynesian models fail to treat relative prices in inter-industry relationships. In this sense, some inflation problems escape the usual Keynesian tools, but there always will be errors of aggregation, and these are no more peculiar to inflation than to deflation.

Newer work on the dynamized Keynesian models containing Phillips curves carry the wage and labor-market analysis of inflation a step further. The wage-push theories are interesting in shifting the focus of attention in treatment of the inflation problem from the money market to the labor market, but they are one-sided in their view of the causal mechanism. They imply that trade unions promote high wages and that these costs lead to high prices. This single cost-push equation is only one in a larger system, and the Phillips curve says that the state of the labor market,

---

[23] S. Weintraub, *A General Theory of the Price Level, Output, Income Distribution and Economic Growth* (Chilton, Philadelphia, 1959).

which is derived from the state of the goods market, affects wage movements. There may also be an effect from previous cost-of-living advances. These may be classified as, at least partly, demand-pull aspects of inflation. The whole group of equations in the labor market — labor demand, labor supply, and wage determination — together with savings–investment and money-market equations, jointly determine the absolute levels of prices and wages. The extended Keynesian system, thus, is capable of dealing with the inflation problem in many ways; through study of the money supply and credit, through consideration of savings–investment balance, and through the state of the labor market. There is no justification for doubting the applicability of the extended Keynesian model to the problems of inflation.

Fast growth: Economists in fast-growing countries — Japan being a typical example — may feel that the forward momentum of their present development will carry them upward at such a pace that they should not use the Keynesian model for analysis. They may feel that the Keynesian system is well suited only for depression economics, and that they have no foreseeable possibilities of depression.

Just as we have argued here that the Keynesian model lends itself well to the analysis of inflation, so does it lend itself well to the analysis of growth. Inflation and growth may seem to go together, but actually they are quite different processes. On a country-by-country basis, there is little correlation in the world economy between growth rate and price change. All combinations seem to be equally frequent.

The Harrod–Domar model of growth is really an extended version of the Keynesian system. It extends the model by bringing in the relationship between capital stock and investment in an essential way. It bases the analysis on the Keynesian concept of savings–investment balance, but it is an extremely simplified version of the theory because it has no price level, wage rate, or interest-rate analysis.

Important ingredients of the modern Japanese growth rate are a high rate of investment, a willingness of the population to save, and the importation of capital. These are all revealed in an extended Keynesian model. The interaction of recent Japanese inflation and high growth rate is better understood if the consumption function is extended to allow for the effects of income distribution and a general upward drift.

Just as American economists have often incorrectly projected a few years' experience into future decades, it is possible that economists in Japan and other fast-growing countries are too optimistic about the future. A slump could occur through the building up of excess capacity in certain lines. The safety margins of the Japanese economy are thin in some areas, and Keynesian analysis of other cycle phases may well be a problem for the future.

The socialist economies are special cases of growing, underdeveloped economies, and I think that it would be unfortunate if they were to be dogmatically doctrinaire in overlooking the possible contributions that Keynesian economics could make to the solution of their problems. Investment may be purely exogenous in fully planned socialism, but its level and sector distribution must be decided upon in an economically efficient manner. The Keynesian aggregative theory will help decide upon the level because it is not appropriate to push capital formation to any extreme whatsoever. There is a best level consonant with stable growth without cycles and severe inflation. Central planners must understand and appreciate the propensity to consume, and failure to do so has, in fact, caused economic trouble for some socialist countries. For public finance under socialism, planners must appreciate saving motives and asset preferences. A truncated Keynesian system with consumption (savings) and liquidity preference treated in some detail would seem to be a natural tool of analysis.

Socialist planners claim that they have eliminated the business cycle. As we know it, the familiar capitalist cycle has not appeared in socialist economies, but there may well be fluctuations. These may come about as the result of the cumulation of internal mistakes in the planning operation or as the result of external disturbances. It is well known, from the great Russian theorist, Slutsky, that random error can easily cumulate into cycles.[24] There will probably be inventory cycles in a socialist economy, and the Metzler extensions of the original Keynesian model would seem to be relevant.[25]

Socialist fluctuations or cycles may exhibit themselves as pauses in upward development or even as downturns. I am not suggesting that there will be a business cycle like ours, but I do argue that a proper understanding of Keynesian economics would help them achieve a smoother growth path.

Underdeveloped countries: Keynesian-type econometric models that have fitted data well in developed industrial countries have also been estimated for India. There may be estimated models for other underdeveloped countries too, but the Indian case may be typical of what to expect. Trade equations are important for India. On the side of export, the demand for basic Indian materials in the world economy dictates the form of the relationship. On the whole, these are specialized goods, and income effects dominate price effects. The same is true of imports; these are largely non-competitive with domestic production, and income effects are the most important among explanatory variables.[26] Thus, the theory must be extended to include foreign-trade multipliers, but the productivity of imports should be explicitly displayed.

Consumption and investment functions exist for India as well as for the advanced countries. The main difference, however, is quantitative. The marginal propensity to consume is much higher for the underdeveloped country. The investment functions of the stock-adjustment or flexible-accelerator type seem to fit well, but we should be very cautious about accepting statistical correlations showing the

---

[24]E. Slutsky, "The summation of random causes as the source of cyclic processes," *Econometrica* **V** (April, 1937), pp. 105–46; see also my paper in the Kalecki anniversary volume, "The role of econometrics in socialist economics," in *Problems of Economic Dynamics and Planning* (PWN, Warsaw, 1964).

[25]L. Metzler, "The nature and stability of inventory cycles," *Review of Economic Statistics* **XXIII** (August, 1941), pp. 113–129.

[26]M. Dutta, "A prototype model of Indian foreign trade," *International Economic Review* **V** (January, 1964), pp. 82–103.

effect of capacity accumulation or utilization on investment in an underdeveloped country. There are so many needs for capital formation that it is hard to envisage an influence of excess capacity on investment. Excess capacity, however, must be understood in an economic and not in an absolute sense. There can be too much industrial capacity in the aggregate to be supported by the effective demand of the whole economy or for a predominantly rural sector. Also there can be partial effects of excess capacity through over-expansion in some area or industry relative to the whole economy.

There is also an asset-preference decision in an underdeveloped country. Studies of Indian liquidity preference yield relations like those in the United States, but for the great mass of individuals there is no possibility of choice. There may be an abnormal preference for gold, other precious metals, and jewels in an underdeveloped country. This would affect the parameters of the function but not its existence.

The wage and price mechanism is likely to be different in under-developed countries. With so much disguised and structural unemployment, it is unlikely that the state of excess supply in the labor market will be a factor in short-run wage determination. Some form of the quantity theory and the savings–investment gap analysis would seem to be more relevant. Import prices are obviously major determinants of the domestic price level.

In fine, a multi-sector Keynesian-type model (agriculture, manufacturing, tertiary, for example) can fit the data of India and other underdeveloped countries. Parameter values and other structural characteristics will be different, but the same general class of models can be expected to apply.

Summary

I look upon the Keynesian theory as essentially a system of equations. While I may have once been satisfied with the explanatory value of a small version of that system expressed in just two or three equations, I now feel that intelligent discussion cannot be carried on unless this system is expanded to include 15 to 20 or even more equations. In current econometric model construction, I am working with some macro-systems that have more than 100 equations.

These larger systems, extended along the lines indicated in this essay, may not be easily recognized as the Keynesian theory, yet I feel that they surely are. They are manifestations of points I have reached, in collaboration with many colleagues, after starting out from the simplest forms of the Keynesian Revolution and working systematically through econometric studies of available data. They are, in a real sense, just extensions of the Keynesian theory in a natural way.

The new versions must have some relative prices, a good theory of price-level determination, dynamic features, a government sector, a trading sector, an effective link to the monetary sector, and a more detailed money market. I think that new advances will be made in these directions and that they will be econometrically based.

A postscript on the role of Keynes in the *Keynesian Revolution* may be in order. Would the Revolution have taken place without Keynes? In the same way that I feel we are now evolving a system, a natural course of intellectual development follows from Keynes' original model. I think that the Keynesian system as a mathematical model would have come into being without Keynes, as a natural outgrowth of the economic discussions of the 1930s.

The dramatic weight of Keynes' personality undoubtedly added much to the speedy acceptance of the theory and was responsible for the philosophical and policy aspects of the *Keynesian Revolution*; but the cold analytical theory would probably have come in any case. The Kalecki model of the business cycle really sets down all the essential ingredients of the simple model, and makes it dynamic in the bargain.[27] Kalecki's mathematical paper in *Econometrica* attracted little attention compared with Keynes' splash, but eventually the theorists would have seen through the matter and given Kalecki's pre-*General Theory* model its full due.

Pronouncements by Frisch and Ohlin on policies for meeting the economic collapse of the early 1930s show clearly that analysis of the situation was congealing along lines that would have led to the same kinds of theoretical models. It was as though these two scholars were interpreting the periods' events in terms of the savings–investment theory of income determination. By a slower, more gradual process their ideas would have merged with Kalecki's formal model into something that is not fundamentally different from the Keynesian system.

Frisch delivered a radio address in 1932 on current economic conditions and took up clearly the role of savings and investment, as separate economic decisions that were interacting to determine the level of economic activity. It is evident, however, that he did not have a closed system of income determination, but he did favor policies that would follow along Keynesian lines.[28]

In 1934, Ohlin reported to the Swedish Unemployment Commission where he outlined a policy to deal with the problems of depression and at the same time presented an analysis of the macroeconomy and business cycles.[29] As in Frisch's analysis, Ohlin gave a clear explanation of the paradox of thrift and the nature of the two-sided savings–investment process. He went further in defining the propensity to save. His theory was not complete enough to develop a well-defined multiplier from a closed system, but he did see the stimulus that would come to economic activity from a rise in either consumption or investment demand. In addition, Ohlin argued against a general wage reduction because of the notion that wages have both cost

---

[27]M. Kalecki, "A macrodynamic theory of business cycles," *Econometrica* **III** (July 1935), pp. 327–344. Cf. L. R. Klein, "The role of econometrics in socialist economics," *op. cit.* Compare also Joan Robinson's contribution to the Kalecki Anniversary Volume, "Kalecki and Keynes," *Problems of Economic Dynamics and Planning* (PWN, Warsaw, 1964), pp. 335–341.

[28]Frisch's ideas were published, belatedly, in *Noen Trekk av Konjunkturlaeren* (Aschehoug, Oslo, 1947).

[29]B. Ohlin, "Monetary theory, public works, subsidies and tariffs as means of unemployment policy," Stockholm, 1934 (tr.).

and demand aspects. He was not like Keynes on the question of wage cuts as a means of alleviating unemployment, but he had good intuition on this subject.

Generally speaking, Ohlin and, possibly, Frisch were more reserved and timid than Keynes on policy recommendations to fight the depression, but they were consistently pointing in the right direction and undoubtedly would have become bolder and more forceful as the magnitude of the world-wide problem became more apparent and persistent. They had substantial pieces of the Keynesian system in their grasp but not a well-articulated complete system that was capable of mathematization. In this respect, Kalecki was far ahead of the Keynesian precursors.[30]

These concluding remarks are not intended to detract from the remarkable Keynesian contribution; they are primarily meant to give proper credit to other scholars and to give comfort in the feeling that good ideas will eventually predominate regardless of any single personality.

Editorial Notes

1. All chapter references and Cf. footnote references are to *The Keynesian Revolution*, unless specified otherwise.
2. General Theory refers to J. M. Keynes, *The General Theory of Employment, Interest, and Money* (Harcourt Brace, New York, 1936).
3. In footnote 2, Hicks, *op. cit.* refers to J. R. Hicks, "Mr Keynes and the 'Classics'; a suggested interpretation," *Econometrica* **V** (1937); Lange, *op. cit.* refers to "The rate of interest and the optimum propensity to consume," *Economica* (1938).
4. In footnote 11, Pigou, *op. cit.* refers to "The classical stationary state," *Economic Journal* **LIII** (1943).
5. *How to Pay for the War* refers to J. M. Keynes, *How to Pay for the War* (Harcourt Brace, New York: 1940).

---

[30] Compare Joan Robinson, *op. cit.*, both on Kalecki's position and on that of the Swedish school.

5

THE NEOCLASSICAL TRADITION OF KEYNESIAN
ECONOMICS AND THE GENERALIZED MODEL[†]

Neoclassical Roots of Keynesian Economics

The introduction of the Keynesian system into economics during the 1930s was, indeed, revolutionary. Almost a half-century later its main structure stands, in spite of claims of counter-revolution. It has, nevertheless, changed, and its future is likely to be evolutionary, in natural extensions of its original base.

In his early classes in Keynesian ecconomics and related subjects, Paul Samuelson consistently emphasized that Keynes was a classical economist schooled in the Cambridge tradition of Marshall and Pigou. More precisely, we should have called him a neoclassical economist. Not only was Keynes a student of the neoclassicists, but he also reasoned in the neoclassical way in developing each block of the structure of his overall macrosystem, as it appeared in the *General Theory of Employment, Interest and Money*.

What do these issues have to do with the original structure of the Keynesian system? Two basic principles of neoclassical economics are (1) the pursuit of optimizing behavior and (2) the clearing of markets. Each piece of the original Keynesian model is based on some form of optimizing behavior. The propensity to consume can be deduced from the theory of consumer behavior, in which a household is viewed as maximizing a utility function subject to a budget constraint. The propensity to invest comes from the schedule of marginal efficiency of capital, in which the equating of the price of an investment to its discounted (marginal) revenue stream is surely an indirect approach to profit maximization by the firm. Finally, the liquidity preference theory of financial asset holding can be readily explained in terms of optimal portfolio choice.

Supply and demand for cash clears the money market in this system, while savings and investment (supply and demand for investment funds) clears the goods market. In the first case the interest rate is presumed to be the equilibrating variable that clears the market, while in the second case it is fluctuating income or output level that clears the saving-investment market.

Behind the three well-known Keynesian functional relationships (propensity to consume, propensity to invest, liquidity preference) lie the supply and demand

---

[†]From *Samuelson and Neoclassical Economics*, ed. George R. Feiwel (Kluwer-Nijhoff, Boston, 1982), pp. 244–262.

functions for labor. This is perhaps the only point at which Keynes diverted from a strict neoclassical position. The neoclassical approach would have labor supply and demand at an equilibrium real wage that occurs at full employment. Keynes' principal point was that a full employment equilibrium does not necessarily exist, and that the economy can become locked into an equilibrium position at less than full employment.

Keynes achieved this result by violating neoclassical homogeneity conditions for the supply function of labor, but there are other approaches to the same results. If there is homogeneity in the supply and demand function — each depending on the real wage — then the market-clearing condition of neoclassical economics would have to be violated in order to achieve the Keynesian result. In any event, Keynes was in the neoclassical tradition for his mode of reasoning and general approach, but he did not become a slave to this point of view in everything he said about the economy of the real world.

Neoclassical theory of behavior deals with micro units, while the corresponding Keynesian concepts refer to macro units — *all* consumers and *all* producers. These two analyses are bridged by the principles of aggregation, which were never carefully explored by Keynes. Among different possible routes to aggregation, one that is straightforward deals with higher moments or parameters of distribution functions. Keynes allowed, in a superficial way, for the effect of income distribution on consumer behavior, but the consequences for his analysis were never carried through. In the case of investment and liquidity preference function, there is practically no consideration of aggregation problems. The same is true of labor supply and demand. In the latter connections the demographic distributions of the labor force are very important and account in a strategic way for shifts in these functions in recent years. These shifts, as will be explained below, have resulted in the most serious criticisms of Keynesian economics as it deals with contemporary issues of full employment, inflation, and instability of the main industrial economies.

Keynesian Economic Policy and Current Economic Problems

The neoclassical tradition shows up clearly in the theoretical structure of the Keynesian system. The associated economic policies known as aggregative demand management follow from the structure of the system but are not necessarily neoclassical in ideology or method. If the Keynesian model is accepted as giving a correct interpretation of aggregative behavior and institutional structure, then the fine-tuning approach to economic demand management looks quite reasonable. For many years this policy technique seemed to work quite well, reaching its zenith in the first half of the decade of the 1960s. It fell into disrepute when inflation became more serious and when a number of other socio-politico-economic events occurred — events that do not seem to be well suited for Keynesian aggregative analysis.

The principal characteristic of Keynesian economic policies is not so much that they focus on demand management as that they are strictly macro policies. In that respect they are consistent with the neoclassical tradition, for they do not concern micro choice and do not interfere with the working of the market mechanism. This aspect is often overlooked. They affect general taxes, general spending, and overall money supply. They let the market mechanism deal with allocation problems. The trouble with their present applicability, however, is that some of the contemporary economic problems are not macro. They deal with situations of particular groups, particular processes, particular markets. Overall macro policy may not reach these issues at all or may do so in a highly inefficient way; therefore, alternative policy approaches must be sought, and theoretical support for these new policy thrusts should come from a system that goes beyond Keynesian macroeconomics.

Let us consider some present structural issues that confront economic policy. The most important single thing wrong with the world's industrial economies is that they have simultaneous high inflation and high unemployment. It is not a case of less-than-full employment equilibrium because the system is in a highly unstable state, with inflation rates varying between 5 percent at the best and 20 percent at the worst. In the early 1960s inflation rates were in the neighborhood of 2 percent in some countries, notably the United States, and unemployment rates were between 5 and 6 percent. That combination seems to be almost out of reach now.

The clearing of labor markets, with nominal wage rates changing to adjust supply and demand for labor, has been affected by demographic distributions. The percentage of youths who are unemployed has risen all over the would. This is partly a consequence of high birth rates just after World War II. It is also a racial matter in the United States and a result of changed attitudes of women toward work outside the home. These demographic shifts have made the clearing of labor markets at reasonable values of nominal wage rate very difficult. In the United States the situation is exacerbated by the institutional nature of minimum wage legislation.

Keynesian-type macro policies of demand management are not very helpful in dealing with this situation. The structure of wages, job training for unskilled youths, and some reconsideration of social insurance benefits are some specific policy problems that come to mind. These are outside the purview of aggregative Keynesian models. If they are introduced the models must be extended considerably in order to explain the enlarged set of endogenous variables associated with demographic structure.

Another dimension of present-day problems occurs in the fields of environment, energy, and food. These three are singled out for attention because they have been so critical on several recent occasions, but they are not unique. Environmental problems developed with congestion, pollution (air, water, solid waste, noise), scarring of terrain, elimination of species, exhaustion of water, and other harmful side effects of intense economic activity. The measures of GNP and similar aggregative magnitudes failed to take account of these "bads" together with "goods" in estimating total output. The aggregative measures were main objective or target variables in the Keynesian model. Either costs of production were underestimated or output was overestimated, and GNP-type indicators gave misleading signals. If policies are to be oriented toward dealing with environmental problems in addition to traditional GNP problems, they will have to look beyond conventional Keynesian macroeconomic policies. The policies must be targeted toward the pricing of specific "bads." Taxation of environmental damage or subsidization of environmental protection call for specific structural policies. Examples are requirements for stack scrubbers in electric power production, restriction of aircraft landings and takeoffs, rerouting of traffic, replacement of terrain after strip mining, and so forth. All these policies lead to higher capital costs and, eventually, to a better environment (better quality GNP).

These are real problems. In a sense, they impose constraints on the straightforward application of Keynesian-type macro policies, but in order to know what the constraints are, it is necessary to extend the theoretical model far beyond the simple Keynesian system. Both policy design and system design go hand in hand.

Energy in a very convenient, inexpensive form was accepted as a fact of life during the development of the Keynesian revolution and during the successful implementation of Keynesian policies during the 1950s and 1960s. There should have been a warning to the industrial world, at the time of the closing of Suez in 1956–1957, that abundant and cheap oil supplies from the Middle East would be subject to risk of limitation. This warning was ignored or not properly interpreted, and Keynesian policies that stimulated growth were pursued with little recognition of the required energy needs.

The oil embargo of 1973–1974 and the subsequent escalation of oil prices have made energy issues chief among economic problems of many industrial nations. Keynesian economic theory and macro policy are almost completely uninformative about meeting this problem through measures that jointly induce conservation and enhance supplies. Specific taxes, subsidies, freeing of market restrictions, and many other structural policies are called for. These policies interact closely with magnitudes in Keynesian models — trade balance, inflation rate, aggregate consumer expenditures — and therefore their implementation must be appropriately integrated with the theoretical system of Keynesian economics. It is not satisfactory to ignore them, and it is not satisfactory to try to compartmentalize theory into an overall macro sector and a specific, independent energy sector. Solving the energy problem is undoubtedly one of the biggest factors in solving the inflation problem. Because of this connection the Keynesian model must be extended to include suitable treatment of energy economics.

Just prior to the onset of the major energy issues that surfaced in 1973, there had been enormous food price rises as a result of Soviet harvest failures, the international food procurement processes, and dietary shifts in fast-growing parts of the world. This was not the first time that food problems (starvation, short supplies, price rises) had come to the forefront of inflationary pressures. Just as the theoretical model showed need for an energy sector, it also showed need for an agricultural sector. Again, it has not been a matter of rejecting the Keynesian macro model, but a matter of extending it to deal with new types of policies — bringing back idle acreages, revamping price support schemes, regulating trading contracts for food exports or imports. In the case of the United States, agricultural exports have become a mainstay of our net external economic position in the face of enormous energy import costs. Ways and means of promoting agricultural exports while maintaining a traditional American role in aiding distressed areas (PL 480) became central policy issues that are far afield from macro fiscal and monetary policy.

To a great extent, the impact of environment, energy, and food on the functioning of the U.S. economy has ultimately manifested itself in declining productivity growth. Keynesian economics is more sympathetic with the relationship

$$\dot{p} = \dot{w} - (\dot{X}/L) \tag{15.1}$$

than with

$$\dot{p} = \dot{M}, \tag{15.2}$$

where $\dot{p}$ = inflation rate $(dlnp/dt)$, $\dot{w}$ = rate of change of unit wage $(dlnw/dt)$, $(\dot{X}/L)$ = rate of change of worker productivity $(dln(X/L)/dt)$, and $\dot{M}$ = rate of change of money supply $(dlnM/dt)$.

The first relationship derives from the approximate constancy of labor's share of total production, an implied relationship in many renditions of Keynesian macroeconomics. The second relationship derives from the crude quantity theory of money, assuming full-capacity production. The quantity theory relationship is contradicted by the Keynesian theory of liquidity preference and plays an important role in anti-Keynesian economics.

Productivity growth is a key factor, according to the first relationship, in offsetting wage gains so as to hold prices steady. To a large extent energy shortfalls or high energy costs have hampered productivity growth in application of the usual techniques of production, and energy policy, together with capital investment policy, forms an important approach to dealing, indirectly, with the problem of inflation. The selection of policies to promote investment may be looked upon as part of general aggregative fiscal policy, but it must be made more specific with industry or sectoral targets, and this requires a theory and model that goes far beyond the scope of aggregative Keynesian theory.

What is true of energy in relation to productivity is also true of job training for unskilled youth, for environmental protection, and for agricultural policy. They all have an impact on productivity in complex ways that cannot be seen through the eyes of Keynesian economics alone.

The simple relationships in Eqs. (15.1) and and (15.2) are not meant to be directly applicable to economic policy or management. They are simply illustrative of ideas. There is no alternative, in my opinion, to the large-scale system that combines the overall thinking of Keynes with the intersectoral thinking of Leontief. In a sense, this combined model aims to approximate in empirical work the Walrasian ideal. We shall never come very close to the enormity of the scope of that system, but we can produce ever-better approximations that provide an increasing amount of micro detail without sacrificing the ability to sum the micro parts into the main aggregate magnitudes that are standard components of Keynesian economics.

These arguments are built on the specific examples of demography, environment, energy, and food; yet the fundamental problem goes far beyond these areas. These are now recognizable problems, and they may remain as problems for some time to come; yet new crises are sure to arise. The objective should be to have a large-scale model with many sectors so that there will be a compartment where the unanticipated new problem can be placed for, at least, preliminary investigation until a more appropriate system can be designed in an evolutionary way.

The large-scale Wharton Model that combines input–output analysis with Keynesian macroeconomics had modest energy sectors prior to 1973. In fact, at the suggestion of industry specialists, it introduced in baseline projections — for a decade or more ahead — an increasing dependence of the United States on oil imports and a consequent worsening of the trade balance. It did not go so far as to incorporate the breakdown of the Bretton Woods system and devaluation/depreciation of the dollar, and it did not foresee the size of the oil price increase, but it did focus on many of the main policy issues during the period 1971–1973. Also, when the energy problem reached crisis proportions in 1973, the model was instrumental in projecting a consequent recession (November 1973). On the whole, the Keynes–Leontief model gave a far better indication of the ensuing substitution against energy than did engineering-type volumetric projections with fixed proportions, which were frequently cited during 1973–1974.

Following this experience, the basic model became much more energy intensive. Coal, oil, and natural gas were separated from mining as a whole. Electric power production was split from delivery of gas and also by type of fuel. Much more detail for energy policy can now be handled in such models. All this is typical of the evolutionary process.

Generalized Model for Generalized Policy

An accounting framework for the Keynes–Leontief system tells a great deal about its equation structure, for the approach is to develop equations to explain the entries in this system of accounts. Chart 15.1 shows the overall structure.

The centerpiece of the chart is the usual input–output system of Leontief. This is true of accounting flows, only. The traditional parameterizing of this system is to treat

$$(X_{ij}/X_j) = a_{ij} \tag{15.3}$$

as a set of technical coefficients, where X_{ij} = flow of real output from sector i to sector j; X_j = total real gross output to sector j (total gross output = total gross input); and a_{ij} = technical coefficient showing requirements of input i per unit of output of j.

Conventional input–output analysis does not treat a_{ij} as strict constants but introduces no systematic way of changing them. There is a resort to technical engineering information in a somewhat informal way. Some formal interpolation schemes, called the RAS method, have been introduced for moving the coefficients a_{ij} through time, but the approach pioneered in the development of Wharton Model is to estimate the a_{ij} as function of relative prices. The ratio X_{ij}/X_j, like price ratios, simply represents endogenous variables of a large model.

Using the Cobb–Douglas theory, the ratios are $X_{ij}/X_{Kj} = \text{const.} \, P_K/P_i$. Using CES theory, another parameter is introduced.

$$\frac{X_{ij}}{X_{Kj}} = \text{const.} \left(\frac{P_K}{P_i}\right)^{\sigma_j} \qquad (15.4)$$

where $\sigma_j = $ elasticity of substitution in the jth sector. Nested CES functions, multilevel CES functions, and translog functions have also been used in further generalizations.

These relationships thus introduce the neoclassical concepts of cost minimization for efficient production, or the elasticity of substitution concept. Accordingly, the production function is generalized to

$$X_j = F_j(X_{1j}, \ldots, X_{nj}, K_j, L_j, t). \qquad (15.5)$$

Both intermediate production flows (the X_{ij}) as well as original factors (K_j and L_j) are used as inputs. This is extremely important for dealing with structural policies, for energy input, various agricultural inputs, and other intermediate inputs are direct arguments in the production function. This gives far greater scope to policy assessment than does the traditional two-factor relationship

$$\text{GNP} = F(K, L, t) \qquad (15.6)$$

in Keynesian models. Gross output of a sector rather than value added is now used as the basic output variable, and intermediate inputs are given explicit consideration.

The two remaining parts of the layout in Chart 15.1 deal with final demand (the right-hand rectangle) and income payments, or value added (the lower rectangle). The deliveries to final demand by each producing sector make up the elements of the final demand matrix. They are the elements of F from the fundamental input–output relationship

$$(I - A)X = F. \qquad (15.7)$$

F is a column vector, each element of which is the sum of deliveries to specific kinds of final demand:

$$F = \begin{pmatrix} F_1 \\ F_2 \\ \vdots \\ F_n \end{pmatrix}$$

$$F_j = f_{j1} + f_{j2} + \ldots + f_{jn}. \qquad (15.8)$$

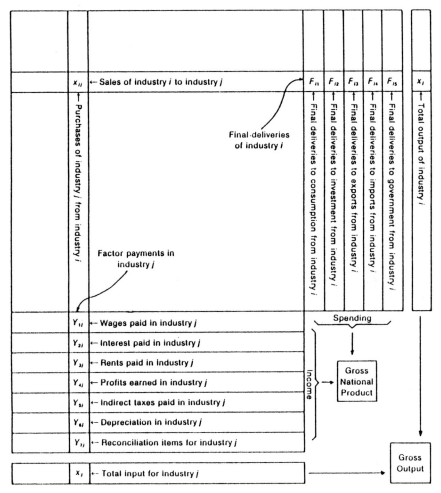

Chart 15.1.　Relationship between Interindustry Transactions, Final Demand, and Factor Payments.

The final demand types are the elements of GNP. In the simplest form they are

$$C_j + I_j + G_j + E_j - M_j \,, \qquad (15.9)$$

which could be interpreted as deliveries by sector j to private consumption, to private capital formation, to government purchases, to net exports (exports minus imports). These are simply a limited number of indicative entries. In reality, there would be many types of consumption, capital formation, public spending, and foreign trade. The number should be suited to the size and complexity of the input–output system.

From an accounting point of view, the important thing to recognize is that the column sums of F form a row whose elements sum to GNP. A macro model explains the column sums directly, as well as their total. Some of the matrix entries in the right-hand rectangle would also be generated directly in a macro model, but rarely would the whole matrix of elements be estimated directly. For this purpose, another matrix expression is constructed:

$$F = CG. \tag{15.10}$$

The elements of C are the entries in the right-hand matrix divided by their column sums:

$$C_{ij} = f_{ij} / \sum_{i=1}^{n} f_{ij}. \tag{15.11}$$

The elements of G are the components of GNP that are explicitly modeled in the macro system.

Within a column, the entries below the input–output system in the bottom rectangle are components of value added in a sector. These are wages, capital rental costs, profits, and indirect taxes (less subsidies). The Keynesian system typically models aggregate income payments as well as final demand. In a complete supply-side analysis, however, the factor payments within a sector are modeled, sector by sector. This means including factor-demand relationships and determination of unit factor costs — wage rates, interest rates, depreciation rates, and tax rates. Profits are residuals. Prices in this system are determined at the industry level and then transformed into final demand prices.

These relations between final demand and industry output or between prices by sector and final demand deflators are

$$(I - A)X + CG. \tag{15.12}$$

The relationship between gross output (X) and value added (Y) is

$$X_j - \sum_{i=1}^{n} X_{ij} = Y_j = \text{value added } (j)$$

$$X_j - \sum_{i=1}^{n} a_{ij} X_j = Y_j$$

$$Y_j / X_j = \left(1 - \sum_{i=1}^{n} a_{ij}\right)$$

$$Y = BX$$

$$B = \begin{pmatrix} 1 - \Sigma_{a_{ij}} & 0 \cdots \cdots 0 \\ 0 & 1 - \Sigma_{a_{i2}} \cdots 0 \\ \vdots & \ddots \quad \vdots \\ 0 & 0 \cdots 1 - \Sigma_{a_{in}} \end{pmatrix}$$

$$(I - A)B^{-1}Y = CG$$

$$Y = B(I - A)^{-1}CG \tag{15.13}$$

This *row* relationship converts the elements of G into elements of Y or components of GNP into the vector of value added by sector. From the relation between Y and X, we can obtain gross output.

The *column* relationship is

$$q'Y = d'G. \tag{15.14}$$

The vector q is the price deflator of value added, while d is the vector of deflators of GNP components. The relationship

$$q'B(I - A)^{-1}CG = d'G \tag{15.15}$$

shows how the elements of the vector d are obtained as column-weighted sums of the elements of q. This relationship is obtained by equating, term by term, the coefficients of elements of G in both sides of the above equation. The matrix equation is

$$d = C'(I - A)^{-1}Bq. \tag{15.16}$$

Corresponding to the transformation of q into d, we have a transformation of p into d:

$$p = A'p + Bq$$
$$q = B^{-1}(I - A')p$$
$$d = C'(I - A)^{-1}BB^{-1}(I - A')P$$
$$d = C'(I - A)^{-1}(I - A')p. \tag{15.17}$$

The sector production functions, wage determination equations, interest rate equations, indirect tax equations, and factor demand functions enable us to complete the explanation of the national income (value added) by sector.

Two further groups of relationships must be added to this system for completion. They are demographic relationships underlying population and labor supply, and flow-of-funds relationships underlying the determination of interest rates, exchange rates, and monetary aggregates.

This is an enormously large model with both supply-side and demand-side content. It is a truly interrelated model in the sense that macro details of the national income and product accounts cannot be determined independently of the structure of production through the input–output system. Conversely, interindustry flows cannot be determined independently of the Keynesian-type explanation of final demand and national income payments. It is neoclassical in spirit; it is a feasible model and has, in fact, been estimated in different variants. It is the system underpinning for contemporary policy. Just as the system is tied together by interdependence, so should policy be so tied together. Macro policy cannot be intelligently set without structural policy, and structural policy needs macro policy. The goals of full employment without inflation cannot be reached by macro policy alone, but, given adequate time, a feasible combination of macro and structural policies can achieve this goal, according to the underlying model, which is long-term in concept.

The Dismissal of Some Fads

The American economy has clearly come into troubled times. We flooded world markets with dollars in supporting the war in Vietnam; we failed to tax properly to finance the war; we suffered price explosions in world commodity markets during the late 1960s and early 1970s; we sold enormous amounts of grain at unfavorable prices after the Soviet harvest failure of 1972; we suffered the oil embargo and price explosions in oil markets. These and other events cumulatively induced an era of inflation with deteriorating growth, rising unemployment, and declining improvement in productivity. Does this sequence of events invalidate Keynesian economic policy of demand management?

It is fair to say that Keynesian thinking and Keynesian policy were inadequate for dealing with these and other major disturbances, but it should not be said that demand management is wrong where it is needed, and it should not be said that an extended model, built around a Keynesian core and integrated with appropriate supply-side relations, cannot cope with the intricacies of the new situation. The theory and model for the 1980s is clearly different from that for the era 1930–1965, but I shall argue that the Keynes–Leontief model is the type needed and not the counter-revolutionary models recently being proposed.

It is not unnatural that when the economy is in trouble, people should seek some fresh ideas, but it is by no means clear that the new ideas need be replacement of a system of thought rather than appropriate revisions and extensions of mainstream thinking. An immediate reaction by some — almost "knee-jerk" in character — might be to seek a new high correlation for a single relationship that appears to explain a great deal in one fell swoop.

This was the approach of the monetarists who, in 1970, with the help of a new U.S. administration that appeared to be sympathetic, rediscovered a high correlation between nominal national income and money supply (in a lag distribution). The graveyard of economic ideas is filled with sudden discoveries or rediscoveries of high correlations that seem to work beautifully in a fairly short sample period and fall apart disastrously when relied on for projection into the future. The simple monetarist formula broke down in the face of the disturbances of the early 1970s. It had no revealing information about commodity or energy prices, nor about harvest conditions or floating currency rates that were governing the overall course of events. In addition to breaking down in the face of disturbances, it was plagued by inherently noisy information in the main monetary aggregates. There have been successions of data revisions because of reporting errors, conceptual errors, and technical progress in the working of financial markets. There has been practically no attempt to model these intricate details adequately in order to rely on the monetarist approach, and there has been inadequate attention to the choice of monetary aggregates ranging all the way from M_1 to M_7 and on to total credit. The more relevant the magnitude, the more difficult it is to control it; thus the monetarist approach may be empty from the viewpoint of policy.

There is no easy way out of the difficult situation into which the United States and other industrial economies have lapsed. The single-equation and single-minded approach of monetarism will not work any better than in the early 1970s, when the St. Louis Model operators had to admit that their system was not suited for short-range forecasting and when it was shown that mainstream, large-scale econometric models outperformed the purely monetarist approach (see Anderson and Carlson, 1976; McNees, 1973a, 1973b).

There has been a beneficial spin-off from the debate with the monetarists. Model builders of comprehensive systems have been induced to pay far more attention to the careful modeling of the financial sector. It is often found that large-scale models of a distinctly nonmonetarist slant, based on the Keynesian concept of liquidity preference, do, indeed, have steady-state solutions that indicate long-run proportionality between money stock and nominal total output value, but this is a *result* for the ratio of two endogenous variables and is not *causal*. It is not suitable for the formation of long-run policy (see Klein, 1978).

Monetarism was reintroduced as a theoretical point of view in order to justify a certain economic policy. The policy recommendation is to propose strict targets for one or more monetary aggregates, to use central banking policy to try to keep within target ranges, as fixed rules, disregarding the consequences for other market characteristics, mainly interest rates, and to let the rest of the economy be as free as possible, with reductions in the amount of government economic activity. A similar point of view has been behind another new fad in macroeconomics — namely, the idea of rational expectations. The promulgators of this viewpoint maintain that economic decision making by households and firms is based on their perceptions of the present and future course of the economy. Their perceptions form the basis for forming expectations of decision variables, such as market prices and income flows. The agents of economic decision making are assumed to have the same information as public authorities, and decision units have already taken account of possible intervention by authorities to improve the economic situation; therefore, public policy actions are fully anticipated in expectations and can do no good.

Generally speaking, the promoters of this fad argue that activist public policy to improve the economy will be in vain. They are not arguing against the use of formal models as much as they are arguing against the pursuit of policy in general. Yet they have specific arguments against the use of econometric models for the formation of policy. In the general model for the economy as a whole,

$$F(Y_t', Y_{t-1}', \ldots, X_t' \Theta') = e_t , \qquad (15.18)$$

where F is a vector of functions, Y is a vector of endogenous variables, X is a vector of exogenous variables, Θ is a vector of parameters, and e_t is an error vector. The proponents of rational expectations argue that elements of Θ are not constant but depend on the policy instruments in X.

$$\Theta = \Theta(X) \qquad\qquad (15.19)$$

such that when policy changes are introduced through changes in X, the values of Θ will change by amounts that will just offset the effects of the policy changes.

This is a highly stylized model, based on implausible assumptions about human behavior. Information is very unevenly spread throughout the population of economic decision units. The information flows available to different private citizens are strongly dispersed, and not randomly so. The information sets available to public authorities are quite different in scope, timing, and accuracy. Different people use information in very different ways. The parameters of economic models are not necessarily constant, but they are very unlikely to depend primarily on X and in just such a way as to nullify public policy actions. In short, it appears to be a contrived theory and to arrive at a no-action outcome. It is hardly intuitive or operational. This approach offers little by way of positive findings and is hardly consistent with evidence that past economic policy moves have affected the economy. The use of expectations is a time-honored activity in economic theorizing and has been used in specific forms in many instances of econometric model building. A body of data on stated expectations already exists, and much of it is built into models that are being used. These data cover investment expectations, consumer purchase expectations, and business expectations about economic activity. These data bases will surely expand in the future and find increasing applicability in econometric model construction. A fruitful research path is to go to expectations material directly and rely less on surrogate variables. There is, however, nothing in existing models that use direct measurement to suggest that activist policy is futile.

The prevalent use of econometric models for the formulation of economic policy is to search for improved economic performance by considering alternative policy simulations or scenarios. This approach is criticized as being inefficient and likely to fall short of potential for the economy. The concept of *optimal control* has been suggested as a more systematic method of searching for the *best* policy combination.

Let us regroup the variables of the general economic model into the following subgroups:

$$Y_1, Y_2, \ldots, Y_{n_1} = \text{target endogenous variables;}$$
$$W_{n_1+1}, W_{n_1+2}, \ldots, W_n = \text{nontarget endogenous variables;}$$
$$X_1, X_2, \ldots, X_{m_1} = \text{instrumental exogenous variables;}$$
$$Z_{m_1+1}, Z_{m_1+2}, \ldots, Z_m = \text{noninstrumental exogenous variables.}$$

Policymakers are assumed to control instruments (X) in order to achieve (as closely as possible) targets (Y).

The policy-making body should optimize a criterion function — maximize gain or minimize loss — subject to the system constraint. The optimization should be implemented over a policy horizon. The procedure would follow the implications of:

$$L((Y_{11} - Y_{11}^*), \ldots, (Y_{n_1 h} - Y_{n_1 h}^*),$$
$$(X_{11} - X_{11}^*), \ldots, (X_{m_1 h} - X_{m_1 h}^*)) = \min, \qquad (15.20)$$

subject to

$$F(Y_t', W_t', Y_{t-1}', W_{t-1}', \ldots, X_t', Z_t', \hat{\Theta}) = 0, \qquad t = 1, 2, \ldots, h.$$

The loss function is written as L; the target variables are Y^*; and the instruments are X. The horizon length is h, and the sample estimate of Θ is $\hat{\Theta}$. This formulation is nonstochastic, with point estimates being used for Θ and $E(e_t) = 0$.

This problem formulation and solution looks good on paper. It does not take into account the politics and time delays of policy implementation, the possibility of using policy to alter the constraint system, the uncertainty of model performance, the uncertainty on the objective function, or the complicated nature of the problem when both n_1 and m_1 are large. It does not appear that public authorities are disposed to let policy formulation be automatic or to give up the prerogatives for altering F. There is little evidence that enormous gains could be realized by going for the "optimum" rather than continuing to make intelligently inspired simulation searches.

Optimal control theory and application teach a great deal about policy methods and about estimated system properties, but they do not stand ready to transform the economic policy problem to a higher plane of achievement at this time. There is no evidence that it has the power to lead us from the present state of stagflation (see Ball, 1978; Hirsch, Hymans, and Shapiro, 1978). This field of scholarly investigation in economics is not a fad, but the notion that it can provide a policy breakthrough is faddish. The approach is, however, system free and is not tied to any particular specification of economic behavior.

Supply-side economics is right in line with the evolutionary nature of the Keynesian system. The Keynes–Leontief model is inspired by the potentials of supply-side economics, and it has a great deal of supply-side content that has already been built into the presently used group of Wharton Models. There is, however, a national preoccupation with one supply-side behavioral characteristic in certain recent policy recommendations for large-scale tax cuts. It is asserted that labor supply is very sensitive to tax reductions. A neoclassical labor supply function could be written as

$$L^s = f\left(\frac{w - t}{p}\right), \qquad (15.21)$$

where w = nominal wage rate before tax, t = marginal tax yield (on an extra hour's pay), and p = price level. This is typically an upward-sloping function, so the lower the rate of taxation, the greater the supply of labor. It is claimed that if workers could retain a larger amount of each unit of gross wage (or other) income, they would be motivated to work harder.

Another tax effect comes from the denominator of the real wage, p. This is the deflator of output at market prices and, therefore, includes the rate of indirect taxation, sales tax, and the like. It also includes the rate of payroll taxation resulting from employer contributions for social insurance because many employers mark up final prices on the basis of total costs, including payroll tax costs. The higher the rate of indirect taxation, the lower the real wage rate.

Models already account for the rate of indirect taxation. The Wharton Model, for example, includes a positive association between labor supply and the real wage rate, before direct taxes are deducted — that is, (w/p) is the included variable instead of $((w - t)/p)$. But the rate of direct taxation, represented by personal income tax, is accounted for by including real disposable income per worker as another variable in the labor supply equation. The striking point, however, is that the sign of the marginal effect is negative!

This result occurs because there are two possible effects of direct taxes, or of take-home pay, in the labor supply function. There is a positive incentive effect, but there is also a negative "target" effect. The closer that workers get to their target levels of income, or the more that they surpass present aspirations, the less they have to work and the more they can enjoy leisure. The work-leisure trade-off gives rise to a well-known and long-accepted concept of labor economics, called the *backward-bending supply curve of labor*. It was frequently cited during World War II as a cause of worker absenteeism in high-wage defense plants. The proponents of massive tax cuts, across the board, must risk having the negative work incentive effect outweigh the positive effect. The Wharton Model results suggest that the negative effects do outweigh the positive, even though they do not prove this in a definitive sense. The work-leisure trade-off leans heavily toward leisure in our affluent community, and the burden of proof is certainly on the shoulders of the specialized brand of supply-side economics. Rather than rest the case on *a priori* reasoning by assertion or even by crude regression analysis, it would seem much more convincing to examine factory records on absenteeism, associated wage changes, deductions from gross pay, and the use of leisure-time activities. It hardly seems possible that subjective motivations resulting from incentives can be discovered without personal interview surveys by sampling techniques. Until more careful investigations are made, it is not reasonable to accept the claims by the supply-side enthusiasts that large and protracted personal income tax cuts will overcome the present stagflation problem.

Another variable in the labor supply function of the Wharton Model, and one that also has strong credentials among labor market economists, is the discouraged worker hypothesis. This idea suggests an inverse correlation between labor supply and unemployment. When labor markets are tight (unemployment low), it is relatively easy to find jobs, and workers are encouraged to be in the market for positions. In periods of high unemployment, the reverse happens, and many potential job seekers are discouraged from looking for work. As taxes are reduced the unemployment rate should fall and labor supply should rise, thus cushioning the inflationary impact of expansion. This aspect of labor market bahavior is already built into mainstream models, where careful simulation analysis indicates that massive tax cuts, across the board, are not adequate by themselves to correct stagflation. This fad provides no adequate basis for overturning received macroeconomic doctrine.

There may be grains of truth in the policies of tax cuts, but they cannot be trusted to do the wonders that their backers claim lie in store for the economy. There is no visible alternative to patient extension of the basic model to include the supply-side fundamentals of the Keynesian–Leontief system and to press steadily for policies that stimulate capital formation, raise the fraction of GNP saved (and invested), improve energy balance, deal with the environment, and ultimately raise the growth rate of productivity improvement. This is a more firmly established policy mix, which eventually leads to improvement of the inflation–unemployment trade-off, according to simulation exercises with estimates of the Keynes–Leontief system (see New York Stock Exchange, 1979).

References

Anderson, L., and K. Carlson, 1976, "St. Louis Model revisited," in *Econometric Model Performance*, eds. L. R. Klein and S. Burmeister (University of Pennsylvania Press, Philadelphia).

Ball, R. J, 1978, *Report of the Committee on Policy Optimisation* (HMSO, London).

Hirsch, A. A., S. H. Hymans, and H. T. Shapiro, 1978, "Econometric review of alternative fiscal and monetary policy, 1971–75," *Review of Economics and Statistics* **60**, pp. 334–345.

Klein, L. R., 1978, "Money in a general equilibrium system: Empirical aspects of the quantity theory," *Economie Appliquée* **31** (**1–2**) pp. 5–14.

McNees, S. K., 1973a, "The predictive accuracy of econometric forecasts," *New England Economic Review* (September/October), pp. 3–27.

———, 1973b, "A comparison of the GNP forecasting accuracy of the Fair and St. Louis econometric models," *New England Economic Review* (September/October), pp. 29–34.

New York Stock Exchange, 1979, *Building a Better Future* (NYSE, New York).

Editorial Note

Prefix number 15 in the equation and chart numberings refer to chapter number 15 of the source, *Samuelson and Neoclassical Economics, op. cit.*

6

THE KEYNESIAN REVOLUTION:
FIFTY YEARS LATER, A LAST WORD[†]

Keynesian theory and policy were being formulated in Cambridge, England almost 60 years ago, and I have already contributed to symposia on Keynesian thinking on the occasion of the 50th anniversary of the publication of *The General Theory of Employment, Interest and Money* (whose preface is dated December 13, 1935).[1] The University of Pennsylvania Economics Department chose as the theme of its annual Economics Day, 1992: "The Keynesian Revolution: Fifty Years Later" which is approximately dated correctly. Although my book was published in 1947, it was conceived and written during 1944 as a doctoral dissertation at MIT.[2] The descriptive title, *Keynesian Revolution*, was used by me, but it undoubtedly occurred previously somewhere in the economics literature. I got the idea for the title from my teacher and thesis supervisor, Paul Samuelson. It serves in the present context as a general description of a body of thought whose role in historical and contemporary discussion of economic analysis is relevant and of interest. In the framework of the present paper, it is used as a vehicle by me to provide my present views on the subject through the medium of responding to constructive critics who commented on my own conception of the Keynesian Revolution at a conference in Philadelphia on April 10, 1992.

There are three facets of macroeconomics that form the basis of the present paper:

(i) **Macroeconomic theory** — I was not the first to use the term *macroeconomics*, but it was not yet accepted as a separate subject of specialization in the study of economics. I used the term in trying to develop aggregation formulas to bridge microeconomics and macroeconomics, but Pieter de Wolff had used it before World War II.[3] Macroeconomics was included in classes on the business cycle. That was my training.

(ii) **Policy formulation** — Keynesian economics was concerned with the problem of the day, namely, how to emerge from the Great Depression. In general, Keynes'

[†]From *Lawrence Klein's The Keynesian Revolution: 50 Years After* (University of Pennsylvania, Philadelphia, 1992), pp. 41–53.
[1]See e.g., "Le politiche economiche Keynesiane: Un analisi retrospettiva," which was the subject of an address to Banco di Napoli, June 26, 1987.
[2]L. R. Klein, *The Keynesian Revolution* (Macmillan, N. Y. 1947; 2nd ed., 1966).
[3] L. R. Klein, "Macroeconomics and the theory of rational behavior," *Econometrica* **XIV** (1946), p. 93.

contributions to economics were developed around contemporary policy issues. The Keynesian revolution tried to develop a systematic and general body of thought, but it had more than a theoretical message. There is both Keynesian theory and Keynesian policy. Professional economists are particularly interested in the former and inquiring citizens in the latter.

(iii) **Macroeconometric modeling** — The first efforts at formal model building were produced by Jan Tinbergen, and he has acknowledged that he was strongly motivated by Keynes' ideas, both in terms of theory and policy. I carried on in the Tinbergen tradition and was obviously stimulated by Keynesian macroeconomics. Macroeconometrics, like all econometrics, is doctrine-free, but there is no doubt that the ready mathematical formulation of Keynesian theory was simply wanting to be put into formal statistical models. Also, Keynes lent great impetus to national income accounting. His own contributions and those of other active pioneer statisticians among economists (particularly Simon Kuznets and Colin Clark) made possible the fitting of Keynesian models to data, which were just becoming available on a large scale in the 1930s.

Responses to Participants in Pennsylvania's Economics Day, April 10, 1992

There are many on-going debates and critiques of the contents of points (i), (ii), (iii) above. They were skillfully brought into the open at the 1992 conference held at the University of Pennsylvania. A systematic summary of major points and references follows.

Edmund Phelps. Ned Phelps raised interesting points about Keynesian analysis, especially in terms of economic theory — extending the analysis to cover micro foundations. His extensions to cover such issues as supply, production, factor demand, and interest rates all sit well with me in the sense that the most productive theoretical research that builds on Keynesian foundations could be more fully described as the Keynesian-neoclassical synthesis. That lengthier phrase better describes my own evolution as a Keynesian. Ned Phelps is, of course, right in pointing out that general equilibrium theory was neglected by Keynes, and there is the possibility that no macroeconomics equilibrium exists (or existed during the Great Depression). Ned surmises that negative interest rates may have been required in order to find a full employment position.

I, personally, tried to handle that problem by introducing, at the next stage of my career, what eventually came to be called the Phillips curve. It showed how wage rates could be determined dynamically, while the economy was in motion, all the while that no stationary equilibrium existed. My own econometric estimates of Phillips curves showed that very large unemployment rates would have been required to stabilize wage rates. Ned Phelps' concept of a natural rate of unemployment and efficiency wages constitute an elegant way of looking at the problem. But I feel very comfortable with my own versions of wage determination equations following labor marker and other conditions.

Ned Phelps is also astute in pointing out that Keynes was overly preoccupied with the short run and also with the mechanics of the closed economy. Roy Harrod, Evsey Domar and others were quick to extend the horizon of analysis to the long run. That proved to be very constructive. Keynes' last contributions were to open his system to international considerations, through his contributions to the establishment of the postwar monetary system. He was a major architect of the Bretton Woods Conference and Agreement. It is odd that an English economist would neglect to emphasize the open aspects of his theories or policy prescription, but that extension was not too long in coming and added to the Keynesian Revolution. Before the breakdown of the Bretton Woods Agreement, I was engaged in extending macroeconometrics, in the Keynesian vein, to the world economy, and most of the applications of the 1950s/1960s were fully aware of the international implications.

In the modern applications of Keynesian-inspired macroeconometrics (in fact, ever since interest rates began to rise in the 1950s), concern with general equilibrium and interest rate determination have been seriously pursued. Although we were taught (and are still teaching) that the public debt was not a significant burden because "we owe it to ourselves," we Keynesians were quick to point out the weight of the burden when internationally held debt became more prevalent, both for the United States, and for many LDCs. In this situation, the financing of U.S. debt was very costly, measured by the high nominal and real interest rates that were realized. Although the United States managed to grow for a long period after 1982, it was at the expense of many people in the debt-burdened LDCs, who experienced a "lost decade." Simple Keynesian economic analysis as it was told in the *General Theory* could not adequately explain what was taking place; it required a more elaborate system that was, in fact, the natural outcome of econometric manifestations of an internationalized Keynesian system, integrated into world models.

Albert Ando. Keynesian economics was under attack from the very beginning of its public release, but the Keynesian Revolution prevailed and dominated macroeconomics for three or more decades. The latest in a series of destructively aimed attacks came from Robert Lucas who has claimed (but not demonstrated) that important parameters in macroeconometric models, including, of course, those that are Keynesian-inspired, are variable and, what is more, functions of economic policy decisions.

Albert Ando argues that the price wage sector of the MPS (MIT–Pennsylvania–Social Science Research Council) Model works very well in an extended mode of a Phillips curve. He recognizes that the early versions of the Phillips curve seemed to go off course during the 1960s.

I agree with Albert Ando's analysis but would make an even stronger statement. If we constructively build a Phillips curve that allows for price movement, and demographic shifts, the relation is stable in the sense that it can be used to make useful econometrically-based judgments. Also, the price-determination part of the system should allow appropriately for productivity changes in addition to wage movements; then there is no insurmountable problem in explaining the inflation of the 1970s. After all, my original version and Phillips' later version both looked at the relation between wage rates (not inflation rates) and labor market conditions. It is no surprise that productivity is variable and plays an important role in the relationship between wages (and other costs) and prices.

As for the Lucas critique, it has been known for years — even decades — that models with variable coefficients in econometric systems may add to explanation of movements in the economy. I investigated such econometric issues in the early 1950s, and they were topics of interest at the Cowles Commission in the 1940s.[4] Of course, coefficients might vary, but who is to decree that their variation can be best represented by simple relationships to economic policy? That, surely, is a contrived argument. To me, as a student of the Keynesian Revolution, it is hard to see how the young group of macroeconomists of the 1980s became so enamored of this viewpoint, without careful resort to substantiating evidence.

Albert Ando introduced three other important issues in connection with an understanding of the Keynesian Revolution, namely, the effects of income distribution, the importance of infrastructure investment in the public sector, and the functioning of automatic stabilizers in the macroeconomy.

Immediately after the publication of the *General Theory* by Keynes, econometricians, just beginning their studies in an entirely new field, tried to estimate aggregate consumption functions. They realized from the start, that income distribution could have something to do with the translation of aggregate income into aggregate consumer spending. Though logically impeccable, they found only modest distributional effects, but decades later after a great deal of "inequitable" progress and the appearance of many very high incomes (of multi-millionaires and billionaires) there is more interest and significance in the effects of income distribution. This is a natural refinement. Also the effects of wealth distribution and income distribution on the implementation of Keynesian policy, in addition to the matter of aggregating micro consumption functions, is of increasing relevance and concern.

Public infrastructure investment was a natural early policy tool when Keynesian ideas were followed by President Roosevelt's Administration during the Great Depression. These ideas received further support during the 1950s and 1960s when the bold planning of the nations' Interstate Highway System was put into place. Meanwhile, what little fiscal policy there has been in the 1980s and today is limited to tax reductions. The beautiful Interstate System has been allowed to deteriorate, along with bridges and other important pieces of public infrastructure. Now, to help us attain full capacity growth again, we are sorely in need of refurbished infrastructure, both for its direct contribution to economic performance and for its

---

[4]L. R. Klein, *A Textbook of Econometrics* (Row, Peterson, Evanston, 1952).

indirect contribution via the Keynesian multiplier. David Aschauer, though he may have exaggerated the magnitude of infrastructure multipliers, extended the original demand-side Keynesian concept to added contributions on the supply side.[5] He argued, quite correctly, that building up of the public infrastructure can provide added support to an anemic economy by facilitating private-sector production activity. Not only do such public works create factor incomes, which then multiply through the economy, but they contribute to better performance in the private sector. Who can argue with the proposition that improved transportation, communication, public health, and other facilities make the private sector perform better?

Not only did President Eisenhower have the advantages of the Interstate construction activity to stimulate the US economy in the 1950s, but he also had the automatic stabilizers silently and efficiently delivering the Keynesian medicine to keep the economy in good working order. Unfortunately, subsequent administrations have eroded this property of our fiscal system. The latest blow was delivered in the tax reform legislation of 1986, when the progressivity of the personal income tax was seriously reduced. This and other stabilizers have been so emasculated that the recuperative powers of the economy have been reduced in the face of a downturn. What is needed is some vintage Keynesian thinking to restore strong effects of automatic stabilization once again. These stabilizers served the US well through many postwar recessions but were mistakenly reduced in the name of tax reform and populist versions of supply-side economics.

Thomas Cooley. It is clear to me that Tom Cooley, as a student, learned what I was trying to convey to him and his colleagues in macroeconomics and econometrics. He is now pursuing new pathways in these subjects beyond what was being taught at Pennsylvania during the 1960s.

His oral remarks, delivered at Economics Day, 1992, and his extremely lucid, well-reasoned written comments prompt three responses.

In the first place, he recognized the formal neoclassical roots of Keynesian economics. By the time I was teaching this subject at Pennsylvania in the 1960s, the views of *The Keynesian Revolution* of the 1940s had changed and evolved. Instead of standing apart as Keynesian economics, the body of material, on the theoretical side, has become a model of the Keynesian-neoclassical synthesis. This is the same point that I made in connection with Ned Phelps' presentation. Tom Cooley clearly recognized the neoclassical foundations, and these are to be expected of a Cambridge University economist like Keynes.

In order to pass from micro foundations of neoclassical behavior embodied in the

— theory of the household (consumer behavior)

— theory of the firm (producer behavior)

— principles of market clearing (price formation)

---

[5]David Aschauer, "Why is infrastructure important?," in *Is There a Shortfall in Public Capital Investment?*, ed. Alicia Munnell (Federal Reserve Bank of Boston, Boston, 1990), pp. 21–50.

it is necessary to deal with aggregation. In the *Keynesian Revolution*, I dealt with this problem as a study in index formation.[6] This work showed that representative agent theory could be used, but only if aggregates or indexes were appropriately defined. This matter is very important but entirely ignored by modern theorists (and scores of students) who use principal agent theory in an uncareful and trivial way without facing up to the index number or aggregation problem. Over the years following the publication of *The Keynesian Revolution*, I have come to think differently about the problem of bridging micro- and macroeconomics. The best procedure is to integrate the microeconomic equations over the joint frequency distribution of explanatory variables and express the resulting macroeconomic equations as functions of the mean and other parameters of the distribution of explanatory variables. This is close, in spirit, to what the early interpreters of Keynes did when they estimated aggregate consumption as a function of aggregate income and Gini or Pareto measures of income inequality. They were doing the right thing in an approximate empirical sense but had no formal theoretical explanation for what they were doing. In any event, they were not using the easy (and wrong) way out by appealing to principal agent theory, as a crutch.

Tom Cooley raised the issue whether postwar business cycles were milder than those that occurred earlier, possibly as a result of Keynesian lessons. We did not return to the conditions of the Great Depression after the Second World War, as many people had thought might occur. My explanation of the reduced amplitude of postwar cycles would be that the automatic stabilizers were, indeed, effective and helped to moderate postwar cycles. This is essentially a repetition of what I said in commenting on Albert Ando's remarks. In addition to the reliance on automatic stabilizers, there was discreet intervention from time to time with Keynesian tools. These, too, helped stabilize the economy after 1947.

Peter Pauly. It is quite right to draw a distinction between macroeconometrics or empirical macroeconomics and the *Keynesian Revolution*. It just happened that the early econometricians were sympathetic with and interested in Keynes' economics of the *General Theory*. It is true that macroeconometrics opens the possibility for active policy formation, and that was Keynes' point of view, as well. *The Keynesian Revolution* provided only a framework for macroeconometrics, albeit a convenient and useful framework. What could not have been foreseen was the massive development of computing. We labored with computing tasks in the early days of macroeconometric model building, but today the investigator is liberated. One can explore more possibilities, and that opened the field to those attracted to other types of systems, besides the Keynesian paradigm.

In the early years of macroeconometric model building, we had hoped that by testing and sifting we would narrow the field to the single model that could be used in a definitive way for policy formation. That was not to be, and, as Peter Pauly observed, there was no convergence. Model building is open to many points of

---

[6]See footnote 3.

view. He looks for new developments in Europe, in contrast with the early emphasis on macroeconometrics in the United States (except for Tinbergen's Holland). He also looks for more international modeling and for guidance from New Keynesian economic theory. These are all constructive viewpoints, with which I can well agree.

Frank Diebold. Coming to the subject in the last 10 years or more, Frank finds a diversity of macroeconomic models to be studied by econometric methods. These are classical, Keynesian, monetarist, neo-Keynesian, and real business cycle models. He properly observes that there was no systematic macroeconomics before Keynes and that the econometric side of the subject received its impetus from Keynesian theory. The econometric methods developed at the Cowles Commission for Research in Economics, the University of Chicago, during the 40s was, in principle, non-doctrinal but was, in practice, identified with Keynesian economics.[7] An important advance, after the Cowles commission thrust, was the contribution of Adelman and Adelman, that showed that a Keynesian type model in a stochastic mode was capable of generating dynamic movements that conformed closely to many aspects of the documented history of US business cycles.[8]

Joel Popkin. Joel participated in the rapid expansion of model applications for interpretation and policy guidance along Keynesian lines. He appreciated the great expansion of macroeconometric modeling but looks now for a slowing down. I believe that slowdowns will occur for large groups of investigators or investigating organizations, but the totality of macroeconometric studies is undoubtedly increasing rapidly because single investigators are so well equipped with versatile, inexpensive hardware, an ample supply of software, and accessible data files. In effect, this set of circumstances puts almost anyone into this field of activity if they are so inclined.

Joel observes that model-based forecasting accuracy is superior but not by a wide margin. The real challenge ahead is to improve accuracy at turning points, but significant improvements will come slowly. He cites, quite appropriately, inventory investment and profits as elusive magnitudes for which we must work very hard to improve accuracy.

Alan Blinder. Although Alan Blinder concentrated on policy issues, he raised very provocative questions about Keynesian economic policy that require theoretical analysis in order to provide answers. In the first place, Alan properly characterized my own thinking at the time of *The Keynesian Revolution* as a blend of activism and optimism. This is quite correct; we thought that Keynesian policy implementation would be easy because it was so obviously the right thing to do and that the public at large-would be readily persuaded. We thought that we had the makings of a good economy right in the palm of our hands. In particular, when I went from MIT with

---

[7]For an interpretation of this period see, Lawrence R. Klein, "Econometric contributions of the Cowles Commission, 1944–47; a retrospective view," *Bance Nazionale del Layoro Quarterly Review,* No. 177 (June 1991), pp. 107–17.

[8]Irma and Frank Adelman, "The dynamic properties of the Klein–Goldberger model," *Econometrica* **27** (October 1959), pp. 596–625.

a fresh Ph.D. in hand, in 1944, to the Cowles Commission, it was ostensibly a move to plan postwar economic policy on the basis of a newly constructed econometric model of the United States, this model being prepared especially for that purpose. Also my tenure at the Cowles Commission, University of Chicago, was used to prepare my Ph.D. thesis, written essentially in 1944, for publication in 1947, as the *The Keynesian Revolution*. The theoretical arguments were worked over, again and again, in debate with my Chicago colleagues, both within and outside the Cowles Commission. In addition, the whole aggregation problem was formulated there, in order to provide good micro foundations for the macro model, and the model was constructed in order to fulfill Jacob Marschak's invitation to me to join the Cowles staff. He said, persuasively to me, "what this country needs is a new Tinbergen model" — to be ready to guide economic policy in the postwar period.

Marschak was optimistic because he thought that the new econometric techniques being developed at the Cowles Commission would turn out to be very powerful. Paul Samuelson and I had just been exposed to a preview at MIT, in a lecture given by Trygve Haavelmo.[9]

Alan points out that forecasts need to be good in order to steer the economy to full employment and keep it there in a stable economic environment. Of course, this was a main objective of my going to Chicago in 1944, and we were involved, at the Cowles Commission, with this very issue when I prepared forecasts, from the first version of the new model, for the Committee for Economic Development to use in their analyses of the postwar economy. We had the forecasted economy right, and prevailing opinions among economists, particularly those of Keynesian persuasion, were wrong, but they would not listen to our case.[10]

Forecasting ability is all important, not only for the proper implementation of Keynesian economic policy, but for any policy. I maintain today, as I did in 1946, that we can in fact make good macroeconomic forecasts for policy guidance through the medium of large-scale econometric models, built along the lines of the Keynesian-neoclassical synthesis. These forecasts are better than any other, although the margin is not huge; the effort requires continuing diligence, persistence, and use of all the new technologies in computing, telecommunications, and provision of economic data.

Modern macroeconomists are all wrong about forecasting failures. The new models of the younger generation or new ideas of modern macroeconomics provide inferior forecasts, by a significant margin, but the advocates have not shown willingness to put their ideas to the test on a highly replicated basis, which is necessary for forecast appraisal.

---

[9] "Abstracts of lectures presented at the Statistics Seminar, MIT, 1942–1943," *Statistical Science* **6** (April 1991), pp. 320–28. See especially the remarks by Lawrence Klein, Paul Samuelson, and the abstract of Trygve Haavelmo's lecture.

[10] When Albert Hart, who was the staff member of the CED cooperating on this project, sent a story about the episode to the editors of *Econometrica* in 1976, after having come across our worksheets while cleaning out his files, they rejected it for publication — showing the same degree of perception as our professional colleagues did in 1946.

Also, standards have changed drastically since 1946. Forecasts now are much more accurate than they were in 1946. We never dreamed, at the Cowles Commission, that we could ever achieve the accuracy standards that we now have, but people's perception of needs for precision have changed, as well. Users of economic forecasts are very demanding; they want pinpoint precision, with almost no delay. Also they want masses of detail now, not simply the predicted movements of the main aggregates that are familiar as macroeconomic indicators. They want industrial market composition, international information, and also broad social science information.

Good forecasting does not come easily or inexpensively, but it can be done, and it can serve the needs of economic policy, far beyond the original concepts of *The Keynesian Revolution*. There are few economists who are willing to undertake the forecasting challenge because of the demanding attention to detail and intensity of effort.

Alan notes that "fine-tuning" is difficult. At the time of *The Keynesian Revolution*, economists did not pay a great deal of attention to such things as steadiness or stability of economic policy. People resent being whipsawed, and politicians often will not pay attention to economic policy needs, on their own merits; these are reasons why fine-tuning is more difficult than was thought at the time of the Keynesian Revolution.

Alan asks whether Keynesian theory is symmetric with respect to inflation. In *The Keynesian Revolution*, I devoted some attention to Keynes' concern about wartime inflation through analysis of the "inflationary gap." This is very useful theorizing about practical problems of policy, but does not have a solid base on the analysis of price determination. It lacks appreciation of speculation, performance of commodity markets, and the role of monetary authorities. In the evolution of macroeconometric models that started with *The Keynesian Revolution* these matters are handled much better, and such models did not fail to anticipate inflation of the 1970s or early 1980s, contrary to the assertions of some modern macroeconomists.

At the time of the writing of *The Keynesian Revolution* we were in the final stages of wartime price control. This was obviously an unusual situation. The controls served their emergency purposes well during the Second World War. My own thinking has certainly been changed, in this respect, from one of support for temporary use in an emergency to substitution of more liberal techniques of income policies for periods of normal functioning of an economy.

Does Keynesian economic policy lead to persistent deficits? Alan poses this question. Deficits should be temporary. Deficits should fluctuate with economic conditions and average to zero over long periods of time. This has been U.S. economic experience until 1980, when the last two administrations have introduced or oversaw policies that have led to unusually large deficits that have persisted for more than one decade. This has not been a period of Keynesian economic policy. One might characterize the tax cuts of 1981–83, which stimulated the economy and helped to generate large deficits, as Keynesian policy, but this would be a careless use of the term. There is nothing in the Keynesian prescriptions to support highly unbalanced policies or excessive reliance on monetary policy to provide economic stabilization. Keynesian policy does not seek a unique combination of tax, public spending, and monetary changes. There were an infinite number of policy alternatives open to politicians during the 1980s that could have put the US economy on a stable path of high employment growth, without accelerating inflation.

A new feature of the U.S. economic situation in the 1980s which was commented on above in connection with Ned Phelps' paper, was the growth of foreign debt as well as domestic debt. Much of the debt, in recent years, has been purchased by foreign investors, and this changes the nature of the interest service burden. It is not a refutation of Keynesian fiscal or public finance policy. It is simply a relevant issue in the extension of the analysis to an open economy.

It is also said that the debt accumulation of recent years has not been a serious matter because the economy continued to grow until 1990, even though debt was growing persistently. A main feature of deficits and associated debt is that if they are unusually large, as has been the case, the funds that the government must float will have to command a high enough interest rate to induce people to buy them — not only domestic citizens or institutions, but also foreigners. The end result is likely to be high interest rates; i.e., U.S. interest rates are higher than they otherwise would have been, had fiscal policy been more prudent and well balanced with monetary policy. Perhaps U.S. rates have been as much as 200 basis points higher than would have been necessary, under more sensible fiscal and other policies.

Not only did high interest rates cause problems for highly indebted developing countries, but they also had severe effects on the U.S. economy. The recession that began in the summer 1990, has been very stubborn and hard on the people of the United States. One reason for the drawn out sluggishness of the U.S. economy has been the high indebtedness with the high interest rates, i.e., higher than they otherwise would have been, had there not been the enormous debt accumulation.

Keynes sought spending, the antithesis of saving, in order to pull the main economies of the world out of the Great Depression. It is well known that he stressed the need for more spending in the United States. After the war, and after Keynes' death, it has not been a persistent issue to find more spending. In very short-run cyclical spurts, it has been important to promote consumer spending, but these are not appropriate long-run policies.

There are times to promote spending and times to promote saving. There is nothing inherent in Keynesian theory or policy to argue that policy should always be the same. Times change and with these changes, policy should appropriately shift. Keynes, throughout his life, dealt with issues of the day, and the *General Theory* was obviously developed from thinking about how capitalism could emerge from the Great Depression. At that time spending was foremost in Keynesian policy makers' minds. There are well-known, and truthful, stories, about the promotion of spending by Keynes, no matter whether such spending was useful or important.

In a sense, he supported "pyramid-building," even though such a measure was far from optimal.

After the War, people were preoccupied with reconstruction and growth. *Saving* was not the enemy once it became evident that the wrong-headed forecasts of return to the conditions of the 1930s were not going to happen. In addition to the changing times, there was extension of the Keynesian theory to deal with growth, by Harrod, Domar and others. There was also extension to deal with international trade. Again, Harrod was prominent, together with others, in promoting this generalization of the narrow Keynesian system. Literal interpretations of the Keynesian Revolution based on strict reading of the *General Theory* and also based on the first formal Keynesian models in mathematical expression can generate unproductive caricatures of the system, but if one looks at the evolving Keynesian-neoclassical synthesis, there is no danger at all in becoming locked into fixed positions that do not apply to a changing economic environment.

Finally, I want to comment on Alan's reference to Social Security as an all inclusive system that would automatically take care of things for which people privately save. One of the more sensational plans for the postwar world, of which there were many in different lines of human needs or behavior, was the Beveridge Plan, labeled as a cradle-to-grave system for all citizens. This was a British plan but similar thinking took place in the United States. In fact, one of my term papers as a MIT student, when I was also working on *The Keynesian Revolution* was to estimate the cost of a similar plan for the United States.[11]

When I first met Lord Beveridge, as a neighbor in Oxford, his remarks to me were complaints that the government was not allowing spectacles to be covered by his system. Some countries went further than others in providing total medical care, retirement benefits, unemployment benefits, higher education and other things for which people privately save. The United States has been a laggard among nations, but I thought, with many of my fellow citizens, during the 1940s, that the postwar era would be one of great social progress. Now, we are forced to be more realistic. People do have to save for supplementary retirement, far and above old age benefits; higher education is very expensive; medical costs are very high; unemployment benefits have severe limitations. We did not fulfill the expectations of Lord Beveridge.

Final comments. One's thesis of nearly 50 years past has usually been put to rest at an early stage. I want to thank the organizers and participants in Economics Day, 1992, for bringing back old memories in a constructive and entertaining way. I truly appreciate the thoughtfulness of all the comments and the stimulus that they provided to re-think many issues or positions taken over the decades in relation to the evolving social system. Keynesian economics has changed with the times — for the better.

---

[11] L. R. Klein, "The cost of a 'Beveridge Plan' in the United States," *The Quarterly Journal of Economics* **LVIII** (May 1944), pp. 423–37.

PART II

ECONOMETRIC MODELS AND METHODOLOGY

The selected papers in Part II are organized under two sections: *Models* and *Methodology*. Lawrence Klein, whose Nobel citation reads "for the creation of econometric models and their application to the analysis of economic fluctuations and economic policies," himself describes the 'antecedents' and the 'prospects' of macroeconometric model-building in two papers listed under *Models*. "Antecedents of macroeconometric models," and "Prospects of macroeconometric modeling," are respectively the first and last chapters of *A History of Macroeconometric Model-Building* (1991), which one reviewer has described as 'a permanent and authoritative reference' book on the subject. The chapter on 'antecedents' traces a number of developments in economic theory that foreshadowed the initiation of macroeconometric models a half-century ago. Klein begins with Leon Walras' elements of pure economics, and Vilfredo Pareto's version of general equilibrium economics. He then moves on to works of Ragnar Frisch and Michal Kalecki, and the arrival of Keynesian macroeconomic theory. The discussion encompasses the earliest experiences in macroeconometric modeling in the 1930s and 40s, particularly the debate between Keynes and Jan Tinbergen, the first Nobel Laureate in Economic Science (with Ragnar Frisch), about presenting a Keynesian macroeconomic system as a set of empirically estimated mathematical relationships.

In the chapter on "prospects," Klein looks ahead to the future development of macroeconometric modeling. He predicts that research activity in the field of model-building will continue to grow, particularly towards expanding the scope of the models by reducing the degree of exogeneity, improving forecasts, refining dynamic elements, more use of control theory applications, construction of flow of funds models, and international modeling. After making a brief rebuttal to the present-day critics of macroeconometric models, his assessment of their future prospects ends on an optimistic note.

"A postwar quarterly model," appearing in the mid-1960s is an important landmark in the history of model-building. It descended from the widely celebrated Klein–Goldberger model and became a forerunner of the Wharton group of models. It was medium in size, and it provided a bridge between small annual models on the one hand and large quarterly models, and models with higher frequency, on the other. Furthermore, it was the first model that was built with an explicit purpose of short-term forecasting of economic activity. The underlying view was to use it as a tool for giving empirically supported understanding of how a 'present-day' economic system works, and for evaluating the impact of alternative economic policies.

Importantly, the simulation calculations of this model were used to obtain guidelines for the historic 1964 tax cut legislation in the United States. It was an enormously successful early experiment in the use of the Keynesian demand management policy.

Also, "The quarterly model" broke new methodological grounds on several points. In it, Klein successfully tested and put into operation new aspects of macroeconometric modeling that he had noted at about the same time in "The Keynesian revolution revisited." Specifically, the model was less aggregative, it described the U.S. economy in more detail; it made use of anticipatory data and realization functions linking actual behavior to expectations; it used the concept and a measure of capacity utilization rate; and it treated the labor market more explicitly. There was also a major breakthrough in linking the real and nominal entities of the system. A generation of students were trained on building and maintaining this model.

"The present debate about macro economics and econometric model specification" is a lecture which Klein delivered to an audience in Taipei, Taiwan, in 1982. For a beginner and one uninitiated in the practice of macroeconometric modeling, it is an absolutely rewarding reading. Herein, in his typical simple style, Klein deals again with major issues involved in the topical debate among economists on macroeconomic theory

and policy, and associated practices of macroeconometric modeling. His analytical main arguments on the fallacy of monetarism, on the rhetoric about the 'newness' of rational expectations, and on the parochial but 'fashionable' interpretation of the so-called supply-side economics are all presented with simple examples that are instructive.

Ever since the breakdown of Bretton Woods system of fixed parities in 1971, the problem of modeling exchange rates between various currencies and explaining capital flows across countries has acquired tremendous significance. At the same time national economies in the world have grown increasingly interdependent; consequently, international coordination of economic policies has become a frontier issue. This has given strong impetus to construction of international models with full intercountry linkage mechanisms.

In his paper, "International models ...," Klein describes the linkage mechanism of the Project LINK system, how it functions, and how it is used regularly to forecast the world economy and evaluate internationally coordinated economic policies. Specific scenarios are generated with respect to coordination of both fiscal and monetary policies, exchange rate coordination and coordination of industrial policy.

Project LINK was initiated by Klein and others in 1968. It was fully described in the paper reprinted in Marquez (1985). Although Project LINK is coming close to celebrating the 30th anniversary of its inception, it continues to be in full and active operation. There is a vast literature available on the LINK system; this paper represents an example of its typical operational use. Several other international models subsequently constructed have also been listed in Klein's paper.

Important methodological aspects of macro-econometric modeling were briefly touched upon in the chapter on "Prospects ...," some are now focused upon in the section on *Methodology* in Part II. Researchers, as well as graduate students of econometrics, should find reading these papers truly rewarding. Four of these papers are 'in-honor' essays. In the opening paper, Klein deals with an accounting system that provides a springboard to model construction. In "Model building to conform to a complete system of social accounts" (1970), he explains the linkage between three separate accounting systems, namely National Income Accounts (NIA), Input–Output (I–O) accounts, and Flow-of-Funds (FF) accounts. The National Income Accounts show balance between aggregate product valuation and income valuation. They are central to macroeconometric models, which primarily concentrate on explaining final demand. In contrast, the I–O accounts show balance between gross output and intermediate output plus final demand. Particularly, for given values of final demand, the I–O models concentrate on explaining either intermediate demand, or gross output (and its sectoral composition) with full recognition of intermediate demand. The NIA, on the other hand, are linked to the Flow-of-Funds accounts through the sources of funds. The sources of funds for net investment, a basic component of NIA system, is found in FF accounts.

Klein schematically shows that the NIA system occupies a central position among the three accounts. In explaining final demand, the NIA system is related to intermediate goods flows of the I–O system, and in explaining savings (sources of investment funding), it is linked to financial flows of the FF system. For a given economy, together, these three accounts explain transactions in goods and services, transactions in financial instruments, and net final transactions that add up to Net National product. He also emphasizes that in order to understand the economy fully, we need to integrate the equations based on these three systems together into one workable model. He gives examples of the Brookings Model and Wharton Models (see the related chapters in *A History of Macroeconometric Model-Building*) in which first steps toward such integration were made.

Importantly, it may be noted that an extended description of full linkage of these accounts is laid out in "Models of the economy as a whole," Chap. 1, of his *Lectures in Econometrics* (1983). But this paper also contains an illustration of one application of an integrated system, and it foreshadows and complements the discussion appearing later in "Econometric aspects of input–output analysis," *Frontiers of Input–Output Analysis*, eds. R. E. Miller, K. R. Polenski, and A. Z. Rose (1989). The students of National Accounting Systems and macroeconometric modeling will find this material immensely interesting.

Written initially for the *International Encyclopedia of Social Sciences* (1968), and later reprinted with some revision in *International Encyclopaedia of Statistics* (1978), "Simultaneous equation estimation," is a lucid and succinct exposition of major econometric techniques of estimating simultaneous equation systems, a standard topic in any advanced textbook of econometrics. This paper is particularly beneficial to graduate students. In simple, but clear, technical terms, Klein analyses the logical and statistical foundations of interrelationship of various estimating techniques by using the maximum likelihood method as a reference point.

A classic problem of *degrees of freedom* is that the number of sample points (T) must be larger than the number of parameters to be estimated. It is dealt with in the paper, "The treatment of undersized samples in econometrics" (1973). This problem generally arises in acute form in estimating a system of equations. Klein shows how, by appropriately recognizing two aspects of counting rules, we can establish necessary conditions for the existence of consistent estimates of parameters. First, the number of data points in a system of n stochastic equations with a sample of size T is nT, and not T; that is, the total number of data points should be counted as equal to "the number of stochastic elements in the joint probability distribution of the system." Second, we should consider the number of *degrees of freedom* in relation to the particular method of estimation used. He then outlines a series of practical ways of coping with the problem of *degrees of freedom* in making consistent estimates of the parameters. And, importantly, he also makes the point that some of the ways he has suggested to deal with the problem of sample size may also be used to handle multicollinearity. The paper should be of immense interest to model-builders.

The next two essays are contributions made respectively in honor of G. L. S. Shackle and A. L. Nagar. Two topical and popular methodological issues of applied econometrics are discussed in these essays. The essay in honor of Shackle, "The treatment of expectations in econometrics" (1972), was written at the onset of what has come to be known as rational expectations economics. It is generally well-recognized that optimal economic decisions are often based on expectation variables which are largely subjective, and difficult to measure for quantitative purposes. In this paper, Klein discusses, with examples, two principal and widely-used methods of dealing with expectations. Both methods have a record of demonstrated success in mainstream applied econometrics. These two methods are: (a) Endogenizing the expectations generating process by using appropriate lag distribution functions (geometric, hump, rational function lag, etc.); and (b) measuring expectation variables exogenously by using sample survey data of households (e.g., consumer buying plans, and their economic expectations), of business firms (e.g., investment plans, and expectations concerning inventory, sales and employment, etc.) and of other economic units. Both methods were utilized in "A postwar quarterly model," an early model in incorporating expectation variables, as is already pointed above.

The essay in honor of Nagar, "The concept of exogeneity in econometrics" (1990), underscores the basic philosophy behind the traditional principle of exogeneity, and the role of exogenous variables in specification and estimation of structural econometric models. The traditional concept of exogeneity is lately being bypassed by other approaches, and quite different concepts have been put forward, either redefining the nature of exogeneity or assuming it away entirely, as in the case of vector autoregressive models. Coming from a master practitioner, Lawrence Klein's paper reminds us in a timely fashion of crucial usefulness of the traditional concept of exogeneity. He makes his argument using several illustrations from recent macroeconometric history.

Traditionally, exogenous variables have been defined as those which "are not in feedback relationship with the model, they are not generated by the economic system being investigated. They are *external* variables." Klein elaborates on the structural role of traditional exogenous variables, and equally importantly, he also offers commentary on the usefulness or non-usefulness, relevance or irrelevance of vector autoregressive models, Granger-causality versus exogeneity, and classification of exogeneity into weak, strong and super exogeneity.

The essay, "Smith's use of data," is a tribute to Adam Smith's legacy and his place in the development of modern economics. The paper was presented at a conference in Edinburgh (July, 1990) where several Nobel Laureates in Economic Science were gathered to mark the bicentenary of Smith's death. In this paper, Klein closely examines Smith's use of systematic data from today's perspective. Particularly, he was interested in Smith's use of a long time series of wheat prices from 1202 to 1764, listed at the end of Chap. XI of *The Wealth of Nations*. Klein develops his analysis around two questions: How did Smith handle or interpret these time series data without the benefit of sophisticated mathematical and statistical techniques of modern economists? What are latent characteristics of these data which may now be discovered by modern time series analysis?

Klein interestingly demonstrates that even without any access to modern computer facilities or insightful statistical techniques, Smith could analyze the real world quite perceptively. He also finds that although Smith's analysis of the wheat price series was mainly descriptive, Smith did comment clearly on several trend phases, major fluctuations from trend, and wheat price movements relative to silver prices. Smith also studied this series after dividing it into 12-year averages. Moreover, in Klein's judgment, Smith's analysis of price determination had all the ingredients of a value-added concept, and his approach was a forerunner of full-cost pricing, his analysis, however, does not seem to entail any consideration of the business cycle.

To probe somewhat deeper into the question of Smith's awareness of the business cycle, Klein then develops a 'what if' scenario, that is, what if modern techniques and computer facilities had been accessible to Smith? He amplifies J. Harold Wilson's work ("Industrial activity in the eighteenth century," *Economica* (1940)) on dating the modern business cycle by subjecting Smith's series to lead-lag multivariate correlation analysis. The inference Klein draws confirms Wilson's finding that there was no discernible movement in various statistical series during the eighteenth century in terms of what might be called a common business cycle. Thus, for Klein, there is little reason to expect that "Adam Smith should have been able to observe business cycles in his professional life." The essay sheds light on the quantitative history of economic thought.

The last paper in Part II is a lecture (1992) prepared in memory of Sukhamoy Chakravarty, an eminent mathematical and economic statistician. The lecture is a sharp commentary on the recent developments that have become currently popular in applied econometrics, in particular, *vector autoregressive models, cointegration, error correction specification,* and the *calibration approach.* Klein examines these developments from at least three modeling perspectives, namely the probability distribution of error, selection of exogenous variables, and specification of economic relationships. He observes critically that much in the forms of these approaches simply reintroduces once-considered, but long abandoned and set aside, ideas of the early history of applied econometrics. He ends his comments by pointing towards some potentially useful lines for new research.

7

ANTECEDENTS OF MACROECONOMETRIC MODELS[†]

1. Introduction

Econometric models have not sprung forth as entirely new creations, like Athene out of the brain of Zeus. Instead, there have been a number of developments in the history of economics that foreshadowed the arrival of these intellectual constructs. In this chapter, we shall focus on four such antecedents which seem particularly important to us. The first is the set of models of general equilibrium, which were first developed by Léon Walras as an abstract system and later extended by Vilfredo Pareto so that, in principle, these models become capable of empirical estimation. The second was the set of two mathematical models of the business cycle in the early 1930s, constructed by Ragnar Frisch and Michal Kalecki, which anticipated the econometric approach. The third major antecedent has been Keynes' *General Theory* and the subsequent development of this approach, of which the operational heritage has been enormous. Indeed macroeconometric models have largely been designed until very recently to implement the Keynesian system, however much these models may have evolved since their beginnings, just prior to the Second World War. The final major antecedent was the empirical literature on Keynesian macroeconomic concepts, particularly on consumption functions, which flourished between the publication of Keynes' *General Theory* (in 1936) and the outbreak of the Second World War (or the publication of Tinbergen's *Business Cycles in the United States of America, 1919–1932*) late in 1939. Before launching into these four major themes, we may examine briefly five related antecedents.

François Quesnay's *tableau économique* was a major accomplishment for his time, and it is reasonable to regard this construct as the first stylized macroeconomic model. Moreover, the *tableau* was both quantitative and dynamic, designed as it was to indicate cyclical (or perhaps secular) improvements or decay. A second related development could be Karl Marx's discussion in *Capital* of the two schemes of simple commodity reproduction and extended commodity reproduction, which easily lend themselves to representations in terms of abstract models. There was, in addition, Marx's concern to measure statistically his own theoretical concepts, such as the rate of surplus value. However, in our view, modern econometric modeling owes relatively little to Karl Marx's theories and method of inquiry, at least directly.

[†]From *a History of Macroeconometric Model-Building* (Edward Elgar, Aldershot, England, 1991), Chap. 1, pp. 3–30; written jointly with Ronald G. Bodkin and Kanta Marwah.

A third subsidiary antecedent is neoclassical theory, particularly the neoclassical theory of the firm, which in several variants has been used to develop theories of the demand for the various factors of production, which have become incorporated into a number of current econometric models. In this regard, it is worth noting that both Jevons and Marshall, two of the founders of the marginalist or neoclassical approach, foresaw an increasing role for measuring the hypothetical concepts of their theories in the evolution of their discipline.[1]

In this connection, we may also cite the work in the 1930s on two-sector models by Griffith C. Evans (1934), which was later extended to an index number interpretation by his student-colleague, F. W. Dresch (1938). Evans, who was primarily a mathematician, developed an interrelated model based on neoclassical theories of production for two sectors, which produced consumption goods and capital goods respectively. With total labor input given exogenously and total capital input constrained by the output of the capital goods sector, the problem was to maximize total consumption output by a suitable allocation of the labor and capital inputs between the two sectors. Dresch then provided the aggregation theory to move from the microeconomic to the macroeconomic plane; this was a development quite apart from Keynes' theory of underemployment equilibrium being developed contemporaneously. Essentially, Dresch showed that Divisia indices of the prices and the quantities for the Evans model satisfied, for the macroeconomy, the same relationships that Evans had postulated for the microeconomy.[2]

A fourth related theme is the thought and work of the German Historical School; here the connection is somewhat indirect, although we shall attempt to make the antecedents more apparent. Although it must be admitted that leading members of this school, such as Wilhelm Roscher and Gustav Schmoller, would probably not have been sympathetic to macroeconometric model-building, it may nevertheless be claimed that the painstaking empirical and statistical work of some of the members

---

[1]Sawyer (1976) has emphasized that Jevons believed strongly in the statistical measurement of his theoretical constructs, particularly at the aggregative level, even though he did not live to have a chance to implement his program. Alfred Marshall, in his celebrated article (1897), "The old generation of economists and the new," stated clearly that one of the tasks of the twentieth-century development of the discipline would be to estimate and to measure, or in other words, to find empirical counterparts to, the theoretical structure that had already been developed by the end of the nineteenth century.

[2]The basic Evans model was also used in two contemporaneous contributions dealing with business cycles, C. F. Roos (1930) and Edward Theiss (1933). (see also Roos' fuller development of his theories in his 1934 book; Roos' global views of the various pieces of a functioning economy anticipate, to a certain extent, macroeconometric model-building.) Building on Evans' approach, Roos (1930) developed a model which gave a differential equation in a typical price, which had cyclical solutions. Indeed, the business cycle was conceived as one of fluctuations in prices in general, with fluctuations in production (and hence employment) as an appendage. Theiss (1933) constructed a similar model of cyclical fluctuations of economy based on Evans' equations of supply and demand. It is interesting to note that Theiss' approach, which consisted of solving linear differential equations of second degree or higher, was intended for empirical application. It is also interesting to note that, for Theiss, the principal source of the business cycle was the long lag in the period of production, which tended to produce over-corrections. (Today we are familiar with this possibility because of the development of cobweb models of agricultural markets.)

of this school, such as the curves of expenditures on various consumption categories of Ernst Engel, would easily fit into a modern econometric model (and indeed they have done so, on a number of occasions). We should not wish to imply that a current model-building is impregnated with *historismus*, requiring a unity of all the social sciences (with due attention paid to the unique characteristics of particular nations) before progress can be made. Nevertheless modern model-building does have a number of characteristics in common with the methods of the German Historical School. In both cases, the subject is the quantitative interpretation of economic history, and so the careful assembling of such data is an essential feature of both approaches. In addition, the typical macroeconometric model uses relationships which are broader than conventional macroeconomic theory. Moreover the relativity of economic laws is well confirmed by practising econometricians; the general experience has been that a typical macroeconometric model cannot be left unmaintained (that is, with unadjusted parameter values) for a period longer than two to four years, or it will go "sour," becoming an unfit tool for purposes of prediction or of policy simulation. Re-estimation is thus an important part of model maintenance.[3]

The fifth and possibly the most important antecedent of macroeconometric modeling was the work on classical statistics around the turn of the twentieth century, when individuals such as R. A. Fisher, Gosset, Karl Pearson and others built on the foundations of probability theory developed earlier by Gauss, Laplace and others. Mary S. Morgan (1984, 1987) has shown that early econometricians did *not* consistently and clearly conceive of their discipline as resting on probabilistic foundations, until Trygve Haavelmo introduced this approach (by means of a stochastic perturbation whose realizations were turned over to the laws of chance) in the early 1940s. Even given its late appearance, it is fair to state that this approach has revolutionized applied econometrics in general and macroeconometric model-building in particular, as well as serving as the basis for numerous propositions in theoretical econometrics.

2. Léon Walras and the Elements of Pure Economics

Econometric models are, above all, logical systems, in which the bahavior of the whole is not always predictable from the nature of the parts which compose the entire system. One of the earliest and clearest views of the economy as a system is that of Léon Walras, in his *Eléments d'économie politique pure*.[4] Walras glimpsed the functioning of a purely competitive economy in static equilibrium as a coherent system that could be represented by a consistent set of equations for prices and

---

[3]It is interesting to note as well that the techniques of econometric modeling have invaded economic history itself, where this approach is called "cliometrics." However, the view of the subject summarized in this paragraph definitely antedates cliometrics.

[4]First published in 1874; *édition définitive*, 1926. All references in this book will be to Jaffé's masterful translation (1954), which furthermore contains a number of collation notes among the several editions of Walras' *Éléments*, as well as some interesting commentaries by the translator of a number of the points under discussion.

quantities, which the market would solve itself by means of the *tâtonnement* process. In Walras' own words (as translated by William Jaffé),

> "And this result is obtained purely and simply by the automatic operation of the mechanism of free competition. The law of supply and demand regulates all these exchanges of commodities just as the law of universal gravitation regulates the movements of all celestial bodies. Thus the system of the economic universe reveals itself, at last, in all its grandeur and complexity, a system at once vast and simple, which, for sheer beauty, resembles the astronomic universe."[5]

In turn, Walras' system has been an inspiration to several generations of econometricians, as they have attempted to find empirical counterparts to his abstract systems of equations. Although we shall argue below that current macroeconometric models are quite different (even in the spirit of the analysis) from Walras' highly abstract models, nevertheless the notion of the economy as a system has been retained and developed.

Accordingly, before presenting some detailed points of Walras' discussion and noting some differences with current econometric models, a review of Walras' development of his view of the economy may be appropriate. After presenting some introductory material (principally definitions), Walras launches into his discussion of the purely competitive economy, which he represents through successively more complicated models. The first model of general equilibrium (in Part II) is one in which stocks of two commodities are exchanged; after this, exchange is generalized (in the second model of general equilibrium, in Part III) to the exchange of fixed stocks of many commodities. In this context, it can be argued that *rareté* (marginal utility, as modified by scarcity or position on the marginal utility schedule)[6] is "the" fundamental "cause" of value in exchange; Walras apparently felt a strong need to vindicate the theory of his father, Auguste Walras, as Willian Jaffé has indicated on a number of occasions. The third model of general equilibrium, which appears in Part IV, is probably the best known of all; here Walras introduces production phenomena and allows land, labor and capital to make their appearance as primary factors of production. Although Walras initially assumed fixed coefficients of production (as in Leontief-style input–output analysis), by the definitive edition he was willing to permit variable coefficients of production, and so the possibility of a marginal productivity theory of output and income distribution was indeed present. Even more interesting are the two final models of general equilibrium. In Part V, the model of general equilibrium is generalized to include individual savings

---

[5]Walras, p. 374. It is interesting to note that this summary view appears at the end of the discussion of the sequence of theoretical models of general equilibrium, before Walras launches into discussions of "applied" topics such as structural changes occurring during economic growth, doctrinal points, monopoly, and some theoretical aspects of taxation.

[6]This is our interpretation of Walras' special use of this term. It should be noted that Jaffé leaves the French word untranslated in his English text.

functions, interpreted as the demand for claims to future income, and also capital formation and the price of capital goods (at times interpreted as share prices on the stock exchanges or *bourses*). Equation-counting criteria are met in this context, but Walras takes some pains to show (in his Lesson 28) that the interaction between the savings and investment functions plays a major role in the determination of the rate of interest, despite the caveat that "(t)heoretically, all the unknowns of an economic problem depend on all the equations of economic equilibrium" (p. 307). Despite the neoclassical orientation of this result, the concern with savings function and the implicit relationships for investment bring us close to a major concern of current-day econometric model-builders. However the underpinning in terms of marginal utility is not lost sight of in the third and fourth models of general equilibrium, as Walras comes back to the maximization of effective utility and the tendency of a purely competitive system to generate at least a relative maximum of the utility functions of its economic agents.

The fifth and final model of general equilibrium may be found in Part VI, "Theory of Circulation and Money." Here Walras permits (in principle) inventories of all commodities, particularly cash balances; this leads him directly into monetary theory and discussions of several sorts of financial markets.[7] Walras makes an attempt to preserve his marginal utility theory of value in this context, by imputing *rareté* to the service of money, which has no direct utility of its own. The discussion of this model comes down to a view of the long-run neutrality of money (the level of prices being strictly proportional to the stock of money, after an exogenous increase in the latter) although, interestingly, there appears to be a short-run effect of the stock of money on interest rates. Discussions of bimetallism and of foreign exchange (including our modern concern, the rate of exchange of a given country's money) conclude this discussion.[8] In particular, money has become a flesh-and-blood commodity fulfilling the standard functions, including a store of value, rather than being no more than a disembodied *numéraire*; in addition, absolute prices, rather than mere relative prices, may now be determined.

It is interesting to note that, on occasion, Walras considered the possibility of an empirical implementation of his system. Thus, in discussing price determination under monopoly (Lesson 41), which significantly comes after the statement of the five models of general equilibrium, Walras speaks of "relat[ing] the rational and rigorously exact equations of exchange and production to the empirical and approximative equation of sales written as a function of price" (p. 440). Earlier, in his discussion of the fifth model of general equilibrium (in the discussion of bimetallism

---

[7]It is very interesting to note that the discussion in article 273 (especially pp. 317–318 suggests that Walras not only had the transactions and wealth (or speculative) motives for holding cash, but also the finance demand for money that Keynes added after the publication of the *General Theory*

[8]In article 314 (p. 374), Walras states clearly the classical price-specie flow mechanism of David Hume, with reinforcing income effects mentioned in earlier editions but deleted by the time of the Definitive Edition.

in particular), he states (article 289, p. 348):

> "If we were to replace the above arbitrary and indeterminate functions
> or curves, in whole or in part, by statistically derived functions or curves
> having concrete coefficients, we could calculate approximately the real
> effects of a resumption of the coinage of silver on the basis of a given legal
> ratio between the values of gold and silver moneys."

This sentence indicates not only the anticipation of the possibility of an econometric
estimation of the parameters of a behavioral equation, but also a recognition that
an estimated model, employed as a complete system, is capable of generating some
tentative and approximate answers to policy issues, in what we now call policy
simulations. Thus it can legitimately be claimed that, despite his rational bias (to
be discussed below), Walras foresaw, at least in part, some of the uses to which the
descendants of his system might be put.

This issue is brought into focus by Walras' treatment of the savings function.
In the first three editions of his work, Walras treated the savings function as an
"empirical datum" in which the utility maximization process was at most implicit;
this is something which has at least a family resemblance to the consumption functions of modern econometric models. By the Definitive Edition, there has been a
slight but significant change in the formulation. New savings are treated like any
other good which is acquired to maximize utility or satisfaction, and the derivation
is "rational" rather than "empirical." Admittedly, the savings function (or the sum
of individual demands for net income, in the Definitive Edition) always depends
on the same arguments, namely the prices of the natural agents, the prices of the
various produced capital goods, the prices of the final goods and services, and the
rate of interest. Noticeably absent from a modern point of view is an income effect (which is appropriate enough, in a full employment economy). The shift from
an empirical relationship to a "rational" one, based on utility maximization over
time (if only implicitly), is probably important as indicating the direction in which
Walras thought that the search for insight should go.[9]

This caveat would almost certainly be underlined by the greatest Walras scholar
of our century, the late William Jaffé, were he able to read (and criticize) the above
interpretation. In reaction to Morishima's treatment of Walras' *Éléments*, Jaffé has
argued that:

> "The *Éléments* was intended to be and is, in all but the name, a real-
> istic utopia, i.e. a delineation of a state of affairs nowhere to be found
> in the actual world, independent of time and place, ideally perfect in

---

[9] On these points, see Lesson 23, especially article 242 (pp. 274–276) and also the attached translator's note h, pp. 587–588 of Jaffé's translation of the Definitive Edition. It is interesting to note
that Milton Friedman (1955) considers this change to be a definite deterioration of the presentation, as he felt that the older Walras was misled by considerations of pure form and "the substance
which the form was to represent was no longer part of him."

certain respects, and yet composed of realistic psychological and material ingredients."[10]

Jaffé also argued that Walras had a vehement dislike for "facts" and the "observation of facts" [statistics?] and that he denounced their manifestations in a number of areas: art, literature, philosophy, science, and, of course, economics. Jaffé goes on to argue that the *Éléments* were intended to be "an abstract expression and rational explanation of the phenomena of the real world,"[11] rather than a slavish reproduction of these real-world data or statistics. In this view, Walras would not have been sympathetic to the interpretation of his system as a mere description of a real-world economy and hence would have been unenthusiastic about econometric estimation of his system.

Indeed the limitations of the Walrasian system as a direct representation of a modern economy should perhaps be given additional emphasis. Upon additional probing, it is clear that the Walrasian model is quite unsuitable for direct econometric estimation, and indeed it is Jaffé's contention that it was never intended to be fitted directly, despite a few passages like the one quoted above, which suggests that Walras himself may have thought of it in this light. Thus the hypothesis of pure competition would appear to be singularly inaccurate as a description of a modern economy, while the amount of detail required for the implementation of any of the last three models described above would appear to be prohibitive. Perhaps the biggest problem is whether the system has any relevance in a context of persistent unemployment; in a seminal article, Robert W. Clower (1966) has argued that Walras' Law will not hold in an underemployment context and that demand (consumption) functions contain quantity variables, such as real income, in such a context.[12] Although Morishima (1980) contends that "... Walras narrowly missed the chance to meet the first Keynesian problem of involuntary unemployment due to overdeterminacy," it seems fair to assert that Walras appears to have been quite neoclassical in his approach to involuntary unemployment.[13] Moreover Clower contends that the acceptance of the Walras paradigm negates the essential message of Keynes' *General Theory*. Even if one does not wish to go this far, it is clear

---

[10] Jaffé (1980), p. 530.

[11] Jaffé (1980), p. 530. The reader may observe that our translation is slightly different from the one presented by Jaffé himself on the following page.

[12] Fundamentally, Walras' Law need not hold in this context, because the aggregative analog to the household budget constraint applies only to the notional or full-employment demand functions, while in an underemployment context the realized or effective demand functions need not be globally consistent with virtual (full-employment) equilibrium. (For example, some households may plan to supply more labor and hence demand more goods than their depressed labor markets may permit.)

[13] The only place in the book where there is (to the best of our knowledge) a discussion of involuntary unemployment appears on pp. 432–423, in the context of the lesson on price fixing and monopoly. Here Walras states the neoclassical view that, if the wage rate is set too high (either because of minimum wage laws or other pressures), the results will be unemployment or underemployment.

that current macroeconometric models cannot be regarded as a direct empirical implementation of the Walrasian system.[14]

To elaborate this point somewhat further, we may note that the Walrasian system is a set of simultaneous equations which is meant to describe the working of the economy; that is, in one interpretation the solution to the system should correspond with observations of the economy. In a similar way, we can think about the set of simultaneous equations that is (arguably) implicit in Keynes' *General Theory* as being a description of the economy. The solution to the Keynesian equation system should also correspond to observations of the economy. There are, however, important differences between the two systems:

1. The Walrasian system generates a set of micro-variables of the economy, while the Keynesian system generates a set of macro-variables.
2. The solution of the Walrasian system as interpreted by K. J. Arrow and G. Debreu (1954), for example, satisfies full economic equilibrium. There is full employment, perfect competition and static equilibrium. The Keynesian system was posed as a simultaneous equation system that did not necessarily have full employment equilibrium, did not necessarily impose the conditions of perfect competition and could generate dynamic as well as static solutions. The Walrasian system in full equilibrium with perfect competition can be shown to satisfy the welfare conditions for a Pareto optimum. The same cannot be said of the solution to the Keynesian system.

As the next paragraph will elaborate, both the Keynesian and Walrasian systems are formulated as a set of simultaneous equations for the whole economy, their principal point of similarity. They are not partial systems.

Does this mean, therefore, that the Walrasian general equilibrium theory has no relevance for current-day macroeconometric modeling? In our view, such an assertion would be far too extreme; Walras' great contribution of the view of the economy as a system (exemplified in the quotation of the beginning of this section) permeates macroeconometric modeling today. This view (akin to the notion of *gestalt* in the school of psychology of that name) is now second nature to econometric model-builders; yet the view was virtually completely absent a century ago and took a long time to become the dominant one in our century. It is in this limited but very important sense that current-day econometric models are descendants of the five models of general equilibrium sketched in the *Éléments*. (Of course, the concept of a system of simultaneous equations should be sharply distinguished from that of equilibrium; examples of one without the other are not difficult to find.) In comparison to this central similarity, the important differences noted above become secondary. Thus detail can be reduced upon suitable aggregation (even though

---

[14]Of course we do not wish to be understood as asserting that the presence of unemployment (whether voluntary or not, whether as an equilibrium phenomenon or not) is essential to a macroeconometric model, as the counter-example of the Sargent model (1976) illustrates in a clear fashion. Rather, the presence of persistent unemployment as explained by the model is characteristic of particular models, especially those constructed in a Keynesian or neoKeynesian framework.

it must be admitted that aggregation itself can be another source of imprecision and error).[15] The hypothesis of pure competition can be regarded as a simple first approximation, to be replaced by more accurate hypotheses as the context under discussion warrants. The price flexibility implied by the *tâtonnements* carried out by the Walrasian *crieur* seems particularly inappropriate in the context of discussions of inflation in the second half of the twentieth century; here one might prefer to substitute the hypotheses of price formation sketched out by the late Arthur M. Okun (1981). And of course the equilibrium described by a current-day econometric model will usually allow for involuntary unemployment, so that consumption (and other expenditure) functions will generally be functions of quantity variables in general and of real income in particular. Another important difference is that the Walrasian models of general equilibrium are generally regarded as static, timeless descriptions of the economy (viewed as purely competitive), while current-day econometric models are dynamic representations for which a static equilibrium position may not even exist.[16] Nevertheless it is our view that these differences are not so important as the essential view of the economy as a global system, one whose behavior as a whole is not readily explicable in terms of the functioning of the various pieces that separately comprise the system. In this way, current econometric models owe a great deal to the French expatriate who held the chair in economics at the Academy of Lausanne, Switzerland, for over 20 years.[17]

3. Vilfredo Pareto's Version of General Equilibrium Economics

Vilfredo Pareto, Léon Walras' successor at Lausanne, developed and refined the latter's general equilibrium analysis. Because we have discussed Walras' models at some length, we shall be relatively brief with regard to Pareto's representations of price formation in a purely competitive economy.[18] Once again, we feel that it is

---

[15]Thus the demands for the myriad of final products aggregate into the consumption functions for households, the investment functions for business enterprises and (in an open economy) export and import demand functions. Realism would also suggest the introduction of another agent making expenditures, namely the public authorities; however, this is not a fundamental modification.

[16]Of course, this position is debatable, as Morishima (1980) claims that Walras' static models can easily be dynamized to encompass a theory of economic growth and possibly also to take cyclical phenomena into account; Jaffé (1980) vigorously challenges Morishima on these points. In any case, the traditional interpretation of the Walrasian system is one of a static model of the competitive process of price formation.

[17]Similarly, Henry W. Spiegel appears to share this view in his text on the history of economic thought (1971), as he argues (p. 556) that modern econometric model-builders are, in one sense, the heirs of Léon Walras and his system of equations. Indeed, Professor Spiegel appears to assert that modern econometric models (along with Leontief's input–output system) go some distance to overcoming the criticism that the Walrasian system is purely formal and not really capable of generating substantive conclusions about the economy (a criticism that goes back at least to Friedman's review of Jaffé's translation, 1955).

[18]Following Jaffé's review (1972) of Ann S. Schwier's translation of Pareto's *Manuel* (the French, not the Italian, version) and the debate among Jaffé, the Schwiers, and Vincent J. Tarascio, in the March 1974 issue of the *Journal of Economic Literature*, we have decided to rely primarily on secondary sources of the Paretian models of general equilibrium, namely Hutchison (1966) and Tarascio (1973) especially pp. 395–403. However we have examined the original Italian version (1906) of the *Manuale*.

the basic concept of the economy as an interdependent system which is important, rather than the specific details of the representation. However there are two differences between Walras' and Pareto's versions of the general equilibrium system that are worth noting here: Pareto's system is more abstract and (paradoxically) appears also to be more oriented towards empirical implementation, at least in principle. Let us take up each of these points in turn.

Pareto's general equilibrium analysis can be found in Chaps. III to VI of the *Manuale* (1906) (and also in the relevant sections of the mathematical appendix). All commentators agree that the analysis is on a very abstract plane. As interpreted by T. W. Hutchison (1966), the model contrasts the tension between tastes on the one hand and obstacles to the satisfaction of human wants on the other, with the equations of general equilibrium describing the markets' resolution (in realistic terms) of this conflict. Tarascio (1973) would appear not to disagree with this characterization, but he adds the interpretation that there appear to be two models of general equilibrium in these four chapters. In Chap. III, there is a very abstract description of the competitive system purely in terms of transformations of economic quantities, while Chaps. IV to VI are concerned with "a less general study of 'tastes' and 'obstacles', their interaction, and equilibrium resulting from such interactions."[19] Accordingly, the Walrasian distinction between exchange, production, capital formation ("*capitalization*") and the formation of prices of financial assets disappear; all economic phenomena display an essential unity. This was just as well for Pareto, as he wished to exorcize those elements of Walras' formulation of general equilibrium theory that were overly subjective in his view, such as the importance of *rareté* (marginal utility) in the determination of exchange value. In addition, Pareto sought to correct a small but important (in his view) error in Walras' theory of production, according to which the coefficients of production (as a group) were sometimes regarded as fixed for purposes of the analysis and sometimes regarded (also as a group) as variable. For Pareto, the truth was that some particular coefficients of productions were always variable when factor prices varied and others (for example, the number of cocoa beans required to produce a chocolate bar of a given size) were largely fixed by technology, at least for all practical purposes.

At the same time, it is interesting to observe that Pareto appears to have designed his system so that it might eventually serve for purposes of empirical or even econometric testing. Thus it might be recalled that his discussion of general equilibrium in the *Manuale* is preceded by an exposition of the "logico-experimental" method in economics and is followed by some interesting discussion in chapters on population, money and applied economics in general. Moreover Pareto himself was not averse to statistically applied work to verify his hypotheses, work that antici-

---

[19]Tarascio (1973), p. 397. In this connection, it may be noted that the concept of "obstacles" is quite general and includes such diverse phenomena as (a) the tastes of other economic agents, (b) barriers of space and time, (c) forms of social organization, and (d) property tenure systems affecting the ownership of complementary factors of production, as well as the more traditional limitations on the stocks of economically produced final goods and services (or, on a slightly longer term perspective, the ease and facility of production).

pates some of the applied econometric research of the current period. Thus, as T. W. Hutchison (1966) notes, among Pareto's most interesting ideas were his applied econometric investigations, in particular those in the *Cours* (1896) where he developed the form of the highly skewed frequency distribution that was meant to be applied to distributions of income and wealth and which has come to be called the "Pareto Law," and also his work on business cycles or crises, which was built on the impressive pioneering work of Clément Juglar with monetary statistics. Indeed, as Tarascio (1973) has pointed out, when Pareto came to apply his equilibrium systems to problems of monetary and unemployment theory he was content to work with aggregates, rather than continuing to deal exclusively with the individual elements of an economy. This is an obvious link to modern macroeconometric modeling.

Finally, Pareto's methodological approach, the so-called "logico-experimental method," appears to have been very much oriented toward empirical testing. Pareto apparently believed in a clear exposition of one's theoretical propositions, eliminating normative content as much as possible, and then confronting the implications of this theoretical framework with the "facts" of experience to the largest extent possible. Tarascio (1968) has made a detailed study of Pareto's methodology and he concludes that not only did Pareto anticipate much of the current discussion of the philosophical underpinnings of economic knowledge,[20] but also that he would have been quite sympathetic to current-day macroeconometric model-building. Accordingly, even more than Walras, Pareto may be claimed as a direct antecedent of current macroeconometric modeling activity.

4. Ragnar Frisch and Michal Kalecki

In the early 1930s, some important work was done in macroeconomic theory in general and on some abstract models of fluctuations in the aggregate economy in particular. This work, which was effected prior to the publication of Keynes' *General Theory* (but after the publication of his *Treatise on Money*) helped lay the groundwork for the construction of the early macroeconometric models. We have already referred to the papers of G. C. Evans (1934), C. F. Roos (1930), and Edward Theiss (1933). However, in our view, the two most important papers were those by Ragnar Frisch (1933) and Michal Kalecki (1935). Additional support for this judgement may be adduced from the fact that Jan Tinbergen's contemporaneous survey piece, in *Econometrica* (1935), devotes considerable attention to the work of both Frisch and Kalecki.

Ragnar Frisch's "Propagation Problems and Impulse Problems in Dynamic Economics" (1933) constructs a simple model of the business cycle which is explicitly dynamic. Investment demand has two components: net investment depends upon the rate of change of the production of consumption goods (the Aftalion or J. M. Clark accelerator), while replacement investment depends upon the

---

[20]Tarascio (1968, p. 136) states, "The economics profession has, to a remarkable extent, adopted Pareto's views on the verification problem, although his contribution has always remained implicit in the technical discussions of his contributions to economics."

current level of output of the consumer goods industries. (Depreciation is viewed as proportional to the initial capital stock; but Frisch assumes a strict proportionality between this capital stock and the related level of output.) A second equation is obtained by taking the desired level of cash balances to be a linear function (with no constant term) of the production of consumer goods and producer goods separately; this might be interpreted as a transactions demand for money. The consumption equation, which is definitely pre-Keynesian, depicts a natural tendency for consumption standards to grow, checked only by the tendency to rein in consumption as the desired level of cash balances increases as well. Finally, Frisch obtains oscillations by making the distinction between investment demand and the production of capital goods. Frisch writes an integral equation which supposes that the production of capital goods lags behind the level of gross investment demand by a constant amount of time. After manipulating his small system of equations, Frisch obtains another small system of mixed difference-differential equations, which he solves by "the method of trial solutions." If "reasonable values" for the structural parameters are substituted, the solution paths are all damped cycles. However Frisch recognizes that the substitution of "reasonable values" for the structural parameters is no substitute for rigorous econometric work. With one of his prescient insights, he declares, "I think, indeed, that the statistical determination of such structural parameters will be one of the main objectives of the economic cycle analysis of the future." His surrounding argument makes it quite clear that he feels that, in order to set forth a full explanation, this kind of work is needed to coordinate and complement the huge mass of empirical or descriptive facts concerning the business cycle already available at the time at which he was writing.[21]

A similar (but distinct) model was presented by Michal Kalecki in the 1933 meetings of the Econometric Society held in Leiden, and published two years later in *Econometrica* (1935). Kalecki's model makes a further distinction: we now have deliveries of capital goods, as well as investment demand and production of capital goods (investment in the national accounts). Kalecki's system is more or less as follows. Investment demand depends positively on realized profits and negatively on the initial stock of capital. Profits (of capitalists) depend only on their own spending (investment goods production and capitalists' consumption), via a sort of multiplier principle which anticipates that of Keynes' *General Theory*. (There is implicitly a capitalists' consumption function in this analysis.) Kalecki has effectively the same equation as Frisch in which capital goods production (investment in a national income accounting concept) is an integral of investment demand experienced for a fixed period between the present and the constant lag in capital goods production. Deliveries of new capital goods lag investment demand (which could be interpreted

---

[21]A related question is whether the business cycle is a real, a monetary, or a mixed phenomenon. It is interesting to note that Frisch argues that his transactions demand for money is only an auxiliary relationship and that his is really not a monetary theory of the cycle. However it is worth noting that, in Frisch's system, without the need for cash as a brake on the dynamic evolution of production, the cycle is eliminated, exactly as it is if the distinction between gross investment and the production of capital goods is obliterated.

as new orders) by exactly the length of this fixed lag. Finally, the rate of change of the capital stock is simply the difference between the deliveries of new capital goods and the level of depreciation, assumed constant in Kalecki's model.

This system (in fullest form, of six dynamic equations in six unknowns) can be reduced to a mixed difference-differential equation in each of the variables of the system. This mixed difference-differential equation may or may not have a cyclical solution. Kalecki then uses rudimentary statistical data of the United States for crude estimates of the parameters of his system, which are the amount of depreciation (its rate), the parameters of the capitalists' consumption function, and the constant lag of deliveries of investment goods behind new orders. He was encouraged to find that "realistic" values of these parameters yielded (maintained) cycles, and also that the period of the cycle was ten years, which he regarded as reasonable. Peripheral discussions in this article consider a multiplier process affecting workers' consumption and incomes, the modification of the model to allow for a growth context, and considerations of financial factors. However, for our purposes, the major significance of Kalecki's pioneering effort is that it appears to represent a step towards an econometric approach to business cycle problems, and hence a step towards the development of macroeconometric model.[22]

5. Keynes, *The General Theory*, and the Revolutions in Macroeconomic Theory and Measurement[23]

The most important single antecedent for the construction of macroeconometric models must be John Maynard Keynes' *The General Theory of Employment, Interest and Money* (1936). Moreover this is a point that would command wide agreement. Thus Richard Stone asserted, in his Keynes Lecture in Economics of 1978:

> "For there is no doubt that in its day Keynes' book had done probably more than any other to encourage the systematic estimation of national accounts magnitudes and the construction of econometric models." (Stone, 1980, p. 62)

Similarly, Don Patinkin (1976) argues:

> "Furthermore, and most important in the present context, the desire to quantify the *General Theory* provided the major impetus for the

---

[22]In this context, it is interesting to note that Frisch, in some prefatory remarks, of which he is the sole author, to Frisch and Holme (1935), a supplementary article, argues that Kalecki should not impose a maintained or neutral (i.e., a non-damped, non-explosive) cycle on the parameter values which he selects for his model but, rather, the parameter values should be "empirically determined." This, too, represents a step towards the construction of a full macroeconometric model. (The bulk of the Frisch-Holme article is devoted to demonstrating a proposition about the existence of a cyclical solution to Kalecki's model which is longer than the fixed lag postulated; this proposition, while true, and its demonstration need not concern us here.)

[23]The major part of the argument of this section has already been published in Bodkin, Klein, and Marwah (1986).

exponentially-growing [sic] econometric work that began to be carried out in the late 1930's on the consumption, investment, and liquidity-preference functions individually and, even more notably, on econometric models of the Keynesian system as a whole." (Patinkin, 1976, p. 1092)

Indeed, it may be noted that for many years macroeconometric models have been constructed as essentially empirical counterparts to the Keynesian system; only in recent years have econometric models based on alternative paradigms (monetarist, radical or post-Keynesian) appeared.[24]

Keynes' *General Theory* itself is worth a cursory review in this context. After six chapters of introductory material, there follow three chapters (grouped together in a section called "Book III, The Propensity to Consume") which treat the consumption function and an associated concept, the multiplier. The notion of consumption as a relatively stable function of a few explanatory variables, including community income, appears to cry for empirical verification and Keynes himself made some preliminary attempts, using early national income data for the United Kingdom developed by Colin Clark and for the United States developed by Simon Kuznets, to verify his hypotheses.[25] However, it must be admitted that the bulk of the work of the empirical testing of the Keynesian system was left for others, particularly after Keynes' severe heart attack in 1937.

Other parts of *The General Theory* contain concepts that are easily put into a theoretical formulation susceptible to econometric testing and estimation without much difficulty. Thus Book IV, entitled "The Inducement to Invest," contains an extended discussion (in Chaps. 11 and 12) of a concept called "the marginal efficiency of capital." Without too much manipulation this discussion can be recast in the form of an investment demand function and so be confronted with statistics on business fixed investment and some of its hypothetical determinants. Book IV also contains an extended discussion of what Keynes called "liquidity-preference" generally, scattered through five chapters (Chaps. 13 to 17 of the work); again, one could attempt to render the liquidity-preference function operational and then to estimate its parameters, which indeed was done by A. J. Brown (1939) and by James Tobin (1947) in the immediate postwar period. Finally, Book V, "Money-Wages and Prices," contains three chapters (Chaps. 19 to 21) and concludes the central theoretical corpus of the work. Depending upon one's preferences, this portion of *The General Theory* could be formulated as an aggregate supply function relating

---

[24]Suggestions for alternative models have come from other sources such as the school of rational expectations (e.g. R. E. Lucas, 1976 or Thomas J. Sargent, 1976) or the time-series, "little theory" approach of Christopher A. Sims (1980).

[25]Keynes' methods of attempting to corroborate his theoretical constructs (an informal examination of the data, grouping the years in pairs) seem rather casual, and it is no surprise to learn that Patinkin (1976) was unable to reproduce Keynes' estimate (between 2.5 and 3) for the U.S. economy. (This might conceivably be the case because Patinkin not unreasonably considered only contiguous years, while Keynes may have carried out his estimation over two more widely separated years.) In any case, in that Keynes then inferred a parameter value of the marginal propensity to consume from the estimated multiplier, it seems likely that he carried out the first instance of reduced form estimation, as Patinkin notes.

real national product to the price level or its rate of change or (corresponding to the breakdown of Book V into three separate chapters) as an employment function (an inverted short-period production function), an equation for the determination of the money wage rate, and an equation for the determination of the aggregative price level.[26] It should be noted that Keynes attempted empirical verification of none of these other relationships, although his theoretical discussion and his example with regard to the consumption function would appear to have pointed the way.

But would Keynes himself have approved of this use of his theoretical apparatus? The answer would appear to be "no," on the basis of two important pieces of evidence: the strictures in *The General Theory* against the representation of his macroeconomic theory as a set of mathematical relationships ("mathematical economics," as he called it) and his September 1939 review of Part I of Tinbergen's study for the League of Nations.

About Keynes' attitude towards mathematically formulated economic theory (which is so essential for econometric modeling of any type, not just macroeconometric models) little need be said.[27] However his review of Tinbergen warrants some comment. Keynes was quite critical of this approach to macroeconomic research,[28] and the tone of his comments suggested that Tinbergen was largely wasting his and the profession's time, if not practising alchemy. The specific criticisms are, in general, reasonably taken, although Keynes' enthusiasts must be embarrassed by the suggestion that linear difference equations may be incapable of generating cyclical fluctuations in themselves, so that (according to Keynes) Tinbergen may be engaged in the task of explaining cycles (in the endogenous variables) by cycles (in the exogenous variables). The other criticisms seem quite reasonable in themselves and appear to have stood the test of time; thus Keynes' various remarks could be interpreted as pointing to single equation bias, the bias of omitted variables, measurement errors in the explanatory variables,[29] the possible mis-specification

---

[26]Thus Keynes appears (in Chap. 21) to have interpreted the marginal productivity condition of neoclassical economics (the equality of the marginal physical product of labor to the ratio of the nominal wage rate to the price of final output) as a relationship for the determination of final goods prices, rather than as a labor demand relationship, at least under conditions of less than full utilization of the labor force.

[27]Stone traces Keynes' views on this subject to his own personality conflicts regarding a lack of success as a research mathematician. Patinkin sees these remarks as a ritualistic continuation of Marshall's attitudes, but also feels that Keynes' comparative advantage did not lie in this field. Presumably Keynes made his peace with mathematically oriented economic theory, as he seems to have acquiesced to Meade's (1936–7) and Hicks' (1937) representations, in fairly tight mathematical terms, of his basic system.

[28]We may note that, in his private correspondence, especially with R. F. Harrod and R. F. Kahn, Keynes showed himself to be even more sceptical than in the published review. See Moggridge (1973), pp. 285–306, for a substantiation of this point.

[29]This point brings us back immediately to the rudimentary character of national income data in Great Britain during the 1930s, and hence this point would appear to have been particularly pertinent at the time of Keynes' review (By contrast, the U.S. Department of Commerce was already producing estimates of national income on a regular basis by 1935.) Whether Keynes contributed to the improvement of this situation or whether, *au contraire*, he hindered some useful developments that were taking place in any case is a point of dispute between Stone (1980) and Patinkin (1976), following some correspondence with Colin Clark.

entailed in assuming linearity throughout the full range (and beyond) of the dependent variable, and (especially) problems of structural change (that is, the possibility that all the past data utilized for parameter estimation may not be homogeneous or may emanate from different universes). Keynes' remarks may also be taken to be a criticism of crude empiricism that may be entailed in the determination of time lags without a suitable theoretical foundation or in the introduction of time trend variables to capture ill-defined secular forces. Keynes also points to the difficulties of an econometric estimation of the effects of an explanatory variable, in the case in which this particular variable has very little movement during a particular historical episode (the influence of the rate of interest on investment expenditures during the 1930s comes to mind as an example). While nearly all of these points are reasonable and most have been (implicitly) incorporated into econometrics textbooks today,[30] Keynes certainly seems to have had relatively little appreciation of the difficult nature of the problems that Tinbergen was attacking and of the generally unsatisfactory nature of non-econometric solutions to this class of problems. Indeed it can be asserted without too much fear of controversy today that intuitive estimates of concepts such as the multiplier or the effect of a certain fiscal policy on the economy are even more likely to be misleading than the econometric estimates, despite the limitations of the latter.[31]

Beyond the specific issues of econometric technique, there is a more general position regarding methodological approach, as Klant (1985), Lawson (1985), and Pesaran and Smith (1985) have pointed out. One can argue that, owing to instability of structures in the social universe, no econometric test is possible; the best that econometricians can do is to *measure* or estimate, as (in this view) testing is a technical impossibility. Klant, Lawson, and Pesaran and Smith argue (with

---

[30] Keynes also appears not to have had a full appreciation of the technique of multiple regression as an artificial manner of holding other influences constant, as he asserts in his review that the technique requires the explanatory variables to be "largely independent" statistically. On the other hand, an apologist for Keynes might interpret his remarks as anticipating the problem of strong multicollinearity, which is so often encountered in applied econometrics.

[31] Opinions on Keynes' performance in this episode have certainly varied among commentators, over the years. Thus, almost 40 years ago, one of us (Klein, 1951) characterized Keynes' review of Tinbergen's work as "one of his sorriest professional performances"; even with the passage of time, Klein sees no reason to revise this evaluation. On the other hand, Patinkin summarizes this same review and concludes that Keynes was more right than incorrect, as well as observing that he (Patinkin) finds it depressing to note how many of Keynes' criticisms are still relevant today. Another evaluation is that of Stone, who, while conceding the validity of some individual points, regards Keynes' review as "a model of testiness and perverseness"; in particular, he argues that Keynes failed to realize that the new technique might have been exactly what might be very helpful "to quantify the multiplier [for example, as in Clark's contemporaneous (1938) article] and other parameters of *The General Theory*." Moreover, Johannes J. Klant, who is generally sympathetic to what he regards as Keynes' basic methodological position, concedes, "Keynes displayed much ignorance and misunderstanding of what Tinbergen had done" (Klant, 1985, p. 91). Finally, Tinbergen himself appears not to have commented again, once he wrote a rejoinder (1940) to Keynes' review. In an article that is generally of an expository nature, written shortly after Keynes' death, Tinbergen (1948) did not comment on Keynes' 1939 critique, perhaps out of respect for a recently deceased intellectual opponent (in this matter). Even in 1986, in reviewing a first draft of this chapter, Professor Tinbergen did not comment specifically on this issue.

differing degrees of emphasis) that this indeed was Keynes' position, and that this is why Keynes reacted so vehemently against Tinbergen's League of Nations study, which was attempting to test alternative theories of the business cycle. By contrast, it is claimed (by Pesaran and Smith) that Keynes would have been far more sympathetic to Tinbergen's earlier work (1937), which put the emphasis on estimation, and solution of practical policy problems.[32] A secondary reason why econometric technique can never test critically a received theory (in this view) is that most (or even all) theories are under-identified or at least ambiguous. Accordingly, for econometric testing, supplementary hypotheses must be provided. But if a theory fails a given econometric test, an ardent proponent of that theory can always claim that the fault lies in the supplementary hypothesis furnished for testing purposes, rather than in the central core of the theory. This critique resembles the "Post-Keynesian" critique of deterministic or econometric models, where it is held that no coherent model, macroeconometric or otherwise, can capture the essential message of Keynes, which in this view is held to be an emphasis on the important role of uncertainty, the uniqueness of particular historical episodes, the under-determination or the indeterminacy of the macroeconomic system, among other points.[33] Nevertheless it would appear that Klant and also Pesaran and Smith (but not Lawson) agree that building forecasting models and econometric research are useful things to do, in the face of serious policy problems. Pesaran and Smith even argue that Keynes would not have been unsympathetic to this approach and that he did something similar in his approach to the practical problems of the day, for example in "How to Pay for the War" and "Can Lloyd George Do It?"

However this should not be regarded as the end of the matter. Richard Stone (1980) argues that, under the pressure of economic policy-making under wartime conditions, Keynes changed his attitudes toward economic statistics ("political arithmetic") and even towards econometric modeling. Moreover Keynes was associated with the "Cambridge Research Scheme" of the National Institute of Social and Economic Research during the period just before the Second World War (1938 and 1939), and much of this research had a strong quantitative and econometric

---

[32] However, Tinbergen in his concluding remarks of *An Econometric Approach to Business Cycle Problems* (1937) clearly mentions testing various received theories as one of the advantages of such an approach. Nor has much changed in this regard. For example, a recent exposition of methodological and philosophical issues in econometric practice (Hendry, 1980) placed great emphasis on econometric techniques as a means of resolving conflicts among rival theories. Hendry, incidentally, reviewed the Keynes–Tinbergen interchanges and expressed great doubt that Keynes could have really meant his apparent position, namely that empirical methods in general and econometric techniques in particular were unsuitable for resolving conflicts among rival economic theories!

[33] Taken to its logical extreme, such a philosophical position would appear to imply that no macroeconomic policies (stabilization policies in particular) are possible, because, if the structure of the economy is so unstable, one can never be sure of what one is doing. In this regard, the proponents of this point of view would appear to join Robert Lucas (1976) and the rational expectations school, who argue that the parameters of the system are highly unstable, at least with a shift in the policy regime itself, thus rendering both economic policy and macroeconometric estimation extremely difficult, if not impossible.

flavor. Stone feels that, in the light of the timing of these activities, "the Tinbergen episode seems even more bizarre." Moreover, both Patinkin (1976) and Stone
note that, when Alfred Cowles first proposed to Keynes that he be President of
the Econometric Society, he first protested that "whilst I am interested in econometric work and have done something at it at different times in my life, I have not
recently written anything significant or important along these lines, which would
make me feel a little bit of an imposter."[34] Thus, as Patinkin rightly points out, we
are entitled to infer that Keynes saw himself as someone who had made important
contributions to econometrics at one stage of his life; we are also probably entitled
to infer that his critical views on econometric modeling had moderated somewhat
by that date (1944). This inference is also indirectly corroborated by the fact that
Stone reports that Keynes delighted in his personal reunion with Tinbergen right
after the end of the Second World War in Europe (in July 1945), speaking enthusi-
astically not only of Tinbergen's personal qualities but also of his work.[35]

Ultimately, however, the issue of Keynes' final views on the econometric developments that his macroeconomic theory to a large extent stimulated is a secondary
issue.[36] It now seems clear that *The General Theory* was a tremendous stimulus, not
only to macroeconomic theory in general, but to macroeconometric model-building
in particular. Indeed, as succeeding chapters will detail, for nearly a generation and
a half after the publication of *The General Theory*, macroeconometric models constructed in the spirit of Keynesian theory dominated the model-building process;
only around the beginning of the 1970s did alternative paradigms of macroeconomic
theorizing begin to be incorporated into the macroeconometric models. Moreover,
Keynes' theorizing completed the steps that Pareto, Evans, Roos, Frisch and Kalecki
had taken away from Walras' microeconomic analysis, allowing researchers to deal
with concepts and quantities that were much easier to measure in practice. This in
turn permitted a return to the sweeping, aggregative concepts of Quesnay's *tableau
économique*, with, however, a much higher degree of precision. This aspect of the
"Keynesian Revolution" opened the field to macroeconometric model-building.

---

[34] Quoted by Stone (1980), p. 63, and by Patinkin (1976), p. 1092 (all but the final phrase, "which
would make me feel a little bit of an imposter").

[35] Stone (1980) concludes his review of the episode by noting that the renewal of the contact had
convinced Keynes that Tinbergen's works should be given "every scope and opportunity," and
he (Stone) asserts, "Nothing could show better the difference between Keynes' first impersonal
impressions and his considered view based on personal experience" (p. 64). At the same time,
we may note that Lawson (1985) has argued that Stone's analysis at most explains the *force* of
Keynes' critique of Tinbergen, without "explaining away" his well-founded (according to Lawson)
logical objections. Moreover it could be argued (as Don Patinkin did in commenting on an earlier
draft of this section) that an emotional reunion right after a cataclysmic war is hardly a set of
circumstances under which a detached, rational reappraisal of a previous opinion can be carried
out.

[36] If Keynes had lived to the ripe old age of his parents, it seems likely that his views would
again have evolved further, under the combined influences of additional evidence and the further
thinking of himself and others about these problems. What direction his further thoughts would
have taken is, at this point, a matter of pure speculation.

6. Statistical Testing of Keynesian Concepts Between the Publication of the *General Theory* and Tinbergen's *Business Cycles in the United States of America, 1919–1932* (1937 to mid-1939)

As noted in the preceding section, a number of the concepts of Keynes' *General Theory* appeared to cry out for empirical verification (or refutation). Most of this discussion centred around the consumption function (or "propensity to consume," as Keynes had termed it). An exception to this generalization was the 1939 study of the "Demand Schedule for Idle Money" by A. J. Brown, which attempted to test the Keynesian theory of liquidity-preference, especially against the alternative loanable funds theory. Although Brown was not able to reject the loanable funds theory (particularly its Wicksellian version), he found evidence also in favor of the theory of liquidity-preference. In particular, the demand for idle money was negatively and significantly related to the long-term rate of interest (that on government consols) and to the rate of change of a price index for final demand; it also appeared to be secondarily related to a measure of business transactions and, possibly, to the transactions of financial institutions.[37] Thus an important concept from *The General Theory*, other than the consumption function, was subjected to empirical scrutiny and found reasonably satisfactory.

A number of studies subjected the consumption function to further statistical examination, and much discussion followed these statistical studies.[38] Hans Staehle (1937) fitted a consumption function in which the average propensity to consume for German wage earners (the proportion of labor income spent in retail sales, smoothed by a four-quarter moving average) was fitted to data over the period 1928–34 and was found to be negatively related both to labor income measured in wage units and also to a measure of the inequality in the distribution of *personal* income. As Staehle insisted on the importance of this latter variable and on his view that others had not taken it into account (at least to the extent that its importance warranted), this generated some controversy. (See Dirks, 1938; Staehle, 1938; Keynes, 1939a; and Staehle, 1939.) We need not comment in detail on this debate, other than to remark that none of the participants in the debate presented alternative regressions to support their alternative interpretations (or to defend their original position).[39] Another early study was that of J. J. Polak (1939), but since his consumption functions for the United States over the period 1919–32 are

---

[37] The significance of the first of these two supplementary explanatory variables suggests that the method of eliminating active balances employed by Brown may not have been completely successful.

[38] Elizabeth W. Gilboy (1939), in a running debate with Professor Acheson J. Duncan of Princeton University (and with Keynes himself), remarked that Keynes' propensity to consume was a statistical, rather than a psychological, law or tendency. This turned out to be prophetic, at least as a general tendency.

[39] Dirks (1938) did put forward the interesting hypothesis that Staehle's results could be explained more simply by income and income change as explanatory variables, owing to what the late T. M. Brown (1952) was to call "habit persistence." In retrospect, it seems clear that most qualified observers would agree with Richard and W. M. Stone that Staehle exaggerated the practical importance of this additional explanatory variable.

virtually identical (as he notes in this article) with those of Tinbergen (1939), which is discussed in the following chapter, we shall content ourselves by merely mentioning this study. Finally, the Stones (Richard and W. M.) published a study (1938–9) in which aggregative consumption functions (with global consumption as a function of aggregate income and of a time trend) were fitted for Germany (two periods), the United Kingdom, the Netherlands, Sweden (two periods) and the United States. Reasonably good fits were obtained, and the Stones felt that their explanation was quite adequate.[40]

The work of Richard and W. M. Stone was oriented, at least in large part, towards gauging the empirical magnitude of Keynes' concept of the multiplier. (The Stones also checked the results of their time series regressions against family budget studies and "Kahn's method of leakages," and, as all three approaches gave similar results, they were encouraged.) Among the leakages distinguished were imports, personal savings and (negatively) reductions in induced government transfer payments (such as the dole) with economic recovery; interestingly, the Stones considered induced taxes as an illegitimate leakage. On the basis of some rough calculations, they estimated that these leakages varied from 0.35 to 0.60 as a proportion of GNP, implying a value of the multiplier, for the developed countries surveyed, from 1.67 to 2.86, largely depending on the degree of openness of the economy in question.[41] Colin Clark, in two articles around the same time (1937, 1938), used impressionistic statistical techniques (based on his pioneering work in developing national income statistics for the British economy) to work up estimates of the expenditures multiplier for two subperiods, 1929–33 and 1934–7. He found that the estimated multipliers were 1.5 and 2.1 respectively (or somewhat higher if a correction were made for a possible autonomous shift in the import demand function), thus confirming Keynes' hypothesis that the multiplier would be greater under depressed conditions. Finally, Michal Kalecki (1939), in the Appendix of Chap. 2, presents estimates of his version of the investment multiplier, for the USA for the period 1919–35, based on Simon Kuznets' national income data for that country.[42] Kalecki

---

[40] Although it was published somewhat later than Tinbergen's League of Nations study, for the sake of completeness we may mention Paul A. Samuelson's 1941 study of "A Statistical Analysis of the Consumption Function." Although Samuelson was not to make his career as an applied econometrician, this study is one of the best of the early work on the aggregative consumption function. Samuelson discusses his variables at length, considering a number of alternatives and defending the specification selected. His best formulation has real, per capita consumption as a linear function of real, per capita "income received" (a sort of disposable income variable) and of real, per capita business savings (which presumably measures increases in household wealth due to increasing claims on the corporate sector); the estimated marginal propensity to consume was 0.81.

[41] The Stones considered, on the basis of some fragmentary evidence, that the multiplier appeared to be largely constant over time, within a given country.

[42] In this connection, we may raise the question of whether Kalecki did develop independently a macroeconomic model that contained all of the essential elements of the Keynesian system. There are legitimate differences of opinion on this subject, but Kalecki's model of the business cycle, his version of liquidity preference and the equations of his system predate the later formal interpretations by Hicks (1937) and Meade (1936–7) of the Keynesian system as a total model. A literal interpretation of the writings of Keynes and Kalecki might lead some scholars, such as Don

estimates a multiplier of 2.25, on the basis of his estimation of a reduced form relationship, with a time lag of roughly four months. It may be mentioned that the time diagram of the calculated and the measured values of national income within the sample period, shows a very tight fit, with turning-points largely reproduced, and Kalecki felt that his theoretical formulation was solidly corroborated.[43]

We may close this section (and this chapter) by reviewing a small macroeconometric model constructed by E. A. Radice (1939) as a dissertation at Oxford University. In this 1939 League of Nations study, Tinbergen not only cites Radice's work but also remarks that, among all the formal macro-theoretical models constructed to represent Keynes' system, only Radice's has all of its parameters estimated (The parameter estimates come from Colin Clark's national income statistics of the U.K. economy, and the sample period is, in general, somewhat longer than that indicated in the title of this article, generally from 1924 to 1936.) In point of fact, Radice's was a very simple model, from the point of structure and specification. There were two identities and four behavioral equations, making six in total. One identity relates GNP to net income paid to individuals, business savings and capital consumption allowances. The behavioral relationships include a personal savings function, a business savings function (with profits plus interest received as the only explanatory variable) and a profits-generating mechanism, linking profits (plus interest received) to gross investment. (All four of the behavioral relationships have only unique explanatory variables, so that the explanations seem fairly simplistic, from a modern perspective. Although this is never stated explicitly, one supposes that the economic variables are deflated for changing price (or wage) levels). The final behavioral equation, the key relationship of the model, is Radice's investment

---

Patinkin, to conclude that Kalecki did not independently develop a mainstream Keynesian model. However the spirit and novelty of Kalecki's contributions are such as to lead one to conclude that it was, indeed, a separate discovery of the same basic system. In this regard, mention might be made of Kalecki's version of the consumption function (which put an explicit emphasis on the functional distribution of income), of Kalecki's investment function (which made the sophisticated distinction between orders and shipments or deliveries), and of Kalecki's alternative to liquidity preference theory, in which the income velocity of money is made an increasing function of the rate of interest. We also know that Kalecki treated these three components as a dynamic system whose solution was meant to describe the economy as a whole.

Apart from the formal question of macroeconometric model-building, it is clear that Kalecki was not able to round out his theory with profound insights into the functioning of financial markets and the formulation of high-level policy, which was the hallmark of Keynes' unusual influence. Kalecki's theory was drafted for a professional audience, while Keynes went far beyond a circle of econometricians and other professional economists. He was talking to major policy- and decision-makers.

[43] Although they were published a few years after Tinbergen's study, mention may be made of Mordecai Ezekiel's two studies (1942a, 1942b). Ezekiel attempted to get an empirical counterpart of the savings and investment functions of macroeconomic theory, and so (by appropriate observation or manipulation) he would have been able to calculate the likely location of possible equilibrium positions and hence the implicit multiplier generated by any possible shift in the investment function. More than half a century later, it is interesting to note that Ezekiel explicitly acknowledged in these articles helpful comments from (among others) Alvin H. Hansen, Paul A. Samuelson, and John Maynard Keynes. Ezekiel's work was criticized at the time by one of us (Klein, 1943), largely on the grounds that (in modern language) Ezekiel had not paid sufficient attention to the problem of identification.

function, a version of the acceleration principle, in which the rate of change of gross investment lags behind a proportional multiple of the second derivative of GNP by a constant time lag, estimated by Radice to be 7 or 8 quarters. More interesting than the simple structure of the model is the associated mathematical analysis. Because of the existence of a mixed differential-difference equation (the function for gross investment), this model can, under some circumstances, produce cycles. In point of fact, this is the case for the fitted values of the parameters obtained. The bulk of the article, indeed, is devoted to a discussion of the character of the cyclical implications of the fitted model. The point estimates suggest a slightly explosive cycle, but Radice feels that neutral or damped cycles would appear to be within the realm of possibility (or, more technically, within the two standard error range of the structural parameter estimates). Sensitivity analysis is carried out in some detail, and the possibility of asymmetrical upswings and downswings is considered. While recognizing the limitations of his statistical base, Radice was encouraged by the close agreement of the estimated periodicity of the cycle generated by his fitted model and the apparent periodicity observed in the British economy. This evaluation seems fair; like Tinbergen's seminal efforts, Radice's attempts should be judged as insightful and pioneering.

References

Arrow, Kenneth J. and Gerard Debreu, 1954, "Existence of an equilibrium for a competitive economy," *Econometrica* **22**, no. 3 (July), pp. 265–290.

Bodkin, Ronald G., Lawrence R. Klein, and Kanta Marwah, 1986, "Keynes and the origins of macroeconometric modeling," *Eastern Economic Journal* **12**, no. 4 (October–December), pp. 442–450. (This piece was also published in O. F. Hamouda and J. N. Smithin (eds), *Keynes and Public Policy After Fifty Years, Volume 2: Theories and Method* (Edward Elgar Publishing Limited, Gloucester, 1988), pp. 3–11.

Brown, A. J., 1939, "Interest, prices and the demand schedule for idle money," *Oxford Economic Papers*, no. 2 (May), pp. 46–69.

Brown, T. M., 1952, "Habit persistence and lags in consumer behavior," *Econometrica* **20**, no. 3 (July), pp. 207–223.

Clark, Colin, 1937, "National income at its climax," *Economic Journal* **47**, no. 186 (June), pp. 308–320.

———, 1938, "Determination of the multiplier from national income statistics," *Economic Journal* **48**, no. 191 (September), pp. 435–448.

Clower, Robert W., 1966, "The Keynesian counter-revolution: A theoretical appraisal," in *The Theory of Interest Rates*, eds. F. H. Hahn and F. P. R. Brechling (St Martin's Press, New York, 1966), pp. 103–125.

Dirks, Frederick C., 1938, "Retail sales and labor income," *Review of Economic Statistics* **20**, no. 3 (August), pp. 128–134.

Dresch, F. W., 1938, "Index numbers and the general economic equilibrium," *Bulletin of the American Mathematical Society* **44** (February), pp. 134–141.

Evans, Griffith C., 1934, "Maximum production studied in a simplified economic system," *Econometrica* **2**, no. 1 (January), pp. 37–50.

Ezekiel, Mordecai, 1942a, "Statistical investigations of saving, consumption, and investment: I, saving, consumption, and national income," *American Economic Review* **32**, no. 1 (March), pp. 22–49.

——, 1942b, "Statistical investigations of saving, consumption, and investment: II, Investment, national income, and the saving-investment equilibrium," *American Economic Review* **32**, no. 2 (June), pp. 272–307.

Friedman, Milton, 1955, " Léon Walras and his economic system," *American Economic Review* **45**, no. 5 (December), pp. 1190–1201.

Frisch, Ragnar, 1933, "Propagation problems and impulse problems in dynamic economics," in *Economic Essays in Honour of Gustav Cassel, October 20th 1933* (Frank Cass and Company Limited, London), pp. 171–205.

——, and Harald Holme, 1935, "The characteristic solutions of a mixed difference and differential equation occurring in economic dynamics," *Econometrica* **3**, pp. 225–239.

Gilboy, Elizabeth W., 1938, "The propensity to consume," *Quarterly Journal of Economics* **53**, no. 1 (November), pp. 120–140.

——, 1939, "Reply" [to comments by Acheson J. Duncan and John Maynard Keynes], *Quarterly Journal of Economics* **53**, no. 4 (August), pp. 633–638.

Hendry, David F., 1980, "Econometrics — Alchemy or science," *Economica* **47**, no. 4 (November), pp. 387–406.

Hicks, John R., 1937, "Mr Keynes and the 'Classics'; a suggested interpretation," *Econometrica* **5**, no. 2 (April), pp. 147–159.

Hutchison, T. W., 1966, *A Review of Economic Doctrines 1870–1929* (Clarendon Press, Oxford).

Jaffé, William, 1972, "Pareto translated: A review article," *Journal of Economic Literature* **10**, no. 4 (December), pp. 1190–1201.

——, 1974, "'Pareto's three manuals': Rebuttal," *Journal of Economic Literature* **12**, no. 1 (March), pp. 88–91.

——, 1980, "Walras' economics as others see it," *Journal of Economic Literature* **18**, no. 2 (June), pp. 528–549.

Kalecki, Michal, 1935, "A macrodynamic theory of business cycles," *Econometrica* **3**, pp. 327–344.

——, 1939, "Investment and income," in *Essays in the Theory of Economic Fluctuations* (Farrar & Rinehart, Inc., New York), Chap. 2, pp. 42–74.

Keynes, John Maynard, 1936, *The General Theory of Employment, Interest and Money* (Harcourt, Brace & Company, New York).

——, 1939a, "Mr. Keynes on the distribution of incomes and the 'propensity to consume': A reply," *Review of Economic Statistics* **21**, no. 3 (August), pp. 128–129.

——, 1939b, "Professor Tinbergen's method," *Economic Journal* **49**, no. 195 (September), pp. 558–568.

Klant, Johannes J., 1985, " The slippery transition," in *Keynes' Economics: Methodological Issues*, eds. Tony Lawson and Hashem Pesaran (Croom Helm, London and Sydney), pp. 80–95.

Klein, Lawrence R., 1943, "Pitfalls in the statistical determination of the investment schedule," *Econometrica* **11**, nos. 3–4 (July–October), pp. 246–258.

——, 1951, "The life of John Maynard Keynes," *Journal of Political Economy* **59**, no. 5 (October), pp. 443–451.

Lawson, Tony, 1985, "Keynes, prediction, and econometrics," in *Keynes' Economics: Methodological Issues*, eds. T. Lawson and H. Pesaran (Croom Helm, London and Sydney), pp. 116–133.

—— and H. Pesaran (eds.), 1985, *Keynes' Economics: Methodological Issues* (Croom Helm, London and Sydney).

Lucas, Robert E., Jr, 1976, "Econometric policy evaluation: A critique," in *The Phillips Curve and Labor Markets*, eds. Karl Brunner and Allan H. Meltzer (North-Holland, Amsterdam), pp. 19–46, Carnegie–Rochester Conference Series on Public Policy, vol. 1, *Supplement* to the *Journal of Monetary Economics*.

Marshall, Alfred, 1897, "The old generation of economists and the new," *Quarterly Journal of Economics* **11** (January), pp. 115–135.

Marx, Karl, 1906, *Capital*, vol. 1, Modern Library Edition (Random House, Inc., New York).

Meade, J. E., 1936–7, "A simplified model of Mr. Keynes' system," *Review of Economic Studies* **4**, pp. 98–107.

Moggridge, Donald (ed.), 1973, *The Collected Writings of John Maynard Keynes*, vol. XIV, *The General Theory and After, Part II, Defence and Development* (Macmillan, London).

Morgan, Mary S., 1984, "The history of econometric thought: Analysis of the main problems of relating economic theory to data in the first half of the Twentieth Century," Ph.D. Thesis, London University, 1984. (This work was also published in 1987 by Cambridge University Press under the title, *The History of Econometric Ideas*.)

——, 1987, "Statistics without probability and Haavelmo's revolution in econometrics," in *The Probabilistic Revolution, vol. 2, Ideas in the Sciences*, eds. L. Krüger, G. Gigerenzer and M. S. Morgan (Bradford Books and MIT Press, Cambridge, Mass., and London).

Morishima, Michio, 1980, "W. Jaffé on Léon Walras: A comment," *Journal of Economic Literature* **18**, no. 2 (June), pp. 550–558.

Okun, Arthur M., 1981, *Prices and Quantities: A Macroeconomic Analysis* (The Brookings Institution, Washington, DC).

Pareto, Vilfredo, 1896–7, *Cours d'économie politique/Professé à l'Université de Lausanne*, vols. 1 and 2 (Lausanne: Rouge). (This work has been republished as volume 1 of the *Oeuvres complètes de Vilfredo Pareto*, G. H. Bousquet and G. Busino (eds) (Droz, Geneva, 1964).

———, 1906, *Manuale di economia politica con una introduzione alla scienza sociale*, no. 13 in the Piccola biblioteca scientifica (Società editrice libraria Milan, 1906). (We have consulted the 1974 reprinting, published in Padova, Italy, by Casa editrice dolt. Antonio Milani.)

Patinkin, Don, 1976, "Keynes and econometrics: On the interaction between the macroeconomic revolutions of the interwar period," *Econometrica* **44**, no. 6 (November), pp. 1091–1123.

Pesaran, Hashem and Ron Smith, 1985, "Keynes on econometrics," in *Keynes' Economics: Methodological Issues*, eds. T. Lawson and H. Pesaran (Croom Helm, London and Sydney).

Polak, J. J., 1939, "Functions in United States consumption, 1919–1932," *Review of Economic Statistics* **21**, no. 1 (February), pp. 1–12.

Radice, E. A., 1939, "A dynamic scheme for the British trade cycle, 1929–1937," *Econometrica* **7**, no. 1 (January), pp. 47–56.

Roos, C. F., 1930, "A mathematical theory of price and production fluctuations and economic crises," *Journal of Political Economy* **38**, no. 5 (October), pp. 501–522.

———, 1934, *Dynamic Economics: Theoretical and Statistical Studies of Demand, Production and Prices*, Cowles Commission Monograph No. 1 (The Principia Press, Inc., Bloomington, Indiana).

Samuelson, Paul A., 1941, "A statistical analysis of the consumption function," in *Fiscal Policy and Business Cycles*, ed. Alvin H. Hansen (W. W. Norton & Company, Inc., New York), Appendix to Chap. 11 (pp. 250–260).

Sargent, Thomas J., 1976, "A classical macroeconomic model for the United States," *Journal of Political Economy* **84**, no. 2 (April), pp. 207–237.

Sawyer, John A., 1976, "Stanley Jevons and the development of scientific method in economics," Working Paper No. 7602 of the Institute for Policy Analysis of the University of Toronto, mimeographed, September.

Schwier, J. F. and Ann S. Schwier, 1974, "Pareto's three manuals," *Journal of Economic Literature* **12**, no. 1 (March), pp. 78–87.

Sims, Christopher A., 1980, "Macroeconomics and reality," *Econometrica* **48**, no. 1 (January), pp. 1–48.

Spiegel, Henry William, 1971, *The Growth of Economic Thought* (Prentice-Hall, Englewood Cliffs, New Jersey).

Stachle, Hans, 1937, "Short-period variations in the distribution of incomes," *Review of Economic Statistics* **19**, no. 3 (August), pp. 133–143.

———, 1938, "New considerations on the distribution of incomes and the 'Propensity to consume'" (partly in reply to M. Dirks), *Review of Economic Statistics* **20**, no. 3 (August), pp. 134–141.

———, 1939, "A rejoinder" (to a reply by John Maynard Keynes), *Review of Economic Statistics* **21**, no. 3 (August), p. 129.

Stone, Richard, 1980, "Keynes, political arithmetic and econometrics," Keynes Lecture in Economics 1978, in the *Proceedings of the British Academy*, London, vol. 64, 1978 (Oxford University Press, Oxford), pp. 55–92.

—— and W. M. Stone, 1938–9, "The marginal propensity to consume and the multiplier: A statistical investigation," *Review of Economic Studies* **6**, pp. 1–24.

Tarascio, Vincent J., 1968, *Pareto's Methodological Approach to Economics: A Study in the History of Some Scientific Aspects of Economic Thought* (The University of North Carolina Press, Chapel Hill).

——, 1973, "Vilfredo Pareto: On the occasion of the translation of his *Manuel*," *Canadian Journal of Economics* **6**, no. 3 (August), pp. 394–408.

——, 1974, "Vilfred Pareto and the translation of his *Manuel*," *Journal of Economic Literature* **12**, no. 1 (March), pp. 91–96.

Theiss, Edward, 1933, "A quantitative theory of industrial fluctuations caused by the capitalist technique of production," *Journal of Political Economy* **41**, no. 3 (June), pp. 334–349.

Tinbergen, Jan, 1935, "Annual survey: Suggestions on quantitative business cycle theory," *Econometrica* **3**, pp. 241–308.

——, 1937, *An Econometric Approach to Business Cycle Problems* (Hermann et Compagnie, Paris).

——, 1939a, *A Method and its Application to Investment Activity*, Part I of *Statistical Testing of Business-Cycle Theories* (Agathon Press Inc., New York, 1968). (Originally published in Geneva by the Economic Intelligence Service of the League of Nations in 1939.)

——, 1939b, *Business Cycles in the United States of America, 1919–1932*, Part II of *Statistical Testing of Business-Cycle Theories* (Agathon Press, Inc., New York, 1968). (Originally published in Geneva by the Economic Intelligence Service of the League of Nations in 1939.)

——, 1940, "On a method of business-cycle research: A reply, " *Economic Journal* **50**, no. 197 (March), pp. 140–154.

——, 1948, "The significance of Keynes' theories from the econometric point of view," Chap. 18 (pp. 219–231) in *The New Economics*, ed. Seymour E. Harris (Alfred A. Knopf, New York).

——, 1986, letter to Ronald G. Bodkin, dated 31 July.

Tobin, James, 1947, "Liquidity preference and monetary policy," *Review of Economics and Statistics* **29**, no. 2 (May), pp. 124–131.

Walras, Léon, 1954, *Elements of Pure Economics* (Richard D. Irwin, Inc., Homewood, Illinois). (A translation, by William Jaffé, of the Edition Définitive of *Eléments d'économie politique pure* (R. Pichon et R. Durand-Auzia and F. Rouge, Paris and Lausanne, 1926).)

8

A POSTWAR QUARTERLY MODEL:
DESCRIPTION AND APPLICATIONS[†][*]

Introduction

The National Bureau of Economic Research has often made the point that annual data are inadequate in business cycle analysis. This is not to claim that they are worthless but merely to recognize that we ought to try to do better. Without going to the extreme that the NBER reaches in doing most of its analysis with monthly data, we in econometric model-building research ought to go at least as far as the construction of quarterly systems. Eventually, we shall build monthly models, but the first step is naturally a quarterly model. There is serious doubt whether suitable data could be found for our methods on a monthly basis. The quarterly national income accounts are now plentiful, though not necessarily ultimately refined, and we have had a good span of time since the end of World War II in which to build up a sample of respectable size.

Some prewar quarterly data stretch back as far as World War I. These have already been exploited in econometric model building by Harold Barger and myself, but our investigation dealt only with a small model to be used for methodological purposes.[1] It might be possible to prepare an approximate set of quarterly series covering the period before as well as after World War II on the scale needed for the present model, but the expenditure of time would be enormous. We made a pragmatic decision to confine the analysis to postwar quarterly data. That alone posed substantial problems of data processing. A possible advantage of this decision was that we obtained a more homogeneous sample, but we lost in terms of richness of experience.

We made another basic decision at the outset, namely, to use seasonally adjusted data. The alternative would have been to introduce explicit seasonal variables, as was done in the recent British model.[2] Consumers of economic data and of the

[†]From *Models of Income Determination, Studies in Income and Wealth*, Vol. 28, ed. Bert G. Hickman (Princeton University Press, Princeton, 1964), pp. 11–36.
[*]Note: The research on this model was supported by the Rockefeller Foundation. Participating at various times over the course of the development of the model was Motoo Abe, R. J. Ball, Hidekazu Eguchi, K. Krishnamurty, Kanta Marwah, Mitsugu Nakamura, Joel Popkin, and Yoichi Shinkai. Harry Eisenpress of the IBM Corporation rendered invaluable computing assistance. Machine time was generously made available to us by IBM.
[1]"A quarterly model for the United States economy," *Journal of the American Statistical Association* (September 1954), pp. 413–437.
[2]Lawrence R. Klein *et al., An Econometric Model of the United Kingdom* (Oxford, Eng., 1961).

results of economic analysis appear to be more receptive to seasonally adjusted than to unadjusted data; therefore, we decided to make our findings available immediately in adjusted form. This freed us from a certain amount of routine work by making the number of variables smaller in each equation. Theoretically, there is much to be said in favor of using seasonal variables with unadjusted data, but an adequate treatment may, in several cases, take us beyond the simple additive process used in the British model.

It may be useful, at the outset, to distinguish the present model from its annual predecessors, using the Klein–Goldberger model as a reference point.[3]

1. The present model is less aggregative. There are more equations in the present model. Some represent obvious decomposition of national product elements; others stem from more subtle theorizing about patterns of behavior.

2. Anticipatory data are used in the present model. In applications of the Klein–Goldberger model to problems of forecasting, frequent use was made of expectations about consumer purchases and investment outlays, but these subjective variables were not built into the models directly. Now we have introduced realization functions which express actual behavior as a function of expectations. In *short-run* forecasting these equations can be used; but since we do not provide an endogenous explanation of expectations, only limited use can be made of such relations. Nevertheless, we feel that this is an important first step in macroeconomic model building.

3. Explicit relations among inventories, sales, backlogs, and order flow appear in the new model. The Klein–Goldberger model slurred over the whole question of inventory investment. Later work has extended that model annually, using more explicit inventory behavior; but the essence of inventory-order patterns probably cannot be discerned with annual data. Our quarterly model is more promising in this respect.

4. The concept of capacity, together with the rate of utilization, is introduced in the new model. It is difficult to define capacity and to measure it. Nonetheless, this concept figures importantly in much economic analysis. We attempt, at the Wharton School, to measure capacity utilization; and, imperfect though our series may be, it appears to be of significance in the structure of our model.

5. The accounting identities are properly expressed in current prices, while the behavioral and technical equations are, save for appropriate exceptions, in real terms, relative prices, or deflated incomes. There was a distortion in the older annual models, caused by requiring the national income identities to hold in real or deflated variables. When prices change by large amounts, these distortions grow in significance.

---

[3]Lawrence R. Klein and A. S. Goldberger, *An Econometric Model of the United States, 1929–1952* (Amsterdam, 1955).

There are other points of difference between the new and the older models, but those above are the differences that motivated the present research. Others will be brought out in the discussion of the equations of the model.

The Model

The sample data include the quarters from I-1948 to IV-1958. For lagged values we used some earlier quarters. Time has elapsed since the model was estimated, and quarterly data for 1959, 1960, and 1961 are now available. Eventually, the whole system will be re-estimated. The estimates are limited-information maximum-likelihood estimates. In some cases two-stage least-squares estimates have been used because of problems of multicollinearity. It has been found that limited information estimates are more sensitive than two-stage estimates to the presence of multicollinearity. In cases where the limited-information method gave obviously nonsensical results, we used two-stage estimates instead. Multicollinearity problems among the set of predetermined variables also proved troublesome, and we estimated the system in two major groups of equations with a somewhat different set of predetermined variables in each group.

List of variables

$^*C_d$	Expenditures on consumer durables, billions of 1954 dollars
$^*C_n$	Expenditures on consumer nondurables, billions of 1954 dollars
$^*C_s$	Expenditures on consumer services, billions of 1954 dollars
$^*Y - T$	Disposable personal income, billions of current dollars
W	Wages, salaries, and other labor income, billions of current dollars
$^*P$	Nonlabor personal income, billions of current dollars
C_d^e	Index of consumer buying plans for durable goods
$^*L$	End-of-quarter cash balances, billions of current dollars
$^*p_d$	Implicit deflator, consumer durables, 1954 = 1.00
$^*p_n$	Implicit deflator, consumer nondurables, 1954 = 1.00
$^*p_s$	Implicit deflator, consumer services, 1954 = 1.00
N	Population, millions of persons
$^*I_p$	Expenditures on private producers' plant and equipment, billions of 1954 dollars
$^*I_h$	Expenditures on nonfarm residential construction, billions of 1954 dollars
$^*I_i$	Inventory investment, billions of 1954 dollars
$^*X$	Private gross national product, billions of 1954 dollars
$^*X_c$	Private gross national product at full capacity, billions of 1954 dollars
I_p^e	Intended investment outlays, billions of 1954 dollars
$^*q_h$	Implicit deflator, nonfarm residential construction, 1954 = 1.00
$^*i_L$	Average yield, corporate bonds, per cent
F_s	Number of marriages, thousands
I_h^s	Number of housing starts

$*h$ Hours worked per week, index

$*i_s$ Average yield, ninety-day commercial paper

$*O$ Manufacturers' new orders, billions of 1954 dollars

$*U$ Manufacturers' unfilled orders, billions of 1954 dollars

$*S_c$ Corporate retained earnings, billions of current dollars

$*P_c$ Corporate profits, billions of current dollars

T_c Corporate income taxes, billions of current dollars

$*q_p$ Implicit deflator, plant and equipment expenditures, $1954 = 1.00$

$*D_r$ Capital consumption allowances, replacement cost, billions of
            1954 dollars

$*N_w$ Number of employees, millions of persons

$*N_g$ Number of government employees, millions of persons

N_e Number of self-employed, millions of persons

W_g Government wages, salaries, and other labor income, billions of
            current dollars

$*p$ Implicit deflator, gross national product, $1954 = 1.00$

$*w$ Average annual wage, current dollars

$*N_L$ Labor force, millions of persons

$*F_e$ Exports of goods and services, billions of 1954 dollars

X_w Index of world production, $1954 = 1.00$

$*F_{im}$ Imports of crude food and materials, billions of 1954 dollars

p_i Implicit deflator, imports of goods and services, $1954 = 1.00$

$*F_{if}$ Other imports, billions of 1954 dollars

R End-of-quarter percentage of total bank reserves held in excess
            of required reserves

i_r Federal Reserve average discount rate

U_d Manufacturers' unfilled orders of durable goods, billions of
            1954 dollars

U_n Manufacturers' unfilled orders of nondurable goods, billions of
            1954 dollars

$*C$ Total consumer expenditures, billions of 1954 dollars

p_w Index of prices of competing exports, $1954 = 1.00$

$*p_e$ Implicit deflator, exports of goods and services, $1954 = 1.00$

G Government expenditures on goods and services, billions of current
            dollars

D_a Capital consumption allowances, accounting prices, billions
            of current dollars

T_i Reconciling item between net national product and national
            income, billions of current dollars

    *Denotes endogenous variable.

    Variables taken from the national income accounts in dollar totals are seasonally
adjusted at annual rates. Most other variables are also seasonally adjusted.

    In the equations written below, the numbers in parentheses under each coefficient
are estimated standard errors. The correlation measures, $\overline{R}$, are computed from

the formula

$$R = \sqrt{1 - \left(\frac{\Sigma r^2}{T - m}\right)\left(\frac{T - 1}{\Sigma x^2}\right)}$$

where r is the residual, x is the dependent variable, and m is the number of parameters in the equation. The equations that have been estimated by the two-stage, least-squares method are marked TSLS below the number.

Estimated equations

$$C_d = -67.1 + 0.363\,\frac{Y - T}{p_d} + 58.4\,\frac{P}{W}$$
$$(51.0)\quad(0.15)\qquad\quad(79.0)$$

$$-1.14\,\frac{1}{8}\sum_{i=1}^{8}(C_d)_{-i} + 0.174\,C_d^e \qquad\qquad \overline{R} = 0.40 \quad (1)$$
$$(0.86)\qquad\qquad\quad(0.093)$$

$$C_n = 27.7 + 0.259\,\frac{Y - T}{p_n} + 8.88\,\frac{P}{W}$$
$$(8.1)\quad(0.044)\qquad\quad(15.0)$$

$$+0.191\,\frac{1}{8}\sum_{i=1}^{8}(C_n)_{-i} + 0.0056\left(\frac{L}{p_n}\right)_{-1} \qquad \overline{R} = 0.99 \quad (2)$$
$$(0.095)\qquad\qquad\quad(0.055)$$

$$C_s = -152.0 + 0.103\,\frac{Y - T}{p_s} + 41.1\,\frac{P}{W}$$
$$(19.0)\quad(0.017)\qquad\quad(6.9)$$

$$+0.0188\,\frac{1}{8}\sum_{i=1}^{8}(C_s)_{-i} + 0.596\left(\frac{L}{p_s}\right)_{-1} + 1.13N \quad \overline{R} = 0.99 \quad (3)$$
$$(0.13)\qquad\qquad\quad(0.024)\qquad\quad(0.16)$$

$$I_p = -8.18 + 32.5\,(X/X_c) + 0.557\,I_p^e \qquad \overline{R} = 0.91 \qquad (4)$$
$$(4.16)\quad(4.76)\qquad\quad(0.0486)$$

$$I_h = -11.3 + 0.0764\,\frac{Y - T}{q_h} - 0.776i_L + 0.0011F + 0.00812\,(I_h^s)_{-1}$$
$$(1.2)\quad(0.0091)\qquad\quad(0.47)\qquad(0.0015)\qquad(0.0007)$$
$$\overline{R} = 0.96 \qquad (5)$$

$$I_i = -48.42 + 0.2675\,(X - I_i) - 0.2997\sum_{j=1}^{\infty}(I_i)_{-j}$$
$$(13.5)\quad(0.0707)\qquad\quad(0.06)$$

$$+269.3\,(p - p_{-1}) + 0.2031U_{-1} \qquad\qquad \overline{R} = 0.99 \text{ (stockform) (6)}$$
$$(75)\qquad\qquad\quad(0.047)$$

$$S_c/q_p = -0.448 + 0.938\,\frac{P_c - T_c}{q_p} - 0.853\,\frac{1}{8}\sum_{i=1}^{8}\left(\frac{P_c - T_c - S_c}{q_p}\right)_{-i}$$
$$(2.5)\quad(0.061)\qquad\quad(0.17)$$
$$\overline{R} = 0.96 \qquad (7)$$

$$P_c = 5.49 + 0.627 \left(P - \frac{1}{3} p_{-1} \right) \qquad \overline{R} = 0.59 \quad (8)$$
$$ (5.1) \quad (0.10)$$

$$D_r = 10.8 + 0.0664X + 0.00599 \sum_{i=1}^{\infty} (I_p + I_h - D_r)_{-i} \qquad \overline{R} = 0.94 \quad (9)$$
$$ (3.10) \quad (0.017) \qquad (0.0034)$$

$$X = 90.9 + 1.758 \left[h(N_w - N_g) + N_e \right] + 0.196 (X/X_c)$$
$$ (60.83) \quad (1.485) \qquad\qquad\qquad\quad (0.062)$$

$$\times \sum_{i=0}^{\infty} (I_p + I_h - D_r)_{-i} + 0.135t \qquad\qquad \overline{R} = 0.99 \quad (10)$$
$$ (0.640) \qquad\qquad\qquad\qquad\quad \text{TSLS}$$

$$X_c = 90.9 + 1.758 N_L + 0.196 \sum_{i=0}^{\infty} (I_p + I_h - D_r)_{-i} + 0.135t$$
$$ (60.83) \quad (1.485) \quad (0.062) \qquad\qquad\qquad\qquad (0.640)$$

$$\overline{R} = 0.93 \quad (11)$$

(residual variance about mean) \qquad TSLS

$$\frac{W - W_g}{P} = 7.19 + 0.254X + 0.254X_{-1} + 0.221t \qquad \overline{R} = 0.99 \quad (12)$$
$$\phantom{\frac{W - W_g}{P} = } (7.4) \quad (0.015) \quad (0.015) \qquad (0.083)$$

$$w - w_{-4} = 169.0 - 38.2 \; \frac{1}{4} \sum_{i=0}^{3} (N_L - N_w - N_e)_{-i}$$
$$\phantom{w - w_{-4} = } (46.0) \quad (15.0)$$

$$+ 2110 \; \frac{1}{4} \sum_{i=0}^{3} (p - p_{-4})_{-i} + 1.56t \qquad\qquad \overline{R} = 0.56 \quad (13)$$
$$ (540.0) \qquad\qquad\qquad (0.80)$$

$$h = 0.721 + 0.320(X/X_c) + 0.00217(X - X_{-1}) - 0.00026t$$
$$ (0.047) \quad (0.052) \qquad\qquad (0.0006) \qquad\qquad (0.00017)$$

$$\overline{R} = 0.51 \quad (14)$$

$$N_L = 61.2 - 0.308 \, (N_L - N_w - N_e) + 0.226t \qquad \overline{R} = 0.99 \quad (15)$$
$$ (0.21) \quad (0.075) \qquad\qquad\qquad (0.0053)$$

$$U = -101 + 2.12O + 111(X/X_c) \qquad\qquad \overline{R} = 0.62 \quad (16)$$
$$ (44) \quad (0.84) \quad (55) \qquad\qquad\qquad \text{TSLS}$$

$$O = 2.56 + 0.0589(X - I_i)_{-1} + 387(p - p_{-1}) \qquad \overline{R} = 0.60 \quad (17)$$
$$ (3.2) \quad (0.0098) \qquad\qquad (72.0)$$

$$F_e = 2.98 + 0.160(X_w)_{-1} \qquad\qquad\qquad \overline{R} = 0.90 \quad (18)$$
$$ (1.112) \quad (0.0115)$$

$$F_{im} = 3.82 + 0.0065X_{-1} - 1.04(p_i/p)_{-1} \qquad \overline{R} = 0.53 \quad (19)$$
$$\phantom{F_{im} = } (0.867) \quad (0.0015) \qquad (0.804)$$

$$F_{if} = 8.11 + 0.039 \frac{Y-T}{p_i} - 24.1 \frac{P}{W}$$
$$\phantom{F_{if} =} (2.62) \quad (0.0082) \qquad\quad (5.3)$$

$$+0.286 \frac{1}{8} \sum_{i=1}^{8} (F_{if})_{-i} \qquad\qquad \overline{R} = 0.97 \quad (20)$$
$$ (0.15)$$

$$\frac{L}{pX + W_g} = 0.815 - 0.0743 i_L - 1.38(p - p_{-1}) \qquad \overline{R} = 0.64 \quad (21)$$
$$\phantom{\frac{L}{pX + W_g} =} (0.058) \quad (0.0131) \qquad (0.92) \qquad\qquad\qquad \text{TSLS}$$

$$i_L = 0.0541 + 0.0497 i_s + 0.959(i_L)_{-1} \qquad \overline{R} = 0.97 \quad (22)$$
$$ (0.15) \qquad (0.034) \qquad (0.060)$$

$$i_s = 0.502 - 0.146 R_{-1} + 1.18 i_r \qquad\quad \overline{R} = 0.96 \quad (23)$$
$$ (0.399) \quad (0.060) \qquad (0.096)$$

$$p_d = 0.548 + 0.422p + 0.00067(U_d)_{-1} \qquad \overline{R} = 0.94 \quad (24)$$
$$ (0.034) \quad (0.039) \qquad (0.00017)$$

$$p_n = 0.346 + 0.618p + 0.00946(U_n)_{-1} \qquad \overline{R} = 0.97 \quad (25)$$
$$ (0.027) \quad (0.024) \qquad (0.0021)$$

$$p_s = 0.716 + 0.000179w - 1.08(C_s/C) \qquad \overline{R} = 0.99 \quad (26)$$
$$ (0.090) \quad (0.000005) \qquad (0.29)$$

$$q_p = -0.508 + 1.52p \qquad\qquad\qquad\quad \overline{R} = 0.99 \quad (27)$$
$$ (0.028) \quad (0.029)$$

$$q_h = 0.492 + 0.000144w \qquad\qquad\qquad \overline{R} = 0.96 \quad (28)$$
$$ (0.021) \quad (0.000006)$$

$$p_e = 0.374 + 0.0688 p_w + 0.572p \qquad\quad \overline{R} = 0.83 \quad (29)$$
$$ (0.063) \quad (0.088) \qquad (0.12)$$

$$p_d C_d + p_n C_n + p_s C_s + q_p I_p + q_h I_h + p I_i + p_e F_e - p_i(F_{im} + F_{if}) + G$$
$$= pX + W_g \qquad\qquad\qquad\qquad\qquad (30)$$

$$W + P + S_c - pX = W_g - D_a - T_i \qquad\qquad\qquad (31)$$

$$hwN_w = W\,10^3 \qquad\qquad\qquad\qquad\qquad\qquad (32)$$

$$W + P = Y \qquad\qquad\qquad\qquad\qquad\qquad (33)$$

$$C = C_d + C_n + C_s \qquad\qquad\qquad\qquad\qquad (34)$$

Discussion of the Equations

To make the system more comprehensible before we discuss applications of the model and its actual performance, we shall comment briefly on each equation or group of equations, comparing it with related work in econometrics.

The consumption equations

Consumer expenditures have been split into three obvious components — durables, nondurables, and services. Starting from the time-honored proposition that consumption (or consumption type) is dependent on aggregate income, we introduce the following qualifications:

1. Income should be adjusted for taxes and transfers. We use disposable income.
2. Relative prices might be relevant when dealing with subgroups of consumption. We deflate disposable income by the price index of the consumption type considered.
3. Income distribution as well as aggregate income may affect consumption. We use a separate variable to measure the ratio of wage to other personal income.
4. There may be lags in consumer behavior. We introduce average consumption (by type) of the past eight quarters to show the effect of the past.[4]
5. Consumer wealth as well as income may influence behavior. We used total stock of cash as a particular wealth variable of strategic importance in consumer spending.
6. Population growth may affect consumption. We introduced an explicit population variable, although we could have measured consumption, income, and cash balances on a per capita basis as an alternative.

We made these adjustments uniformly to all three consumption functions, but in the end settled for selective use of certain variables in certain equations. This was an empirical selection that has been used throughout the model. Many experimental calculations were made for each equation. We finally settled upon a set of parameter estimates for each equation that looked reasonable. Reasonableness was based on *a priori* notions about sign and order of magnitude of coefficients. The degree of experimentation was limited because we committed ourselves to a set of predetermined variables for the whole group of calculations by the method of limited information. We introduced one special variable in the equation for consumer durables. This variable is an index of consumer buying plans for new cars and other household items. We do not explain this variable within the system.

The investment equations

Capital formation is divided into producers' plant and equipment, residential construction, and inventory investment. In the plant and equipment equation, investment intentions are introduced explicitly. These are the data of the Office of Business Economics — Securities and Exchange Commission on first intentions deflated

---

[4]In the Barger–Klein quarterly model, last quarter's consumption was used, in direct analogy to the successful use of last year's consumption in the annual models. There is so much pure autocorrelation that this kind of quarterly relation was not satisfactory. If past consumption is to represent a standard or norm from which adjustments to current conditions take place, it seems better to use average consumption of the recent past. All these schemes using past consumption are transformations of distributed lag processes.

by the price index of capital goods as of the (future) date to which the intentions refer. One may justifiably argue that we should deflate them as of the date at which the intentions are expressed. A similar anticipatory variable appears in the residential construction equation. It is the lagged value of starts.

The system is open with respect to these two anticipatory variables; i.e., we offer no endogenous explanation of investment intentions or housing starts; therefore, the extrapolation period for the model is limited. Our treatment here is parallel to that in the equation for consumer durables, where we introduce the index of consumer buying plans. In the inventory investment equation, we have proceeded somewhat differently. We have the backlog of orders as a kind of anticipatory variable there, but we attempt to give, at a later stage in the model, an endogenous explanation of unfilled orders, bringing new orders into the system as well.

The positive correlation between inventory investment and unfilled orders may seem to be strange, for businessmen ought not to be accumulating stocks while they still have backlogs of unfilled orders on hand. Our disaggregation was not carried far enough in this system to distinguish among inventories of raw materials, goods in process, and finished goods. The first two ought to be positively associated with unfilled orders, while the third ought to be negatively associated. A similar result is found by Duesenberry, Eckstein, and Fromm in their quarterly model.[5]

In the housing demand equation we use a long-term interest rate variable to show the effect of credit terms, and a marriage variable to show the effect of demographic pressures on facilities.

The capacity variable, which we have estimated with considerable expenditure of research effort, appears to be highly significant in the equation for plant and equipment.

The inventory equation, apart from the usual transactions and stock adjustment terms, contains an indication of price speculation. We did not separate farm from nonfarm inventories. This is another direction in which future disaggregation ought to go.

The elements of nonwage income

There are three equations for nonwage income components. One covers corporate saving; one relates noncorporate (excluding wages) to corporate income; and one deals with depreciation. The fundamental national accounting identity equating national income to national product, with appropriate reconciling items, requires the separate explanation of corporate saving. In the explanation of corporate saving a variable measuring corporate income, as distinct from other nonwage income, must be used. This necessitates an equation. Finally, depreciation in the system must be explained; for the capital formation variables are measured gross, and they must be cumulated for measurement of capital stock.

---

[5] James S. Duesenberry, Otto Eckstein, and Gary Fromm, "A simulation of the United States economy in recession," *Econometrica* (October, 1960), pp. 749–809.

Corporate savings are made to depend on corporate income (after taxes) and lagged dividend payments of the past eight quarters. The explanation of the particular lag scheme here is the same as in the consumption equations.

When we use depreciation variables in the model for the purposes of measuring capital stock, we reckon depreciation at replacement costs. In other instances, we reckon in accounting prices. Here, we are interested in relating depreciation to the accumulated stock of fixed capital and the rate of economic activity.

The relation between corporate and total nonwage income is purely empirical. It may be wiser to separate dividend and interest income from the nonwage non-corporate amounts, explaining this slow-moving component by a simple trend or autoregression, and to relate corporate income to income from noncorporate self-employment. The particular combination of variables used in the estimation of this empirical relation has been chosen so as to avoid some complications of multi-collinearity.

Production functions

The ordinary version of the production function is estimated by Eq. 10. There we have a relationship between real private output [GNP less government wages and salaries, deflated by the GNP deflator (see Eq. 30)], the input of labor, the input of capital, and a technological time trend. Labor input is measured as private employment $(N_w - N_g)$ adjusted by an index of hours worked (h) plus the number of self-employed (N_e). Since h is an index value on a unit base, we express adjusted employees and self-employed in conformable units: $h(N_w - N_g) + N_e$. Capital input is measured as the accumulated stock of capital, based on statistics of net investment in fixed capital, times the rate of utilization of capacity. Strictly speaking, we would want to have the rate of utilization of capital as the multiplying factor, but lacking a direct estimate of capital utilization we use an overall measure of capacity utilization.

Capacity as expressed in Eq. 11 must be explained.[6] It is an important, but elusive, concept in its own right, and it plays an important role in this model. By capacity output, in the aggregate, we mean a *point* on the macroeconomic production function corresponding to full utilization of inputs — labor and capital in this case. We might write

$$X_c = \alpha_0 + \alpha_1 N_L + \alpha_2 K + \alpha_3 t + \nu$$

where X_c = capacity output
N_L = labor force
K = stock of capital [shorthand for $\Sigma_{i=0}^{\infty}(I_p + I_h - D_r)_{-i}$]
ν = random error.

---

[6]The discussion of capacity and the production function bears heavily on ideas put forward by Professor Morishima of Osaka University.

Perhaps we should write $0.97(N_L - N_g)$, or some other high fraction of the private labor force, for full-utilization labor input in order to allow for frictional unemployment and public employment. In this paper, $1.0N_L$ is used, since the applied work to be described was based on this value.

This is not an independent relationship. Its parameters should be the same as those of the ordinary production function, expressed in terms of actual output, employment, and utilized capital. Two separate linear functions might be used to approximate a single nonlinear production surface — one linear function approximating actual operations and the other approximating full-capacity operations. In the actual process of equation estimation we found difficulties in estimating the full-capacity version of the production function, because N_L, K, and t are obviously strongly intercorrelated. They are all smooth trends. The problem in estimating the ordinary production function directly is that direct estimates of capital utilization cannot be obtained. We have direct estimates for labor in the form of employment and hours statistics. We approximated the solution of this problem by estimating

$$X = \alpha_0 + \alpha_1[h(N_w - N_g) + N_e] + \alpha_2(X/X_c)K + \alpha_3 t + u.$$

We were able to do this because we had independent estimates of X/X_c.

These independent estimates have come to be known as the Wharton School index of capacity utilization. The index is constructed in the following way: Each of thirty major components of the Federal Reserve index of industrial production is plotted on time charts. Seasonally adjusted monthly series, averaged to quarters, are plotted. Trend lines through peaks are established. These are linear segments connecting pairs of successive peaks. Peaks are established by inspection, with minor or temporary peaks eliminated. Some simple rules are established for recognizing peaks. From the last peak in a series, the trend lines are continued linearly with the same slope as the last completed segment. When actual production is rising and goes above the extrapolated trend, we increase the slope of the extrapolated line until a definite peak is established. When the trend lines are revised, we revise capacity calculations back to the last previous peak. The ratios of actual production to trends drawn through peaks give us figures on the percentage of capacity utilized by industry. The industry figures are averaged with weights into a national figure. The weights are those used to combine the Federal Reserve output series in its national index of production.

It would require an extensive argument and documented research study to give full justification to this method of estimating capacity utilization rates. In this paper, we merely want to describe our procedures and definitions of variables in the model. Many criticisms could obviously be raised about our method of measuring capacity. In our use of this measure we have implicitly assumed that industrial capacity, as we measure it from the FRB index components, is indicative (in an index sense) of capacity to produce private national product.

Using our estimates of the production function in (10), we find that the same coefficients inserted into (11) produce calculated values of X_c that are also close to those independently derived by our method of trends through peaks.

The relation between (10) and (11) may be further clarified by multiplying the production function, on both sides, by X_c/X. We then transform

$$X = \alpha_0 + \alpha_1[h(N_w - N_g) + N_e] + \alpha_2(X/X_c)K + \alpha_3 t + u$$

into

$$X_c = \alpha_0(X_c/X) + \alpha_1(X_c/X)[h(N_w - N_g) + N_e] + \alpha_2 K \\ + \alpha_3(X_c/X)t + (X_c/X)u.$$

The employment variable, in brackets, is marked up by the factor X_c/X. This should bring it close to N_L or $0.97(N_L - N_g)$. The coefficients of α_0, α_3, and u make this form differ slightly from the full-capacity version

$$X_c = \alpha_0 + \alpha_1 N_L + \alpha_2 K + \alpha_3 t + \nu$$

with which we started this discussion.

Wages, hours, and labor force

Associated with the technical conditions of production are the demand for labor and hours of work. Labor demand is converted into wage payments through valuation of employment by the wage rate.

The private wage bill, deflated by the general price index, is made a linear function of current and lagged output, with an upward time trend. This is a straightforward generalization of the constancy of labor's share. To avoid problems of collinearity between X and X_{-1}, we make their coefficients equal before estimating the equation.

The wage rate (quarterly earnings at an annual rate) is made to depend on the state for the labor market, the general price level, and a trend. This is a familiar interpretation of the "law of supply and demand" used in the annual models that preceded the present work. Wage changes (over a four-quarter span) are made to depend on unemployment (averaged over the past four quarters), price changes (over a four-quarter span, averaged over the past four quarters), and a trend.

Unemployment is the residual difference between labor force and employment; therefore, we need an equation for labor force. We considered the standard hypothesis that makes labor supply depend upon the real wage rate, but found no satisfactory relationship. Labor force follows a smooth trend that we represent by a purely chronological variable. There is, however, an elastic cyclical element in the labor supply. This is largely accounted for by housewives, students, and semi-retired people. They appear to swell the ranks of the labor force when jobs are plentiful and to withdraw when jobs are scarce. In our equation we represent this by a negative association between labor supply and unemployment.

Orders and backlogs

The inventory equation discussed above contained a variable representing unfilled orders. In the endogenous explanation of unfilled orders we use the rate of capacity operation and the flow of new orders. This requires an additional equation to explain new orders, which we do in terms of recent sales and price changes. Our orders series are limited to the manufacturing sector, and eventually we would want to extend this part of the model on a disaggregated basis to nonmanufacturing sectors.

Foreign trade

In a formal sense, both imports and exports are endogenous in this model. The explanation of exports is carried no further than to relate it directly to world production. Relative prices, as we have been able to measure such a magnitude, have not been found to be of significance in this equation. Overseas reserves, trade liberalization, and other variables may eventually prove to be important in a more detailed study of exports. In the applications we have made with the model, exports have been set at predetermined levels, and the export equation used here has been purely formal.

Import demand, however, has been more closely geared to the domestic economy. We divide imports into two classes, imports of unfinished and imports of finished goods. The former are determined directly from statistics of crude food and material imports. Imports recorded in the GNP accounts less these crude food and material imports are called "finished" imports. They are a residual, consisting of goods and services. We treat them like consumer goods. Equation 20, therefore, is simply an import analog of the consumption equations.

Money and interest

Demand for cash balances, which appears as a variable in the consumption equations, is made to depend on the long-run interest rate as a standard formulation of the doctrine of liquidity preference. One version of that theory is to assume that velocity, instead of being a constant, is a function of the interest rate. We have made the reciprocal of velocity our dependent variable. We have extended the dependence of cash holdings to price movements as well as the level of the interest rate.

In most versions of the modern theory of employment, the monetary authorities are assumed to control the stock of cash directly. Our assumption here is that they influence or control bank reserves and the discount rate. These influence the short-term rate, which then has a bearing on the long-term rate. These lines of reasoning are brought out in Eqs. 22 and 23. The long-term rate is assumed to be a Koyck-type distributed lag function of past short-term rates. After transformation, this becomes a linear relation with the current short rate and the lagged long rate as explanatory variables.

Prices

In various individual equations of the system, specific price levels occur. For example in Eqs. 1, 2, and 3, there are three separate consumer prices. We follow a general rule on all the specific price variables. Each specific price is related to the general price or wage level and possibly to some particular factor affecting that price.

Our system is interrelated; nevertheless, we can pick out certain main lines of causation. For a given output level, including a rate of capital formation as a component, the production function (10) shows labor requirements. Equation 13 is responsible for wage rate determination, and Eq. 12 can be transformed into a mark-up of price over unit labor costs. Thus, both the general price level and the wage rate are determined in the system. In Eqs. 24 through 29, specific prices are related to one of these two general variables. The backlog variables used in (24) and (25) are subclasses of total unfilled orders. While the total is explained within the system, the components are not. The coefficient of C_s/C, the fraction of total consumption accounted for by services, is statistically significant but negative. This does not appear to be a reasonable result.

Identities

The remaining equations in the systems are identities. Components of national product, valued in current prices, add to the total. This is expressed as private GNP (pX) plus government wages and salaries (W_g) In the next identity, the components of net national income $(W + P + S_c)$ are equated with GNP $(pX + W_g)$ less depreciation (D_a) and a reconciling item (T_i), which consists of indirect taxes less subsidies, the statistical discrepancy, and other small items. In this relation, depreciation is valued at accounting prices. We do not give an explicit relation between accounting price and replacement cost depreciation in the model, but we do use some simple proportions between these two for short-period applications.

Equation 32 expresses the wage bill as the product of employment, hours, and the wage rate. The final two equations are self-evident.

Applications — 1961 forecasts

In the first trial calculations using this model, we extrapolated beyond the terminal sample date, IV-1958, for predictions of the first three quarters of 1961. These calculations were started in March 1961, and were completed in April. Results for the first quarter were not known but could be guessed in broad outline.

To keep the algebra of solution simple we fixed values over the forecast period for some variables in order to make the system linear. This required the assignment of prices. We were not generally satisfied with Eqs. 24 through 29, in any case, and thought that prices could be predicted *a priori* for the three quarters of 1961 as well as they could be predicted by these equations. We also set the general price level at predetermined values. Interest rates and exports were similarly fixed at predetermined levels.

In order to solve the remaining equations linearly, we needed to fix values P/W in (1)–(3) and (20). This required the suppression of Eq. 13. Capacity output was estimated from (11), using last period's labor force and capital stock with the constant item adjusted so as to make the computed value agree with the first quarter's observation, I-1961; and the denominator of X/X_c could thus be computed in advance of the other variables for each forecast solution. This, too, was done to preserve linearity. We added three equations, determined from recent observations, on tax-transfer variables.

$$T = -45.16 + 0.198Y$$
$$T_c = -4.59 + 0.599P_c$$
$$T_i = -39.86 + 0.213pX$$

Using the values of predetermined variables in Table 1, we solved the system for endogenous variables in I-1961. First, however, we made estimates of variables in this model from a starting point in the fourth quarter of 1960.

We reduced the system algebraically to two equations in I_i and X. One was directly obtained from the inventory equation (6) with predetermined values substituted for the other variables. The other was obtained by substitution and algebraic reduction of the other variables in (30). This gave a residual equation in I_i and X. We adjusted the constant terms of each equation so that they gave us the correct values, simultaneously, for I_i and X corresponding to our best estimates of these in the observation period, IV-1960. Keeping these adjustments in the constant terms of the two equations in I_i and X, we solved the system sequentially in I-, II-, III-1961. We used computed values from one quarter as lagged inputs for successive quarters. *We did not adjust individual equations, apart from the two relations between I_i and X, which kept a constant adjustment throughout the time sequence of solutions.* Some component series of national product may therefore be biased, but the quarter-to-quarter variation should not be seriously distorted. *Some of our computed components do not add to national totals.* Selected results are given in Table 2.[7] Actual values are in Table 3.

On the surface, this appears to have been a good forecast. The prediction of an upturn in the economy after the low point in the first quarter of 1961 was not surprising. Opinion was much divided, however, on the magnitude of the recovery. There is no doubt that many persons were surprised (in government and business) by the magnitude of our increments from first to second quarter and from second to third quarter. This is not to say that we were alone in predicting a substantial improvement in real output, but the model came out in the correct neighborhood when there were great doubts in the minds of many persons that the recovery would be this strong. It is also important to note that the prediction was for a surprisingly

---

[7]This table was circulated privately to more than 100 technicians in April 1961. It was a genuine forecast.

Table 1. Predetermined variables used in 1961 forecasts.

Variables	Value Assumed			Actual Value*		
	I	II	III	I	II	III
P/W	0.36	0.36	0.36	0.36	0.35	0.35
$\frac{1}{8}\Sigma(C_d)_{-i}$	41.0	computed		41.3		
C_d^e	110.0	110.0	110.0	117.0	110.0	113.0
$\frac{1}{8}\Sigma(C_n)_{-i}$	140.6	computed		140.3		
$(L/p_n)_{-1}$	227.7	228.5	229.0	227.7	231.1	238.9
$\frac{1}{8}\Sigma(C_s)_{-i}$	111.5	computed		112.1		
$(L/p_s)_{-1}$	210.8	211.5	212.0	212.4	214.8	219.9
N	182.5	183.3	184.1	182.5	183.2	(183.95)p
I_p^e	28.5	28.0	28.0	28.9	27.9	(28.6)p
i_L	4.64	4.60	4.50	4.59	4.59	4.72
F	296.0	450.0	461.0	291.0	430.0	(430.0)p
$(I_h^s)_{-1}$	1,003.0	1,050.0	1,100.0	1,003.0	1,016.0	1,100.0
X_{-1}	394.0	computed		395.0		
t	61.0	62.0	63.0	61.0	62.0	63.0
q_p	1.22	1.22	1.22	1.23	1.23	(1.23)p
$\frac{1}{8}\Sigma\frac{1}{q_p}$ $\times(P_c - T_c - S_c)$	11.2	computed		11.3		
P_{-1}	102.9	computed		101.7		
W_g	51.0	52.0	53.0	50.4	51.3	52.1
$p^\dagger$	1.153	1.153	1.153	1.156	1.158	1.164
$\Sigma(I_i)_{-j}$	239.3	computed		246.4		
$(X - I_i)_{-1}$	396.4	computed		396.2		
$(p_i/p)_{-1}$	0.841	0.840	0.840	0.841	0.835	0.830
$\frac{1}{8}\Sigma(F_{if})_{-i}$	19.72	computed		19.0		
G	103.0	104.0	105.0	105.0	107.3	108.5
p_e	1.085	1.085	1.085	1.105	1.204	(111.0)p
F_e	25.0	25.0	25.0	25.0	21.9	(24.0)p
D_a	44.5	45.0	45.5	44.2	45.0	45.5
p_d	1.045	1.045	1.045	1.048	1.055	1.055
p_n	1.085	1.085	1.085	1.085	1.081	1.081
p_s	1.175	1.180	1.185	1.167	1.174	1.174
q_h	1.170	1.170	1.170	1.170	1.170	(1.175)p
p_i	0.97	0.97	0.97	0.97	0.96	(0.96)p
N_e	9,200.0	9,200.0	9,200.0	9,410.0	9,100.0	8,820.0
N_g	8,600.0	8,700.0	8,800.0	8,670.0	8,700.0	8,450.0
$\Sigma(I_p)_{-i}$	2,224.86	computed		2,224.86		
$\Sigma(I_h)_{-i}$	1,006.27	computed		1,006.27		
U_{-1}	44.6	computed		44.3		

p = preliminary.

* Available at later date — after the forecast.

† The value for IV-1960 was estimated to be 1.152.

Table 2. Selected forecast values, 1960–61 (billions of 1954 dollars unless otherwise stated).

Variable	Starting Value 1960 (IV)	Estimate 1961 (I)	Forecast 1961 (II)	Forecast 1961 (III)
C_d — durable consumption	43.5	41.4	43.4	47.9
C_n — nondurable consumption	144.7	143.9	145.4	148.2
C_s — services consumption	115.0	115.5	116.9	118.7
I_p — plant and equipment	36.4	35.4	35.4	36.3
I_h — residential construction	18.2	17.7	18.2	19.9
I_i — inventory investment	−2.4	−4.4	−2.7	0.7
X — private GNP	394.0	388.4	396.2	412.1
GNP (current prices)	503.8	498.8	508.8	528.2
X/X_c (capacity rate)	0.89	0.87	0.88	0.90

Table 3. Actual values of selected, forecast variables, 1960–61 (billions of 1954 dollars).

Variable	1960 (IV)	1961 (I)	1961 (II)	1961 (III)
C_d — durable consumption	41.6	37.6	39.8	40.3
C_n — nondurable consumption	141.3	141.6	142.6	145.2
C_s — services consumption	116.6	117.8	119.2	121.4
I_p — plant and equipment	38.5	36.3	36.9	36.6
I_h — residential construction	17.5	16.5	17.6	19.9
I_i — inventory investment	−1.1	−3.2	2.9	3.9
X — private GNP	395.1	389.6	401.4	407.0
GNP (current prices)	504.4	500.8	516.1	525.8
X/X_c (capacity rate)	0.88	0.86	0.90	0.92

large increase in output associated with quite modest increments in our estimate of capacity utilization.

While our estimate of GNP for the third quarter is close to the outcome, the model underestimated the growth from the first to the second quarter and overestimated it from the second to the third. We had too little inventory investment and too much durable consumption. Our other errors were less remarkable.

These are only surface observations. A more detailed appraisal requires two considerations: (1) data revision and (2) accuracy of assumptions. We made our forecast for the second and third quarters on the basis of preliminary estimates of the fourth quarter of 1960 and informed guesses about the first quarter of 1961, which had just passed. Data were not fully collected for the first quarter of 1961, and many of the fourth quarter estimates for 1960 were highly tentative. Our base period (IV-1960) estimates of output were too high by approximately $1 billion, and our inventory estimates were too low by the same magnitude. These two variables were forced by our adjustment process to give the "correct" values as we estimated them at the time for the base period. *We did not adjust the other component equations of the model;* therefore, in the "back" solution, which gives the distribution of values of individual variables, all the identities do not necessarily hold; and we may start off from biased values in the base period. This bias is not serious, though, since we can see its magnitude in IV-1960. C_d is, for example, overestimated by about \$2.0 billion in the base period. This bias value in C_d is not adequate to account for the large value of durable consumption in the third quarter. We definitely overestimated the rise in C_d. Apart from the underestimate of inventory change, no other GNP component is seriously enough distorted in the forecast to merit special consideration. Our index of capacity utilization was revised in the summer of 1961.[8] Although it is not apparent in the comparison of the values for IV-1960, the new index tends to run about one or two points above the old one that was used in the forecast.

One of the drawbacks of the model is that it contains so many predetermined variables that a large amount of nonmodel forecasting is necessary before the model can be used in forecasting. A month's work at data processing and extrapolation of exogenous variables is required in preparation for a forecast. The large number of predetermined variables in Table 1 indicates the magnitude of initial input. There are many variables, covering many aspects of the economy here. It is easy to be right on some values, too high on some, and too low on others. We underestimated the growth in money supply. Government spending was set too low in the initial period and grew slightly less than was actually the case. The interest rate should have risen slightly instead of declining by a small amount. Housing starts were actually fixed in advance. Price increases were too low. Population growth was closely estimated, and so on.

Major sources of error in the forecast are not to be sought in the assumptions made for predetermined variables or in data revisions. The model is only a statistical estimate of reality and is subject to error. Imperfect knowledge of the true relationships in the economy and some large disturbances probably account for the great part of the forecast error. Strikes and hurricane damage in the third quarter probably had substantial effects on changes in variables between the second and third quarters.

Applications — The Recessions of 1953–54 and 1957–58

Models can be tested by *ex post* as well as by *ex ante* forecasts. In the previous section, we described *ex ante* forecasting. In this section we shall summarize the results of a simulation study prepared for the Joint Economic Committee of the

---

[8]The index was computed from the FRB indexes on a 1957 base in the revision. The older indexes on a base of 1947–49 had been previously used.

Congress of the United States.[9] This is an example of *ex post* forecasting and has the advantage of controlling error in the assumptions for predetermined variables. Since it is an application after the event, good estimates of the predetermined variables are available.

Ex post extrapolations of a model outside the sample data to which the model is fitted provide better tests than do *ex post* calculations using internal sample data. The present example uses internal data and is, therefore, not as stringent a test as we hope, eventually, to apply. At the moment this example is cited as an interesting application.

The problem posed in this application was how to determine, from the model, whether and how much specific dampening of inventory fluctuation in past recessions would have contributed to total output stabilization. This is a hypothetical problem, exemplifying how models can be used in policy formulation, and is not a test of the model. However, the first step in attacking the inventory stabilization issue was to let the model run through the course of each of the two recessions considered to see whether it duplicated actual output fluctuations. Predetermined variables were inserted into the equations for the first quarter of 1953 (and the first quarter of 1957). The system was then successively solved as a dynamic model through the fourth quarter of 1954 (and the fourth quarter of 1958). Exogenous variables were assigned their actual values for each quarter's solution, but lagged endogenous variables were generated within the model after starting from given initial conditions. As in the case of the 1961 forecasts, the two equations were adjusted in I_i and X, so that correct values were obtained for the starting quarter of each simulation. New tax equations were determined for the simulation periods, and the changes in revenue laws during 1954 required the use of different tax equations for the quarters of 1953 and of 1954. The results are given in Table 4.

Table 4. Actual and simulated values of X, 1953–54 and 1957–58 (billions of 1954 dollars).

Quarter	1953–54		1957–58	
	Actual	Computed	Actual	Computed
I	334.72	334.72	371.90	371.90
II	338.87	337.64	373.03	369.82
III	335.69	332.65	373.24	367.90
IV	329.64	331.29	366.76	368.94
I	326.43	328.18	353.72	365.98
II	325.35	341.27	355.02	378.10
III	327.40	343.62	360.25	388.62
IV	335.33	349.23	370.89	397.91

---

[9]Lawrence R. Klein and Joel Popkin, "An econometric analysis of the post-war relationship between inventory fluctuations and changes in aggregate economic activity," *Inventory Fluctuations and Economic Stabilization*, 87th Cong., 1st sess. (December, 1961), III, pp. 69–89.

Computed output turns up one quarter earlier than output in 1954, and the recovery is stronger. In 1958, the timing is coincident, but the downswing started earlier and was interrupted by a temporary advance in the fourth quarter of 1957. The sharpness of the 1957–58 recession is not duplicated in the computed data. The fall is not as great as the actual output decline, and the revival is stronger. The revival is also stronger in the computed than in the actual output for 1954.

The time paths of other variables can be seen in the tables and charts of the JEC study paper referred to earlier. The policy application of the model made in the study paper can be summarized by noting that if inventory fluctuations are autonomously reduced in amplitude, fluctuations in output, employment, and other variables are also reduced. The model results show that if inventory fluctuation (deviations above and below zero inventory investment) can be reduced by a factor of one-quarter, output fluctuations are moderately reduced. At the cycle troughs, we estimated multiplier values of four to five, i.e., the trough of the production cycle is raised by four or five dollars (1954 prices) for every dollar reduction in the absolute value of inventory investment at the trough. If inventory stabilization is much greater, say, a dampening of fluctuations by a factor of three-quarters, the ordinary business cycle in computed output vanishes.

Self-criticism

This is only another one in a series of American models. There will be more to come. The ancestors of this model have been used to make a number of helpful forecasts, provide a setting for computational experiments, and provide tailor-made subjects for critical doctoral dissertations. They have all had a measure of intellectual attack. In anticipation of some points of attack on the present system, the system might be appraised here and now. This will set the stage for work on the models to come.

By the time data are collected, parameters are estimated, and models are tested for performance, ideas about the detailed structure of the economy can change drastically. At the end of this time-consuming process (about three years in the present case) we usually decide that we would have built the system differently if we were starting the project freshly. The price and interest rate equations are the poorest of the lot in the model, and these need revision.[10] It would be possible to use the present price and interest rate equations in a more essential way in forecasting from the present model, but a good and simple computing routine for coping with the nonlinearities caused by these is not fully prepared.

As in past models, we have looked for a balanced estimate of equations as a whole and systems as a whole. Goodness of fit, randomness of residuals, signs of coefficients, approximate magnitude of coefficients, and standard errors have all been used together in deciding whether to accept or reject estimated equations. In

---

[10]In a joint project supported by the work of many scholars, and sponsored by the Social Science Research Council, a new model is being built which appears to be much stronger on the side of price estimation. The price formation equations are quite different.

these decisions many candidates are accepted for which individual coefficients do not meet some standard test — say a t-test for significance at the 5 percent level. Some of our standard errors are large. If the model were brought up to date and re-estimated with twelve more observations, some of these insignificant results might be changed.

In specific equations there are definite possibilities for improvements. Population might be directly introduced in the consumption equations by expressing all variables in per capita terms. The empirical relation between P_c and P can be improved by extracting dividend and interest income from P, estimating that component separately by some simple autoregressive scheme, and relating only entrepreneurial elements of P to P_c. This relation can be refined even more if farm entrepreneurial income is taken out of P as well.

Inventories should be subdivided by farm and non-farm category. In addition the non-farm category should be disaggregated by stage of process and type of holder (seller versus manufacturer). These disaggregations all call for a substantially larger model. Many of these things are already being done in the Social Science Research Council model referred to in footnote 10. In the equation for residential construction, housing starts are an important variable. Starts are not really independent in their relation and certainly not for as many time periods ahead as we have tried to use them in applications. In fact, construction expenditure series are prepared by the phasing-in of starts data, using an average construction lag. We should have an equation explaining starts, another showing how construction data are built from starts data, and another on unit structure value.

Similarly, investment intentions and consumer buying plans are not really independent data in our system, although we use them in that way. We need separate equations explaining these expectations, in addition to equations showing how expectations are transformed into realizations.

The government sector is purely exogenous except for the simple tax-transfer equations used in applications of the model. There is much useful work that can be done in distinguishing between induced government expenditures like those for highways and education and purely autonomous categories like defense. Some equations can be developed for the induced parts, and some realization functions associating expenditures with budget appropriations can be constructed. Many more things can be done on the side of government receipts. Tax equations using income distribution and internal revenue reports can be greatly improved. Major transfer items could be usefully separated from taxes and estimated in new equations. All these improvements require substantial research work, but they are all feasible and can easily be added to the basic framework presented here.

9

THE PRESENT DEBATE ABOUT MACROECONOMICS AND ECONOMETRIC MODEL SPECIFICATION[†][*]

Conventional Views Under Attack

It is almost 50 years since the introduction of the Keynesian models and modes of thinking about macroeconomics; therefore, what was considered to be revolutionary in the 1930s or 1940s is now taken to be a conventional view. The fierce debate in professional economic circles about macroeconomics — theory and policy — turns up a great deal of criticism of the conventional view, but it often seems as though the attack is upon the practices of econometric model building as much as upon macroeconomic thought as a whole. This may not be surprising since econometric model building took its inspiration from the Keynesian system, and the early attempts can be considered to be exercises in bringing empirical content to the Keynesian models, both estimating and testing them.

The older debates of Keynes vs. the classics had a great influence on the speci-fication of econometric models, and it may be useful to review that development at this time. The mathematical formulations of the Keynesian system by J. R. Hicks and O. Lange were elegant and attractive. After S. Kuznets developed a database that contained statistical series on the main concepts, it was only natural that there would be attempts to build complete models of the system, or to estimate relation-ships for the fundamental components, such as consumption (or savings) function, investment function, and liquidity preference function.

It is difficult to capture the movement of the economy in small systems built on the interrelationships of this limited group of equations. A prototype model, known as Klein Model I, that I put together in 1946, served as a useful pedagogical or indicative research tool in many econometric studies, but that small system of 3 stochastic equations plus 3 identities would not do as a working model to interpret actual movements of the economy. Indeed, it would not be adequate for the implementation of Keynesian type economic policy in the form of aggregative demand management.

As models grew in order to cope with the problems of the day, they evolved into what are now the *mainstream* econometric systems, often consisting of more than 1,000 simultaneous equations. From a technical point of view, the advent of

---

[†]From *Chung-Hua Series of Lectures by Invited Distinguished Economists, No. 5* (The Institute of Economics, Taiwan, 1982), pp. 3–20.
[*]Delivered in Taipei, Republic of China, July 24, 1982.

the electronic computer, harnessed to the needs of econometrics, made possible the evolution from the tiny macro model of the Keynesian system — into the large mainstream models that are presently in use all over the world.

The evolution went in the direction of the neoclassical synthesis of Keynesian economics. Production functions, first-order conditions for optimization, clearing of markets, equations of portfolio choice, factor supply relationships were all introduced in the neoclassical spirit, reflecting the fact that Keynes was trained by Marshall, Pigou and other neoclassical economists. He was always a neoclassical economist, and apart from dropping an assumption of automatic tendencies towards full employment equilibrium, his system of thought reflected this kind of professional upbringing.

From the viewpoint of economic theory, the skeleton systems of Hicks and Lange were extended in a neoclassical direction, and these systems became larger because they contained many sectors, each receiving neoclassical treatment. But the systems, in the interests of realism, were also extended in some other directions. They were "opened up" for trade, again in terms of neoclassical reasoning. Public sectors were added for government economic activity, regulation, taxation, subsidization, transfer mechanisms. Institutional detail was added, as were stochastic and dynamic components.

Flippant equating of present mainstream models with purely Keynesian systems is a loose use of language that conveys an entirely incorrect impression about the content of the systems. They should, more properly, be called neoclassical Keynesian syntheses. To call them "eclectic" is not very informative, but it is more revealing to note that they combine many of the neoclassical ideas of Keynes' teachers with Keynes' views, narrowly conceived, from the *General Theory*.

The sources of criticism

The mainstream econometric model has a well-known and distinctive genealogy. It is being criticized, and I shall not dwell on the motivation for that criticism. That is a subject that I have dealt with in some other lectures this year. I shall focus on the impact of the criticism on the specification of mainstream econometric models.

Monetarism

The doctrinaire versions of monetarism have inspired research on econometric model building in the direction of constructing monetarist models. At the simplest and crudest levels, the fundamental equation of exchange:

$$Mv = PX$$

is made a key part of the model specification; so much so that control over M by the monetary authorities, combined with stable parameter v, implies control over the nominal value of output PX. This stands at the apex of the monetarist model, and other things follow from it. In fact, Milton Friedman has often observed that the distinction between monetarism and Keynesianism is that the former determines PX directly and deduces the components of total spending from it. It is a top-down approach. By way of contrast, he notes that the latter determines PX as the sum of its components, which are first determined in the Keynesian model. It proceeds from:

$$PX = C + I + G + E - M .$$
$$C = \text{private consumer spending}$$
$$I = \text{private capital formation}$$
$$G = \text{public spending}$$
$$E = \text{exports}$$
$$M = \text{imports} .$$

It is a bottom-up approach.

What is wrong with the simplistic quantity equation?

1. In the first place, M is an endogenous variable and is extremely difficult for the authorities to control. The monetarists have done a great disservice by emphasizing control over M and arguing that it can be effectively targeted. It is definitely not an exogenous variable.
2. The velocity coefficient v is not a parameter; it is a variable. It is best expressed as the ratio of two endogenous variables PX/M.

Econometrics is often inconclusive about tests of economic hypotheses. When it comes to testing the existence of a stable relationship, even in stochastic form, with additive error e:

$$MV = PX + e, \qquad V = \text{const}$$

the data will reject this specification. It will reject it as decisively as it rejects the crude acceleration principle either in stock or in flow form:

$$K = \alpha X + u$$
$$I = \alpha \Delta X + e$$
$$K = \text{capital stock}$$
$$u, e = \text{random errors} .$$

The flexible accelerator or the generalized investment function are more acceptable from an econometric point of view, but they involve time lags (dynamic specifications) and the introduction of other variables (capital rental, capacity ceilings, other factor costs, liquidity).

In a similar vein, the quantity equation for money needs to be generalized. Friedman generalized it, much along the lines of the flexible accelerator, by introducing lags in prices and in output. He specified[1]:

$$MV_t = \left(\sum_{i=0}^{17} \lambda^i P_{t-i}\right)^{\alpha} \left(\sum_{i=0}^{17} \lambda^i X_{t-i}\right)^{\beta} e_t.$$

But even this extension is not acceptable as a stable econometric relationship. Further generalizations to determine the demand for money in relationships that have both dynamics and other variables (interest rates, inflation rates, wealth) are proving to be quite elusive in the United States. The instability of the money demand function has been quite marked recently and is often cited as a primary reason why control over M has been so poor. It has led the President of the Federal Reserve Bank of Boston to be very pessimistic about the possibility of making monetarism operational.[2]

The monetarist position may be stated in the extreme that money alone matters. Through their insistence on this point even through the turbulent period in the

---

[1] In Milton Friedman's article "The demand for money: Some theoretical and empirical results," *JPE* (August, 1959), he writes:

$$\text{equation (1)} \qquad \frac{M}{NP_p} = \gamma \left(\frac{Y_p}{NP_p}\right)^{\delta}.$$

This equation is estimated by him (equation (9)) to have coefficients:

$$\gamma = 0.00323$$
$$\delta = 1.810$$

This is the same as my equation (on this page) except that I do not have per capita money balances M/N and per capita income Y_p/N.

His value of δ corresponds to my β. His coefficient (exponent) for P_p is 1.0, while mine is α. His estimate of γ stands for $1/v$ in my notation.

His footnote 13, after equations (9) and (10) in his article, explains how Y_p and P_p are estimated. You can see that he applied equation (8) in his article to both, but equation (8) is a continuous function with exponential weight, which is approximated by:

$$\sum \lambda^i X_{t-i},$$

as he did it in *A Theory of the Consumption Function*. Actually, he did not deflate nominal income by price and then perform the moving average. He applied the moving average formula to nominal income and to price separately. He then divided long run nominal income by long run price to get long run real income. I can re-state my equation to come closer to what he actually did, but the "spirit" of my formulation is correct.

On pp. 143–147 of the *Theory of the Consumption Function*, he states how he estimates Y_P. In the table at the end of these pages he writes down the annual weights for a 17-year discrete approximation to integral. Those weights follow approximately a geometric distribution with ratio 3:2 between successive weights.

[2] Frank Morris, "Do monetary aggregates have a future as targets for federal reserve policy?" Paper presented to the Conference on *Supply Side Economics in the 1980s,* Federal Reserve Bank Atlanta, March 17, 1982. See also A. M. Solomon (President of the Federal Reserve Bank of New York) "Financial innovation and monetary policy," speech before the American Economic Association and American Finance Association, December 28, 1981, Washington, D.C.

United States when President Nixon intervened with his new Economic Policy, and when the whole world was shocked by the oil embargo of 1973 followed by OPEC pricing of oil, they convinced econometricians that money does matter, even though their strict models provided little guidance for the economies of the world through those difficult times.

The end result has been that the mainstream econometric model has a great deal more monetary and financial detail. At the beginning, models introduced aggregative money demand functions; some made velocity a function of endogenous variables instead of treating it as a parameter. At the outset, the monetarist view of the authorities having control over money supply was introduced, but this idea soon gave way to detailed explanation of money supply generated from reserve identities and the institutional operating rules of a country's banking system.

Demand and supply of money were used in order to determine a representative short-term interest rate as a market balancing factor. The term structure of rates has then been used to determine the spectrum of rates, covering both intermediate and long-term rates. This is the mechanism of the financial system in the Wharton Model, heavily influenced by the research of Ando and Modigliani for the Federal Reserve Model.

But recently, the Wharton Model team has introduced a new concept, namely, a complete flow-of-funds model, to depict in much more detail the workings of the financial sector. In the flow of funds model, financial assets and liabilities in five different sectors were modeled separately:

> households
>
> non-financial businesses
>
> commercial banks
>
> thrift institutions
>
> life insurance and other financial sectors.

The central banking sector and treasury are also modeled, and work is in progress to round out the picture for the international sector (balance of payments).

Flows of different financial instruments into and out of these sectors are estimated and have important impacts on behavioral relationships in the real sector.

An ultimate goal, from my point of view, is to estimate the yields (interest rates) on the different financial instruments that flow among these sectors. Such estimates would produce the spectrum of rates through the clearing of financial markets, in place of the term structure relationships that are used. It is not yet known whether this approach would provide more accurate estimates of interest rates, but it will undoubtedly provide much information and understanding about the working of financial markets.

It should be clear, therefore, that monetary-financial analysis plays an important role in mainstream econometric models, and we model builders do have a debt to monetarists for calling our attention to the importance of such basic research.

Rational expectations

The concept of expectations runs through many chapters of Keynes' *General Theory*.[3]

> "Thus the behavior of each individual firm in deciding its daily output will be determined by its *short-term expectations* — expectations as to the cost of output in various possible scales and expectations as to the sale-proceeds of this output..."

Keynes also devotes an entire chapter to long-term expectations in connection with the inducement to invest. The whole discussion of Keynesian economics, which laid the foundation for the first macroeconometric models, focused strongly on expectations. It is almost as though the people who "wrote the book" on expectations in macroeconomics are being told by a new generation of the importance of expectations in economic analysis, particularly macroeconomic theory and policy.

At a conference sponsored by the Federal Reserve Bank of Boston in 1978, it was left to Benjamin Friedman to point out to the proponents of rational expectations that my own early models developed equation specifications directly in terms of *expectations* of key market variables.[4]

Expectations are important, and they have always been carefully considered in econometric model design. The question is how to express these subjective magnitudes in an objective way. In the mainstream econometric models, two approaches have been used. The first and most common method is to assume:

$$\text{expected } y_t = \sum_{i=0}^{n} W_i y_{t-i}$$

namely, that the expected value of an economic variable is a distributed lag in the present level and *history* of that variable. Thus, one is assumed to look at the current standing of an expected magnitude, its rate of change, its acceleration, etc., using as high an order difference as seems necessary or possible, to get at the historical effect.

As a practical matter, this formulation is probably not bad. It is highly realistic. It has the effect of introducing *dynamics* into the model specification.

A second approach is to use people's own expressions of their expectations as determined in sample surveys. The trouble with expectations is that they are not generally observed in the same way that transactions quantities or prices are in economics, and we have a weak base for validating theories of expectations. But it seems straightforward to me to go right to the source of expectations, to the very

---

[3] J. M. Keynes, *The General Theory of Employment, Interest, and Money* (Harcourt Brace, New York, 1936), p. 47.

[4] B. Friedman, "Discussion" on Robert E. Lucas and Thomas J. Sargent's "After Keynesian macroeconomics," in *After the Phillips Curve: Persistence of High Inflation and High Unemployment*, Conference Series No. 19 (Federal Reserve Bank of Boston, 1978). See also L. R. Klein, *Economic Fluctuations in the United States, 1921–1941* (Wiley, N.Y, 1950).

people who hold the expectations as a basis for economic decision making, and to find out directly what the expectations are.

At first, expectations were used, as reported, for advance indication of subjective variables over short horizons, say 3 to 6 months ahead. Now, the goals are more ambitious, and the model building is more intricate. Expectations are treated as endogenous variables and generated by behavioral equations. These equations are testable, for they are based on observed data, some of which are objective answers to survey questions.

Not having an existing economic theory to account for expectations, the proponents of rational expectations invented a theory that provides them with answers that they found attractive. Economic theory is basically static. From optimizing theory of the household or of the firm, static equation specifications are derived. They are then made dynamic by assuming that expected values are given by lag distributions or some other dynamic process.

The theory of rational expectations assumes that all economic agents have the same comprehensive fund of information about the economy, and that this fund is processed efficiently so as to come up with objective (estimated) magnitudes for the expectational variables. In the limiting case, the theory of rational expectations assumes that people, on average, know (explicitly or implicitly) the working system of the economy, and that they generate expected values from estimates of the true structure of the economy. Thus, if an econometric model renders a valid (approximate) estimate of the performance of the economy, then typical citizens generate the same values, on average, of the endogenous magnitudes of the model, including the expectations variables.

Another operational method of introducing rational expectations into model specification is to assume:

$$\text{expected } y_{t+1} = y_{t+1};$$

therefore *actual* future values are used in place of *expected* values for a future value of a variable. Instead of assuming that history gives a basis for projection of an expected magnitude, a future value is used. This is possible in the sample period when all values are available, both historical and future, for each sample data point.

In an extreme form of rational expectations theory, it is argued that economic policy, apart from the imposition of fixed rules, is futile because people, acting with the same model and information set as the public authorities, will outguess, in advance, the effects of policy action by the authorities and will already have taken their policies into account in reaching their behavioral decisions. The authorities, then, simply validate the expectations that people are assumed to be using as a basis for their own economic decisions.

How might rational expectations theory work out in practice? Let us consider a simple cobweb model of demand and supply, which has a time honored place in economic analysis. The cobweb theory can be interpreted, in non-stochastic form, as:

$$X_t^s = \alpha + \beta p_t^e$$
$$p_t = \gamma + \delta X_t^d$$
$$X_t^s = X_t^d = X_t .$$

This simple model asserts that supply depends on *expected* price and that price is determined by market demand, with the provision that markets are cleared, namely, that supply equals demand. This is thought to be a good model for a perishable seasonal crop. Basically, the cobweb model fits well in practice, with some inventory and scrap enhancements, to a wide variety of commodity models in primary sectors — agriculture, forestry, fishing, and mineral extraction.

The conventional specification, well suited to the thinking in mainstream model building, is to assume:

$$p_t^e = p_{t-1} ,$$

i.e., producers look at last season's price, their latest piece of information about prices, and produce accordingly. In an agricultural market, they would be assumed to commit acreage to a crop by planting on the basis of last season's price. This setup produces well-known dynamic equations:

$$X_t = \alpha + \beta p_{t-1}$$
$$p_t = \gamma + \delta X_t$$

leading to the reduced (and final autoregressive) form:

$$X_t = \alpha + \beta\gamma + \beta\delta X_{t-1}$$
$$p_t = \gamma + \delta\alpha + \delta\beta p_{t-1} .$$

The steady state solutions are:

$$X_t = \frac{\alpha + \beta\gamma}{1 - \beta\delta}$$
$$p_t = \frac{\gamma + \delta\alpha}{1 - \beta\delta} .$$

If the supply slope is positive and the demand slope negative, there is "sawtooth" oscillation (probably damped) about this steady state solution. In a stochastic environment, there are random shifts that tend to keep the oscillations alive. This is the reality.

An eminent economic theoretician has remarked that "this model is an affront to man's intelligence." Yet, it seems to agree well with market facts.

In a world of rational expectations, it would be assumed that the well-informed producer would form price expectations by knowing that price would be set at an amount that would clear the market:

$$p_t^e = \gamma + \delta X_t .$$

If he were to shun the world of the mainstream model builder, he would have:

$$X_t = \alpha + \beta(\gamma + \delta X_t), \text{ or}$$
$$X_t = \frac{\alpha + \beta\gamma}{1 - \beta\delta},$$

which is the steady-state value. The rational expectations model would move immediately to the steady state, but, in reality, the system takes time to get there and may not even reach it on account of random disturbances. If, in forming expectations, producers look at a weighted combination of last period's prices and the projected market clearing prices:

$$p_t^e = w_1(\gamma + \delta X_t) + w_2 p_{t-1},$$

then we will have the modified cobweb system:

$$X_t^s = \alpha + \beta\left[w_1(\gamma + \delta X_t) + w_2 p_{t-1}\right]$$
$$p_t = \gamma + \delta X_t^d$$
$$X_t^s = X_t^d = X_t.$$

This would lead to the same reduced form equations as in the cobweb case, but the coefficients would have different meanings:

$$X_t = \alpha + w_1\beta\gamma + w_1\beta\delta X_t + w_2\beta\gamma + w_2\beta\delta X_{t-1}$$
$$p_t = \gamma + \delta\frac{\alpha + w_1\beta\gamma}{1 - w_1\beta\delta} + \delta\frac{w_2\beta}{1 - w_1\beta\delta}p_{t-1}.$$

In this situation, we find that there is a lack of identification. From a statistical point of view, the conventional cobweb and the rational expectations version look alike to the statistician; so what is new?

If price expectations were to be dependent on government policy for things like price supports or subsidies, the mainstream model, which is very keen on the use of institutional information, would have exogenous policy variables, as would the rational expectations models, for they emphasize the use of a complete information set. We should, therefore, have the same lack of identification and not be able to distinguish between them.

The versions of the rational expectations hypothesis that argue that policy is impotent have another view of the link between exogenous policy instruments and the behavioral model. They assert that reaction coefficients in models are functions of the policy instruments. In other words, we would have the following:

$$\alpha(Z_t), \beta(Z_t), \gamma(Z_t), \delta(Z_t)$$

where Z is a policy instrument. It makes sense to generalize the mainstream econometric model toward new research on parameter variation. The reaction coefficients may depend on the phases of the business cycle, on stochastic processes, on technical progress; but why should they depend on policy instruments? They may or may not, but it is surely contrived to make them depend on Z_t in precisely such a way as to leave policy impotent. While it is commonplace to emphasize change and to argue that surely the reaction coefficients change, it is my belief, on the basis of consideration of scores upon scores of economic relationships, that continuity and stability of coefficients are more prevalent characteristics than change. Many basic parameters survived World War II, and they will surely survive the much milder impact of OPEC pricing and analogous recent events.

Economic relationships are all approximations to the underlying true system, and it is probably just as good an approximation to write:

$$X_t^s = \alpha + \beta p_{t-1} + \varepsilon Z_t$$
$$p_t = \gamma + \delta X_t^d + \eta Z_t$$
$$X_t^s = X_t^d = X_t$$

as it is to write, in an unspecified way:

$$X_t^s = \alpha(Z) + \beta(Z) p_{t-1}$$
$$p_t = \gamma(Z) + \delta(Z) X_t^d$$
$$X_t^s = X_t^d = X_t \,.$$

There is a big difference in policy analysis to argue that exogenous variables take on new values, than to argue that parameters have changed because public authorities change the values of Z_t.

When all is said and done, the arguments by the proponents of rational expectations have led us to consider, more or less carefully, the structure of lags in mainstream models and also to consider other elements in the information set besides own history of a given variable. It has also encouraged model builders to take a more serious look at expectation variables from sample surveys to integrate them more fully into mainstream models.

Supply side economics

The meaning of supply side in economics is often poorly understood. Keynesian economics is frequently referred to as being concerned solely with demand side of the economy. This can hardly be correct, since Keynes, at an early stage of the *General Theory*, introduced the concept of the aggregate supply function. Since Keynesian economic policy focuses on the concept of aggregate demand management, people sometimes overlook the supply side aspects of the Keynesian model; nevertheless, the Keynesian system, for all its recognition of the supply side, gives inadequate attention to supply.

The popular meaning of supply side economics, in the present day United States, is understood to be tax incentives having an expected effect on savings, investment, and productivity. In particular, if the marginal rate of taxation (income tax) is lowered, the proponents of SSE expect to find significant, favorable responses in savings, investment, and worker effort.

From the viewpoint of consumer behavior, the appropriate variables for savings and labor force participation equations should be:

$$r(1-t) - \frac{d\ln p}{dT} \qquad \text{real interest rate after tax}$$

$$\frac{w(1-t)}{p} \qquad \text{real wage rate after tax}.$$

The first variable consists of the interest rate (r), the marginal tax rate (t), and the price level (p). The first term in this expression defines nominal interest rate after tax, and the second subtracts the inflation rate to obtain the real, aftertax, interest rate. The second variable consists of the nominal wage rate (w), the marginal tax rate (t), and the price level (p). The numerator defines the nominal wage rate after tax, and the denominator converts the nominal wage rate to the real wage rate.

For business investment behavior, the corresponding variable to consider is:

$$\frac{PK(r+\delta)}{(1-tc)}(1 - itc - \delta_{pv}(tc))$$

PK = price deflator of capital goods
r = interest rate
δ = depreciation rate
tc = corporate tax rate
itc = investment tax credit rate
δ_{pv} = present value of depreciation.

This variable is known as the user cost or rental price of capital. For some time, this variable has been used as a key explanatory factor in investment decisions in econometric models. It, together with its reaction coefficient, shows the sensitivity of investment to the corporate tax rate, the special incentives given by the investment tax credit rate, and the guideline length of life for capital goods under the corporate tax code; this last mentioned variable being a part of the present value of depreciation (δ_{pv}). The formula is stated in terms of the American tax system.

At an earlier stage of macroeconometrics, it was argued that investment decisions were relatively insensitive to business taxes because business behavior should be the same whether it was maximizing 100 percent of profits or a fraction (after tax) of profits. The only avenue for corporate tax rates was in using profits (after tax) as a liquidity factor in investment decisions. It was also felt that business investment was relatively insensitive to interest rate fluctuations, but this result was largely empirical. D. W. Jorgenson used neoclassical profit maximization to derive the formula for user cost of capital, in which business taxation and interest rate were both combined with other variables in the above expression, and it was found that user cost was an important factor in investment decisions.

By the mid-1960s, the Jorgenson formula, or variations of it, were standard parts of macroeconometric models; therefore, this aspect of supply side economics has a long history in models of the aggregate economy. It is interesting to note how it gradually worked its way into model specification. It is in the Keynesian spirit of marginal efficiency of capital, but its use represented a modification, or amplification of the standard Keynesian model. It shows, in a real sense, that the neoclassical modification of Keynes defines the present mainstream model, not the pure early renditions of the *General Theory*. This point is ill understood by some supply side advocates.

It also emphasizes that investment demand is actually a supply side phenomenon, because demand for capital becomes important in establishing the conditions for production, particularly for technically changing conditions for production.

While tax incentives are abundantly visible in the investment function, they are less clear in the savings and labor supply equations. In those two cases, the arguments of the supply side advocates have been taken seriously, and marginal tax rates have been appropriately inserted into the relevant equations. The empirical findings are weak and indefinite. There are some moderate effects of tax rates on saving and worker effort, but they are hard to establish; they are both small and slow in temporal build-up. From the viewpoint of United States economic policy, their beneficial effects have been grossly overstated, but they do occupy logical places in macroeconometric models and should be kept there, in spite of their relatively weak effects.

If that were the whole of supply side economics, we might conclude that it is not particularly fruitful for deeper research investigation. On the other hand, there is a more general interpretation of supply side economics, where there is a great deal to be done to add to the present fund of knowledge about this subject.

The economic conditions of supply must surely encompass such things as:

— techniques of production
— availability of basic materials
— environmental conditions
— demographic structure of population, work force, and employment
— industrial composition of production .

Large scale models with inter-industry (input–output) modules, sector modules, and demographic distributions are called for. They result in what I have elsewhere called the Keynes–Leontief Model.[5] This is becoming the mainstream model. It consists, in the Wharton version, of more than 2,000 equations. It is hardly a Keynesian model, based on size alone, and it goes far beyond the considerations of Keynes, although it is not incompatible with the Keynesian system.

---

[5]L. R. Klein, "The supply side," *American Economic Review* **68** (March 1978), pp. 1–7.

At the time of the oil embargo, followed by high OPEC prices for crude oil, there was much discussion of the issues and problems of energy economics. One could well criticize mainstream models for not having energy sectors. Fortunately, the Wharton large scale model was in existence, with the rudiments of an energy sector. As the national debate continued, model builders were forced to heed the discussion and add detailed energy content to their systems. This was an early discussion about supply side economics, and it resulted in highly beneficial model re-specification.

At the present time, there is great energy detail, both on the side of production and consumption of fuel and transformed energy, in the annual inter-industry version of the Wharton Model. Other sectors could be similarly investigated. This has been a profound contribution on the supply side and appears to be more productive than present analysis of tax incentives.

The Model of the Future

Since any model is but an approximation to the real thing, we may well ask what the next generations of models will be like, and to what extent they will bear the imprint of the contemporary debate.

Models will, as I have indicated in the previous sections, show adaptation and modification as a result of the debates now taking place in macroeconomic theory. There will be more financial detail, better lead–lag structures, and more explicit tax systems. These are ongoing and are likely to be dwarfed by some new tendencies in model design.

The most frequent use of macroeconomic models is in scenario analysis — scenarios of change *with and without* some strategic policies, or variables, or concepts. In order to make concise comparisons — *with and without* — models should be modular in design. If they are modular, more sector detail can, when needed, be inserted by removing more superficial modules and focusing attention on details of change in the newly installed module. In connection with the recent hearings on steel subsidies from abroad, we at Wharton Econometrics found it convenient to develop a steel sector model in some detail and then link this subsystem to the total Wharton Model, so that the present small steel sector would be effectively overridden and replaced with one that has the requisite specificity.

The U.S. economy is now recognized to be *open*. Over the years more trade disaggregation has been introduced, but now balance of payments accounts need to be fully integrated. This is actually part of a larger flow-of-funds sector. It includes the foreign flows. But the single most impressive challenge to model builders comes in the form of research for endogenous generation of exchange rates, under the influence of the present managed float. Exchange rate study is going on in several centers, all over the world, but the proximity of project LINK to Wharton Econometrics means that results worked out for one group may also be useful for the other. It is now routine to generate effective dollar rates in the Wharton Model and for the world economic system. Both in LINK and in Wharton Econometrics, complete systems of bilateral rates are obtained for the major countries.

Out of the small Keynesian Kernels — the IS-LM diagram or the 45-degree line diagram — grew the systems of economic relationships that are used daily for important problems. Although there is a great deal of professional dialog, with much contrary opinion, about the usefulness of large scale systems, there is such thirsting for information that we have no way to go except to control the ever larger systems that are evolving. The efficient computer makes it increasingly easy to handle and use large scale systems.

A few years ago, the introduction of control theory techniques in econometrics was cited as a breakthrough that would greatly change the way models are used. The impact was originally felt to be as important as advocates now think that monetarism, rational expectations, and supply side economics will be in shaping models for the next generation.

Control theory applications have much relevance for macroeconometrics and will tell us things about models that would not otherwise be noticed or examined. In this respect, control theory methods will add much to the improvement of quality of models. They will not, however, revolutionize our subject; they will surely be helpful, though.

Emphasis will be on comparative scenario analysis, but, as ever, great interest will remain in pure forecasting. In this respect, I am still attached to the proposition that *the test* of an economic theory or method is its ability to predict.

Over the years, especially since the end of World War II, when systematic attempts have been made to predict the national and international economy through the medium of econometric models, significant gains have been made. When we embarked on this venture in the late 1940s, we never dreamed that we could consistently track the economy as well as we have, nor did we believe that we could score so many successes in foreseeing changes or turning points in the overall economic situation. This is not to say that we had only successes and no failures, but the *replicated* record, in a statistical sense, is what counts.

Particularly large gains in predictive accuracy were made when economists harnessed the power of the electronic computer (in the 1960s) and were able to draw upon the improvements in data availability, during this protracted period.

Gains were made and the record has been amply documented, but there were many times when we thought that significant breakthroughs were just ahead.[6] We thought that quarterly or monthly data would lead to great improvements over models constructed from annual data. We also thought that the use of sample surveys and cross section data would help. We looked to advances in the methods of mathematical statistics, to better understanding of the problem of identification, to new developments in economic theory (game theory, programming methods, risk

---

[6]One important source of records are the tables of errors for several U.S. models maintained by Stephen McNees of the Federal Reserve Bank of Boston and published from time to time in the *New England Economic Review*.

theory, etc.). It has rarely been a case of big jumps forward. Instead, progress has been steady and slow. At the present time, the existing gap between our accuracy standards for applications of developing economy models and of developed economy models shows the distance that we have come in some 35 or more years. We have moved, for the main aggregates, from errors of 5 to 10 percent to errors of 1 to 5 percent.

Now, as we look at the churning discussions about macroeconomic theory, we might well ask whether the resolution of the debate will bring us significantly nearer to the truth? I personally doubt that the present debate is constructive enough to accomplish much along that line of analysis. In this sense, I do not believe that the present challenges will strongly survive the tests of predictive power. At this stage, there is little, in an objective or concrete sense, to show.

It has been my experience that highly doctrinaire models or theories do not fare well in the rough and cruel world of economic forecasting. They may do well for short periods of time, but if pursued on a highly repetitive basis, their weaknesses show up badly when underlying circumstances change. This is what happened when doctrinaire monetarism in the United States was confronted by President Nixon's control programs of 1971–73 and then by the oil embargo and changes in the terms of trade vis-á-vis oil exporting nations. Monetarism could not cope effectively with these big changes in the real economy. On the other hand, slow steady progress was made by the large mainstream models.

As these models are modified by the present debates, but definitely not replaced, they should improve by small degrees. Continuity in small improvements in accuracy can be expected, but not large steps forward.

10

INTERNATIONAL MODELS FOR FORECASTING
AND POLICY FORMATION†

1. The Link System

Even the most isolated of countries in the world economy have opened to trade and capital movements to an increasing extent so that we can truly say that the world is becoming more interdependent. Interdependencies lend themselves well to modeling; therefore, it is not surprising that more and more attention is being paid to international models as time goes by.

To a large extent this paper will draw upon the experience of working with project LINK ever since its beginning in 1968, but other approaches to international model building are appearing more frequently; therefore, an attempt will be made to refer to other projects in this expanding area.

Besides the LINK project, the following other international models have been reported and are now well known:

The Federal Reserve Multi-Country Model
The INTERLINK Model of OECD
The EURO-LINK Model of the Common Market
COMET of the Common Market
DESMOS (Greek for LINK) of the six original Common Market countries
The World Market of the Japanese Economic Planning Agency
The FAIS Model of Tsukuba University of Japan
The FUGI Model of Soka University of Japan
The World Model of Wharton Econometric Forecasting Associates (WEFA).

These are all econometric models in which conventional estimation methods are used for fitting each country's (area's) equations to aggregative time series data, and trading relationships are established in order to tie the various models together into a single system of interdependent relationships.

These are *mainstream* international models, but other types also exist. Some are based on general equilibrium systems with parameter values that are imposed *a priori*, are determined from simple ratios, or other isolated observations. There are also internationally linked input–output models and some very global models, i.e., models that interrelate broad regions of the globe. These are usually very compact models. One such version built for three regions — developed, developing, and

---

†From *Prévision et Analyse économique* (Cahiers du GAMA) **4**, 3 (September, 1983), pp. 93–113.

centrally planned — consists of just 37 equations for the whole world. The global models focus on medium to long term growth and are useful in generating trend simulations for 20 to 30 years. From this point forward, they take us through the 80s, 90s, and into the 21st Century.

The most important feature of international models that distinguishes them from national models is the linkage mechanism. Most of the models are based on the use of one or more world trade matrices. The matrix of trade shares (bilateral cell entries as fractions of associated total imports) is used to transform imports, endogenously explained in each country (area), into exports. Exports are exogenous, to a first approximation, in national economy models but endogenous in international modeling.

As an alternative to the use of the trade matrix for transforming imports into exports, some international models are built directly upon relationships for bilateral trade flows:

$$\frac{X_{ij}}{X_{\cdot j}} = f\left(\frac{p_{ij}}{p_{\cdot j}}\right)$$

X_{ij} = trade flow from i to j

$X_{\cdot j}$ = total imports of j

p_{ij} = price of X_{ij}

$p_{\cdot j}$ = price of $X_{\cdot j}$.

All variables are understood to be expressed in a common monetary unit (usually U.S. dollars) and other variables, including lags, may be introduced in order to round out the explanatory power of such equations.

The LINK formula uses the matrix of ratios:

$$A = (a_{ij}) \ , \ a_{ij} = \frac{X_{ij}}{X_{\cdot j}}$$

to transform an import vector M into an export vector X by the expression:

$$X = AM \ .$$

A primary emphasis of the LINK models, at its conception, was to explain world trade flows and the international transmission mechanism. Coming at a time when the world economy had just gone through an enormous expansion of world trade, it is not surprising that thinking about international economic relationships was based on trade flows, bilateral and total, but now we see much of the transmission mechanism transcending trade flows. International finance, exchange rate determination, and capital flows seem to be at least as important, if not more so, in determining the state and development of the world economy. Recycling of the petrol deficit (in payments), coping with exchange fluctuations, and servicing international debt are such massive problems that threaten world stability, that attention has shifted towards those aspects of model building that treat these phenomena. Concretely, this means that each component model needs financial equations for the working of domestic money markets, exchange rate equations, capital flow equations, and other international financial equations.

A point of view of the LINK system is that each resident model builder in a home country knows his (or her) area best and can do a superior modeling job to what any distant outsider can. The LINK project is thus designed to be an amalgamation of individual models from each of several countries, tied together in a consistent way by the standardized treatment of the foreign trade sector working through trade shares matrix. The EURO-LINK system, which is much smaller in scope, proceeds in this way too. The other models are all international in coverage but are constructed at arms length everywhere except in a home country. They treat each country uniformly by preparing the data, estimation, and application all in one phase. This has obvious advantages but lack the insight and expertise that come from the individual countries.

When the LINK system was first built, the Bretton Woods scheme of fixed parities was in force; therefore the model was originally predicated upon a system of fixed (exogenous) exchange rates. The breakdown of the system of fixed parities in 1971 and the introduction of the floating rate system with many modifications, made it imperative for us to introduce equations that generate endogenous exchange rates that are determined simultaneously, with the rest of the system.

A second major development was the large change in the terms of trade for the developed world versus the developing world or for oil-importing countries versus oil-exporting countries. This required that we look into the problem of recycling the large external deficits for a number of oil-importing countries vis-á-vis the oil exporters. This necessitates balance-of-payment modeling, and an extension to problems of international finance.

These two major developments have had large impacts on the structure and use of the LINK system. Many of the applications of the model have to do with problems created by the oil embargo (with high/rising oil prices), debt rescheduling, and fluctuations in exchange rates.

The models that have been mentioned thus far all involve the developed industrial countries in a crucial way. They are either world-wide in scope or restricted in emphasis to a few industrial countries. The Common Market models (EURO-LINK, COMET, DESMOS) are all sublinkages in that they link together countries in only a part of the world economy, but they do not pay close attention to the developing countries. Professor S. Ichimura, on the other hand, has put together a model of the developing countries of the Pacific Basin and Southeast Asia in a sublinkage that emphasizes the role of the newly industrialized economies, together with other developing economies in the region. It is not, however, purely a model of developing countries because it contains models of the two largest developed trading partners of the bloc, namely Japan and the United States. There is much potential for further research along these regional sublinkage lines, especially in Latin America and

Eastern Europe. The latter area introduces a new dimension, that of modeling the centrally planned economies. This is a task that is being undertaken on a country-by-country basis, and, indeed, models of the socialist countries are included in the LINK system, but they are not fully integrated into a well articulated bilateral trade network. That is to say, a well documented set of trade matrices, by commodity class is not explicitly incorporated into the system for individual socialist countries. At present, there are separate trading cells for CMEA countries, as an aggregated group and for the People's Republic of China as a separate country.

2. Some International Specifications

The reactions to the oil embargo of 1973–74 and again to the second oil shock of 1979–80 have demonstrated the force of synchronized movement in the international economy. Some economists believe that the present world economic crisis results from an underappreciation of the international ramifications of setbacks in major parts of the world. This may necessitate a high degree of policy coordination in order to bring about a sustained recovery.

A cursory examination of some simple model properties shows this international flavor of the world economy. Consider the kind of two-country trading models introduced 40 years ago by Lloyd Metzler (1942) to treat international problems in the context of the Great Depression:

$$y_1 = d_1 y_1 + m_2 y_2 - m_1 y_1 + g_1$$

$$y_2 = d_2 y_2 + m_1 y_1 - m_2 y_2 + g_2$$

y_i = country i's production (real GDP)

$d_i y_i$ = country i's private domestic expenditures (on home and foreign goods/services)

d_i = marginal propensity to spend (on consumer and producer goods /services) in country i

$m_i y_i$ = country i's imports of goods/services

m_i = marginal propensity to import of country i

g_i = country i's exogenous public expenditures (and exogenous demand).

Each equation expresses a country's GDP as the sum of private and public domestic spending plus exports minus imports, recognizing, in a two-country world, that one country's exports are the other's imports.

Let us further define, in the usual single country analysis, the domestic multipliers as:

$$M_1 = \frac{1}{1 - d_1 + m_1} \; ; \; M_2 = \frac{1}{1 - d_2 + m_2}.$$

Both of these expressions allow for import linkages, but they do not take further account of international repercussions. They show, in the usual way, how a unit of public expenditure (Δg_i) is multiplied into M_i units of ΔGDP_i. The same multipliers would be used for translation of unilateral export increases into GDP increases.

If we *reduce* the system to expressions that show how GDP in each country depends on exogenous expenditures in either country, we have:

$$y_1 = \frac{M_1(g_1 + m_2 M_2 g_2)}{1 - m_1 m_2 M_1 M_2}, \quad y_2 = \frac{M_2(g_2 + m_1 M_1 g_1)}{1 - m_1 m_2 M_1 M_2}.$$

It is likely that:

$$1 > 1 - m_1 m_2 M_1 M_2 > 0;$$

therefore if one country increases its public expenditures Δg_1 (for g_2 held fixed), the multiplier effect in country 1 (Δy_1) will exceed M_1. Correspondingly, there will be an effect in country 2 as well. We shall have:

$$\Delta y_2 = \frac{m_1 M_1 M_2}{1 - m_1 m_2 M_1 M_2} \Delta g_1.$$

If we take account, properly, of international relationships, we shall find that the increase in 1's activity stimulated more imports from 2, which raised y_2 by the export multiplier. At the same time, 2's added activity contributed to additional imports from 1, etc. The expanded multiplier formulas take all this into account.

But if the policies are coordinated so that both 1 and 2 are increasing public expenditures together, then each has an extra impact. The extra impact for 1 is:

$$\frac{\Delta y_1}{\Delta g_2} = \frac{m_2 M_2 M_1}{1 - m_1 m_2 M_1 M_2},$$

and the extra impact for 2 is:

$$\frac{\Delta y_2}{\Delta g_1} = \frac{m_1 M_1 M_2}{1 - m_1 m_2 M_1 M_2}.$$

A purpose of international model building is to estimate m_i and M_i for all countries and take account of the appropriate interaction effects when changes occur, either unilaterally or in a coordinated manner. In both cases there is an international effect over and above the standard contributions from domestic multiplier coefficients, M_i.

This example is purely indicative. It would have to be generalized in at least three ways in order to deal with realistic problems. It would have to be extended to an n-country system; it would have to allow for endogenous exchange rates; it would have to introduce prices, interest rates and many other variables in order to qualify as a suitable model in any single country before being tied together in a world system.

In terms of the simple expenditures model, there is no problem in generalizing the 2-country case to an n-country case, and all the principles hold, namely, that the multipliers change when international feedback effects are taken into consideration and that various coordination scenarios are possible in policy implementation.

The extent and degree of coordination is quite open. Also, taxes can be readily introduced into this kind of system as well as import restrictions; therefore, coordination of tax, in addition to expenditure policies can be treated on the fiscal side. Similarly protectionism (vs liberalization) can be investigated as an alternative type of policy.[1]

The simple model for two countries is written as though both accounting systems are in homogeneous units. Actually, the imports (into 1 from 2 or into 2 from 1) for each country needs to be converted from the currency units of the exporting country into those of the importing country. This is no problem if the exchange rate is exogenous or if the system is real and the conversion is done at a fixed rate that prevailed for the base period that is used in evaluating constant priced GDP.

In a more general system, exchange rates are variable, not fixed, and exchange rate equations for bilateral currency pairs must be introduced. Exchange rate fluctuations have been unusually wide since 1973, particularly since 1977, and have had a great deal to do with inflation, availability of goods, and service/capital flows between countries.

But exchange rates depend on inflation rates, interest rates, current balances, and international capital flows. All these other variables must be introduced together with the endogenous treatment of exchange rates. The problem of stagflation in the world economy reflects these joint movements of exchange rates, prices, and interest rates. The systems, therefore, must be extended. They must have financial markets in each of the major country models.[2] They must also have production relations, factor demands, price/wage equations, and other equations that make up a large system. A large national model in LINK may have as many as 1,000 equations (the Wharton Model of the United States and the Metric Model of France, e.g.). The total system has about 8,000 equations. Realistic models of the world economy are far different from the 2-equation system used to illustrate first principles. They are large and complicated. They have large data bases and must be managed in a very systematic and formal way.

3. Validation

Before any model is applied, it should be tested — against sample data, other historical data, in extrapolation exercises, in sensitivity analysis (multipliers). There have been no comprehensive validation studies of international models comparable with those that have been designed for national models, but some accuracy studies have been made of LINK forecasts, and it is useful to present them here.

The LINK Model is very large, as indicated above, and it is necessary to be highly selective in any testing procedures. There are two kinds of tests: (1) test of predictive power for world totals and (2) tests of predictive power for selected

---

[1] For analytical treatment of income taxes in this framework, see Johnson and Klein (1974), and Klein and Su (1979).

[2] The Federal Reserve's Multi-Country Model is particularly strong in this respect, but covers only five main national economies (U.S., Japan, Germany, U.K., France).

country or area statistics. In both cases, there will be an examination of production, price changes, and trade flows. There is not enough experience yet with exchange rate forecasting to test in this area, too.

An exhaustive survey of the forecast record has never been prepared, for different variables and for different time horizons. The forecasts made each year are for three year horizons.

Following a regular spring forecast meeting of project LINK a forecast was estimated for 1976, 1977, and 1978, including the year 1975 on an ex post basis. This forecast was prepared in July 1976. Some world aggregates are reported in Table. 1.

Table 1. Actual and predicted values, world trade, world GDP and GDP deflator, 1975–78. (percent variations)

		1975	1976	1977	1978
World Trade					
value	P	1.5	10.8	13.1	15.1
	A	4.5	12.5	13.5	15.5
volume	P	− 5.0	4.1	6.8	11.0
	A	− 4.0	11.0	5.0	5.5
price	P	6.1	6.4	5.9	3.6
	A	8.5	1.5	8.5	10.0
World GDP					
	P	− 0.2	5.5	5.5	5.2
	A	− 0.2	4.7	4.6	4.3
GDP Deflator	P	10.5	8.1	7.2	5.9
(industrial countries)	A	11.2	7.4	7.6	7.5

P = predicted

A = Actual

Trade and GDP deflator from *World Economic Outlook*, IMF, Washington, D.C., June 1981;

World GDP, Wharton Econometric Forecasting Associates.

Such forecasts and comparisons with actual data are not easy to prepare. Data are regularly being revised; there are conflicting estimates produced by the different international organizations for world totals. Scope, units, and concepts vary markedly. These tables are by no means exhaustive, but they do provide a look, with some depth, at a LINK forecast. As the system is evolving, this is the forecast for the country components as they existed in 1976. On earlier occasions, some other forecasts validations were made [see Klein (1976), Johnson and Klein (1979)].

When all the separate results are added to make world totals, the overall accuracy is better. There are two deficiencies in the system, however, shown in Table 1. In the first place, the separation of world trade totals into a price component and

Table 2. Actual and predicted values, trade balances, GDP and GDP deflator, 13 LINK countries, 1976–78.

		1976		1977		1978	
		P	A	P	A	P	A
Australia	Trade balance	0.4	2.1	0.8	1.0	0.9	0.1
	GDP/GNP	4.7	4.0	7.2	0.5	5.0	3.2
	PGDP/PGNP	14.0	13.2	12.9	9.6	14.0	7.2
Austria	Trade balance	−1.7	−2.5	−0.7	−3.8	−0.8	−3.2
	GDP	4.3	4.6	3.5	4.4	6.0	0.5
	PGDP	7.5	5.5	8.0	5.3	7.1	5.3
Belgium	Trade balance	−1.4	−1.7	−0.3	−3.1	2.4	−2.9
	GDP	1.9	5.3	4.1	1.0	4.6	3.2
	PGDP	11.6	7.7	7.8	7.1	7.1	4.1
Canada	Trade balance	0.1	1.7	0.4	2.9	0.6	3.9
	GDP	3.1	5.8	6.3	2.4	7.0	4.0
	PGDP	9.1	9.3	4.6	7.2	3.5	6.5
Finland	Trade balance	−1.0	−0.6	−0.5	0.5	0.2	1.2
	GDP	0.9	0.3	3.0	0.4	2.6	2.3
	PGDP	10.2	12.6	8.1	10.1	14.0	7.7
France	Trade balance	−0.9	−4.8	−7.4	−3.0	−8.9	0.5
	GDP	4.9	5.2	7.2	3.1	6.5	3.7
	PGDP	10.1	9.8	8.4	9.0	5.8	9.5
W. Germany	Trade balance	23.8	16.1	25.8	19.6	24.2	24.7
	GDP	6.2	5.2	4.9	3.0	6.6	3.2
	PGDP	5.9	3.3	4.5	3.8	5.7	3.8
Italy	Trade balance	−2.9	−4.3	−4.0	−0.1	−2.3	2.9
	GDP	2.6	5.9	2.9	1.9	4.9	2.7
	PGDP	14.6	18.0	11.5	19.1	6.0	13.9
Japan	Trade balance	11.1	9.8	9.9	17.2	12.5	25.3
	GDP	8.4	5.3	7.4	5.3	6.4	5.0
	PGDP	9.9	6.4	9.8	5.7	5.3	4.6
Netherlands	Trade balance	−1.4	1.3	−1.3	−0.3	0.9	−1.5
	GDP	4.2	5.3	4.3	2.4	6.7	2.7
	PGDP	4.9	8.9	5.9	6.3	4.9	5.2
Sweden	Trade balance	0.3	0.2	−0.1	0.2	1.7	2.6
	GDP	1.7	1.2	1.5	−2.0	4.0	1.3
	PGDP	8.5	11.6	9.4	10.7	4.0	10.0
U.K.	Trade balance	−8.0	−7.0	−1.3	−3.9	−4.9	−2.9
	GDP	3.6	3.6	3.3	1.3	3.0	3.3
	PGDP	14.6	14.6	11.2	14.0	4.4	10.9
U.S.	Trade balance	−2.6	−9.4	6.3	−30.9	10.4	−33.7
	GDP	6.0	5.4	5.5	5.4	4.2	4.4
	PGDP	6.2	5.2	6.2	6.0	5.4	7.4

Trade balance: billions of U.S. dollars. GDP or GNP: percent variation.
PGDP or PGNP: percent variation. P = predicted. A = actual.

volume component have much error, while the nominal values are projected closely, in line with observations. Secondly, the GDP volume changes tend to be overestimated, while the price changes tend to be underestimated. The underestimation of the degree of inflation has been a problem. In the country estimates (Table 2), this can be seen in a few key cases, but it is not uniform. But in the two far-out years (1977–78), there was a tendency to overestimate GDP growth.

As forecasts and applications with the LINK system progress, there will be more archival research in documenting the validation statistics. Regular forecasts exercises and validation of other international models has not been reported on any systematic basis.

Estimation of the standard error of forecast is, in principle, possible with models of this size and complexity, but such estimates have never been produced. A possible procedure would be to generate stochastic simulation from which to study a distribution of forecasts. The problem of stochastic simulation of an international model like LINK, has been investigated, and the stochastic elements have effects on the simulation, but the computational problems are formidable, and the actual cases have been worked out only for small prototype systems.

4. Policy Analysis

Validation is only exploratory; so we cannot say that we have a validated system about which we could be confident for purposes of policy application. We are still proceeding on an act of faith.

Policy applications of the LINK system have been made on several occasions, but among those selected for comment, I want to emphasize the applications concerning some form of coordinated policy. Also, I shall refer to protectionist scenarios, which are just the opposite of policy coordination.

Among coordinated policies the most notable are:

fiscal coordination,
monetary coordination,
exchange coordination,
industrial policy.

These simulations have been made over the years and are relevant to the policy problem of generating a revival from the world recession, but with reference to those policy scenarios that have already been completed it can readily be seen how coordinated policies may work. Two scenarios will be examined:

(A) Fiscal stimuli to three large economies — Germany, Japan, and the United States. For Japan we also programmed a personal tax cut (¥ 2.6 trillion on a base of ¥ 13 trill). For Germany we assumed a tax reduction for wage earners (DM 20 billion on a base of DM 235 bill.). In the case of the U.S. steady increases of $ 10 billion in defense were implemented.

(B) In addition to the fiscal stimulus, exchange rates were changed by 10 percent upward valuations of the DM and Yen. The DM was changed (1977, 1978) from 2.45 DM/\$ to 2.23. The Yen was changed (1977, 1978) from 290.1 ¥/\$ to 263.9.

Before considering the results, let us discuss the changes, especially in the light of present (1982) considerations. In today's depressed world the United States, Germany, and Japan are again being asked to reflate; the United States, to save itself from slipping into a much more serious recession (or depression) and the others as countries that are in a position to take stimulative measures. The United States already has enormous military expenditures planned, and because of large pending budget deficits, is practically precluded from taking fiscal action. Today, the principal request is for monetary easing to bring down interest rates.

Germany and Japan will undoubtedly follow the United States' lead in reducing interest rates as a result of easier monetary policy, but those countries can also use some fiscal stimulus although they tend to resist prodding on that issue. The main point is that they should seek recovery through domestic stimulus rather than through increasing exports.

As for the added policies in scenario (B), they are right in line with present discussions about an overvalued dollar via-á-vis undervalued DM and Yen. Up evaluations of 10 percent are about the right magnitude.

The results of these two policy scenarios are given in Table 3.

Modest tax cuts and expenditure increases can be expected to add more than one-half percentage point to the volumes of world trade and developed world production. These gains, especially the gains in trade, are much larger if the dollar falls in relation to the DM and Yen.

Table 3. Aggregative simulation results, coordinated fiscal and exchange rate policies. (1977–78, percentage deviations from baseline case)

	Scenario A		Scenario B	
	1977	1978	1977	1978
World Trade (nominal)	0.6	0.8	4.1	4.8
World Trade (real)	0.5	0.7	1.3	1.6
GDP (real) (13 LINK OECD countries)	0.6	0.8	0.8	0.8

Under the first set of policies, the three stimulus countries enjoy the largest gains, averaging about a full percentage point. The gain for policy passive partner countries is much smaller, but they generally gain by 0.2 or 0.3 percentage points in production. The gains in trade volume would spread to the benefit of the developing countries who need a strongly growing volume of trade so that their exports can expand.

Table 4. Coordinated monetary policy, world summary. (Change over baseline)[1]

	GDP					PDP			
	1980	1981	1982	1983		1980	1981	1982	1983
OECD	0.5	1.1	1.3	1.4	OECD	0.0	−0.1	−0.2	−0.2
CPE	0.0	0.0	0.0	0.0					
Developing countries	0.1	0.2	0.2	0.3					
World	0.3	0.7	0.9	0.9					

	Trade balance ($ US billion)[2]					Trade volume			
	1980	1981	1982	1983		1980	1981	1982	1983
OECD	−0.9	−3.4	−5.0	−7.9	OECD	0.5	1.4	1.6	1.7
CPE	0.4	1.0	1.5	2.0	CPE	0.3	0.7	0.9	1.1
Developing countries	0.4	1.9	3.1	4.1	Developing countries	0.4	0.9	1.4	1.4
World	—	—	—	—	World	0.5	1.2	1.4	1.6

[1]For the trade balance the figures refer to the arithmetic change in the level from the control solution, i.e., (SOL-BASE) in $ US billions. For all other variables the percentage difference in level is reported [i.e., (SOL-BASE) * 100/BASE].
[2]Because of changes in the model for « rest of the world », which closes the LINK system, the changes reported in trade balances for each year need not sum to zero.

The up valuation of the DM and Yen in the second scenario pulls back, slightly, the GDP growth in Germany and Japan, but the gains are quite large elsewhere.

Monetary policy coordination has been investigated under the LINK system more recently. In 1981, we simulated coordinated reductions in interest rates, while what we have had is reductions of the rates in the United States followed by corresponding reductions elsewhere [see Klein, Simes and Voisin (1981)]. In actual fact, rates have come down by many more points than in our simulations, but the simulations were controlled. Only rates changed, from the baseline case. Other variables were held to a fixed course. In the real world, development did not follow this pattern.

To carry out the coordinated scenario of easier monetary policy, with a target of lowering interest rates by 2 full percentage points during the 4-year period 1980–83 we made the following kinds of model adjustments:

(i) Some concept of money supply was increased — United States, Canada, Switzerland.

(ii) Key interest rates, except where exogenous, were shocked with endogenous liquidity variables — Germany, France, United Kingdom.

(iii) With substantially exogenous financial sectors, interest rates and liquidity variables were directly adjusted — Australia.

Table 5. Coordinated monetary policy, OECD countries in LINK, fourth year results. (Changes over baseline)[1]

	Interest rate[2]	Money supply[2]	Private fixed investment	Private consumption	Trade balance	Consumption deflator	GDP
Australia	−2.0	3.0	0.4	2.8	0.1	−0.2	1.6
Austria	−2.0	1.8	5.2	0.8	−0.4	−0.6	1.5
Belgium[3]	−2.0	n.a.	3.6	1.9	−0.2	0.4	2.0
Canada	−2.3	11.9	6.1	1.3	−0.1	0.7	1.4
Denmark[3]	n.a.	n.a.	6.2	0.8	−0.1	0.0	1.3
Finland[3]	−2.0	n.a.	3.3	1.8	−0.3	0.7	2.1
France	−2.0	4.4	2.5	0.0	−0.5	−0.5	0.5
Germany	−1.5	0.6	13.3	1.0	−2.6	0.1	3.0
Greece[3]	−2.0	5.4	3.3	0.5	0.0	0.0	0.9
Italy	−2.0	1.6	5.1	0.4	0.5	0.1	1.2
Japan[3]	0.0	n.a.	4.3	0.5	−0.6	0.6	1.1
Netherlands[3]	n.a.	n.a.	4.8	1.1	−0.1	−0.1	1.6
Norway[3]	n.a.	n.a.	3.0	0.0	0.0	0.0[4]	1.1
Spain[3]	n.a.	n.a.	4.2	1.5	−0.5	−0.7[4]	1.8
Sweden	−2.0	3.6	0.6	0.3	0.5	0.2	0.6
Switzerland	−0.7	10.0	17.7	3.4	−3.2	1.0	4.3
United Kingdom	−1.7	5.0	1.3	0.1	−0.2	0.4	0.1
United States	−2.0	3.6	2.8	1.2	−1.1	−1.2	1.4

[1] For interest rates and the trade balance (in $ US billions) the reported figures refer to the arithmetic change in the level from the control solution (i.e., SOL-BASE). For all other variables the percentage difference in level is reported [i.e., (SOL-BASE) * 100/BASE].

[2] The definitions for the reported interest rate and money supply variables may differ across countries.

[3] Private fixed investment in this country was directly shocked. See text.

[4] The figures relate to the GDP deflator rather than the consumption deflator.

(iv) If no financial sector was available, investment was shocked by an amount corresponding to a change in rates of 2 percentage points — Belgium, Denmark, Finland, Greece, Japan, Netherlands, Norway, Spain.

The version of the LINK system used in 1981, for this simulation, was considerably expanded in country coverage and tabular displays.

This coordinated policy adds more than one per cent to GDP of the industrial counties, after the first year of the simulation, and helps the developing countries, particularly because world trade volume improves by even more, in percentage terms, than does GDP. On the whole, trade balances improve for the developing countries, at the expense of the OECD countries. As far as inflation is concerned, it is not increased and is possibly trimmed because of productivity gains.

Individual country results are better, as far as real growth is concerned, throughout the industrial world, in the fourth year of this simulation. The gains over baseline GDP in the fourth year range up to 4.0 per cent.

In 1981 and 1982, interest rates have fallen by even more than 2 percentage points. In the United States, some short term rates have fallen by as much as 10 points, but on average the fall has been closer to about 7 to 8 points. Long term rates have declined by about 3 to 5 points. Other countries followed suit by lowering their rates soon after the rates were lowered in the United States. In some cases the American decreases were matched, and in others they were partially matched. They were rarely, if ever, exceeded. But, as was noted above, in the actual world many other things happened; so it may not appear that the favorable results of this simulation were realized, but if rates had not been reduced, the world economic situation would probably have been much worse, by a wide margin, and that is what really matters in this analysis.

Industrial policy programs based on supply-side improvements are not easy to quantify apart from their interpretation as specific fiscal or monetary policies. Many supply side policies might be associated with changed regulatory rules, implementing training schemes, funding research, introducing specific technological developments, or controlling production of basic materials.

The LINK system has not been used for the study of comprehensive industrial policies but has been used for examining fiscal policies that are designed to raise the level of investment which, in turn, leads to productivity gains. [See Klein, Bollino and Fardoust (1982)]. By emphasizing policies that enhance productivity we attempt to hold inflation in check while pursuing better growth performance.

The LINK system was simulated in two basic modes for the decade of the 1980s. One had a policy stimulus for the United States alone. This is a ≪ locomotive ≫ scenario. The other was coordinated among 13 LINK industrial countries and is called a ≪ convoy ≫ scenario. We also considered the two types of scenarios under fixed and floating exchange rate regimes.

The assumptions imposed on the two basic modes are shown in Table 6. It can been seen that each country's model was stimulated to produce more fixed investment. It is thus a specialized case of coordinated fiscal policy. The results for key economic variables are shown in Tables 7 and 8.

They show that if the United States act alone through targeted tax cuts (increases in the investment tax credit) there are significant gains in the United States and moderate gains elsewhere. With all countries acting in concert, the overall gains are larger, and they are spread over all the partner countries. There are impressive gains in productivity and no increase in overall inflation. There are some modest gains for the developing countries.

These policies were studied more than one year ago (today, December 1982), but their relevance is more salient now than ever, for much of the world is looking towards a leading (locomotive-type) role to be played by the United States in helping to extricate the world economy from its present precarious position. But it is also generally recognized that it will not be satisfactory for the United States to try to be a sole locomotive and that the more satisfactory solution is for all the major

Table 6. Industrial policy simulations — Project LINK policy assumptions (Pre-linkage).[1]

	Target variable	Target variable[2] as % of total investment	Locomotive (local currency)	Convoy (local currency)	Nature of exogenous shock
Australia	Private investment in equipment	58.1	—	5816.00 mil	+ Increased capital tax allowance − Decreased corporate tax rate
Austria	Private investment in equipment	47.4	—	13.50 bil.	− Decreased corporate tax rate
Belgium	Private investment in equipment	73.9	—	279.87 bil.	+ Increased call money interest rate + Increased autonomous investment
Canada	GFCF in machinery	39.2	—	25.31 bil.	− Lower user cost of capital
Finland	Total Investment	100	—	20709.00 mil.	− Lower implicit corporate tax rate + Increased autonomous investment
France	Total investment	100	—	344.60 bil.	− Lower fiscal pressure on investment price − Lower corporate tax rate + Increased autonomous investment
Germany	Private fixed investment	100	—	498.66 bil.	− Lower implicit corporate tax rate + Increased autonomous investment
Italy	Private investment	100	—	24510.00 bil.	− Lower implicit corporate tax rate + Increased autonomous investment
Japan	Private investment	100	—	63749.00 bil.	+ Increased government transfer to firms + Increased implicit depreciation rate + Increased autonomous investment
Netherlands	Investment in equipment	91.6	—	23.44 bil.	+ Increased total depreciation + Increased autonomous investment in equipment
Sweden	Investment in equipment (manufacturing)	36.4	—	18.12 bil.	− Lower local government corporate tax rate − Lower central government corporate tax rate + Increased autonomous investment in equipment
U.K.	Private investment	100	—	45.62 bil.	− Lower marginal corporate tax rate + Increased autonomous investment in equipment
U.S.	Nonresidential investment	75.1	214.42	214.42 bil.	+ Increased investment tax credit

[1] Cumulative additional nominal investment for the period 1982–90 over the base solution.
[2] Average 1982–90.

Table 7. Industrial policy simulations key economic varibles.[1]

| | Real GDP growth rate[2] | | Consumption deflator rate of change | | Labor productivity rate of change | |
| | 1980–90 | | 1980–90 | | 1980–90 | |
	L	C	L	C	L	C
Canada	0.15	0.32	−0.02	0.30	0.05	0.25
France	0.02	0.41	−0.0	−0.01	0.0	0.27
Germany	0.01	0.30	0.04	0.62	0.0	0.20
Italy	0.01	0.09	0.0	−0.02	0.23	0.48
U.K.	0.02	0.21	−0.01	−0.05	0.0	0.25
U.S.	0.45	0.42	−0.32	−0.30	0.15	0.20
Japan	0.10	0.48	0.0	0.19	0.38	0.56
OECD[3]	0.20	0.40	−0.1	−0.0		
Developing countries (non-oil)	0.05	0.10	−0.0	−0.0		
World	0.10	0.20	−0.0	−0.0		

[1] All figures are differences in percentages: scenario — control.
[2] L = locomotive. C = convoy.
[3] 13 LINK OECD countries.

Table 8. Industrial Policy Simulations Real Growth Rates of Exports and Imports.[1]

| | Exports[2] 1980–90 | | Imports 1980–90 | |
	L	C	L	C
Canada	0.37	0.41	0.02	0.72
France	0.1	0.36	+ 0.0	−0.32
Germany	0.1	0.32	+ 0.0	−0.32
Italy	+ 0.0	0.26	+ 0.0	0.15
U.K.	+ 0.0	0.16	0.40	0.43
U.S.	0.23	0.39	0.10	0.56
Japan	0.4	0.60	0.20	0.40
OECD[3]	0.2	0.4		
Developing countries				
Oil exporters	0.0	0.4	0.0	0.0
Oil importers	0.2	0.3	0.3	0.4
Centrally planned[4]	0.0	0.2	0.0	0.2
World	0.1	0.3	0.1	0.3

[1] All figures are differences in percentages: scenario — control.
[2] L = locomotive. C = convoy.
[3] 13 LINK OECD countries.
[4] Eastern Europe and U.S.S.R.

Table 9. Industrial policy simulation — flexible and fixed exchange rate regimes.[1]

	Consumption deflator[2] 1980–90		Real GDP growth 1980–90	
	L	C	L	C
U.S.	0.01	−0.0	0.11	0.12
Japan	0.19	0.2	0.35	0.38
OECD Europe	−0.3	−0.4	−0.1	0.0
OECD[3]	0.0	0.0	0.1	0.15
Developing non-oil	0.7	0.5	0.0	0.0
World	0.1	0.1	0.0	0.1

[1] All figures are in percent differences: flexible — fixed.
[2] L = locomotive. C = convoy.
[3] 13 LINK OECD countries.

industrial countries to act in concert. The convoy case, therefore, is the appropriate one for the present situation.

Fixed exchange rates are used in the industrial policy simulations reported so far. A more realistic approach is to introduce equations for flexible (endogenous) exchange rates. Short term, quarterly, exchange rate equations are used for extrapolations of 3 to 5 years length, but for these longer term simulations of about one decade it is required to have exchange rate equations that pick out exchange rate changes along a trend path. For this purpose, we have used a version of purchasing power parity as estimated and tested [see Klein, Fardoust and Filatov (1981)].

The imposition of a PPP rule for exchange rate adjustment does not have a great effect on the system simulation. It leads to moderately higher growth rates in both locomotive and convoy scenarios. It also leads to slightly higher inflation rates, but not uniformly so.

Industrial policies may take many forms; therefore, policy analysis can be reformulated to interpret other kinds of changes besides those induced by fiscal changes that are closely associated with increasing capital formation.

Finally, in this summary of policy analysis at the international level, it may be useful to review some LINK estimates of system sensitivity to oil price changes. These are not, strictly speaking, policy scenarios. They are more in the nature of sensitivity to external disturbance. The point of using model analysis in these situations is to determine the magnitude of the system response and then devise policies accordingly to offset the ill effects.

From the time of the initial large jump in oil prices in 1974 and again in 1979–80, the LINK system has repeatedly been used to analyze the impact of rising oil prices on both activity levels and inflation rates. After many trials these calculations settled into a pattern. Simulations of the LINK system for a general rise in world oil prices, 10 percent above a base path in which oil prices are held to a zero

Table 10. Effects of a sustained increase of 10 percent in world oil prices, 1982–1985. (Deviations of growth rate from the baseline solution)

	1982	1983	1984	1985
Real exports of goods	−0.3	−0.5	−0.4	0.2
Export price (unit value)	2.1	2.4	2.4	2.3
Real GDP (1970 $)	−0.4	−0.5	−0.5	−0.4
Price deflator of consumer expenditures (OECD)	0.5	0.6	0.7	0.5
Real exports of mineral fuels	−0.4	−0.5	−0.4	− 0.2

real growth rate, are shown in Table 10. The simulation is performed over the period 1982–85.

These simulations suggest that a 10 percent rise in oil prices would result in a decline in the world growth rate of 0.4 to 0.5 percentage points. Real exports would decline by about the same amount, but the sign reverses in 1985. The inflation rate in industrial countries would be expected to rise by 0.5 percentage points and then start to decline after three years. The associated decline in exports of SITC 3, mineral fuels, implies an elasticity coefficient of about 0.04 to 0.05 in the short run, declining to about 0.02.

It may seem strange to be considering oil price rises at a time when they are almost stationary and expected to fall soon. The model, simply designed for a scenario of decline, produces just about the opposite effect of a price rise. This high degree of symmetry may turn out to be implied by the model structure when solved in a fairly mechanical way. But in actuality there may be significant asymmetries. We have seen crisis situations caused by price declines in 1981–82 that showed signs of spreading in a harmful way throughout the world economy. In order to produce asymmetric results, some strong *a priori* assumptions will have to be built into the scenario design. The asymmetrical results, affecting Mexico, Venezuela, Nigeria, Indonesia and other oil exporters with debt problems, may not show unless price declines exceed 25 per cent or more.

5. Conclusions

The international dimension in models changes the response mechanism, generally increasing sensitivity of the world economy, as a result of national economies acting upon one another to produce indirect effects that must be added to direct effects.

Combinations of fiscal, monetary and exchange rate policies lend richness to the response mechanism. These effects make synchronized downswings much worse than isolated downswings. But it also means that corrective policies will be more efficient if combined with other countries' policies in a mutually reinforcing manner.

In LINK simulations, over the past 12–14 years, various combinations of policies have been worked out to get specific results. At the present time, the world awaits a careful search for new policy combinations that have promise for lifting us from world-wide recession.

References

Johnson, K. and L. R. Klein, 1974, "Stability in the international economy: The LINK experience," in *International Aspects of Stabilization Policy*, eds. A. Ando, R. Herring and R. Marston (Federal Reserve Bank of Boston, Boston.), pp. 147–188.

Johnson, K. and L. R. Klein, 1979, "Error analysis in the LINK models," in *Modelling the International Transmission Mechanism*, ed. J. Sawyer, (North Holland, Amsterdam), pp. 45–71.

Klein, L. R. 1976, "Five-year experience of linking national econometric models and of forecasting international trade," in *Quantitative Studies of International Economic Relations*, ed. H. Glejser, (North Holland, Amsterdam), pp. 1–24.

———— , 1981 "The LINK project," in *International Trade and Multicountry Models*, ed. R. Courbis (Economica, Paris), pp. 197–209.

———— , C. A. Bollino, and S. Fardoust, 1982, "Industrial policy in the world economy: medium term simulations," *Journal of Policy Modeling* **4** (2), pp. 175–189.

———— , S. Fardoust, and V. Filatov, 1981, "Purchasing power parity in medium term simulation of the world economy," *Scandinavian Journal of Economics* **83** (4), pp. 479–496.

———— , R. Simes, and P. Voisin, 1981, "Coordinated monetary policy and the world economy," *Prévision et Analyse économique* **2** (3), pp. 75–105.

———— and V. Su, 1979, "Protectionism: An analysis from project LINK," *Journal of Policy Modeling* **1** (1), pp. 5–35.

Metzler, L. A., 1942, "Underemployment equilibrium in international trade", *Econometrica* **10** (2), pp. 97–112.

11

PROSPECTS FOR MACROECONOMETRIC MODELING[†]

In the past 16 chapters, we have looked at the history of macroeconometric model-building, both in terms of individual developments and also in terms of more general developments. It is now time to look at prospective future development, for the remainder of the current century and into the next. Of course, some of the discussion of the preceding chapter contained implicit forecasts of prospective future developments; but it is time to be more explicit. One point should be made clear: we have no explicit "model" of the development of technology in the subdiscipline of macroeconometric modeling, so our "forecasting" in this chapter is definitely of the impressionistic variety (and hence contrary to what we should recommend in the case of a "real-world" national economy!).

1. A Growth Sector

During the great build-up of constructive applications of econometric models of the macroeconomy during the 1960s and 1970s, which coincided with the rapid introduction of the electronic computer, econometrics, in a commercial sense, became known as a growth industry. An entire industry was founded in the form of econometric consulting firms, but growth concept extended beyond the expansion of sales of econometric services in the market place. Scholarly econometric activity also expanded commensurately with the growth of the industry. Scholarly journals (such as the *Journal of Econometrics, Empirical Economics, Journal of Quantitative Economics, Economic Modelling* and *Journal of Policy Modeling*) were founded, and the econometric content of other, more general journals expanded.

The recession of the early 1980s, the election of a government in the United States that appeared hostile to the modeling concept and the spread of competition in the market-place gave the impression to some observers that the expansion curve had leveled off. But the seeming slowdown of growth was only temporary. As far as commercial activity is concerned, significant growth remains to be captured in international modeling, in areas outside the United States (especially Europe, Japan and the developing countries) and in new areas of research, the market for foreign exchange being a notable case. Good samples of data, the grist for the econometrician's mill, are just becoming available in the field of exchange rate estimation,

---

[†]From *A History of Macroeconometric Model-Building* (Edward Elgar, Aldershot, England, 1991), Chap. 17, pp. 536–557; written jointly with Ronald G. Bodkin and Kanta Marwah.

since the period of floating rates dates only from 1973. After the recession of 1981–2, commercial activity in econometrics resumed its strong upward course again (up to the present time: autumn 1989).

Scholarly activity is also growing, especially in developing and centrally-planned economies. Model-building is a natural tool for development planning in these countries. A misleading opinion that there was too much exogeneity and too little market influence for the successful application of econometric models, let alone their meaningful construction, in such economies has been refuted by the preparation of models for most of the centrally-planned and developing countries. Two bottlenecks have been the lack of availability of usable statistical samples and the shortage of trained personnel. Over a time-span of some 20 or more years, both these obstacles have been overcome. There is now a fair, though far from adequate, data base and a good cadre of econometricians — some self-educated and some trained in institutions of North America, Japan, Europe, Australia and elsewhere. This growth area may prove to be very large in the years to come.

A reason why some people may have thought that they detected a leveling-off in growth rate of activity in macroeconometrics is that the methodology is becoming so widely accepted. In earlier days, when the econometric approach was struggling for attention, its take-off was quite apparent. Now this approach is taken for granted. The current generation of students is almost completely computer-oriented and, with the computer, the building of models is a natural, straightforward step. It is almost second nature for them to formulate a problem in a quantitative mould, program its analysis on the computer (either the mainframe or the personal computer), and try to work out a solution. Facilities are now so favorable for the econometric approach that it is almost effortlessly implemented. People do an accepted and expected thing; so the growth aspect goes unnoticed.

The econometrics industry achieved greatest commercial growth through the delivery medium of time-sharing, that is, by remote terminal access to a large mainframe computer. In the present era and the period ahead, time-sharing will continue to be used for some problems but probably not as a commercial growth sector. Instead, there is already a marked shift to distributed processing through the medium of microprocessors, used either in a self-contained fashion or in a downloading and up-loading relationship with large mainframe computers.

The spread of commercial growth will be different because microprocessing is much less expensive. But in terms of econometric activity there is bound to be enormous growth because the microprocessor opens so many easily accessible horizons to the model-builder.

2. Two Extremes

Tinbergen's first model of the United States (not his first model, as indicated in Chap. 6) was bigger than textbook models, although not large by modern standards. Klein's early models, reverting to the Keynesian paradigm, tended to be smaller.

Then models expanded greatly in size. As we noted in the preceding chapter, the computer made this possible.

There will be a continuing tendency for econometricians to build large models — larger and larger to meet the highly diversified needs of the user community, where specificity together with the macro picture is very demanding. But at the same time a new development in computation has occurred, and it is having some effect on the scope of model-building. There is a distinct tendency to prepare small models, of approximately 10 equations (or fewer) for treatment on a micro computer. Management of data files, sophisticated estimation methods, simulation and many other analytical statistics for the behavior of models can be readily and speedily implemented. The inexpensive, accessible and self-contained nature of this process is very attractive for the complete econometric treatment of small models, with ever-informative graphic and tabular displays.

While the micro computer is ideal for the study of small models in both research and teaching, it should be noted that it is getting more and more powerful, but not necessarily larger — in size or in cost. The significance of these facts is that fairly large models can also be handled well on the personal computer. It is fully recognized that the models of 50 or more equations tend to become "black boxes" and not readily understood visually. Intensive personal use on the small computer with good graphics can lend transparency to the "black box," and so promote understanding through experience. The computer power of the microprocessor is enlarging the capability of model analysis to systems of up to 1000 equations.

There are these reasons to look for more work to be done with small systems and continuing work with conventionally sized systems. But there are also arguments for going to the other extreme, namely the construction and use of the very large system, now considered to be a model of some 10000 or more equations. A major case of such a large system is an international model like that of Project LINK, consisting of many standard-sized models of individual countries.[1] It is called the multi-model system. This is not the only large-scale computing problem that goes with a large model; systems that make extensive use of input–output relations tend to be quite large and impose heavy computer requirements. At the same time, their large size is primarily associated with the need to provide industry detail with overall economic performance, and this need is both continuing and growing. Computer developments are expected to be accommodating.

The multi-model problem for international and interregional systems, as well, has been handled progressively over the past few years with conventional mainframe computers. However more can be done with large multi-model systems if an order of magnitude improvement in computer analysis takes place. At the other extreme from the microprocessor we have the supercomputer. Many versions of the super-computer have an architecture that is well suited to the multi-model problem; it is an architecture of parallel processing. Each model, in the multi-model system, can

---

[1] See Klein, Pauly, and Voisin (1982). See also the discussion of Chap. 15.

be simultaneously processed, instead of being done in a serial fashion; this is a key for speeding up the calculation of the world system, on the basis of the individual country components.[2]

3. Errors of Forecasting

In connection with large-scale computer needs, the problem of error in the presentation of forecasts was mentioned and briefly discussed. This problem deserves lengthier consideration in its own right.

It is now routine to have probability limits accompany weather forecasts, and public opinion results often have measures of statistical significance of the point spread presented. In a close election contest, the pollster will frequently say that the estimated outcome is "too close to call," meaning that the point spread between candidates is less than the width of the associated error band. Political pollsters have had their "knuckles rapped" so severely in cases of large mistakes in U.S. elections (for example, Landon vs. Roosevelt, 1936; Dewey vs. Truman, 1948) that they have found it essential to report the error band associated with a forecast. This error band may be substantially widened by the fact that a non-trivial number of the respondents may be unable or unwilling to state a preference, and there is no guarantee that these non-respondents mirror at all the committed portion of the population.

Results from macroeconometric model simulations should be routinely presented as

$$\hat{y}_{T+F} \pm k\hat{S}_y$$

where $\hat{y}_{T+F}$ is the forecast value of y in period F, after the end of the sample T, and k is a multiple associated with a given degree of probability (the higher the probability of enclosing the "true" value, the larger the value of k). $\hat{S}_y$ is an estimate of the standard error of forecast.

The formulas for estimated standard errors of forecast are formidable for large systems. In principle they take into account the errors associated with (1) random disturbances, (2) sampling variability of the system's parameter estimates (variance and covariance), and (3) the magnitude of exogenous or lagged endogenous variables. For small systems, it is possible to use the formulas developed by Goldberger, Nagar and Odeh (1961). For large systems, it seems best to use the Monte Carlo approach of George Schink (1971). In any event, non-linearity would suggest a Monte Carlo approach.

From time to time, forecast errors have been evaluated for main magnitudes of individual models; this is helpful in an indicative sense, but it would be more satisfactory to have all forecast error estimates of all the endogenous variables and an appropriate degree of probability.

---

[2]See also the discussion of stochastic simulations and optimal control problems, in the context of large models, in the two preceding chapters.

The ability to do this, at least in principle, is one of the great advantages of the econometric modeling approach. Some other methods of forecasting or policy analysis are not well suited to the presentation of error bands. The formula for the variance of forecast error for a projection of an endogenous variable from a linear model is:

$$Var\,\hat{y}_{T+F} = F_{T+F}\Omega_\pi F'_{T+F} + \sum_\nu$$

where F_{T+F} is an $n \times mn$ matrix display of exogenous variables at forecast period $T + F$, $\Omega\pi$ is an $mn \times mn$ covariance matrix of derived estimated reduced form coefficients ($\pi = A^{-1}B$), and $\sum_\nu$ is an $n \times n$ covariance matrix of reduced form disturbances ($A^{-1}e_t$). The associated model is $Ay_t + Bx_t = e_t$. There are n endogenous variables (y_t) and m exogenous variables (x_t). (It is assumed that there are no lagged endogenous variables appearing in the model, which is obvious limitation, but one that could be taken into account.)

The system may be approximated linearly in the neighborhood of the solution value, and then the formula can be evaluated for that approximate system, or replicated stochastic simulation techniques can be used to generate a whole distribution of forecasts, and the variance of this distribution can be computed. Either approach will be very computer-intensive, but this should be done with every forecast in the future in order to know what is expected with regard to accuracy.

At the same time, a comprehensive record has been compiled by Stephen McNees and associates for a wide variety of variables and models covering the period (by quarters) since 1970.[3] From these tabulations we can compute absolute and squared deviations from actual values, appropriately averaged. This gives experienced error, not expected error based on estimated distributions of stochastic elements. Probability measures to be associated with McNees's tabulations are not known, but his records are extremely valuable in showing what can be learned from experience.

4. Control Theory Applications

Control theory applied to economic systems is, like error analysis, interesting in its own right, quite apart from the computational issues involved. It is not necessarily the case that control theory will be used to try to control the actual economy or make policy directly, in an optimal way. The principal contribution of control theory to macroeconometric modeling is to teach us something about the properties of estimated systems. By pushing a system towards stringent target values, we learn whether or not it behaves well under stress and whether the optimal values of instrument variables make sense. If the system produces unacceptable results, in terms of extreme values for instruments, or if it is pushed into forbidden territory (violating limits of non-negativity, for example), we may have reason to question the specification or estimated structure of the system.

---

[3] A recent publication in this series of studies is McNees and Ries (1983).

Also, we have little guidance for the choice of exogenous inputs into the medium (five year) or long-run (ten or more years) forecasts. Control theory methods can be used to find *baseline* values of the inputs (exogenous instrument variables) which will bring the system towards *balanced growth paths* or paths with well established long-run properties, such as:

1. real growth rate = real interest rate;
2. labor's share = constant;
3. personal saving rates = constant.

In connection with the multi-model problem for the LINK system, an interesting application of control theory was used in order to determine numerically the degree of perceived "overvaluation" of the U.S. dollar in 1984. During the closing years of the Bretton Woods system of fixed parities among currencies, the exchange rates for each country were taken as exogenous variables — fixed by international agreement. An approach for estimating exchange rates is to set a series of targets for current account or trade balances for each country and to ask, through the methods of control theory, what estimated exchange rate values would bring the countries of the world to their balance of payments targets simultaneously over a period of two years. This is the special case, first pointed out by Jan Tinbergen (1956), where the number of targets and instruments are equal. If the control theory calculation is done appropriately, we should find a zero value for the loss function

$$L(y_1 - y_1^*, y_2 - y_2^*, \ldots, y_n - y_n^*)$$

where $L(0, 0, \cdots, 0) = 0$ and y_i^* is the target for the ith variable $y_i, i = 1, 2, \cdots, n$. Calculation of this problem was done in 1984, and existing trade balances were modified by reducing the surplus positions of Japan and West Germany considerably and by allocating about one-half of this reduction towards the improvement of the U.S. balance and the remaining portion to the remaining trading partners. The control theory calculation seemed to suggest that the U.S. dollar was overvalued by roughly 30 per cent in 1984, a very plausible result, given the large number of other independent calculations which also came to this approximate value.[4]

When these and other control theory applications have been made routine in model testing, estimation and use (application), we shall have made an important step forward. There is every reason to expect this to happen in the near future.

5. Lags and Expectations

Of all the refinements in econometric methodology, none is more important in contributing to better results than the elaborate and sophisticated use of economic dynamics in specifying the structure of economic systems. Deep and extensive exploration of lag structure has done at least as much, and probably more, good in

---

[4]We note with some satisfaction the adjustment in the exchange value of the U.S. dollar between early 1985 and the time of writing (autumn 1989).

improving econometric model performance than all other refinements in estimation procedure or methodology.

Over the years we have progressed from using one, two, or three period lags, freely estimated, to using geometric lags (applying Koyck transformations), to Almon polynomial lag distributions, Shiller lag distributions, Pascal lag distributions, and rational polynomial lag distributions. These are all important steps, some more general than others, but each contributing to our better understanding of dynamic structure.

The advances were made possible through the exploitation of the computer because search or iteration is usually involved. The most important aspect of the advance has been the freeing of our ability to estimate lags in several variables simultaneously. The general expression for a single equation (the ith equation of a system) is:

$$\alpha_i(L)y_t + \beta_i(L)x_t = \gamma_i(L)e_t$$

where:

α_i, β_i and γ_i = row vectors of parameters associated with equation i;

y_t = column vector of endogenous variables;

x_t = column vector of exogenous variables;

e_t = column vector of lagged values of the scalar variable e_{it}, the error term associated with equation i at time t; and

L = lag operator, that is, $L^j z_t = z_{t-j}$.

In a sense, if we can search, with the computer, for the best Box–Jenkins estimate of the ith relation, in the sense that *equilibrium* or steady-state form of the equation satisfies *a priori* economic restrictions, then we shall have good system dynamics.

Economic theory is often fairly explicit about the foundations for the equilibrium form of the equation but offers practically no guidance about the underlying dynamics. That part is empirical and therefore computer-intensive. The importance of lag distribution specification is that it restricts the parameter space for the feasible set of estimates and therefore conserves degrees of freedom, as well as offering some protection against multicollinearity.

A school of thought about the structure of lag distributions is the so-called "rational expectations" school, who assert that economic agents use the dynamic model solution to project their own expected values, thus implying a specific lag distribution. As suggested in the preceding chapter, however, there is an identification problem, which makes it unlikely that we shall be able to discriminate in specification between the lag distributions generated by "rational expectations" and those generated by assuming one of the well-known *a priori* distributions.

To the extent that economic behavior establishes agents' reactions to *expected* values, we might try to estimate explicitly, rather than implicitly, the lag distributions associated with the formation of expectations. In this respect, a promising area of research is the collection of agents' stated expectations from sample surveys, and the estimation of the relevant equations for relationships of reaction as well as the relationships showing how the stated expectations are determined by empirical equations containing lag distributions.

In a simple case, we should have:

$$y_{1t} = f(y_{2t}^*) + e_t$$
$$y_{2t}^* = g(y_{1,t-1}, y_{1,t-2}, \ldots, y_{2,t-1}, y_{2,t-2}, \ldots, y_{3,t-1},$$
$$y_{3,t-2}, \ldots, y_{n,t-1}, y_{n,t-2}, \ldots) + u_t,$$

where y_{2t}^* is expected value of y_{2t}. In this illustrative example, y_{2t}^* is made to depend on the chronological evolution of many variables, not simply on its own history.

A great deal of effort has been spent on estimating such equation from consumer and business surveys. Expectation equations generated from such sources are used in some macroeconometric models and future exploitation of these ideas is likely to be one of the coming developments of our subject.

6. Use of Cross-Section Data

In a broader sense the collection of stated expectations from individual agents can be used in cross-section as well as time-series variation. There is all too little use of cross-section data in the construction of macroeconometric models.

There is a long history of the use of family budget data to estimate Engel curves and associated elasticities. Similarly, inter-establishment or inter-industry data have been used extensively to estimate production functions. These microeconomic relationships may, under some simplifying assumptions, be used for the estimation of aggregative relationships. The key bridging relationship in the aggregation procedure is the underlying distribution function, such as the distribution of income among households or the size distribution of firms.

New advances in understanding and estimating the distribution functions can lend great richness in the specification of macro-models because it enables one to go behind the aggregates and make some estimates of distribution factors. Further work in this direction has the potential of enabling us to build better and more useful models.

The supplementation of aggregative time-series samples with data from cross-sections can lead to a significant improvement in our understanding of behavior and in developing model structure, but it cannot be a breakthrough. It will simply be incremental. These types of data have been used frequently in the past; so we are not entering an unexplored field of statistical analysis. It is simply a case of not having fully integrated cross-section samples and the associated relationships estimated from them into macroeconometric models as fully as possible.

Every new piece of information helps, and a few pieces may be picked up through our carefully considering micro data from individual economic agents.

7. Flow-of-Funds Models

A good deal of progress has been made in adding financial detail to macro-models. As we saw in part in Chap. 2, the earliest attempts by Tinbergen put much effort into financial modeling for the United States (and for the United Kingdom). In particular, he investigated the boom–bust cycle of the stock market in the United States during the 1920s and 1930s. He also looked at the development of the UK economy in the era of the gold standard.

Preoccupation with the fiscal structure of Keynesian models diverted some attention from financial aspects, but, in the past quarter-century, when credit crises (or crunches) have had such visibly large effects on macroeconomic performance, it has become imperative to pay more attention again to the financial side of economic structure.

Keynesian models always had a financial sector, and Keynes was personally occupied with financial transactions of a sophisticated nature, but some of the early models, apart from Tinbergen's study of the United States in the 1920s and 1930s, had loosely connected financial and real sectors.

In the reconstruction period following the Second World War, the real economy dominated the situation through the process of demobilization, implementation of the Marshall plan in Europe, and the waging of war in Korea. Once the reconstruction period was completed, interest rates moved in a wide range, and financial markets assumed greater importance.

Many models with elaborate financial content have been built for the Federal Reserve System, for other central banks outside the United States and for non-banking institutions also. Mention must be made of the DRI contribution (Eckstein, Green and Sinai, 1974; Eckstein, 1983), which employed the data in the flow-of-funds accounts. These accounts serve as an elaborate data base for financial models in the same sense that national income accounts and input–output accounts serve real sector models, including real sector models with moderately detailed production sectors.[5]

The flow-of-funds accounts do not have as long a history as do the national income accounts and they contain more data gaps. In general, they are less accurate and less well developed than the national income accounts; nevertheless they are very important and play a strategic role in gaining an understanding of financial behavior. These accounts attempt to show the flow of transactions involving financial instruments on a "from-whom"/"to-whom" basis. Financial instruments have issuing agents and holding agents, in stock or level form. The first differences of these stocks are the flows of financial assets and liabilities among the main groups of the domestic macro economy:

commercial banks,

thrift institutions,

---

[5]It may be noted that, in recent years even without explicit use of flow-of-funds accounts, many standard macroeconometric models have contained moderately detailed financial sectors.

the central bank,

the treasury,

insurance companies,

other financial businesses,

non-financial businesses,

households, and

rest-of-the-world.

The process of equating supplies and demands for all instruments determines a set of asset prices. These, in turn, determine interest rates. The "perpetuity" asset has a simple reciprocal relationship to interest rates:

$$p = l/r \, .$$

Finite length bonds and other instruments are related to interest yields in more complicated formulas. But the important issue is that the spectrum of interest rates is determined by the spectrum of instrument prices. This is more specific, and more complicated, than the usual procedure of explaining only a key rate by market equations and spinning off the spectrum of rates through equations of the term structure.

It is more fundamental and ultimately easier to take account of specific institutional features of the financial system to determine rates on mortgages, commercial paper, broker loans, certificates of deposits, retirement accounts, municipal bonds, corporate bonds, bank loans and other instruments by employing supply and demand equations in each of these markets than by doing it in only one (short-term) market and relating other rates to such a key rate.

A full flow-of-funds model is not complete by itself. It needs to be integrated with both national income and input–output models. It appears from the writings of Eckstein and associates (cited above) that this is precisely what has been done in the DRI Model of the U.S. economy, although it has been somewhat difficult to judge, as the description of the individual sectors is sometimes sketchy. In any case, it may be asserted that a complete treatment of the financial sector by means of a flow-of-funds submodel may well be one of the most important contributions that has been made in macroeconometric modeling.

It is worth elaborating a special aspect of the flow-of-funds accounts. Record-keeping has been generally good for international transactions, especially in current price terms. Often it is hard to obtain the associated real and price series that accompany the current value flows. But model-building for the balance of payments is perhaps better known and established.

First, we must account for the flows of imports and exports. This is routine in mainstream macroeconometric models. In world trade or multi-country models, such as Project LINK, the additional detail of bilateral trade flow estimates is also generated by the model. The new feature, however, is the modeling of exchange rates. These rates have been (largely) market-determined for more than a decade; before then, the Bretton Woods system of fixed parities determined exchange rates.

Many of the relevant variables for explaining exchange rates are readily available from macro-models of the real economy and for world trade. But large and volatile capital flows between pairs of countries are not yet very well understood. Why does financial capital leave some shores and enter others? This is inherently a difficult question and we do not have good answers yet. We do not even have good data on bilateral capital flows between nations.[6]

Special modeling of international capital flows and estimation of exchanges rates from the equating of supply and demand for currencies are problems that are attracting a great deal of attention from econometricians and are sure to result in some new knowledge.[7] A partial filling of the gaps remaining in flow-of-funds modeling will be taken care of by this research, and the solution of problems of building international macro-models will be advanced. In a limited way, it is possible that a breakthrough could occur here.

8. International Modeling

The capital flow/exchange rate problems discussed in connection with flow-of-funds model-building represent but one of several different directions being followed in international model-building. Work will continue in Project LINK, the OECD Interlink Model, the Japanese EPA model of the world economy, the Federal Reserve Multi-Country Model, and others with much attention focused on the OECD (industrial market) economies. Two other groups of countries will also be the subject of both national model-building efforts and internationally linked efforts. These are the developing countries (LDC) and the centrally-planned economies (CPE).[8] In the case of China, there are joint aspects of LDC and CPE model-building.

For the most part, data for the LDCs and the CPEs are less available and less reliable. The usual time frame is annual, with data spans existing over two or three decades. The problem is thus constrained, but headway is being made. All the socialist countries of Eastern Europe, the USSR and China have had models estimated for their economies.[9] Many, but not all, developing countries have been modeled. There are sure to be more than 90 different developing countries for which models are available.[10]

These models have special features. The socialist systems must be built around the planning process. The LDC models must be sensitive to special export lines

---

[6] An attempt has been made in this direction by Kanta Marwah and L. R. Klein (1983).

[7] See Marwah (1985) and the references contained in this paper.

[8] See Chaps. 11 and 12 above, for a historical treatment of macroeconometric model-building in the case of two groups of LDCs. In the case of the CPEs, we were unsuccessful in an attempt to furnish a historical account of these developments.

[9] See W. Welfe (1983).

[10] Goetz Uebec *et al.* (1988) list approximately 90 LDCs (depending upon the classification) for which macroeconometric models are available.

(often primary commodities), migrant workers, essential imports (capital and materials), servicing of external debts, and income distribution. The econometric study of individual countries in the CPE or LDC categories has progressed far and will continue to improve with the study of single countries. Within Project LINK, the most recent research step has been to add some 30 or 40 LDC Models to those of the OECD and CPE regions already present on an individual country basis, and to integrate these models into the linkage mechanisms. In the spring of 1988, the matrices of trade in the worldwide LINK system consisted of 79 rows and columns, a formidable undertaking. There are many good years of research activity which remain to be taken up in polishing and augmenting models for developing countries; therefore this looks like an attractive direction for future work.

9. The Reduction of Exogeneity

Economic behavior is a major part of societal behavior; however it is obvious that the explanation of economic behavior can fruitfully be expanded along research lines established in other disciplines. Promising work in neighboring disciplines span demography, criminology, health, psychology, and engineering.

Demography already appears in macro-models and has been considered for a long time — since Malthus, in a sense, or since model-builders recognized at an early stage that per-capita formulations of economic relationships were advantageous. But, generally speaking, population size and composition were introduced as exogenous variables that had impacts on the economy without there being adequate analysis to explain population dynamics in their own right. Now there is much more concern with modeling population characteristics through birth rates, fertility rates, death rates, rates of immigration and emigration, and age–sex–race distributions of labor force, employment, income or wage earnings. The beginnings of an endogenous treatment of demography are in place, but much more needs to be done, and it can be expected that future models will go much further in this regard. Endogenous treatment of population should contribute to an overall improvement in accuracy and, for long-term models, this is a necessity. This is especially true in model-building for developing countries, where population characteristics are of predominant importance. But, most of all, the generation of population variables in econometric applications — projections, scenarios, policy simulations, multiplier analysis — will be another manifestation of the tendency to provide immediately useful information for users of model results. In specific industries, economic analysts need to know about the size of the infant, teenage, adult or aged population. Government policy — for social security retirement programmes, Medicare, unemployment compensation, disability pay — leans heavily on demographic projections, which ideally should go hand-in-hand with economic projections.

While demography may be the first externally related area to be incorporated endogenously into macroeconometric models, it is certainly not the only one. Criminal activity is already in the data base, implicitly, as crime in the form of shoplifting or theft from businesses shows up as a transfer payment (business to household sector) in the national income accounts, while the under-reporting of income from criminal operations may be partially embedded in the statistical discrepancy of the accounts. (Of course, conceptually the income from criminal activities does not form a part of national income, while the social costs of law enforcement are indeed a part of GNP, on both the expenditures and the income sides of the national accounts.) Crime is influenced by the state of the economy and has some feedback on the macro economy; therefore an explanation of its influence, together with related economic variables, should be integrated into models. The financial sums associated with crime are far from trivial. Since they play roles in day-to-day economic life, they must be explained, together with legitimate income sources, or, in other words, they must become conventional endogenous variables of macro-models.[11]

Health expenditures are closely associated with ageing, the raising of children, and other aspects of the life cycle; accordingly, a full endogenous treatment of demography would implicitly include health. There are, however, many aspects of health economics that arise, apart from the association with demography.

The health sector of the economy is an important producing sector. In a large-scale model with many inter-industry relationships (an input–output system), the health industry figures importantly because it is fast-growing; it is one of the high-technology sectors that figures importantly in future economic growth; it absorbs many people who gravitate towards the service industries; it is a sector where costs have been rising by unusually large amounts; and it is an important and growing sector of consumption. These and other aspects argue for its full explanation and integration into the equation systems of macroeconomics. When it is integrated, there should be careful attention paid to the professional medical side in order to capture technical progress.

Social psychology has played an important part in developing the use of sample surveys of human populations for the analysis of consumer and business behavior. The writings of George Katona were replete with efforts to bring psychological methods and theory into economics. This has been done in large measure through the survey approach, which asks people about their plans, expectations and perceptions of the economy, as well as their own positions. The survey instrument provided some lead time from which to infer psychological influences on economic behavior, but the "shelf-life" of these pieces of information is only of a few months. In order to bring them effectively into models for longer time periods it is necessary to develop a theory or model of subjective attitudes, clearly a psychological problem, but also a problem with effect on, *and feedback from*, the economy.

An exposition of the way this problem has been handled in the past is provided by descriptions of the "anticipations version" of the Wharton Model.[12] The new interest in the generation of expectations in economic models provides added in-

---

[11] Gary Becker's seminal article (1968) on the economics of crime has already inspired a number of econometric studies in this area.
[12] See F. G. Adams and L. R. Klein (1972).

centive to turn to the problem of introducing psychology into economic models and developing endogenous explanation of many psychological magnitudes. Eventually this theoretical excursion should take up such problems as the spread of economic panic, imitative behavior, fashion, fads and general bandwagon or contagion effects, as well as an investigation of whether expectations are "rational."

The entire input–output system, dealing with the laws of production, has strong engineering foundations. This extends to the concept of the production function — macro, micro or inter-industry. In medium- to long-term econometric applications, there is a strong engineering aspect to the study of technical progress.

In connection with the energy crisis, starting in 1973, the engineering foundations of energy analysis became important. Economists had to learn something about engineering aspects of energy before they could make a proper assessment of the impact of changing terms of trade for energy products. A proper technical or engineering treatment of energy supply and energy production became essential and finally emerged. Production functions of macroeconometric models shifted in great measure from:

$$X_{\nu a} = f(L, K, t),$$

to

$$X_g = g(K, L, E, M; t), \quad \text{where}$$

$$
\begin{aligned}
X_{\nu a} &= \text{real valued added;} \\
L &= \text{labor input;} \\
K &= \text{capital input;} \\
X_g &= \text{real gross input;} \\
E &= \text{energy input;} \\
M &= \text{material input;} \\
t &= \text{chronological time.}
\end{aligned}
$$

This latter type of production function (the so-called "KLEM" production function) is an important, fundamental change in econometric specification and is engineering-based. The endogenous treatment of E and M is essentially an engineering problem, and we can look upon these two variables as a type of engineering variables because they are related to the structure of production.

In some models the analysis has been carried much further by introducing energy type and materials type. Types of labor and capital are also disaggregated. The engineering production function is capable of traveling far in the direction of disaggregation.

Finally, the explanation of technical progress, not just the statistical estimation of time trend effects, requires the introduction of engineering information. In moving forward over decades or more one needs the generation of technical progress, which is, to a large extent in one view, an exercise in engineering. In another view, technical progress is an endogenous phenomenon reflecting managerial considerations, particularly profitable opportunities for innovation.

10. Macroeconomic Model-Building Under Attack

In recent years, macroeconometric model-building has come under severe criticism from knowledgeable observers. Thus Hendry (1980) raises the question of whether applied econometric is closer to "alchemy" than to "science," while Leamer (1983) suggests, "Let's take the 'con' out of econometrics." In addition Sims (1980) suggested that current macroeconometric models are badly under-identified and that an alternative approach (based on employing unrestricted reduced forms which treat *all* variables as endogenous) be used.

Space does not permit a detailed comment on any of these three challenging papers. One can interpret Leamer's paper as reminding us that pure macroeconometric modeling can never replace judgement in the formulation of wide economic policies, or even in the tentative assessment of the state of the world.[13] Hendry, while he begins with an example of a regression that is quite spurious (but not much worse than many in the literature, he claims), argues that best-practice econometric (characterized by heavy testing, particularly within the sample, of the fitted relationships) can go far to making applied econometrics (which presumably includes macroeconometric modeling) respectable.[14] Sim's critique is perhaps the most difficult of all, yet paradoxically perhaps the easiest with which to come to grips. Sim's arguments about under-identification really seem to be philosophical issues, about which reasonable scholars can indeed differ.[15] Moreover the constructive alternative that Sims proposes seems most unattractive for large systems, of the type that Sims appears to recognize are needed for policy purposes. The reluctance to impose some structure, in a large system, would appear to guarantee in advance that useful results could not be obtained. In terms of needed useful simplifications, we prefer our own (the orthodox variety) to those suggested by Sims.

The most formidable critique to the use of macroeconometric models as a guide to aggregative economic policy would appear, however, to originate with the "ratio-

---

[13]Of course, there is slightly more to Leamer's article than this. As a Bayesian, Leamer argues strongly for a Bayesian approach to the use of econometric tools to obtain new knowledge.

[14]Hendry also comments that the then existing macroeconometric models "broke down" in the face of the oil price shocks of 1973-4, which he implies would not have happened had the model-builders followed the "best practice" that he recommends. We should only comment that this "break-down" was a relative matter, as some models were able to function (make predictions and policy analyses) with suitable adjustment of the constant terms. But, wherever one stands in this evaluation, surely it is legitimate to allow model-builders to learn from past mistakes, particularly when the external environment shifts. One of our major themes in this book is the continuing (if not monotonic) progress in model-building, which of course implies that one will learn from the mistakes of the past.

[15]As Sims recognizes, the argument is very similar to that put forward by T. C. Liu (1960) a generation ago. One of us (Klein) considered that point of view at that time and found it unattractive, from a philosophical point of view. Sim's repackaging of the argument has not led us to change our minds in this matter.

nal expectations hypothesis" and the related "Lucas critique" of macroeconometric model-building (Lucas, 1976). Briefly stated, the argument would appear to be the following: economic agents have preferred plans of action, and so they will take into account *any* systematic action of policy-makers. Accordingly, this will mean (Lucas gives several extended examples in the paper cited) that the parameters of the system are dependent on the policy regime in force when the relationships of the system were estimated. This would also imply that, were a new set of policies to be implemented (generally with the goal of improving economic welfare as the policy-makers see matters), the parameters of the system *will shift* systematically. Thus the system would break down and in particular would no longer permit a sound prediction (even a conditional prediction) of the likely consequences of a new policy action.[16] Obviously this would be quite a severe criticism of macroeconometric modeling in general — if the argument could be sustained.

However one can argue that the *empirical* significance of such a criticism is not terribly important. If this were the case, then (minor) regime changes from this source could easily be absorbed into the disturbance terms of the stochastic equations of the model, and previous techniques of using macroeconometric models could continue more or less as before. In his 1983 book, Otto Eckstein made an extensive study of past forecasting errors with the DRI Model of the U.S. economy, to see whether he might detect a systematic tendency, on the part of the model, to produce greater forecasting errors when macroeconomic policy was undergoing obvious regime changes. His conclusion was negative: "So far, the evidence suggests that changes in policy regimes are not among the principal causes of simulation error, that forecast error is largely created by other exogenous factors and the stochastic character of the economy" (Eckstein, 1983, p. 51). Instead, Eckstein points to other sources of regime change, such as wars, civil disturbances and OPEC oil price shocks. Indeed it is a somewhat contrived argument to claim that parameters in macroeconometric models are very particular functions of policy choices. In variable parameter systems that we attempt to deal with through non-linearities and equation shifts, other sources of parameter variation undoubtedly dominate policy changes.

Moreover one can criticize the Lucas critique and the associated rational expectations view of the macroeconomy on the theoretical grounds also. One aspect of the Lucas critique asserts that the economic agents use all the information available, in order to produce expectations (or forecasts) of the endogenous variables that are unbiased. This is often interpreted to assert that, if one is using a macroeconomic model (econometric or other kind) for purposes of analysis, one should assume that the agents in general will have this information available to them. (In a complicated, non-linear model, it is not clear to us that this is equivalent to supposing

---

[16]In the monetary area, this has come to be known as "Goodhart's Law," after Charles Goodhart, a British monetary economist. As summarized by Goodhart himself (1986), this law asserts, "Any statistical regularity, notably in the monetary area, will break down when pressure is placed upon it for control purposes."

that the agents have the ability to produce unbiased forecasts.) In criticizing this view, we may remark, following Klein (1982), that it is difficult to imagine a typical citizen, untrained in macroeconomics, coming to the same specific conclusions as a professional economist on an issue of macroeconomic policy, let alone following the same specific steps in the reasoning process.[17] The general statement that economic agents base their decisions on all the information available to them at the time that these choices are made is an excellent point that most model-builders have had in mind and have tried to implement for some time. There is nothing very special about rational expectations theory that proves that this way is the only way to interpret the behavior of agents. Such an interpretation can be done in an infinite variety of ways, one of which has been extensively pursued by model-builders for more than 40 years, namely to generate sample survey response indicators as endogenous variables of models by relating them to many other endogenous variables that are available at the time decisions are made. In addition, two other considerations, pointed out by Eckstein, suggest limitations of the theoretical underpinning of the rational expectations hypothesis. Work with macroeconometric models in general (and the DRI model in particular) suggests that the hypothesis of continuous market-clearing is a quite inadequate description of the historical record. Second, more than first moments of subjective probability distributions may matter, if economic agents are risk-averse. Because both household and business decision-makers appear to be risk averters, the expected variances of outputs and prices may play a role, with agents reducing their planned spending on consumption and investment if the expected variance increases. (This is Eckstein's explanation of the apparently surprising result that the partial effect of increased inflation may be to *diminish* real consumption expenditure.) Accordingly, while the challenge raised by the rational expectations school has raised some important questions about the dynamics of the macroeconomy (in particular, with the nature and characteristics of expectations formation and also the kinds of lag distributions appropriate for macroeconomic variables), we doubt that this critique is applicable in its present form.

11. Structural Change

A dilemma for econometricians in both micro and macro analysis has been that large samples of time-series data spanning periods of 50 to 100 years run the risk of encountering changes in the economic environment that induce structural changes in models; whereas confinement to small, short samples of time-series data, while preserving homogeneity of structure over the sample span, provides too few degrees of freedom for reliable statistical inference.

---

[17]Of course, this assumes not only that the model in question is the true one, but also that the typical agent recognizes this and has no doubts on this score. (Mitigated conclusions follow if the typical agent considers the possibility that two or more models may be the "correct" one; see Holden, Peel and Thompson (1982), Chap. 6.) But if professional economists cannot decide what is the true model, is it "rational" (in the non-technical sense of this word) to expect the general public to be able to do so?

This is not an easy problem to resolve, but our tastes are for having as much information as possible in time-series that are as long as possible. If there is solid evidence of structural change, then this aspect of economic life should be incorporated into model structure. But we also take the view that there is more stability than volatility in economic behavior. (In particular, we argued in the preceding section that changes in policy regimes are unlikely to produce *major* structural changes.) There is good evidence that fundamental economic behavior survived the enormous upheaval of the Second World War. Interwar relationships from the much studied period of the 1920s and 1930s returned, after a transitional reconstruction period, to old patterns in the 1950s or at least by the 1960s. This was true in many countries — in North America, Europe and the Far East — where long time-series are available.

This issue is relevant in this forward-looking chapter, concluding our historical survey of macroeconometric model-building, because some people claim that we are now in a new era where the structure of the economy is different because we might have:

1. persistently large public deficits,
2. persistent trade imbalances,
3. unusual international currency alignments,
4. higher (than previous) levels of unemployment, and
5. stagflation.

Most of these new environmental conditions are manifestations of disequilibrium. It is not likely that they will persist indefinitely. But the most important thing to be pointed out is that individuals do not show evidence of changing fundamentally over long historical stretches. It is remarkable that some recent estimates of Engel curves from modern China (1982) (Hu *et al.*, 1984) show characteristics that are remarkably close to those reported by Houthakker (1975) for China of the 1920s in his article on the centenary of Engel's Law.

Politicians cannot repeal the laws of economics; they can distort them for relatively short periods of time. Short-run macroeconometric models should take account of these distortions and should also take account of new goods or new technical processes, but they should not be hasty in following fads that would try to negate the persistence of the patterns of fundamental human behavior.

12. Conclusions

As this chapter suggests, we feel that there are a number of interesting, even fascinating, research problems that remain to be tackled. The current generation of young macroeconometricians have a number of challenges in front of them. There is no need for boredom or indifference in the face of the tasks which remain.

At the same time, we feel optimistic with regard to the solution of most, if not all, of the challenges outlined in this chapter. Models of the future will be better models, in part because most of the challenges outlined above will have been solved. New developments, as yet unforeseen, will also undoubtedly contribute to the improvement of future generations of macroeconometric models. We see these improvements as occurring not only in the realm of scientific discourse but also in the domain of practical applicability, for purposes of public policy and commercial applications. Thus it is our view that builders of macroeconometric models can face the future with hope and enthusiasm, both in terms of the contributions that will be made and also in terms of the demand for their services. As indicated in the initial section of this chapter, we see a continuation of growth, at least for the next decade or so, in the macroeconometric model-building industry.

References

Adams, F. G. and L. R. Klein, 1972, "Anticipations variables in macro-econometric models," in *Human Behavior in Economic Affairs*, eds. B. Strumpel, J. N. Morgan and E. Zahn (Elsevier, Amsterdam), pp. 289–319.

Becker, G. S. , 1968, "Crime and punishment: An economic approach," *Journal of Political Economy* **76**, no. 2 (March/April), pp. 164–314.

Eckstein, Otto, 1983, *The DRI Model of the U. S. Economy*, (McGraw-Hill, New York).

Eckstein, O., E. W. Green, and A. Sinai, 1974, "The data resources model: Uses, structure and analysis of the U.S. economy," *International Economic Review* **15**, no. 2 (October), pp. 595–615.

Goldberger, A. S., A. L. Nagar, and H. S. Odeh, 1961, "The covariance matrices of reduced form coefficients and of forecasts of a structural econometric model," *Econometrica* **29**, no. 4 (October), pp. 556–573.

Goodhart, C. A. E., 1986, "Autobiographical sketch", in *Who's Who in Economics*, 2nd edn., ed. Mark Blaug (MIT Press, Cambridge, Mass.) pp. 322–333.

Hendry, D. F., 1980, "Econometrics — Alchemy or Science?," *Economica*, N. S. **47**, no. 188 (November), pp. 387–406.

Holden, K., D. A. Peel, and J. L. Thompson, 1982, *Modelling the UK Economy: An Introduction* (Martin Robertson & Company, Oxford).

Houthakker, H. S., 1957, "An international comparison of household expenditure patterns, commemorating the centenary of Engel's law," *Econometrica* **25**, no. 4 (October), pp. 532–550.

Hu, Teh-wei, Bai Jushan, and Shi Shuzhong, 1984, "Household expenditure patterns in a large Chinese city" (unpublished), Pennsylvania State University and Nankai University, Tianjin.

Klein, L. R., 1982, "The present debate about macro economics and econometric model specification," *Chung-Hua Series of Lectures by Invited Eminent Economists*, no. 5 (Institute of Economics, Academia Sinica, Taipei, Taiwan, July).

————, P. Pauly and P. Voisin, 1982, "The world economy — A global model," *Perspectives in Computing* **2** (May) pp. 4–17.

Leamer, E. E., 1983, "Let's take the con out of econometrics," *American Economic Review* **73**, no. 1 (March), pp. 31–43.

Liu, T. C., 1960, "Underidentification, structural estimation and forecasting," *Econometrica* **28**, no. 4 (October), pp. 855–865.

Lucas, R. E. Jr, 1976, "Econometric policy evaluation: A critique," in *The Phillips Curve and Labor Markets*, eds. A. H. Meltzer and K. Brunner, (North-Holland, Amsterdam,) pp. 19–46; Carnegie–Rochester Conference Series on Public Policy, vol. 1, *Supplement* to the *Journal of Monetary Economics*; also reprinted in his (1981) *Studies in Business-Cycle Theory* (MIT Press, Cambridge, Mass.), pp. 104–130.

Marwah, K., 1985, "A prototype model of the foreign exchange market of Canada: forecasting capital flows and exchange rates," *Economic Modelling* **2**, no. 2 (April), pp. 93–124.

————, and L. R. Klein, 1983, "A Model of foreign exchange markets: Endogenizing capital flows and exchange rates," in *Capital Flows and Exchange Rate Determination*, eds. L. R. Klein and W. E. Krelle, Supplementum **3**, *Zeitschrift für Nationalökonomie/Journal of Economics*, pp. 61–95.

McNees, S. K. and J. Ries, 1983 "The track record of macroeconomic forecasts," *New England Economic Review*, (Nov./Dec.), pp. 5–18.

Schink, G., 1971, "Small sample estimates of the variance–covariance matrix of forecast errors for large econometric models: The stochastic simulation approach," unpublished PhD thesis, University of Pennsylvania, 1971.

Sims, C. A., 1980 "Macroeconomics and reality," *Econometrica* **48**, no. 1 (January), pp. 1–48.

Tinbergen, J., 1952, *On the Theory of Economic Policy* (North-Holland, Amsterdam).

————, 1956, *Economic Policy: Principles and Design* (North-Holland, Amsterdam).

Uebe, Goetz, Georg Huber, and Joachim Fischer, 1988, *Macro-Econometric Models: An International Bibliography* (Gower, Aldershot).

Welfe, W., 1983, "Models of the socialist economy," in L. R. Klein, *Lectures in Econometrics* (North-Holland, Amsterdam, New York and Oxford), Appendix, pp. 197–227.

Editorial Notes

Chapter references are to *A History of Macroeconometric Model-Building*.

12

MODEL BUILDING TO CONFORM TO
A COMPLETE SYSTEM OF SOCIAL ACCOUNTS[†]

1. Three Accounting Systems

National income and product accounting has a long and established historical position in the quantitative analysis of the macroeconomy. These accounts, invaluable as they are, give only a partial picture of the economic process and need to be supplemented by interindustry (input–output) accounts and the flow of funds (sources and uses) accounts.

National income and product accounts: The primary function of the national income accounts (NIA) is to show two equivalent valuations of aggregate social product. On the one hand, we obtain an aggregate valuation on the *product* side as the total amount of money spent on newly produced goods and services in a given accounting period. This is called the gross national product (GNP) or the net national product (NNP) depending on whether or not we subtract capital consumption for the accounting period.

On the other hand, we obtain an aggregate valuation on the income side as the total payments to the factors of production that are employed in producing the totality of products in the accounting period. This is called the national income (NI). By accounting convention, profit or surplus must be regarded as a factor payment in order to make the two valuations come to the same total.

Were it not for various institutional arrangements, accounting delays, and errors of observation we would always have the equality

$$\text{NNP} = \text{NI}. \tag{1.1}$$

Instead, we use in practical work, the modified relationship

$$\text{NNP} = \text{NI} + (\text{Reconciling items}). \tag{1.2}$$

The reconciling items in the American case consist of indirect taxes, subsidies, surplus of public enterprises, business transfers, and of course the statistical discrepancy. In model building, the reconciling items are individually estimated by simple institutional relationships, as in the case of indirect taxes, or treated as exogenous. Ignoring the existence of the statistical discrepancy, we use (1.2) as an accounting equation for the determination of profit; i.e., this total is treated as a residual item.

[†]From The Symposium on National Economy Modeling, Novosibirsk, USSR, June 1970, p. 31.

Accounting balance equations occur in other places in the construction of macro-economic equation systems. The main instances are

$$S + C = Y \qquad \text{household account} \qquad (1.3)$$

S = personal saving

C = personal consumption expenditures

Y = personal income

$$T + D = G \qquad \text{government account} \qquad (1.4)$$

T = tax and other public receipts

D = deficit

G = government expenditures on goods and services

$$M + B = E \qquad \text{external account} \qquad (1.5)$$

M = imports of goods and services

B = trade balance

E = exports of goods and services.

Separate aggregate accounts may be set up for different units of economic activity, in this case for households, public authorities, and foreigners. The balance equations for each account insure that total receipts just match total outlays, provided a balancing item (S, D, or B) is placed in each account. By analogous reasoning, Eq. (1.1) is an accounting identity for the aggregate production account of firms in the economy, and this account is balanced by the residual item called "profit."

The four accounting identities associated with the four NIA sectors determine four balance variables, once the other variables are determined, but it is the whole point of macroeconomic analysis to show how the other variables are, in fact, determined. The virtue of the accounting analysis is to lay out in a neat and systematic way all the variables to be determined.

In a double entry accounting system, every item is entered twice, once as a receipt entry and once as an expenditure entry; but the mathematical analysis of behavior associated with each entry need not be in duplicate. The subcomponents of the entries in each account indicate the member and types of equations that will be needed in a model to build a complete deterministic system.

The components of NNP are consumer expenditures (also in the household account), business capital expenditures, exports and imports (also in the trade account), and government expenditures (also in the government account). The components of NI are wages (also in the household account). A principal objective of macroeconometric model building is to construct a system that gives a complete explanation of all the components of NNP and NI. From the main identity (1.2) and the other identities, balance items are determined. Such a model "explains" all the entries in the national income and product accounts. The size of the model depends on the degree of decomposition of account entries and that is partly a matter of the degree of disaggregated detail in the accounts, which in turn depends on the objectives of the model user.

The fact that the accounting system forms the basis for model construction does not mean that the model builder is confined to NIA data for constructing his system; he should go outside the NIA system for whatever seems relevant. In practice, this means using price variables, wage rate variables, money market rate variables, demographic variables, pressure of demand variables, capacity limitation variables and others that may be relevant for explaining behavior within the complex of variables that make up the NIA system.

In the main production account, there is one special entry that dóse not have a double entry duplicate elsewhere in the system, that is the *net* investment entry. This represents capital goods produced during the accounting period but not wholly consumed during the period. Similarly the balance items in each account, defined in the equations above, do not have double entry counterparts unless a separate account is set up to provide just this property. In addition to the receipt/expenditure account corresponding to the existence of separate groups of economic agents, a *capital* account is needed. This may also be called a *sources and uses* account. Its entries for *uses* of funds are the components of net investment. Its entries for *sources* of funds are the balance items displayed in the equations. The addition of the S&U account provides complete double entry coverage. The S&U account establishes the link between the NIA system and the flow-of-funds system that will be discussed below.

Input–output accounts (I–O). Models that are motivated by and based on the NIA system are called *final demand* models and should be distinguished from *intermediate* demand models. A guiding principle in the construction of major aggregates from NIA entries is that double counting should be avoided; i.e, NNP represents the total of "value added" at each stage of the economic process, and the expenditure accounts that total to NNP represent sales to final purchasers. Final purchases are of inherent interest in economics as are the NIA entries, but that is not to say that we should overlook intermediate transactions. Such transactions may be of unusual significance even though their sum total may exceed NNP because they involve some double counting. The classic formulas of I–O analysis

$$(I - A)X = F \tag{1.6}$$

I = identity matrix

$A = (a_{ij})$

a_{ij} = amount of production of sector i
used to produce one unit of output in sector j

$X = (x_1, x_2, \ldots, x_n)'$ = output vector for n sectors

$F = (f_1, f_2, \ldots, f_n)'$ = demand vector for n sectors

relates intermediate to final production. The elements of X are gross output values for each sector. Their sum exceeds NNP because it includes double counting. An element of X includes value added by each sector and the value of intermediate goods used in the production process.

The accounting base for (1.6) is derived from the identities

$$x_i = \sum_{j=1}^{n} x_{ij} + f_i \qquad i = 1, 2, \dots, n \qquad (1.7)$$

where x_{ij} are deliveries from sector i to sector j and f_i are deliveries to final demand. The matrix flow elements, x_{ij}, are values of intermediate deliveries. The relationship of I–O variables to NNP is

$$\text{NNP} = \sum_{i=1}^{n} f_i + (\text{Reconciling item}). \qquad (1.8)$$

The reconciling item is needed to account properly for the treatment of imports. If the trade entry for each f_i is *net* exports, the identity in (1.8) holds without need for a reconciling item. If, however, competitive imports are distributed to using industries together with similar domestic output, an import reconciling item is needed in (1.8).

Traditionally, I–O analysis has concentrated attention on properties of $(I - A)X$, and $(I - A)^{-1}$. For given values of F, properties of X can be derived. Macroeconometrics has concentrated on models that explain elements of F expressed as

$$\sum_{i=1}^{n} f_{ij'} \qquad j = 1, 2, \dots, m$$

where final demand for each sector is split into m categories such as consumer purchases, fixed investment, inventory investment, exports, and government purchases. The sector composition of such sums has been more or less ignored.

If I–O and macroeconometric analysis are to be fully integrated, relationships between techniques that "explain" F and techniques that "explain" X (given F) must be worked out. One of the tasks of the present paper is to indicate how this is being done in present research studies and to consider alternative approaches. A full integration of final demand and I–O analysis was first attempted in the Brookings Econometric Model Project.[1] In a later section, new developments along these line will be discussed.

The flow of funds accounts (FF). Behind the sources and uses of funds that appear in the final capital account of the NIA system are many intermediate financial transactions that may be relevant to an understanding of economic behavior

---

[1] *The Brookings Quarterly Econometric Model of the United States*, Chap. 17 and *The Brookings Model: Some Further Results*, Chap. 4 and Chap. 11, eds. J. Duesenberry *et al.* (North Holland, Amsterdam, 1965 and 1969).

and the working of the macroeconomy. These transactions are displayed in the FF accounting system.

The sources of funds in the NIA system may be classified as personal saving, business saving, government saving, and foreign saving. These savings flows can be developed, as in Eqs. (1.1)–(1.5), as the difference between an income stream and an outlay stream. An alternative approach to the same savings totals can be made directly through changes in assets and liabilities of the corresponding economic agents. Each agent grouping — households, businesses, governments, foreigners, or financial institutions — can engage in the following savings transactions:

change cash holding (currency or deposits)

change insurance reserves

change pension reserves

buy or sell securities (equities or bonds)

increase or repay indebtedness

change equity in noncorporate business.

Underlying these acts of saving or dissaving, there may be many intermediate transactions, some in existing assets or liabilities and some new assets or liabilities. Such financial transactions may be reported net or gross. If they are reported gross they reveal more about the transactions that are taking place in the money market.

If a model is built with the objective of "explaining" the total of sources available to finance net capital formation and if the "explanation" proceeds through direct estimates of savings, rather than the residual estimates in the NIA system, it is necessary to build a model that explains the composition of the entire balance sheets of each major grouping of economic agents. Having their balance sheet items for the end of each accounting period, we may estimate savings as the net total of asset and liability changes from one time period to the next.

The NIA system occupies a central position. It has been the fountainhead for most macroeconometric model projects. Through the explanation of final demand, it is related to the intermediate goods flows in an I–O system and through the explanation of savings it is related to gross financial flows in an FF system. All three systems together explain transactions in goods, transactions in financial instruments, and final transactions that add to NNP in the whole economy. This provides the accounting background for complete system modeling of an economy.

2. Historical Developments in Model Building

Final demand systems: The first econometric models were those of Tinbergen for the Netherlands and U.S. economies. They were brilliant pioneering efforts and interesting in their distinctive features, but less adapted to the exposition of complete social accounting systems than are the postwar generation of models. A system that has frequently been used in experimental calculation and which is revealing in the connection to social accounting systems is the one known as Klein's

Model I.[2] A particular numerical representation of that system (full-information–maximum-likelihood estimates, diagonal covariance case) is

$$C = 16.78 + 0.02\pi + 0.23\pi_{-1} + 0.80(W_1 + W_2) \tag{2.1}$$

$$I = 17.79 + 0.23\pi + 0.55\pi_{-1} - 0.15K_{-1} \tag{2.2}$$

$$W_1 = 1.60 + 0.42(Y + T - W_2)$$
$$+ 0.16(Y + T - W_2)_{-1} + 0.13(t - 1931) \tag{2.3}$$

$$Y + T = C + I + G \tag{2.4}$$

$$Y = \pi + W_1 + W_2 \tag{2.5}$$

$$K_t - K_{t-1} = I_t \tag{2.6}$$

C = consumer expenditures in billions of 1934 dollars
π = nonwage national income in billions of dollars, deflated by index on 1934 base
W_1 = private wage income in billions of dollars, deflated
W_2 = public wage income in billions of dollars, deflated
I = net investment in billions of 1934 dollars
K = end-of-year stock of capital in billions of 1934 dollars
$Y + T$ = net national product in billions of 1934 dollars
G = government expenditures and net exports in billions of 1934 dollars
Y = net national income in billions of 1934 dollars.

The coefficients are estimated from sample time series, 1920–1941. The six dependent variables are C, I, W_1, π, Y, K. The independent variables are W_2, T, G, t. The basic NIA identity is exemplified here by Eqs. (2.4) and (2.5). Together they imply

$$C + I + G = \pi + W_1 + W_2 + T.$$

This is equivalent to (1.2), with T as the reconciling item. When the exogenous variables G, W_2, and T are determined, it can be seen that model solutions for C, I, W_1 from other equations lead to determination of π from (2.4) and (2.5). Profits (nonwage income) are the residual income payments determined by the accounting system.

From

$$Y - C$$

where these two variables are determined separately in the system, we have an expression for S, personal and business savings.[3] This is the accounting relationship (1.3), but S is used only implicitly and not explicitly in this simple economy.

---

[2]L. R. Klein, *Economic Fluctuations in the United States, 1921–1941* (Wiley, New York, 1950), Chap. III.
[3]Since Y is national income and not just personal income in this system, business savings are implicitly combined with personal savings here.

The expression

$$G - T$$

gives a combined estimate of D and B from (1.4) and (1.5) because the net foreign balance has been included with total government expenditures, in this simplified system, as a single independent (exogenous) variable. In more sophisticated systems, exports and imports are both treated separately from government expenditures. Also, the reconciling variable, associating national income and national product includes only indirect taxes. In a more complete and detailed system direct taxes and nontax receipts would also have to be explicitly introduced.

Finally, the identity in (2.6) is another form of the sources and uses expression of the equivalence between savings and investment. The left hand side ΔK is a direct estimate of national savings as the change in real wealth. From the expression

$$I = \pi + W_1 + W_2 - C + T - G$$
$$= (Y - C) + (T - G)$$

we can see that investment is also equated to the indirect or residual measure of personal, government, foreign, and business savings.

It is evident that the three accounting identities (2.4–2.6) are not enough to close the system. Behavioral equations are also needed. General macroeconometric analysis must be called upon to supply these parts of the model specifications, in the accounting framework, but beyond the scope of pure accounting relationships. Equation (2.1) is the equation of consumer behavior, sometimes called the *propensity to consume*, linking consumer spending to income receipts. Similarly (2.2) is the investment equation or *propensity to invest*. Finally (2.3) is a distribution equation, showing how the income side of the national accounts are distributed between wage and nonwage income. Since the government sector is treated exogenously, *private* wages W_1 are related to private national product, $(Y + T - W_2)$. The lag structures and other behavioral properties of this compact equation system are more fully discussed in the original reference.[4] The point to be emphasized here is the way that this macroeconometric system fits into the social accounting schemes discussed above.

The public sector, especially on the revenue side, is only perfunctorily treated in this system. In serious applied work with models, it is necessary to distinguish between *personal* and *national* income, to introduce more kinds of taxes and transfer payments and to separate those government spending decisions that are linked to overall economic performance from those that are purely exogenous.

Klein's Model I is in the category of what might be called *pedagogical models*. These are useful for illustrating principles — in this case, some simple principles of macromodel building in the framework of social accounting and alternative methods

---

[4] See L. R. Klein, *op. cit.*

of system estimation — but they are not suitable for serious or realistic application to actual macroeconomic problems. Larger and more complex U.S. models generated by Tinbergen's original League of Nations effort are the

Klein–Goldberger Model, 1953
Wharton Model, 1960
Office of Business Economic Model, 1963
Brookings Model, 1964
Federal Reserve Board–MIT–Penn Model, 1967.

These are listed by date of first concrete research results. They are all associated with continuing research activities and are always being revised. They have given rise to off-shoot model projects, and the field is being invaded by new models of recent vintage. Also, substantial model building projects are being carried out in a number of developed and developing economies. These non-U.S. models are of the same family as far as account structure is concerned and fully consistent with the discussion of the present paper.

The main point about the structure of this array of U.S. models in relation to social accounting systems is that they are all final demand models, developed mainly to explain in more detail the components of the separate accounts. They are all larger, ranging in size from the 20-equation Klein–Goldberger type system to the 300 Brookings type system. In place of overall expenditures, they often explain types of consumer expenditures (durables, nondurables, goods, services), types of capital formation (business investment in fixed capital, residential investment, inventory investment), imports, and exports. They also provide more detailed explanation of income payments by types such as wages and salaries, transfer payments, social insurance contributions by employers, self employment income, rentier income, and corporate dividends.

A consequence of expanding such systems towards a more detailed explanation of NIA components is that there must be an order of magnitude enlargement of the whole model. Overall consumption, investment and similar large social aggregates may be insensitive to *relative* price movements. The larger systems cannot overlook relative prices, and this necessitates the introduction of several market price variables into the models. Explanatory equations must be introduced for these separate variables. In addition, if there are several price variables, it must be recognized that the NIA identities *hold only in current prices*, and there must be separate equations for *unit income variables* such as wage rates and interest rates. There must also be separate equations for physical or constant-prices aggregates. In such models, there are

market equations for prices, wage rates, interest rates;
technical equations for physical outputs and factor inputs.

These are in addition to the accounting and behavioral relationships of the simpler models. Legal relationships to represent the tax-transfer system and other imposed constraints on the economy are also in such large working models, but these might also be introduced in pedagogical systems.

Equations to determine absolute price level and interest rate variables are sure to involve the financial and money markets of an economy; thus the larger models must integrate the financial sectors involved in the FF accounts with the NIA sectors in the usual final demand models. Rudimentary monetary sectors were present in the Klein–Goldberger, Wharton, and OBE Models at an early stage, but a much larger financial sector was introduced in the Brookings Model, and this approach reached a flowering in the FRB–MIT–Penn Model, which makes more extensive use of the FF account system. By way of historical interest, it is useful to point out that a significant feature of Tinbergen's original U.S. Model for the League of Nations was based on an elaborate financial sector and attempts to portray the important influence of the American stock market in the cyclical swings of the 1920s and 1930s. The second generation models, typified by Klein's Model I and the Klein–Goldberger Model concentrated more on final demand and the NIA system. The Brookings Model is perhaps representative of a third generation system and brings us full-circle back to much of Tinbergen's original inspiratorial message.

Input–output systems: Interindustry models of the flows of goods that are entries in an I–O accounting system have been treated by Leontief as largely self-contained and not closely linked to macroeconometric models of final demand or financial flows. This is not to say that final demand, F, in Eq. (1.6) is ignored, but much more attention is paid in interindustry analysis to study of $(I - A), (I - A)^{-1}$, and X than to F. Essentially, the overall level of final demand and its composition is assumed in interindustry analysis and consequences for X are determined on the basis of estimates of $(I - A)^{-1}$. By itself such a model is not fully predictive; it is conditionally predictive.

The composition of final demand, by type of final purchaser and by supplying sector, is generally not known as an economic time series for many periods except in the basic periods for which the I–O systems are drawn up, and this is infrequent in many cases. I–O accounting systems and models exist for the USA and many other countries. The flow of statistical material is uneven, however. In some countries, there is an annual table and in others there are tables for only selected years. The U.S.A., which is usually rich in statistical data about the economy, has basic tables in the postwar years for only selected periods — 1947, 1958, and 1963.

There has been a major methodological difference in the econometrics of model construction for final demand and for interindustry analysis. The former has been inferential, stochastic, and based on the modern theory of mathematical statistics. The latter, by contrast, has been arithmetical and direct. The major problem of statistical estimation, after the I–O accounting system has been developed, has been the calculation of

$$a_{ij} = x_{ij}/x_j \, .$$

The a_{ij} are treated as parameters and estimated from a single pair of observations

(x_{ij}, x_j). In the language of statistical inference there are no degrees-of-freedom associated with such estimates. As more instances of I–O accounts become available for different years, there may be a few sample observations on (x_{ij}, x_j), but not enough to make computation of a_{ij} a proper estimation problem using the principles of statistical inference. This does not mean that the two kinds of models cannot be consistently integrated within a larger system, but it does mean that econometric analysis must be more flexibly structured and utilized in order to build the full system. The Brookings Model was the first to try to make a full model involving both final demand from the NIA system and intermediate demand from the I–O accounting system. This and alternative approaches will be discussed below.

Leontief extended his interindustry models in several different directions, of which three merit special consideration:

(i) The system is made dynamic by the addition of a capital matrix

$$(I - A)X + BX = F^* \tag{2.7}$$

where

$B = (b_{ij})$

b_{ij} = amount of ith type of fixed capital used to produce one unit of output sector j.

$F^* = (f_1^*, f_2^*, \ldots, f_n^*)'$ = final demand vector for n sectors, deleting investment in fixed capital.

(ii) The system is written in terms of prices rather than production. This requires some assumption about unit profit margins.

$$(I - A')P = R, \tag{2.8}$$

where $P = (p_1, p_2, \ldots, p_n)'$ = price vector for n industries,

$\quad\quad R = (r_1, r_2, \ldots, r_n)'$ = vector of gross operating profits per unit of output for n industries.

(iii) The system is written of a localized geographical unit smaller than our entire nation. In such a system, flows of goods must be designated by both industry and areas of origin and industry and area of destination.

Local interindustry models for a state or metropolitan area are now being used in economic analysis in the USA.

Flow of funds systems: It is only in recent years, not much before the decade of the 1960s, that regular and comprehensive FF accounts have become a regular part of the economic statistician's annals. It is, therefore, not surprising that model building has been less influenced by this accounting system than by the other two. A rudimentary sources and uses account for the economy as a whole, with little provision for second hand financial transactions, has always been present in the form of a savings-investment equality for macroeconometric models based on the NIA system. Also an overall equation or small group of equations for holding of money balances and interest rate determination have been present in such systems, but the monetary sectors of models have been small, modest, and poorly linked to the "real" sectors.

The large scale Brookings Model had a detailed and a condensed monetary sector. Much of this analysis was carried over to the Federal Reserve Board–MIT–Penn Model, which changed the usual proportions between monetary and real sector equations of a complete system. That Model is fundamentally a financial model, with a small real sector that closes the system. The Bank of Canada Model is similarly detailed in the financial sector. The Brookings and FRB–MIT–Penn Models differ from earlier macroeconometric models in being more sensitive to changes brought about by monetary policies.

In the newest version of the Wharton Model, now under construction, the financial sector is approached in a new way. The system is being built to explain the complete or main entries of balance sheets of

Commercial banks
Savings banks
Savings and loan associations
Life insurance companies.

This is a major step towards completeness, but does not include brokerage firms, property and casualty insurance companies, nonfinancial companies, and the balance of payments.

In dealing with the balance sheets of the covered parts of the financial sector it will be necessary to explain deposit liabilities of all forms of banks, assets in the form of securities, mortgage loans, business loans. For life insurance companies, cash security investments, mortgage holdings, and policy reserves must be separately explained. Associated with these asset and liability items are short term (bill) rates (public and private), long term (bond) rates (public and private), mortgage rates, federal funds rates, and Euro-dollar rates.

Most models treat imports, exports and the net trade balance endogenously. Few go on to consider explicit treatment of capital flows — long, short, public, private, direct or portfolio. All these items are, however, treated endogenously and explicitly in a new sector being developed for the Brookings Model.

Recent American experience with "credit squeezes" in 1966 and 1969 show how important Euro-dollar balances, mortgage investments, bank loans to business, and interest rates are to macroeconomic performance. It is thus urgent to draw upon data in the FF accounts to build a complete monetary sector that is compatible with real economy models that have long histories of study and performance. Work done on the Brookings, FRB–MIT–Penn, and new Wharton models show that equations based on data in the FF accounts can be fully integrated with equations based on data in the NIA system and I–O accounts.

3. Complementarity Between Macroeconometrics and I–O Model Building

Research work will progress in the direction of explaining the whole model of three accounting systems, but some analytical problems and preliminary results with the merging of the first two (NIA and I–O systems) are sufficiently interesting in their own right that separate treatment is suggested.

Brookings Model linkage: The combination of I–O and conventional macro analysis of final demand has two objectives in the Brookings Model:

(a) to relate prices by industry of origin to price deflators of GNP components

(b) to decompose total real GNP into GNP by industry of origin.

The price decision or price formation equation in the Model is hypothesized as a mark-up on unit costs, especially unit labor costs,

$$P_i = \alpha_i \frac{W_i L_i}{X_i} \qquad i = 1, 2, \ldots, n \tag{3.1}$$

$P_i = i$th sector's output price
$W_i = i$th sector's wage rate
$L_i = i$th sector's labor input
$X_i = i$th sector's value added.

The actual price equations are more complicated in short run dynamics; they distinguish between "normal" and actual unit costs; they contain some lag adjustments; and they contain some pressure-of-demand variables. These equations may variously be looked upon as price formation, labor demand, or factor income share equations.

GNP components in final demand equations of macromodels involve relative price deflators of the components and deflated expenditure totals. In the NIA identities, the same GNP components must be expressed in current prices. It is, therefore, necessary to explain both composite prices for GNP component deflators and prices in behavior equations like (3.1). The implicit deflator of a GNP component is a weighted average of the P_i with the weights being proportional to the fraction of each sector's real output delivered to the final demand category (GNP component) in question. Columns of a conversion matrix

$$F = (f_1, f_2, \ldots, f_n)' \qquad \text{final demand vector} \tag{3.2}$$

$$C = \begin{pmatrix} C_{11} & (C_{1m}) \\ \vdots & \vdots \\ (C_{n1}) & C_{nm} \end{pmatrix} \qquad \text{conversion matrix}$$

$$G = (g_1, g_2, \ldots, g_m)' \qquad \text{GNP components}$$

are weights used in the price index formulas

$$q_j = \sum_{i=1}^{n} C_{ij} P_i \tag{3.3}$$

to obtain a deflator for the jth component of GNP (q_j) from the prices by industry of origin (P_i). The column sums of C are normalized to be unity.

The coefficients C are obtained by regression of each of the time series $(I - A)X_t$ on G_t. It is done this way because time series of F are not generally available by direct estimate.

In order to determine P_i from equations of the form (3.1), it is necessary to know X_i, output in individual sectors. Similarly in factor demand equations for fixed capital formation (investment) and working capital formation (inventory change) it is also necessary to have estimates of X_i. The equation

$$X = (I - A)^{-1} F = (I - A)^{-1} CG \tag{3.4}$$

shows the relation between GNP determination (by components) and individual industry output determination.

It happens, by the structure of the Brookings Model, that the vectors G and X must be simultaneously determined. It is a complete feedback system. It is possible to have a pure GNP type model to determine G and then use (3.4) to determine X, but the Brookings Model does not function in this way because the capital formation elements of G depend on individual elements of X. In a system of any degree of sophistication this is likely to be the case.

It should be pointed out that the vector X in I–O analysis is a vector of *gross* outputs, while the variables X_i in (3.1) and in capital formation equations of the Brookings Model are *values added*. Another transformation is needed

$$X^* = DX \tag{3.5}$$

where D is a diagonal matrix to convert elements of the value added vector X to elements of the gross output vector X^*. These diagonal elements are mark-up factors. In the Brookings Model, the I–O matrix $I - A$ is condensed to eight highly aggregative sectors; thus there is not much interindustry content in the model. The procedure used is largely experimental. The coefficients in $(I - A)$ are not estimated by methods of statistical inference; they are simply taken from the 1947 or 1958 tables of I–O coefficients. The elements of D are average mark-up factors, but the elements of C are regression estimates.

An interesting experimental calculation with the model reveals that extrapolations to 1961–62 with the model based on the 1947 I–O compare favorably with those based on the 1958 I–O table. In some parts of the model, one set of calculations outperforms the other, but on an overall basis there is not a great deal to choose between the two systems.[5]

---

[5] See *The Brookings Model: Some Further Results, op. cit.* Chap. 11.

The elements of $(I - A)$ and D are determined at specific sample time points or may be time averages in the case of D. The coefficient matrix C is, in the Brookings Model, a regression estimate and therefore, is subject to sampling fluctuation. The elements of C are estimated with a recognition that error is present, and are obtained so as to minimize error in some well defined sense, while $(I - A)$ and D are obtained so as to make an exact transformation of variables between F and X^* in some base period. In periods outside the base period, error is present. The point to be emphasized is that the linkage between macroeconometric and I–O models in connecting GNP and sector output variables or GNP deflators and sector prices is subject to error. The error may be viewed as sampling fluctuations in elements of $(I - A)$, D and C or as error due to the neglect of significant variables, say in the statistical relationship between F and G in (3.2).

An attempt has been made in the Brookings Model formulation to deal with error by making autoregressive corrections in price and output conversion from GNP to I–O bases. In (3.4), observed values may be inserted on the right-hand side of the equation for elements of G, and these may be used for computation of $\hat{X}$. Autoregressive error corrections of the form

$$X_{it} = \alpha_0 + \alpha_1 \hat{X}_{it} + \alpha_2 X_{i,t-1} \tag{3.6α}$$

$$X_{it} = \beta_0 + \beta_1 \hat{X}_{it} + \beta_2 (\hat{X}_{i,t-1} - X_{i,t-1}) \tag{3.6β}$$

$$X_{it} = \gamma_0 + \hat{X}_{it} + \gamma_1 (\hat{X}_{i,t-1} - X_{i,t-1}) \tag{3.6γ}$$

may be estimated over the sample period for each sector and used to keep computed values of X_{it} from wandering. In an analogous way, autoregressive corrections can be developed for the relationships between q_{it} and $\hat{q}_{it}$ defined in (3.3). The form (3.6β) was found to be most satisfactory in the case of the Brookings Model.

A mixture of trend and autoregressive shift between X_{it} and $\hat{X}_{it}$ or q_{it} and $\hat{q}_{it}$ can also be used. This would modify (3.6β) to the form

$$X_{it} = \beta_0 + \beta_1 \hat{X}_{it} + \beta_2 (\hat{X}_{i,t-1} - X_{i,t-1}) + \beta_3 t.$$

Another correction factor that can be considered is the addition of a second order autoregressive factor such as $(\hat{X}_{i,t-2} - X_{i,t-2})$.

Part of the trend drift may be ascribed directly to changes in elements of $(I - A)$ and D. If these matrices are calculated from direct ratios at isolated points of time, we may construct simple interpolations and trend extrapolations of these matrices to see if the interpolated and extrapolated estimates of these two matrices give better estimates of X_{it} and q_{it} obviating the necessity for using the autoregressions in (3.6) or reducing their significance. In a dynamic economy, however, it is evident that static relationships in (3.2)–(3.4) will not be adequate for price and output conversion.

Wharton Model linkage: Regression estimates of (3.2) should be determined under the restriction that column sums of C are unity. This is not always easy to obtain with the added restriction that elements of C be positive. A more direct estimate of C has been devised by R. S. Preston.[6] He splits the final demand vector

$$F = (f_1, f_2, \ldots, f_n)'$$

into m types of final demand associated with each sector.

$$F = (f_1, f_2, \ldots, f_n)' = \begin{pmatrix} f_{11} & f_{12} & \cdots & f_{1m} \\ f_{21} & f_{22} & \cdots & f_{2m} \\ \cdot & \cdot & & \cdot \\ \cdot & \cdot & & \cdot \\ \cdot & \cdot & & \cdot \\ f_{n1} & f_{n2} & \cdots & f_{nm} \end{pmatrix}. \tag{3.7}$$

The final demand types are the usual demand categories for GNP components on the expenditure side, such as consumer expenditures, fixed capital formation, inventory investment, net foreign trade, government expenditures, all decomposed again into finer categories — consumer durable goods expenditures, etc. In the base year for which input–output data are collected, the elements of the final demand matrix in (3.7) are observed. A normalized version of F is

$$F^* = (f_{ij}^*) = \left(\frac{f_{ij}}{\sum_{i=1}^{n} f_{ij}} \right) = \left(\frac{f_{ij}}{g_j} \right) \tag{3.7}$$

where g_j is the jth column sum of F. Each element of F^* is obtained by dividing each element of F by its corresponding column sum. This gives a matrix of percentages showing the composition of final demand. The column sums are observable in periods other than the I–O base; they are GNP components such as consumer expenditures, fixed capital formation, etc.

The matrix product

$$F(g_1, g_2, \ldots, g_m)' = F^* G \tag{3.8}$$

provides an estimate of F for periods other than the I–O base on the assumption that the sector composition of final demand, by type, does not change. The Eqs. (3.8) are used by Preston instead of the regression estimates of (3.2). His approach guarantees accounting consistency between I–O and NIA systems since the columns of F^* sum to unity, by construction.

In Preston's model, there can be drift or other change in $(I - A)$, D, or F^*. He, therefore, needs trend and autoregressive corrections as in (3.6) for sector price and output estimates. In the same way that direct interpolations can be made between independent estimates of $(I - A)$ or D for different time periods, such interpolations can also be made for independent estimates of F^*. This may lessen the burden placed on mechanical autoregressive and trend correction.

---

[6]R. S. Preston and M. K. Evans, "A new way of using aggregate economic models: Industry forecasts with econometric models," Discussion Paper No. 138, Department of Economics, University of Pennsylvania, Philadelphia, 1969.

In the Brookings Model linkage, there is feedback between the I–O and final demand macro model because equations of the latter system depend explicitly on individual output values from the former and implicitly on the individual prices from the former. The I–O part of the model cannot be solved without final demand estimates, and the macroeconometric parts of the model cannot be solved without I–O variable estimates. This is a truly interrelated system with feedback.

A new version of the Wharton I–O linkage system is being built on the feedback principle, but a preliminary estimate is being used that has no feedback. This is possible if Eqs. (3.8) are used at the linkage point because they need not be so specific as to disaggregate the macro model to the point where it must depend on I–O variables. In getting regression estimates of the matrix in (3.2), the final demand macro model must be sufficiently disaggregated to explain separate elements of X, the output vector. Disaggregation of the final demand model, in turn, forces the econometrician to introduce fairly specific price and output variables. This form of interdependence is, in a sense, avoided (or evaded) if the F^* matrix is assumed to be constant. In that case, a fairly aggregative final demand model can be used to determine broad categories of GNP. This gives estimates of G. Final demand F is estimated from (3.8) and X from (3.4). In this kind of system, there is no feedback. The macro model based on the NIA system determines overall activity levels, and the interindustry model based on the I–O system determines its distribution among individual lines of production.

A study of intermediate range economic growth in the United States (1970–1975) has just been completed by Preston using the no-feedback linkage system.[7] There are three basic parts to this calculation.

(i) Assumptions about exogenous variables for the macro model, 1970–75.
(ii) Dynamic simulation 1970–75 of the macro model from fixed initial conditions, 1969 and earlier.
(iii) Solution of the I–O system for individual sector outputs, 1970–75.

These results are set out in Tables 1, 2, and 3 respectively. The assumptions for solution of the medium term macro model used here are made to correspond for the first two years with those used in the short term econometric forecasts regularly made with the Wharton Econometric Forecasting Model (quarterly). The solution of the annual macro model agrees quite closely with the annual averages of the quarterly solution. There is thus a great list of macroeconometric input into the final interindustry model solution.

Current vs. constant price I–O systems: The standard interindustry model is based theoretically on a "real" interpretation of $(I - A)$. It is assumed that the

[7]R. S. Preston and L. R. Klein, "The 1970s: An economic scenario for the decade," *Wharton Quarterly* (Summer, 1970).

Table 1. Main assumptions: Annual Macro model 1969–1975.

	1969	1970	1971	1972	1973	1974	1975
Government expenditures billions of dollars (current prices)	214.7	224.8	236.8	254.9	276.6	299.4	321.2
Government expenditures billions of dollars (1958 prices)	149.8	149.4	151.8	158.0	165.0	172.0	178.0
Exports billions of dollars (1958 prices)	48.4	53.1	57.1	60.0	63.0	66.4	69.4
Armed forces (millions)	3.503	3.340	3.100	3.000	3.000	3.000	3.000
Federal personal tax rate (percent)	13.938	12.715	12.394	11.994	11.794	11.694	11.694
Federal corporate tax rate (percent)	42.842	43.291	43.173	43.598	44.023	44.448	44.873
State and local indirect tax rate (percent)	8.788	9.270	9.739	9.800	9.900	10.000	10.000
Federal transfer payments billions of dollars (current prices)	50.400	57.300	61.000	66.000	71.000	76.000	81.000
Bond yield (percent Moodys AAA)	7.03	7.85	7.68	6.50	6.00	5.50	5.00
Contribution for social insurance (billions of dollars, current prices)	54.400	58.200	62.600	69.600	73.400	60.000	84.000

Source: Wharton Econometric Forecasting Associates, March 12, 1970 Release.

I–O coefficients in (1.6) are estimated from

$$a_{ij} = \frac{X_{ij}}{X_j},$$

and that these are estimates of stable parameters. Associated with this assumption is the implied assumption that each sector produces only one good and that relative prices are invariant under changes in final demand. In this kind of economic world, the matrix $(I - A)$ should be estimated from ratios of input and output expressed in constant prices since individual sectors do, in fact, produce more than one good. The elements of X are assumed to be in constant prices. These are the units in which the solution values of Table 3, are expressed.

An alternative assumption is that each sector produces many goods and that a_{ij} are computed from the ratios of two values — the ratio of the value of input in current prices to the value of output in current prices.[8] The model that goes with

---

[8]L. R. Klein, "On the interpretation of Professor Leontief's system," *Review of Economic Studies* **XX(2)**, (1952–53), pp. 131–136; see also M. Morishima, "The interpretation of Leontief's system," and L. R. Klein, "The interpretation of Leontief's system — A reply," *Review of Economic Studies* **XXIV(1)**, (1956–57), pp. 69–70.

Table 2. Gross national product, 1969 and projections for 1970–1975. (Billions of dollars, 1958 prices)

	1969	1970	1971	1972	1973	1974	1975
Gross national product	727.7	730.1	747.9	805.6	855.6	890.9	925.7
Federal government purchases	76.1	71.8	69.7	70.0	71.0	72.0	73.0
State and local government purchases	73.7	77.6	82.1	88.0	94.0	100.0	105.0
Personal consumption expenditures	466.0	474.5	486.9	524.9	556.0	579.1	603.1
Gross private investment	111.9	106.2	109.2	122.7	134.6	139.0	144.0
Business fixed investment	81.5	82.3	78.1	84.3	94.4	100.5	104.0
Residential structures	23.5	21.0	25.0	25.8	26.7	27.0	27.3
Other investment	6.9	2.9	6.1	12.6	13.9	12.3	12.5

Source: Wharton Econometric Forecasting Associates, March 12, 1970 Release.

Table 3. Gross National Product by major industrial sector. (Billions of dollars, 1958 prices)

	1969	1970	1971	1972	1973	1974	1975	1975/1969
Gross National Product	727.7	730.1	747.9	805.6	855.6	890.9	925.7	4.1%
Agriculture	25.0	28.3	28.2	26.1	27.0	29.4	30.0	3.5%
Mining	16.7	16.0	16.4	18.3	19.3	19.8	20.4	3.4%
Contract construction	25.1	23.1	23.8	25.0	27.6	29.4	30.9	3.5%
Manufacturing	227.3	223.2	229.1	255.2	272.5	281.5	291.6	4.2%
Non durable goods	89.1	89.9	92.4	99.9	106.0	110.3	114.7	4.3%
Durable goods	138.2	133.3	136.6	155.3	166.8	171.2	176.9	4.2%
Transportation	33.8	34.4	35.1	36.9	38.8	40.4	41.7	3.6%
Communications	19.2	19.7	20.4	21.7	23.0	24.0	25.0	4.5%
Electric, gas, water, sanitary	20.0	20.6	21.3	22.8	24.1	25.2	26.3	4.7%
Trade	124.0	125.7	128.4	138.2	146.6	152.6	158.4	4.2%
Finance and insurance	21.7	22.1	22.7	24.3	25.8	27.0	28.1	4.4%
Real estate	77.2	79.8	82.2	88.2	93.8	98.5	103.0	4.9%
Services	67.6	69.3	71.4	76.5	81.2	85.0	88.8	4.7%
Government	69.5	68.6	69.0	71.4	74.1	76.7	78.9	2.1%
Other	0.6	−0.6	−0.1	1.0	2.1	1.4	1.8	

Source: Wharton Econometric Forecasting Associates, March 12, 1970 Release.

(Cont'd)

Table 3 (Cont'd). Gross National Product — manufacturing durables. (Billions of dollars, 1958 prices)

	1969	1970	1971	1972	1973	1974	1975	1975/1969
Lumber and wood products	4.5	4.4	4.5	4.6	4.9	5.1	5.3	2.8%
Furniture and fixtures	3.1	3.0	2.9	3.3	3.7	3.8	3.9	2.8%
Stone, clay, and glass	6.7	6.5	6.6	7.1	7.7	8.0	8.3	3.0%
Primary iron and steel	10.6	9.3	9.4	11.4	12.3	12.3	12.5	2.8%
Primary non-ferrous metals	5.8	5.6	5.7	6.4	6.9	7.1	7.3	3.9%
Fabricated metal products	14.2	13.5	13.9	15.7	16.8	17.3	17.9	3.9%
Machinery, except electrical	22.8	21.8	21.9	25.6	27.7	28.3	29.0	4.09%
Electrical machinery	24.9	24.4	25.2	28.5	30.6	31.5	32.6	4.6%
Non auto transportation	15.5	15.5	16.3	18.5	19.9	20.7	21.6	5.7%
Auto and equipment	21.5	20.5	21.2	24.4	25.8	26.2	26.9	3.8%
Instruments and related products	5.4	5.5	5.6	6.2	6.6	6.9	7.1	4.7%
Miscellaneous durable man.	3.3	3.3	3.3	3.6	3.9	4.1	4.3	4.5%
Food and kindred products	20.2	21.0	21.3	21.9	22.8	23.9	24.7	3.4%
Tobacco manufactures	3.4	3.4	3.6	4.0	4.3	4.5	4.7	5.5%
Textile mill products	6.6	6.2	6.4	7.3	7.8	8.0	8.2	3.7%
Apparel and related products	7.2	7.0	7.2	8.3	9.0	9.3	9.7	5.1%
Paper and allied products	8.4	8.4	8.7	9.4	9.9	10.4	10.8	4.4%
Printing and publishing	9.6	9.7	10.0	10.7	11.4	11.9	12.4	4.4%
Chemicals and allied products	20.1	20.5	21.3	23.0	24.4	25.5	26.6	4.8%
Petroleum and related industries	5.0	5.0	5.2	5.7	6.1	6.3	6.5	4.5%
Rubber and plastics	7.0	6.9	7.1	7.8	8.3	8.6	8.9	4.1%
Leather and leather products	1.7	1.8	1.8	1.9	2.0	2.1	2.2	4.4%

Source: Wharton Econometric Forecasting Associates, March 12, 1970 Release.

the estimation of the a_{ij} as value ratios of the current priced sum of inputs from a sector to current priced sum of outputs by a sector is one in which each sector has the following extended Cobb–Douglas technology:

$$X_i = A_i e^{\delta_i t} \left(\prod_{j=1}^{n} x_{ji}^{\alpha_{ji}} \right) L_i^{\beta_i} K_i^{\gamma_i} \tag{3.9}$$

L_i = labor input for the ith sector

K_i = capital stock of the ith sector.

If net returns are maximized, subject to this technology we obtain

$$\alpha_{ji} = \frac{P_j X_{ji}}{P_i X_i} \tag{3.10}$$

$$\beta_i = \frac{w_i L_i}{P_i X_i} . \tag{3.11}$$

The ratios in (3.10) are the value I–O coefficients, and the ratios in (3.11) are wage shares of the value of total output. If we impose the usual homogeneity restriction

$$\sum_{j=1}^{n} \alpha_{ji} + \beta_i + \gamma_i = 1 , \tag{3.12}$$

the capital share ratio is determined, from (3.10), (3.11), and (3.12) as a residual.

In separate tests of I–O models with current vs. constant price value ratios, Watanabe and Tilanus and Rey have found that the coefficients tend to be more stable from current than from constant price ratios.[9] Watanabe's results of greater stability for value coefficients are centered in manufacturing. A study of the model (3.10)–(3.11) in expanded form with a more complete system of equations for the whole economy has been made by M. Saito.[10] The I–O parameters were estimated from a table with current value ratios; the other parameters in (3.9) and the other macro equations of the complete system were estimated by general econometric methods of regression analysis.

4. Prospects for Building the Complete System

The Brookings Model and the newer systems of Preston and Saito show that large scale models that fully integrate I–O and macroeconometric models can in fact be constructed and used in problems of economic analysis. In this section, we consider the possibility of building the entire system, effectively linking a completed set of entries in NIA, I–O, and FF accounting systems.

To develop the complete system, it would require building on a Preston or Saito type model that is already large or a full explanation of the changes in separate assets and liabilities of financial institutions (banks, thrift institutions and insurance companies), public treasury, foreigners, nonfinancial companies. The complete system would provide estimates of total savings flows and investments in the economy and also the underlying intermediate financial transactions in the exchange of existing assets and liabilities.

The full system has not in fact been built, but there is every reason to believe that it is possible. Some unpublished research on a complete model of assets and

---

[9]T. Watanabe, "A test of the constancy of input–output coefficients among countries," and C. B. Tilanus and G. Rey, "Input–output volume and value predictions for the Netherlands, 1948–1958," *International Economic Review* **II** (September, 1961), pp. 340–350 and **V** (January, 1964), pp. 34–45.

[10]M. Saito, "An interindustry study of price formation," *Review of Economics and Statistics*, forthcoming.

liabilities of financial and nonfinancial institutions, compatible with the Wharton Model shows that the NIA and FF systems can be fully integrated.[11] The fact that pairs of the three basic accounting systems can be fully integrated suggests that it is feasible to combine all three into one self-contained system. In terms of U.S. data, it may not be possible to obtain suitable statistical series for all the necessary variables on a quarterly basis for a uniformly long sample period. It appears that large scale I–O models are most readily constructed on an annual basis, considering data limitations, that FF models may be constructed on a quarterly basis but for a shorter sample period say, for the last decade; that NIA models can be constructed either quarterly or annually for a long sample span — going back at least as far as 1948. Some combinations of unit data period and sample length can be used for the whole model. Although it is more straightforward to use a common data base for all relationships in the complete system simultaneously; there is no reason, in principle, why a mixture of data bases cannot be used for the different parts of a large system.

The potential uses of the large unified system are manifold. While it appeared for some time that the NIA system served the needs of economic policy formation and business forecasting adequately, it has become evident that new use of monetary controls and the appearance of new monetary instruments require the use of models based on FF systems of account. The issue of certificates of deposit, Euro-dollar balances, and bank issues of unsecured paper have changed the analysis of monetary economics in tracing the availability of funds for capital formation. The FF model must give a complete picture of assets and liabilities of financial institutions that contain these new instruments.

The influence of the Vietnam War on the American economy has caused a distortion in the normal pattern of resource use and the mix of output among sectors. The plausible way of getting at the influence of this distortion in the economy is through the use of an I–O model, but for completeness it should be used together with the NIA model. This kind of combined model can show how the economy will change under demobilization — cease fire conditions. It should also show how technical change will work its way through the economy. These are typical kinds of problems that can be attacked with the complete model.

---

[11] D. S. Swamy, "An econometric study of United States financial markets," unpublished Ph.D. dissertation, University of Pennsylvania, 1970.

13

SIMULTANEOUS EQUATION ESTIMATION[†]

The distinction between partial and general equilibrium analysis in economic theory
is well grounded (see Arrow, 1968). Early work in econometrics paid inadequate attention to this distinction and overlooked for many years the possibilities of improving statistical estimates of individual economic relationships by embedding them in
models of the economy as a whole [see "Econometric Models," "Aggregate"]. The
earliest studies in econometrics were concerned with estimating parameters of demand functions, supply functions, production functions, cost functions, and similar
tools of economic analysis. The principal statistical procedure used was to estimate
the α's in the relation

$$y_t = \sum_{i=1}^{n} \alpha_i x_{it} + u_t, \qquad t = 1, 2, \ldots, T,$$

using the criterion that $\sum_{t=1}^{T} u_t^2$ be minimized. This is the principle of "least
squares" applied to a single equation in which y_t is chosen as the dependent variable and $x_{1t}, \ldots, x_{nt}$ are chosen as the independent variables. The criterion is the
minimization of the sum of squared "disturbances" (u_t) which are assumed to be
unobserved random errors. The estimation of the unknown parameters α_i is based
on the sample of T observations of y_t and $x_{1t}, \ldots, x_{nt}$. This is the usual statistical
model and estimation procedure that is used in controlled experimental situations
where the set of independent variables consists of selected, fixed variates for the
experimental readings on y_t, the dependent variable. [See "Linear Hypotheses,"
article on "Regression."]

However, economics, like most other social sciences, is largely a nonexperimental
science, and it is generally not possible to control the values of $x_{1t}, \ldots, x_{nt}$. The
values of the independent variables, like those of the dependent variable, are produced from the general outcome of economic life, and the econometrician is faced
with the problem of making statistical inferences from nonexperimental data. This
is the basic reason for the use of simultaneous equation methods of estimation in
econometrics. In some situations $x_{1t}, \ldots, x_{nt}$ may not be controlled variates, but
they may have a one-way causal influence on y_t. The main point is that least
squares yields desirable results only if u_t is independent of $x_{1t}, \ldots, x_{nt}$, that is, if
$E(u_t x_{it}) = 0$ for all i and t.

[†]From *International Encyclopaedia of Statistics*, Vol. 2, eds. William H. Kruskal and Judith M.
Tanur (The Free Press, New York, 1978) pp. 979–994.

Properties of estimators. If the x_{it} are fixed variates, estimators of α_i obtained by minimizing $\sum u_t^2$ are *best linear unbiased* estimators. They are linear estimators because, as shown below, they are linear functions of y_t. An estimator, $\hat{\alpha}_i$, of α_i is called unbiased if

$$E\hat{\alpha}_i = \alpha_i \,,$$

i.e., if the expected value of the estimator equals the true value. An estimator is best if among all unbiased estimators it has the least variance, i.e., if

$$E(\hat{\alpha}_i - \alpha_i)^2 \leqslant E(\tilde{\alpha}_i - \alpha_i)^2 \,,$$

where $\tilde{\alpha}_i$ is any other unbiased estimator. Clearly, the properties of being unbiased and best are desirable ones. These properties are defined without reference to sample size. Two related but weaker properties, which are defined for large samples, are *consistency* and *efficiency*.

An estimator, $\hat{\alpha}_i$, is consistent if plim $\hat{\alpha}_i = \alpha_i$, that is, if

$$\lim_{T \to \infty} P\left(|\hat{\alpha}_i - \alpha_i| < \epsilon\right) = 1, \qquad \text{for any } \epsilon > 0 \,.$$

This states that the probability that $\hat{\alpha}_i$ deviates from α_i by an amount less than any arbitrarily small ϵ tends to unity as the sample size T tends to infinity.

Consider now the class of all consistent estimators that are normally distributed as $T \to \infty$. An *efficient* estimator of α_i is a consistent estimator whose asymptotic normal distribution has a smaller variance than any other member of this class. [See "Estimation."]

Inconsistency of least squares. The choice of estimators, $\hat{\alpha}_i$, such that $\sum_{t=1}^{T}\left(y_t - \sum_{i=1}^{n} \alpha_i x_{it}\right)^2$ is minimized is formally equivalent to the empirical implementation of the condition that $E(u_t x_{it}) = 0$, since the first-order condition for a minimum is

$$\sum_{t=1}^{T}\left[\left(y_t - \sum_{i=1}^{n} \alpha_i x_{it}\right) x_{it}\right] = 0$$

On the one hand, the α_i are estimated so as to minimize the residual sum of squares. On the other hand, they are estimated so that the residuals are uncorrelated with $x_{1t}, \ldots, x_{nt}$. The possible inconsistency of this method is clearly revealed by the latter criterion, for if it is assumed that the u_t are independent of $x_{1t}, \ldots, x_{nt}$ when they actually are not, the estimators will be inconsistent. This is shown by the formula

$$\text{plim } \hat{\alpha}_i = \alpha_i + \text{plim} \frac{1}{|M|} \sum_{j=1}^{n} m_{uj} M_{ji} \,,$$

where M is the moment matrix whose typical element is $\sum_t x_{it} x_{jt}$; $|M|$ is the determinant of M; m_{uj} is $\sum_t u_t x_{jt}$; and M_{ji} is the j, i cofactor of M. The inconsistency in the estimator is due to the nonvanishing probability limit of m_{uj}. In a nonexperimental sample of data, such as that observed as the joint outcome of the uncontrolled simultaneous economic process, we would expect many or all the x_{it} in a problem to be dependent on u_t.

Identifying restrictions. Since economic models consist of a set of simultaneous equations generating nonexperimental data, the equations of the model must be *identified* prior to statistical estimation. Unless some restrictions are imposed on specific relationships in a linear system of simultaneous equations, every equation may look alike to the statistician faced with the job of estimating the unknown coefficients. The economist must place *a priori* restrictions, in advance of statistical estimation, on each of the equations in order to identify them. These restrictions may specify that certain coefficients are known in advance — especially that they are zero, for this is equivalent to excluding the associated variable from an economic relation. Other restrictions may specify linear relationships between the different coefficients.

Consider the generalization of a single equation,

$$y_t = \sum_{i=1}^{m} \alpha_i z_{it} + u_t \,,$$

where $E(z_{it} u_t) = 0$ for all i and t, to a whole system,

$$\sum_{j=1}^{n} \beta_{ij} y_{jt} + \sum_{k=1}^{m} \gamma_{ik} z_{kt} = u_{it}, \qquad i = 1, 2, \ldots, n,$$

where $E(z_{kt} u_{it}) = 0$ for all k, i, and t. Every variable enters every equation linearly without restriction, and the statistician has no way of distinguishing one relation from another. Zero restrictions, if imposed, would have the form $\beta_{rs} = 0$ or $\gamma_{pq} = 0$, for some r, s, p, or q. In many equations, we may be interested in specifying that sums or differences of variables are economically relevant combinations, i.e., that $\beta_{rs} = \beta_{ru}$ or that $\beta_{rv} = -\gamma_{rw}$ or, more generally, that

$$\sum_{s=1}^{n_r} w_s \beta_{rs} + \sum_{s=1}^{m_r} v_s \gamma_{rs} = 0 \,.$$

The last restriction implies that a homogeneous linear combination of parameters in the rth equation is specified to hold on *a priori* grounds. The weights w_s and v_s are known in advance.

If general linear restrictions are imposed on the equations of a linear system, we may state the following rule: an equation in a linear system is identified if it is not possible to reproduce by linear combination of some or all of the equations in the system an equation having the same statistical form as the equation being estimated.

If the restrictions are of the zero type, a necessary condition for identification of an equation in a linear system of n equations is that the number of variables excluded from that equation be greater than or equal to $n - 1$. A necessary and sufficient condition is that it is possible to form at least one nonvanishing determinant of order $n-1$ out of those coefficients, properly arranged, with which the excluded variables appear in the $n-1$ other equations (Koopmans *et al.*, 1950).

Criteria for identifiability are stated here for linear equation systems. A more general treatment in nonlinear systems is given by Fisher (1966). [See "Statistical Identifiability."]

Alternative Estimation Methods

Assuming that we are dealing with an identified system, let us turn to the problems of estimation. In the system of equations above, the y_{jt} are *endogenous* or *dependent* variables and are equal in number to the number of equations in the system, n. The z_{kt} are *exogenous* variables and are assumed to be independent of the disturbances, u_{it}.

In one of the basic early papers in simultaneous equation estimation (Mann & Wald, 1943), it was shown that large-sample theory would, under fairly general conditions, permit lagged values of endogenous variables to be treated like purely exogenous variables as far as consistency in estimation is concerned. Exogenous and lagged endogenous variables are called *predetermined* variables.

Early econometric studies, for example, that of Tinbergen (1939), were concerned with the estimation of a number of individual relationships in which the possible dependence between variables and disturbances was ignored. These studies stimulated Haavelmo (1943) to analyze the consistency problem, for he noted that the Tinbergen model contained many single-equation least squares estimates of equations that were interrelated in the system Tinbergen was constructing, which was intended to be a theoretical framework describing the economy that generated the observations used.

The lack of independence between disturbances and variables can readily be demonstrated. Consider the two-equation system

$$\beta_{11} y_{1t} + \beta_{12} y_{2t} + \sum_{k=1}^{m} \gamma_{1k} z_{kt} = u_{1t}$$

$$\beta_{21} y_{1t} + \beta_{22} y_{2t} + \sum_{k=1}^{m} \gamma_{2k} z_{kt} = u_{2t} \, .$$

The z_{kt} are by assumption independent of u_{1t} and u_{2t}. Some of the γ's are specified to be zero or are otherwise restricted so that the two equations are identified. Suppose we wish to estimate the first equation. To apply least squares to this equation, we would have to select either y_1 or y_2 as the dependent variable. Suppose we select y_1 and set β_{11} equal to unity. We would then compute the least squares regression of y_1 on y_2 and the z_k according to the relation

$$y_{1t} = -\beta_{12}y_{2t} - \sum_{k=1}^{m} \gamma_{1k}z_{kt} + u_{1t},$$

which incorporates all the identifying restrictions on the γ's.

For this procedure to yield consistent estimators, y_{2t} must be independent of u_{1t}. The question is whether the existence of the second equation has any bearing on the independence of y_{2t} and u_{1t}. Multiplying the second equation by u_{1t} and forming expectations, we have

$$E(y_{2t}u_{1t}) = -(\beta_{21}/\beta_{22})E(y_{1t}u_{1t}) + (1/\beta_{22})E(u_{1t}u_{2t}).$$

From the first equation (with $\beta_{11} = 1$), we have

$$E(y_{1t}u_{1t}) = -\beta_{12}E(y_{2t}u_{1t}) + E(u_{1t}^2).$$

Combining these two expressions, we obtain

$$E(y_{2t}u_{1t}) = \frac{E(u_{1t}u_{2t}) - \beta_{21}E(u_{1t}^2)}{\beta_{22} - \beta_{21}\beta_{12}}.$$

In general, this expression does not vanish, and we find that y_{2t} and u_{1t} are not independent.

The maximum likelihood method. The maximum likelihood method plays a normative role in the estimation of economic relationships, much like that played by perfect competition in economic theory. This method provides consistent and efficient estimators under fairly general conditions. It rests on specific assumptions, and it may be hard to realize all these assumptions in practice or, indeed, to make all the difficult calculations required for solution of the estimation equations.

For the single-equation model, the maximum likelihood method is immediately seen to be equivalent to ordinary least squares estimation for normally distributed disturbances. Let us suppose that $u_1, \ldots, u_T$ are T independent, normally distributed variables. The T-element sample has the probability density function

$$p(u_1, \ldots, u_T) = \left(\frac{1}{\sqrt{2\pi}\sigma}\right)^T \exp\left(-\frac{1}{2\sigma^2}\sum_{t=1}^{T}u_t^2\right).$$

By substitution we can transform this joint density of $u_1, \ldots, u_T$ into a joint density of $y_1, \ldots, y_T$, given $x_{11}, \ldots, x_{n1}, x_{12}, \ldots, x_{n2}, \ldots, x_{nT}$, namely,

$$p(y_1, \ldots, y_T | x_{11}, \ldots, x_{nT}) = \left(\frac{1}{\sqrt{2\pi}\sigma}\right)^T \exp\left[-\frac{1}{2\sigma^2}\sum_{t=1}^{T}\left(y_t - \sum_{i=1}^{n}\alpha_i x_{it}\right)^2\right].$$

This function will be denoted as L, the likelihood function of the sample, and is seen to depend on the unknown parameters $\alpha_1, \ldots, \alpha_n$ and σ. We maximize this function by imposing the following conditions:

$$\frac{\partial \log L}{\partial \alpha_i} = -\frac{1}{\sigma^2} \sum_{t=1}^{T} \left[\left(y_t - \sum_{j=1}^{n} \alpha_j x_{jt} \right) x_{it} \right] = 0, \qquad i = 1, \ldots, n,$$

$$\frac{\partial \log L}{\partial \sigma} = -\frac{T}{\sigma} + \frac{1}{\sigma^3} \sum_{t=1}^{T} \left(y_t - \sum_{j=1}^{n} \alpha_j x_{jt} \right)^2 = 0.$$

These are recognized as the "normal" equations of single-equation least squares theory and the estimation equation for the residual variance — apart from adjustment for degrees of freedom used in estimating σ^2.

In a system of simultaneous equations, we wish to estimate the parameters in

$$\sum_{j=1}^{n} \beta_{ij} y_{jt} + \sum_{k=1}^{m} \gamma_{ik} z_{kt} = u_{it}, \qquad i = 1, \ldots, n.$$

Here we have n linear simultaneous equations in n endogenous and m exogenous variables. The parameters to be estimated are the elements of the $n \times n$ coefficient matrix

$$\mathbf{B} = (\beta_{ij}),$$

the $n \times m$ coefficient matrix

$$\mathbf{\Gamma} = (\gamma_{ik})$$

and the $n \times n$ variance–covariance matrix

$$\mathbf{\Sigma} = (\sigma_{ij}).$$

The variances and covariances are defined by

$$\sigma_{ij} = E(u_i u_j).$$

A rule of normalization is applied for each equation,

$$\beta_i \mathbf{\Sigma} \beta_i' = 1.$$

In practice, one element of $\beta_i = (\beta_{i1}, \ldots, \beta_{in})$ in each equation is singled out and assigned a value of unity.

The likelihood function for the whole system is

$$L = \mathrm{mod}|\mathbf{B}|^T \left(\frac{1}{\sqrt{2\pi}} \right)^{Tn} |\mathbf{\Sigma}|^{-T/2} \exp \left\{ -\frac{1}{2} \sum_{t=1}^{T} [(\mathbf{B} y_t' + \mathbf{\Gamma} z_t')' \mathbf{\Sigma}^{-1} (\mathbf{B} y_t' + \mathbf{\Gamma} z_t')] \right\},$$

where $y_t = (y_{1t}, \ldots, y_{nt})$, $z_t = (z_{1t}, \ldots, z_{mt})$, $|\mathbf{\Sigma}|$ is the determinant of $\mathbf{\Sigma}$, and mod $|\mathbf{B}|$ is the absolute value of the determinant of $\mathbf{B}$ (Koopmans *et al.*, 1950).

The matrix $\mathbf{B}$ enters this expression as the Jacobian of the transformation from the variables $u_{1t}, \ldots, u_{nt}$ to $y_{1t}, \ldots, y_{nt}$. The problem of maximum likelihood estimation is to maximize L or $\log L$ with respect to the elements of $\mathbf{B}$, $\mathbf{\Gamma}$, and $\mathbf{\Sigma}$. This is especially difficult compared with the similar problem for single equations shown above, because $\log L$ is highly nonlinear in the unknown parameters, a difficult source of nonlinearity coming from the Jacobian expression mod $|\mathbf{B}|$.

Maximizing $\log L$ with respect to $\mathbf{\Sigma}^{-1}$, we obtain the maximum likelihood estimator of $\mathbf{\Sigma}$, which is

$$\hat{\mathbf{\Sigma}} = (\mathbf{B}\,\mathbf{\Gamma})M(\mathbf{B}\,\mathbf{\Gamma})',$$

where M is the moment matrix of the observations, i.e.,

$$M = \frac{1}{T} \left[\begin{array}{ccc} y_{11} & \cdots & y_{1T} \\ \vdots & & \vdots \\ y_{n1} & \cdots & y_{nT} \\ \hline z_{11} & \cdots & z_{1T} \\ \vdots & & \vdots \\ z_{m1} & \cdots & z_{mT} \end{array}\right] \left[\begin{array}{ccc|ccc} y_{11} & \cdots & y_{n1} & z_{11} & \cdots & z_{m1} \\ \vdots & & \vdots & \vdots & & \vdots \\ y_{1T} & \cdots & y_{nT} & z_{1T} & \cdots & z_{mT} \end{array}\right]$$

$$= \left[\begin{array}{cc} M_{yy} & M_{yz} \\ M_{zy} & M_{zz} \end{array}\right].$$

Substitution of $\hat{\mathbf{\Sigma}}$ into the likelihood function yields the *concentrated form* of the likelihood function

$$\log L = \text{Const.} + T \log \text{mod}|\mathbf{B}| - (T/2) \log |\hat{\mathbf{\Sigma}}|,$$

where Const. is a constant. Hence, we seek estimators of $\mathbf{B}$ and $\mathbf{\Gamma}$ that maximize

$$\log \text{mod}|\mathbf{B}| - \frac{1}{2} \log |\hat{\mathbf{\Sigma}}| = \log \text{mod}|\mathbf{B}| - \frac{1}{2} \log |(\mathbf{B}\mathbf{\Gamma})M(\mathbf{B}\mathbf{\Gamma})'|.$$

In the single-equation case we minimize the one-element variance expression, written as a function of the α_i. In the simultaneous equation case, we maximize $\log \text{mod}|\mathbf{B}| - \frac{1}{2} \log |\hat{\mathbf{\Sigma}}|$, but this can be shown to be equivalent (Chow, 1964) to minimization of $|\hat{\mathbf{\Sigma}}|$, subject to the normalization rule

$$|\mathbf{B}M_{yy}\mathbf{B}'| = C,$$

where C is a constant. This normalization is direction normalization, and as long as it is taken into account, scale normalization (such as $\beta_{ii} = 1$, cited previously) is arbitrary. Viewed in this way, the method of maximum likelihood applied to a system of equations appears to be a natural generalization of the method of maximum likelihood applied to a single equation, in which case we minimize σ^2 subject to a direction-normalization rule.

Recursive systems. The concentrated form of the likelihood function shows clearly that a new element is introduced into the estimation process, through the presence of the Jacobian determinant, which makes calculations of the maximizing values of $\mathbf{B}$ and $\boldsymbol{\Gamma}$ highly nonlinear. It is therefore worthwhile to search for special situations in which estimation methods simplify at least to the point of being based on linear calculations.

It is evident that the concentrated form of the likelihood function would lend itself to simpler methods of estimating $\mathbf{B}$ and $\boldsymbol{\Gamma}$ if $|\mathbf{B}|$ were a known constant. This would be the case if $\mathbf{B}$ were triangular, for then, by a scale normalization, we would have $\beta_{ii} = 1$ and $|\mathbf{B}| = 1$. If $\mathbf{B}$ is triangular, the system of equations is called a recursive system. We then simply minimize $|\hat{\boldsymbol{\Sigma}}|$ with respect to the unknown coefficients; this can be looked upon as a generalized variance minimization, an obvious analog of least squares applied to a single equation.

If, in addition, it can be assumed that $\boldsymbol{\Sigma}$ is diagonal, maximum likelihood estimators become a series of successive single-equation least squares estimators. Since the matrix $\mathbf{B}$ is assumed to be triangular, there must be an equation with only one unlagged endogenous variable. This variable (with unit coefficient) is to be regressed on all the predetermined variables in that equation. Next, there will be an equation with one new endogenous variable. This variable is regressed on the preceding endogenous variable and all the predetermined variables in that equation. In the third equation, another new endogenous variable is introduced. It is regressed on the two preceding endogenous variables and all the predetermined variables in that equation, and so on.

If $\boldsymbol{\Sigma}$ is not diagonal, a statistically consistent procedure would be to use values of the endogenous variables computed from preceding equations in the triangular array instead of using their actual values. Suppose one equation in the system specifies y_1 as a function of certain z's. We would regress y_1 on these z's and then compute values of y_1 from the relation

$$\hat{y}_{1t} = \sum_{k=1}^{m} \hat{\gamma}_{1k} z_{kt} \, ,$$

where the $\hat{\gamma}_{1k}$ are the least squares regression estimators of the γ_{1k}. (Some of the γ_{1k} are zero, as a result of the identifying restrictions imposed prior to computing the regression.) Suppose a second equation in the system specifies y_2 as a function of y_1 and certain z's. Our next step would be to regress y_2 on $\hat{y}_1$ and the included z's and then compute values of y_2 from the relation

$$\hat{y}_{2t} = \hat{\beta}_{21} \hat{y}_{1t} + \sum_{k=1}^{m} \hat{\gamma}_{2k} z_{kt} \, .$$

The procedure would be continued until all n equations are estimated.

Methods of dealing with recursive systems have been studied extensively by Wold, and a summary appears in Strotz and Wold (1960). A recursive system without a diagonal Σ-matrix is found in Barger and Klein (1954). One of the most familiar types of recursive systems studied in econometrics is the cobweb model of demand and supply for agricultural products [see "Business Cycles: Mathematical Models"].

Limited-information maximum likelihood. Another maximum likelihood approach that is widely used is the limited-information maximum likelihood method. It does not hinge on a specific formulation of the model, as do methods for recursive systems; it is a simplified method because it neglects information. As we have seen, identifying restrictions for an equation takes the form of specifying zero values for some parameters or of imposing certain linear relations on some parameters. The term "Limited information" refers to the fact that only the restrictions relating to the particular equation (or subset of equations) being estimated are used. Restrictions on other equations in the system are ignored when a particular equation is being estimated.

Let us again consider the linear system

$$\mathbf{B}\mathbf{y}'_t + \mathbf{\Gamma}\mathbf{z}'_t = \mathbf{u}'_t.$$

These equations make up the *structural form* of the system and are referred to as structural equations. We denote the *reduced form* of this system by

$$\mathbf{y}'_t = -\mathbf{B}^{-1}\mathbf{\Gamma}\mathbf{z}'_t + \mathbf{B}^{-1}\mathbf{u}'_t$$

or

$$\mathbf{y}'_t = \mathbf{\Pi}\mathbf{z}'_t + \mathbf{v}'_t.$$

From the reduced form equations select a subset corresponding to the n_1 endogenous variables in a particular structural equation, say equation i, which is

$$\sum_{j=1}^{n_1} \beta_{ij} y_{jt} + \sum_{k=1}^{m_1} \gamma_{ik} z_{kt} = u_{it}.$$

The summation limit m_1 indicates the number of predetermined variables included in this equation; we have excluded all zero elements in γ_i and indexed the z's accordingly. Form the joint distribution of $v_{1t}, \ldots, v_{n_1 t}$ over the sample observations and maximize it with respect to the unknown parameters in the ith structural equation, subject to the restrictions on this equation alone. The restrictions usually take the form

$$0 = \sum_{j=1}^{n_1} \beta_{ij} \pi_{jk}, \qquad k = m_1 + 1, \ldots, m,$$

where there are m predetermined variables in the whole system; that is, the $\gamma_{ik}, k = m_1 + 1, \ldots, m$, are specified to be zero. The estimated coefficients, $\hat{\beta}_{ij}, \hat{\gamma}_{ik}$, and $\hat{\sigma}_i^2$, obtained from this restricted likelihood maximization are the limited-information estimators. Methods of obtaining these estimators and a study of their properties are given in Anderson and Rubin (1949).

Linear regression calculations are all that are needed in this type of estimation, save for the extraction of a characteristic root of a matrix with dimensionality $n_1 \times n_1$. A quickly convergent series of iterations involving matrix multiplication leads to the computation of this root and associated vector. The vector obtained, properly normalized by making one coefficient unity, provides estimates of the β_{ij}. The estimates of the γ_{ik} are obtained from

$$\hat{\gamma}_{ik} = -\sum_{j=1}^{n_1} \hat{\beta}_{ij}\hat{\pi}_{jk}, \qquad k = 1, \ldots, m_1,$$

where the $\hat{\pi}_{jk}$ are least squares regression coefficients from the reduced form equations.

It is significant that both full-information and limited-information maximum likelihood estimators are *essentially* unchanged no matter which variable is selected to have a unit coefficient in each equation. That is to say, if we divide through an estimated equation by the coefficient of any endogenous variable, we get a set of coefficients that would have been obtained by applying the estimation methods under the specification that the same variable have the unit coefficient. Full-information and limited-information maximum likelihood estimators are invariant under this type of scale normalization. Other estimators are not.

Two-stage least squares. The classical method of least squares multiple regression applied to a single equation that is part of a larger simultaneous system is inconsistent by virtue of the fact that some of the "explanatory" variables in the regression (the variables with unknown coefficients) may not be independent of the error variable. If we can "purify" such variables to make them independent of the error terms, we can apply ordinary least squares methods to the transformed variables. The method of two-stage least squares does this for us.

Let us return to the equation estimated above by limited information. Choose y_1, say, as the dependent variable, that is, set β_{i1} equal to unity. In place of $y_{2t}, \ldots, y_{n_1 t}$, we shall use

$$\hat{y}_{jt} = \sum_{k=1}^{m} \hat{\pi}_{jk} z_{kt}, \qquad j = 2, \ldots, n_1,$$

as explanatory variables. The $\hat{y}_{jt}$ are *computed* values from the least squares regressions of y_j on all the z_k in the system ($k = 1, \ldots, m$). The coefficients $\hat{\pi}_{jk}$ are the computed regression coefficients. The regression of y_1 on $\hat{y}_2, \ldots, \hat{y}_{n_1}, z_1, \ldots, z_{m_1}$ provides a two-stage least squares estimator of the single equation. All the equations of a system may be estimated in this way. This can be seen to be a generalization, to systems with nontriangular Jacobians, of the method suggested previously for recursive models in which the variance–covariance matrix of disturbances is not diagonal.

We may write the "normal" equations for these least squares estimators as

$$
\begin{bmatrix} \sum_{t=1}^{I} y_{1t}\hat{\boldsymbol{y}}_t' \\ \sum_{t=1}^{I} y_{1t}\hat{\boldsymbol{z}}_t^{*\prime} \end{bmatrix} = \begin{bmatrix} \boldsymbol{M}_{\hat{y}\hat{y}} & \boldsymbol{M}_{\hat{y}z^*} \\ \boldsymbol{M}_{z^*\hat{y}} & \boldsymbol{M}_{z^*z^*} \end{bmatrix} \begin{bmatrix} -\boldsymbol{b}' \\ -\boldsymbol{c}' \end{bmatrix}.
$$

In this notation $\hat{\boldsymbol{y}}_t$ is the vector of computed values $(\hat{y}_{2t}, \ldots, \hat{y}_{n_1 t})$; $\boldsymbol{z}_t^*$ is the vector $(z_{1t}, \ldots, z_{m_1 t})$;

$$
\begin{bmatrix} \boldsymbol{M}_{\hat{y}\hat{y}} & \boldsymbol{M}_{\hat{y}z^*} \\ \boldsymbol{M}_{z^*\hat{y}} & \boldsymbol{M}_{z^*z^*} \end{bmatrix} = \begin{bmatrix} \hat{y}_{21} & \cdots & \hat{y}_{2T} \\ \vdots & & \vdots \\ \hat{y}_{n_1 1} & \cdots & \hat{y}_{n_1 T} \\ \hline z_{11} & \cdots & z_{1T} \\ \vdots & & \vdots \\ z_{m_1 1} & \cdots & z_{m_1 T} \end{bmatrix} \begin{bmatrix} \hat{y}_{21} & \cdots & \hat{y}_{n_1 1} & x_{11} & \cdots & z_{m_1 1} \\ \vdots & & \vdots & \vdots & & \vdots \\ \hat{y}_{2T} & \cdots & \hat{y}_{n_1 T} & z_{1T} & \cdots & z_{m_1 T} \end{bmatrix};
$$

$\boldsymbol{b}$ is the estimator of the vector $(\beta_{i2}, \ldots, \beta_{in_1})$; and $\boldsymbol{c}$ is the estimator of the vector $(\gamma_{i1}, \ldots, \gamma_{im_1})$. It should be noted that $\boldsymbol{M}_{\hat{y}z^*} = \boldsymbol{M}_{yz^*} = \boldsymbol{M'}_{z^*y}$. It should be further observed that

$$
\boldsymbol{M}_{\hat{y}\hat{y}} = \boldsymbol{M}_{yz}\boldsymbol{M}_{zz}^{-1}\boldsymbol{M}_{zy}.
$$

In this expression the whole vector $\boldsymbol{z}_t = (z_{1t}, \ldots, z_{mt})$, which includes all the predetermined variables in the system, is used for the evaluation of the relevant moment matrices.

k-Class estimators. Theil (1958) and Basmann (1957), independently, were the first to advocate the method of two-stage least squares. Theil suggested a whole system of estimators, called the k-class. he defined these as the solutions to

$$
\begin{bmatrix} \sum_{t=1}^{T} y_{1t}\boldsymbol{y}_t' - k\sum_{t=1}^{T} y_{1t}\hat{\boldsymbol{v}}_t' \\ \sum_{t=1}^{T} y_{1t}\boldsymbol{z}_t^{*\prime} \end{bmatrix} = \begin{bmatrix} \boldsymbol{M}_{yy} - k\boldsymbol{M}_{yz}\boldsymbol{M}_{zz}^{-1}\boldsymbol{M}_{zy} & \boldsymbol{M}_{yz^*} \\ \boldsymbol{M}_{z^*y} & \boldsymbol{M}_{z^*z^*} \end{bmatrix} \begin{bmatrix} -\boldsymbol{b}' \\ -\boldsymbol{c}' \end{bmatrix}.
$$

In this expression $\hat{\boldsymbol{v}}_t$ is the vector of residuals computed from the reduced form regressions of $y_{2t}, \ldots, y_{n_1 t}$ on all the z_{kt}. If $k = 0$, we have ordinary least squares estimators. If $k = 1$, we have two-stage least squares estimators. If $k = 1 + \lambda$ and λ is the smallest root of the determinantal equation

$$
|\boldsymbol{M}_{yz}\boldsymbol{M}_{zz}^{-1}\boldsymbol{M}_{zy} - \boldsymbol{M}_{yz^*}\boldsymbol{M}_{z^*z^*}^{-1}\boldsymbol{M}_{z^*y} - \lambda(\boldsymbol{M}_{yy} - \boldsymbol{M}_{yz}\boldsymbol{M}_{zz}^{-1}\boldsymbol{M}_{zy})| = 0,
$$

we have limited-information maximum likelihood estimators. This is a succinct way of showing the relationships between various single-equation methods of estimation.

Of these three members of the k-class, ordinary least squares is not consistent; the other two are.

•Three-stage least squares. The original derivation of two-stage least squares estimates was obtained by an application of Aitken's generalized method of least squares. The equation to be estimated will be written as

$$y_1 = -Y_i\beta_i - Z_i\gamma_i + u_i,$$

where

$$y_1 = \begin{bmatrix} y_{11} \\ y_{12} \\ \vdots \\ y_{1T} \end{bmatrix}; \quad Y_i = \begin{bmatrix} y_{21} & y_{31} & \cdots & y_{n_11} \\ y_{22} & y_{32} & \cdots & y_{n_12} \\ \vdots & \vdots & & \vdots \\ y_{2T} & y_{3T} & \cdots & y_{n_1T} \end{bmatrix}; \quad \beta_i = \begin{bmatrix} \beta_{i2} \\ \beta_{i3} \\ \vdots \\ \beta_{in_1} \end{bmatrix}$$

$$\gamma_i = \begin{bmatrix} \gamma_{i1} \\ \gamma_{i2} \\ \vdots \\ \gamma_{im_1} \end{bmatrix}; \quad Z_i = \begin{bmatrix} z_{11} & z_{21} & \cdots & z_{m_11} \\ z_{12} & z_{22} & \cdots & z_{m_12} \\ \vdots & \vdots & & \vdots \\ z_{1T} & z_{2T} & \cdots & z_{m_1T} \end{bmatrix}; \quad u_i = \begin{bmatrix} u_{i1} \\ u_{i2} \\ \vdots \\ u_{iT} \end{bmatrix}.$$

Form the product

$$Z'y_1 = Z'Y_i\beta_i - Z'Z_i\gamma_i + Z'u_i,$$

where Z_i is a submatrix of Z, which is the data matrix for the whole set of exogenous variables. As long as $m > n_1 - 1$, the overidentified case (necessary condition), we can regard this setup as implying the regression of the moment quantity $\Sigma_{t=1}^{T} z_{it}y_{1t}$ on $\Sigma_{t=1}^{T} z_{it}y_{jt}$ and $\Sigma_{t=1}^{T} z_{it}z_{kt}$ ($j = 2, \ldots, n_1; k = 1, 2, \ldots, m_1$). The data set for the regression runs from 1 to m. The disturbance has variance $\sigma^2 X'X$. The formulas for the generalized least squares regression with the indicated variance reduce to those for two-stage least squares estimation of β_i and γ_i.

$$\text{est} \begin{bmatrix} -\beta_i \\ -\gamma_i \end{bmatrix} = [(Z'Y_iZ'Z_i)'(Z'Z)^{-1}(Z'Y_iZ'Z_i)]^{-1}(Z'Y_iZ'Z_i)'(Z'Z)^{-1}Z'y_1$$

$$= \begin{bmatrix} Y_i'Z(Z'Z)^{-1}Z'Y_i & Y_i'Z_i \\ Z_i'Y_i & Z_i'Z_i \end{bmatrix}^{-1} \begin{bmatrix} Y_i'Z(Z'Z)^{-1}Z'y_1 \\ Z_i'y_1 \end{bmatrix}.$$

These are standard formulas for two-stage least squares estimators, using data matrix notation.

▶ The method of three-stage least squares is a natural extension of the method of generalized least squares as applied to the previous case. The complete system of equations can be written as

$$\begin{bmatrix} y_1 \\ y_2 \\ \vdots \\ y_n \end{bmatrix} = \begin{bmatrix} X_1 & 0 & \cdots & 0 \\ 0 & X_2 & \cdots & 0 \\ \vdots & \vdots & & \vdots \\ 0 & 0 & \cdots & X_n \end{bmatrix} \begin{bmatrix} \delta_1 \\ \delta_2 \\ \vdots \\ \delta_n \end{bmatrix} + \begin{bmatrix} u_1 \\ u_2 \\ \vdots \\ u_n \end{bmatrix},$$

where
$$X_i = (Y_i \; Z_i),$$
$$\delta_i = -\begin{bmatrix} \beta_i \\ \gamma_i \end{bmatrix}.$$

Now form the equations

$$\begin{bmatrix} Z'y_1 \\ Z'y_2 \\ \vdots \\ Z'y_n \end{bmatrix} = \begin{bmatrix} Z'X_1 & 0 & \cdots & 0 \\ 0 & Z'X_2 & \cdots & 0 \\ \vdots & & & \\ 0 & 0 & \cdots & Z'X_n \end{bmatrix} \begin{bmatrix} \delta_1 \\ \delta_2 \\ \vdots \\ \delta_n \end{bmatrix} + \begin{bmatrix} Z'u_1 \\ Z'u_2 \\ \vdots \\ Z'u_n \end{bmatrix}.$$

The three-stage least squares estimator of δ is the Aitken generalized least squares estimator of this system.

$$\text{est}\,\delta = [X'(S^{-1} \otimes Z(Z'Z)^{-1}Z')X]^{-1} X'(S^{-1} \otimes Z(Z'Z)^{-1}Z')y,$$

where S is the estimated covariance matrix of residuals from the two-stage least squares estimate of each single equation. We can write this out as

$$\text{est} - \begin{bmatrix} \beta \\ \gamma \end{bmatrix} = \begin{bmatrix} S^{11}X'_1 Z(Z'Z)^{-1}Z'X_1 \cdots S^{1n}X'_1 Z(Z'Z)^{-1}Z'X_n \\ \vdots \qquad\qquad \vdots \\ S^{n1}X'_n Z(Z'Z)^{-1}Z'X_1 \cdots S^{nn}X'_n Z(Z'Z)^{-1}Z'X_n \end{bmatrix}$$

$$\times \begin{bmatrix} \Sigma S^{1i}X'Z(Z'Z)^{-1}Z'y_1 \\ \vdots \\ \Sigma S^{ni}X'Z(Z'Z)^{-1}Z'y_i \end{bmatrix},$$

where $(S^{ij}) = S^{-1}$.

▶ Both two- and three-stage least squares estimators can thus be interpreted as Aitken estimators, one for single equations in a system and one for whole systems of equations. This class of estimators was first derived by Theil and Zellner (see Zellner & Theil, 1962).

Theil and Zellner termed their method three-stage least squares because they first derived two-stage least squares estimators for each single equation in the system. They computed the residual variance for each equation and used these as estimators of the variances of the true (unobserved) random disturbances. They then used Aitken's generalized method of least squares (1935) to estimate all the equations in the system simultaneously. Aitken's method applies to systems of equations in which the variance–covariance matrix for disturbances is a general known positive definite matrix. Theil and Zellner used the two-stage estimator of this variance–covariance matrix as though it were known. The advantage of this method is that it is of the full-information variety, making use of restrictions on all the equations of the system.

Other methods. If the conditions for identification of a single equation are such that there are just enough restrictions to transform linearly and uniquely the reduced form coefficients into the structural coefficients, an indirect least squares method of estimation can be used. Exact identification under zero-type restrictions would enable one to solve

$$0 = \sum_{j=1}^{n} \beta_{ij}\pi_{jk}, \qquad k = m_1 + 1, \ldots, m,$$

for a unique set of estimated β_{ij}, apart from scale normalization, given a set of estimated π_{jk}. The latter would be determined from least squares estimators of the reduced forms. Since there are $n_1 - 1$ of the β_{ij} to be determined, the necessary condition for exact identification here is that $n_1 - 1 = m - m_1$.

If there is *underidentification*, i.e., too few *a priori* restrictions, structural estimation cannot be completed but unrestricted reduced forms can be estimated by the method of least squares. This is the most information that the econometrician can extract when there is lack of identification. Least squares estimators of the reduced form equations are consistent in the underidentified case, but estimates of the structural parameters cannot be made.

Instrumental variables. The early discussion of estimation problems in simultaneous equation models contained, on many occasions, applications of a method known as the method of instrumental variables. In estimating the ith equation of a linear system, i.e.,

$$\sum_{j=1}^{n_1} \beta_{ij}y_{jt} + \sum_{k=1}^{m_1} \gamma_{ik}z_{kt} = u_{it},$$

we may choose $(n_1 - 1) + m_1$ variables that are independent of u_{it}. These are known as the instrumental set. Naturally, the exogenous variables in the equation $(z_{1t}, \ldots, z_{m_1t})$ are possible members of this set. In addition, we need $n_1 - 1$ more instruments from the list of exogenous variables in the system but not in the ith equation. For this problem let these be denoted as $x_{2t}, \ldots, x_{n_1t}$. Since $E(z_{st}u_{it}) = 0, s = 1, \ldots, m_1$, and $E(x_{rt}u_{it}) = 0, r = 2, \ldots, n_1$, we can estimate the unknown parameters from

$$\sum_{j=1}^{n_1} \beta_{ij} \sum_{t=1}^{T} y_{jt}x_{rt} + \sum_{k=1}^{m_1} \gamma_{ik} \sum_{t=1}^{T} z_{kt}x_{rt} = 0, \qquad r = 2, \ldots, n_1,$$

$$\Sigma_{j=1}^{n_1}\beta_{ij} \sum_{t=1}^{T} y_{jt}z_{st} + \Sigma_{k=1}^{m_1}\gamma_{ik}\Sigma_{t=1}^{T}z_{kt}z_{st} = 0, \qquad s = 1, \ldots, m_1.$$

With a scale-normalization rule, such as $\beta_{i1} = 1$, we have $(n_1 - 1) + m_1$ linear equations in the same number of unknown coefficients. In exactly identified models there is no problem in picking the x_{rt}, for there will always be exactly $(n_1 - 1)z$'s excluded from the ith equation. The method is then identical with indirect least squares. If $m - m_1 > n_1 - 1$, i.e., if there are more exogenous variables outside the ith equation than there are endogenous variables minus one, we have overidentification, and the number of possible instrumental variables exceeds the minimum needed. In order to avoid the problem of subjective or arbitrary choice among instruments, we turn to the methods of limited information or two-stage least squares. In fact, it is instructive to consider how the method of two-stage least squares resolves this matter. In place of single variables as instruments, it uses linear combinations of them. The computed values

$$\hat{y}_{jt} = \sum_{k=1}^{m} \hat{\pi}_{jk} z_{kt}, \qquad j = 2, \ldots, n_1,$$

are the new instruments. We can view the method either as the regression of y_1 on $\hat{y}_2, \ldots, \hat{y}_{n1}, z_1, \ldots, z_{m_1}$ or as instrumental-variable estimators with $\hat{y}_{2t}, \ldots, \hat{y}_{n_1 t}$, $z_{1t}, \ldots, z_{m_1 t}$ as the instruments. Both come to the same thing. The method of instrumental variables yields consistent estimators.

Subgroup averages. The instrumental-variables method can be applied in different forms. One form was used by Wald (1940) to obtain consistent estimators of a linear relationship between two variables each of which is subject to error. This gives rise to a method that can be used in estimating econometric systems. Wald proposed that the estimator of β in

$$y_t = \alpha + \beta x_t,$$

where y_t and x_t are both measured with error, be computed from

$$\hat{\beta} = \frac{\displaystyle\sum_{t=\frac{T}{2}+1}^{T} y_t - \sum_{t=1}^{\frac{T}{2}} y_t}{\displaystyle\sum_{t=\frac{T}{2}+1}^{T} x_t - \sum_{t=1}^{\frac{T}{2}} x_t}.$$

He proposed ordering the sample in ascending magnitudes of the variable x. From two halves of the sample, we determine two sets of mean values of y and x. The line joining these means will have a slope given by $\hat{\beta}$. Wald showed the conditions under which these estimates are consistent.

This may be called the method of subgroup averages. It is a very simple method, which may readily be applied to equations with more than two parameters. The sample is split into as many groups as there are unknown parameters to be determined in the equation under consideration. If there are three parameters, for example, the sample may be split into thirds and the parameters estimated from

$$\bar{y}_1 = \alpha + \beta \bar{x}_1 + \gamma \bar{z}_1,$$
$$\bar{y}_2 = \alpha + \beta \bar{x}_2 + \gamma \bar{z}_2,$$
$$\bar{y}_3 = \alpha + \beta \bar{x}_3 + \gamma \bar{z}_3.$$

The extension to more parameters is obvious. The method of subgroup averages can be shown to be a form of the instrumental-variables method by an appropriate assignment of values to "dummy" instrumental variables.

Subgroup averages is a very simple method, and it is consistent, but it is not very efficient.

Simultaneous least squares. The simultaneous least squares method, suggested by Brown (1960), minimizes the sum of squares of all reduced form disturbances, subject to the parameter restrictions imposed on the system, i.e., it minimizes

$$\sum_{t=1}^{T}\sum_{i=1}^{n} v_{it}^2,$$

subject to restrictions. Suppose that the v_{it} are expressed as functions of the observables and parameters, with all restrictions included; then Brown's method minimizes the sum of the elements on the main diagonal of Σ_v, where Σ_v is the variance–covariance matrix of reduced form disturbances, whereas full-information maximum likelihood minimizes $|\Sigma_v|$.

Brown's method has the desirable property of being a full-information method; it is distribution free; it is consistent; but it has the drawback that its results are not invariant under linear transformations of the variables. This drawback can be removed by expressing the reduced form disturbance in standard units

$$v'_{it} = v_{it}/\sigma_{v_i}$$

and minimizing

$$\sum_{t=1}^{T}\sum_{i=1}^{n} (v'_{it})^2.$$

Evaluation of Alternative Methods

The various approaches to estimation of whole systems of simultaneous equations or individual relationships within such systems are *consistent* except for the single-equation least squares method. If the system is recursive and disturbances are independent between equations, least squares estimators are also consistent. In fact, they are maximum likelihood estimators for normally distributed disturbances. But generally, ordinary least squares estimators are not consistent. They are included in the group of alternatives considered here because they have a time-honored status and because they have minimum variance. In large-sample theory, maximum likelihood estimators of parameters are generally efficient compared with all other estimators. That is why we choose full-information maximum likelihood estimators as norms. They are consistent and efficient. Least squares estimators are minimum-variance estimators if their variances are estimated about estimated (inconsistent) sample means. If their variances are measured about the *true*, or population, values, it is not certain that they are efficient.

Limited-information estimators are less efficient than full-information maximum likelihood estimators. This should be intuitively obvious, since full-information estimators make use of more *a priori* information; it is proven in Klein (1960). Two-stage least squares estimators have asymptotically the same variance–covariance matrix as limited-information estimators, and three-stage (or simultaneous two-stage) least squares estimators have the same variance–covariance matrix as full-information maximum likelihood estimators. Thus, asymptotically the two kinds of limited-information estimators have the same efficiency, and the two kinds of full-information estimators have the same efficiency. The instrumental-variables or subgroup-averages methods are generally inefficient. Of course, the instrumental-variables method can be pushed to the point where it is the same as two-stage least squares estimation and can thereby gain efficiency.

A desirable aspect of the method of maximum likelihood is that its properties are preserved under a single-valued transformation. Thus, efficient estimators of structural parameters by this method transform into efficient estimators of reduced form parameters. The apparently efficient method of least squares may lose its efficiency under this kind of transformation. In applications of models, we use the reduced form in most cases, not the individual structural equations; therefore the properties under conditions of transformation from structural to reduced form equations are of extreme importance. Limited-information methods are a form of maximum likelihood methods. Therefore the properties of limited information are preserved under transformation.

To obtain limited-information estimators of the single equation

$$\sum_{j=1}^{n_1} \beta_{ij} y_{it} + \sum_{k=1}^{m_1} \gamma_{ik} z_{kt} = u_{it},$$

we maximize the joint likelihood of $v_{1t}, \ldots, v_{n_1}t$ in

$$y_{jt} = \sum_{l=1}^{m} \pi_{jl} z_{lt} + v_{jt}, \qquad j = 1, \ldots, n_1,$$

subject to the restrictions on the ith equation. In this case only the n_1 reduced forms corresponding to $y_{1t}, \ldots, y_{n_1 t}$ are used. It is also possible to simplify calculations, and yet preserve consistency (although at the expense of efficiency), by using fewer than all m predetermined variables in the reduced forms. In this sense the reduced forms of limited-information estimation are not necessarily unique, and the same endogenous variable appearing in different structural equations of a system may not have the same reduced form expression for each equation estimator. There is yet another sense in which we may derive reduced forms for the method of limited information. After each equation of a complete system has been estimated by the method of limited information, we can derive algebraically a set of reduced forms for the whole system. These would, in fact, be the reduced forms used in forecasting, multiplier analysis, and similar applications of systems. The efficiency property noted above for limited and full information has not been proven for systems of this type of reduced forms, but this has been studied in numerical analysis (see below).

Ease of computation. Finally we come to an important practical matter in the comparison of the different methods of estimation — relative ease of computation. Naturally, calculations are simpler and smaller in magnitude for single-equation least squares than for any of the other methods except that of subgroup averages. The method of instrumental variables is of similar computational complexity, but for equations with four or more variables it pays to have the advantage of symmetry in the moment matrices, as is the case with single-equation least squares. This is hardly a consideration with modern electronic computing machines, but it is worth consideration if electric desk machines are being used.

The next-simplest calculations are those for two-stage least squares. These consist of a repeated application of least squares regression techniques of calculation, but the first regressions computed are of substantial size. There are as many independent variables in the regression as there are predetermined variables in the system, provided there are enough degrees of freedom. Essentially, the method amounts to the calculation of parameters and computed dependent variables in

$$\hat{y}_{jt} = \sum_{k=1}^{m} \hat{\pi}_{jk} z_{kt}, \qquad j = 2, \ldots, n_1.$$

Only the "forward" part of this calculation by the standard Gauss–Doolittle method need be made in order to obtain the moment matrix of the y_{jt}. In the next stage we compute the regression

$$y_{1t} = -\sum_{j=2}^{n_1} b_{ij} \hat{y}_{jt} - \sum_{k=1}^{m_1} c_{ik} z_{kt}.$$

Two important computing problems arise in the first stage. In many systems $m > T$; i.e., there are insufficient degrees of freedom in the sample for evaluation of the reduced forms. We may choose a subset of the z_{kt}, or we may use principal components of the z_{kt} (Kloek & Mennes, 1960). Systematic and efficient ways of choosing subsets of the z_{kt} have been developed by taking account of the recursive structure of the model (Fisher, 1965). In many economic models m has been as large as 30 or more, and it is often difficult to make sufficiently accurate evaluation of the reduced form regression equations of this size, given the amount of multicollinearity found in economic data with common trends and cycles. The same procedures used in handling the degrees-of-freedom problem are recommended for getting round the difficulties of multicollinearity. Klein and Nakamura (1962) have shown that multicollinearity problems are less serious in ordinary than in two-stage least squares. They have also shown that these problems increase as we move on to the methods of limited-information and then full-information maximum likelihood.

Limited-information methods require all the computations of two-stage least squares and, in addition, the extraction of a root of an $n_1 \times n_1$ determinantal equation. The latter calculation can be done in a straightforward manner by iterative matrix multiplication, usually involving fewer than ten iterations.

Both limited information and two-stage least squares are extremely well adapted to modern computers and can be managed without much trouble on electric desk machines.

Three-stage least squares estimators involve the computation of two-stage estimators for each equation of a system, estimation of a variance–covariance matrix of structural disturbances, and simultaneous solution of a linear equation system of the order of all coefficients in the system. This last step may involve a large number of estimating equations for a model of 30 or more structural equations.

All the previous methods consist of standard linear matrix operations. The extraction of a characteristic root is the only operation that involves nonlinearities, and the desired root can quickly be found by an iterative process of matrix multiplication. Full-information maximum likelihood methods, however, are quite different. The estimation equations are highly nonlinear. For small systems of two, three, or four equations, estimates have been made without much trouble on large computers (Eisenpress, 1962) and on desk machines (Chernoff & Divinsky, 1953). The problem of finding the maximum of a function as complicated as the joint likelihood function of a system of 15 to 20 or more equations, is, however, formidable. Electronic machine programs have been developed for this purpose. The most standardized sets of full-information maximum likelihood calculations are for systems that are fully linear in both parameters and variables. Single-equation methods require linearity only in unknown parameters, and this is a much weaker restriction. Much progress in computation has been made since the first discussion of these econometric methods of estimation, in 1943, but the problem is far from solved, and there is no simple, push-button computation. This is especially true of full-formation maximum likelihood.

Efficient programs have recently been developed for calculating full-information maximum likelihood estimates in either linear or nonlinear systems, and these have been applied to models of as many as 15 structural equations, involving more than 60 unknown parameters.

Generalization of assumptions. The basis for comparing different estimation methods or for preferring one method over another rests on *asymptotic* theory. The property of consistency is a large-sample property, and the sampling errors used to evaluate efficiency measures are asymptotic formulas. Unfortunately, samples of economic data are frequently not large, especially time series data. The amount of small-sample bias or the small-sample confidence intervals for parameter estimators are not generally known in specific formulas. Constructed numerical experiments, designed according to Monte Carlo methods, have thrown some light on the small-sample properties. These are reported below.

Another assumption sometimes made for the basic model is that the error terms are mutually independent. We noted above that successive least squares treatment of equations in recursive systems is identical with maximum likelihood estimation when the variance–covariance matrix of structural disturbances is diagonal. This implies mutual independence among contemporaneous disturbances. In a time series model we usually make another assumption, namely, that

$$E(u_{it}u_{jt'}) = 0, \qquad t \neq t', \text{ for all } i, j.$$

The simplest way in which this assumption can be modified is to allow the errors to be related in some linear autoregressive process, such as

$$u_{it} = \sum_{j=1}^{n}\sum_{k=1}^{p} \rho_{ijk}u_{j,t-k} + e_{it}, \qquad i = 1, 2, \ldots, n,$$

where $E(e_{it}e_{jt'}) = 0$ $(t \neq t',$ for all $i, j)$. In a formal sense joint maximum likelihood estimation of structural parameters and autoregressive coefficients, ρ_{ijk}, can be laid out in estimation equations, but there are no known instances where these have been solved on a large scale, for the estimation equations are very complicated. For single-equation models or for recursive systems which split into a series of single-equation regressions, the autoregressive parameters of first order have been jointly estimated with structural parameters (Barger & Klein, 1954). The principal extensions to larger systems have been in cases where the autoregressive parameters are known *a priori*. Then it is easy to make known autoregressive transformations of the variables and proceed as in the case of independent disturbances. [See "Time Series."]

Related to the above two points is the treatment of lagged values of endogenous variables as predetermined variables. The presence of lagged endogenous variables reflects serial correlation among endogenous variables rather than among disturbances. In large samples it can be shown that for purposes of estimation we are justified in treating lagged variables as predetermined, but in small samples we incur bias on this account.

Another assumption regarding the disturbances in simultaneous equation systems is that they are mainly due to neglected or unmeasurable variables that affect or disturb each equation of the model. They are regarded as errors in behavior or technology. From a formal mathematical point of view, they could equally well be regarded as a direct error in observation of the normalized dependent variable in each equation, assuming that the system is written so that there is a different normalized dependent variable in each equation. There is an implicit assumption that the exogenous variables are measured without error. If we change the model to one in which random errors enter through disturbances to each relation and also through inaccurate observation of each individual variable, we have a more complicated probability scheme, whose estimation properties have not been developed in full generality. This again has been a case for numerical treatment by Monte Carlo methods.

The procedures of estimating simultaneous equation models as though errors are mutually independent when they really are not, and as though variables are accurately measured when they really are not, are *specification* errors. Other misspecifications of models can occur. For simplicity we assume linearity or, at least, linearity in unknown parameters, but the true model may have a different functional form. Errors may not follow the normal distribution, as we usually assume. [See "Errors," article on "Effects Of Errors In Statistical Assumptions."]

Full-information methods are sensitive to specification error because they depend on restrictions imposed throughout an entire system. Single-equation methods depend on a smaller set of restrictions. If an investigator has particular interest in just one equation or in a small sector of the economy, he may incur large specification error by making too superficial a study of the parts of the economy that do not particularly interest him. There is much to be said for using single-equation methods (limited information or two-stage least squares) in situations where one does not have the resources to specify the whole economy adequately.

There are numerous possibilities for specifying models incorrectly. These probably introduce substantial errors in applied work, but they cannot be studied in full generality for there is no particular way of showing all the misspecifications that can occur. We can, however, construct artificial numerical examples of what we believe to be the major specification errors. These are discussed below.

Sampling experiments. The effect on estimation methods of using simplified assumptions that are not fully met in real life often cannot be determined by general mathematical analysis. Econometricians have therefore turned to constructing sampling experiments with large-scale computers to test proposed methods of estimation where (1) the sample is small; and (2) there is specification error in the statement of the model, such as (a) nonzero parameters assumed to be zero, (b) dependent exogenous variables and errors assumed to be independent, (c) imperfectly measured exogenous variables assumed to be perfectly measured, or (d) serially correlated errors assumed to be not serially correlated.

So-called Monte Carlo methods are used to perform the sampling experiments that conceptually underlie sampling error calculations. These sampling experiments are never, in fact, carried out with nonexperimental sources of data, for we cannot relive economic life over and over again; but we can instruct a machine to simulate such an experiment.

Consider a single equation to be estimated by different methods, for example,

$$y_t = \alpha + \beta x_t + u_t, \qquad t = 1, 2, \ldots, T.$$

Fix α and β at, say, 3.0 and 0.5, respectively, and set $T = 30$. This would correspond to the process

$$y_1 = 3.0 + 0.5x_1 + u_1$$

$$\vdots \qquad \vdots \qquad \vdots \qquad \vdots$$

$$y_{30} = 3.0 + 0.5x_{30} + u_{30}.$$

We also fix the values of the predetermined variables $x_1, x_2, \ldots, x_{30}$ once and for all. We set $T = 30$ to indicate that we are dealing with a 30-element small sample. A sample of 30 annual observations would be the prototype.

Employing a source of random numbers scaled to have a realistic standard deviation and a zero mean, we draw a set of random numbers $u_1, \ldots, u_{30}$. We then instruct a machine to use $u_1, \ldots, u_{30}$ and $x_1, \ldots, x_{30}$ to compute $y_1, \ldots, y_{30}$ from the above formulas. From the samples of data $y_1, \ldots, y_{30}$ and $x_1, \ldots, x_{30}$, we estimate α and β by the methods being studied. Let $\hat{\alpha}$ and $\hat{\beta}$ be the estimated values. We then draw a new set of random numbers, $u_1, \ldots, u_{30}$, and repeat the process, using the same values of $x_1, \ldots, x_{30}$. From many such repetitions, say 100, we have sampling distributions of $\hat{\alpha}$ and $\hat{\beta}$. Means of these distributions, when compared with $\alpha(= 3.0)$ and $\beta(= 0.5)$, indicate bias, if any, and standard deviations or root-mean-square values about 3.0 or 0.5 indicate efficiency. From these sampling distributions we may compare different estimators of α and β.

What we have said about this simple type of experiment for a single equation can readily be extended to an entire system:

$$\mathbf{B}y'_t + \mathbf{\Gamma}z'_t = u'_t, \qquad t = 1, 2, \ldots, T.$$

In this case we must start with assumed values of $\mathbf{B}$ and $\mathbf{\Gamma}$. We choose a T-element vector of values for each element of z_t, the predetermined variables, and *repeated* T-element vectors of values for each element of u_t. The random variables are chosen so that their variance–covariance matrix equals some specified set of values. As in the single-equation case, $T = 30$ or some likely small-sample value. The z_t are often chosen in accordance with the values of predetermined variables used in actual models. In practice, Monte Carlo studies of simultaneous equation models have dealt with small systems having only two, three, or four equations.

Two sets of results are of interest from these studies. Estimates of individual elements in $\mathbf{B}$ and $\mathbf{\Gamma}$ can be studied and compared for different estimators; estimates of $\mathbf{B}^{-1}\mathbf{\Gamma}$, the reduced-form coefficients, can be similarly investigated. In addition, we could form some overall summary statistic, such as standard error of forecast, for different estimators.

The simplest Monte Carlo experiments have been made to test for small-sample properties alone; they have not introduced measurement errors, serial correlation of disturbances, or other specification errors. Generally speaking, these studies clearly show the bias in single-equation least squares estimates where some of the "independent" variables in the regression calculation are not independent of the random disturbances. Maximum likelihood estimators (full or limited information) show comparatively small bias. The standard deviations of individual parameter estimators are usually smallest for the single-equation least squares method, but this standard deviation is computed about the biased sample mean. If estimated about the true mean, least squares sometimes does not show up well, indicating that bias outweighs efficiency. Full-information maximum likelihood shows up as an efficient method, whether judged in terms of variation about the sample or the true mean. Two-stage least squares estimators appear to have somewhat smaller variance about the true values than do limited-information estimators, and both methods measure up to the efficiency of single-equation least squares method when variability is measured about the true mean.

Asymptotically, limited-information and two-stage estimators have the same variance–covariance matrices, and they are both inefficient compared with full-information estimators. The Monte Carlo results for small samples are not surprising, although the particular experiments studied give a slight edge to two-stage estimators.

When specification error is introduced, in the form of making an element of Γ zero in the estimation process when it is actually nonzero in the population, we find that full-information methods are very sensitive. Both limited-information and two-stage estimators perform better than full-information maximum likelihood. Two-stage estimators are the best among all methods examined in this situation. Limited-information estimators are very sensitive to intercorrelation among predetermined variables.

The principal result for Monte Carlo estimators of reduced form parameters is that transformed single-equation least squares values lose their efficiency properties. Being seriously biased as well, these estimates show a poor overall rating when used for estimating reduced forms for a system as a whole. Full-information estimators, which are shown in these experiments to be sensitive to specification error, do better in estimating reduced form coefficients than in estimating structural coefficients. Their gain in making use of all the *a priori* information outweighs the losses due to the misspecification introduced and, in the end, gives them a favorable comparison with ordinary least squares estimators of the reduced form equations that make no use of the *a priori* information and have no specification error.

If a form of specification error is introduced in a Monte Carlo experiment by having common time trends in elements of z_t and u_t, so that they are not independent as hypothesized, we find that limited-information estimators are as strongly biased as are ordinary least squares values. If time trend is introduced as an additional variable, however, the limited-information method has small bias.

When observation errors are imposed on the z_t, both least squares and limited-information estimators show little change in bias but increases in sampling errors. In this model, it turns out as before that the superior efficiency of least squares estimators of individual structural parameters does not carry over to the estimators of reduced form parameters.

A comprehensive sampling-experiment study of alternative estimators under correctly specified and under misspecified conditions is given in Summers (1965), and Johnston (1963) compares results from several completed Monte Carlo studies. This approach is in its infancy, and further investigations will surely throw new light on the relative merits of different estimation methods.

For some years economists were digesting the modern approach to simultaneous equation estimation introduced by Haavelmo, Mann and Wald, Anderson and Rubin, and Koopmans, Rubin, and Leipnik, and there was a period of little change in this field. Since the development of the two-stage least squares method by Theil, there have been a number of developments. The methods are undergoing interpretation and revision. New estimators are being suggested, and it is likely that many new results will be forthcoming in the next few decades. Wold (1965) has proposed a method based on iterative least squares that recommends itself by its adaptability to modern computers, its consistency, and its capacity to make use of *a priori* information on all equations simultaneously and to treat some types of nonlinearity with ease. Also, excellent recent books, by Christ (1966), Goldberger (1964), and Malinvaud (1964), greatly aid instruction in this subject.

[See also "Linear Hypotheses," article on "Regression."]

Bibliography

Aitken, A. C., 1935, "On least squares and linear combination of observations," *Proceedings* **55**, (Royal Society of Edinburgh), pp. 42–48.

Anderson, T. W. and Herman Rubin, 1949, "Estimation of the parameters of a single equation in a complete system of stochastic equations," *Annals of Mathematical Statistics* **20**, pp. 46–63.

Arrow, Kenneth J., 1968, "Economic equilibrium," in *International Encyclopaedia of the Social Sciences*, Volume 4, ed. David L. Sills (Macmillan and Free Press, New York), pp. 376–389.

Barger, Harold, and Lawrence R. Klein, 1954, "A quarterly model for the United States economy," *Journal of the American Statistical Association* **49**, pp. 413–437.

Basmann, R. L., 1957, "A generalized classical method of linear estimation of coefficients in a structural equation," *Econometrica* **25**, pp. 77–83.

Brown, T. M., 1960, "Simultaneous least squares: A distribution free method of equation system structure estimation," *International Economic Review* **1**, pp. 173–191.

Chernoff, Herman and Nathan Divinsky, 1953, " The computation of maximum-likelihood estimates of linear structural equations," in Cowles Commission for Research in Economics, *Studies in Econometric Method*, eds. William C. Hood and Tjalling C. Koopmans (Wiley, New York), pp. 236–269.

Chow, Gregory C., 1964, "A comparison of alternative estimators for simultaneous equations," *Econometrica* **32**, pp. 532–553.

Christ, C. F., 1966, *Econometric Models and Methods* (Wiley, New York).

Eisenpress, Harry, 1962, "Note on the computation of full-information maximum-likelihood estimates of coefficients of a simultaneous system," *Econometrica* **30**, pp. 343–348.

Fisher, Franklin M., 1965, "Dynamic structure and estimation in economy-wide econometric models," in James S. Duesenberry *et al.*, *The Brookings Quarterly Econometric Model of the United States* (Rand McNally, Chicago), pp. 589–635.

———, 1966, *The Identification Problem in Econometrics* (McGraw-Hill, New York).

Goldberger, Arthur S., 1964, *Econometric Theory* (Wiley, New York).

Haavelmo, Trygve, 1943, "The statistical implications of a system of simultaneous equations," *Econometrica* **11**, pp. 1–12.

Johnston, John, 1963, *Econometric Methods* (McGraw-Hill, New York).

Klein, Lawrence R., 1960, "The efficiency of estimation in econometric models," in Ralph W. Pfouts, *Essays in Economics and Econometrics: A Volume in Honor of Harold Hotelling* (Univ. of North Carolina Press, Chapel Hill), pp. 216–232.

——— and Mitsugu Nakamura, 1962, "Singularity in the equation system of econometrics: Some aspects of the problem of multicollinearity," *International Economic Review* **3**, pp. 274–299.

Kloek, T. and L. B. M. Mennes, 1960, "Simultaneous equations estimation based on principal components of predetermined variables," *Econometrica* **28**, pp. 45–61.

Koopmans, Tjalling C., Herman Rubin, and R. B. Leipnik (1950) 1958, "Measuring the equation systems of dynamic economics," in *Statistical Inference in Dynamic Economic Models*, Cowles Commission for Research in Economics, Monograph No. 10, ed. Tjalling C. Koopmans (Wiley, New York), pp. 53–237.

Malinvaud, Edmond (1964) 1966, *Statistical Methods of Econometrics* (Rand McNally, Chicago) (First published in French).

Mann, H. B. and Wald, Abraham, 1943, "On the statistical treatment of linear stochastic difference equations," *Econometrica* **11**, pp. 173–220.

Strotz, Robert H. and Herman Wold, 1960, "A triptych on causal chain systems," *Econometrica* **28**, pp. 417–463.

Summers, Robert, 1965, "A capital intensive approach to the small sample properties of various simultaneous equation estimators," *Econometrica* **33**, pp. 1–41.

Theil, Henri (1958) 1961, *Economic Forecasts and Policy*, 2d ed., rev. (North-Holland Publishing, Amsterdam).

Tinbergen, Jan, 1939, *Statistical Testing of Business-cycle Theories*, Volume 2: Business Cycles in the United States of America: 1919–1932 (League of Nations, Economic Intelligence Service, Geneva).

Wald, Abraham, 1940, "The fitting of straight lines if both variables are subject to error," *Annals of Mathematical Statistica* **11**, pp. 284–300.

Wold, Herman, 1965, "A fix-point theorem with econometric background," *Arkiv für Matematik* **6**, pp. 209–240.

Zellner, Arnold and Henri Theil, 1962, "Three-stage least squares: Simultaneous estimation of simultaneous equations," *Econometrica* **30**, pp. 54–78.

Postscript

Work has continued in several fruitful directions for estimation of systems of simultaneous equations. The principal directions concern generalization to deal with serially correlated errors, dynamic structures, and iterated instrumental variables estimators. The method of two-stage least squares has been applied to estimation of single equations in complete systems with errors satisfying

$$u_{it} = \sum_{j=1}^{n} \sum_{k=1}^{p} p_{ijk} u_{j,t-k} + e_{it},$$

$$E(e_{it} e_{jt'}) = 0, \qquad\qquad t \neq t', \text{all } i, j.$$

Usually these methods are restricted to the case where $p_{ij} = 0$ if $i \neq j$. Most work has been done with two-stage least squares estimators for the serially correlated case, but results have been developed for other methods as well.

The case of serially correlated errors has been treated, where lagged endogenous variables are present in the equation. Additionally, lag distributions have been considered for individual equations, with or without the presence of serially correlated errors.

A natural outgrowth of Wold's fixed point method, in which ordinary least squares estimators are iterated, is one in which instrumental variables are determined from estimated reduced forms, with all restrictions on parameters imposed, and used iteratively in the estimation of each single equation. Such methods provide consistent estimates and have the desirable properties of using up degrees of freedom quite economically and also being easy to use in nonlinear systems. Given an initial estimate of the individual equations of a system with coefficient matrices $\mathbf{B}^{(0)} \mathbf{\Gamma}^{(0)}$, instruments are determined as

$$y_t^{(1)} = -(\mathbf{B}^{(0)})^{-1} \mathbf{\Gamma}^{(0)} Z_t.$$

The included predetermined variables and components of $y_t^{(1)}$ (corresponding to included endogenous variables) are used as instruments, equation by equation. New estimated equations are solved in reduced form to generate new instruments and the process goes on iteratively in an obvious way. Some investigators are iterating these instrumental variable estimators until convergence is obtained, while others are stopping after one or two iterations. The method is being investigated for the case of dynamically generated instruments from system simulation over time. These methods appear to be quite promising, but no conclusive verdict is yet available.

Additional Bibliography

Brundy, J. M. and D. W. Jorgenson, 1971, "Efficient estimation of simultaneous equations by instrumental variables," *Review of Economics and Statistics* **53**, pp. 207–224.

Chow, Gregory C., 1968, "Two methods of computing full-information maximum likelihood estimates in simultaneous stochastic equations," *International Economic Review* **9**, pp. 100–112.

Dhrymes, Phoebus J., 1970, *Econometrics: Statistical Foundations and Applications* (Harper, New York).

——, 1971, *Distributed Lags: Problems of Estimation and Formulation* (Holden-Day, San Francisco).

——, 1972, "Simultaneous equations inference in econometrics," *Institute of Electrical and Electronics Engineers Transactions on Automatic Control* **17**, pp. 427–438.

Dutta, M. and E. Lyttkens, 1974 "Iterative instrumental variables method and estimation of a large simultaneous system," *Journal of the American Statistical Association* **69**, pp. 967–986.

Eisenpress, Harry and John Greenstadt, 1966, "The estimation of nonlinear econometric systems," *Econometrica* **34**, pp. 851–861.

Fair, Ray C., 1970, "The estimation of simultaneous equation models with lagged endogenous variables and first order serially correlated errors," *Econometrica* **38**, pp. 507–516.

Hendry, D. F., 1971, "Maximum likelihood estimation of systems of simultaneous regression equations with errors generated by a vector autoregressive process," *International Economic Review* **12**, pp. 257–272.

Klein, Lawrence R. (1973) 1974, *A Textbook of Econometrics*, 2nd ed. (Prentice-Hall, Englewood Cliffs, N.J.).

Theil, Henri, 1971, *Principles of Econometrics* (Wiley, New York).

Editorial Note

These [" "] refer to other articles in the *International Encyclopaedia of Statistics* with different authorships.

Acknowledgment

"Simultaneous Equation Estimation" by Lawrence R. Klein. Reprinted/Translated with permission of Macmillan Library Reference USA, a Division of Simon & Schuster, from *International Encyclopaedia of Statistics*, William H. Kruskal and Judith M. Tanur, Editor. Vol. 2, pp. 979–994.
Copyright © 1968 by Crowell Collier and Macmillan, Inc.
Copyright © 1978 by The Free Press.

14

THE TREATMENT OF UNDERSIZED SAMPLES
IN ECONOMETRICS[†]

1. The Degrees of Freedom Problem

One straight line can be passed through two points; one three-dimensional plane through three points; and one n-dimensional hyperplane through n points. These simple geometric facts imply, in linear correlation theory, a perfect fit of an n-parameter relationship to n sample points. The statistical inference problem does not arise unless there are more data points than parameters to be estimated. *Degrees of freedom* must be available in order to give rise to an inference problem.

In single equation regression analysis, the degrees of freedom problem does not generally arise in acute form since we rarely deal with more than ten or so unknown coefficients in a single equation and usually have more than ten data points. In fitting high order polynomials, the nonlinear function being estimated really falls under the heading of linear regression analysis since transformations of variables re-cast the problem in linear form, as far as parameter estimation is concerned, and shortage of degrees of freedom restrains the statistician from forcing a close or perfect fit by inclusion of more and more powers of regressor variables. The same situation prevails for lag distributions; more and more lag terms with unknown coefficients can force the fit of the regression equation. The use of orthogonal polynomials and few-parameter lag distributions are ways of coping with the degrees of freedom problems while obtaining estimates of high order terms.

In the case of equation systems the degrees of freedom problem is more serious and more common. The number of parameters in the system is often actually as large as or greater than the number of data points. Although this is not the proper way of looking at the numbers situation for calculation of degrees of freedom, it does raise the possibility of trouble in the estimation process. I assert that appropriate estimates can usually be made, even though there are fewer data points than system parameters, yet the argument is lengthy and round about.

That the pure counting problem is different in single equation linear regressions and in complete systems can be indicated by a simple pair of examples.

[†]From *Econometrics Studies of Macro and Monetary Relations*, eds. A. A. Powell and R. A. Williams (North-Holland, Amsterdam, 1973), pp. 3–26.

(i) The single equation

$$y_t = \alpha_1 x_{1t} + \alpha_2 x_{2t} + \cdots + \alpha_m x_{mt} + e_t \qquad (t = 1, 2, \ldots, T) \qquad (1.1)$$

must be estimated from a sample (of size T) with more than m data points, i.e.,

$$T > m;$$

otherwise a perfect fit can be obtained.

Write Eq. (1.1) for each data point

$$y_1 = \alpha_1 x_{11} + \alpha_2 x_{21} + \cdots + \alpha_m x_{m1} + e_1$$
$$y_2 = \alpha_1 x_{12} + \alpha_2 x_{22} + \cdots + \alpha_m x_{m2} + e_2$$
$$\vdots$$
$$y_T = \alpha_1 x_{1T} + \alpha_2 x_{2T} + \cdots + \alpha_m x_{mT} + e_T. \qquad (1.2)$$

If $T = m$, there is a vector $a' = (a_1, a_2, \ldots, a_m)$ that estimates $\alpha' = (\alpha_1, \alpha_2, \ldots, \alpha_m)$ with zero residuals

$$y = Xa + 0; \qquad X = (x_{ij}), \qquad (1.3)$$

provided det.$X \neq 0$.

If $T < m$, a perfect fit can be obtained in an infinite number of ways by assigning $(m - T)$ arbitrary values to elements of a and solving for the remaining T elements from

$$y_1 - a_{T+1}^0 x_{T+1,1} - \cdots - a_m^0 x_{m1} = a_1 x_{11} + a_2 x_{21} + \cdots + a_T x_{T1} + 0,$$
$$y_2 - a_{T+1}^0 x_{T+1,2} - \cdots - a_m^0 x_{m2} = a_1 x_{12} + a_2 x_{22} + \cdots + a_T x_{T2} + 0,$$
$$\vdots$$
$$y_T - a_{T+1}^0 x_{T+1,T} - \cdots - a_m^0 x_{mT} = a_1 x_{1T} + a_2 x_{2T} + \cdots + a_T x_{TT} + 0. \quad (1.4)$$

If

$$\det. \begin{bmatrix} x_{11} & \cdots & x_{T1} \\ \vdots & & \vdots \\ x_{1T} & \cdots & x_{TT} \end{bmatrix} \neq 0,$$

there will exist a truncated estimate $(a_1, a_2, \ldots, a_T)$ giving zero residual variation for any choice $a_{T+1}, \ldots, a_m$. This holds for any ordering of the coefficients.

(ii) The equation system

$$Ay_t + Bx_t = e_t \qquad (1.5)$$

with typical equation

$$\sum_{j=1}^{n} \alpha_{ij} y_{jt} + \sum_{j=1}^{m} \beta_{ij} x_{jt} = e_{it} \qquad \begin{aligned} & (i = 1, 2, \ldots, n) \\ & (i = 1, 2, \ldots, T) \end{aligned} \qquad (1.6)$$

can be estimated with coefficients (a_{ij}) and (b_{ij}) that produce zero residuals if nT does not exceed the number of unknown parameters, provided the determinant of the appropriate data matrix does not vanish.

There are two specific aspects of this proposition that should be stressed. In the first place, the number of data points is not simply T; it is nT. This is the number of stochastic elements in the joint probability distribution of the system. It combines both the number of equations and the number of points at which sample observations are taken. Secondly, the number of unknown parameters in the system is not given by the number of elements (A, B). From these $(n^2 + nm)$ elements we must subtract n for the rule of units normalization, i.e., the choice of one element of y_t to have a unit coefficient in each equation. We must also subtract the number of identifying restrictions on the equations of the system. This issue does not arise in the single equation regression model. The implicit effect of the identifying restrictions is to impose *a priori* values on some of the system's coefficients. If we write out each equation for each sample point, we shall have the nT equations

$$\alpha_{11}y_{11} + \cdots + \alpha_{1n}y_{n1} + \beta_{11}x_{11} + \cdots + \beta_{1m}x_{m1} = e_{11} ;$$

$$\vdots \qquad \qquad \vdots \qquad \vdots \qquad \qquad \vdots \qquad \vdots$$

$$\alpha_{11}y_{1T} + \cdots + \alpha_{1n}y_{nT} + \beta_{11}x_{1T} + \cdots + \beta_{1m}x_{mT} = e_{1T} ;$$

$$\vdots \qquad \qquad \vdots \qquad \vdots \qquad \qquad \vdots \qquad \vdots$$

$$\alpha_{n1}y_{11} + \cdots + \alpha_{nn}y_{n1} + \beta_{n1}x_{11} + \cdots + \beta_{nm}x_{m1} = e_{n1} ;$$

$$\vdots \qquad \qquad \vdots \qquad \vdots \qquad \qquad \vdots \qquad \vdots$$

$$\alpha_{n1}y_{1T} + \cdots + \alpha_{nn}y_{nT} + \beta_{n1}x_{1T} + \cdots + \beta_{nm}x_{mT} = e_{nT} . \qquad (1.7)$$

If there are nT or more unknown coefficients (α_{ij}) and (β_{ij}), we shall be able to find a set of estimates (a_{ij}) and (b_{ij}) that produce a perfect fit. This is obviously a different criterion than applied in the case of the single equation, and it does not involve a simple comparison of T with n, m, or the number of unknown coefficients.

A point that is not usually appreciated is that the number of degrees of freedom should be considered in relation to the method of estimation used. Some methods are more economical than others in the use of degrees of freedom. Let us first take up single-equation methods of estimating equations in complete interdependent systems.

The first stage calculation for either limited information (maximum likelihood) single equation (LISE) estimates or two-stage-least-squares (TSLS) estimates is the regression of each dependent variable on all the independent variables of the system. From (1.5), we obtain

$$y_t = -A^{-1}Bx_t + A^{-1}e_t \qquad (1.8)$$

which is written as

$$y_t = \Pi x_t + \nu_t. \tag{1.9}$$

The first-stage regression calculations ignore the identities

$$\Pi = -A^{-1}B, \tag{1.10}$$

$$\nu_t = A^{-1}e_t, \tag{1.11}$$

and simply estimate the unrestricted regressions

$$y_{it} = \pi_{i1}x_{1t} + \cdots + \pi_{im}x_{mt} + \nu_{it} \quad \begin{aligned} (i &= 1, 2, \ldots, n) \\ (t &= 1, 2, \ldots, T). \end{aligned} \tag{1.12}$$

From preceding arguments, it is evident that we must have $T > m$. If this inequality does not hold, we can obtain a perfect fit for (1.9), in which case the second stage of TSLS or LISE will collapse into ordinary single equation regression by the method of least squares (OLS).

This is, by far, the most commonly encountered problem of shortage in degrees of freedom, since many econometric systems now have large values for m if all the lagged values of dependent variables are classified as *predetermined* variables and placed in the x-vector for this calculation. We frequently find that $m > T$, in practice.

Another way of looking at this problem is to observe that

$$\det. (X'X) = 0,$$

where $X'X$ is the moment matrix of predetermined variables. The regression estimate of π_i in (1.12) is given by

$$\text{est. } \pi_i = (X'X)^{-1}X'y_i \; ; \tag{1.13}$$

therefore it is essential that $X'X$ be nonsingular.

It is instructive to look at the degrees of freedom problem from this point of view, since multicollinearity among elements of x_t also causes $X'X$ to be singular or at least "ill-conditioned."[1] Methods that will be suggested in Sec. 2 for coping with a shortage of degrees of freedom will also be used for coping with the problem of multicollinearity. Both problems are manifestations of basic singularities.

So far, we have shown that for OLS calculations, the degrees of freedom restriction is

$$T > m_i,$$

---

[1] See Klein and Nakamura (1962).

where m_i is the number of regressors (unknown coefficients) in the ith single equation. For TSLS or LISE calculations we must have

$$T > m.$$

This is a much stronger condition since $m \geqslant m_i$. The number of predetermined variables in a complete system will almost always be greater than the number in a single equation. In today's systems, the discrepancy between m_i and m is large.

Other methods of estimation, particularly three-stage-least-squares (3SLS) and full-information-maximum-likelihood (FIML) impose even stronger degrees of freedom requirements on a system. These will be examined now.

An important matrix in the calculation of full information estimators (3SLS and FIML), and indeed a matrix that is important by itself for stochastic simulation, evaluation of forecast error and other uses, is the estimated variance/covariance matrix of structural disturbances,

$$\text{est.} \sum = \text{est.} \ (E(e_{it}e_{jt})). \tag{1.14}$$

The covariances of sample residuals form the estimate of the Σ-matrix,

$$\text{est.} \sum = \left[\frac{1}{T} \sum_{t=1}^{T} (\text{res.})_{it} (\text{res.})_{jt} \right]. \tag{1.15}$$

This matrix appears directly in the concentrated likelihood function

$$\log{(\det. A)} - \frac{1}{2}\log{(\det. \Sigma)}$$

that is maximized for FIML estimates. The "normal equations" of 3SLS estimation make use of the elements of est. Σ^{-1} as weighting factors. It is evident, therefore, that est. Σ must be nonsingular in order that the likelihood function be finite or that the inverse of est. Σ exist. A necessary condition for the nonsingularity of est. Σ is

$$T > n.$$

The restriction

$$T > m$$

is obviously necessary for 3SLS estimation as long as that method uses TSLS estimation for the calculation of est. Σ^{-1}. It can easily be shown that the same restriction holds for FIML estimation. We may write

$$\text{est.} \sum = \text{est.} \frac{1}{T} \sum_{t=1}^{T} (Ay_t + Bx_t)(Ay_t + Bx_t)'. \tag{1.16}$$

Define

$$
W = (Y|X) = \begin{bmatrix} y_{11} & \cdots & y_{n1} & x_{11} & \cdots & x_{m1} \\ \vdots & & \vdots & \vdots & & \vdots \\ y_{1T} & \cdots & y_{nT} & x_{1T} & \cdots & x_{mT} \end{bmatrix}, \tag{1.17}
$$

$$
\Gamma = (A|B) = \begin{bmatrix} \alpha_{11} & \cdots & \alpha_{1n} & \beta_{11} & \cdots & \beta_{1m} \\ \vdots & & \vdots & \vdots & & \vdots \\ \alpha_{n1} & \cdots & \alpha_{nn} & \beta_{n1} & \cdots & \beta_{nm} \end{bmatrix}. \tag{1.18}
$$

It follows that

$$
\text{est.} \sum = \text{est.} \ -\frac{1}{T}(\Gamma W'W\Gamma'). \tag{1.19}
$$

The moment matrix $W'W$ must be positive definite in order for the matrix in (1.19) to be nonsingular. In order for $W'W$ to be positive definite, we must have

$$
T > m + n.
$$

Since $Y'Y$ and $X'X$ are both principal minors of $W'W$, they must be positive definite. This implies the inequality

$$
T > m,
$$

which is the same one that holds for LISE and TSLS.

All the methods of estimation considered except OLS require that the number of predetermined variables be fewer than the number of sample points. In addition, the full information methods require that the number of equations (endogenous variables) also be fewer than the number of sample points. These are highly restrictive conditions.

These are not purely formal conditions. In large macroeconometric systems it is likely that we shall find a shortage of degrees of freedom in the sense that

$$
n > T, \quad m > T.
$$

In systems with large numbers of observations, these restrictions may not be consequential, but there are many situations in which they are effectively having an influence on estimation procedures. In the estimation of the Brookings Model (Dusenberry *et al.*, 1965), we have a case where there are fewer than 100 time series observations (quarters since 1948) ($T < 100$) but more than 200 equations ($n > 200$). Counting lag variables, there are more than 200 predetermined variables ($m > 200$). In a situation like this, straightforward applications of FIML, 3SLS, TSLS, and LISE are all precluded. There is, however, nothing to prevent OLS estimation of each equation. The Wharton Model and several others with 50–100 simultaneous stochastic equations usually violate one of the two restrictions, or come close to it.

Econometricians are usually loath to use data from the period of the Korean War and post World War II reconstruction or reconversion; therefore most samples effectively begin after 1953, and (limiting ourselves to consideration of quarterly models) this cuts significantly into sample size. Data are available for models like the Klein–Goldberger Model for a longer time period, but these are necessarily annual models and consist of no more than 35–40 observations.[2] In microeconomic cross section samples there are thousands of degrees of freedom, but not enough information to estimate a complete system.

For the near term, econometricians must face the fact that there is a shortage of degrees of freedom. In the case of the developing countries where model building is rapidly gaining popularity for planning growth, the degrees of freedom are even scarcer because samples are rarely available before 1950 and are only annual. In these cases and in the cases of large models for the industrial economies, application of FIML or 3SLS methods seem to be out of the question unless the whole model is split into mutually orthogonal blocks. These methods can be applied within small blocks provided one is prepared to make the strong assumption of block diagonality in the covariance matrix of errors. It seems more plausible, however, to modify single equation methods such as LISE or TSLS for the usual type models. These are the procedures that we take up in the next section.

2. Ways of Coping with Undersized Samples

To many econometricians it seems strange to work hard at getting estimates by consistent and efficient methods when degrees of freedom are scarce, data are often of dubious quality, and differences in numerical magnitudes of individual coefficients are often small. Because there are such great needs for improvement, I contend that we should be on the lookout for even modest gains wherever possible; all avenues should be explored. It also appears that small differences in individual coefficients may become magnified into significant differences in complete system solutions. Also, small inconsistencies or biases in complete system solutions may build up over time in dynamic simulations. This point is especially significant in striving for consistent estimation for models of the developing countries. The main issue is to make long run analyses, and in decade-length simulations there is much chance for error build-up to occur. There will always be build-up of *random* errors; it is avoidance of *bias* error build-up that is being pursued in the construction of consistent estimates for developing country models.

2.1. *Deletion of variables*

The simplest method of obtaining consistent estimates of the TSLS or LISE types for systems that have too few degrees of freedom in that

$$T < m$$

---

[2]See Klein (1969).

is to select subsets of predetermined variables to be used as regressors in the first-stage calculations.

From

$$\{x_{1t}, x_{2t}, \ldots, x_{m_1 t}, x_{m_1+1,t}, \ldots, x_{mt}\}$$

a subset

$$\{x_{1t}, x_{2t}, \ldots, x_{m_1 t}\}$$

is selected for which

$$m_1 < T.$$

Included in the selected subset are the predetermined variables that explicitly appear in the single equation to be estimated. This means that the first-stage regressions cannot be done once and for all for the whole system; they must be tailored to the estimation of specific structural equations.

This is an old procedure and was always in the "oral tradition" discussions at the Cowles Commission in the early days of development of simultaneous equation methods. It was then used for LISE calculations of the first postwar U.S. model and received formal justification (consistency) in the basic paper on LISE by Anderson and Rubin (1950).[3]

The drawback to this method is its arbitrariness and lack of uniqueness; there are many ways in which subsets of predetermined variables, sufficient for the estimation of any single equation, can be selected, and there is no simple criterion to indicate where to stop in this solution process. If it was feasible to search over all possible subsets for each equation, we could choose that combination of equation estimates that provided the best system simulation performance, measured by some summary statistic, but this does not seem to be a practical suggestion for large systems.

Where collinear variables alone are omitted, i.e., where the omitted variables are highly correlated with retained variables, there should be little effect on the estimated residual variances and covariances in the reduced form. The two systems

$$y_{it} = \sum_{j=1}^{m} p_{ij} x_{jt} + (\text{res.})_{it}, \tag{1.20}$$

and

$$y_{it} = \sum_{j=1}^{m_1} p'_{ij} x_{jt} + (\text{res.})'_{it}, \tag{1.21}$$

will give rise to approximately the same covariance matrix

$$\text{est. } \Sigma_\nu = \left[\frac{1}{T} \sum_{t=1}^{T} (\text{res.})_{it} (\text{res.})_{jt} \right], \tag{1.22}$$

---

[3]For an application see Klein (1950).

using either (1.20) or (1.21) as the estimates of the reduced forms in (1.12), if the omitted variables $x_{m_1+1,t}, \ldots, x_{mt}$ are highly correlated with $x_{1t}, \ldots, x_{m_1,t}$. If the collinearity is strong enough and if the omitted set is large enough, both the problems of collinearity and shortage of degrees of freedom could be handled jointly by the appropriate deletion of first stage regressors. This is only a special case and is not typical, however.

2.2. *Principal components*

If instead of regressing on all the predetermined variables independently we were to carry out the first stage regressions on restricted combinations of predetermined variables we may be able to get round the degrees of freedom problems and the collinearity problem in a systematic way that is not open to personal choice or arbitrariness. Kloek and Mennes (1960) proposed the use of principal components of predetermined variables as a procedure for dealing with a shortage of degrees of freedom. They suggested alternative ways of doing this, either by forming principal components of variables excluded from a given equation, principal components of certain residuals, or principal components of all the predetermined variables in the system. The last way has the advantage that the components need to be evaluated only once for an entire system.

Principal components of $x_{1t}, \ldots, x_{mt}$ expressed as linear combination of the x's

$$(PC)_{it} = \sum_{j=1}^{m} q_{ij} x_{jt} \qquad (i = 1, 2, \ldots, m), \tag{1.23}$$

are mutually orthogonal and have the same generalized variance (in total) as that of the original set of variables. That is to say, the components each contribute to an "explanation" of the generalized variance of the x's. If we order them by percentage of variance accounted for individually, we may be able to find a small number of principal components that account for a large portion of the generalized variance of the predetermined variables. Principal component analysis may be regarded as a *data reduction* technique, by enabling us to replace a large number of predetermined variables by a small number of linear functions of these variables. The replacement set preserves, to a large extent, the generalized variance of the original set, and if the number of elements in the replacement set is small, as usually happens, we are likely to find that they do not exhaust the available degrees of freedom in the system when used as first stage regressors. They have the additional advantage of being orthogonal; therefore they are not collinear regressors.

Principal components have the disadvantage of not being invariant under a change in units of measurement of the original predetermined variables. If, however, we adopt a convention that they shall be evaluated as characteristic vectors of a correlation matrix

$$\left[\frac{\displaystyle\sum_{t=1}^{T}(x_{it} - \bar{x}_i)(x_{jt} - \bar{x}_j)}{\sqrt{\displaystyle\sum_{t=1}^{T}(x_{it} - \bar{x}_i)^2(x_{jt} - \bar{x}_j)^2}} \right] = R \,, \tag{1.24}$$

$$|R - \lambda I| = 0 \,, \tag{1.25}$$

we have a definite rule to follow that is independent of the units of measurement of the individual x_{it}.

Principal components, being linear functions of the original x_{it}, as in (1.23), can often be associated with particular types of movements in the variables that are responsible for movement of the economy. One component may give big weight, through large values of q-coefficients, to trend variables in $x_{1t}, \ldots, x_{mt}$; another to short-cycle variables; and still others to long-cycle variables; etc. In short, the data reduction methods of principal components analysis enable us to pick out leading groupings within $x_{1t}, \ldots, x_{mt}$. The fact that several variables among the predetermined set account for each of the dominant aspects of economic movement means that data reduction through principal component analysis enables us to pick out a small number of leading characteristics associated with a few principal components. This is the reason why collinearity is avoided at the same time that degrees of freedom are conserved.

2.3. *Restricted reduced forms*

The identifying restrictions on a system leave many "holes" or restrictions on elements in A and B, the matrices of the economy's structure. When the reduced form is derived as in (1.8)

$$y_t = -A^{-1}Bx_t + \nu_t \,,$$

there will be corresponding restrictions on $-A^{-1}B$. These are ignored in the first stage regressions for TSLS or LISE estimators, and that is a basic reason why degrees of freedom considerations look so large, as do the multicollinearity problems as well. If we had some preliminary estimates of A and B, say $\hat{A}$ and $\hat{B}$, the estimated restricted reduced forms[4]

$$\hat{\hat{y}}_t = -\hat{A}^{-1}\hat{B}x_t \tag{1.26}$$

would provide values of y_t that could be used as regressors or instruments in the subsequent stages of TSLS or LISE estimation calculations.

---

[4]In (1.26), we denote computed values as $\hat{\hat{y}}_t$ instead of $\hat{y}_t$, since the latter are customarily the values obtained from unrestricted reduced form regressions $\hat{y}_t = \hat{\Pi}x_t$.

If few degrees of freedom are used up in estimating each row of $(A|B)$, and (1.26) is derived from the row by estimates of the whole system, then the values of $\hat{y}_t$ can be used at a final stage for the estimation of each single equation without using many degrees of freedom. All the economic information on coefficient structure is used in this approach. In that sense it is a full-information procedure, but covariance information on the structure of the random errors is not used; therefore this method is not as efficient as FIML or 3SLS, yet it makes few demands on degrees of freedom and in that sense has much to recommend it as a kind of full information method.

There are many ways of getting preliminary estimates $\hat{A}$, $\hat{B}$ for the calculation of instruments or regressors from (1.26). Three possible methods are[5]

(i) instrumental variables;
(ii) TSLS (or LISE) with arbitrarily selected subsets of predetermined variables;
(iii) TSLS (or LISE) with principal components of predetermined variables.

The method of instrumental variables is taken here to mean the arbitrary selection of n_{i-1} instruments for the formation of the "normal equations"

$$\sum_{t=1}^{T} y_{1t} z_{kt} = -\sum_{j=2}^{n_i} \alpha_{ij} \sum_{t=1}^{T} y_{jt} z_{kt}$$

$$-\sum_{j=1}^{m_i} \beta_{ij} \sum_{t=1}^{T} x_{jt} z_{kt} \quad (k = 2, 3, \ldots, n_i),$$

$$\sum_{t=1}^{T} y_{1t} x_{\ell t} = -\sum_{j=2}^{n_i} \alpha_{ij} \sum_{t=1}^{T} y_{jt} x_{\ell t}$$

$$-\sum_{j=1}^{m_i} \beta_{ij} \sum_{t=1}^{T} x_{jt} x_{\ell t} \quad \begin{array}{l}(\ell = 1, 2, \ldots, m_i); \\ (m_i \leqslant m; n_i \leqslant n).\end{array} \qquad (1.27)$$

The outside instruments are $z_{2t}, \ldots, z_{n_i t}$; while the inside instruments are $x_{1t}, \ldots, x_{m_i t}$. The first dependent variable is assumed to have a normalized unit coefficient ($\alpha_{i1} = 1$), and the identifying restrictions are implied by the fact that n_i and m_i do not cover all dependent and independent variables of the system.

Since the selection of z_{kt} is arbitrary except for the fact that these variables must qualify as being proper instrumental variables, the preliminary estimates of A, B are inefficient. The procedure using the restricted forms may be iterated, however, and this should lessen dependence on the starting estimates. Nevertheless, it is important to have good starting estimates that are economically plausible.

The method of instrumental variables applied as in (i) to single equations, one at a time, is simple, straightforward and no more demanding on degrees of freedom than is OLS, but it gives a *consistent* starting estimate. It is only slightly more

---

[5]OLS estimates of structural equations, though inconsistent, would also be suitable initial estimates and need not lead to inconsistency of the final estimates.

laborious to use method (ii) in place of (i) for a starting estimate. Since TSLS (or LISE) can be given instrumental interpretations, (i) is a special case of (ii). Estimates based on starting values provided by (ii) should be more efficient than those based on (i) and somewhat less arbitrary because there are fewer ways in which subgroups of instruments appropriate to (ii) can be chosen than there are ways in which separate instruments for Eq. (1.27) can be chosen.

A preferred way of obtaining preliminary estimates for the computation of values from restricted reduced forms is by estimating the entire system by TSLS (or LISE) using principal components of predetermined variables. The arbitrariness of selection of the components can be reduced by fixing a required percentage of total variance to be accounted for by the principal components or a minimal number of degrees of freedom to be preserved for the estimation of unrestricted reduced forms.[6]

The estimates of A and B obtained by (iii) are useful in themselves as estimates of the entire system, but there is some evidence that they can be improved upon through the use of restricted reduced forms. Asymptotically, we shall not be able to improve upon TSLS efficiency through iterative use of the restricted reduced forms, but there is some evidence that sample simulation performance of complete systems is improved in terms of mean square error if the ordinary estimates are iterated once. There is some evidence as well that post sample extrapolative performance is also improved, but that evidence is less impressive.[7]

2.4. *Causal ordering*

Soon after the introduction of the simultaneous equations approach to inference in econometric systems by the Cowles Commission, Bentzel and Wold (1946) pointed out the enormous simplification in the whole procedure in the case where the model has the structure of the cobweb theory. For example, the system

$$q_t = \beta_0 + \beta_1 p_{t-1} + e_t$$
$$p_t = \alpha_0 + \alpha_1 q_t + u_t \tag{1.28}$$

can be efficiently estimated by regressing (OLS) q_t on p_{t-1} and p_t on q_t, separately, provided e_t and u_t are independent. The main feature of this system is that it is fully recursive, namely, the matrix of coefficients of dependent variables is triangular

$$A = \begin{bmatrix} 1 & 0 \\ -\alpha_1 & 1 \end{bmatrix},$$

and the covariance matrix of disturbances is diagonal

$$\Sigma = \begin{bmatrix} \sigma_e^2 & 0 \\ 0 & \sigma_u^2 \end{bmatrix}.$$

---

[6] When principal components are used as first stage regressors, in place of predetermined variables, there are, in fact, some restrictions placed on the reduced forms, but these are not economic theoretic restrictions.

[7] See Johnston *et al.* (1974).

In this kind of system, through a proper recursive ordering of equations we can always form a set of efficient OLS estimates. These use no more degrees of freedom per equation than the number of unknown coefficients in each individual equation. There is, generally speaking, no degrees of freedom problem in estimating this system. Even if Σ is not diagonal, a variation on TSLS and OLS can be devised which is highly economical in the use of degrees of freedom. In this case, the first equation to be estimated by OLS is the one that has only one unlagged dependent variable and one or more predetermined variables. This would be the first equation in (1.28). In the second equation p_t should be regressed on the values of q_t computed from the first equation rather than observed q_t values. This, in fact, uses a restricted reduced form. Even if there were other predetermined variables in the second equation, these would not be used in the computation of q_t values for OLS purposes in the second; this is the sense in which a restricted reduced form is being used. Fisher (1965) generalized the concept of a recursive system into one in which

A is block triangular;

Σ is block diagonal.

Within blocks the usual methods (OLS, TSLS, LISE, FIML, 3SLS) are to be used, but blocks may be small enough so that degrees of freedom problems are not serious. The predetermined variables of a block are those that appear explicitly in equations of the block and dependent variables that come from prior blocks in the recursive ordering. If the Σ matrix is block diagonal, actual values of dependent variables may be taken from prior blocks, but if Σ is not block diagonal, computed values of dependent variables may be taken from prior blocks. The dependent variables taken from prior blocks are added to the list of predetermined variables within a block.

If the Brookings Model or the Wharton Model is to be estimated by FIML or 3SLS techniques, some block decomposition must be introduced in order to satisfy the degrees of freedom restrictions. The same considerations hold for ordinary TSLS or LISE methods. Fisher's method, called Structurally Ordered Instrumental Variables (SOIV) takes account of the causal structure both from the point of view of economic lines of relationship and dynamics. Implicitly, however, this is done automatically when restricted reduced forms are used in the iteration of TSLS or LISE methods. The advantage of the latter methods based on the restricted reduced forms is that they do not require extensive prior searching for the recursive ordering into an optimal block structure lay out. Something like the SOIV method will be necessary for the application of FIML methods to large systems, but single-equation methods are probably better handled by the use of principal components and restricted reduced forms.

3. Some Practical Problems

One of the most important aspects of contemporary model building has been the extensive and intensive use of lag distributions to capture the economic dynamics of the system. It is no longer satisfactory to introduce simple delays of one or two periods for some leading variables. Similarly, we can do better than make simplifying transformations, as in the well-known Koyck case, by casting the specification into a linear problem with short lags. The issue has been to estimate lengthy complicated lag distributions on several variables simultaneously, and this has greatly improved the explanatory power of single equations. The preferred procedure has been to specify an equation such as an investment function

$$I_t = \sum_{i=0}^{s} w_i \left[\frac{P}{C}\right]_{t-i} + \sum_{i=0}^{u} q_i x_{t-i} + \sum_{i=0}^{v} r_i K_{t-i} + e_t \qquad (1.29)$$

and find distributed lag weights w_i, q_i, r_i together with length of lag s, u, v that minimize

$$\sum_{t=1}^{T} \hat{e}_t^2.$$

It has been a significant advance to be able to do this by search or iteration methods, and the results appear to be gratifying. Methods have not been extended yet to simultaneous equation systems, but even on a single equation OLS basis, much research was required in order to devise workable procedures for simultaneous estimation of several lag distributions within one equation. Simple Koyck transformations are not capable of putting this case into linear from. Working directly with the untransformed specification, we have not complicated the structure of the error term.

As a practical matter the estimation of equations like (1.29) and indeed all the preliminary specifications of a complete model have been explored by OLS methods. The usual procedure is to estimate by consistent methods after the preliminary specification by OLS methods. This is less than satisfactory, but it is the way models of any complexity are, in fact, constructed.

Two lag distributions that are capable of showing the types of dynamic reactions that we hypothesize for economic behavior are the rational polynomial and the (Almon) finite polynomial. The latter will form the basis of the present discussion. It will be assumed that w_i, q_i and r_i lie along polynomials

$$\begin{aligned}
w_i &= \alpha_0 + \alpha_1 i + \alpha_2 i^2 + \alpha_3 i^3 + \cdots ; \\
q_i &= \beta_0 + \beta_1 i + \beta_2 i^2 + \beta_3 i^3 + \cdots ; \\
r_i &= \gamma_0 + \gamma_1 i + \gamma_2 i^2 + \gamma_3 i^3 + \cdots .
\end{aligned} \qquad (1.30)$$

The OLS estimates are obtained by searching the parameter space for values of $s, u, v, \alpha_j, \beta_j, \gamma_j$, and the degrees of the polynomials. There are customarily some end point restrictions on w_i, q_i, and r_i.

What has all this to do with the problem of undersized samples? It is simply that when we come to the stage of developing TSLS or other consistent estimates for a large model with comparatively few sample points, we are going to be starting from a specification that is based on long lag distributions, for which we have OLS estimates. It is not practical to consider each lag variable

$$(P/C)_{t-1}, (P/C)_{t-2}, \ldots; \quad x_{t-1}, x_{t-2}, \ldots; \quad K_{t-1}, K_{t-2}, \ldots; \text{ etc.,}$$

as separate predetermined variables and search again for optimal parameter values in the context of consistent estimation methods. There are likely to be several long lags, and this will enormously extend the list of predetermined variables. There are two alternative simplifications that serve to reduce the computing burden associated with lag distributions in the context of consistent estimation. The composite variable

$$\sum_{i=0}^{u} q_i x_{t-i}$$

can be written as

$$q_0 \sum_{i=0}^{u} \frac{q_i}{q_0} x_{t-i} = q_0 x_t + q_0 \sum_{i=1}^{u} \frac{q_i}{q_0} x_{t-i},$$

$$= q_0 x_t + q_0 z_t . \tag{1.31}$$

The variable z_t will be constructed from lag values of x_t with coefficients (q_i/q_0) estimated from the OLS values and will appear as one single predetermined variable of the system. The scale parameter q_0 will be re-estimated by consistent methods, taking account of the fact that x_t and z_t are constrained to have identical coefficients.

The alternative procedure is to rewrite the equation being estimated as[8]

$$I_t = \alpha_0 \sum_{i=0}^{s} \left[\frac{P}{C}\right]_{t-i} + \alpha_1 \sum_{i=0}^{s} i \left[\frac{P}{C}\right]_{t-i} + \alpha_2 \sum_{i=0}^{S} i^2 \left[\frac{P}{C}\right]_{t-i} + \cdots$$

$$+ \beta_0 \sum_{i=0}^{u} x_{t-i} + \beta_1 \sum_{i=0}^{u} i x_{t-i} + \beta_2 \sum_{i=0}^{u} i^2 x_{t-i} + \cdots$$

$$+ \gamma_0 \sum_{i=0}^{v} K_{t-i} + \gamma_1 \sum_{i=0}^{v} i K_{t-i} + \gamma_2 \sum_{i=0}^{v} i^2 K_{t-i} + \cdots$$

$$+ e_t . \tag{1.32}$$

---

[8]This suggestion was made by Robert Rasche.

The predetermined variables are:

$$\sum_{i=1}^{s} i \left[\frac{P}{C}\right]_{t-i}, \sum_{i=1}^{s} i^2 \left[\frac{P}{C}\right]_{t-i}, \ldots;$$

$$\sum_{i=1}^{u} i x_{t-i}, \sum_{i=1}^{u} i^2 x_{t-i}, \ldots;$$

$$\sum_{i=1}^{v} i K_{t-i}, \sum_{i=1}^{v} i^2 K_{t-i}, \ldots.$$

These are more numerous than in the previous case. Also, the estimation of $\alpha_j, \beta_j, \gamma_j$ by consistent methods will re-introduce some searching again. To keep the number of predetermined variables from growing unusually large and to limit the amount of computation, the first alternative should be chosen. The method of principal components and restricted TSLS estimation applied to this kind of model is feasible.

An earlier version of the Wharton family of models was estimated by constructing 12 principal components of predetermined variables, regressing dependent variables on these principal components, and using the computed regressands as regressors in the second stage regressions of each structural equation. These estimates have also been iterated once by computing a new set of values from restricted reduced forms and using them as regressors in structural equations again. These are all feasible calculations in a system with 50 structural equations and 68 quarterly observations. The newer version of this model will have many more lags, a few more equations, and a few more variables. The methods of restricting the lag distributions by ratios of OLS estimates will be used. This method has been applied to the Wharton Annual and Industry Model, which has 150 structural equations and only 18 annual observations. Seven principal components were found to account for more than 75% of the variance of predetermined variables. Dependent variables were regressed on these, together with included predetermined variables from each equation. The computed regressands were then used as second stage regressors.

If the dependent variables of a system are regressed on a fixed set of principal components for an entire system, and on no other variables, in the first stage, the computed regressands should be used as instrumental variables in the second stage; otherwise consistency will not be obtained. If, however, the first stage regressions contain the included predetermined variables, the computed regressands may be used as either regressors or instruments in the second stage.

This issue arises in another way for LISE estimates. In that method, a difference between two covariance matrices is used

$$B = (Y'X)(X'X)^{-1}(X'Y) - (Y'X_i)(X_i'X_i)^{-1}(X_i'Y). \qquad (1.33)$$

The matrix B is the difference between the covariance matrix of unrestricted reduced form residuals using only the components of x_t appearing explicitly in the ith equation and the same covariance matrix using all the components of x_t. Of course the first set of residuals dominate the second in the sense that B is positive semi-definite. If we replace the whole set of x_t by principal components, denoted as a data matrix P, we cannot be sure that

$$(Y'P)(P'P)^{-1}(P'Y) - (Y'X_i)(X_i'X_i)^{-1}(X_i'Y)$$

will be positive semi-definite. This problem can be avoided if P is augmented by x_i, i.e., if the first stage regressions contain the included predetermined variables for each structural equation, as well as the principal components.

Even though $X'X$ is singular or ill-conditioned, either through a shortage of degrees of freedom or collinearity, both of which are likely to occur in large dynamic systems, we can still extract principal components. Care must be taken to use much computational accuracy and to watch for multiple or close characteristic roots. Since it is not known in an absolute sense just how many roots to extract, we should experiment to the extent allowable by computing facilities to see which set of principal components gives the best system estimate, based on some overall statistic of simulation performance. Average (RMSE/mean) would seem to be a good indicator of performance. It has been found that a modest number of principal components seems to produce TSLS estimates that simulate best.

References

Anderson, T. W. Jr. and H. Rubin, 1950, "The asymptotic properties of estimates of the parameters of a single equation in a complete system of stochastic equations," *Annals of Mathematical Statistics* **21** (December), pp. 570–582.

Bentzel, R. and H. Wold, 1946, "On statistical demand analysis from the viewpoint of simultaneous equations," *Skandinavisk Aktuarictidskrift*, pp. 95–114.

Duesenberry, J. *et al.*, 1965, *The Brookings Quarterly Econometric Model of the United States* (Rand McNally, Chicago).

Fisher, F. M., 1965, "Dynamic structure and estimation in economy-wide econometric models," in *The Brookings Quarterly Econometric Model of the United States,* eds. J. Duesenberry *et al.* (Rand McNally, Chicago).

Johnston, H. N., L. R. Klein, and K. Shinjo, 1971, "Estimation and prediction in dynamic econometric models," in *Econometrics and Economic Theory*, ed. W. Sellekaerts (Macmillan, London), pp. 27–56.

Klein, L. R., 1950, *Economic Fluctuations in the United States, 1921–1941* (John Wiley and Sons, New York).

——, 1969, "Estimation of interdependent systems in macroeconometrics," *Econometrica* **37** (April), pp. 171–192.

—— and M. Nakamura, 1962, "Singularity in the equation systems of econometrics: some aspects of the problem of multicollinearity," *International Economic Review* **3** (September), pp. 274–299.

Kloek, T. and L. B. M. Mennes, 1960, "Simultaneous equations estimation based on principal components of predetermined variables," *Econometrica* **28** (January), pp. 45–61.

Editorial Note

Prefix number 1 in the equation numbering refers to chapter number 1 of the source, *Econometric Studies of Macro and Monetary Relations, op. cit.*

15

THE TREATMENT OF EXPECTATIONS IN ECONOMETRICS[†]

1. Specification of Econometric Models

To a large extent, econometric analysis builds on an economic theory base. This is particularly true in the specification of econometric models; whether micro or macro, whether partial or complete. The prominent role assigned to expectations in economic theory must surely carry over, then, to econometric analysis. Theoreticians like Professor Shackle have made the point in a telling way that economic units use expectations when making optimal economic decisions. In some versions of theory, economic units are assumed to optimize expected profits or expected satisfactions. These optimization schemes are planned in terms of expected market variables, such as expected output price, expected interest rate, expected wage rate or even expected tax rate. Expected income levels, expected activity levels, expected factor inputs are also highly relevant in model building.

This is all clear enough and rightfully enriches theoretical reasoning in economics, but what of econometrics, where it is not appropriate to reduce a problem to various contingencies about the outcome of expectations? In econometrics, we need definite measurement and fully testable model formulations. The trouble with expectations variables is that they are subjective, personal, and not easily measured for numerical statistical analysis.

For as long as most living econometricians can remember, an attempt has been made to introduce lags in econometric model specifications as surrogates for expectations. In my first model building venture, for the Cowles Commission in the middle 1940s, I specified the equations of the models being constructed in terms of anticipated values and used recently realized values of a variable as indicators of anticipated values.[1] I wrote, "... the immediate past level, rate of change, acceleration, etc., of prices would be a likely set of data on which to form expectations of future prices." Other authors, of course, had also used lags or distributed lags of variables to represent expectations and to bring other aspects of dynamics into econometric models. Apart from expectations, lags might appear in econometric equations because of construction periods, delays in decision making, adaptations to new situations, and stock/flow definitions. All lag distributions are

---

[†]From *Uncertainty and Expectations in Economics,* eds. C. F. Carter and J. L. Ford (Blackwell, Oxford, 1972), pp. 175–190.
[1]L. R. Klein, *Economic Fluctuations in the United States, 1921–1941* (Wiley, New York, 1950), p. 16.

not indicative of expectations, and, as I shall argue later, all expectations are not represented as lag distributions; nevertheless the most common way to quantify and measure expectations variables is through the use of lags.

The simplest example of a model using time lags for expectations is the familiar cob-web. This system is assumed to be descriptive of agricultural markets for perishable commodities. The model is well known,

$$q_t^s = \alpha_0 + \alpha_1 p_{t-1} + e_t \qquad \text{supply} \qquad\qquad (1)$$

$$q_t^d = \beta_0 + \beta_1 p_t + u_t \qquad \text{demand} \qquad\qquad (2)$$

$$q_t^s = q_t^d \qquad\qquad\qquad \text{market clearing} \qquad (3)$$

$$e_t, u_t = \text{error}.$$

Since the commodity is perishable, by assumption markets are effectively cleared, as asserted in (3). The model states that producers supply (plant) a good (agricultural commodity) on the basis of expected price and put the whole amount (crop yield) on the market for whatever price it will fetch. Anticipated price, which forms the basis for supplier decisions, is not objectively measured, but an indicator of expected price is used instead. In the typical agricultural case, the farmer has little basis for forming expectations about price when he has to decide upon acreage and seeding. He knows the price at that time, but not at the time of marketing, because he doesn't know the volume to be marketed. In the absence of *a priori* knowledge about subsidies, price supports, or other price information, the best judgment about future price is last season's price.

Objective data could be collected for this model, and it could be estimated by standard econometric techniques. The estimated system would then generally imply the periodic cob-web cycle. The system need not be linear but the lag structure serving as a surrogate for expectations should be the same for a nonlinear version of the model.

This kind of dynamic system seems to fit data for many different markets in a reasonably good manner. It is, however, considered by many theoreticians to be an affront to producer intelligence and the general theory of rational behavior. If the oscillation were predetermined as it comes out of this simple model, producers would act on the oscillatory information and speculate the pattern out of existence. If we complicate the model by permitting storage and crop carry-overs, inventory speculation on the basis of expected prices might introduce a more complicated lag structure through the use of longer and more detailed lag distributions. This may also affect "expected" price in the supply equation.

Are lags, either in the simple form of last period's value or in lag distribution form, always good measures of anticipations? In the case of price, it seems that the recent historical existence of an unusual period (closing of the Suez Canal, worldwide devaluation, outbreak of war, etc.) would produce some highly atypical values that would be poor indicators of expectations in situations where it is known that the unusual factors will not be present. It seems to be wrong for the econometrician to be a "slave" to past values, no matter how unusual they are, as indicators of expectations.

The American economy has just come through a period in which previous price movements were distorted by a major strike which has been settled. The strike (General Motors, autumn, 1970) distorted the weights in forming the GNP deflator, which is often used as a general price variable in econometric models. Since the index number for cars happens to be below the average index value for all GNP and since it received a small weight during the historical strike period, this biased the whole index upward for the particular quarter. There will be a corresponding downward bias in the strike recovery period. This suggests that lagged price is a poor indicator of current price. This defect is not remedied by using an entire lag distribution instead of a simple lag value for expected price.

Another approach to dynamic economic modeling for the purpose of representing expected values was followed at an early stage by Metzler in his construction of inventory models.[2] His schemes are all translated into terms of observable time series and have been statistically estimated. In simplest form, using Metzler's own notation, the system is

$$u_t = \beta y_{t-1} \qquad \text{consumption function} \qquad (4)$$

$$s_t = \beta(y_{t-1} - y_{t-2}) \qquad \text{inventory investment function} \qquad (5)$$

$$y_t = u_t + s_t + v_0 \qquad \text{definition of national income} \qquad (6)$$

$$y_t = \text{national income}$$

$$u_t = \text{consumer expenditures}$$

$$s_t = \text{production for inventory}$$

$$v_0 = \text{exogenous investment.}$$

In this system, consumption is made to depend on lagged income. This is a behavioral or adjustment delay. The inventory equation is based on the idea that production for inventory should be the difference between actual and normal stocks of the preceding period, where the difference in the two stock levels is determined by the difference between actual and expected sales of period $t-1$. Actual sales for consumption are

$$\beta y_{t-1},$$

while anticipated sales are

$$\beta y_{t-2};$$

therefore, production for inventory is

$$s_t = \beta y_{t-1} - \beta y_{t-2}.$$

[2] L. A. Metzler, "The nature and stability of inventory cycles," *The Review of Economic Statistics* (August 1941), pp. 113–129.

Equations (4)–(6) make up a small self-contained dynamic system, depending on observed data, since lag values have been used in place of expected values. The model has been extended by Metzler by introducing expected income (from past values) in the consumption function and making a stock adjustment form of the inventory investment equation.

Inventories and inventory models are hard to estimate and determine well, in an econometric sense, yet the Metzler model stands up as an outstanding contribution which performs as well as alternatives in a difficult sector. Much of the good performance of the Metzler model stems from his use of expectations in the form of lag variables.

2. Two Approaches

There are two principal methods of dealing with expectations in econometrics. One is an extension of the older idea of using lagged values, as indicated in the cob-web and inventory cycle models cited above. The other is by direct measurement from sample surveys of individual respondents.

Lag distributions

The extension in the use of lagged values is the use of lag distributions. A simple but indirect way of introducing a lag distribution is to start from the assumption that expectations are formed from the adjustment hypothesis.

$$p_t^e - p_{t-1}^e = \lambda(p_{t-1} - p_{t-1}^e). \tag{7}$$

This states that the change in an expected value (price expectations in this case, p_t^e) is adjusted with coefficient $\lambda(0 < \lambda < 1)$ to the discrepancy between the previous period's actual and expected value. The integral of this finite difference equation in expected values is

$$p_t^e = \lambda \sum_{i=1}^{\infty}(1 - \lambda)^{i-1}p_{t-i}. \tag{8}$$

This dynamic adjustment process of expectations formulation is, therefore, equivalent to assuming that expected price is a weighted average of past prices, where the weights are proportional to the geometric series $1, (1-\lambda), (1-\lambda)^2, (1-\lambda)^3, (1-\lambda)^4$, etc. Since the sum of these terms is given by

$$\sum_{i=1}^{\infty}(1 - \lambda)^{i-1} = \frac{1}{1 - (1 - \lambda)} = \frac{1}{\lambda}$$

we can write

$$\lambda \sum_{i=1}^{\infty}(1 - \lambda)^{i-1}p_{t-i} = \sum_{i=1}^{\infty}w_i p_{t-i}$$

where

$$\sum_{i=1}^{\infty}w_i = 1.$$

If (7) is a stochastic relation, but not directly observable, with random error u_t, the integral in (8) has an error term of the form

$$v_t = \sum_{i=0}^{\infty} (1 - \lambda)^i u_{t-i}.$$

The series v_t is autocorrelated. On the other hand if expectations are assumed to be formed directly as a weighted average of past prices, as in (8), with a random error term, the associated error derived for (7) will be autocorrelated.

The idea of assuming expected values to be weighted averages of past values is now common in econometric work. It is formally the same as assuming that *permanent* or *long run* values stand for expected values, where long run values are defined as weighted averages of past values. This is the idea behind the various empirical, time-series formulations of the permanent income hypothesis for saving or consumption. It is used for the specification of agricultural supply functions, dependent on *long run* price, and in the version of the quantity theory of money equation in which *long run* price and *long run* income are the joint explanatory variables that are associated with movements in the money stock.

In the theory of the term structure of interest rates, it is asserted that the long term rate is a moving average of expected short term rates. This gets expressed as

$$(r_L)_t = \alpha \sum_{i=0}^{\infty} \mu^i (r_s)_{t-i} + u_t \tag{9}$$

or in some closely related variant. Equation (9) is often estimated from

$$(r_L)_t = \alpha (r_s)_t + \mu (r_L)_{t-1} + v_t \tag{10}$$

or

$$(r_L)_t = \alpha (r_s)_t + \mu (r_L)_{t-1} + \beta (r_s)_{t-1} + v_t. \tag{10}'$$

Equation (10) or (10)$'$ is directly estimated from observed data, but interpreted as an estimate of (9). In the latter form it can be seen to have expectational content.

A similar idea occurs in the various stock adjustment formulations of economic behavior, the most celebrated being the stock adjustment form of the accelerator equation

$$K_t - K_{t-1} = I_t = \lambda (K_t^* - K_{t-1}) + e_t. \tag{11}$$

The expression in (11) implies that capital, K_t, is changed over its previous value, giving net investment, I_t, in proportion to the discrepancy between *desired* capital stock and actual capital stock of the previous period. If desired stock is proportional to output, K_t, we have

$$I_t = \lambda (\alpha X_t - K_{t-1}) + e_t \tag{12}$$
$$= \lambda \alpha X_t - \lambda K_{t-1} + e_t.$$

Equation (12) can also be written as

$$K_t = \lambda \alpha X_t + (1 - \lambda) K_{t-1} + e_t$$

whose integral is

$$K_t = \alpha \lambda \sum_{i=0}^{\infty} (1 - \lambda)^i X_{t-i} + u_t . \qquad (13)$$

In this form we can interpret the right hand explanatory variable as *long run* or *permanent* production level, which determines capital stock. This is, therefore, a form of expectations explanation of capital stock. The econometrician usually estimates (12) from current and lagged data, but the parent hypothesis is (13).

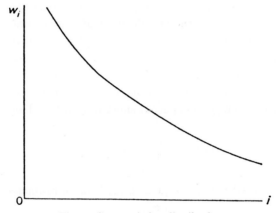

Fig. 1. Geometric lag distribution.

All the expressions used so far to represent lag distributions are of the geometric type. The typical shape is shown in Fig. 1. More general lag distributions, particularly of the unimodal humped type, are also important in econometric analysis. They, too, justify interpretation in terms of expectations. In planning economic decisions that take several periods (months, quarters, years) to formulate and execute, the lag distribution is likely to be of the hump type. This is typical of large scale investment planning and is just the kind of situation in which the use of expectations analysis in the sense of Professor Shackle is most appropriate. Econometric analysis of investment now generally assumes that expectations of activity levels and market conditions at the most remote stage, when the project is being first considered, have little weight but grow in relative significance as the time approaches for making final commitments. There is a peak (lag) period of effect and a steadily declining degree of influence as the time approaches for final delivery or installation. Since investment projects are often large and lumpy, only limited changes in the whole scheme can be instituted after a certain point of work has been passed. In the case of a building, decoration, furnishing, and equipping can be changed as the final date approaches.

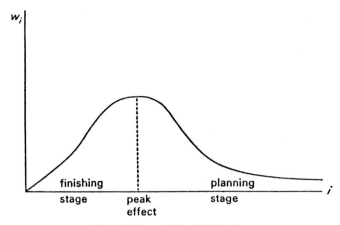

Fig. 2. Humped lag distribution.

Expectations of market or activity conditions have some effect, but they become comparatively small as the final date approaches. The lag distribution should thus have the form in Fig. 2. To illustrate this kind of lag distribution in the context of investment functions, we write

$$I_t = \sum_{i=0}^{p} w_i X_{t-1} + \sum_{i=0}^{r} q_i K_{t-i} + e_t \tag{14}$$

where w_i and q_i follow distribution patterns with the general shape given in Fig. 2. A special case, however, would be a monotonically falling distribution curve in Fig. 1. Possibilities for graduation of w_i and q_i are polynomial lag functions or rational polynomials, both of which are being used in current work.[3]

$$w_i = \alpha_0 + \alpha_1 i + \alpha_2 i^2 + \alpha_3 i^3 \tag{15}$$

or

$$\frac{N(L)}{D(L)} = \frac{n_0 + n_1 L + n_2 L^2 + \cdots}{1 + d_1 L + d_2 L^2 + d_3 L^3 + \cdots} \tag{16}$$

$$L^j X_t = X_{t-j} .$$

In the first case, we say that the w_i or the q_i lie along polynomials which can have a prescribed shape over a finite range. The statistical estimation of the polynomial coefficients provides a basis for calculating the weights in the lag distribution from (15). In (16) we form a ratio of two operator polynomials, where L is the lag (displacement) operator and the investment function has the form

$$I_t = \frac{N_1(L)}{D_1(L)} X_t + \frac{N_2(L)}{D_2(L)} K_t + e_t .$$

---

[3]S. Almon, "The distributed lag between capital appropriations and expenditures," *Econometrica* (January 1965), pp. 178–196; D. W. Jorgenson, "Rational distribution lag functions," *Econometrica* (January 1966), pp. 135–149.

The estimation of the coefficients in the numerator and denominator polynomials provides a basis for computing the weights in the relevant lag distribution.[4] Estimation problems are more difficult to handle for (16) than for (15), but the former distribution forms are more general.

The rational function lag distributions may appear to be quite arbitrary, but L. Taylor has tried to show how they might arise from an optimization process by an economic decision maker.[5] The geometric lag distributions are special cases of this form when

$$\frac{N(L)}{D(L)} = \frac{n_0}{1 + d_1 L}.$$

The polynomial lag distribution is very convenient and tractable, but it serves more as a graduation formula than a process that is derived from theoretical economic analysis.

To summarize, in applied dynamic econometrics, expectations are widely represented by the use of lag distributions that attempt to portray the conditions of the economy at the time decisions are being made about significant economic variables. The use of lag distributions is growing rapidly and being extended to cover a wide variety of parametric specifications.

Direct measurement

An entirely different approach to the econometric treatment of expectations is taken in sample survey investigations. Instead of trying to infer people's expectations from lag variables, the survey researcher goes directly to the respondent and ascertains his expectations. For the United States, we have regular surveys of households, business firms, and other economic units. Expectations are ascertained by questionnaire on

consumer buying plans
consumer income, price, and financial expectations
business capital expenditures
business inventory, sales, and employment expectations
area building plans.

The consumer surveys actually pose three kinds of questions:

1. buying plans for specific goods (or services); 2. expectations about incomes and market prices; 3. general attitudes towards the state of the economy and the state of personal economic situations. There is a dispute among economists on the comparative importance of specific buying plans against attitudes and expectations, but all three seem to be relevant in careful analysis.

These kinds of survey data are quite universal. Many countries have had long experience with surveys of investment plans, inventory expectations and sales ex-

---

[4]P. Dhrymes, L. R. Klein, and K. Steiglitz, "Estimation of distributed lags," *International Economic Review* (June 1970), pp. 235–250.

[5]L. Taylor, "The existence of optimal distributed lags," *Review of Economic Studies* (January 1970), pp. 95–106.

pectations. Such data are used in several ways for econometric analysis. In single cross-section samples they may be used to determine effects of expectations or subjective variables generally on decisions together with more objectively measured variables on actual performance. For example consumer spending may depend on actual income and expected income levels as in

$$C_i = f_i(Y_i, Y_i^a) + e_i \qquad i = 1, 2, \ldots, N.$$

Price anticipations may be used to study both buying and portfolio decisions on the part of consumers or other economic units. This is of some interest because prices and other market variables are effectively held constant for a single cross section sample, but price expectations may vary widely across such a sample.

When direct questioning for expectation variables is done in sample surveys, these schemes often become regularized and a whole time series of expectations across successive survey samples may be constructed. Indices of attitudes, buying plans, and investment outlays are now available in the U.S. and elsewhere. These can be used as supplementary economic variables like other time series statistics in the estimation of econometric relationships. Instead of trying to represent expected prices and incomes by surrogates in the form of lag distributions, such variables may be directly represented by time series of sample indices. In a closely related way, realization relationships based on time series data can be estimated from variables that try to explain the discrepancy between actual and expected performance.

A principal problem with all these applications of directly estimated expectations, taken from sample surveys, is that they are primarily used only in a single direction, i.e., their effect on objective variables is studied. The missing link is an explanation of the generating process of the expectations themselves. They were primarily introduced for predictive purposes and are constructed to have some lead time over actual economic performance. Much research has been devoted to using expectations indices as indicators of actual buying or actual economic activity in specific lines of endeavor. They are treated as *predetermined* variables to use the language of econometrics. A natural step to follow is to try to build an explanation of the generation of expectations, or to *endogenize* the subjective variables.

There are two noteworthy attempts to "explain" expectations. Jorgenson has hypothesized that expected investment, measured by sample survey intentions data, have the same explanation as observed investment, but the explanatory variables should simply be dated for earlier occurrence.[6] By this approach we would replace

$$I_t = \frac{N_1(L)}{D_1(L)} X_t + \frac{N_2(L)}{D_2(L)} K_t + e_t \tag{17}$$

by

$$I_t^e = \frac{N_1(L)}{D_1(L)} X_{t-2} + \frac{N_2(L)}{D_2(L)} K_{t-2} + u_t \tag{18}$$

---

[6]D. W. Jorgenson, "Anticipations and investment behavior," *The Brookings Quarterly Econometric Model of the United States*, eds. J. Duesenberry *et al.* (Rand McNally, Chicago, 1965), pp. 33–92.

where I_t^e are expectations of I_t, two periods (six months) in advance. A statistical procedure would be to estimate I_t^e from (18) and then phase I_t^e into I_t either by using (17) together with (18) or by establishing an empirical relationship between I_t and I_t^e of the sort that would be an implied specification of (17) and (18) together. The empirical relationship implied, in parametric form, between I_t and I_t^e is

$$I_t = \sum_i w_i I_{t-i}^e + \nu_t. \qquad (19)$$

This is the kind of relationship estimated by Shirley Almon in her celebrated paper, except that she used capital *appropriations* instead of *expectations*.[7]

Yet another possibility is to use the approach of R. Eisner in developing capital realization equations that explain $(I_t - I_t^e)/I_t^e$ in terms of such variables as changes in sales, profits, orders and previous deviations between expected and actual investment.[8] All the effects of explanatory variables are estimated from lag distributions. A combination of equation types (18) with either (19) or realization equations estimated by Eisner seem to offer promise for future model building work.

Jorgenson's Eq. (18) provides a formal method for endogenizing expectations, but it may be less satisfying to research workers than a systematic empirical search guided by economic theory to the extent possible, for a good (best) statistical relationship between subjective expectations and objective economic variables. An attempt has been made by S. Hymans to derive a stable statistical relationship between the Survey Research Center's (University of Michigan) index of consumer attitudes and other macro variables of the economy that would be generated in a large scale model.[9] Hymans' study of consumer expenditures makes two significant contributions to the econometrics of expectations. Not only does he generate endogenously, but he also has an improved way of using expectations to predict consumer behavior. He "filters" expectations by requiring the index to change by a minimum amount or to change consecutively, in one direction for several periods before its value is counted as non-zero in affecting consumer expenditure decisions. In this way, small erratic movements that do not come up to threshold values are filtered out of the relationship. This seems to improve the predictive performance of the index. Other filtering devices may also be used. T. Juster recommends scaling of the intensity or probability of consumer buying plans in constructing an index of intentions.

The endogenous generation of expectations may be investigated empirically at the micro or macro level. At the level of individual decision-making such variables may be used in cross-section regression estimates, particularly to establish whether

[7] S. Almon, *op. cit.*
[8] R. Eisner, "Realization of investment anticipations," *The Brookings Quarterly Econometric Model of the United States,* ed. J. Duesenberry *et al.* (Rand McNally, Chicago, 1965), pp. 93–128.
[9] S. Hymans, "Consumer durable spending: Explanation and predictions," *Brookings Papers on Economic Activity* **2** (1970), pp. 173–206.

such variables are important or not.[10] Hymans, on the other hand, explains expenditures at the macro level in a way that is fully compatible with aggregative model structure.

There is a drawback, however, to Hymans' results in explaining an index of consumer sentiment, namely, that he makes use of stock market variables for part of his explanations. Econometricians, unsurprisingly, have been singularly weak in explaining stock market averages in macroeconometric models. Such variables probably have a large element of personal attitudes which is the thing to be explained. Results similar to Hymans', from the point of view of degree of correlation, for explanation of consumer attitudes have also been obtained by Adams and Green, although they use mainly labor market variables in their statistical equations.[11]

A second issue that arises particularly in the case of consumer expectations is the mixture between attitudes and buying plans in an overall index. Economists at the Survey Research Center, led by G. Katona, claim that general consumer attitudes revealed by their subjective appraisals of national and personal economic conditions are more significant than specific buying plans in predicting actual consumer behavior. The empirical result is that buying plans correlate well with actual behavior in cross-section samples but not in aggregative time series studies, unless possibly "filtered."[12]

The present *Index of Consumer Sentiment* has five component attitude measures of responses to questions on:

   (i) Business conditions during the next 12 months.
  (ii) Business conditions during the next 5 years.
 (iii) Evaluation of present financial situation.
 (iv) Expected personal financial situation during the next 12 months.
  (v) Whether it is a good or bad time to buy consumer durables.

Formerly a scaling of buying plans was also included in the Index. Answers to other questions have been considered at one time or another. These are for price and income expectations. Stable, reliable results appear to come principally from the five-point Index.

To round out the presentation of materials on direct questioning of respondents on expectations, we have had some results with other variables or processes, such as sales, inventory, and employment expectations and forward commitment variables such as orders or building starts. The latter two serve the same role as expectations in providing short run predictions of behavior, but they are less subjective and derived from different kinds of samples. They are not obtained from depth

---

[10]See L. R. Klein and J. B. Lansing, "Decisions to purchase consumer durable goods," *The Journal of Marketing* (October 1955), pp. 109–132.

[11]F. G. Adams and E. W. Green, "Explaining and predicting aggregative consumer attitudes," *International Economic Review* (September 1965), pp. 275–293.

[12]See F. G. Adams, "Consumer attitudes, buying plans and purchases of durable goods: A principal components, time series approach," *The Review of Economics and Statistics* (November 1964), pp. 347–355.

interviews with persons as respondents. To a large extent, they are derived from regular records. The Munich business test data have been extensively analyzed by Theil for predictive content, and the U.S. series on inventories and sales do not have a long enough record to make a dull assessment of their usefulness, but the prospects are not particularly bright.[13]

To what do these several investigations and results with the direct approach add in terms of future econometric model building? I have tried to formulate the Wharton Econometric Forecasting Model on a two-track system, one track with some equations entirely in objective form with the usual variables on income flows, stock levels, relative prices, etc., and the other track with these equations replaced by statistical equations that add expectations variables to all the others present.

> The Index of Consumer Sentiment in consumption equations for cars and other durables.
> Investment intentions in the equations for capital formation.
> Housing starts in the equations for residential construction.

The result is that short-run ex-post forecasts, within the sample period of fit, for the system as a whole perform better when the expectations track equations are included for one and two period forecasts than when they are excluded in favor of the other track.[14] This is only a preliminary result. It must be extended systematically to post-sample data; it must try equations on the expectations track one-at-a-time with the rest of the system; it must examine some forms of filtering. Yet it is quite suggestive. Careful direct measurement of expectations may help in prediction, and if Hymans' results can be extended they can be included on a self generating basis.

3. Uncertainty in Econometric Application

A good deal of the work in applied econometrics is devoted to prediction — using estimated systems to extrapolate into the future. In this way expected magnitudes are estimated and then used in economic decision-making. The role of uncertainty in such applications has long been recognized and dealt with. Sampling error and estimated variance of random disturbances have been combined into a formula for standard error of forecast. The uncertainty surrounding econometric prediction has been recognized and dealt with through the construction of tolerance intervals associated with point forecasts. Although the relevant magnitudes are difficult to estimate in large econometric systems, the principles of their use in deriving appropriate forecast intervals or regions are well known. The calculus of uncertainty for this application is an established procedure drawn from statistical theory.

Another aspect of uncertainty in econometric applications is the uncertainty on the state of the world determining the exogenous inputs to a complete, estimated model. In the repeated (quarterly) forecast applications of the Wharton Model in

---

[13]H. Theil, *Economic Forecasts and Policy* (North-Holland Publishing Co., Amsterdam, 1958).
[14]See L. R. Klein, *An Essay on the Theory of Economic Prediction* (Markham, Chicago, 1971).

the United States a set of practices has been developed for dealing with uncertainty. We have considered the range of plausible alternatives for exogenous variables and parameters. These may cover a range from bullishness to bearishness; or from the assumption of occurrence of a labor disturbance to absence of such a disturbance, etc. Many alternatives are possible at any one time. Because the computerized models are so simple to recompute (solve again) and so quickly re-evaluated, uncertainty is handled by providing the economic decision-makers with separate calculations for each of the several exogenous readings.

Now, many of the large industrial companies and policy-making public bodies make regular use of the Wharton Model or other econometric forecasting devices. For the future, this is the way that expectations are likely to be formed, whether they are for prices, incomes, sales or other economic variables. Expectations and forecasts will become synonymous, and such forecasts will be in an interval whose size is governed by uncertainty considerations.

The models, with internal dynamics, will be based on the translation of a theory of expectations into lag distributions as discussed above, and these estimated systems will then become the basis from which expectations will be formed for individual producer, consumer, or public authority decision-making in economics. At this time, the Wharton Model serves as a forecasting device for more than one hundred users, whose economic activities are carried out on a large scale. Econometrics and the analysis of expectations are, therefore, necessarily closely allied.

A complication is due to arise on the issue of self-fulfilling (or defeating) expectations. If the larger corporations whose decisions are of predominant importance for the functioning of the American Economy, act on the econometric results of a given model, the model is likely to have a great bearing on the outcome of the economy's performance. This bearing would be predictable if we could estimate the "feedback" effects of a model solution on business or public behavior. Econometricians took the view for a long time that their work was largely experimental and would not be used for direct action by economic decision-makers. With the large development and improvement of econometric model building in recent years, it is no longer correct to regard econometric forecasts as purely experimental; they are seriously used for determining expected future values on a large scale. It is now necessary to turn attention to the feedback problem to try to estimate relationships that explicitly show the effects of econometric predictions on economic behavior. It is logically possible to close the system this way; econometricians simply have not tried extensively.

16

THE CONCEPT OF EXOGENEITY IN ECONOMETRICS[†]

This paper is concerned with the concept of exogeneity of variables in structural econometric models. Examples from recent economic history are presented which illustrate their generation and their importance for prediction. The relationship of exogenous variables to vector autoregressive models and the notion of Granger-causality is also discussed.

1. Variable Classification and Meaning

The standard approach to econometric model specification begins with the classification of variables. There are, to begin with, three kinds of variables used in model construction:
(1) endogenous, (2) exogenous, (3) random error.

The intuitive meaning of these three types is:

Endogenous — These variables have an influence on the economic model and are affected by the economic model; i.e., there is feedback between the model and endogenous variables. In other words, the endogenous variables are *generated* by the economic system being investigated. They are *internal* variables.

Exogenous — These variables have an influence on the economic model but are not affected by the economic model. They are not in feedback relationship with the model, and they are not generated by the economic system being investigated. They are *external* variables.

Random error — These are variables that are generated by "nature" and have an effect on the functioning of the economic model. The errors, e, are correlated with endogenous variables, y, but the joint probability distribution of e is not affected by the economic system being investigated. They are *external*, not directly observable, and follow a well defined probability distribution. They are governed by the laws of chance.

In a linear static system, the variables appear as in Eqs. (1) and (2)

$$Ay + Bx = e \tag{1}$$

$$\Gamma x = u \tag{2}$$

[†]From *Contributions to Econometric Theory and Application, Essays in Honour of A. L. Nagar*, eds. R. A. L. Carter, J. Dutta, and A. Ullah (Springer-Verlag, New York, 1990), pp. 1–22.

y is an n-element column vector of *endogenous* variables

x is an m-element column vector of *exogenous* variables

e is an n-element column vector of random errors

A is a nonsingular $n \times n$ matrix of coefficients

B is a rectangular $n \times m$ matrix of coefficients

Γ is a nonsingular $m \times m$ matrix of coefficients

u is an m-element column vector of random errors.

The econometric model is (1), in which all three variable types appear. Equation system (2) exists and is responsible for explaining or generating x, but does not have economic content. If we write (2) as

$$0y + \Gamma x = u$$

the concept of no-feedback from y to x via the economic system is more obvious,

$$x = \Gamma^{-1}(0y + u).$$

If y were not multiplied by a null matrix, there could be a direct feedback from y to x. In this formulation, x is stochastic because it depends on u, but the economic model with x classified as exogenous would be perfectly acceptable if x were simply a vector of fixed variables (known numbers) and not stochastic, but according to the concepts of economic models, y must be stochastic.

The enlarged system consisting of (1) and (2) together is block recursive because the matrix

$$\begin{bmatrix} A & B \\ 0 & \Gamma \end{bmatrix}$$

has a block triangular structure. It is said to be *fully* recursive if e and u are statistically independent so that the $(n + m) \times (n + m)$ covariance matrix

$$\begin{bmatrix} Eee' & Eeu' \\ Eue' & Euu' \end{bmatrix}$$

is block diagonal, i.e., if Eue' and Eeu' are both zero. The block diagonality of the covariance matrix usually simplifies the statistical inference problem for estimating the coefficient matrices because the joint probability density functions of e and u can be factored into a product of the probability densities of e and of u

$$p(e_1, \ldots, e_n, u_1, \ldots, u_m) = f(e_1, \ldots, e_n)g(u_1, \ldots, u_m).$$

If the parameter set of f and g are non-overlapping, the maximum likelihood estimation of the system factors into separate maximization of f and of g (after transformation of variables) from e_t to y_t and x_t and from u_t to x_t.

In the linear case, regardless of whether e and u are jointly normal, the least squares estimate of the reduced form of (1)

$$y_t = -A^{-1}Bx_t + A^{-1}e_t$$
$$= \Pi x_t + v_t$$

provides consistent estimates of Π.

$$\hat{\Pi} = \left\|\sum_t y_t x_t'\right\| \left\|\sum_t x_t x_t'\right\|^{-1}$$

$$\text{if } \| Ev_t x_t' \| = 0$$

which would hold in the block diagonal covariance case.

If x_t is non-stochastic, then the above condition on the covariance of v_t and x_t' automatically holds.

This formulation generalizes to nonlinear systems of the form

$$F(y', x', \theta') = e, \tag{1'}$$

$$G(x', \phi') = u. \tag{2'}$$

F and G are vector functions. The variables y, x, e, and u are as previously defined. The parameters of the system θ and ϕ replace A, B, Γ.

Inference in (1') and (2') is more complicated than in (1) and (2), but the ideas that x is generated by (2') and that y has no effect on x still prevail.

The concepts and definitions that have been introduced are well known, and the exposition appears to be pedantic. This is familiar textbook material. It is, however, being restated in connection with a re-examination of the concept of exogeneity because some quite different concepts are being put forward in econometrics, either changing the nature of exogeneity or doing away with it entirely; so it is useful to restate basic premises in arguing for the usefulness of the standard concepts.

T. C. Koopmans made these points clear for the general model — the triangularity of the Jacobian matrix, the diagonality of the covariance matrix, the factorization of the likelihood function. In the oral discussions at the Cowles Commission, these ideas were used to show how variables could be treated as though they were exogenous in partial systems or in single equations provided they were not correlated with the disturbance terms of the equation(s) in question, even though such variables are not strictly exogenous from the point of view of an entire model of the economic system.[1]

There are two important extensions of the model (1)–(2) that should be mentioned. The stated model is static, but in both the linear and nonlinear forms, dynamics may be entered. The linear dynamic form is

$$A(L)y_t + B(L)x_t = \Delta(L)e_t, \tag{3}$$

$$\Gamma(L)x_t = E(L)u_t. \tag{4}$$

All the matrix expressions are written as matrix polynomials in the operator L

$$L^s y_{it} = y_{i,t-s}$$

and similarly when operating on $x_t, e_t,$ or u_t.

---

[1] T. C. Koopmans (1950).

The stochastic terms e_t and u_t need not be the only conduit for probability to enter the system. The variables, whether endogenous or exogenous, could be written as

$$y_t = y_t^* + v_t$$

$$x_t = y_t^* + z_t$$

where y_t^* and x_t^* are "true" unobserved values of the measured magnitudes y_t and x_t. The random variables v_t and z_t are errors of measurement or observation. Unless there are strong assumptions made about the probability structure of v_t and z_t, we are confronted with a basic lack of identification in the system that combines the two sources of error, and the most conventional model does not use error of measurement in the stochastic specification, even though the idea is quite realistic. There are, indeed, well known measurement errors in economic statistics; but the complications that arise by recognizing them explicitly do not play a crucial role in the debates about exogeneity, although they are not wholly irrelevant.

2. Examples of Exogenous Variables

In the preceding section we have introduced some concepts, and in this section, we shall attempt to give substance to the basic ideas by citing some realistic examples. The best examples of exogenous variables are associated with the general phenomenon of weather. Crop yield in agriculture, production and sales of seasonal goods, electric power use and many other economic activities are significantly related to weather. There are many dimensions to this variable. We must consider rainfall, temperature, wind, hours of sunshine, and monthly (or shorter period) distributions of these magnitudes. In a strongly agricultural economy, weather can be enormously important. In more advanced societies with less strategic reliance on agriculture and many means of compensating for weather variables (irrigation, refrigeration, air conditioning, flood control, etc.) it may be possible to soften the extreme effects of weather variation, but such softening has only partial effect.

In general, the economy does not affect the weather (or climate). Over long periods of time, the functioning of the economy may affect the atmosphere and thereby change natural conditions, but this is not yet clear for purposes of economic modeling. In the short run there can be cloud seeding, but, here again, there are debates about its effect and its effectiveness.

The measurable characteristics of weather serve as excellent examples of exogenous variables, but weather effects are so diverse and unknown that it is difficult to obtain precise measurement. For example, we may have excellent statistics on inches of rainfall, but what rainfall should be measured for estimating crop yield — when and where? Weather indexes are approximations that are subject to error. This is a case of measurement or observation error. The index values may be accurate, but they are probably inaccurate in measuring the "true" weather effect that is needed for a particular problem. Also, extreme weather in the form of storms has great economic impact, but it occurs almost randomly.

If an exogenous variable is under control, it can be measured accurately, say temperature in a controlled experiment. But if weather is generated by the laws of meteorology according to equation system (2) it may have a large error, since we know that meteorology does not provide highly accurate information for time periods of one month or longer. The "noise-to-signal" ratio is large in meteorology, just as it is in economics.

Indian economists in 1985, 1986, and early 1987 were generally optimistic and confident about their country's economic progress. They were basing their judgment on econometric model performance, recent experience and an (exogenous) assumption that weather would continue to be normal. By mid year 1987 it became obvious that a severe drought was at hand, and that their model inputs were wrong, leading to incorrect model outputs. Just one year later, we experienced the same thing in the United States. A severe drought caused a food and grain crop shortfall of more than 25%. This changed farm income, government support, food price inflation, and world market prices very much. These are cases of stochastic exogenous variables that contain no system feedback from the economy.

It is interesting to note that the overall GNP statistics for an economy as large and as industrial as the United States show clearly the adverse effects of the drought in the summer quarter's reports because of the large drawing down of farm inventories. It is also noteworthy that end-of-year (1988) projections for 1989 generally assumed normal conditions for the next crop and harvest, because there was very little information available on weather conditions as much as six months in advance. Moreover, some of the most sophisticated projections anticipated that the official body responsible for the government's GNP statistics would allocate a *seasonally adjusted* increase in farm production for the first quarter of 1989 in advance of knowing whether or not weather conditions were going to be normal in the 1989 crop year. The early 1989 reports on the behavior of the economy would, it was assumed, contain an allocation of activity that had not yet occurred, and this decision was wholly unrelated to the performance of the economy in any sector. That surely describes a variable that has no feedback effect from the economy.

In general, major noneconomic events are candidates for classification as exogenous variables. The most pervasive is war, but embargoes, interdictions of transport, strikes, or perhaps the stock market crash of October 19, 1987, are major events that impact the economy yet are not explicable by systematic econometric analysis.

In some systems of thought, Marxist and other, a total interpretation of history must include economics, politics, social forces, and other phenomena all together. According to this view of the world, everything except natural events should be endogenous. At one extreme, by the economic interpretation of history, an economic model should treat war, strikes, and other major events as endogenous variables explained by the model. There is, however, an econometric argument against this view. Econometrics, as opposed to theoretical economics, has a statistical base, and for variables to be explained by the model there must be a statistical sample. Many of the major events are one-time occurrences. There are not enough wartime observations or other unusual events to establish a good sample for estimating or testing theory building related to such events. A usual procedure in econometrics is either exclude sample points with such events from the data base to be used, to use some direct exogenous measurement of the event, or to introduce a surrogate ("dummy") variable to try to estimate an effect of the event, regarding it as an exogenous variable. Data are usually not contaminated in every possible dimension by such events; therefore it is rare to throw away observations for such circumstances. World War II was so pervasive and disruptive nearly everywhere, that the affected period is usually deleted from statistical samples and no theory specification is attempted for this event. The Korean, Vietnam, or Iran–Iraq Wars, horrible though they may be, do not necessarily justify deletion from sample information for many kinds of investigations. But they are *exogenous* events.

The oil embargo and changes in terms of trade for energy products are usually not modeled explicitly. There have been some recent attempts to build a model of the energy markets and "explain" oil prices, but they are not very successful, and certainly not as successful as are modeling exercises for other primary product markets. During the period of great OPEC influence it would have been virtually impossible to predict oil prices from an econometric model, yet oil prices played important exogenous roles in econometric models. The situation is changing, now that OPEC is losing control to market forces, but until recently, the recommended procedure was to regard oil prices as exogenous variables.

The stock market crash of October 19, 1987, is a very interesting case. First, is it possible to explain the crash, or what is the same, build a model that did or could project the path of equity prices during 1986, 1987, 1988? Secondly, can the effect of equity price movements, during this period, on economic bahavior be explained?

The run-up of stock prices during 1986 and the first nine months of 1987, like the run-up of the U.S. dollar until 1985, was probably a great speculative spree fostered by new trading instruments, new hardware, new software, permissive attitudes of regulators, some breaking of rules. It was very much an economic event, but should it be endogenous? The random error, e_t, in econometric models, is made up of that myriad of factors that are not explicitly measured and put into the model; they are omitted variables, and it seems that the underlying factors shaping the crash fall into this category.

It has been extremely difficult to assess the effect of the crash. There is no discernible effect on macro behavior as far as consumer spending or producer investing are concerned. Real demand, except for some kinds of consumer spending and residential investment in the United States, has not responded. There are, however, economic effects. Investment portfolios have definitely shifted proportions away from equity holdings. Markets remain very sensitive to "news." Economic activity in the finance, insurance, and real estate sector fell and had not recovered within one year. With the help of monetary authorities, interest rates were held down for the greater part of one year after the crash, but public policy was complemented by investor preferences for safer investments in high quality debt instruments and official monetary intervention to keep markets calm during an election year.

The Crash was a one-time event; its full effect on the economy has not yet been realized; and it does not fit into the category of variables that we usually call endogenous. It was a one-time exogenous event and can be measured through many surrogate indicators, but we are not yet very sure about its effect. It is interesting to remark that Jan Tinbergen, in one of the first macroeconometric models ever built, provided an endogenous explanation of equity prices in his model of the U.S. and found great significance for the Crash of 1929 in bringing consumer and investment spending to the low levels of the Great Depression.[2]

Together with weather, one of the most important groupings of exogenous variables in macroeconometric models is public policy, covering use of both fiscal and monetary instruments. Tax collections and transfer payments are endogenous, but the setting of tax rates and formulas for transfers are in the hands of public authorities — a minister, an executive in government, or a legislature. Decision making of individual people and even legislative bodies is too personal and too much dependent on choices by a small group of people whose actions are not statistically predictable to be based on a statistical sample. If thousands or millions make decisions, which we econometricians analyze, in market behavior, that constitutes a proper statistical sample whose regularity we study through interrelationships connecting endogenous and exogenous variables. In a sense, economics and econometrics are not "clinical" subjects; they are "field" subjects.

What has been said for tax and transfer payment policy can also be said for expenditure policy for public services, military, and other functions of government. Behavior of central bank governing boards that determine official participation in financial markets does not have statistical regularity. It reflects the decisions of a few people. And these decisions frequently vary a great deal between regimes.

It is my opinion that fiscal and monetary policies (also trade or commercial policies) of governments are exogenous decisions of just a few people, but it is popular now in model building to include *reaction* functions. These are designed to show how official bodies will react to the economy. In particular, they would attempt to show how the Federal Reserve Open Market Committee would "lean against the wind" or follow some other strategy that the model builder thinks is appropriate for their behavior. It is perfectly legitimate to explore various assumptions about official behavior, each being portrayed by separate reaction functions, but I regard this kind of exploratory analysis only as interesting examination of assumed alternatives. It does not justify the classification of official policy variables as endogenous. Together with weather and other natural phenomena, official policy variables should also be exogenous.

---

[2] J. Tinbergen (1939).

Demographic variables are frequently classified as exogenous in econometric model investigation. Like political decisions, demographic decisions could be assumed to be generated by a model that is apart from the economic model being investigated. If x_t represent population size, births, deaths, migration, participation in the work force, and many other demographic magnitudes, we might be tempted to assume that they satisfy the structure of Eq. (2)

$$0y_t + \Gamma x_t = u_t \,. \tag{2}$$

This assumes that demographic variables are stochastic but generated by their own model, without feedback form y_t. This is probably a poor assumption. It is quite apparent that many economic decisions are affected by demographic variables; x_t does affect y_t, but it is probably not true that demographics can neglect the feedback effects of economic variables y_t on x_t.

Demographic variables often move slowly. In short run cyclical models, demographic variables may be approximately classified as exogenous. All the people who are to be in the next decade's work force are already born and available, although an estimated number may die during the coming period. A more volatile component of the work force comes from immigration, and all the potential immigrants are not at hand. There is less and less justification for putting demographic variables in the exogenous category. There is much feedback from economic variables to demographic variables, and econometricians must undertake the research task of shifting demographics to the endogenous category.

One demographic variable is age. If we deal with age cohorts, life cycle decisions, and interaction with medical care, we find that age is a complicated variable or group of variables. Frequently it is measured as chronological age, which advances by one unit each year. In this narrow sense it is an exogenous variable, but that does not give a satisfactory treatment of age in economics. Similarly, chronological time is often used as a trend variable standing for technical change, growth, aging, or a variety of processes. Technically, chronological time is regarded as an exogenous variable, but that is only because it is an unspecified proxy for our ignorance. Some investigators use chronological time as an exogenous *instrument* for estimation by the method of instrumental variables or some closely related methods such as two-stage-least squares. This is hardly a recommended choice for an instrument, particularly if it is to be a major instrument.

3. Alternative Approaches

The issue of the concept of exogeneity is only partly a matter of taking up long standing debates that have been referred to already and re-examining them. Our capabilities are now greater. We have better information, more information, more powerful computer facilities, and more experience with econometric models. One form of improvement is to reduce the scope of exogeneity (in practice) because it frequently has been used to avoid work or to seek a seemingly easy way out when analyzing specific problems. If a variable is classified as exogenous, the investigator does not have to face up to the effort of explaining it.

But the concept is now at issue because there are challenges from other approaches. Let us consider first the approach of time series analysis, in that form that minimizes the use of economic theory in econometric model specifications.

Christopher Sims has suggested and promoted use of the following model, known as the vector-autoregressive-model (VAR)

$$y_t = A(L)y_{t-1} + e_t,$$

$$y_t \text{ and } e_t \text{ are } n\text{-element column vectors.}$$

(5)

Each variable y_{it} is expressed as a linear function of previous *own* values and previous *other* values with additive error. The system could be generalized. Simultaneity could be allowed; exogenous variables could be used; and the error terms could be generated by moving average or autoregressive processes. For our purposes, in the present discussion, the most interesting and relevant idea is that no exogenous variables are used. This is Sims' own choice.

This is a general system, but it has been mainly applied to macro models. In these formulations, monetary and fiscal variables are in the y_t-vector and therefore differ in concept from the point of view put forward earlier that variables decided upon by a small number of people lack statistical regularity.

Since the VAR system has little (or no?) economic theory, there is unusually heavy reliance on empirical information for the structure of the system. In many respects, this approach could be called "Measurement without Theory," which is a well-known criticism by Tjalling Koopmans of time series analysis of the National Bureau of Economic Research.[3] Since few economic theoretical restrictions are used and since y_t includes both conventional endogenous and exogenous variables, the number of economic processes that can be investigated is rather small. A mainstream macroeconometric model would have hundreds or even thousands of elements in y_t, while Sims has about 10 or, at most, 20. Other VAR systems of fewer than 10 variables have also been suggested for some macroeconometric applications.

Given an econometric model, either (1) in the linear mode or (1') in the nonlinear mode, there are two driving forces in a structural model. One set of forces are the random errors, which also provides the probability base for statistical inference in the system, and the other set of forces are the exogenous variables. Key sensitivities in the model are the multipliers, i.e., the partial derivatives

$$\frac{\partial y_{it}}{\partial x_{jt}}, \text{ given } x_{kt^*}, k \neq j,$$

which show how y_{it} varies when x_{jt} changes, with all other x_{kt} held to unchanged values. In the VAR system, the only driving forces are in the error terms, unless one or more of the system's relationships undergoes shift.

---

[3]T. C. Koopmans (1947).

The VAR system is dynamic; so an imposed change on any $y_{it'}, t' < t$ at an earlier time point can induce a change in y_{it} at the later time period. Earlier change becomes a force for later change. This property holds in the mainstream model (3), too. For many statistical purposes we treat historical values of y_{it} as though they were exogenous. The broader term, *predetermined* variable, includes both previous values of endogenous variables and values, contemporary or previous, of exogenous variables.

Exogenous variables and prior values of endogenous variables acting as forces in a model make up the causal structure, apart from random errors. In the context of dynamic systems, Clive Granger has defined causality as indicating that prior values of one variable (in this case y_{t-j}) are significantly correlated with x_i, as in

$$x_t = \sum_{j=1}^{m} a_j x_{t-j} + \sum_{j=1}^{m} b_j y_{t-j} + e_t. \tag{6}$$

This means that the history of y_t provides information about x_t that is not provided by x_t's own history.[4] Similarly, he would conclude that x causes y if some prior values of x_t are significantly related to y_t in

$$y_t = \sum_{j=1}^{m} c_j x_{t-j} + \sum_{j=1}^{m} d_j y_{t-j} + u_t. \tag{7}$$

In a general model such as (3), the associated reduced form would be

$$y_t = -A_0^{-1} A_1(L) y_t - A_0^{-1} B(L) x_t + A_0^{-1} \Delta(L) e_t.$$

If both some b_j in (6) and some c_j in (7) are not zero, as could happen in practice, then x_t and y_t are said to be in feedback relation with each other. A_0 is the matrix of coefficients of $L_0 (= I)$ in $A(L)$; $A_1(L)$ is the polynomial matrix of coefficients of $L, L^2, \ldots$, etc. The reduced form implies that y_{it} depends linearly on $y_{i,t-j}$ (all i, j), on $x_{k,t-p}$ (all k, p) and on moving sums of errors. Empirically, it is quite possible that lagged values of some particular x_{kt} are significantly correlated with y_{it} even though the correct relationship is the reduced form equation, in which y_{it} has significant correlations with other variables too. These other variables may be predominant, and would crowd out the correlation with lags of x_{kt} if they were included in the model and in empirical tests, using the model as a guide. Also, in moderate or large models there are usually not enough degrees of freedom to estimate unrestricted reduced form types of equations, although there are, if restrictions are imposed. These restrictions are closely associated with the classification of variables in the exogenous or endogenous category. They come, to a large extent, by bringing economic theory to bear on system specification, something that is missing in the empirical time series approach to testing for causality. Causality should be studied within the context of a total system and not by pairwise lead-lag correlations,

---

[4]C. W. J. Granger (1969).

unless there happens to be some particular recursive structure in (3) that implies a bivariate relationship between y_{it} with its own lags and those of x_{kt}. This is a very special case in which the two approaches (time series analysis and structural model analysis) converge, but does not provide a general concept. The economic system is basically complicated and highly multivariate, whether being represented in microeconometric or macroeconometric models. It is highly unlikely that simple bivariate relationships will provide adequate representation of economic complexity. Particular samples may show some impressive (or impressionistic) correlations, but they always break down when repeatedly applied in an outside-sample context.

Granger causality has some empirical interest, but it is not a general concept, and it is not the same thing as causality or exogeneity as the concept has traditionally been used in econometrics. Exogeneity deals with decomposition of the joint probability distribution of the sample or, in linear systems, with the correlation between measured variables of the model and the error terms of the individual equations, whether the measured variable being considered is present in a particular equation or not.

In an interesting exploration of the concept of exogeneity, Robert Engle, David Hendry, and Jean-Francois Richard introduce the concepts of weak, strong, and super exogeneity.[5] Their concept of weak exogeneity is essentially the same as that of Koopmans, in which the likelihood function can be factored appropriately for estimation purposes.

They define strong exogeneity as weak exogeneity plus Granger noncausality. This is surely unfortunate, because Granger causality or noncausality is not related to a model of the economy; it is purely an empirical aspect of a sample of data.

In the linear case, exogeneity in the usual, time-honored definition is based on the correlation between the variables classified as exogenous and the unobserved random errors of the system. The significance of these correlations can be tested, and a statistic can be constructed that shows the strength or weakness of the concept. This would seem to provide a more appropriate way to define strong exogeneity. Since the authors remark that Granger noncausality is neither necessary nor sufficient for weak exogeneity, it is hard to see why the two unrelated concepts are put together to extend the standard concept.

Super exogeneity, on the other hand, does extend the standard concept, for it deals with the case in which the parameters of the model being considered undergo structural change. The treatment of variable parameter models is interesting. Super exogeneity defines variables whose changes do alter the parametric structure of the first factor of the likelihood function

$$f(e_1, e_2, \ldots, e_n),$$

which they call the conditional model. This extension of the concept is intended to

---

[5]R. Engle A., D. Hendry, and J-F Richard (1983).

deal with what is called the Lucas critique, by which it is asserted that the response parameters of the macro model are functions of the exogenous policy variables.[6]

References

Engle, Robert, David Hendry and Jean-Francois Richard, 1983, "Exogeneity," *Econometrica* **51**, pp. 277–304.

Granger, C. W. J., 1969, "Investigating causal relations by econometric models and cross-spectral methods," *Econometrica* **37**, pp. 424–438.

Koopmans, T. C., 1947, "Measurement without theory," *The Review of Economic Statistics* **29**, pp. 161–172.

————, 1950, "When is an equation system complete for statistical purposes?," in *Statistical Inference in Dynamic Economic Models*, ed. T. C. Koopmans (John Wiley, New York), pp. 393–409.

Lucas, R. E., 1976, "Econometric policy evaluation: A critique," in *Carnegie–Rochester Conferences on Public Policy*, eds. K. Brunner and A. Meltzer (North–Holland, Amsterdam), pp. 19–46.

Tinbergen, J., 1939, *Business Cycles in the United States of America, 1919–1932* (League of Nations, Geneva).

---

[6]R. E. Lucas (1976).

Nobel Laureates in economics remember Adam Smith on the bicentennial of his death, July 1, 1990. Gathered at the grave of Adam Smith in the Canongate Kirkyard in Edinburgh are (left to right) Wassily Leontief — the 1973 Nobel laureate; Lawrence Klein — 1980; James Buchanan — 1986; Franco Modigliani — 1985; Maurice Allais — 1988; James Tobin — 1981; and James Meade — 1977.

17

SMITH'S USE OF DATA[†*]

Adam Smith was a professor of moral philosophy, and he is appropriately remembered for the underlying philosophical foundations that he provided for modern economics, yet *The Wealth of Nations* is full of quantitative analysis that is not explicitly philosophical, and I propose to look into his digressions into economic time series, in particular his analysis of wheat prices and related matters in Chap. XI, "Of the rent of the land" which rounds out Book I.

In terms of modern economic discourse, one might say that Smith's argument is decidedly "anecdotal." He draws on a vast treasure of interesting facts, many of which are quantitative, down to numerical details. He refers (I, xi, b, 16) to the price of butcher's meat paid by Prince Henry (who died on 6 November, 1612). He quotes a price of £9 10s. for 4 quarters of an ox weighing 600 pounds (31s. 8d. per hundred pounds weight). The argument of much of the book is supported by reference to many facts like these, some in precise numerical terms and some in general, such as the relation between the price of rice in China and the price of wheat in Europe. The philosophical base of *The Wealth of Nations* is implicit in all the explicit reasoning about the real world, which Smith has observed in minute detail, both contemporaneously and historically. My emphasis in this essay is, however, on Smith's use of systematic data in much the same way that modern quantitative economists look at such evidence.

At the end of Chap. XI, there is an extensive time series listing of wheat prices from 1202 to 1764. I am not going to analyze his use of data elsewhere, but simply will concentrate on this tabulation of wheat prices, although I do want, eventually, to relate this discussion to other statistical series of the eighteenth century in England in order to try to gain some perception of this appreciation of dynamic economics of his times.

The wheat data were not collected and prepared by Adam Smith. In modern parlance we would say that they are a secondary data listing, taken from two main sources: Bishop Fleetwood, *Chronicon Preciosum* (1707: 77–124) and supplemented by the accounts of Eton College. Two issues are of some interest. 1) How did Smith handle or interpret the data? 2) What are characteristics of these data that can be determined by modern time series analysis?

[†]From *Adam Smith's Legacy*, ed. Michael Fry (Routledge, London, 1992), pp. 15–28.
[*]Ms Matild Horvath supplied invaluable research support for this investigation.

Smith did some very good and perceptive things with these data, but he also did some questionable things. First, it must be stressed that Smith realized the problem of changes in purchasing power when studying the behavior of prices over long periods of time. Accordingly, he presented Fleetwood's time series of wheat prices in two modes, as nominal prices and as *real* prices. The latter mode was termed "The average price of each year in money of the present times." Very early in *The Wealth of Nations* (Chap. V, "Of the real and the nominal price of commodities, or of the price in labour, and their price in money," he wrote,

> Labour, therefore, is the real measure of the exchangeable value of all commodities. (I, v, 1)

> Labour, like commodities may be said to have a real and a nominal price. Its real price may be said to consist in the quantity of the necessaries and conveniences of life which are given for it; its nominal price, in the quantity of money. The labourer is rich or poor, is well or ill rewarded, in proportion to the real, not to the nominal price of this labour. (I, v, 9)

Fleetwood's nominal wheat prices were apparently transformed into real prices by using the table by Martin Folkes (*Table of English Silver Coins*. 1745:142) The editorial notes of Edwin Cannan remark that the transformation was very approximate, with some margin of error.

Apart from some degree of numerical error, the main controversial aspect of Smith's use of these data is his splicing of the Fleetwood series, which ended with the entry for 1597. The entries for the next four years — 1598, 1599, 1600 and 1601 — were taken directly, without adjustment from the Eton College account. These prices were from Charles Smith (*Tracts on the Corn Trade*, 1766). The problem is that the Eton College quotations refer to the Windsor quarter, which consisted of 9 bushels; whereas a standard quarter was equal to 8 bushels. Also the Windsor market prices are for the best or highest priced wheat, and Smith makes no mention of quality differences. The splicing of the two series of wheat prices is not a major issue, however, because only four values are added to the Fleetwood time series, and the Eton College series are then tabulated separately from 1595 to 1764. Smith did not transform the Eton College series to real prices.

Smith's analysis of this price series was mainly descriptive. He commented on trend phases, some notable fluctuations (departures from trend) upwards or downward, and movements in relation to silver prices. He also commented from time to time about price movements in relation to prices of livestock or livestock products, but there are no lengthy or systematic listings of other prices in *The Wealth of Nations*.

Smith divided the series into 12-year averages and followed the smoother movements of the latter. He saw a declining trend in wheat prices from the thirteenth century to the middle of the sixteenth century and then rising towards the end of the sixteenth century. Fleetwood believed that silver was falling in value, but Smith attached much importance to the wheat prices and felt that they provided a better measure of value than prices of any other commodity. He also noted divergent movements of wheat and silver prices in various epochs and turned to such events as discoveries of new sources of precious metals in America as explanations for the divergences. His analysis of supply–demand balance in price determination was quite perceptive. He also invoked such events as Civil War, bounty on corn export, and debasement of coins as additional special factors that influenced the supply–demand balance for commodities.

Smith analyzed price movements of the seventeenth and eighteenth centuries in relation to each other, to silver prices, and unusual supply factors, affecting either grain yields or availabilities of precious metals. In an earlier chapter, however, he provided a nice general analysis of price determination. He broke price into four components — intermediate materials component, a wage (labour) component, a profit component and a rent (land) component. He then worked with what amounts to a value-added concept of production and implicitly subtracted materials costs from gross output value. He was then left with three familiar inputs — land, labour and capital. The reward to land was rent, to labour was wage, and to capital (termed "inspection and direction") was profit. This way of decomposing price into factor rewards was used for commodities such as corn and flax, but was also well suited for manufactured goods. This approach is the forerunner of present attachment to full-cost pricing in which all the factor costs are covered.

Let us suppose that Adam Smith had access to the facilities of modern hardware and software and also to the insightful techniques of twentieth-century statistical method. What might have been the kind of presentation at the end of Book I of *The Wealth of Nations*?

First, we can examine time series graphs of nominal and real prices, 1202–1594. These all come from Fleetwood. Nominal prices of wheat over this span of nearly four centuries show no decisive trend. There is an unusual peak at about 1270 and an intermediate peak near the end of the sixteenth century. There are fluctuations during this near 400-year period and more will be said of that below, but there is no trend and that may seem to be unusual to us who have lived in an inflationary era. We generally expect nominal prices to rise over very long stretches of time.

Smith wisely and daringly chose a very long time span, within which he analyzed price movements. We can see from Figs. 2.1–2.4 that prices rose *and* fell over several centuries. Nowadays, economists become overly preoccupied with short-run phenomena and translate recent experience to very long time periods — possibly forever. The general impression now is that prices rise endlessly. Some economic historians write about large inflationary bouts in sixteenth-century Spain or other European centers. It is truly remarkable that both the real and the nominal series examined by Smith showed no long-term trend. He could comment on specific short-term movements in price, but he was not confronted with an implicit time graph that moved relentlessly upwards on a trend path.

Real prices of wheat, quoted in prices of Smith's time in the eighteenth century, are larger in value than the main run of nominal prices but the fluctuations are not very different. The same early peak that is found in the nominal series is plainly

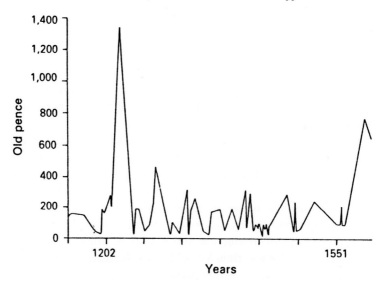

Fig. 2.1. Nominal prices 1202–1594.

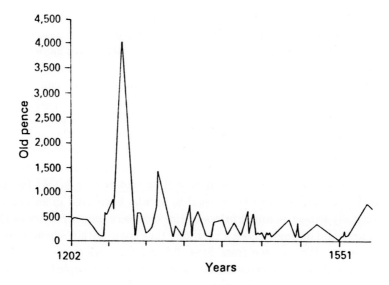

Fig. 2.2. Real prices 1202–1594.

visible, but the tendency of the series to run up to an intermediate peak at the end of the sixteenth century is much subdued. In the later period 1594–1764 there are fewer missing annual observations and the data are not transformed into real prices. Again there is no pronounced trend, but if all the nominal data are put together in one time series diagram, it is clear that there are two statistical universes. The price graph from 1594–1764 is distinctly on a higher level than that part of the graph from 1202–1594.

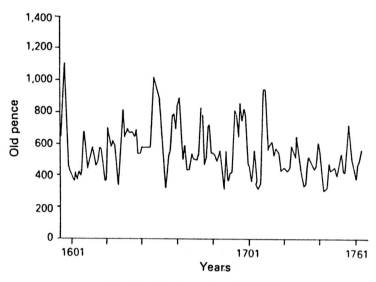

Fig. 2.3. Nominal prices 1594–1764.

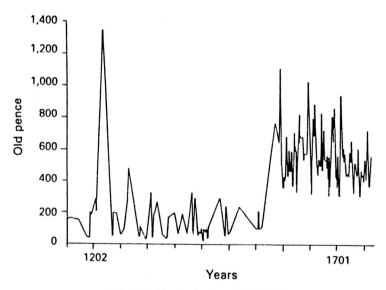

Fig. 2.4. Nominal prices 1202–1764.

What do these price data show? Interestingly enough, they show consistent systematic movement. A periodogram analysis of the Windsor wheat quotations from 1594–1764 (Fig. 2.5) shows 3 peaks, at cycle lengths of 2–3 years, 6 years (the dominant peak) and at 42 years. A medium-term price cycle of 6 years seems to be plausible. Adam Smith commented on various particular price movements but he did not cite or notice empirical cyclical regularities. Although his data series show little sustained trend, they do have distinct cyclical properties. There are too many

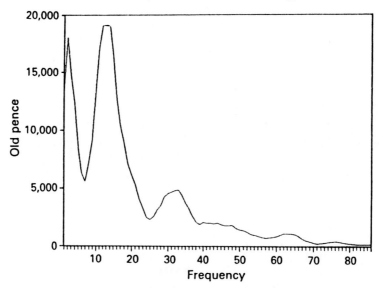

Fig. 2.5. Periodogram: wheat price 1594–1764.

missing yearly values in the longer span of the other series, 1202–1594, to support a similar periodogram analysis.

It is interesting to focus on Smith's own century, the eighteenth. A subject of some consequence but one that is not taken up in depth by Adam Smith is the issue of cyclical regularity. As far as price is concerned, periodicity of fluctuation was present. Extensive documentation of the nineteenth century reveals deeply ingrained cyclical fluctuations. Smith commented at great length on particular movements in the price series but not to the point of drawing conclusions about regularity or commodity of fluctuations among many different series. The concept of "the business cycle" came much later. It had its origins in the nineteenth century, and it is worthwhile inquiring when this economic phenomenon first appeared and why it did not seem to occur earlier. There are many studies of business cycle movement beginning with the nineteenth century, mainly after 1850. In the United States, the period around the Civil War generally marks the start of serious quantitative research on business cycles. In Japan, the Meiji Restoration generally provides a convenient starting point. To a large extent, data availability is the primary constraining factor. In his encyclopedia article on "Business Cycles," Arthur F. Burns cites cyclical turning points for four countries[1]:

United States, beginning 1834;

Great Britain, beginning 1792;

Germany, beginning 1866;

France, beginning 1840.

In all cases, monthly dating precision begins after the middle of the century.

---

[1] Arthur F. Burns, "Business cycle," in David Sills (ed.), *International Encyclopedia of the Social Sciences* **2** (Macmillan, New York, 1986), pp. 226–245.

Sir William Beveridge (later Lord Beveridge) investigated the British trade cycle in the period before 1850. He found cyclical evidence in terms of physical production during the period 1785–1850.[2] His former research assistant J. H. Wilson (later Lord Wilson) reported a remarkable study on the period from 1717 to 1786.[3] Wilson raised some intriguing issues. If Beveridge and others had established the existence of the trade cycle, as we know it and analyze it in modern times, did it exist in similar form in the eighteenth century, in particular, in Adam Smith's time? Wilson did not relate his investigation to Adam Smith, rather to the eighteenth century, however, in the terms of reference of this paper, I am raising the question of the existence of the phenomenon in Smith's economic environment.

Both Beveridge and Wilson confined their investigation to physical indices of production and the latter notes specifically "In no case have prices, or total values involving prices, been used." It is, accordingly, interesting in the present context to examine the wheat price series used by Adam Smith for the corresponding period of the eighteenth century in relation to the output series of J. H. Wilson.[4]

Adam Smith, as noted above, was a keen observer of the economic events of his day and has an enormous grasp of economic history. Should one therefore have expected him to anticipate the industrial changes that were just beginning at the end of the eighteenth century and the characteristics of the economic system that they generated, in particular the business cycle? In a sense, these fluctuations are the outgrowth of the market economy whose foundations were being laid by Smith. Also, if there were regular rhythmical fluctuations with links distributed in time across many sectors of the economy, should they have been treated in more detail by Smith?

It is interesting that J. H. Wilson found no evidence of the business cycle in the eighteenth century comparable to that found by Sir William Beveridge in the nineteenth century. Wilson dated the modern cycle from the 1760s. He concluded: "In the eighteenth century, fluctuations there were, but they were, in the main, localized to particular areas, or confined to individual industries." Indeed, Adam Smith noted aspects of fluctuations in wheat prices in general and also other *particular* fluctuations in certain countries, areas or economic sectors. This is fully in keeping with our finding a significant periodicity in eighteenth-century wheat

---

[2] Sir William H. Beveridge, "The trade cycle in Britain before 1850," *Oxford Economic Paper* **3** (February, 1940), pp. 74–109.

[3] J. H. Wilson, "Industrial activity in the Eighteenth Century," *Economica*, n.s. **7** (May, 1940), pp. 150–60.

[4] Wilson, *op. cit.*, notes that a satisfactory price index of the eighteenth-century period was being calculated on the basis of Sir William Beveridge's price tables in *Prices and Wages in England (The Mercantile Era)* but was not ready for the *OEP* article (see n.b above). Of course, the standards of statistical information and precision would have been much higher than is exhibited in Smith's use of the Eton College accounts with respect to Windsor market prices, but the issue being investigated is Smith's data analysis, and this is what is being related to eighteenth century economic conditions.

price movements. Not only do we find significant periodicities in the wheat price series used by Smith, but we also find evidence of periodicities in Wilson's series. He extracted trends from the series, and they show the following periodicities as illustrated in Figs. 2.6–2.10:

> Industrial index 4.4 years
> (average of series) 2.3
> Coal 5.0
> 2.3
> Iron and steel 3.3
> Textiles 2.4
> Others 1.1.

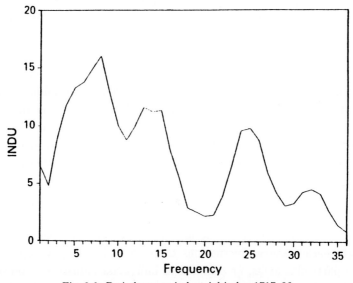

Fig. 2.6. Periodogram: industrial index 1717–86.

To substantiate his observation that a general business cycle in the modern sense did not exist prior to the late 1700s, Wilson calculated the correlation matrix for coal, iron and steel, and textiles. Of the six bivariate correlations, he found only one to be significant, namely, that between coal and textiles. This lack of correlation shows that there is not a general tendency among different series to fluctuate together, in a general business cycle pattern.

To amplify Wilson's work, I have considered the following additional calculations:

(i) Lead–lag correlation among interrelated series that are typical of modern business cycle movements.

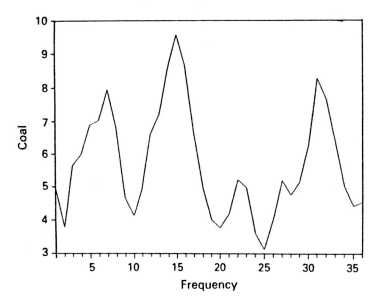

Fig. 2.7. Periodogram: coal 1717–86.

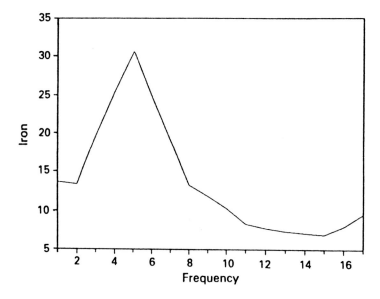

Fig. 2.8. Periodogram: iron 1717–49.

(ii) The possible existence of general (multivariate) linear relationships among the
    variables instead of exclusively bivariate relationships.

(iii) Correlations between the wheat price data found in Smith's volume and various
      series from Wilson on physical production.

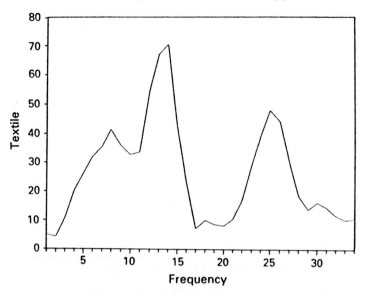

Fig. 2.9. Periodogram: textile 1720–86.

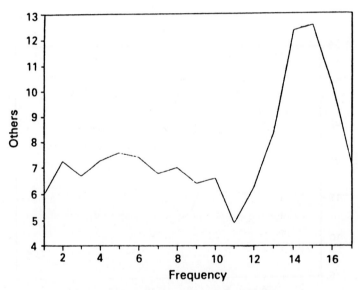

Fig. 2.10. Periodogram: others 1717–49.

The significant correlation between textiles and coal production can be extended to the general lag relationship:

$$T_i = \alpha 0 + \sum_{i=O}^{3} \alpha_i C_{t-i} + u_t \, .$$

In this equation, textiles production (T), a finished manufactured good, is related to prior inputs of coal (C) as a fuel or intermediate good in the manufacturing process. It is natural to look for a time lag here. For the period 1723–1786, I confirm Wilson's finding of a significant relationship:

$$T_t = -27.24 + 0.51C_t + 0.38C_{t-1} + 0.26C_{t-2}$$
$$(-0.59) \quad (2.78) \quad (2.78) \quad (2.78)$$

$$+ .13C_{t-3} \quad R^2 = 0.097$$
$$(2.78) \quad DW = 1.82.$$

t^- statistics are in parentheses below coefficient estimates, and they indicate that the estimated distributed lag coefficients differ significantly from zero.

On the other hand, iron and steel production is not significantly related to coal production, even with trial specifications of various time lags. Wilson constructed a broader measure of "industrial" output, which averages coal, iron and steel, textiles, and *other* series. His industrial index series was correlated with the Eton College wheat price series, 1718–1763, to see if there was any relationship between two cyclical series, one related to food prices and the other related to industrial output, broadly defined. There is no discernible relationship. Correlations estimated from

$$I_t = \alpha + \beta(WP)_{t-\theta} + u_t \quad \theta = 0, 1, 2$$

or from

$$(WP)_t = \gamma + \delta I_{t-\theta} + v_t \quad \theta = 0, 1, 2$$

show low correlation, high serial correlation of residuals, and very low t^- statistics for any of the parameter estimates $\hat{\alpha}, \hat{\beta}, \hat{\gamma}$ and $\hat{\delta}$. In this notion I_t stands of an index of industrial output, WP for wheat price; u_t and v_t are error terms.

Wilson smoothed the industrial index series with a three-year moving average. We, similarly, smoothed the wheat price series with a three-year moving average, but the smoothed series were no more closely correlated than the non-smoothed series.

Finally, the series from Wilson, on the one hand, and from Smith on the other, were considered from another point of view. The separate series for coal, iron and steel, textiles, and *other*, were analyzed by the method of principal components, to see if there was a "common factor" in these series that would be related in a cyclical sense to fluctuations in wheat prices, 1721–1749. Here, the sample size is a lowest common denominator among the four which do not have identical observations points in all cases. The cumulative fractions of overall variance accounted for by the successive principal components are:

PC1	0.377
PC2	0.628
PC3	0.828
PC4	1.0.

There is no single factor that can be identified with the concept of the business cycle that accounts for an overwhelming fraction of the variance. The four components are mutually orthogonal, and I regressed the wheat price on these as four independent variables

$$(WP)_t = 453.93 + 17.59PC1 + 19.15PC2$$
$$(27.64) \qquad (1.05) \qquad\quad (1.15)$$

$$+ 8.07PC3 + 8.03PC4 \qquad R^{-2} = 0.00$$
$$(0.48) \qquad\quad (0.48) \qquad\quad DW = 0.97.$$

No PCi is significant; the overall correlation is nonexistent; and the residual are serially correlated. The same equation with an estimated autoregressive transformation, or with a lagged dependent variable is no better in establishing an empirical relationship between wheat price and any principle component.

From this analysis, I draw the same conclusion as J. H. Wilson; there is no discernible common tendency for various statistical series to move together during the eighteenth century in what might be called a common business cycle, and the addition of wheat price to the set of production statistics does not alter that conclusion. There is little evidence that Adam Smith should have been able to observe business cycles in his professional life time. It is an open question as to whether he should have been able to see the makings of a business cycle in what was coming in the industrial age of the nineteenth century.

Editorial Note

Prefix number 2 in the figure numbering refers to chapter number 2 of the source, *Adam Smith's Legacy, op. cit.*

18

SOME TENDENCIES IN MODERN ECONOMETRICS[†]

1. Background Notions

All analytical subjects, probably all scholarly fields of investigation, for the matter, should be exploring new avenues of research and seeking new findings. In economics, generally, there is an explosion of research activity, associated with new information, new devices, new scholarly journals, and new professional opportunities. Econometrics, which greatly expanded as a sub-discipline of economics in the second half of this century, is presently branching out in many directions, some of which appear to be fruitful and some of which do not.

There are now several books and articles on historical development of econometrics from sparse early roots in the 19th century and much more significant growth activity in the 20th century. It is worth while to reconsider some earlier research, in relation to recent developments.

The subject grew quite naturally as formal economics and mathematical statistics expanded, but a breakthrough occurred that came to be known as the "Haavelmo Revolution." A manuscript authored by Trygve Haavelmo circulated among academic economists and statisticians in the late 1930s and early 1940s; it was published as a supplement to *Econometrica* in 1944.[1] An important interpretation of Haavelmo's contribution, viewed largely from the side of mathematical statistics, has been published by Theodore W. Anderson on the occasion of the award of the prize in memory of Alfred Nobel to Haavelmo in 1989.[2]

In order to assess some recent developments in econometrics, I want to emphasize a few important aspects of Haavelmo's contribution, which indeed has many facets. Essentially, Haavelmo placed econometric methodology in the midst of developments that were taking place, or had already taken place, in statistical inference. Statistics in economics, which was already well established, but under development at the time of Haavelmo's work, was largely concerned with descriptive statistics. The main problems were those of describing the economy in quantitative terms. Haavelmo's approach showed how to relate mathematical specifications of economic relationships to probability interpretations of statistical estimates of the specified relationships.

[†]From *Indian Economic Review, Special Number in Memory of Sukhamoy Chakravarty* (1992) pp. 5–14.
[1]Haavelmo (1944).
[2]Anderson (1991).

All econometrics does not deal with the estimation of behavioral relationships or economic decision-making, but a large portion of the discipline is involved in analyzing economic behavior, and this forms the focus for the present discussion. To show how probability and economic relationships are involved together, let us consider the fundamental, but general, model that formed the basis for Haavelmo's approach.

$$F(y'_t, y'_{t-1}, \ldots, y'_{t-p}, x'_t, x'_{t-1}, \ldots, x'_{t-q}, \Theta') = e_t \tag{1}$$

$$y_t = \begin{pmatrix} y_{1t} \\ y_{2t} \\ \vdots \\ y_{nt} \end{pmatrix}; x_t = \begin{pmatrix} x_{1t} \\ x_{2t} \\ \vdots \\ x_{mt} \end{pmatrix}; \Theta = \begin{pmatrix} \Theta_1 \\ \Theta_2 \\ \vdots \\ \Theta_s \end{pmatrix}; e_t = \begin{pmatrix} e_{1t} \\ e_{2t} \\ \vdots \\ e_{nt} \end{pmatrix}$$

y_t = dependent (endogenous) variables
x_t = independent (exogenous) variables
Θ = parameters
e_t = random errors
F = n-element vector of functions

In this system, there are n equations that determine the time paths of n endogenous variables, given initial values for the endogenous variables, initial and contemporaneous values for the exogenous variables and the parameter values for Θ. The equations are not necessarily linear, and all variables or all parameters are not present in each equation.

To estimate the parameters, Θ, from a T-element sample of data for y_t and $x_t (t = 1, 2, \ldots, T)$, we first specify the joint probability of e_t and then transform it into a joint probability distribution of y_t, given x_t and Θ. This is a crucial transformation

$$\Pr(y_{1t}, \ldots, y_{nt} | y_{1t-1}, \ldots, y_{nt-p}; x_{1t}, \ldots, x_{mt-q}; \Theta_1, \ldots, \Theta_S) dy_{1t}, \ldots, dy_{nt}$$

$$= \Pr(e_{1t}, \ldots, e_{nt}) \left| \frac{\partial(e_{1t}, \ldots, e_{nt})}{\partial(y_{1t}, \ldots, y_{nt})} \right| dy_{1t}, \ldots, dy_{nt} \quad t = 1, 2, \ldots, T \tag{2}$$

By direct substitution of (1) into the term on the rhs of (2) we have an expression in terms of data on y_t and x_t, dependent on Θ. The second term on the rhs is simply the Jacobian of the transformation from e_t to y_t (via F)

$$\frac{\partial(e_{1t}, \ldots, e_{nt})}{\partial(y_{1t}, \ldots, e_{nt})} = \begin{pmatrix} \frac{\partial f_1}{\partial y_{1t}} & \cdots & \frac{\partial f_1}{\partial y_{nt}} \\ \vdots & & \vdots \\ \frac{\partial f_n}{\partial y_{1t}} & \cdots & \frac{\partial f_n}{\partial y_{nt}} \end{pmatrix}$$

The joint probability distribution over the entire sample can be formed by combining the probabilities for all $t = 1, 2, \ldots, T$. In the simple case in which the e_t mutually independent in t (e.g., no serial correlation), the joint probability distribution over the whole sample is the T-fold product of the probabilities in (2). Further simplifications can be introduced by assuming F to be linear and also by assuming that all the e_{it} are mutually independent at time t.

The main point is not the actual implementation of the techniques of statistical inference that are based on particular simplifications but the logic and philosophy of the approach. The probability structure of the e_{it} is at the foundation of the whole system. The important thing for the econometrician to do is to specify

$$\Pr(e_{1t}, \ldots, e_{nt}) \text{ and } F$$

in great detail and to be sure that the procedures that are followed are in agreement with these specifications.

It can be seen that there are three fundamental aspects of this way of looking at the econometric model:

 (i) The probability distribution of error
 (ii) The values for the exogenous variables (and initial conditions)
(iii) The specification of the economic relations in F.

These three elements *drive* the system.

There are other important aspects of the "Haavelmo Revolution" but I regard these to be the most important. There also are the problems of simultaneity of equations, degrees of freedom for estimation, nonlinearity structural change, and identification, but these aspects are not strategic in assessing present tendencies in econometrics. At one time or another, they have been intensively studied.

2. The Probability Distribution of Error

The importance of assumptions about the error terms, their probability distribution, and their relationship to the economic variables of the system through the Jacobian are evident from the exposition of the previous section. This prompted specification of autocorrelation and homoscedasticity properties for e_t. In the fundamental paper by Mann and Wald on the extension of the new ideas to systems of finite difference equations, assumptions about the mutual independence of the e_t (e.g., serial correlation of error) and the finite covariance matrix of error, were made at the very beginning of the reporting on new developments.[3] Mann and Wald also assumed that the characteristic roots of the system of finite difference equations were less than unity in absolute value. These, for linear equations, were assumptions about the parameters.

An important aspect of these assumptions is that they are made about the random errors and not directly about the economic variables themselves. All properties of the variables are implied from the relationships in (1) and (2). This is in contrast with the approach in quantitative economics or the older versions of economic statistics, where attempts were made to characterize the properties of the economic variables directly.

---

[3]Mann and Wald (1943).

Associated with equation (1) are the reduced forms of the system, the final solution form, and, for linear systems, the final autoregressive form. For linear versions of (1), these equations can be derived in closed form expressions. For nonlinear systems they must, in general, be approximated in closed form or implied by numerical solutions.

Symbolically, (1) can be stated in reduced form as

$$y_t = G(y'_{t-1}, \ldots, y'_{t-p}, x'_t, \ldots, x'_{t-q}, \Theta', e_t). \tag{3}$$

Equation (3) merely states that each element of y_t is some function of previous values of y_t, values of x_t, the parameters of the system, and the errors of all the equations of the system. If G could be explicitly evaluated, then, the solution time paths of y_t could be computed given the exogenous variables inputs (past, present, and future), previous values of all the elements of y_t, estimates of Θ, estimates of e_t. The last mentioned variables could be evaluated at their means or any other set, to which some probability of occurrence could be attached.

After the mid 1940s, the emphasis shifted to estimation of values of y_t, as point values or in regions with associated probability, from the entire systems in (1) and (2) and to accept these estimates if our assumptions about

$$\Pr(e_{1t}, \ldots, e_{nt}) de_{1t}, \ldots, de_{nt}$$

were not violated. We would not accept patently counter-intuitive values for y_t, but intuitive conditions were imposed very sparingly. We would not accept negative quantities or prices, where we knew that values should be positive. For the most part, we would not accept explosive values for y_t. That meant that the characteristic roots of linear versions or approximations to (1) should satisfy

$$|\lambda_i| < 1.$$

We estimated systems and then extracted roots to see if fluctuations occurred and were bounded, but we did accept growth trends. Except for dominant trends, we assumed dynamic stability for the outcome. If the solutions did not exhibit this property, we examined the structure of the model for explanation and possible respecification. Mann and Wald imposed dynamic stability on their difference equation systems because that implied finite values for the second order moments of the economic variables, as $T \to \infty$. We also examined steady-state or long-run properties of the elements of y_t. We looked for key ratios or correspondences among variables that were known to prevail in descriptive statistics.

Extensive discussion evolved in the early years of econometrics whether attempts should be made to estimate (1) and derive from the estimated system the dynamic features of the economic entity being studied or to go directly to the final solution forms (or final autoregressive forms) and study the dynamic properties, bypassing structural estimation of (1).

The approach of examining the "final" relationships among the elements of y_t was rejected for several reasons. Important among the reasons were:

(i) There is an inherent lack of understanding or explanation in simply studying the covariation among the elements of y_t, with lags, as well as contemporaneous values.

(ii) In deriving a final form from (1) the properties of the error terms get transformed, often in unknown or unrecognizable ways, especially in the case of nonlinear equation systems.

If we search merely for relationships among elements of y_t, unguided by some systematic structure, we are likely to draw false conclusions that hold only for a particular sample and not in the all-important process of extrapolation. There will be a tendency to draw conclusions that are oversimplified, without deeper exploration for underlying relationships. This appears, to me, to be crude empiricism.

The error structure of final forms is not merely complicated by nonlinearities, so that the error terms have a complicated impact on the system, but even for linear dynamic models, such system reduction is well known to introduce serial correlation in the additive errors of the final form.[4]

3. Consideration of Some Recent Proposals

A currently popular form of dynamic analysis in econometrics is the estimation of vector autoregressive systems (VAR). These take the form

$$y_t = A(L)y_{t-1} + e_t \tag{4}$$

where y_t is an n-element column vector, $A(L)$ is an $n \times n$ matrix polynomial in the displacement operator, L

$$L^j y_{it} = y_{i,t-j}$$

and e_t is an n-element column vector of error. The error process may or may not be specified with some serial correlation properties.

Superficially, equation system (4) looks like a linear version of (1), but there are exceptions. There is no economics in (4), it is just a plausible collection of variables that constitute the components of y_t. No economic theory, no inherent knowledge of economic institutions are called upon to constitute the identifying restrictions on (4). It is essentially an empirical system. It is expressed in linear form, but could, in principle, be extended to nonlinear systems. But without theoretical guidance, it is hard to see how meaningful nonlinearities can be built into the system.

The system in (4) has no exogenous variables. It is, indeed, presumptuous to assert that a small, modest system like that in (4) can explain policy action by a limited group of officials, such as central bank executives or bureaucrats, or parliamentarians. Such small groups of personalities do not constitute a statistical sample,

---

[4]Hurwicz (1944).

where we can rely on the laws of large numbers. Also natural and other external events have their own mechanisms, quite separate from the laws of economics.

Of course, exogenous variables could be added, to form

$$y_t = A(L)y_{t-1} + B(L)x_t + e_t \tag{5}$$

but this does not seem to find a place in the research agenda of VAR investigations.

There are some excellent possibilities of using VAR or ARIMA procedures in collaboration with structural models such as (1). They are quite useful in making interim short-run adjustments to estimated systems like (1) for extrapolation purposes.[5]

Another direction that is being pursued in modern econometrics is to test for cointegration. The time series vector y_t is differenced element-by-element ($\Delta^r y_{it}$) to achieve stationarity. If $\alpha' y_t$ is stationary, then α is a cointegrating vector and series y_t are said to be cointegrated. In the model building approach, equation system (1) is estimated and the "residuals" obtained from the fit, or lack of fit, to sample data must satisfy the properties of random variables following a joint probability distribution. There are no *a priori* restrictions imposed on the elements of y_t and x_t, only on the probability distribution of e_t and their relationship to y_t, x_t as expressed in (2).

Mann and Wald imposed the restriction that the characteristic roots lie in the unit interval

$$|\lambda_i| < 1.$$

This guarantees dynamic stability and is a property of Θ in a linear system. It also implies a finite asymptotic limit for the moments of y_t. The imposition of dynamic stability is conventional but questionable. For a linear system it implies that the business cycle must be damped, unless kept alive by stochastic shocks. This is a plausible representation, but a number of properties and procedures have been worked out for systems in which

$$\lambda_i = 1 \text{ for some } i.$$

The theory and practice of cointegration *assumes* that economic series must be reduced to *stationarity* before being used in linear equation systems with coefficients to be estimated. Economic data are not necessarily *stationary* and should not have to be differenced until stationarity is obtained in a statistical sense. The only objective in econometric inference should be to separate F from e_t (the "signal" from the "noise") in a way that provides estimates of the probability distribution of e_t that conform to assumptions about e_t — not about y_t.

The decision whether or not to form relations among y_t and x_t as specified in (1) should be based on properties of e_t and not y_t (or x_t).

---

[5]Klein and Sojo (1989).

These issues have come up time and again in econometrics, and automatic manipulation of y_t, x_t in advance of estimation has been set aside but the methods of cointegration (with or without error correction) are trying to reintroduce the once-abandoned ideas, and there is a danger that the profession could be misled.

According to the variate-difference method, each economic series could be represented as a polynomial in t, and the r-th differences of the r-th degree polynomial are known to be constant.

$$\Delta^r \left(\sum_{i=0}^{r} \alpha_i t^i \right) = \text{const.}$$

This method was abandoned since the polynomial representation of economic series is dubious.

Similarly, automatic transformation to first differences (or to some low order difference for certain variables) was once recommended as an automatic technique for avoiding serial correlation of residuals. The importance of paying attention to serial correlation of residuals has been recognized as important in order to get good properties for

$$\Pr(e_t)$$

but general Cochrane–Orcutt transformations or other techniques have been used for this purpose instead of automatic differencing of data series.

For linear systems with simple polynomial trends (mainly linear trends), Frisch and Waugh demonstrated early on in econometrics that one obtains the same results by estimating[6]

$$y_t = \alpha + \beta x_t + \gamma t + e_t,$$

using OLS, as by estimating

$$(y_t - a_0 - a_1 t) = \beta(x_t - b_0 - b_1 t) + e_t.$$

Where $a_0 + a_1 t$ is an OLS trend fitted to data on y_t
$b_0 + b_1 t$ is an OLS trend fitted to data on x_t.

This is similar to the procedures for dealing with cointegration, but it does not use differencing in order to obtain stationarity.

The interesting interpretation of the Frisch–Waugh result is that if both y_t and x_t have linear trends, it does not matter whether the series first have trends extracted and are then correlated or whether the series are (multiple) correlated with t as an added variable. This suggests it is not wrong, in any sense, to estimate a relationship with nonstationary variables y_t and x_t, provided one does the obvious and sensible thing, namely, to include their common trend as a third variable. The classical procedure is perfectly valid: Obtain the right data set (in this case, y_t, x_t, and t)

---

[6] Frisch and Waugh (1933).

and estimate a relationship but making sure that $\Pr(e_t)$ has appropriate properties. One such property is lack of serial correlation, which would probably not be found if t were not included and if the trends for y_t and x_t were quite different.

I stress these points because the present generation of economics students is being misled into thinking that they must automatically form differences of the variables they may be examining. They should be taught instead to think carefully about specification of F in (1), the underlying economic mechanism, and should try to isolate residuals that have good probability properties. Instead they are being frightened by a specter of "spurious" correlation.

By generalization of the Frisch–Waugh theorem and sensible model specification, one can proceed in the usual way to build a model like (1) with specifications that may call for some nonstationary variables in the F relations. It is then possible to estimate these equations as we always have in econometrics with proper inclusion of exogenous or endogenously induced trends, examine the distribution of residuals, and, if all tests come out well, proceed with applications of the model so estimated.

There is nothing incorrect about cointegration, but it is not an essential first step for the analysis of multiple time series.[7] It may give some useful information, but it does not really tell us much about model building, and if the multiple time series do not include all the relevant variables in F it may lead the uncareful student to think that a proper relationship has been established on the basis of an empirical correlation among a limited group of variables.

Next, let us consider error correction, which has been closely linked to cointegration analysis. The idea is simply that a fraction of disequilibrium (indicated by a computed residual) in one period is corrected in the next period. This could be a plausible dynamic adjustment process, but it is nothing more or less than that. Its importance and use should be judged with stock adjustment or various adaptive procedures. They are all particular ways of imposing lag structures on a system and should, in principle, be no more powerful than general systems of lag distributions, all of which are simplified approximations to realistic dynamics. The dual concepts of cointegration and error correction have been put forward as special approaches to econometrics with a high degree of generality, but they are actually very special ways of dealing with common trends or common factors and dynamics. They have yet to demonstrate superior powers of extrapolation which is, after all, the ultimate test, but are leading economists away from analytical model building into a highly empirical model of analysis. This looks to me like a backward step, and like those that have previously been considered in the early history of econometrics and set aside until recently.

The idea of treatment of common factors is long established in quantitative economics and econometrics. Allowance for seasonal variation is a case in point,

---

[7] Federal Reserve researchers argue that cointegration tests encounter the problem that the vector α is not unique in sign or magnitude. In the older day this was considered as grounds for rejecting recommended procedures, which again questions some model tendencies. See Swamy, Muehlen, and Mehta (1989).

and the Frisch–Waugh theorem has been used in that connection too for the understanding of the handling of linear additive seasonals. In cross-section samples, where mechanical differencing is out of the question, size factors are eliminated by "dividing-them-out" (per person, per equivalent adult, per acre, per asset value, etc.). There are many ways of taking common factors into account; cointegration analysis could be useful, but it is being applied now in a nondiscriminating way that could lead to false or misleading inferences.

Another new line of analysis in model econometrics is called *Calibration*. Rather than estimating parameters of a model through examining the residuals or errors associated with every data point through some well established estimation and testing method, builders of models try to choose parameter values in accord with a highly selected set of system characteristics.

The general model to which calibration methods can be applied should, in principle, be no different from that of (1). In practice, however, the models that have been used for the application of calibration method are fairly small and adhere very closely to tightly (rhymes with 'rightly') reasoned economic specifications. In older times econometric modeling was often linked to special versions of economic analysis — Keynesian, neoclassical, Walrasian, etc. — but the subject should be applicable for a very wide spectrum of theory. There is no reason for calibration to be confined.

In calibration studies some well established descriptive values are singled out. These may be:

key ratios

> savings ratio
> wage share of output
> velocity of circulation of cash balances
> money multipliers
> capital–output ratio

or, key balances

> growth rate vs. interest rate
> market clearing
> net assets and money supply

Some coefficients or parameter values are set by personal judgment of the investigator or by expert information (scientific laws).

Parameter values are determined (calibrated) so that the system exhibits long run properties — values for key ratios, conforms to established business cycle patterns, observes institutional restraints.

This approach is in contrast to mainstream econometric model building, where systems like (1) are fit to *all* sample data points, treated as a completer set. *A priori* information, if it is very firm, can be built in from the beginning or equations can be specified so that key ratios are reached in a steady state. Also, the results are tested in long-run simulations to see whether or not conventionally estimated systems take on well established properties in both the long and short runs. This is different from enforcing these values at the specification stage.

Except for rigorously determined accounting and other identities, all equations in (1) are stochastic. Some calibration practitioners have allowed for very sparse use of stochastic equations. They have been known to reserve the stochastic terms for the generating of exogenous variables. Whereas the stochastic formulation is of supreme importance in specification and analysis of (1), it plays a relatively small role in some calibration studies.

The long standing controversy of large vs. small models is still an issue. Many of the exponents of the new approaches mentioned here, the calibration school in particular, opt for small systems. They make their tight reasoning for so-called representative agents who are supposed to stand for millions of economic decision-makers all treated alike in a handful of equations. They optimize for the whole society or perhaps for single markets.

Again, as with other new methods, there is widespread usage, without the backing of established performance records in extrapolation.

4. The Challenge and Opportunities for Econometrics

There are three fundamental areas in which the environment for new econometric research has definitely improved. Data sources are much more plentiful in this *information* age. We have data on more aspects of the economy, larger samples (both time series and cross sections), more frequent reports, and better information about international magnitudes. Also the computational hardware and associated software are much better.

The pure time series methods, which do have a great deal of promise if pursued carefully, have become more attractive to scholars because of the large increases in data availability as well as more tractability for computational purposes. The advances in data availability, hardware, and software undoubtedly account for the intensive pursuit of time series analysis.

But we need thinking and analysis to go along with the above improvements. For better and deeper analysis of the model in (1) we should be turning more and more attention to

  (i) data accuracy (error of observation).
 (ii) structural change.
(iii) error analysis of uncertain inference.

  (i) A key factor in treatment of observation error is our ability to decompose total error variance into that part associated with overall disturbance and that part associated with imprecise observation. Within observation error, itself, we need information on relative accuracy of many variables — prices, money market conditions, types of product and income flows, capital transfers, etc. We are gradually learning about observation error and may some day be able to make some headway with error decomposition. But this is an extremely important area of weakness. It is one where we should be undertaking the digging work necessary in order to make progress.

(ii) Structural change is always potentially taking place. Perhaps analysis of variable parameter models offers some hope for improvement. This is, at any rate, an area of research that is very much needed. The tests for detection of structural change, its prediction, and incorporation of change in model structure are all important areas of investigation. Disequilibrium analysis and careful watching of restructuring economies are both promising kinds of investigation that should be further encouraged.

(iii) Finally, in this brief look forward, I should mention decision-making under uncertainty, where the latter is quantified by econometric study, is an area where we econometricians can probably do the most good for the users of our results. Before a careful calculus for users can be designed, it is necessary to determine how large error bands or joint error regions are together with the probabilities of their occurrences.

Interval or regional area methods of inference and methods of presentation are made much more possible through large scale computer use. The main tool seems to be stochastic simulation, about which a great deal has become known in the last decade or so. Stochastic simulation depends, of course, on our ability to separate signal from noise and estimate the variance–covariance matrix of error. This is why we should stick with the general kind of formulation in (1) and try to make it ever more applicable, relevant, and meaningful.

There are many lines of new research that are potentially fruitful, but these are the main ones that appeal to me now. They unfortunately do not command the attention of the coming generation of scholars who appear to be looking in a different direction, as I have outlined in the previous section.

References

Anderson, T. W., 1991, "Trygve Haavelmo and simultaneous equation models," *Scandinavian Journal of Statistics* **18**, pp. 1–19.

Frisch, R. and F. V. Waugh, 1933, "Partial time regressions as compared with individual trends," *Econometrica* **1**, pp. 387–401.

Haavelmo, Trygve, 1944, "The probability approach in econometrics," *Econometrica*, Supplement to Vol. 12.

Hurwicz, Leonid, 1944, "Stochastic models of economic fluctuations," *Econometrica* **12**, pp. 114–124.

Klein, L. R. and E. Sojo, 1989, "Combination of high and low frequency data in macroeconometric models," in *Economics in Theory and Practice: An Eclectic Approach*, eds. L. R. Klein and J. Marquez (Kluwer, Dordrecht).

Mann, H. B. and A. Wald, 1943, "On the statistical treatment of linear stochastic difference equations," *Econometrica* **11**, pp. 173–220.

Swamy, P. A. V. B., Peter von zur Muehlen and J. S. Mehta, 1989, "Cointegration: Is it a property of the real world?," *Finance and Economics Discussion Series,* No. 96, Federal Reserve Board, Washington, D.C.

PART III
APPLIED ECONOMETRICS

Fourteen papers (#19–32) assembled in Part III, Applied Econometrics, are organized under four themes: *Anticipations and Forecasting* (4), *Phillips Curve* (2), *International Economics and Finance* (7), and *Growth* (1). Two of the papers on *Anticipations and Forecasting* were published in the early 1970s and the other two, most recently in 1993 and 1994.

The first paper (with F. G. Adams, 1972) was written in honor of George Katona, renowned pioneer in behavioral economics. It deals with the role of consumer attitudes and expectations in predicting consumer expenditure and residential construction and in forecasting aggregate economic activity in the United States. The role of anticipations is methodologically cast in two alternative formulations, one as exogenously measured auxiliary explanatory variables, and the other as endogenously determined through a realization–expectation framework. Both formulations were analytically touched upon in a related methodology paper, as we have seen earlier in Part II, dealing with the treatment of expectations in econometrics.

Specifically, the paper focuses on the central question concerning the extent to which attitudes and buying intentions anticipate aggregate activity and the relation of these variables to other variables of the system. The subjective variables on attitudes and anticipations, when treated exogenously, are obtained from data collected by household surveys conducted by the University of Michigan. The paper concludes that anticipatory variables are indeed useful in making economic forecasts, but only in a modest way. Furthermore, these variables must be properly integrated into the structural equations of the model "in a logical and specific way." "Consumer attitudes help to explain consumption; investment anticipations relate to various types of investment; and housing starts signal the movement of residential construction."

In his paper, "The precision of econometric prediction: standards, achievement, potential" (1973), Klein indeed cites the use of endogenous anticipatory variables for consumer spending, business fixed investment, and housing construction as one of the factors which have led to error reduction in GNP forecasts. In this paper, he explains how our standards of precision governed by both user requirements and professional ability have shifted over time. Highlighting series of instances of well-known faulty predictions and how they led to incorrect policies in the early history of forecasts (e.g., predictions of post-war recession in 1946, Colin Clark's prediction of post-Korean War economic collapse, underestimation of recovery in 1961 during the early Kennedy Administration, and later the effect of the Vietnam

War on the economy, and the miscalculation of predictions for 1971 by the Nixon Administration), Klein emphasizes the importance of making correct forecasts (*the importance of being right*). A comparative record of error statistics from actively maintained mainstream U.S. models of the time is also presented.

Much has been achieved over time where precision is concerned as conventional forecast error bounds have fallen substantially. Today's tolerable error limits for key economic variables are: GNP, 1%; aggregate price level, 1 index point; unemployment rate, 1/2 percentage point; and short-term interest rate, 100 basis point. As far as future scope is concerned, there exists an asymptotic limit to precision. The paper reminds model-builders and forecast users of an *uncertainty principle*, there "is an irreducible error margin that we shall probably never be able to penetrate."

Klein attributes enhancement in forecast precision to more data, better data, better economic and statistical theory, larger models (more sectors, more nonlinearities, more attention to changing institutions) and the use of anticipatory data. One form of better and increasingly informative data flow for forecasting purposes are data with high-frequency intervals (monthly, weekly, and even daily) which have become available in the information age. The exploitation of such data, to good advantage in economic forecasting, is demonstrated in Klein's next two recent papers, "Economic forecasting at high-frequency intervals" (with J. Y. Park, 1993), and "Economic forecasting and decision-making under uncertainty" (1994). These papers provide a bridge to model-building in the information age.

In these two papers, Klein shows how mainstream econometric models — annual or quarterly — with all the necessary structural details, in combination with an information flow from time-series (ARIMA, VAR, or VARMA) models built with higher-frequency data but limited in structure, can yield predictions with much greater accuracy. The large information flow is unequal; some data are available at extremely high frequency, other vital series at no more than a quarterly frequency. As a way out, as far as forecasting work in the United States is concerned, Klein explains the techniques he has used for filtering high-frequency data regularly into rolling, repetitive forecasts of low-frequency models — quarterly, semestral or annual. Thus comprehensive economic forecasts can be reinterpreted and recalibrated on a more accurate basis as more, even partial, information flows become available. He also explains how one can, as he has, combine a "portfoilo" of forecasts based on different approaches to reduce the variance of forecasting error.

His reflections on predictive accuracy of structural econometric models continue in his paper on forecasting and decision making under uncertainty in honor of his former student, Sir James Ball. Klein lays out the main sources of errors and reminds decision makers that they must forecast, like it or not, and that "attempts to look into the future are error prone." The model-builders who must continue making forecasts, albeit subject to error, in order to advise decision makers, can find an important message that alternative approaches such as methods of optimal control, generating model consistent expectations, and using more efficient or more sophisticated statistical techniques of inference have been pursued intensively in recent years to reduce forecast errors and noise-to-signal ratio. But none has succeeded in making any significant sustained improvement. His suggestion on model improvement still is, "To me, it means adding more detail, treating individual economic sectors more carefully, improving the data base, and staying in close touch with developments in the economy." The avenues of research that look promising are forecasting at higher frequencies, rolling forecasts with improved data, and combining forecasts.

The two papers on the Phillips Curve were written after the Phillips Curve concept came under unjustified sharp attacks in the mid-seventies. Graduate students of macroeconomics should find these short papers particularly illuminating. Their central message is that the concept of the Phillips Curve is much "maligned and misunderstood" and its "criticism is ill-founded on superficial and inadequate analysis." It is clearly demonstrated quantitatively that the Phillips Curve "is very much alive, in tune with modern data," and capable "of coping with labor market changes that have been occurring since the 1950s."

A common view that Phillips Curve implies a trade-off relationship provides a misleading interpretation of this concept. The Phillips curve is essentially a *structural* relationship in contrast to a trade-off, which is a *derived* form. A *structural* relationship is based on fundamental behavior according to accepted principles of economics; a *derived* form refers to a relation between two endogenous variables that are generated by a complete system. Various structural relationships, combined and consolidated by a process of substitution and elimination, enter into a *derived* form relationship.

Specifically, the Phillips Curve is a multivariate structural relationship between wage change, rate of inflation, unemployment rate and other variables. It is based on a market clearing adjustment process of the labor market. This was made quite clear in Phillips' celebrated article. A simple bivariate relationship between the two variables, inflation rate and unemployment rate, in isolation from other system variables is a highly misspecified relationship; it is neither a Phillips curve nor a trade-off relationship. And, whether trade-off between inflation and unemployment occurs depends on the type of shock administered to the economic system. Properly interpreted and analyzed, both Phillips Curve and trade-off relationships are seen to have remained stable, at least in the case of the United States economy.

In "The longevity of economic theory" (1977), we are given the clearest and simplest exposition of the Phillips Curve and the trade-off relationship that I have come across in the literature. The analytical discussion is supported by three sets of quantitative estimates of *derived* relationships between inflation and unemployment for the U.S. economy. The path of the U.S. economy is projected for the period 1975–1985 by simulating the Annual and Industry (Wharton) Model under three different shocks: (i) An increase in real government spending, (ii) an increase in farm prices, and (iii) an increase in the price of oil imports. The results obtained, as *a priori* expected, in case (i) show a trade-off (negative) relation between inflation and unemployment, but in (ii) and (iii), there is no trade-off, the inflation difference and the unemployment difference triggered by the policy shocks are of the same sign. Thus it is demonstrated that the appearance of a trade-off relationship between inflation and unemployment depends critically on the choice of the policy shock.

In the second paper, "The Phillips curve in the U.S." (1982), Klein reinforces his argument by presenting updated estimates of structural Phillips Curves for the U.S. for seven industry groups. He also goes into a short quantitative history of this structural relationship, predating A. W. Phillips' work, tracing it to works of Jan Tinbergen in the 1930s and his own in the 1940s.

Important international economic issues of our increasingly interdependent world economy are the subject of several following papers. The first two papers, "Protectionism" (with V. Su, 1979), and "Disturbances to the international economy" (1979), deal with issues of an historic time, the stagflationary 1970s, when the Keynesian paradigm was faced with challenges. The papers also show early applications of a full international econometric model. These two papers virtually initiated exercises of international policy evaluations that continued later with the work on coordination of international economic policies. (See *Editorial ii*)

During the 1970s when the world economic environment had turned stagflationary, many countries were attracted by protectionist policies. They took many forms, such as tariffs, quotas, reference pricing, and antidumping, etc. By using the transmission mechanism of the world trading system embodied in Project LINK, Klein, in the essay on protectionism, analyzed the impacts of protectionist policies, in various combinations, among the world trading countries. Since the operational LINK system is highly disaggregated, dynamic, nonlinear, and strongly multilateral, Klein presents a simple pedagogical two-country model of protection at the beginning of the paper. The mechanism by which protectionist policies impact GNP of both countries is explained with and without the assumption that the second country retaliates in beggar-thy-neighbor policies, and also for cases when people do and do not distinguish between their spending on domestic and foreign goods. The pedagogical model is laid out in terms of elementary parameters of total spending and mutual trade relationships of the two countries.

For a typical open economy, studied in isolation, exports are a *driving* force, but in the structure of the LINK system of multimodels, imports enter as a *driving* force which generates an *amplification* effect on the supply side. The impacts from simulated scenarios of protectionist policies on total world trade, in value and volume, GNP, growth rates and inflation rates of 13 OECD countries are tabulated. The results confirm the view that, taken as a whole, the world loses under protectionist environments; they validate benefits of liberalization, "the original wisdom of Adam Smith."

In "Disturbances to the international economy" (1979), Klein first identifies nine (actual) episodes or potential disturbances as shocks to the world economy of the early 1970s, and then assesses the effects of these shocks on price and output for various countries, and for the world as a whole. The list of specific shocks he considered included the Smithsonian agreement on exchange rates, Soviet grain purchases and rising food prices, the oil embargo of 1973 (followed by raising of oil prices), capital transfers, a wage offensive, debt default, commodity and currency speculations, a large-scale crop failure, etc. Once again, the vehicle of analysis is the LINK system, and Klein briefly explains the procedure used in linking various econometric models of countries, regions, and major traded commodities. Examples of impacts are tabulated. The paper adds tremendously to our understanding of that turbulent period; it underscores that oil price increases were major sources of mid-1970s stagflation in the industrial countries.

Also, substantial shifts were being noted in the structure of the world trade matrix during the decade of 1970. Klein provides a review of international competitiveness over this period through cross-country comparisons of productivity, unit labor costs and prices in "International productivity comparisons" (1983). This paper was written for audiences across disciplines, and has been technically presented in a simple form. After explaining the concept of factor productivity (and total factor productivity) at the beginning of the paper, he outlines the methodology of measurements, nonparametric and parametric, of factor productivity at the national level, and for the purpose of international comparisons. In the approach using parametric measurement, he alternatively uses Cobb–Douglas and CES production functions with multiple factor inputs, entered singly and in nested combinations. Both students of economics and researchers in applied econometrics will find this paper particularly interesting for understanding and dealing with the highly intractable productivity concept.

The earlier structure of the LINK model had one major weakness, namely, that exchange rates across currencies and multilateral capital flows across nations, by and large, were not determined endogenously in the system.

All capital transactions in the balance of payments accounts were treated in a rudimentary way. Klein, in the next two papers (1981, 1983), devotes his attention to the foreign exchange markets.

The long-run movements of exchange rates are examined in "Purchasing Power Parity ...," a paper written jointly with Shahrokh Fardoust and Victor Filatov (1981). Exchange rates provide a system of adjustment mechanisms that tend to bring the world economy into equilibrium. This paper examines the principle of purchasing power parity as performing an equilibrating function. Specifically, it examines: (a) Are movements in exchange rates determined by the purchasing power parity rule?; and (b) does the PPP principle generate convergent solutions? How do these solutions differ from the baseline solutions obtained without imposing this principle?

The estimates with the annual data (1972–1980) from a pooled time series of a cross-section of countries show that the PPP doctrine holds, on the average, in the long run. That is, they show that "purchasing power parity movements in exchange rates and export prices were approximately realized during the 1970s, after exchange rates were allowed to fluctuate." Furthermore, when the LINK system was simulated by adding exchange rate equations according to the principle of PPP for each country in order to estimate the values of exchange rates endogenously, the results shifted in plausible directions. It emerged clearly that PPP doctrine is "workable as far as modeling and simulation are concerned." And, also, "it does constitute a convergent dynamic process."

In the short run, exchange rates respond to many other factors besides prices, such as interest rates differentials, capital flows, current account balances and related fundamental factors. In our joint paper, "A model of foreign exchange markets ..." (1983), we tackle the problem of simultaneous determination of international capital flows and exchange rates. This paper was presented at the LINK meeting, September 1982, Wiesbaden, Germany, in a special session held at the Deutsche Bundesbank, Frankfurt. In the model, both capital flows and exchange rates are endogenized. The econometric analysis is conducted with the time series (1972–1979) of annual data pooled across six countries — Canada, France, Germany, Japan, U.K., and the U.S.

Using balance of payments statistics of the IMF, the *net* capital flows are disaggregated into *nine* categories by functional type and ownership. These *nine* categories are: Direct investment; portfolio investment; resident official long-term capital, short-term capital; deposit money banks long-term capital, short-term capital; other long-term capital, short-term capital; and errors and omissions. The theoretical underpinnings of the model are neither purely a portfolio nor purely a monetary approach, but basically embody a balance of payments structural model. Both "interest parity" and "price parity" deviations are explicitly recognized; strict conformity to either of these rules is simply not presumed. By and large, various categories of net capital flows are shown as being determined by optimizing rates of return, risk, and uncertainty factors. The adjustment process determining the exchange rate implicitly embodies a government intervention function. This process is specifically relevant for a system of managed float whose two adjacent polar regimes of fixed and flexible exchange rates simply become special cases.

The quantitative results are interesting and revealing. For instance, it appears that "exchange rate gyrations are basically determined by long-term flows." A number of comparable experiments with alternative specifications are also presented. The final model is tested by simulation.

Interested readers may also see his follow-up work, "Bilateral capital flows and the exchange rate, the case of the U.S.A. vis-a-vis Canada, France, West Germany, and the U.K." (with K. Marwah and R. G. Bodkin), *European Economic Review* **29** (1985), in which an analysis of aggregate (gross) capital flows, at a bilateral level, based on similar theoretical underpinnings is presented. This work on capital flows led to further research by me on Canadian forward and spot currency rates. (See K. Marwah, "A prototype model of foreign exchange market of Canada, forecasting capital flows and exchange rates," *Economic Modelling* **2**, April 1985.)

"Global monetarism" was Klein's contribution to a volume (1988) in honor of Colin Clark. Here, Klein investigates the question, "Does the monetarist model prevail on a world scale?" The answer is sought by testing a central tenet of the monetarist model over an aggregate of countries; specifically, whether the relationship between velocity and interest rate is statistically significant at this global level. The central notion of stability of velocity in the monetarist model is known to have failed for country after country. Although, for non-monetarists, this phenomenon was by no means unexpected, Klein provides yet another test at the aggregate level which is potentially more favorable to the monetarist model. At the global level, there exists a possibility of "significant error cancellation across countries."

Unfortunately, results do not lend support to the monetarist model. Velocity, even in the context of country grouping, does not emerge as a stable parameter. It remains a variable that depends upon the interest rate as predicted by non-monetarist specifications, such as the Keynesian liquidity preference theory, or Kalecki's J-curve for velocity.

"Restructuring of the world economy" contains Klein's retrospective and critical perspective views on the ongoing structural change and adjustment process taking place in the world economy. He also provides some guidelines and policy recommendations. Klein looks at the process of restructuring of the world economy from various dimensions including shifts in the sectoral composition of international production, employment and trade flows, the slow down of productivity growth, especially in the aftermath of the energy shock of 1973, debt burdens, trade and financial imbalances with their implications for international competitiveness and for adjustments in the foreign exchange markets, and the emergence of newly industrialized economies on the world stage.

His core recommendations include greater emphasis on long-term productivity growth and improved economic efficiency, use of industrial policy to promote competitiveness, establishment of an appropriate balance between monetary and fiscal policy within each country, along with international policy coordination between countries, support for capital formation and increased investment in education and research, and less reliance on major swings in macroeconomic policy or exchange rate policy. His message is clear that all macroeconomic policy instruments should be used in coordination "to achieve steadiness in exchange rates, interest rates, inflation, growth, and employment."

The final paper in Part III, coauthored with Y. Liang, is a small pedagogical two-gap model calibrated to the macroeconomic data of the Chinese economy. It appears as the lead article in the inaugural issue of the *China Economic Review* (1989). The model is an open-economy variant of the basic Harrod–Domar growth model, in which the two gaps are the saving–investment and export–import gap. These two gaps are always equal to each other in size by a national income accounting relationship; however, the mode of interactions between them is pertinent in distinguishing a model of a developing country from that of a fully industrialized economy. This is particularly significant with respect to the role of imports as the system moves from one point of equilibrium to another. For instance, in the case of an industrialized economy, "imports displace domestic activity," but, *ceteris paribus*, in a model for the developing economy, imports, by making foreign capital or materials accessible, may "enable the system to reach higher levels of activity." The paper is a simple illustrative exercise done with data of a real economy; it can be readily used in classroom discussions.

19

ANTICIPATIONS VARIABLES IN MACROECONOMETRIC MODELS[†,*]

The Role of Anticipations

For many generations economists have made use of such subjective concepts as "expected," "anticipated," "desired," or "planned" and have usually represented these magnitudes by distributed lags or other surrogates on the grounds that direct objective measurements were not available. Not so with the research programs of George Katona, who takes the approach that since consumer expectations, attitudes, and other subjective feelings are important for economic behavior, we, as economists, should go directly to the agents of action and ask them what these subjective variables are at regular intervals of time.

Measurement of subjective variables associated with economic units (firms, households, bureaus) received large impetus from George Katona's work, and grew to a status that would not otherwise have been achieved. It is the purpose of this essay to look into the independent contribution of anticipatory variables in forecasting with econometric models. We are not arguing for either the survey approach or the formal model-building approach, but for their joint use to improve the contributions of both to the overall objective of getting more forecast accuracy for the economy.

Although George Katona's principal work has been with attitudinal variables obtained from consumer surveys, we are going to look further afield into investment surveys and statistics of advance commitments — consumer attitudes, investment intentions, and housing starts. We are aware of inventory expectations, sales expectations, employment expectations, and price expectations; but these variables are not going to be used in our present investigation, partly because they are not very reliable and partly because they do not appear to be productive in getting us to our main objective. Orders variables are already in our models and appropriations variables could be similarly introduced but have not been used in the Wharton Model, which forms our basic econometric point of reference.[1]

[†]From *Human Behavior in Economic Affairs*, eds. Strumpel *et al.* (Elsevier, Amsterdam, 1972), pp. 289–319; written jointly with F. Gerard Adams.
[*]The authors wish to thank Vijaya Duggal for help beyond the call of duty. Nariman Behravesh provided valuable research assistance.
[1]Wharton Models have been formally used in regular forecasting exercises since 1963, but in this paper we are going to use the new, 1971, version of the Model, called Wharton Mark III. It is our third generation of Wharton Models.

The most important aspect of the anticipatory variables that we are going to deal with is their *lead time*. They involve answers to questions about the future or about things that indicate future developments. To some extent, we shall use variables that include some future commitments. In a dynamic economy like ours where big changes can occur on short notice, certainly within one year, it cannot be assumed that anticipatory variables remain firm as indicators for more than three to six months. They are mainly of use as predictors for short-run business cycle analysis. At most they are indicative of some aspects of the economy for one year, but are more likely to be valid for a shorter period. Consumer attitudes probably erode faster than business investment intentions and housing starts. Investment planning deals with major time-consuming projects that need much advance planning. They also have some degree of commitment, possibly contractual. This gives them firmness and less flexibility than consumer attitudes. Housing starts are physically evident commitments but are usually phased into completion in less than one year.

Anticipatory variables provide a short look ahead and can be compiled without much delay. George Katona and his colleagues at the Survey Research Center can ascertain consumer attitudes on a nationwide basis in less than one month with good information on a horizon of up to six months. Housing starts are regularly reported every month on the basis of data collections with no more than a month's delay. Investment surveys, like consumer surveys, are usually quarterly and take no longer to execute. We therefore have a quick resource for short-run analysis.

Another dimension of anticipatory variables, related to their lead time, is their degree of firmness. The anticipatory variables in the consumer sector are the least firm of those used in economic forecasting. Opinions or attitudes could, under pressure, change almost overnight, and buying plans frequently appear to be statements of purchase probability rather than firm intentions. There is enough stability in many of these data so that they are good predictors, but they are not as firmly based as are other anticipatory variables. Orders can be cancelled; construction plans can be either curtailed or expanded. Therefore investment intentions, even if measured by contracts or appropriations, are not fixed until completion. They are subject to revision, but probably less frequently than consumer attitudes. A housing start is probably more fixed than investment intentions, but even in this case revision is possible through partial cancellation or modification of building plans.

Anticipations are going to be used in the present study in as structural a way as possible. They are not going to be used simply as broad indicators of behavior in the economy as a whole; they are going to be related to specific types of behavior. At impact they will be highly localized, but their complete system effects will be traced through the whole economy by solving simultaneous dynamic equations.

In the case of consumer attitudes, the measured subjective variables will be related to consumer expenditures and residential constructions. We shall not draw any direct inferences about the effect of consumer attitudes on total production, employment, or income — only on specific types of consumer expenditures, which, in turn, will have some effects on aggregate activity.

Similarly, investment intentions will be studied in direct relation to capital formation. It will be through econometric analysis of an entire equation system that the effect of intentions in the economy as a whole will be inferred. Housing starts will be studied in relation to residential construction outlays, and their broader influence on the whole economy will have to be transmitted through residential construction expenditures.

Alternative Schemes for Using Anticipations

One of the main features of the present study is that anticipations will be used, if possible, in a closed system. Most frequently, these variables have been used as *predetermined* indicators because of their well-known lead time. This has been a passive use of such variables. Given their quantitative standing on some date and their approximate lead time, they have been used as indicators of specific types of behavior up to the end of their valid horizons.

In contrast with the use of anticipatory variables as predetermined variables over the duration of their (brief) lead time, we shall try to "explain" anticipations as well as actual behavior. One such scheme to be considered is a prediction-realization sequence.

In the initial phase, equations are developed to explain anticipations. In the received theory of investment, actual capital outlays are made a function of current and past values of production, relative price of output and capital rental, stock of capital. The equation may be written as

$$I_t = \sum_{i=0}^{p} w_i X_{t-i} + \sum_{i=0}^{q} x_i \left(\frac{P}{c}\right)_{t-i} + \sum_{i=0}^{r} y_i K_{t-i} + e_t.$$

If anticipations have a lead time of six months (two quarterly time units in the scale of t), they might be explained by

$$I_t^a = \sum_{i=0}^{p} w_i X_{t-i-2} + \sum_{i=0}^{q} x_i \left(\frac{P}{c}\right)_{t-i-2} + \sum_{i=0}^{r} y_i K_{t-i-2} + e_t.$$

This is the same equation that is used to explain I_t, except that everything occurs two quarters earlier. If this equation can be established as an estimate using data on $I_t^a, X_{t-i-2}, (\frac{P}{c})_{t-i-2}, K_{t-i-2}$, we can compute the system by adding a realization equation that explains $I_t - I_t^a$ as a function of $X, p/c, K$, their historical changes, and other variables. The two equations — one explaining I_t^a and the other explaining $I_t - I_t^a$ — provide enough equations to keep the system in which they are included closed. This scheme has been seriously considered previously but not fully implemented.[2] This general scheme is somewhat modified in our specification estimated below for investment. Investment intentions are estimated as in the equation just given for I_t^a but as there are two anticipations for each quarter's investment

---

[2] See the chapters by Dale Jorgenson and Robert Eisner in Duesenberry *et al.* (1965).

in the SEC–OBE surveys — one with two quarters' lead time and one with one quarter's lead time — we have made the second anticipations variable for a given quarter a function of the first anticipations variable, as well as distributed lags in the usual objective explanatory variables.[3]

Instead of specifying a *realization* equation directly, we make actual investment outlays a function of distributed lags in first and second anticipations and of current values in the usual objective variables.

A related scheme, but one that is less formal in the association between equations that explain the standard objective variable and the corresponding anticipatory variables, is one that simply tries to explain anticipations by other endogenous variables — not necessarily lagged and not necessarily the same ones that explain corresponding expenditure behavior. The endogenous explanation of consumer attitudes may appear to be a considerably different equation from that explaining consumer durable expenditures, but that is no problem from the viewpoint of generating all endogenous variables in a closed system.

In a previous attempt to introduce anticipatory variables in the Wharton Model, we developed equations in which anticipatory variables played an *auxiliary* role; i.e., they were simply included as additional variables together with standard objective variables to determine if the subjective factors have an independent (supplementary) explanatory contribution to make (Evans and Klein, 1968). A consumer attitudes index, investment intentions, and housing starts were introduced as separate variables in consumption, investment, and housing equations respectively.

The auxiliary type relationships were used only for short solutions over the two-quarter lead time of the anticipations. In the present study such equations will be one of the alternatives considered. They will be used in longer extrapolations together with equations for the anticipatory variables.

The appropriate scheme for integrating anticipatory variables into the demand equations of a macro-model depends on the nature of the anticipations and on the demand category to be considered.

Consumption does not depend firmly on buying plans, and nonspecific consumer sentiment data can be seen as supplementing the objective determinants of consumer spending. Adams and Green (1965) have explained attitudes in terms of changes in labor market conditions. Hymans (1970) has linked such functions to endogenous explanation of consumer purchases. For the explanation of consumer attitudes, Hymans has used such variables as changes in disposable income, stock prices, and consumer prices. His results are moderately good, but leave much error in the endogenous generation of consumer attitudes. This will show up in solutions beyond the lead time of one or two quarters. Our procedure will be along the same lines for the consumer sector, but the equation for endogenous treatment of consumer

---

[3]Throughout this paper we will refer to the anticipations variable with two-quarters lead time as "first anticipations," and the variable with one quarter lead time as "second anticipations." These traditional names will be used despite the fact that anticipations expressed still earlier are now available at times.

attitudes is a transformation of a distributed lag in changes in unemployment and consumer prices. To some extent, these equations for consumer attitudes are purely empirical, for a widely accepted theory to explain them is not available.

With regard to business fixed investment, the OBE Model has relied on investment intentions for predictions of capital formation (Liebenberg *et al.* (1966). Subsequently, the OBE econometricians developed an independent investment function that depended only on standard objective variables. They used this equation for longer simulations. They also tried the following procedure: For the first two quarters of a forecast, use the anticipations variables

$$I_t = I_t^a$$

where I_t^a is taken with lead time from an earlier survey of intentions. They used the first anticipations from the previous quarter's survey to predict investment two quarters ahead and the second anticipations to predict investment one quarter ahead.[4] For the third and future quarters ahead, they used the standard function with only objective variables. The difficulty with this approach is that it may provide a discrete jump at the switching point between the second and third quarters ahead. This difficulty is avoided in our approach by using the same investment functions for all prediction periods, feeding into them actual values of the anticipations when they are available or endogenously estimated values when actuals are not available.

In some of our equations, we have also adopted Jorgenson's suggestion (Duesenberry *et al.*, 1965) of investment as a distributed lag on anticipations and as noted above, we made use of a modified realization approach.

The well-known housing model of Sherman Maisel established particular relationships between starts and capital expenditures on residential construction.[5] There are many detailed aspects to Maisel's model, but the principal idea is that starts depend on income, credit market conditions, relative prices, and possibly other standard objective variables of a macro-model. Similarly average value per start depends on objective economic variables. Expenditures are estimated from

$$(I_h)_t = \sum_{i=0}^{p} w_i V_{t-i}(H_s)_{t-i}; \qquad \sum_{i=0}^{p} w_i = 1$$

where I_h = capital outlays for residential construction
   V = average value per start
   H_s = housing starts
   w_i = weight factor

In this equation, expenditures are expressed as a moving average of the value of starts. Presumably this is approximately the same formula that national income

---

[4] Friend and Thomas (1970) have argued that such direct use of the investment anticipations compares favorably with other formulations in prediction. It is not clear, however, why this should be so.

[5] See the chapter by Sherman Maisel in Duesenberry *et al.* (1965).

statisticians use for phasing-in starts to get expenditures. An alternative approach is to estimate the distributed lag coefficients of residential construction on starts (Fair, 1971). Brady's work (Brady, 1970) has suggested that it may be important to distinguish between various classes of housing starts.

Our variation of the Maisel model is both more and less detailed. Single family starts are separated from multi-family starts. In this respect our model is more disaggregated than Maisel's, but not as much as Brady's, and introduces what seem to be important behavioral differences between owner-occupiers and landlords. Otherwise, our model is more aggregative and somewhat cruder than Maisel's. Expenditures on residential construction, in constant prices, are made a function of income, credit terms, and relative prices as standard objective variables.

Credit availabilities have been measured by a proxy based on the differential between long and short interest rates. These variables are available from the financial sector of the Wharton Model; whereas more specific flows of funds to lending institutions, such as those used by Fair and Brady, are not. We take a further step into the realm of anticipatory variables by including the index of consumer attitudes, for these are relevant to house buying as well as to purchases of cars or other consumer durables. Single family starts are specified to depend on income, credit conditions, relative prices, consumer attitudes, and trend. Multiple family starts depend on the same class of variables but are not directly related to the index of consumer attitudes.

Two variants of equations have been run. One explains total non-farm residential construction directly; introduces starts as "auxiliary" variables in the sense explained above; and uses Maisel's fixed time phasing for the independent variables. The other distinguishes between construction of new homes and additions and alterations and estimates the time lag between starts and residential construction put-in-place.

In all three sectors — consumption, business fixed capital formation, and residential construction — we have joint explanation of anticipatory variables and the corresponding GNP component. We are thus able to make use of anticipatory lead time for very short run predictions and then to generate future estimates of the anticipatory variables for prediction beyond the lead-time horizon. The various alternative approaches outlined here will all be tested in complete system solutions.

The basic alternatives compared below are:

Version I. — Objective variables version: Consumption, investment, and residential construction are explained entirely in terms of objective variables using the standard equations of the Mark III Wharton Model.

Version II. — Anticipations as auxiliary variables: Anticipations have been introduced into the equations simply as supplements to the other variables in the equations as in earlier versions of the Wharton Model.

Version III. — Anticipations in a realizations framework: Anticipations have been used in this version as direct forecasters of the fixed investment in a realizations type format. This has not been possible for consumer purchases of automobiles, where the Version III equation simply drops the unemployment variable. Version III may also be characterized as the approach which puts greatest weight on the anticipations variables.

Single Equation Results

The equations incorporating anticipations variables are evaluated from a single equation point of view in this section. In view of space limitations, only the standard errors, $\bar{R}^2$, and Durbin–Watson statistics of the Version I equations, those in the standard version of the Mark III model, are shown. An alphabetic index of variables is presented in the Appendix.

Consumption

The numerous empirical studies of consumer attitudes and buying plans have produced consensus, if not agreement, with regard to the usefulness of this material in consumption functions. On the basis of earlier work and some additional empirical experimentation, it appears that attitudinal variables contribute particularly to the explanation of consumer purchases of cars, but have little or no effect on other consumer purchases. Broad consumer anticipations like the SRC Index of Consumer Sentiment, and surrogates for them, have been useful in time series but buying plans variables have shown considerably less promise (Adams, 1964).[6]

The direct use of buying plans as predictors and their integration into realization functions do not appear warranted. Empirical analysis was focused on the use of the SRC *Index of Consumer Sentiment* (CSI) and other anticipatory variables as auxiliary variables in the automobile purchases equation.

Numerous equations were tested incorporating the CSI variable, and/or other objective variables which could influence consumer anticipations. Stock prices were not used, however, since they pose forecasting difficulties in their own right. Strangely, the filtered version of the CSI variable used by Hymans (1970) works less well over the time period considered here than does the CSI index in its original form. Other proxies for attitudes, for example weekly hours in manufacturing industry, make a contribution to explaining auto purchases but generally are not as statistically significant as the CSI variable.

---

[6] Juster's recent work with purchase probabilities is conceptually between explicit "plans to buy" and broad attitudinal measures. Unfortunately there is not yet a sufficiently long time series of the purchase probabilities index to allow serious simulation tests.

The best equations obtained were[7]:

Table 1. Automobile Purchasing Functions.

Version II

$$CA\text{-}MHTR = 0.06612 * (Y\text{-}TR/PC) + 29.9426 * LIQUID \qquad\qquad (1)$$
$$\phantom{CA\text{-}MHTR = }(5.98) \phantom{* (Y\text{-}TR/PC) + } (2.32)$$
$$- 4.3000 * DS + 1.023 * CR$$
$$(4.39) (1.27)$$
$$- 10.380 * (PA/PC) - 0.2552 * UN$$
$$(1.23) (1.27)$$
$$+ 0.2814 * (CA\text{-}MHTR)_{-1} + 0.8877 * (IL/IS)_{-4}$$
$$(2.71) \phantom{* (CA\text{-}MHTR)_{-1} + } (1.43)$$
$$+ 0.0525 * CSI_{-1} + 0.0831 * \Delta CSI_{-2} - 21.094$$
$$(1.54) \phantom{* CSI_{-1} + } (1.44) \phantom{* \Delta CSI_{-2} - } (1.24)$$
$$\overline{R}^2 = 0.9714 \; SE = 1.091 \; DW = 1.760$$

Version III

$$CA\text{-}MHTR = 0.0653 * (Y\text{-}TR/PC) + 34.8092 * LIQUID \qquad\qquad (2)$$
$$\phantom{CA\text{-}MHTR = }(5.89) \phantom{* (Y\text{-}TR/PC) + } (2.81)$$
$$- 4.3779 * DS + 0.9136 * CR$$
$$(4.45) (1.14)$$
$$- 10.5138 * (PA/PC) + 0.3214 * (CA\text{-}MHTR)_{-1}$$
$$(1.24) (3.24)$$
$$+ 0.8019 * (IL/IS)_{-4} + 0.0697 * CSI_{-1}$$
$$(1.29) \phantom{* (IL/IS)_{-4} + } (2.22)$$
$$+ 0.08122 * \Delta CSI_{-2} - 27.239$$
$$(1.40) \phantom{* \Delta CSI_{-2} - } (1.65)$$

$$\overline{R}^2 = 0.9711 \; SE = 1.096 \; DW = 1.851$$

Version I Statistics $\qquad\qquad \overline{R}^2 = 0.9688 \; SE = 1.316 \; DW = 1.593$

Except for the consumer sentiment variables, Equation (1) is exactly as in Version I, the standard Wharton Model. When the CSI variables are included, the contribution of unemployment becomes nonsignificant and this variable has been omitted in Equation (2). The other coefficients are not much affected by the presence of the anticipations variable. The CSI variable results in only very modest improvement in the explanatory power of the auto equation.

In the explanation of CSI, as well, numerous alternative formulations and variables were explored. As above, we did not use stock prices despite the evidence that they could be useful on a single equation basis. Surprisingly a simple formulation:

---

[7]Definitions of variables are given in the Appendix. The estimation period for all equations is 1953.3 to 1970.1.

$$CSI = 0.7565 \ CSI_{-1} - 3.4625\Delta UN - 93.1000(PC\text{-}PC_{-3}) \qquad (3)$$
$$(13.44) \qquad\qquad (4.09) \qquad\qquad (4.02)$$
$$+ 24.5840$$
$$(4.58)$$

$$\overline{R}^2 = 0.8351 \ SE = 2.3529 \ DW = 1.6737$$

where CSI is simply a distributed lag function of change in unemployment and consumer prices, works best. This version of the equation is used to explain forward values of CSI endogenously.

As in the original version of the Wharton Model, separate investment equations have been estimated for three industrial categories, mining and manufacturing, regulated industries, and commercial and others.

In the Version II formulation, the anticipations variables have simply been added to existing equations, testing whether they contribute information not already incorporated in the objective determinants of investment. For this purpose it has been assumed that the prediction period of the OBE-SEC investment anticipations corresponds to their time lead, two quarters for the so-called "first anticipations" and one quarter for the "second anticipations" and that businessmen make an accurate allowance for change in prices of capital goods. This means that the anticipations can be introduced as single values (not distributed lags) with the indicated time lag and deflated by the capital goods deflator of the time the investment is effected.

The general form of the equation is:

$$I_t = f(\lambda_i(\theta)Z_i, EP1_{t-2}, EP2_{t-1})$$

where

$$I_t - \text{investment at time } t,$$
$$\lambda_i(\theta)Z_i - \text{distributed lags of } i \text{ objective variables, and}$$
$$EP1_{t-2} \text{ and } EP2_{t-1} - \text{OBE-SEC first and second investment anticipations,}$$
$$\text{deflated by business fixed investment deflator for time } t.$$

Empirically such an equation could turn out to be equivalent to a realizations function. Suppose the effect of the lag terms of the objective variables is absorbed by the anticipations, the equation would indicate that investment depends on anticipations as modified by those terms of the objective variables which intervene between the time anticipations are formulated and investment is put in place. In other words, realized investment would be a function of plans and of realizations of the anticipated objective variables. However, the empirical results, Table 2, do not support such a notion.

Inclusion of anticipations reduces the standard error of estimate in these equations for IPMM and IPR. In the IPC equation, the effect of anticipations is not significant, and the Version II equation is marginally worse than the Version I formulation. The coefficient of the anticipations is statistically significant in the

Table 2. Version II Business Fixed Investment Functions.[8]

$$IPMM = -3.765 + 7.238 * CPMM_{-1} \tag{4}$$
$$ (1.73) \quad (3.24)$$
$$+ \, 0.5770 * EPMM2_{-1} + 0.2048 * EPMM1_{-2}$$
$$(4.83) \qquad\qquad\qquad (1.78)$$
$$+ \sum_{i=0}^{5} a_{4i} XMM_{-i} + \sum_{i=0}^{15} b_{4i}(UCCMM/PMM)_{-i}$$
$$[0.0238] \qquad\qquad [-14.7732]$$
$$P = 0.0058 \qquad\quad P = -3.1864$$
$$i = -4 \qquad\qquad\quad i = -3$$

$$\overline{R}^2 = 0.9919 \; SE = 0.4473 \; DW = 1.413$$
Version I Statistics $\qquad\qquad \overline{R}^2 = 0.9811 \; SE = 0.6830 \; DW = 0.6079$

$$IPR = -2.356 - 0.0244 * KR_{-1} + 0.7764 * EPR2_{-1} + 0.0630 * EPR1_{-2} \tag{5}$$
$$ (1.48) \quad (1.96) \qquad\qquad (3.63) \qquad\qquad\quad (0.337)$$
$$+ \sum_{i=0}^{35} a_{5i} XR_{-i} + \sum_{i=0}^{4} b_{5i} XMF_{-i}$$
$$[0.2923] \qquad\quad [0.0427]$$
$$P = 0.0148 \qquad P = 0.0131$$
$$i = -11 \qquad\quad\; i = -1$$

$$\overline{R}^2 = 0.9915 \; SE = 0.3423 \; DW = 1.399$$
Version I Statistics $\qquad\qquad \overline{R}^2 = 0.9845 \; SE = 0.4625 \; DW = 1.1040$

$$IPC = 2.553 + 0.02792 * KC_{-1} + 0.1923 * EPC2_{-1} \tag{6}$$
$$ (3.30) \quad (8.56) \qquad\qquad (1.33)$$
$$+ \sum_{i=0}^{7} a_{6i} XC_{-i} + \sum_{i=0}^{15} b_{6i}(UCCC/P)_{-i}$$
$$[0.7246] \qquad\quad [-341.9020]$$
$$P = 0.1258 \qquad P = -49.6543$$
$$i = -3 \qquad\qquad i = -4$$

$$\overline{R}^2 = 0.9671 \; SE = 0.9593 \; DW = 0.6510$$
Version I Statistics $\qquad\qquad \overline{R}^2 = 0.9679 \; SE = 0.9475 \; DW = 0.6910$

---

[8]The sum of the distributed lag coefficients is shown in square brackets. Underneath the sum is shown P, the peak absolute value of the lag coefficients, and i, the timing of the peak value. Due to space limitations, the lag coefficients and their t-values are not included in the text. They are available from the authors on request.

other equations, but it is smaller than unity[9] even in the cases (IPR and IPMM) where the categories of investment covered and the anticipations variables correspond. In contrast to the realizations interpretations, the lagged objective variables continue to have a significant effect. The anticipations must consequently be seen as auxiliary variables in this scheme.

Version III forces the investment equations into a realizations function mold. Following Jorgenson it is assumed that investment is a distributed lag function of the anticipations in contrast to the typical realization function formulation which takes the anticipations as direct predictors (with an implied coefficient of 1.0) of investment. However, investment plans may be modified after they have been made so that it is appropriate to introduce intervening variables, objective variables which provide information on the period between the formulation of investment plans and their realization. The general functional form used here is

$$I_t = f(\lambda_{1,2}(\Theta)EP_{1,2}, Z_i)$$

where $\lambda_{1,2}(\Theta)EP_{1,2}$ are distributed lags of the first and second investment anticipations and Z_i are objective variables occurring after the anticipations are formed. In contrast to Version II, the distributed lag here applies to the anticipations which are forced to account for lagged values of the objective variables, since only current (or briefly lagged) values of the latter are used. These functions put much heavier weight on the anticipations than the Version II formulation. The Version III investment functions, shown in Table 3, also improve on functions without anticipatory variables. But in comparison to the Version II equations, the equation for IPMM is an improvement; whereas for IPR and IPC the realization formulation is not quite as good. The distributed lag coefficients of the anticipations carry negative signs in some instances. It should be remembered that the first and second anticipations are in effect two readings, one quarter apart (at time $t-2$ and $t-1$), on the same investment to be carried out at time t. The inclusion of both anticipations means that the interpretation of the coefficients is somewhat precarious. In the case of the equation for IPMM (Eq. 7) the sum of the coefficients over the entire lag period for EPMM1 is -0.297 and for EPMM2 it is 1.103. Writing in terms of the first anticipation, the effect is $(-0.297 + 1.103)$ EPMM1 + 1.103 (EPMM2 – EPMM1).

The first anticipation has an impact of .806 and a revision of the anticipations has a somewhat greater effect of 1.103. In the case of IPR the effect of the first anticipation can be calculated as .890 but revisions of anticipations only have a small effect of .060.

The objective variables in these equations, intended to catch the impact of changes in the investment after investment plans are made, have been included only when the results had directions of effect in agreement with prior notions.

---

[9] In view of multicollinearity, statistical considerations determined whether first or second anticipations or both were included.

Table 3. Version III Realization Investment Function.

$$IPMM = 3.268 - 7.701 * UCCMM/P + 6.113 * CPMM_{-1} + 0.01627 * XMM \tag{7}$$
$$(3.07)\quad(2.43)\qquad\qquad(4.67)\qquad\qquad(4.26)$$

$$+\sum_{i=0}^{4} a_{7i}\,EPMM1_{-2-i} + \sum_{i=0}^{4} b_{7i}\,EPMM2_{-1-i}$$

$$[-0.2972]\qquad\qquad[1.1029]$$
$$P = -0.0831\qquad\qquad P = 0.5134$$
$$i = -1\qquad\qquad i = -1$$

$$\overline{R}^2 = 0.9951\ \ SE = 0.3479\ \ DW = 1.586$$

$$IPR = -0.3786 + 0.2066 * XR - 0.0111 * KR_{-1} \tag{8}$$
$$(0.763)\quad(4.74)\qquad\quad(2.43)$$

$$+\sum_{i=0}^{4} a_{8i}\,EPR2_{-1-i} + \sum_{i=0}^{4} b_{8i}\,EPR1_{-2-i}$$

$$[0.8307]\qquad\qquad[0.0595]$$
$$P = 0.2800\qquad\qquad P = 0.4581$$
$$i = -3\qquad\qquad i = 0$$

$$\overline{R}^2 = 0.9878\ \ SE = 0.4096\ \ DW = 1.296$$

$$IPC = -3.920 + 0.0823 * XC - 14.297 * UCCC/PCOM + 0.0065 * KC_{-1} \tag{9}$$
$$(0.624)\ (2.31)\qquad\quad(0.512)\qquad\qquad(0.472)$$

$$+\sum_{i=0}^{4} a_{9i}\,EPC2_{-1-i} + \sum_{i=0}^{4} b_{9i}\,EPC1_{-2-i}$$

$$[-0.5517]\qquad\qquad[0.70108]$$
$$P = -0.4201\qquad\qquad P = 0.2461$$
$$i = -4\qquad\qquad i = -1$$

$$\overline{R}^2 = 0.9620\ \ SE = 1.0302\ \ DW = 0.686$$

Equations to explain the anticipations variables themselves have been formulated in the same way as in the model equations for investment. It is assumed that investment plans are a function of objective variables for activity, user cost, and capital stock or capacity utilization. The function for the second anticipations includes the first anticipations as a variable. They may be considered a form of "revisions of anticipations" equations. The functions selected are shown in Table 4.

The equations explaining the first anticipations are quite similar with regard to coefficients and lag structure to the original equations explaining investment in terms of objective variables only. In the equations for the second anticipations the objective variables remain statistically significant, but, as we would expect, these coefficients are much smaller since the first anticipations are included in the

Table 4. Function for Investment Anticipations.

$$EPMM2 = -2.648 + 0.7624 * EPMM1_{-1} + 4.0512 * CPMM_{-2} \tag{10}$$
$$(1.03) \quad (8.81) \qquad\qquad (1.74)$$

$$+ \sum_{i=0}^{5} a_{10i}(XMM_{-1})_{-i} + \sum_{i=0}^{15} b_{10i}(UCMM/PMM)_{-1-i}$$

$$[0.0343] \qquad\qquad [-12.8062]$$
$$P = 0.0106 \qquad\qquad P = -2.8030$$
$$i = -1 \qquad\qquad i = -3$$

$$\overline{R}^2 = 0.9901 \ SE = 0.5070 \ DW = 2.241$$

$$EPMM1 = -10.169 + 16.236 * CPMM_{-3} \tag{11}$$
$$(2.35) \quad (5.64)$$

$$+ \sum_{i=0}^{5} a_{11i}(XMM_{-2})_{-i} + \sum_{i=0}^{15} b_{11i}(UCMM/PMM)_{-2-i}$$

$$[0.1401] \qquad\qquad [-49.3650]$$
$$P = 0.0313 \qquad\qquad P = -8.0960$$
$$i = -2 \qquad\qquad i = -3$$

$$\overline{R}^2 = 0.9715 \ SE = 0.8523 \ DW = 0.647$$

$$EPR2 = 1.7259 - 0.00996 * KR_{-2} + 0.6666 * EPR_{-1} \tag{12}$$
$$(1.44) \quad (0.984) \qquad\qquad (7.17)$$

$$+ \sum_{i=0}^{36} a_{12i}(XR_{-1})_{-i} + \sum_{i=0}^{33} b_{12i}(UCCR/PXR)_{-1-i} + \sum_{i=0}^{4} C_{12i}(XMF_{-1})_{-i}$$

$$[0.3233] \qquad\qquad [-39.7899] \qquad\qquad [-0.0075]$$
$$P = 0.0128 \qquad\qquad P = -2.1591 \qquad\qquad P = -0.0053$$
$$i = -18 \qquad\qquad i = -10 \qquad\qquad i = -4$$

$$\overline{R}^2 = 0.9912 \ SE = 0.2296 \ DW = 2.591$$

$$EPR1 = 2.196 - 0.05765 * KR_{-3} \tag{13}$$
$$(1.12) \quad (3.76)$$

$$+ \sum_{i=0}^{36} a_{13i}(XR_{-2})_{-i} + \sum_{i=0}^{33} b_{13i}(UCCR/PXR)_{-i} + \sum_{i=0}^{4} c_{13i}(XMF_{-2})_{-i}$$

$$[1.0100] \qquad\qquad [-94.2582] \qquad\qquad [0.0490]$$
$$P = 0.0401 \qquad\qquad P = -4.2204 \qquad\qquad P = 0.0224$$
$$i = -17 \qquad\qquad i = -13 \qquad\qquad i = -1$$

$$\overline{R}^2 = 0.9775 \ SE = 0.3894 \ DW = 1.907$$

$$EPC2 = 1.086 + 0.00858 * KC_{-2} + 0.6179 * EPC1_{-1} \tag{14}$$
$$(1.99) \quad (4.40) \qquad\qquad (6.49)$$

$$+ \sum_{i=0}^{10} a_{14i}\Delta(XC_{-1})_{-i} + \sum_{i=0}^{15} b_{14i}\Delta(UCC/PCOM)_{-1-i}$$

$$[0.3393] \qquad\qquad [-166.5655]$$
$$P = 0.0434 \qquad\qquad P = -18.1043$$
$$i = -6 \qquad\qquad i = -4$$

$$\overline{R}^2 = 0.9679 \ SE = 0.6402 \ DW = 2.365$$

(Cont'd)

Table 4. (continued)

$$EPC1 = 4.813 + 0.01866 * KC_{-3} \tag{15}$$
$$(12.6) \quad (14.4)$$

$$+ \sum_{i=0}^{10} a_{15i}\Delta(XC_{-2})_{-i} + \sum_{i=0}^{15} b_{15i}\Delta(UCC/PCOM)_{-2-i}$$

$$[0.7936] \qquad\qquad [-507.3583]$$
$$P = 0.0999 \qquad\qquad P = -58.3565$$
$$i = -5 \qquad\qquad i = -4$$
$$\overline{R}^2 = 0.9355 \ SE = 0.8498 \ DW = 0.914$$

equation. Here again the empirical evidence suggests that the first anticipations play an "auxiliary" role and that the coefficients do not fully describe a "revision" of anticipations process.

Residential construction

Two alternative approaches to explaining residential construction have been tested. As before, Version II seeks simply to add supplementary anticipations variables — single and multiple housing starts and CSI — to the present Wharton Model residential construction equation. The alternative Version III approach establishes a more direct estimated distributed lag relationship between construction of new housing and includes separate treatment of additions and alterations.

$$IH = 14.656 + 0.0088 * Y \ 0.6047 * \sum_{i=0}^{2} w_i(IL\text{-}IS)_{-i} \tag{16}$$
$$(2.84) \quad (2.66) \qquad (2.83)$$

$$+ 9.692 * \sum_{i=0}^{2} w_i HSM_{-i} + 7.954 \sum_{i=0}^{2} w_i HS1_{-i}$$
$$(9.90) \qquad\qquad (11.35)$$

$$+ 0.06230 * \sum_{i=0}^{2} w_i CSI_{-i} - 13.7470 * \sum_{i=0}^{2} w_i(PH/PR)_{-i}$$
$$(3.52) \qquad\qquad (2.998)$$

$$\overline{R}^2 = 0.9129 \ SE = 0.5853$$
$$DW = 0.786$$

$$w_0 = 0.41$$
$$w_1 = 0.49$$
$$w_2 = 0.10$$

Version I Statistics $\qquad\qquad \overline{R}^2 = 0.5777 \ SE = 1.289 \ DW = 0.3968$

The original Wharton Model residential construction equation uses Maisel's average time phasing relationship between housing starts and construction-put-in-place as weights for Fisher type distributed lags on the monetary tightness and the relative price terms. The same weighting scheme has been applied to the anticipations variables added to this equation. The Version II equation shows significant coefficients for multiple starts and single starts and for CSI. The objective variables continue to be statistically significant but with substantially smaller coefficients. The degree of explanation achieved is spectacularly higher than in equations without anticipations variables.

The Version III approach equations use a different disaggregation, one more appropriate for relating residential construction and housing starts. Total residential construction is broken down:

$$IHT = INHU + AA$$

where $INHU$ = construction of new houses and AA = additions and alterations and non housekeeping residential construction are explained separately. Note that $INHU$ includes farms since the current housing starts statistics usually include farm housing.[10] The value of new residential construction (in 1958\$) is explained in terms of single and multiple starts and the lagged average real value per start.

$$INHU = -12.447 + 1.0224 * \left(INHU_{-i} \Big/ \left(\sum_{i=1}^{3} w_i HST_{-1} \right) \right) \qquad (17)$$
$$\quad\quad\ (7.12) \quad\ (8.88)$$

$$+ \sum_{i=0}^{3} a_{17i} HS1_{-i} + \sum_{i=0}^{3} b_{17i} HSM_{-i}$$

$$\qquad\quad [12.4672] \qquad\qquad [11.7426]$$
$$\qquad\quad P = 5.4413 \qquad\quad P = 4.7054$$
$$\qquad\quad i = 0 \qquad\qquad\quad i = 0$$

$$\overline{R}^2 = 0.9534 \ \ SE = 0.3990 \ \ DW = 2.314$$

$$w_0 = 0.41$$
$$w_1 = 0.49$$
$$w_2 = 0.10$$

This is a statistical approximation of the OBE procedure of translating starts into construction put in place.

It is interesting to note that the distributed lag for single and multiple starts is practically the same and conforms closely to the phasing used in the Version

---

[10] Since nonfarm residential construction is contained in the model, it is obtained by subtracting farm residential construction, as exogenous variable, from IHT.

II equation.[11] The lagged average value per start (in 1958$) carries a coefficient slightly greater than unity, indicating an upward trend in real value per start. As a result of the inclusion of this variable the coefficients of single and multiple starts are of about equal value.

Additions and alterations, a residual item which poses some seasonal adjustment problems, is explained very simply in terms of a time trend, a seasonal correction dummy, the consumer sentiment index, and the distributed lag on housing construction prices.

$$AA = 23.493 + 0.0269 * TIME + 1.0 \ PAA \qquad (18)$$
$$\quad (11.1) \quad (13.8)$$

$$+ \sum_{i=0}^{5} a_{18i}(PH/P)_{-i} + \sum_{i=0}^{5} b_{18i} CSI_{-i}$$

$$[22.2411] \qquad [0.0303]$$
$$P = 6.1478 \qquad P = .0098$$
$$i = -1 \qquad i = -1$$
$$\overline{R}^2 = 0.8705 \ SE = 0.2143 \ DW = 0.7307$$

Interestingly, the short term fluctuation of residential additions and alterations are picked up by a distributed lag on consumer sentiment, which has a highly significant effect in this equation.

The explanation of housing starts is visualized in terms similar to those used to explain residential construction in the Version I equation. Since the factors affecting single starts are likely to differ from those affecting multiple starts, the two classes of starts have been considered separately.

The equations used are:

$$HS1 = -1.427 + 0.0056 * (Y\text{-}TR/PC) \qquad (19)$$
$$\quad (1.48) \quad (5.08)$$
$$- 0.02277 * TIME - 0.09703 * TIGHT$$
$$\quad (7.028) \qquad \qquad (2.32)$$

---

[11]The phasing is as follows:

Distributed Lag Weights

Quarter		HSI	HSM	Version II Phasing
	t	0.44	0.40	0.41
	$t-1$	0.42	0.40	0.49
	$t-2$	0.18	0.20	0.10

$$+ \sum_{i=0}^{8} a_{19i}(IL\text{-}IS)_{-i} + \sum_{i=0}^{8} b_{19i}(PH/P)_{-i} + \sum_{i=0}^{4} c_{19i} \Delta CSI_{-i}$$

$$\begin{array}{ccc} [0.2348] & [1.3255] & [0.0144] \\ P = 0.0368 & P = -0.9554 & P = 0.0064 \\ i = -5 & i = -1 & i = -1 \end{array}$$

$$\overline{R}^2 = 0.9057 \; SE = 0.0644 \; DW = 1.326$$

$$HSM = 1.9196 - 0.1249 * TIGHT + 0.00233 * (Y\text{-}TR/PC) \tag{20}$$

$$\begin{array}{ccc} (2.50) & (3.90) & (7.26) \end{array}$$

$$+ \sum_{i=0}^{8} a_{20i}(IL\text{-}IS)_{-i} + \sum_{i=0}^{8} b_{20i}(PR/P)_{-i}$$

$$\begin{array}{cc} [0.1745] & [-2.5017] \\ P = 0.0267 & P = -0.4677 \\ i = -5 & i = -2 \end{array}$$

$$\overline{R}^2 = 0.8761 \; SE = 0.0643 \; DW = 0.510$$

Both kinds of starts are sensitive to monetary tightness. This has been indicated here by a nonlinear effect of the interest rate differential as a proxy variable. The difference between the long and the short interest rate is introduced with a distributed lag, and it enters once again in the form of the "TIGHT" dummy which catches those unusual periods of monetary crisis when the short rate exceeds the long rate. Both equations have an income effect. The price effect is on the price of houses for single starts and on the price of rentals in the case of multiples. Single housing starts have a negative time trend in accord with recent developments. Remarkably, the single starts are significantly affected by changes in consumer sentiment, multiple starts are not. The degree of explanation achieved is quite good.

System Simulation Results

Full system dynamic simulations of the anticipations equations as part of the Wharton Model were carried out for the period 1960.1 to 1970.1. The simulations make use of the entire model except for the tax functions; taxes are treated as exogenous.[12] Runs embodying Version II equations (1), (3), (4), (5), (6), (10), (11), (12), (13), (14), (15), (16), (19), (20) and Version III equations (2), (3), (7), (8), (9), (10), (11), (12), (13), (14), (15), (17), (18), (19), (20) are compared with Version I,

---

[12]Exogenizing taxes tends to increase the errors of the model as compared to a simulation of the complete system since errors in the endogenous tax estimates would tend to offset errors elsewhere in the system. However, the comparisons made here are not likely to be affected. No constant adjustments, which would also tend to reduce forecast error, were made.

Table 5. Simulation Results.

		Version I				Version II				Version III			
		Forecast Period (Quarters)												
		1	2	3	4	1	2	3	4	1	2	3	4
CA	RMSE	1.137	1.275	1.359	1.393	1.061	1.172	1.315	1.381	1.063	1.140	1.267	1.331
	$\lvert\%E\rvert$	3.122	3.652	3.948	4.019	3.019	3.499	3.864	4.039	3.086	3.498	3.846	3.900
	$\overline{E}$	0.183	0.252	0.282	0.315	0.105	0.147	0.205	0.245	0.061	0.094	0.153	0.198
IP	RMSE	1.679	1.871	2.071	2.223	1.243	1.479	2.041	2.138	1.092	1.297	1.800	2.167
	$\lvert\%E\rvert$	2.305	2.668	2.908	3.058	1.579	1.938	2.830	2.921	1.481	1.766	2.407	3.005
	$\overline{E}$	0.070	0.249	0.303	0.360	-0.002	0.052	0.065	0.156	-0.028	-0.018	-0.078	-0.084
IPMM	RMSE	0.706	0.840	0.942	1.015	0.469	0.767	0.944	0.956	0.358	0.438	0.739	0.972
	$\lvert\%E\rvert$	2.940	3.481	3.838	4.173	1.770	2.105	3.755	3.944	1.517	1.711	2.924	3.914
	$\overline{E}$	0.084	0.219	0.228	0.240	0.035	0.057	0.030	0.077	0.007	0.021	-0.006	-0.004
IPR	RMSE	0.429	0.422	0.438	0.475	0.323	0.352	0.416	0.445	0.356	0.400	0.450	0.461
	$\lvert\%E\rvert$	2.190	2.186	2.317	2.459	1.596	1.822	2.198	2.240	1.828	2.017	2.241	2.313
	$\overline{E}$	0.025	0.038	0.054	0.068	0.011	0.024	0.046	0.052	0.022	-0.017	-0.006	0.010
IPC	RMSE	1.025	1.087	1.126	1.158	0.953	1.046	1.134	1.191	0.949	1.013	1.092	1.208
	$\lvert\%E\rvert$	4.045	4.338	4.578	4.702	3.810	4.203	4.650	4.825	3.610	3.870	4.370	4.850
	$\overline{E}$	-0.039	-0.008	0.021	0.051	-0.048	-0.028	-0.010	0.028	-0.012	-0.022	0.065	-0.090
IH	RMSE	1.431	1.443	1.496	1.682	0.730	1.089	1.248	1.292	0.636	1.240	1.744	2.087
	$\lvert\%E\rvert$	5.521	5.572	5.622	6.552	2.680	3.661	4.283	4.586	2.374	4.634	6.756	8.237
	$\overline{E}$	-0.084	-0.078	-0.088	-0.027	-0.028	-0.034	0.013	0.101	0.026	0.048	0.023	-0.144

Table 5 (Continued)

		Version I				Version II				Version III			
						Forecast Period (Quarters)								
		1	2	3	4	1	2	3	4	1	2	3	4
GNP$	RMSE	4.141	6.117	7.756	8.474	3.785	5.716	7.597	8.365	3.739	5.383	7.131	7.984
	$|\%E|$	0.485	0.730	0.939	1.020	0.445	0.687	0.938	1.014	0.441	0.656	0.888	0.972
	$\overline{E}$	0.350	0.541	0.776	1.191	0.167	0.189	0.413	0.876	074	0.039	0.186	0.537
1958$													
GNP	RMSE	4.068	5.506	6.434	6.707	3.741	5.009	6.125	6.425	3.653	4.720	5.680	6.006
	$|\%E|$	0.532	0.699	0.839	0.878	0.487	0.634	0.808	0.864	0.474	0.605	0.767	0.804
	$\overline{E}$	0.916	1.180	1.473	1.888	0.736	0.817	1.069	1.516	0.640	0.659	0.845	1.195
P	RMSE	0.0027	0.0036	0.0043	0.0055	0.0027	0.0035	0.0042	0.0054	0.0027	0.0042	0.0042	0.005
	$|\%E|$	0.204	0.265	0.332	0.413	0.199	0.266	0.325	0.404	0.201	0.261	0.321	0.392
	$\overline{E}$	-0.001	-0.001	-0.002	-0.002	-0.001	-0.001	-0.002	-0.002	0.0009	-0.0013	-0.0016	-0.001
C	RMSE	2.349	0.3009	3.857	3.987	2.240	2.803	3.396	3.830	2.229	2.728	3.248	3.645
	$|\%E|$	0.474	0.609	0.765	0.831	0.461	0.573	0.720	0.807	0.461	0.571	0.697	0.765
	$\overline{E}$	0.416	0.631	0.783	0.958	0.314	0.463	0.617	0.793	0.256	0.383	0.523	0.687
W$	RMSE	1.946	3.178	4.200	4.830	1.906	3.113	4.151	4.840	1.905	3.093	4.101	4.783
	$|\%E|$	0.386	0.710	0.919	1.017	0.382	0.691	0.912	1.041	0.384	0.686	0.900	1.006
	$\overline{E}$	0.170	0.378	0.544	0.807	0.135	0.294	0.437	0.704	0.116	0.256	0.383	0.640
UN	RMSE	0.261	0.450	0.584	0.659	0.254	0.435	0.573	0.656	0.254	0.431	0.564	0.643
	$|\%E|$	4.102	7.542	10.233	12.290	3.977	7.166	9.895	11.999	3.961	7.001	9.568	11.619
	$\overline{E}$	-0.203	-0.027	-0.029	-0.034	-0.16	-0.010	-0.003	-0.005	-0.012	-0.001	0.009	0.012

$RMSE$ = Root Mean Square Error; $|\%E|$ = Percent Absolute Error; $\overline{E}$ = Mean Error

the standard version of the Model. Results for forecast simulations for one-quarter, two-quarter, three-quarter, and four-quarter forecasts are summarized in Table 5.

Looking first at the GNP components which are directly affected by the equation changes (shown in the first page of the Table) substantial improvements are apparent in the predictions for investment and housing. For consumer purchases of automobiles there is also an improvement but it is relatively smaller.

The additional information provided by anticipations data is most important for the early quarters when the actual data on anticipations are used in the equations. As the forecast is extended beyond this point, the estimates of anticipations used are themselves endogenous and the gain in accuracy diminishes.

The modest gain obtained in the simulation of CA is not surprising in view of the analogous single equation result. Consumer sentiment has a net effect in reducing RMSE in Version III, particularly, where the unemployment variable has been omitted entirely. But, of course, consumer sentiment is closely related to the employment situation so that much of the impact of consumer attitudes has already been incorporated in the unemployment variable used in the Version I equation. It is interesting however to note that the formulation using the attitude variable shows less positive bias (a lower mean error, $\bar{E}$) than the Version I equation.

In the case of business fixed investment, the greatest improvement occurs with IPMM. RMSE is reduced almost by one-half in the one- and two-quarter forecasts and remains a little lower even in the third and fourth quarter. The realizations function formulation (Version III) gives consistently better results in this case. Again the anticipations appear to reduce bias. The results are less clear for IPR and IPC. Beyond the first quarter forecasts the gains are quite small, and while Version III is best for IPC, the "auxiliary" Version II works best for IPR. As was apparent in the single equation results as well, the anticipations data seem to be less firmly linked to investment in these categories than they are for manufacturing and mining.

With regard to residential construction, the anticipations equations reduce RMSE almost by one half for the one-quarter predictions and by lesser amounts in subsequent quarters. Some improvement remains even in the four-quarter predictions. Surprisingly, however, the more disaggregated Version III equations do less well after the one-quarter forecasts than the Version II equations, and after two quarters even less well than the version I formulation. Why this should be so is not clear. There is reason to question the validity of the underlying data breakdown, and that may explain the failure of the more disaggregated equations in Version III to give as good results as the simpler versions.

Results of the forecast simulations for aggregative statistics are shown on the second page of Table 5. In view of the considerable improvement for the GNP components, we might have hoped for a larger decrease in the error statistics for the GNP aggregate. Despite the effects of offsetting error,[13] we do find a systematic reduction in Version II and III below the error statistics of the Version I simulation that makes no use of anticipations variables. This improvement ranges from $.4 to $.8 billion in the RMSE for GNP in current and constant dollars (Version II compared to Version I). It is noteworthy that the reductions in error, though modest, are sustained for as long as four quarters. We fully expected to find most of the impact of anticipations in the first two quarters. At the same time the bias of the forecasts is reduced particularly in Version III.

There is almost no impact on the price forecasts, and the improvement in the estimates for unemployment is very small.

The separate effect of the anticipatory variables for consumption, investment, and residential construction is shown in Table 6. For these simulations, only the equations introducing anticipations relevant to one GNP component at a time have been changed (using Version III equations for consumption and investment and Version II equations for residential construction). Other equations remain as in Version I. The results show that in each case the use of anticipations variables results in a small improvement in the forecast of aggregate GNP.

Conclusions

The survey data on consumer sentiment pioneered by George Katona are only one type of anticipatory material on economic developments. We have suggested in this study that these data must be fitted into the structure of econometric models in a logical and specific way, not as broad cyclical indicators. Consumer attitudes help to explain consumption; investment anticipations relate to various types of investment; and housing starts signal the movement of residential construction. While the forecasting horizon of the anticipations themselves may be limited, we have fitted them into the model endogenously, using the actual data when available and the endogenous estimates of the anticipations for later periods. The anticipations have been cast in the role of auxiliary variables in one formulation and into a realizations equation framework in another.

We conclude from these calculations that the anticipatory variables are indeed useful in prediction. On a single equation basis and in full system simulations, the inclusion of the anticipations improves prediction for the relevant components of GNP, particularly for one- and two-quarter predictions. The net contribution of the consumer attitudes is relatively modest. This does not mean that consumers fail

---

[13] One offset is related to the inventory determination equations of the Wharton Mark III model. The latter explain the movement of inventories in terms of an approximation of the identity

$$\text{Inventory Change} = \text{Production} - \text{Sales}.$$

If current production exceeds sales, inventories are being accumulated; if sales exceed production, inventories are being reduced. The approximation to this identity substitutes GNP final demand components to take the role of sales. On the production side of the identity, proxies for investment demand enter with lags. This means that in the very short run a change in the prediction for IP, or IH, is partially translated into an offsetting change in inventories.

Table 6. Separate Effects of Anticipatory Variables.

Anticipations Variables in :

		CA (Version III equations)				IP (Version III equations)				IH (Version II equations)			
						Forecast Period (Quarters)							
		1	2	3	4	1	2	3	4	1	2	3	4
GNP$	RMSE	3.963	5.836	7.507	8.337	4.029	5.928	7.700	8.494	4.018	5.888	7.431	8.08
	$|\%E|$	0.474	0.718	0.945	1.030	0.471	0.695	0.932	1.021	0.474	0.710	0.903	0.98
	$\overline{E}$	0.124	0.149	0.319	0.749	0.301	0.424	0.629	1.038	0.338	0.497	0.708	1.09
GNP	RMSE	3.880	5.157	6.070	6.366	3.948	5.281	6.341	6.692	3.983	5.348	6.193	6.42
1958 $	$|\%E|$	0.513	0.669	0.819	0.868	0.511	0.666	0.816	0.879	0.522	0.683	0.808	0.83
	$\overline{E}$	0.663	0.744	0.973	1.399	0.874	1.059	1.294	1.673	0.925	1.175	1.458	1.85

RMSE = Root Mean Square Error;   1%E = Percent Absolute Error; $\overline{E}$ = Mean Error.

to react to their feelings about economic prospects. Rather it reflects the presence of a proxy for attitudes, the unemployment rate, in the original consumer purchases of autos equation. The impact of anticipatory variables is greater in the business fixed investment and housing equations where anticipatory information is likely to be more firm. For aggregate GNP, the improvement in RMSE amounts to $.4 to $.8 billion and persists even in four-quarter forecasts.

The last word has not been said on the usefulness of anticipations data in macro-economic models. This study suggests that, properly integrated into the framework of structural equations, anticipations variables can make an important contribution to improved prediction of the components of GNP and to a lesser extent to the prediction of aggregate economic activity.

APPENDIX

List of Variables

C	**	PERSONAL CONSUMPTION EXPENDITURES
CA	**	PERSONAL CONSUMPTION EXPENDITURES ON AUTOS & PARTS
CDA$		NONPASSBK. SAVINGS OF PUBLIC AT MEMBER BANKS
CPMM		WHARTON CAPACITY INDEX, MFG & MINING
CR		DUMMY: CONSUMER CREDIT–REG W
CSI		MICH CONSUMER SENTIMENT INDEX
CUR$		CURRENCY COMPONENT OF MONEY SUPPLY, SA
DAA		DUMMY FOR BAD SEASONAL; NONZERO IN 68.2,69.2,69.3,70.1
DD$		DEMAND DEPOSIT COMPONENT OF MONEY SUPPLY, SA
DS		DUMMY: AUTO SUPPLY SHORTAGE 48.1–2,48.3–4,49.1,53.3
EPC1	*	1ST INVEST ANTICIPATION, COMMERCIAL – ADVANCED 2 QTR
EPC2	*	2ND INVEST ANTICIPATION, COMMERCIAL – ADVANCED 1 QTR
EPMM1	*	1ST INVEST ANTICIPATION, MFG+MINING – ADVANCED 2 QTR
EPMM2	*	2ND INVEST ANTICIPATION, MFG+MINING – ADVANCED 1 QTR
EPR1	*	1ST INVEST ANTICIPATION, REGULATED – ADVANCED 2 QTR
EPR2	*	2ND INVEST ANTICIPATION, REGULATED – ADVANCED 1 QTR
HS1		SINGLE UNIT NEW PRIVATE HOUSING STARTS INCL FARM, SA
HSM		TOTAL NEW MULTIPLE UNIT HOUSING STARTS, SA
IH	**	FIXED INVESTMENT IN NONFARM RESIDENTIAL STRUCTURES
IHAA	**	INVESTMENT IN RESIDENTIAL ADDITIONS & ALTERATIONS, SA
IHT	**	FIXED INVESTMENT IN TOTAL RESIDENTIAL STRUCTURES, SA
IL		MOODY'S TOTAL CORPORATE BOND YIELD
INHU	**	INVESTMENT IN NEW RESIDENTIAL STRUCTURES
IP	**	IPC+IPMM +IPR
IPC	**	COMML & OTHER P+E INVEST.
IPMM	**	MINING+MFG. P & E INVESTMENT
IPR	**	INVEST IN REG P & EQUIP.
IS		RATE ON 4-6 MO. PRIME COMM'L PAPER
KC	**	CAPITAL STK IN COMMERCIAL & OTHER
KR	**	CAPITAL STK IN REGULATED IND
LIQUID		(CUR$+DD$+TD$-CDA$)/(Y*PC)
MHTR	**	MOBILE HOMES & TRAVEL TRAILERS PURCHASES
P		IMPLICIT PRICE DEFLATOR FOR GNP
PA		AUTOS & PARTS DEFLATOR

PC		IMPLICIT DEFLATOR FOR PCE
PCOM	**	COMM. AND OTHER GPO DEFLATOR
PH		IMPLICIT DEFLATOR FOR NONFARM RES. STRUCT.
PMM	**	MANUF. AND MINING GPO DEFLATOR
PR		RENTAL COMPONENT OF CPI
PXR		REGULATED GPO DEFLATOR
TD$		TIME DEPOSITS SA
TIGHT		INTEREST RATE DUMMY = 1.0 WHEN IS > IL; 0 OTHERWISE
TIME		TIME TREND, 1948.1 = 1
TR		TRANSFER PAYMENTS RECEIVED BY PERSONS
UCCC		USED COST OF CAPITAL, COMMERCIAL INDUSTRIES, EQUIP'T
UCCMM		USER COST OF CAPITAL, MFG. & MINING, EQUIPMENT
UCCR		USER COST OF CAPITAL, REGULATED INDUSTRIES, EQUIP'T
UN		UNEMPLOYMENT RATE, ALL CIVILIAN WORKERS
W$		COMPENSATION OF EMPLOYEES
XC	**	GPO, COMMERCIAL AND OTHER
XMM	**	GPO IN MINING, MFG.
XR	**	GPO IN REGULATED IND.
Y		DISPOSABLE PERSONAL INCOME DEFLATED BY PC

* Investment anticipations are deflated by deflator for business fixed investment at time investment is to be put in place.

**1958$

References

Adams, F. G., 1964, "Consumer attitudes, buying plans and purchases of durable goods," *Review of Economics and Statistics*, November.

—— and E. W. Green, 1965, "Explaining and predicting consumer attitudes," *International Economic Review*.

Brady, E. A., 1970, "An econometric analysis of the U.S. residential housing market," Working Paper #11, Federal Home Loan Bank Board, Washington, D.C., November 30.

Duesenberry, J. *et al.* (eds.) 1965, *The Brookings Quarterly Econometric Model of the United States* (Rand McNally, Chicago).

Evans, M. K., and Lawrence R. Klein, 1968, *The Wharton Econometric Forecasting Model*, 2nd rev. ed. (Economics Research Unit, University of Pennsylvania, Philadelphia).

Fair, R. C., 1971, *A Short-Run Forecasting Model of the U.S. Economy* (D. C. Heath and Company, Lexington, Massachusetts), Chap. 5.

Friend, I., and W. C. Thomas, 1970, "A reevaluation of the predictive ability of plant and equipment anticipations," *Journal of the American Statistical Association*, June.

Hymans, S. H., 1970, "Consumer durable spending: Explanation and prediction," *Brookings Papers on Economic Activity* **2** (The Brookings Institution, Washington, D.C.).

Liebenberg, M., A. Hirsch, and J. Popkin, 1966, "A quarterly econometric model of the U.S.: A progress report," *Survey of Current Business*, May.

20

THE PRECISION OF ECONOMIC PREDICTION: STANDARDS, ACHIEVEMENT, POTENTIAL[†]

I. The Importance of Being Right

The two major factors governing current standards of precision in economic forecasting are user requirements and professional ability. In this presentation, I am going to be concerned primarily with *econometric* prediction, where the standards of precision in forecasting are often set both by the objective of out-performing most other types of forecasters as well as serving the needs of a variety of users.

Econometric forecasting at a macro level began essentially during World War II. With low standards and high aspirations, it fared badly at first, but fortunately it has come a long way since that era. The users at that time were principally government departments and the Federal Reserve. Major corporations were just beginning to become interested in systematic forecasting. Of course, people have tried to forecast the economy since the time of Joseph in Egypt, but systematic methods, and especially econometric methods, have a much shorter history.

At the beginning, econometric forecasters were strongly influenced by the 20s and 30s, when there had been wide swings in economic activity in short run periods. It is difficult to say just what our standards were at that time, but many people would probably have responded favorably to the thought that errors in predicting GNP and its main components could be held to a range of ± 5 to 10 percent, most of the time, say 90 percent of the time. Since those early attempts GNP has flowed on much like "Ole Man River," and annual prediction errors of more than 1.0 percent in level form are now intolerable. The annual change in GNP is now about as large as the total used to be in the 30s and currently an error of 10 percent in predicting this change is not uncommon and at the limit of the range of respectability. Let us say that an extreme allowable error in predicting GNP change at today's order of magnitude is thus $10 billion. Similar errors for other variables are:

aggregate price index	1 index point
aggregate unemployment rate	1/2 percentage point
short-term interest rate	100 basis points

[†]From *The Economic Outlook for 1973* (RSQE University of Michigan, Department of Economics, Ann Arbor, 1973), pp. 91–111.

I cannot document these limits and they may seem somewhat arbitrary, but they are my judgement of both what users require and the profession has generally achieved. In a sense figures like these have come to be expected.

How have these conventional error bounds arisen? The most frequent source of information is the recognition of past mistakes. The past 25 years is full of records of faulty predictions that led to incorrect policies, embarrassment, lack of credibility, and/or foregone profits. The biggest mistakes are well known; others are more difficult to list systematically. The predictions of postwar recession in 1946 are among the most celebrated errors. The unemployment rate rose from 1.9 percent in 1945 to 3.9 percent in 1946 and 1947, but the predictions of 6 million people unemployed as a result of the postwar let-down, implying an unemployment rate of 10 percent, was clearly wide of the mark by an excessive margin.

We might commemorate these meetings with a reference to the opening forecasts in October 1953, when Mr. Colin Clark had frightened the world with a forecast, based on econometric studies, of an economic collapse like that of 1929. Fortunately, the first Michigan Model came out with an accurate forecast of a small post-Korean decline to save the day for econometrics, but the Clark forecast was widely believed and had an impact on economic thinking of the time.

During the early Kennedy Administration, the extent of the recovery in 1961 from the 1960–61 recession was seriously underestimated by administration economists which in turn led to an over-reaction in predicting 1962, incorrectly. In this case, it was soon discovered that an error of only $5 billion (at an annual rate) in GNP forecasts in a given quarter was enough to switch a budget surplus or balance into deficit. This gives a critical value.

Underestimation of the order of magnitude of the effect of the Vietnam war on the economy of 1965 led to a failure to recognize certain inflation dangers and culminated in the incorrect forecasts of the effect of the 1968 tax surcharge. Real GNP was predicted by the Wharton Model within close range, as stated by William Chartener at these meetings in 1969, but the price index was underestimated by 3 whole index points. This is an outside estimate and did introduce a credibility gap for econometric models.

The last in this series of selected big mistakes was the celebrated "1065" prediction for 1971 by the Nixon Administration. I cannot say that the figure obtained was an econometric prediction, for the consensus of respectable models was in a very different range. The Administration figure was substantially outside the $10 billion range that I have arbitrarily set, and tends to confirm the plausibility of the arbitrary error figure that I have chosen.

The importance of these extreme errors is not widely recognized. It is not possible to say what the world would have been like if the errors had been avoided, but it is possible to discern immediate consequences. At the end of World War II, we were not prepared to cope with an era of inflation at unemployment levels far lower than the average of the prewar decade. Being wrong at the beginning of the postwar period was probably not decisive, but it delayed our ability to deal with the inflation problem. It is sometimes said that Sweden concluded an unfavorable trade agreement with Soviet Russia on the basis of erroneous predictions of the U.S. economy by her advisers.

It is hard to point to disastrous consequences in the case of the 1953–54 recession. The parallel with 1929 was not a view of the U.S. government although many U.S. business corporations were unduly pessimistic, but it was a popular view in the U.K. and Western Europe. It is even rumored that clever followers of Keynes made poor portfolio decisions for their colleges on the basis of bad forecasts of the U.S. cycle and its impact abroad.

Residual accounts like profits, saving, surplus, or deficit are very sensitive to error. Some of these are politically strategic, although shifts towards redefinitions of balance items have so confused the issues that particular plus or minus figures do not have the same importance that they had 10 or 20 years ago. Nevertheless, the projected budget deficit is still an important figure and is very sensitive to projections of overall economic activity. Sound budget planning at all levels of government requires that estimates of tax and expenditure bases, which are the main statistical measures of aggregate activity, should be estimated well within 1.0 percent errors for levels and between 5 and 10 percent for changes. Thus at the national level, projected GNP and profit figures should be accurate within $\pm$ $2.0 billion for good estimation of deficits or surpluses. The miscalculations in 1962 were not disastrous for the government, but they did give rise to cynicism on the part of the public and a lack of credibility, which grew to be much more serious in later years.

The miscalculations in 1968 left the country exposed to unnecessary additional rounds of inflation. Had the full magnitude of the inflationary problem been seen in the summer of 1968, it is not certain that appropriate counter policy could have been obtained, but it is possible that the inflationary movement and subsequent recession could have been avoided.

The unjustified prediction of "1065" in 1971 stood in the way of policies needed to alleviate unemployment and turn the economy quickly around after the recession turning point, but its greatest damage was undoubtedly to econometric method. I would not want to call this an econometric forecast, but unfortunately some non-professionals have done so. It is a hopeful sign, however, that the model approach that produced this kind of estimate has been pushed into the background and practically forgotten.

The above discussion of standards has looked at the issue mainly from the viewpoint of public policy users of forecasts. Other users are large industrial corporations, banks, world organizations, and individual speculators. The large corporation predicting its own profits and associated variables must be as sensitive to forecast errors in national aggregates as government. Company performance balances are often sensitive to the main national economy balances, and it is important that they have the same standards of precision for variables describing the national economy that big government has. The models for individual firms or industries are, however, less well established, more dependent on special factors, and based on poorer samples so that final errors are likely to be larger in percentage terms. Eventually, the same standards might apply for both business and government users, but at this stage, business standards are not generally as high. There are, however, exceptional cases where standards are higher for some magnitudes, physical production being one.

World organizations, who must make judgements about the future of the U.S. economy are in much the same position as the U.S. government, but much of their use is concentrated on trade and those domestic variables interrelated with many other economies. There are few countries of the world, although there are some, where current standards are as high as in the U.S. For this reason, international bodies may use lower standards than does the U.S. government. This is a changing situation, and the time can be foreseen when most industrial countries will use common standards of accuracy.

As for small business, personal speculators, investors, and other users of economic forecasts, it is probably not critical for them to achieve the highest standards mentioned above. Forecasts of direction and approximate rate of change of the major economic magnitudes at the national level provide the important background information they require. Their time is better spent in understanding their special circumstances than in achieving high standards of accuracy of prediction.

Turning points are particularly important for the individual investor or speculator. They are also important in avoiding great surprises for government policy makers and big business advisers. Turning points, however, are the hardest to predict, and in the neighborhood of turning points, our standards must be much less severe. The main issue is to catch the turn, but we should realize that our error bands may be practically twice as large in these circumstances.

Another approach towards the setting of standards is to use the statistical formula for the standard error of forecast. In an important study of a linear model, A. S. Goldberger, A. L. Nagar, and H. S. Odeh[1] used the following structural model

$$Ay_t + Bx_t = e_t \qquad t = 1, 2, \dots, T$$

with reduced form

$$y_t = -A^{-1}Bx_t + A^{-1}e_t$$

to compute the standard error of forecast

$$S^2_{y^f_{T+1}} = F_{T+1}\Omega F'_{T+1} + \sum .$$

---

[1]A. S. Goldberger, A. L. Nagar, and H. S. Odeh, "The covariance matrices of reduced form coefficients and of forecasts for a structural econometric model," *Econometrica* **29** (October, 1961), pp. 556–573.

In these formulas

A = nonsingular square matrix of structural coefficients of dependent variables
B = rectangular matrix of structural coefficients of independent variables
y_t = vector of dependent variables
x_t = vector of independent variables
e_t = vector of random errors
y^f_{T+1} = value forecast for y_t at time $T + 1$
F_{T+1} = properly constructed matrix of independent variables at time $T + 1$
Ω = covariance matrix of reduced form coefficients
Σ = covariance matrix of reduced form errors.

The variance of the forecast error computed by this formula is seen to depend on the variance of the residual error, uncertainty about parameter values, and the magnitude of the independent variables. It is a formidable job to evaluate this formula for large modern macro models. Goldberger, Nagar, and Odeh provide some approximations in order to simplify the calculations but even in the relatively simple case they tried the errors turn out to be quite large. For a national income value of about \$100 billion in 1940, they estimate the standard error of forecast to be \$12.6 billion. This is just one standard error, yet it is large for a one-year forecast by today's standards, especially in percentage terms.

In a research study at the Wharton School, George Schink has used numerical simulation techniques to get round the difficulties in computing $S^2_{y^f_{T+1}}$ and has obtained values that appear to be better approximations to the standard error of forecast.[2] The Schink method allows for nonlinearity in the original equation structure, time dependence of errors and the dynamics involved in a multiperiod forecast. In these respects, his system is a generalization of that used by Goldberger, Nagar, and Odeh. His numerical results are extended to the case of a large model, in this instance the Wharton Model.

In a sampling experiment, Schink obtains 100 replicated estimates of the model and from each estimate makes multiperiod extrapolations, quarter-by-quarter. He finds that one standard error of GNP is approximately \$7 billion and rises to a total of \$10 billion in four quarters. This experiment provides us with an objective reason for putting an outside limit of \$10 billion as a "standard" for a one-year forecasting error in GNP for modern econometric forecasting.

It is not a purely nominal or arbitrary slip to reckon error in terms of *one standard* error of forecast. Given the imprecision of social science findings and the applications of social policy, one standard error is about all we can aspire to in constructing tolerance intervals for error. This may seem like a low standard, especially in comparison with error bands tolerated in some natural science fields and engineering, yet it is realistic. Social policy must be set with an idea of the

---

[2] G. R. Schink, "Small sample estimates of the variance–covariance matrix of forecast error for large econometric models: The stochastic simulation technique," Ph.D. dissertation, University of Pennsylvania, 1971.

probability of being wrong much more frequently than 5, 10, or even 25 percent of the time.

It is my opinion that within the standards suggested here, governments can make indicative plans, i.e. use indirect policy controls of the sort generally associated with our economy, and do a reasonably good job of economic management. Given the margin of errors committed and likely to be committed, such planning should be flexible, in the sense that once mistakes in forecasting have been recognized, they can be corrected. The "New Economics" of the postwar world was optimistic that adequate precision could be attained to carry out policies intelligently. Some of the larger mistakes have shaken that belief, and there is no doubt that the dominant view was one of over optimism, but the mistakes have been instructive and show that we are not locked in forever to policies that are misguided by poor forecasts.

Some economists have tried to shun responsibility by claiming that forecasting mistakes do not really matter in a crucial way. They feel that intelligent policy can proceed even in the face of large mistakes in forecasting. I disagree with this view, and argue that careful forecasting is good enough to form a basis for policy. It is even possible that some improvements can be made. These will be discussed in Sec. III below.

Finally, let me close this section on standards by noting that fixed rule policies, such as steady growth in money supply, also require forecast precision. Money supply is an endogenous variable that is affected in a complicated way by many indirect actions of the central monetary authorities. Their precision in attaining targets is no better than the general forecaster's precision in helping a broad range of policy makers stabilize the economy. No matter what approach is used to formulate economic policy, it just will not be possible to avoid the necessity for making good forecasts.

II. Some Actual Error Statistics

The standards talked about in the previous section are only crudely indicative of some limits. Best practice quickly influences new standards and, in fact, econometric forecasting is often more accurate than has been suggested. In this Sec. I want to analyze why actual forecasts are better than would be suggested by calculation of the standard error of forecast and show how much better they are.

Errors may conveniently be examined from three viewpoints, (1) Ex-post, within sample, (2) Ex-post, outside sample, and, (3) Ex-ante. Within-sample errors are naturally the smallest. They have the comforting advantage of being related, at least on a single equation basis, to the parameter estimates of models. The parameters are not generally estimated so that multiperiod system prediction errors are minimized; they are, in most cases, chosen so that single equation estimates of one-period errors are minimized. The transition from single equations to complete systems and from single periods to dynamic paths results in an enlargement of error, but nothing like the enlargement associated with extrapolation.

In a working seminar supported and sponsored by NSF/NBER, a group of model proprietors have standardized a set of error statistics. The results of within sample simulations for leading variables are shown in Table 1. In the very short run, GNP is estimated within \$2.0–\$4.0 billion, rising gradually to a level near \$10.0 billion in two years. These seemingly precise estimates of production are associated with errors of no more than about 20 basis points in interest rates, 50 basis points in unemployment rate, and one-half an index point in price levels. It is remarkable that all these models conform to a narrow range at this time.

Ex post forecasts outside the sample period are based on the correct inputs of all predetermined variables. Performance, however, is markedly less precise once we shift from interpolation to extrapolation (Table 2). The same models show error statistics that are nearly twice as large when simulation occurs outside the sample period. They are still indicative of good performance but they are much larger than in Table 1. It should be noted, though, that the extrapolation period is short and occurs at a difficult time when severe moves were under way in monetary policy.

The various models are not as similar for extrapolation as for interpolation error properties. The main discrepancies occur for GNP extrapolations beyond one year. The smallness of the extrapolations sample, however, imparts instability to the average squared errors.

Record keeping on ex-ante forecasting is considerably less prevalent. This has not been an objective of the NSF/NBER seminar; so results are not available on a uniform basis across models, but they are available for the Wharton Model. The results in Table 3 cover the period 1967.1–1972.2. In ex ante prediction, we face a serious problem of data revision that is not apparent in ex post analysis on a fixed set of historical data that are accepted as observed without change for the period of analysis. In order to cope with data revision we adjust the revised observations by the discrepancy between actual and extrapolation value in the last period before the beginning of the extrapolation. The adjusted (observed) series is thus

$$y^a_{T+j} = y^u_{T+j} + (y^e_T - y^u_T)$$

$j = 1, 2, \ldots$

$T = $ last period before extrapolation

$a = $ adjusted

$u = $ unadjusted

$e = $ extrapolated .

In other words, we make extrapolated and observed (revised) series equal in the last period before extrapolation and make the same constant adjustment to the observed series throughout the extrapolation period.

In the very short run, ex ante forecast errors are not much larger than those in Tables 1 and 2, but they grow much faster than the interpolation errors in Table 1.

Table 1. Simulation Error, Within Sample Period (Root-mean-squared error).

BEA Model, 1961.1–1967.4

Quarters ahead

	1	2	3	4	5	6	7	8
Nominal GNP ($ bill)	2.39	4.68	6.57	7.81	8.95	9.99		
Quarterly change	2.39	3.86	4.15	4.21	4.24	4.50		
Real GNP ($ bill, 1958)	1.97	3.99	5.68	6.94	8.12	8.94		
Quarterly change	1.97	3.28	3.68	3.78	3.76	3.98		
GNP deflator (1958:100)	0.21	0.33	0.41	0.50	0.55	0.59		
Unemployment rate (%)	0.22	0.25	0.31	0.32	0.32	0.34		
Corporate bond yield (%)	0.13	0.17	0.21	0.20	0.21	0.23		

(Serial correlation of residuals, as estimated in sample, used to adjust solution values)

Brookings Model, Condensed Version, 1959.1–1965.4

	1	2	3	4	5	6	7	8
Nominal GNP ($ bill)	4.08	5.38	5.83	5.85	5.78	5.72	5.66	5.80
Quarterly change	4.08	3.29	3.37	3.49	3.72	3.66	3.64	3.66
Real GNP ($ bill, 1958)	3.70	4.66	5.01	5.13	5.19	5.25	5.32	5.57
Quarterly change	3.70	2.96	3.13	3.26	3.43	3.38	3.37	3.33
GNP deflator (1958:100)	0.20	0.32	0.39	0.44	0.46	0.46	0.48	0.47
Unemployment rate (%)	0.25	0.34	0.38	0.38	0.39	0.40	0.40	0.41
Bond yield* (%)	0.10	0.10	0.13	0.16	0.17	0.17	0.18	0.20

(No adjustments of residuals)

*Long term U.S. government security yield (%)

DHL-III Model, 1961.1–1967.4 (Michigan Model)

	1	2	3	4	5	6	7	8
Nominal GNP ($ bill)	3.30	4.85	7.30	8.38	9.42	10.18	10.61	10.39
Quarterly change	3.30	5.34	7.55	6.51	7.00	7.24	7.00	6.50
Real GNP ($ bill, 1958)	3.03	4.96	7.32	8.52	9.64	10.41	10.80	10.58
Quarterly change	3.03	5.39	6.94	6.22	6.70	6.92	6.65	5.98
GNP deflator (1958:100)	0.16	0.26	0.36	0.47	0.56	0.64	0.71	0.79
Unemployment rate (%)	0.16	0.31	0.45	0.52	0.54	0.56	0.58	0.56
Corporate bond yield (%)	0.11	0.17	0.21	0.22	0.24	0.26	0.28	0.29

(No adjustment of residuals)

(Cont'd)

Table 1 (continued).

Ray Fair Model, 1962.1–1967.4 (excl. 1964.4, 1965.1, 1965.2)

	Quarters ahead							
	1	2	3	4	5	6	7	8
Nominal GNP ($ bill)	2.80	4.12	4.49	4.56	4.00			
Quarterly Change	2.80	3.13	3.47	3.50	3.76			
Real GNP ($ bill, 1958)	2.81	4.14	4.32	4.22	3.61			
Quarterly Change	2.81	2.81	3.15	3.33	3.51			
GNP deflator (1958:100)	0.18	0.29	0.35	0.37	0.37			
Unemployment rate (%)	0.21	0.32	0.43	0.51	0.52			

(No adjustment of residuals; observed sample data on anticipatory variables used for input values)

Federal Reserve Bank of St. Louis Model, 1961.1–1967.4

	1	2	3	4	5	6	7	8
Nominal GNP ($ bill)	3.16	4.51	5.52	6.34	6.93	7.55	8.51	9.60
Quarterly change	3.16	3.16	3.16	3.16	3.16	3.16	3.16	3.16
Real GNP ($ bill, 1958)	2.88	4.09	4.77	4.98	4.68	4.33	4.43	4.72
Quarterly Change	2.88	2.90	2.91	2.92	3.02	3.03	2.90	2.92
GNP deflator (1958:100)	0.19	0.31	0.38	0.45	0.55	0.68	0.82	0.98
Unemployment rate (%)	0.23	0.27	0.32	0.35	0.32	0.24	0.17	0.19
Corporate bond yield (%)	0.16	0.17	0.16	0.16	0.16	0.16	0.19	0.22

(No adjustment of residuals)

M. P. S. Model, 1961.1–1967.4

	1	2	3	4	5	6	7	8
Nominal GNP ($ bill)	2.53	3.57	4.97	5.50	6.61	6.58	6.64	6.59
Quarterly Change	2.53	3.30	3.73	3.97	3.86	4.08	4.15	4.20
Real GNP ($ bill, 1958)	2.63	3.67	3.98	4.36	5.50	5.90	6.30	6.70
Quarterly Change	2.63	3.07	3.27	3.52	3.52	3.71	3.77	3.77
GNP deflator (1958:100)	0.22	0.28	0.38	0.47	0.59	0.63	0.65	0.68
Unemployment rate (%)	0.31	0.39	0.44	0.45	0.45	0.47	0.49	0.47
Corporate bond yield (%)	0.11	0.12	0.13	0.14	0.14	0.12	0.12	0.11

(Serial correlation of residuals, as estimated in the sample, used to adjust solution values; no other adjustments, stock market endogenous)

(Cont'd)

Table 1 (continued).

Wharton Mark III Model, 1961.1–1967.4

	Quarters ahead							
	1	2	3	4	5	6	7	8
Nominal GNP ($ bill)	3.14	4.70	6.05	6.62	6.98	7.04	7.02	6.82
Quarterly change	3.14	4.16	4.04	4.12	4.05	4.03	4.04	4.03
Real GNP ($ bill, 1958)	3.08	3.91	4.32	4.52	5.05	5.43	5.62	5.82
Quarterly change	3.08	3.51	3.42	3.60	3.62	3.62	3.62	3.67
GNP deflator (1958:100)	0.23	0.28	0.34	0.47	0.59	0.67	0.77	0.88
Unemployment rate (%)	0.21	0.38	0.50	0.54	0.59	0.63	0.64	0.64
Corporate bond yield (%)	0.15	0.23	0.24	0.29	0.28	0.31	0.33	0.35

(No adjustment of residuals)

H-C Annual Model, Stanford University 1961–66

	Years ahead				
Nominal GNP ($ bill)	11.17	15.16	15.51	15.35	15.02
Annual Change	11.17	10.22	9.69	9.60	9.50
Real GNP ($ bill, 1958)	10.57	14.14	14.37	14.32	14.06
Unemployment rate (%)	0.92	1.08	1.06	1.11	1.10

(No adjustment of residuals; (prices, interest rate, wage rate exogenous, except for compositional effects on GNP deflator.)

Wharton Annual Model, 1961–67

Nominal GNP ($ bill)	4.97	5.74	10.33	14.32	23.57
Annual change	4.97	4.27	6.39	9.96	12.71
Real GNP ($ bill, 1958)	6.20	7.08	6.37	8.84	10.87
Annual change	6.20	7.41	8.44	10.52	10.32
GNP deflator (1958:100)	0.70	0.64	1.52	2.74	3.89
Unemployment rate (%)	0.63	0.97	1.20	1.60	1.92
Corporate bond yield (%)	0.19	0.32	0.42	0.56	0.63

After one year, the quarterly GNP error exceeds $12 billion. If we average quarterly forecasts within a year, taking advantage of error cancellation, the annual forecast error is only $7.75 billion in the first year.

The particular forecast period chosen for analysis of ex ante error covers a difficult phase, as did the ex post extrapolations, and this undoubtedly biases the error statistics upwards. Also, if we evaluate a bias component of the root-mean-square-

Table 2. Extrapolation Error, Outside Sample Period (Root-mean-squared error).

BEA Model, 1969.1–1971.2

Quarters ahead

	1	2	3	4	5	6	7	8
Nominal GNP ($ bill)	4.30	12.47	18.21	20.78	21.13	19.72		
Quarterly change	4.30	11.31	6.40	4.04	4.09	4.43		
Real GNP ($ bill, 1958)	3.51	9.05	11.54	11.02	8.42	6.83		
Quarterly change	3.51	7.93	3.38	3.48	5.56	6.81		
GNP deflator (1958:100)	0.25	0.34	0.57	0.98	1.65	2.44		
Unemployment rate (%)	0.35	0.86	1.23	1.39	1.40	1.26		
Corporate bond yield (%)	0.42	0.52	0.60	0.68	0.75	0.79		

(Serial correlation of residuals, as estimated in sample, used to adjust solution values; no other adjustment except for GM strike in 1970.)

Brookings Condensed Model, 1966.1–1970.4

	1	2	3	4	5	6	7	8
Nominal GNP ($ bill)	6.74	11.36	16.08	20.94	25.69	29.54	33.18	39.77
Quarterly change	6.74	7.61	8.32	7.94	8.44	7.11	7.08	8.01
Real GNP ($ bill, 1958)	5.86	9.64	13.40	16.41	18.78	20.45	21.24	24.22
Quarterly change	5.86	6.30	6.90	6.47	6.84	5.75	5.81	6.34
GNP deflator (1958:100)	0.42	0.65	0.80	0.91	0.96	1.08	1.30	1.70
Unemployment rate (%)	0.26	0.51	0.81	1.02	1.16	1.26	1.14	1.21
Corporate bond yield (%)*	0.28	0.40	0.45	0.51	0.54	0.61	0.69	0.76

(Constant term of each equation adjusted by average residual in 4 quarters prior to extrapolation)
*Long term U. S. government security yield.

DHL-III Model, 1968.1–1970.4 (Michigan Model)

	1	2	3	4	5	6	7	8
Nominal GNP ($ bill)	6.06	10.25		17.03				
Quarterly change	6.06	7.72		9.25				
Real GNP ($ bill, 1958)	5.04	8.39		12.26				
Quarterly change	5.04	6.55		7.75				
GNP deflator (1958:100)	0.41	0.61		0.88				
Unemployment rate (%)	0.24	0.53		0.80				
Corporate bond yield (%)	0.23	0.32		0.44				

(No adjustments of residuals)   (Cont'd)

Table 2 (continued).

Ray Fair Model, 1965.4–1969.4

	Quarters ahead							
	1	2	3	4	5	6	7	8
Nominal GNP ($ bill)	2.91	4.35	4.52	6.77	9.89			
Quarterly change	2.91	3.76	4.32	4.50	4.49			
Real GNP ($ bill, 1958)	3.12	4.74	4.71	5.40	6.61			
Quarterly change	3.12	3.15	3.23	3.03	2.98			
GNP deflator (1958:100)	0.21	0.39	0.57	0.76	0.97			
Unemployment rate (%)	0.36	0.68	0.90	1.08	1.23			

(Parameters re-estimated with data prior to each extrapolation period)

Federal Reserve Bank of St. Louis Model, 1970.1–1974.4

	1	2	3	4	5	6	7	8
Nominal GNP ($ bill)	10.29	14.88	13.83	11.69	11.15	16.11		
Quarterly change	10.29	10.89	11.56	12.62	13.13	10.75		
Real GNP ($ bill, 1958)	6.81	8.54	8.36	10.25	8.33	10.86		
Quarterly change	6.81	7.04	7.62	8.18	7.77	5.33		
GNP deflator (1958:100)	0.48	0.81	0.90	0.76	0.71	0.70		
Unemployment rate (%)	0.22	0.23	0.29	0.36	0.34	0.30		
Corporate bond yield (%)	0.50	0.52	0.45	0.32	0.34	0.37		

(No adjustment of residuals)

Wharton Mark III Model, 1970.2–1972.1

	1	2	3	4	5	6	7	8
Nominal GNP ($ bill)	9.90	19.46	27.16	31.09	35.60	41.89	44.94	48.85
Quarterly change	9.90	10.71	10.39	9.34	10.40	9.51	2.83	0.93
Real GNP ($ bill, 1958)	10.39	16.89	22.02	24.58	26.97	28.81	27.79	26.33
Quarterly change	10.39	7.67	6.99	5.50	5.77	3.80	2.63	1.77
GNP deflator (1958:100)	0.93	0.88	0.96	0.94	0.66	0.10	0.82	1.28
Unemployment rate (%)	0.65	1.21	1.73	2.14	2.54	2.98	3.27	3.41
Corporate bond yield (%)	0.27	0.40	0.42	0.51	0.59	0.67	0.75	0.84

(No adjustment of residuals)

Table 3. Ex Ante Forecast Error.

Wharton Model, 1967.1–1972.2 (Root-mean-square error)

Quarters ahead

	1	2	3	4	5	6	7	8
Nominal GNP ($ bill)	3.98	7.88	11.11	12.34	16.11	20.16	25.58	29.91
Quarterly change	3.98	6.64	7.88	7.15	8.62	8.77	9.43	9.74
Real GNP ($ bill, 1958)	3.02	6.09	7.66	7.83	8.57	10.66	14.55	18.58
Quarterly change	3.02	5.07	5.86	5.76	6.23	6.84	7.39	7.52
GNP deflator (1958:100)	0.43	0.76	1.34	1.92	2.49	3.23	4.06	4.90
Unemployment rate (%)	0.21	0.43	0.69	0.89	0.99	1.13	1.24	1.45
Corporate bond yield (%)	0.24	0.43	0.59	0.75	0.91	1.07	1.22	1.38

error statistic

$$\frac{1}{F} \sum_{j=1}^{F} e^2_{T+j} = \frac{1}{F} \sum_{j=1}^{F} (e_{T+j} - \bar{e})^2 + \bar{e}^2$$

$$e_{T+j} = y^a_{T+j} - y^f_{T+j}$$

$$\bar{e} = \frac{1}{F} \sum_{j=1}^{F} e_{T+j}$$

y^a_{T+j} = adjusted value in j-th forecast period
y^f_{T+j} = predicted value in j-th forecast period
$\bar{e}^2$ = (bias)^2

we find that much of the most serious recent error in the second year of prediction is due to bias. This is especially true of nominal GNP and price forecasts.

In a period shorter than one year, ex ante forecasts are much smaller than George Schink's estimates of the standard error of forecast. This is particularly true of short forecasts of one or two quarters' duration. One standard error, however, is not much bigger than the error involved in longer ex ante forecasts. This difference between actual performance and formula evaluation of error in the very short run compared to the differences in the extended run is not surprising. For the immediate future, we are able to use a great deal of extra-statistical information based on most recent economic performance, large unique disturbances, parameter drift, and similar *a priori* model inputs that are capable of being quantified. After two quarters, the model takes over more of the forecasting job by itself and performs about as well as formula analysis says it should. In many respects, this is comforting to the econometrician and should be linked with the result that econometric forecasts show a clearer superiority over pure judgmental forecasts in projection horizons of one year or more.

Econometric forecasting covers a wide range of variables. Many of the large models regularly project one hundred or more variables but only some representative magnitudes have been examined in this presentation. The variables selected are among the most important and are representative, but among others there is a fair amount of dispersion. Inventories, profits, the net foreign balance, and personal saving are difficult to predict — either because they are volatile, rest on a poor data base, or are estimated as small residual values. Consumer spending, wage payments, and employment are comparatively easy to predict. Systematic studies of ex post or ex ante prediction have not been made for the whole range of variables, but enough have been examined in detail so that I feel that the impressions given in this paper faithfully represent the broader situation.

III. Asymptotic Limits to Improvement

Some promising sources of improvement in economic prediction are (1) better data, (2) better economic and statistical theory, (3) larger models, and (4) the use of anticipatory data.

(1) *Better Data.* There can be no doubt that the relative strength of our current position vis-a-vis the first exercise at the end of World War II and the early 1950s, is due in part to the enormous advances in data preparation, data quality, and data volume. The ever shortening delay in the provision of preliminary estimates is extremely helpful in diagnosing the current situation and in preparing for ex ante forecasting. Many series are now simply more accurate in measuring what they are supposed to measure and are in a form that can be made to correspond better with concepts of economic analysis. These facts enhance predictive accuracy.

(2) *Economic and Statistical Theory.* If not used slavishly, economic theory is a good guide to model specification, especially for steady-state or equilibrium functioning of models. Perhaps even greater help has come from the theoretical treatment of distributed lags, serial correlation, nonlinearities, and equation system methods of estimation. On the frontiers of econometric theory, work being done on methods of variable parameter estimation and iterates of restricted reduced forms looks quite promising. I do not expect enormous improvements from these developments, but if $0.5 or $1.0 billion can be shaved from the Root-Mean-Squared-Error (RMSE) of GNP forecasts, I would like to take advantage of such a gain. Similarly 10–20 basis point improvements in the RMSE of unemployment rate, interest rate, or inflation rate would be welcome, if not of the "break-through" category.

(3) *Larger Models.* "Bigger" is by no means "better." In one sense, we might argue that if models can be enlarged to provide more economic information without losing accuracy, there is justification in building bigger models. Some people feel that

bigger models place greater strain on data sources, open up more possibilities for model management error, and tend to breed specification error across equations of an entire system. There is something to most of these points, yet I would argue that there are potential gains in the construction of bigger systems and that it is not only a question of doing at least as well with large systems; we can, in fact, do better. I have often claimed that small systems may do seemingly better in goodness-of-fit statistics, sample period simulations, and a few favorable true forecast situations, but that they will always come to situations in which important things not explicitly represented in small systems will play a large role.

Small models fared poorly in the period nominated by the General Motors strike of 1970. It is not impossible, but it is awkward to factor *a priori* strike information into small models. This is not a nit-picking matter and it is not defensible to accept the practice of small model proprietors who averaged two quarters to wash out the strike effects. It was a critical period, in the midst of recovery from the 1969–70 recession, and judgment was required on the issue whether the economy was suffering a relapse into secondary recession or simply responding to a strike of a \$15 billion GNP component as it ought to be responding. The small models were singularly uninformative on the underlying state of the economy in late 1970.

It is not surprising that the small models did poorly in forecasting 1972 after the introduction of President Nixon's New Economic Policy (NEP). They contain few entry points for import surcharge, exchange rates, wage freeze, price freeze, phase II controls, investment tax credit, and many other policies associated with NEP.

(4) *Anticipatory Data.* In the shadow of the Survey Research Center and the honorific events concerned with George Katona's retirement, it is good to be able to report some optimistic findings on the use of anticipatory data. For one- and two-quarter predictions, without feedback, it has been evident for some time that consumer attitudes and investment plans have been significant variables in econometric models in the sense that they improve forecast performance. Following the lead of Saul Hymans, Gerard Adams and I have found that it is possible to extend previous results by endogenizing anticipatory variables so that the forecast horizon can be extended beyond two quarters.[3] Adams and I find evidence of modest reduction in RMSE, approximately \$0.5 billion in GNP forecasts, if endogenous anticipatory variables are introduced for consumer spending, fixed business investment, and housing. For the past two years, ex ante forecasts have regularly been made using this system, with some notable successes for specific areas of the economy, but the experience is too brief for the development of reliable ex ante error measures at this stage.

Improvements are certainly desired, needed, and feasible, yet in the best of situations they are likely to be modest. There is an irreducible error margin that

---

[3]Saul H. Hymans, "Consumer durable spending: Explanation and prediction," *Brookings Papers on Economic Activity* **2** (1970) pp. 173–199.

we shall probably never be able to penetrate. Most of the models discussed in connection with the error statistics in Tables 1 and 2 look fairly similar. No one model dominates in all periods for all variables. Given many uncertainties, we might say that they are all bunched together near what looks like the asymptotic limits of reliability.

At a decade review meeting on the Brookings Econometric Model project, Paul Samuelson suggested the idea that there may be an *uncertainty principle* in economics, establishing an asymptotic limit to attainable precision. His suggestion gives rise to our thinking about why this limit exists, if it does, and about how an *uncertainty principle* is peculiar to economics.

Lack of full reliability of data is one reason why an asymptotic limit to precision may exist. If we are not sure exactly what we are estimating, in numerical terms, and if the degree of unsureness is of the order of magnitude of reported errors, it seems clear that we cannot expect to reduce significantly the errors that we are now making. The size of error cannot be precisely determined if we lack knowledge of the true benchmark magnitudes. There are, however, some pieces of indirect evidence that are strongly indicative of lower bounds to the absolute size of error. For example, the statistical discrepancy between the income and expenditure sides of the NIA measure of aggregate activity should be zero if both income and expenditure items are correctly determined. The discrepancy has reached quarterly absolute values (annual rate) as large as $6.5–7.0 billion. A more usual range would be ± $3.0–5.0 billion. This does not mean that the true value of either national income or national product is incorrectly measured by the full amount of the discrepancy, but I would say that it is fully likely that errors on one side or the other are as large as the maximum discrepancy at some time or other. Another indication is given by the magnitude of the data revisions. An official agency of the U.S. government, using the best techniques, personnel, and facilities, sees fit to revise its estimates of GNP frequently by as much as ± $1.0 billion and occasionally by as much as ± $5.0–7.0 billion.

The statistical discrepancy and the extent of data revisions are, at worst, larger than very short run estimates of error of prediction; therefore, it seems implausible to believe that we can really decrease prediction error by an appreciable amount. It may not even be as small as we think it is, given that it is estimated against an uncertain benchmark. In addition, even if we were able to observe economic phenomena accurately, our models will always only approximate specifications of reality. There will be residual error, distributed with finite variance, and that variance parameter will, in fact, be an objective of estimation. Being a finite variance parameter, it will not vanish with increasing sample size; therefore we can count on imprecision in prediction by at least that amount — Σ in the formula described above for standard error of forecast. As specification of models improves over the years, we may reduce diagonal elements of Σ, but we shall never be able to eliminate them entirely.

The uncertainty principle in physics is different, but some of its consequences are similar. The physical principle concerns uncertainty of measurement (observation). This occurs in the form of a trade-off, reminiscent of the inflation–unemployment trade-off in economics. In physics, it is stated that it is impossible to specify simultaneously both the position and velocity of a particle as accurately as it is wished. One of the two variables may be fixed as accurately as desired, only at the cost of lack of precision in the other.

This is expressed as

$$\Delta x \Delta p_x \geq \frac{h}{4\Pi}$$

where Δx and Δp_x denote uncertainty in x and p_x respectively; and h is a constant.

Since h is small, physical uncertainty may not be a practical matter of concern. This is unlike the situation in economics. Quoting from the *Encyclopedia Britannica*, we read "... if the initial position and velocity are known, together with the forces acting, then a particle's path can be computed for all future time. On the other hand, the uncertainty principle prevents specification of the initial conditions in quantum mechanics, and as a result the future of a particle cannot be definitely predicted. Because of this, the law of cause and effect ceases to apply, though the ambiguity is, of course, important only on the atomic scale."

One is struck by the strong parallel with imprecision in the prediction of paths of economic variables in dynamic systems. The rub is, of course, that our lack of certainty is much more significant and prevails at both the super and atomic levels. Our trade-offs in the economic sphere are not between degrees of precision but between degrees of achievement of goals, precisely or imprecisely measured. In spite of the differences in interpretation, however, the principle of uncertainty is a fruitful concept if only to render us humble in the face of the gigantic task that we undertake in trying to predict human behavior in the economic sphere of life. Today's forecast hero should bear in mind the strong likelihood that his day of reckoning is just around the corner.

21

ECONOMIC FORECASTING
AT HIGH-FREQUENCY INTERVALS[†]

Forecasting on the basis of the daily flow of monthly or more frequent statistical reports on the economy can enhance the predictive accuracy of quarterly structural models. The high degree of serial correlation in economic data can be used advantageously in quarterly forecasting for a horizon as long as 6 months — perhaps somewhat longer. The model used for high-frequency (weekly) forecasting of the U.S. economy has a national accounting structure and tries to follow the choice of indicators that are used in preparing early estimates of national income and product accounts (NIPA). Estimates are separately generated for the income side and the product side of NIPA. At the level of GDP and closely related aggregates a third prediction is also generated from estimates of the principal components of major monthly indicators. A simple average of three estimates of GDP, together with detail on NIPA components and scores of monthly indicators has been produced every weekend, summarizing the business week's flow of information. This procedure is followed not only for producing a steady stream of high-frequency forecasts but also for providing adjustment factors that can be used for model recalibration, without judgemental input. The tracking of the U.S. economy is illustrated for the period starting before the invasion of Kuwait until the end of the Gulf War.

Keywords: High-Frequency Forecasting, The Quarterly National Income and Product Accounts (NIPA), Monthly Economic Indicators, Mixing Frequencies, Combining Forecasts, ARIMA, Box–Jenkins Methods, Transfer Functions, Principal Components, Business Cycles, The 1990–1991 Recession of the U.S.A.

Review of Time Units of Forecasts

Econometric and other statistical techniques of economic forecasting are significantly constrained by data availability. More informal methods, particularly methods that treat individual economic series or relationships without accounting for their interrelatedness, have long used monthly time series and made monthly forecasts. More formal econometric methods that rely on systematic data collection of scores, hundreds, thousands of economic series have usually chosen the "lowest common denominator" (LCD), as far as selection of the basic time unit of observation is concerned.

At the beginning of econometric modeling for forecasting, that LCD choice usually meant that annual data were used, mainly because the principal social accounts — the national income and product accounts (NIPA) — were fully available only at annual intervals. During the late 1950s and early 1960s a number of

---

[†]From *Journal of Forecasting* **12** (1993), pp. 301–319; written jointly with J. Y. Park.

countries, mainly the advanced industrial ones, were able to provide a large base of quarterly data and, particularly, quarterly social accounts.

In those days, low frequency meant annual data and high frequency meant quarterly data. Most, but not all, industrial nations have by now a suitable quarterly data base, and few developing countries, or formerly centrally planned economies, have them. On a world basis, the LCD is annual; and on an OECD basis, it is (practically) quarterly.

The less formal methods and those formal methods that use single or very few equations (such as vector autoregressive systems) have a monthly LCD, at least among industrial countries. The situation is changing rapidly in this "Information Age." We are being deluged with a very large supply of information. It comes to us monthly, weekly, daily, hourly, and in near-continuous *real time*. The highest-frequency information comes from financial and commodity markets, where global trading results are monitored on a 24-hour basis as economic transactions take place. This large information flow is unequal; some data are available at extremely high frequency but others that are vital for an understanding of the total economic picture are not available at a higher frequency than quarterly, and then even with some time delay.

Profits, which are crucial for the understanding of the market economy, are available in the information-oriented U.S. economy only quarterly, and the first estimates (very approximate) only one month later than the other items in the national income and product accounts. Of course, large companies, and others too, report individually on a more prompt schedule, but these results are very "noisy" for formal examination. Countries that have no quarterly, or very delayed reporting of quarterly accounts do provide some indirect pieces of information on, for example, industrial production, crop yields, or international trade more promptly, and these can be used for approximate calculations, but such stratagems are not very satisfactory.

Comprehensive economic forecasts can be reinterpreted, usually on a more accurate basis, as partial information flows become available. These are usually high-frequency flows, and there may also be staggered reporting of fairly low frequency flows, but they do provide useful forecasting information on a rolling basis as the facts become available.

The purpose of the present paper is to analyze how the increasingly informative data flow, with which we are provided on a daily or more frequent interval, can be used to good advantage in economic forecasting. In very practical terms we shall refer to quarterly forecasts, which are now quite common, as low-frequency forecasts and to monthly forecasts as high-frequency ones. The latter may be monthly forecasts of monthly magnitudes or concepts, or they may be monthly restatements of quarterly forecasts (using latest information in the ongoing flow).

The ever-improving and expanding information flow represents a gain that is virtually asking to be exploited by econometricians, but nothing is easily achieved in the field of economic forecasting, and many problems must be faced in the attempt to make scientific progress. In the first place, the higher-frequency data flows (monthly, weekly, daily, etc.) are prone to high serial correlation. This is both a benefit and a cost. High serial correlation provides a basis for extrapolation but it introduces inefficiency in parameter estimates.

A particularly vexing matter that complicates the use of high-frequency information is the accounting for seasonal movements. At the frequency level of annual data analysis, seasonality is not a problem, although it is for semestral and quarterly data. It is even more of a problem at the high-frequency level of monthly, weekly, or daily data because we must deal, for example, with very short-run weather changes that often occur (an unusually severe spell of winter, unusual drought in summer, or sudden storms) and such quirks of the calendar as Easter or long holiday weekends.

A seemingly convenient way to deal with the seasonal problem is to use officially adjusted data. The alternative is to use unadjusted or own-adjusted data. The latter alternative does not seem to be attractive because most governments can put more resources into seasonal measurements than can individual or small team researchers. The use of unadjusted data may seem to be recommended on grounds of purity but the main issue is not how people behave theoretically but how they do, in fact, behave.

It seems much safer to assume that people react to officially cited data and base their decisions on data that are officially adjusted no matter how poor the official adjustment procedure may seem to be in comparison with what one might do with own procedures. Experience seems to support that most explicit seasonal estimates in equations using unadjusted data are either based on very restrictive assumptions or are so heavily parameterized as to be far from actual behavioral choices, so that the preferred procedure would be to use official data, adjusted for seasonal variation.

Some Proposed Approaches

At Wharton Econometrics we used to maintain two separate models of the U.S. economy. One was a quarterly model that focused on short-run dynamics in order to interpret business cycle developments. It was based on data reaching as far back as the 1950s by quarters (seasonally adjusted at annual rates). A second model was annual and was used primarily to interpret medium-term developments, over decades at a time, and also to explore the sectoral composition of output through an integrated input–output system. Both models were in the tradition of the Keynesian–neoclassical synthesis although the latter was several times larger than the former by virtue of the fact that it contained an imbedded input–output model for some 65 sectors of the economy. The distribution of sectoral production across industries was a central feature of the system's output. Both models were built and estimated in the usual way, based on time-series samples, and closely integrated into the country's social accounting system. The first two years of the longer-run industry models were forced to agree, at annual frequencies, with the values estimated by the quarterly model. In this way, high- (quarterly) and low-

(annual) frequency systems were combined, although both systems were similarly estimated. A main objective, however, was to show how quarterly results could be used for short-run guidance of an annual model that was widely used for decade-length projections. After the first 2 or 3 years, the annual model had a life of its own in extrapolation.

When oil shipments were embargoed, during autumn 1973, the annual model, through its input–output module, was used in order to adjust the quarterly model for oil shortfalls (Klein, 1974). This was done because the input–output system had explicit energy sectors, where adjustments could be readily applied on the basis of *a priori* information about the embargo and its effects.

Another approach that is fundamentally quite different was presented by Liu and Hwa (1974). They used an extensive collection of monthly time series in order to interpolate quarterly data from the National Income and Product Accounts into a system of accounting totals at monthly frequencies. They then estimated a monthly macro model for the U.S. economy from the sample of synthetic monthly data.

Most countries do not publish monthly data on national income or product. Canada, for example, is an exception and publishes monthly data on GNP but not on many other entries in the social accounts. The United States produces monthly estimates of consumer spending and personal disposable income, but not monthly GNP. Years ago, statisticians in the Department of Commerce refused to prepare monthly series on GNP for the use of Chairman Arthur Burns of the Federal Reserve System. The Commerce statisticians argued that they could not approve the quality of the monthly series.

The Liu–Hwa model, based on interpolated data, was successful and showed promising predictive power, but it was not maintained after T. C. Liu's death. The Federal Reserve Research Division made analogous interpolations and produced a small monthly econometric model for estimating and predicting monthly GNP (Corrado and Haltmaier, 1988).

T. C. Liu's approach to high-frequency forecasting was through structural analysis, and there is much to be said in favor of this as a fundamental technique that draws heavily on economic analysis for specification of relationships among variables. Its disadvantages are the paucity and imprecision of the underlying data. It must trade off analysis for data quality and work basically with interpolated statistical series.

There are, at least, three other approaches to the problem, all of which are better grounded in the high-frequency data set and which make some use of time series properties of the high-frequency data.

If the economy could be described by a set of linear simultaneous equations, any variable could be expressed in final autoregressive form as

$$y_{it} = f_i\left(y_{i,t-1}, y_{i,t-2}, \ldots, X_{1t}, X_{1,t-1}, X_{1,t-2}, \ldots, X_{mt}, X_{m,t-1}, X_{m,t-2} \ldots\right)$$
$$+ \rho_{i10}e_{1t} + \rho_{i11}e_{1,t-1} + \cdots + \rho_{in0}e_{nt} + \rho_{in1}e_{n,t-1} + \cdots.$$

All lags are finite in this expression and the functions f_i are linear. For the matrix expression of the model, we have

$$A(L)y_t + B(L)X_t = C(L)e_t$$

where L is the time-displacement operator. The final autoregressive form is

$$\|\Delta(L)\|y_t = -a(L)B(L)X_t + a(L)C(L)e_t$$

where

$$a(L) = \text{adjoint of } A(L)$$
$$\Delta(L) = \text{det.} A(L).$$

The vector variables y_t are endogenous; X_t are exogenous; and e_t are random errors.

In a very proximate sense, if we neglect the fact that economic systems are non-linear, neglect the influence of exogenous variables, and neglect the multivariable aspect of the error terms for each y_{it}, we can say that every variable could be empirically estimated by an ARIMA equation. This could also be generalized to a VAR or VARMA system. These are only first approximations, and eventually the systems can incorporate many of the cross-effects from elements of X_t on elements of y_t in transfer function relationships. It should be noted that in a linear system, the autoregressive part is identical for every variable.

The method of high-frequency modeling developed at the University of Michigan starts from the premise that both a VAR time-series model and a quarterly structural model have some distinctive contribution for the explanation of behavior of the economy in the current quarter. Therefore a combination of results from the two systems contains more information than either one alone (Howrey, 1991).

The VAR system, like most other renditions of that form for the macroeconomy, contains some *a priori* restrictions, but these are not closely related to economic analysis. Also, the VAR systems tend to be quite modest in size, i.e., no more than about ten equations. They tend to be highly aggregative.

The University of Pennsylvania approach is different from the others explained so far. It has, however, a time-series aspect. It is based, mainly, on two sets of variables: monthly indicators ($I_{i\tau}$) and quarterly entries in the National Income and Product Accounts (N_{it}) (Klein and Sojo, 1989). The values of $I_{i\tau}$ are estimated from ARIMA equations

$$I_{i\tau} = \sum_{k=1}^{P} \alpha_{ik} I_{i,\tau-k} + \sum_{k=0}^{q} \beta_{ik} e_{i,\tau-k}.$$

Transfer functions and VARMA systems could also be used. The fundamental idea, here, is that careful ARIMA estimates of almost all economic variables generated by a modern market economy exhibit a great deal of serial correlation that comes from the final autoregressive form. As an empirical generalization, we might argue that most, if not all, major economic variables can be projected from fitted ARIMA equations quite well over 6-month horizons. Longer projections tend to build up error and wander from observed data series.

A second set of equations in the Pennsylvania system are called "bridge" equations. They relate items in the NIPA system(N_{it}) to corresponding variables among the indicators. The simplest expression is

$$\ln N_{it} = \alpha_i + \beta_i \ln I_{it} + e_{it}$$

where the I_{it} are obtained from 3-month (quarterly) averages of $I_{i\tau}$.

These "bridge" equations are not simply arbitrary; they adhere as closely as possible to prevailing practice in the actual construction of NIPA systems. For example, if N_{it} represents wage payments to workers in the economy, the statisticians who prepare the NIPA estimates follow monthly figures on average working hours per week, hourly wage rates, and number of workers. Their joint product approximates quite closely the corresponding NIPA items. For nearly every item in the NIPA system reporting, coverage and timing are inexact; therefore the triple product does not precisely generate observations for N_{it}.

We have drawn up a correspondence between monthly indicators series that the NIPA statisticians use in order to create the quarterly accounts, item by item. There are a few items where no specific indicators are used, but in most cases accounting for major NIPA items the indicators are well defined.

The "bridge" equations are not theoretical; they are practical expressions of what is presumably done. These equations are expressed in log–log form, because good indicators should be related to NIPA values with

$$\alpha_i = 0$$
$$\beta_i = 1.0$$

In other words, *percentage* changes in N_{it} should be well estimated by *percentage* changes in I_{it}.

The $I_{i\tau}$ are mainly produced in current prices; therefore current valued NIPA measures are correlated with current valued indicator variables. Similar correspondences between monthly price indexes and quarterly deflators in the NIPA system enable us to estimate real NIPA magnitudes.

A feature of the Pennsylvania high-frequency models is that they follow these procedures for both the expenditure and income sides of the national income and product accounts. We, therefore, generate two values for GNP. At present, we average the totals for the two sides with equal weight. The expenditure side totals are available in both current and constant prices, but the income side totals can be obtained only in current prices. To estimate real GNP from the income side we form

$$\frac{\sum_i N_{it}^{\text{I}}}{\text{PDGNP}_t^{\text{E}}}$$

where $N_{it}^I = i$th income item in national income and $PDGNP_t^{\text{E}}$ = price deflator of *GNP* on the expenditure side.

For the grand total of either side, *GNP*, a third estimate can be made. This is based on such informative monthly aggregates as industrial production, personal income, money stock, new orders, shipments, interest rates, inflation rates, hours worked per week, etc. In many respects these are like the major leading indicators used by the National Bureau of Economic Research and Geoffrey Moore, the colleague of Arthur Burns and Wesley Mitchell. This NBER program was originally presented in Burns and Mitchell (1947).

In a purely empirical approach, real GNP_t is correlated (quarterly) with the most important principal components of total production indicators:

$$\text{GNP}_t = \sum_j \Pi_j^G PC_{jt}^G$$

where PC_{jt}^G is the jth principal component of production indicators. Usually five or six principal components are used in this calculation in order to have 95% of the overall variance accounted for by the reduced set. Each variable is expressed in normalized form:

$$\frac{X_{it} - \bar{X}_i}{\text{SD}(X_{it})}$$

before the principal components are estimated. A similar equation is estimated for

$$\text{PDGNP}_t = \sum_j \Pi_j^P PC_{jt}^P.$$

Two valuable indicator series used by the NBER now, in their experimental index construction, are interest rate spreads:

(1) Long Treasury rate — short Treasury rate;
(2) Private commercial paper rate — short Treasury rate.

The first shows something about the slope of the yield curve, which is very sensitive to the business cycle. The second shows something about risk — the difference between a private market and a sovereign rate. They are both valuable new indicators. Some testing is presently being undertaken at the Pennsylvania group to find some new indicators. It should be pointed out, however, that indicators of the yield curve slope have been in Wharton Econometric Models for more than two decades.

At the most aggregative level, the GNP and overall inflation forecast, for the short run, is thus averaged over three estimates — from the expenditure side, the income side, and principal components of indicators. It should be remembered that the idea of forming principal components of NBER indicators is not new. It has been examined previously as a preferred way of combining diverse pieces of indicator information.

It can be said that the use of time-series methods — formal or informal, as the case may be — is an exercise in "measurement without theory." (For a review of Burns and Mitchell, 1947, see Koopmans, 1947.) Formal time-series methods that are now being intensively pursued supply mathematical statistical theory to cyclical measurement, but they do not supply economic theory. The latter kind is contained in structural models. Of the techniques investigated here, T. C. Liu's and Carol Corrado's methods try to introduce macroeconomic theory into high-frequency analysis.

The most compelling reason for not introducing formal theoretical systems of economic analysis is that the data base is deficient at the high-frequency end of the time spectrum. It is adequate to support pure time-series analysis, but it has to be worked upon; perhaps excessively, in order to provide a statistical sample for formal model construction.

This is a debatable issue. Should one make the main compromises at the data end of the problem or at the theoretical specification end? The Pennsylvania method attempts to find a compromise position. Time-series methods, such as ARIMA estimates, are used, together with principal component and conventional regression methods, but there is not an intensive use of economic theory. There is, however, one branch of economic analysis that is used, namely social accounting. There are many rules and conventions that are specific to social accounting. In addition, we try to follow the good judgements of the NIPA statisticians in determining which high-frequency indicator variables are to be used for the preparation of a well-balanced NIPA system. We must watch not only the specific indicators that the NIPA statisticians have designated but also the implied accounting balances, with special attention to residual entries. Also, the fact that we deal separately with the expenditure side and the income side means that we approach the all-important aggregate measure of activity (GNP or GDP) from two positions. We are keenly aware of the economic concept of "money illusion" in emphasizing the real values and inflation estimates in our results. These matters do not involve deep theory, but they do draw on established economic practice. In this sense, we do not have a case of "measurement without theory."

There is also another sense in which we are being guided by the theory of economic science. We are seeking a method of making objective adjustments to models that will line them up to recent economic facts. If we force the lower-frequency models to line up with the high-frequency indicator-based models we are implicitly choosing a limited number of adjustment factors that successive generations of econometricians could, in principle, also generate. Subjective judgements are eliminated. In effect, a quarterly structural model is forced to have the same strategic values as the *current* (and *next*) *quarter* models. The latter are based on the rapid flow of monthly indicators.

Data are scarce in econometrics, no matter how much we try to get ever-larger samples. The objective of all the methods is to take advantage of the increased amount of high-frequency information in order to improve our forecasting and analytic abilities.

Some Results

It is an objective of present research activities in high-frequency modeling to build an international network of such systems and also to try at all times to introduce more analysis and interrelatedness into the models. Naturally our greatest experience is with the U.S. case. Models have been built, however, for Canada, Japan, and the U.K. A near-term objective is to complete models for all Summit Countries by adding some for Germany, France, and Italy. They all have advanced data bases and can be modeled along the lines outlined above. Other countries have substantial flows of monthly performance characteristics; so they too can be brought into the world study of business cycles by the methods proposed in this paper. Some developing countries as well as smaller developed ones have enough information to carry the work further.

At the international level of analysis some cross-country correlations can be introduced into what are now ARIMA equations. For example, U.S. industrial production could be related with Canadian production of kilowatt hours of electricity and vice versa. International capital flows should correspond, to some extent, with partner countries' trade/payments balances or imbalances. International interest rate spreads can also be used for the estimation of capital flows.

Not only are cross-country relationships to be explored, as we gain more experience with the systems presently in use, but also there can be some interrelationships within the equation system for any one country. Consumer purchases of furniture, furnishings, and appliances should be related to change in housing starts, an important indicator variable for residential construction as it appears on the expenditure side of the NIPA system. There are many such cross-relationships to be explored. In their own way, they bring structure to the systems, and do it at a high-frequency level. There are, however, two specific areas that need further statistical work, namely, to relate actual expenditures and incomes of households to consumer attitudes that are determined monthly in sample surveys. The second cross-correlation concerns business surveys, which can similarly be related to business spending for plant and equipment, hiring, production, and inventory decisions. The household and business surveys are determined monthly, for attitudinal horizons of a few months at a time.

In the United States a special survey made by business purchasing agents is now being examined for relationship to inventory investment and other vexing issues in business behavior. The surveys are subjective and perhaps fickle. Immediately after the victory in the Gulf War by the Coalition Forces in January 1991 consumers expressed very favorable attitudes. The high values in consumer indexes did not lead immediately to high spending at retail. There is information in subjective survey responses, but it is not always firm or lasting.

A further source to be explored in much greater detail is that contained in daily market reports on *futures* prices. The spread between spot and futures prices in relation to stock positions or the explanatory power of futures prices for estimating spot prices should be part of the research program in the very near future, in the interest of improving the systems.

For a few years the U.S. Current Quarter Model has been brought up to date frequently — now practically weekly and certainly on the occasion of a major data release. Not only are the equations extrapolated to fill in the months of the current quarter and to estimate the succeeding quarter, but also the entire set of equations is re-estimated with new data, including both the added observations and revisions of historical series.

Unusual importance is placed on the GNP estimates so the first tables summarize features of these, as well as some closely related aggregates. In addition to GNP, we present

$$\text{Total demand} = C + I + G + X$$
$$= GNP + M \text{ (imports are added back)}$$
$$\text{Domestic demand} = C + I + G$$
$$= GNP + M - X \text{ (exports are subtracted)}$$
$$\text{Domestic final demand} = C + I + G - \Delta H \text{ (inventory change is subtracted)}$$

keeping in mind the identity

$$GNP = C + I + G + X - M$$

where

C = consumer expenditures,
I = gross investment,
G = government expenditures,
X = exports,
M = imports, and
ΔH = inventory change.

Total demand was first considered after Iraq's invasion of Kuwait in August 1990 because it was felt that oil prices reflected in import valuation did not correspond with those charged in spending by consumers, businesses, or government. Domestic demand is interesting in its own right, especially when the U.S. economy is out of business cycle phase with other major economies. Final sales are often considered by subtracting inventory change from GNP. In the present context, the change in inventories is taken from domestic demand rather than total GNP. Although the alternative aggregative concepts were introduced in order to provide a different picture of the overall economy after the disruptions in the Gulf. It has been thought that they are useful and informative; so they are being retained at present.

On the first page of the U.S. report, timing is provided for the data of the latest new releases being incorporated. There is also a running history of previous forecasts, week by week. Similar results are given for total demand and domestic demand. GNP and the two aggregate demand concepts are then averaged — in real terms, by deflator, and in nominal terms; always keeping in mind the identity

$$GNP * PGNP = GNP\$$$

price $*$ quantity $=$ value

The various components of real GNP, the components of nominal GNP, and thus deflators, follow, for the expenditure side of NIPA. Finally, nominal accounts are presented for GNP from the income side. The first three columns, by quarters, present historical observations, while the next two columns present forecasts. In the case of the current quarter some monthly observations are known, on a preliminary basis, before the quarter is over. Thus tables are completed by the monthly indicators used. Entries to the left of bold vertical lines are latest reported observations.

There is much to digest in a complete report, but a pictorial view shows how the projections for GNP and the deflators have evolved, in the aggregate. These are presented in Appendix 1.

A case study: U.S. forecasts of the business cycle phases 1990–91

For some time, the techniques explained in this paper have been used for actual forecasting exercises. As software and data management techniques improve, it has been found possible to make frequent forecasts when new information becomes available, and, as noted in the previous section, updated forecasts are made weekly. Prior to the onset of the Gulf crisis and the invasion of Kuwait, several forecasts were made — not yet weekly — and all during the war and its aftermath weekly reports were issued.

Since there is some substantive question about the nature of the 1990–91 recession concerning its possible unusual characteristics and since there is some doubt whether the extrapolative time-series techniques can pick up the influence of strong exogenous disturbances, it is useful to trace the forecast history and interpret the model's message at each of several stages of this cyclical process.

Did the Gulf crisis cause the recession in the United States? Could public authorities have used monetary policy to prevent the recession if Iraq's invasion of Kuwait had not occurred? Will the recovery be "normal" or will it be temporary and turn into an early secondary recession? These are all points of great substantive interest. Also, during the recession, many people asked whether a deep depression was about to occur.

As early as August 1990 the model showed a definite slowing of the American economy, with practically zero growth in the third quarter of 1990. By September 1990 it was projecting, negative change in real GNP for 1990Q4. During October and November the model projections fluctuated between 0% and 1.4%, but at the beginning of December they turned decisively negative. Members of the cycle-dating committee of the National Bureau of Economic Research, the unofficial arbiters, declared almost 5 months later, on 25 April 1991, that the downturn started in

July 1990. Thus, as far as GNP measurements are concerned, the model stated several months earlier than the NBER committee that real growth was positive in the third quarter and negative in the fourth quarter. In July 1992, revisions of estimated GDP indicated a decline from the second to the third quarter, 1990. That implies a peak during July, August, and September, which is consistent with the NBER decision, but the model's results for many other variables, together with GNP, correctly indicated a turning point much earlier than mid-quarter. It should be noted that some members of the NBER committee implied, individually, that a summer peak would be the current date. Both this kind of information and the model's results indicate that the recession began before the invasion of Kuwait. The model's projections for earlier quarters showed that the turning point was being approached in the months of the second quarter; so a great deal of business cycle information was being generated by the model, and this information was not directly related to the Gulf crisis.

In retrospect, the early period of the conflict brought uncertainty, higher energy prices, and fear of inflation. These events reacted adversely on financial markets and probably made the recession that had already begun rather worse than it might have been. The early period was followed by mobilization, deployment, and current defence spending that has always brought some form of economic stimulus to the United States. It was "military" Keynesianism. After the Allies' victory, there was a resurgence of confidence, a complete abandonment of uncertainty, large transfers from abroad to cover the actual war outlays; yet the recession continued to run its course in the usual way. After slightly less than one year, production gained; employment turned up; retail sales started to recover; and the normal process of recovery got under way. The Gulf crisis was a "wash" event. There were a few months on the negative side, followed by a few on the positive side. The recession was not unusual. It was affected by the crisis but not caused by it.

The model projected the first negative movement of quarterly output before it occurred and before it was first reported (late January 1991). It projected positive change in output for the second quarter of 1991Q2 around the middle of May before any dating by the NBER, reports of second-quarter GNP, or before talk of prolonged, "double-dip" or anaemic recovery had ceased.

As high-frequency reports became available, often in both favorable and unfavorable directions, the model served as an informative filter that charted the near-term development of the economy in a useful way.

It is interesting to examine the flow of information about inflation. As always, many factors were at work, but the predominant influence was the volatility of the price of crude oil. It went very high in August and September 1990 after the invasion of Kuwait. The model had no inkling of this movement, but daily spot and futures prices showed developments without delay. Since the model does not translate inflationary price movements instantaneously after a sudden shock and since it does not have cross-effects from structural demand and supply equations, it is interesting to see how the high oil prices and resulting high overall price indexes (producer and consumer price indexes) interpreted economic dynamics during August, September, and October, 1990.

The mathematical and statistical structure of the model reveals the high *positive* serial correlation that is found in most, but not all, economic series. Inventory investment frequently shows *negative* serial correlation, and this is quite understandable, but inflation tends to have strong positive serial patterns. As soon as the speculators drove up crude oil prices in August 1990, the sensitive components of the producer and consumer price indexes (PPI and CPI) quickly reflected the increases. Therefore with one or, at most, two months' delay the ARIMA equations for oil-sensitive prices began to drive up inflation rates. The high prices for consumer expenditures on oil, coal, and gas induced lower outlays, and this was observable in model performance. There was a short delay, in this case only one month, and then the external disturbance was in the model contributing to a more intense economic contraction than had been building up naturally. The higher the frequency of information used, the sooner will shock effects be revealed; that is how model performance can be improved in the information age, provided such allowance is built into model specification. Personal judgement of model builders is not involved, merely the readings of the market.

New Directions

Experience with the Pennsylvania and other approaches to the use of high-frequency data in forecasting economic tendencies is promising but far from leading to the full potential of this line of research. There are new data to be explored, new model specifications, some of which have already been discussed, and new techniques to be used.

A particular source of data that merits considerable research are the futures markets. These exist mainly for key primary commodities, where functioning markets for futures already exist. These data are for prices and volumes of futures contracts. They are already widely used by people who make transactions in these markets but are mainly confined to judgements about trading in specific commodities. In the Gulf conflict it was seen how trading in the oil market had a total economy effect. If the oil price equation of the model were to be based, in part, on the futures price, there would be virtually no delay in feeding information about unusual price movements into the price equation with system-wide effects. What is true about the oil market is also potentially the case for food, feed, fibre, metal, other fuels, other industrial materials. Price movements in these commodities are useful early warning indicators in their own right, but they are also useful for predicting movements in some more general price indexes.

An interesting equation which has been examined recently is

$$\Delta \ln P_{st} = \alpha + \beta \Delta \ln P_{f,t-k} + \gamma S_{t-k} + e_t$$

where

P_{st} = spot price,

$P_{f,t-k}$ = futures price for a contract expiring at t but reported k time units in advance, and

S_{t-k} = inventory position at $t - k$.

This model performed well for the crude oil market but could be studied for many others as well. The precise specification in first differences of logarithms is only suggestive; other specifications could also be examined, with various transformations of inventory data possible. This equation goes beyond pure ARIMA treatment for indicator variables and introduces more economic analysis. One can go a step further, and use futures market information to get a better estimate of inventory behavior. One of the weakest components of all economic models with short-run business-cycle content are the inventory relationship. Therefore more work on this item is suggested, and futures markets may turn out to be quite helpful.

In many respects, futures markets serve as indicators of *expectations*, which have always been important for business cycle analysis. Another source for information on expectations are readings of consumer and producer responses from sample surveys. An index of consumer sentiment is a component of the U.S. index of leading economic indicators. It also is used as an (endogenous) variable in some macroeconometric models.

Consumer expectations surveys have a long history in the United States, going back at least 50 years, but the country has lagged behind Europe in the development of surveys on business expectations, especially on a replicated and fully representative basis. A survey that has been watched for a long time but is not adequately represented in formal models is the survey conducted monthly by the National Association of Purchasing Management mentioned earlier in this paper. This provides anticipatory information in the form of a diffusion index, on many items of business decision making — inventories, production, shipments, sales, employment, etc. It can help to improve upon the ARIMA equations in various parts of the high-frequency model, particularly in the case of inventory investment (see Appendix 2).

Another direction for model research, already mentioned, is in the international treatment of high-frequency data. Since models are now available for a few countries, with more to come, it is worth considering cross-country relationships. This, too, should improve upon the ARIMA equations for indicators. At high frequency, the most evident cross-country relationships to consider are those in the financial sector, where information and reaction flows occur almost continuously in real time. This is equally true of basic commodity markets and trading in futures contracts.

One methodological procedure, which has long been researched in connection with analysis of macroeconometric models, is the use of stochastic simulation for the purpose of constructing probability-based confidence intervals for forecasts. The random errors in both the indicator equations and the bridge equations for the

Pennsylvania Model can be generated under the constraint of estimated parameter values of well-known distribution functions. Distributions of forecasts can be used for the numerical estimation of probability values associated with forecasts. This can add a fresh dimension to the business-cycle analysis of high-frequency modeling and forecasting.

Appendix 1: U.S. Current Quarter Model: Forecast Summary

How to interpret the graphs

Currently, forecasts from the U.S. Current Quarter Model are updated on a weekly basis. The following two graphs (Figs. 1 and 2) trace Real GNP growth rates and inflation rates of the GNP deflator from the weekly forecasts. The horizontal axis of the graph is the date on which a forecast is estimated and the vertical axis is the percentage (%) change of seasonally adjusted annual growth rates. Starting points of arrows in the graphs indicate the current quarter while ending points indicate the next quarter. The horizontal length of arrows indicates one quarter. Therefore arrow movements are expected to show continuous information flows on the economy through changes in various monthly economic and financial indicators.

Recall that the first release of quarterly figures on the National Income and Product Accounts (NIPA) is available 3 weeks after the end of that quarter. Jumps between arrows represent data revisions of the successive quarterly releases or movements of the current quarter to the next quarter due to the NIPA data release for the current quarter.

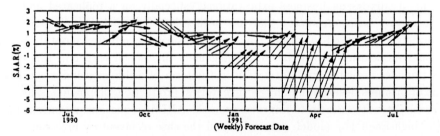

Fig. 1. Forecasted growth rates of real GNP.

(University of Pennsylvania Current Quarter Model for the U.S.)

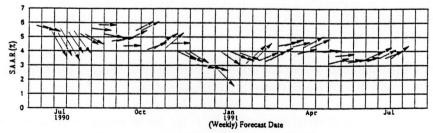

Fig. 2. Forecasted inflation rates — GNP deflator.

(University of Pennsylvania Current Quarter Model for the U.S.)

Forecast summary

This forecast incorporates the following National Income and Product Accounts:

GNP   (1)Q   2nd
Personal Income and Outlays   (4)M   −1M

The forecast adds additional information on the following monthly economic indicators to the most recent previous forecast:

Mfgs. Ships, Inv, and Orders	( )M	−2M	5/31
New Construction	( )M	−2M	6/03
Employment	( )M	−1M	6/07
Comsumer Instalment Credit	( )M	−2	6/07
Producer Price Index	( )M	−1M	6/13
Retail Sales	( )M	−1M	6/13
Consumer Price Index	( )M	−1M	6/14
Industrial Production Index	( )M	−M	6/14
Trade Inventories	( )M	−2	6/15
Housing Starts	(5)M	−1M	6/18
International Merchandise Trade	(4)M	−2M	6/19
Export/Import Trade Index	( )M	−1M	6/27

The forecasts from the Current Quarter Model for the U.S. record the following growth rates of Real GNP (RGNP) and GNP Deflator (PGNP):

	1990Q4		1991Q1		1991Q2		1991Q3		
	RGNP	PGNP	RGNP	PGNP	RGNP	PGNP	RGNP	PGNP	
JAN04	−2.22	4.05	−0.51	−3.47]					
JAN14	−2.24	3.97	−0.52	3.34	0.65	3.98			
JAN17	−2.52	3.93	−0.53	3.42	0.43	4.33			
JAN23	−2.37	3.88	−0.57	3.43	0.42	4.44			
JAN29	[−2.13	2.75]	0.79	3.18	0.56	4.44			⇐1st 90Q4
FEB04			0.68	3.25	0.63	4.60			
FEB11			−0.18	3.29	0.91	3.93			
FEB19			−1.14	3.26	1.18	4.08			
FEB25			−1.27	3.44	1.06	4.27			
MAR04	[−1.95	2.75]	−4.52	4.36	0.65	4.71			⇐2nd 90Q4
MAR11			−4.43	4.41	0.75	4.82			
MAR18			−4.47	4.29	0.11	4.67			
MAR25			−4.13	3.84	0.58	4.16			
APR01	[−1.58	2.75]	−5.03	4.29	−0.65	5.04			⇐3rd 90Q4
APR08			−5.23	4.23	−0.99	4.89			
APR15			−4.93	4.05	−0.12	4.09			
APR22			−4.65	3.95	−0.13	4.06			
APR30			[−2.81	5.52]	−0.47	3.16	0.46	3.50	⇐1st 91Q1

MAY06	−0.45	3.66	0.44	3.77		
MAY13	−0.26	3.34	0.81	3.46		
MAY20	0.07	3.24	0.97	3.42		
MAY30	[−2.57	5.21]	0.11	3.34	0.78	3.58	⇐ 2nd 91Q1
JUN10	0.09	3.49	1.14	4.00		
JUN17	0.21	3.47	1.26	4.20		
JUN24	0.24	3.48	1.38	4.16		

Forecasted growth rates of Real Total Demand (RTD) and TD Deflator (PTD):

2	1990Q4		1991Q1		1991Q2		1991Q3		Official release
	RTD	PTD	RTD	PTD	RTD	PTD	RTD	PTD	
JAN23	−2.10	5.26	−0.40	3.27					
JAN29	[−2.73	5.06]	1.02	2.94	0.97	4.01			⇐ 1st 90Q4
FEB04			0.88	2.99	1.04	4.01			
FEB11			0.06	3.03	1.25	3.60			
FEB19			−1.22	3.01	1.35	3.76			
FEB25			−1.35	3.19	1.24	3.93			
MAR04	[−3.07	4.78]	−3.78	3.28	1.15	3.97			⇐ 2nd 90Q4
MAR11			−3.74	3.33	1.21	4.06			
MAR18			−4.05	3.16	0.63	3.85			
MAR25			−3.69	2.81	1.05	3.41			
APR01	[−3.07	4.83]	−4.14	2.64	0.61	3.38			⇐ 3rd 90Q4
APR08			−4.32	2.59	0.27	3.25			
APR 15			−3.94	2.40	1.15	2.36			
APR22			−4.46	2.46	1.03	2.38			
APR29			[−3.38	3.07]	0.32	2.10	0.81	3.09	⇐ 1st 91Q1
MAY06					0.24	2.53	0.79	3.32	
MAY13					0.41	2.24	1.12	3.04	
MAY20					0.29	2.33	1.10	3.22	
MAY30			[−3.80	2.83]	0.40	2.37	0.93	3.33	⇐ 2nd 91Q1
JUN10					0.39	2.50	1.26	3.74	
JUN17					0.50	2.49	1.38	3.88	
JUN24			1.32	2.33	1.39	3.86			

Forecasted growth rates of Real Domestic demand (RDD) and DD Deflator (PDD):

	1990Q4		1991Q1		1991Q2		1991Q3		Official release
	RDD	PDD	RDD	PDD	RDD	PDD	RDD	PDD	
JAN23	−3.42	5.66	−0.59	3.45					
JAN29	[−4.23	5.84]	1.08	2.50	0.89	4.18			⇐ 1st 90Q4
FEB04			0.73	3.20	0.98	4.25			
FEB11			−0.24	3.22	1.23	3.77			
FEB19			−1.35	3.19	1.39	3.93			
FEB25			−1.48	3.37	1.27	4.11			

MAR04	[−4.52	5.31]	−4.06	3.54	1.22	4.15			⇐ 2nd 90Q4
MAR11			−3.94	3.58	1.33	4.24			
MAR18			−4.16	3.42	0.80	4.06			
MAR25			−4.22	3.13	1.19	3.58			
APR01	[−5.05	5.34]	−4.84	2.96	0.71	3.57			⇐ 3rd 90Q4
APR08			−4.94	2.92	0.49	3.44			
APR15			−4.51	2.72	1.57	2.56			
APR22			−4.72	2.73	1.55	2.56			
APR29			[−3.84	3.88]	0.81	2.19	0.77	3.32	⇐ 1st 91Q1
MAY06					0.70	2.61	0.74	3.55	
MAY13					0.91	2.28	1.12	3.23	
MAY20					0.95	2.29	1.02	3.34	
MAY30			[−3.98	3.66]	0.91	2.39	0.86	3.47	⇐ 2nd 91 Q1
JUN10					0.99	2.50	1.24	3.83	
JUN17					1.13	2.48	1.39	4.02	
JUN24					1.09	2.49	1.31	4.02	

Forecast summary: gross national product (billions of dollars, SAAR)

	1990Q3	1990Q4	1991Q1	1991Q2	1991Q3
Real GNP					
(i) Expenditure Side GNP	4170.0	4153.4	4126.5	4137.0	4172.0
% Previous Q, AR	1.44	−1.58	−2.57	1.03	3.43
% Year before	0.98	0.49	−0.58	−0.43	0.05
(ii) Income Side GNP	4170.0	4153.4	4126.5	4116.9	4115.6
% Previous Q, AR	1.44	−1.58	−2.57	−0.92	−0.13
% Year before	0.98	0.49	−0.58	−0.92	−1.31
(iii) Principal Components est. GNP	4170.0	4153.4	4126.5	4132.9	4141.7
% Previous Q, AR	1.44	−1.58	−2.57	0.62	0.86
% Year before	0.98	0.49	−0.58	−0.53	−0.68
Average Real GNP	4170.0	4153.4	4126.5	4128.9	4143.1
% Previous Q, AR	1.44	−1.58	−2.57	0.24	1.38
% Year before	0.98	0.49	−0.58	−0.63	−0.64
GNP Deflator (1982 = 100)					
(i) Expenditure Side PGNP	132.2	133.1	134.8	135.9	137.1
% Previous Q, AR	3.71	2.75	5.21	3.28	3.75
% Year before	4.26	3.98	4.09	3.73	3.74
(ii) Income Side PGNP: Same as (i)	132.2	133.1	134.8	135.9	137.1
% Previous Q, AR	3.71	2.75	5.21	3.28	3.75
% Year before	4.26	3.98	4.09	3.73	3.74
(iii) Principal components est. PGNP	132.2	133.1	134.8	136.1	137.8
% Previous Q, AR	3.71	2.75	5.21	3.88	4.98
% Year before	4.26	3.98	4.09	3.88	4.20

Average GNP Deflator	132.2	133.1	134.8	136.0	137.3
% Previous Q, AR	3.71	2.75	5.21	3.48	4.16
% Year before	4.26	3.98	4.09	3.78	3.90
Nominal GNP					
(i) Expenditure Side GNP$	5514.6	5527.3	5561.7	5621.9	5721.9
% Previous Q, AR	5.34	0.92	2.51	4.40	7.31
% Year before	5.27	4.50	3.47	3.28	3.76
(ii) Income Side GNP$	5514.6	5527.3	5561.7	5594.6	5644.4
% Previous Q, AR	5.34	0.92	2.51	2.39	3.61
% Year before	5.27	4.50	3.47	2.78	2.35
(iii) Principal Compo. est.GNP$	5514.6	5527.3	5561.7	5624.3	5705.3
% Previous Q, AR	5.34	0.92	2.51	4.58	5.88
% Year before	5.27	4.50	3.47	3.33	3.46
Average Nominal GNP	5514.6	5527.3	5561.7	5613.6	5690.5
% Previous Q, AR	5.34	0.92	2.51	3.79	5.59
% Year before	5.27	4.50	3.47	3.13	3.19

Forecast summary: total demand $(C + I + G + X)$ (billions of dollars, SAAR)

	1990Q3	1990Q4	1991Q1	1991Q2	1991Q3
Real TOTAL DEMAND (TD)					
(i) Expenditure Side TD	4847.0	4809.4	4763.1	4793.1	4830.9
% Previous Q, AR	2.28	−3.07	−3.80	2.55	3.19
% Year before	1.27	0.35	−1.06	−0.55	−0.33
(ii) Income Side TD	4847.0	4809.4	4763.1	4772.4	4772.6
% Previous Q, AR	2.28	−3.07	−3.80	0.78	0.02
% Year before	1.27	0.35	−1.06	−0.98	−1.53
(iii) Principal Components est. TD	4847.0	4809.4	4763.1	4770.5	4782.0
% Previous Q, AR	2.28	−3.07	−3.80	0.63	0.97
% Year before	1.27	0.35	−1.06	−1.02	−1.34
Average Real TOTAL DEMAND	4847.0	4809.4	4763.1	4778.7	4795.2
% Previous Q, AR	2.28	−3.07	−3.80	1.32	1.39
% Year before	1.27	0.35	−1.06	−0.85	−1.07
TD Deflator (PTD, 1982 = 100)					
(i) Expenditure Side PTD	128.5	130.0	130.9	131.6	132.8
% Previous Q, AR	14.35	4.83	2.86	2.06	3.50
% Year before	4.04	4.43	3.91	3.52	3.31
(ii) Income Side PTD: Same as (i)	128.5	130.0	130.9	131.6	132.8
% Previous Q, AR	4.35	4.83	2.86	2.06	3.50
% Year before	4.04	4.43	3.91	3.52	3.31
(iii) Principal Components est. PTD	128.5	130.0	130.9	131.9	133.4
% Previous Q, AR	4.35	4.83	2.86	2.88	4.58
% Year before	4.04	4.43	3.91	3.73	3.78

Average TOTAL DEMAND Deflator	128.5	130.0	130.9	131.7	133.0
% Previous Q, AR	4.35	4.83	2.86	2.33	3.86
% Year before	4.04	4.43	3.91	3.59	3.47

Nominal TOTAL DEMAND (TD$)

(i) Expenditure Side TD$	6228.6	6253.5	6237.1	6308.5	6413.3
% Previous Q, AR	6.73	1.61	−1.05	4.66	6.81
% Year before	5.36	4.80	2.80	2.95	2.97
(ii) Income Side TD$	6228.6	6253.5	6237.1	6281.2	6335.8
% Previous Q, AR	6.73	1.61	−1.05	2.86	3.52
% Year before	5.36	4.80	2.80	2.50	1.72
(iii) Principal Compo. est. TD$	6228.6	6253.5	6237.1	6291.4	6377.5
% Previous Q, AR	6.73	1.61	−1.05	3.53	5.59
% Year before	5.36	4.80	2.80	2.67	2.39
Average Nominal TOTAL DEMAND	6228.6	6253.5	6237.1	6293.7	6375.5
% Previous Q, AR	6.73	1.61	−1.05	3.68	5.30
% Year before	5.36	4.80	2.80	2.70	2.36

Forecast summary: domestic demand $(C + I + G)$ (billions of dollars, SAAR)

	1990Q3	1990Q4	1991Q1	1991Q2	1991Q3
Real DOMESTIC DEMAND (DD)					
(i) Expenditure Side DD	4216.5	4162.2	4120.0	4139.6	4173.0
% Previous Q, AR	1.61	−5.05	−3.98	1.91	3.26
% Year before	0.54	−0.45	−1.57	−1.43	−1.03
(ii) Income Side DD	4216.5	4162.2	4120.1	4119.4	4116.3
% Previous Q, AR	1.61	−5.05	−3.98	−0.06	−0.31
% Year before	0.54	−0.45	−1.57	−1.91	−2.38
(iii) Principal Components est. DD	4216.5	4162.2	4120.1	4134.7	4145.1
% Previous Q, AR	1.61	−5.05	−3.98	1.43	1.00
% Year before	0.54	−0.45	−1.57	−1.55	−1.69
Average Real DOMESTIC DEMAND	4216.5	4162.2	4120.1	4131.3	4144.8
% Previous Q, AR	1.61	−5.05	−3.98	1.09	1.31
% Year before	0.54	−0.45	−1.57	−1.63	−1.70
DD Deflator (PDD, 1982 = 100)					
(i) Expenditure Side PDD	131.8	133.5	134.7	135.4	136.6
% Previous Q, AR	4.87	5.34	3.66	2.08	3.62
% Year before	4.50	4.82	4.31	3.98	3.67
(ii) Income Side PDD: Same as (i)	131.8	133.5	134.7	135.4	136.6
% Previous Q, AR	4.87	5.34	3.66	2.08	3.62
% Year before	4.50	4.82	4.31	3.98	3.67
(iii) Principal Components est. PDD	131.8	133.5	134.7	135.8	137.4
% Previous Q, AR	4.87	5.34	3.66	3.30	4.82
% Year before	4.50	4.82	4.31	4.29	4.28

Average DOMESTIC DEMAND Deflator	131.8	133.5	134.7	135.5	136.9
% Previous Q, AR		4.87	5.34	3.66	2.49	4.02
% Year before		4.50	4.82	4.31	4.08	3.87
Nominal DOMESTIC DEMAND (DD$)					
(i) Expenditure Side DD$		5555.9	5556.1	5549.6	5604.7	5700.3
% Previous Q, AR		6.56	0.02	−0.47	4.03	7.00
% Year before		5.07	4.35	2.66	2.49	2.60
(ii) Income Side DD$		5555.9	5556.1	5549.1	5577.3	5622.8
% Previous Q, AR		6.56	0.02	−0.47	2.02	3.30
% Year before		5.07	4.35	2.66	1.99	1.20
(iii) Principal Compo. est. DD$		5555.9	5556.1	5549.6	5614.7	5695.4
% Previous Q, AR		6.56	0.02	−0.47	4.78	5.87
% Year before		5.07	4.35	2.66	2.68	2.51
Average Nominal DOMESTIC DEMAND		5555.9	5556.1	5549.6	5598.9	5672.8
% Previous Q, AR		6.56	0.02	−0.47	3.60	5.39
% Year before		5.07	4.35	2.66	2.39	2.11

Appendix 2: Inventory Estimators Using Sample Survey Resources by the National Association of Purchasing Managers

The NAPM's inventories index has been recently examined and added to the ARIMA model of manufacturing inventories as a predictor series by using a transfer function that specifies the relationship between the predictor series and the output series. The monthly level of manufacturing inventories as the output series is given as:

$$\bar{I}_{\text{inv},\tau} = \frac{U(L)}{S(L)} \bar{I}_{\text{NAPM},\tau-b} + N_\tau$$

where $\bar{I}_{\text{NAPM}}$ is the pre-whitened NAPM inventories index and $\bar{I}_{\text{inv}}$ is the pre-whitened level of manufacturing inventories of the Department of Commerce, $U(L)/S(L)$ is the transfer function, b is the number of periods of time delay between $\bar{I}_{\text{NAPM}}$ and its predictive effect on $\bar{I}_{\text{inv}}$ and N_τ is any noise process (including an ARIMA model).

Based on the data for the period, 1982Q1 through 1991Q4, the final model was estimated to be:

$$(1 - 0.262\ L^1 - 0.267\ L^2)\bar{I}_{\text{inv},\tau} = -7.469 + (0.091 - (0.87L^2)\ \bar{I}_{\text{NAPM},\tau-1} \quad (1)$$
$$(0.096) \qquad (0.097) \qquad\qquad (1.800) \quad (0.036) \qquad (0.036)$$

$$+ (1 + 0.200L^6)e_\tau \qquad\qquad\qquad (2)$$
$$(0.105)$$

where standard errors are given in parentheses.

Both I_{inv} and I_{NAPM} were pre-whitened by the filter with an autoregressive factor of $(1 - 0.16838L^1)$ and a moving-average factor of $(1 - 0.206L^6)$. The delay parameter is estimated to be 1, which is consistent with the 5 weeks' delay in the data release of manufacturing inventories.

All parameter estimates are significant and the residuals of the model are not different from white noise. The SEE of 1.261 is less than the pure ARIMA value of 1.304 and the Akaike's information criterion (AIC) is reduced to 365.83 from 378.01. Our introduction of the National Association of Purchasing Management (NAPM's) inventory survey as the predictor series appears to show promise for enhancing the estimates of the quantity data on manufacturing inventories of the Department of Commerce.

References

Burns, A. F. and W. C. Mitchell, 1947, *Measuring Business Cycles* (National Bureau of Economic Research, New York).

Corrado, C. and J. Haltmaier, 1988, "The use of high-frequency data in model-based forecasting at the Federal Reserve Board," Finance and Economic Discussion Series, 24.

Howrey E. P., 1991, "New methods for using monthly data to improve forecast accuracy," in *Comparative Performance of U.S. Econometric Models*, ed. L. R. Klein (Oxford University Press, New York), pp. 227–249.

Klein, L. R., 1974 "Supply constraints in demand oriented systems: an interpretation of the oil crisis," *Zeitschrift für Nationalökonomie* **34**, pp. 45–56.

——— and E. Sojo, 1989, "Combinations of high and low frequency data in macroeconometric models," *Economics in Theory and Practice: An Eclectic Approach*, eds. L. R. Klein and J. Marquez (Kluwer, Dordrecht) pp. 3–16.

Koopmans, T. C., 1947, "Measurement without theory," *Review of Economics and Statistics* **29** (August), pp. 161–172.

Liu, T. C. and E. C. Hwa, 1974, "A monthly model of the U.S. economy," *International Economic Review* **15**, pp. 328–365.

22

ECONOMIC FORECASTING AND
DECISION-MAKING UNDER UNCERTAINTY[†]

Introduction — Errors and their Sources

Decision-makers in private firms or households and in public office must realize that a great deal of uncertainty accompanies many of their future commitments. All too often people act as though present or recently discernible conditions will prevail endlessly, and that is hardly ever the case. Often businessmen blame failed strategies on some stage or other of the trade cycle, but they should know that cycle phases have come and gone for at least two centuries. In the energy field, people acted in the 1950s as though oil would remain plentiful and cheap for ever; then in the 1970s and 1980s many people were trapped by their assumptions that prices would rise forever.

Birth rates, spending patterns, investment needs, and many other aspects of modern economic life, are always undergoing change. When important decisions are being made, it is unavoidable to try to take future change into account if intelligent decisions are to be made. Sometimes, the decision-maker is lucky enough to have some flexibility or room to maneuver and correct mistakes in mid-course, but even then account must be taken of possibilities that can occur in the next stage.

Like it or not, decision-makers must forecast, and attempts to look into the future are error prone. In this opening section, an attempt will be made to lay out the sources of error in order to gain enough understanding to guide decision making under uncertainty.

In order to point out the sources of error, it is useful to show the model that is being used:

$$F(\mathbf{y'_t}, \ldots, \mathbf{y'_{t-p}}, \mathbf{x'_t}, \ldots, \mathbf{x'_{t-q}}, \Theta') = \mathbf{e_t} , \tag{9.1}$$

or, in explicit reduced form:

$$\mathbf{y_t} = G(\mathbf{y'_{t-1}}, \ldots, \mathbf{y'_{t-p}}, \mathbf{x'_t}, \ldots, \mathbf{x'_{t-q}}, \Theta', \mathbf{e_t}) \tag{9.2}$$

where:

y_t is an n-element column vector of dependent variables
x_t is an m-element column vector of independent variables
Θ is an r-element column vector of parameters
e_t is an n-element column vector of errors.

[†]From *Money, Inflation, and Employment, Essays in Honor of James Ball*, ed. S. Holly (Edward Elgar, Aldershot, England, 1994), pp. 183–193.

$$F = \begin{pmatrix} f_1 \\ f_2 \\ \vdots \\ f_n \end{pmatrix} \qquad G = \begin{pmatrix} g_1 \\ g_2 \\ \vdots \\ g_n \end{pmatrix}.$$

If all $f_i(i = 1, 2, \ldots, n)$ are linear, then the g_i functions will be linear with additive errors that are linear combinations of the elements of $\mathbf{e_t}(e_{1t}, e_{2t}, \ldots, e_{nt})$.

Forecasts from this system are error-prone for four reasons:

1. Random errors, $\mathbf{e_t}$, are always disturbing the system; they are not observed, but properties of their probability distribution are estimated, and their mean value (zero) is customarily used for forecasts. If the zero-mean is not used, some other value is assigned, and may not be correct. (It *will not*, in general, be correct.)
2. The parameters are not observed and estimates are used. These estimates are based on a sample and are subject to sampling error.
3. In order to compute elements of $\mathbf{y_t}$ from Eq. (9.2), input values must be used. These are initial conditions for $\mathbf{y_{t-1}, y_{t-2}, \ldots, y_{t-p}}$ and values for the independent variables $\mathbf{x_t, \ldots, x_{t-q}}$. Economic data are always imperfectly observed; so there are errors of observation for both historical values of $\mathbf{y_t}$ and $\mathbf{x_t}$ and values for $\mathbf{x_t}$ in the projection period.
4. The model may be misspecified.

Not knowing the population distribution from which the $\mathbf{e_t}$ were drawn (by 'NATURE'), econometricians usually assume that they are distributed according to a multivariate normal distribution. This is not a bad assumption, but it need not be correct. The problem can be dealt with if the $\mathbf{e_t}$ are generated by another distribution, provided it is known — up to particular values. The latter can be estimated. In the case of the normal distribution, with zero mean, the investigator must estimate the variance–covariance error of the joint distribution of $\mathbf{e_t}$, over the sample. In practice, these are the statistics that are needed. If (9.1) is linear and $\mathbf{e_t}$ is normal, then the error term for (9.2) will be an additive linear combination of $\mathbf{e_t}$. Its variance–covariance matrix will be made up of terms that are linear combinations of terms in the variance–covariance matrix of $\mathbf{e_t}$.

In large samples, the normality assumptions ought to provide good approximations, but in small samples the estimation of contributions to forecast error from the $\mathbf{e_t}$ must be tailored to the particular distribution that is relevant.

In a linear system, the estimates of Θ, denoted as $\hat{\Theta}$, will be linear functions of the errors $\mathbf{e_t}$. The normal distribution has reproductive properties; so the sampling distribution of $\hat{\Theta}$ will also be normal. Again, in large samples, the assumption of normality for $\hat{\Theta}$ will be plausible. For small samples, the distribution of $\hat{\Theta}$ will be functions of the distribution of $\mathbf{e_t}$. There are formulae that can be used for the evaluation of functions of random variables.

The econometrician never knows the true values for initial conditions or for independent variables in the projection period. Economic data get revised for years and years, decades and decades. Presumably, after a few rounds of revisions, estimated values for these variables should improve, but they are never completely correct. This is especially true for the macroeconomy or aggregated markets. Occasionally revisions may be as large as 10 or 20 per cent, but usually, in the industrial world, they are no more than about 5 per cent. For developing countries and for world totals, the revisions are often large. The degree of revision tells us something about departures from true values, but they rarely tell us the exact amount of the discrepancy. We therefore do not know the exact amounts of this type of error to allow for. Some approximations will be discussed below.

Finally, we may be using the wrong model and thus committing specification error. Within the universe of linear models, the principal form of misspecification will be the deletion or inclusion of elements of x_t or y_t. If elements of y_t are missing, we must enlarge the model in order to keep the system complete. Since the error term, e_t, is additive, as are x_t or y_t (with coefficients), the concept of misspecification in a linear model means the separation of a random variable from terms involving x_t and y_t. The latter are observable; the e_t are not. If we can isolate an estimate of the distribution of e_t, and if these estimates satisfy the properties of a probability distribution of errors, we have some confidence that we have made the correct specification. This concept is testable, but we cannot be sure that the test result is not accidental. We can measure (imperfectly) elements of y_t and x_t, including additional elements that were not used in the original specification, to see if they are correlated with $\hat{e}_t$, the sample residuals of the estimated system in (1). If the correlations are negligible, we have some degree of reason to feel that the specification is satisfactory, but if there are large correlations, we must consider respecification of the system.[1] In the nonlinear case, there is no general procedure to test for misspecification, except through forecasting with repeated checking of accuracy. Although there are four sources of error generally, we shall focus attention on the first three.

It should also be remarked that the economy functions in a changing environment. Political systems, institutional systems, technology and other aspects of the economic environment, are always undergoing some degree of change. We would detect this in a change of Θ. Again, there is no fixed rule for detecting change of this type when it occurs, except to keep repeating model usage and to keep looking for evidence of discrepancies that could signal a change of regime. There are well-known tests for parameter change, and these can be implemented when we uncover signals that such changes are contributing to discrepancies.

---

[1] In systems that are estimated by single-equation methods, the residuals in a given equation are exactly uncorrelated with "right-hand side" variables of that same equation, but this property does not necessarily hold with respect to right-hand side variables in other equations.

The linear form of (9.2) is:

$$y_{it} = \sum_{j=1}^{N} \pi_{ij} z_{jt} + v_{it} \qquad (9.2)'$$

where z_{jt} is an element of the vector of all predetermined variables of the system, combining the vectors:

$$y_{t-1}, y_{t-2}, \ldots, y_{t-p}, x_t, x_{t-1}, x_{t-2}, \ldots, x_{t-q}$$

and v_{it} is a linear combination of $e_{1t}, \ldots, e_{nt}$. From (9.2)' it is possible to derive:

$$estvar(y_{it}) = \sum_{j=1}^{N} \sum_{k=1}^{N} s_{jk}^{\pi} \left(z_{jt} - \bar{z}_j \right) \left(z_{kt} - \bar{z}_k \right) + \sum_{j=1}^{N} \sum_{k=1}^{N} s_{jk}^{z} \pi_j \pi_k + s_{vt}^{2}. \qquad (9.3)$$

In (9.3): s_{jk}^{π} is the jk term of the covariance matrix of the estimates of π_{ij} and π_{ik}; s_{jk}^{z} is the jk term of the covariance matrix of estimates of the (observation) errors of z_{jt} and z_{kt} (observation errors and errors of choice of independent variables in the projection period);

s_{vt}^{2} is the estimated variance of the random error v_{it}.

Goldberger *et al.* (1961) showed how to estimate (9.3) directly from sample data, but assumed that all elements of z_{jt} were known accurately. Feldstein (1971) showed how to allow for error in choice of z_{jt}.

The first term on the right-hand side of (9.3) accounts for error in parameter estimation, the second term for input error in initial conditions or independent variables, and the third term for disturbance error in the structural equations of the model.

The formula in (9.3) is instructive and helps us to understand error sources, but it is only an asymptotic approximation for linear systems. By using simulation techniques it will be shown how it is possible to deal with error in nonlinear models estimated from finite samples.

Of course, many decision-makers do not use formal models. They make subjective estimates of future magnitudes of y_t, for use in making policy or strategy decisions. Whether or not they have formal models in mind they are subject to the same errors; the only difference is that they lack the general means of identifying the sources of their errors and individual quantifications of the various kinds of error. They lack an error framework.

The Reduction of Error in Decision-Making under Uncertainty

Error will be present, and in economic decision-making it will be present in large degree. It is generally true that the noise-to-signal ratio is large in economics, but it can be reduced through careful work. In order to improve decision-making, it is extremely important to keep error as low as possible.

For the model-builder, who will be making forecasts (subject to error) in order to advise decision-makers, the obvious suggestion is to improve the model. This is easily said but not easy to execute. It is like telling a country that desires to become more competitive in international markets that it should improve economic efficiency, or become more cost-effective, or raise productivity. These are all worthy goals, but suggestions are somewhat (not entirely) empty unless they are accompanied by additional suggestions about how to do so.

The implication, however, is not to work in the direction of using existing models more effectively; it is definitely to build a better model. This means different things to different people. To me, it means adding more detail, treating individual economic sectors more carefully, improving the data base, and staying in close touch with developments in the economy. These are very different directions for model improvement than:

1. Using methods of optimal control.
2. Generating model consistent expectations.
3. Using more efficient or more sophisticated methods of statistical inference.

Many of the points implied by (1)–(3) have been pursued intensively and extensively in recent years, yet I can detect no sustained improvement from any of them in reducing forecast error or in reducing the noise-to-signal ratio significantly. There are many claims and expressions of (false) hopes, but no systematic documentation that establishes the gains.

As far as work in the United States is concerned, with the elaboration of the *mainstream* model, with more data, better data, more sectors, more nonlinearities, close attention to structural change, and more attention paid to changing institutions, there has been a trend improvement in prediction error from the beginning of the 1950s to the beginning of the 1990s. This improvement has been cited by Stephen McNees (1988), the unofficial judge of predictive accuracy.

The U.S. record is cited because it is carefully documented and has been studied over time by Stephen McNees. In a general way, it can be said that all over the world there has been an improvement in the accuracy of economic forecasts. For the U.K., Sir Terence Burns (1986) shows how medium-term forecasts have improved.

At the end of the Second World War, some serious attempts at systematic economic forecasting were initiated and fared worse than subsequent efforts. The latter showed definite improvement, with gains in experience as well as facilities.

The trends in economic model building that lay stress on points (1)–(3) above are very popular with the present generation of forecasters and general econometricians. It is not that they are wrong; it is simply that they have not led to discernible improvement by way of error reduction or gains in credibility.

There are, however, avenues of research that do look promising. They are:

1. Forecasting at higher frequencies, using better techniques for estimating the time-shape of economic reactions.

2. Forecasting with improved data bases at high frequency on a rolling, repetitive basis.
3. Combining forecasts from different approaches to reduce the variance of error.

The degree of uncertainty, measured by the variance of forecast error, can be improved. While Sir Terence Burns focuses attention on the medium term — say, three to five years — the short term, or high frequency interval, is meant to be one to six months. There are definite possibilities for improvement at this end of the forecasting spectrum, and these improvements can be used to recalibrate models at the quarterly frequency, with cumulative predictive power of one to two years.

First, let us consider high-frequency forecasting under point (1) above. Significant improvements have been made over the last decades in estimating the time-shape of economic reactions. In general, we are much better prepared to estimate lag distributions with monthly and higher frequency data either by spectral techniques or in the time domain. The data samples are much more plentiful and up to date, with no more than one or two months' delay at the most. There is much serial correlation in economics statistics, and this is fundamental. Time-series methods are well designed to capture that serial correlation.

The existence of serial correlation can be shown in the liner version of Eq. (9.1):

$$\mathbf{A}(L)\mathbf{y_t} + \mathbf{B}(L)\mathbf{x_t} = \mathbf{e_t} \qquad (9.1)'$$

L is a displacement operator, $L^i\mathbf{y_t} = y_{t-i}; L^j\mathbf{x_t} = x_{t-j}$
$\mathbf{A}(L)$ and $\mathbf{B}(L)$ are matrix polynomials in powers of L.
The general solution to this system of linear dynamic equations is:

$$\mathbf{y_t} = \mathbf{K}\lambda^t - [\mathbf{A}(L)]^{-1}\mathbf{B}(L)\mathbf{x_t} + [\mathbf{A}(L)]^{-1}\mathbf{e_t}$$

where:

$\mathbf{K}$ is a matrix depending on initial conditions
λ is the vector of eigenvalues of $(9.1)'$
$[\mathbf{A}(L)]^{-1}(-\mathbf{B}(L)\mathbf{x_t} + \mathbf{e_t})$ is a particular solution of the system of finite difference equations.

Even if the elements of $\mathbf{e_t}$ are serially uncorrelated, those of $[\mathbf{A}(L)]^{-1}\mathbf{e_t}$ will be serially correlated. They are likely to be highly serially correlated.

In practice, we find a great deal of serial correlation among economic magnitudes. The structure of (9.1) shows why this is likely to be so, and in fact the real world, which can be better approximated by the general nonlinear system in (9.1) is likely to retain the same correlated error properties that are evident in (9.1).

Equations of the sort:

$$a_i(L)\mathbf{y_{it}} + b_j(L)x_{jt} = c_i(L)e_{it} \qquad (9.4)$$

can be estimated by Box–Jenkins and related techniques to get at the serial properties of $\mathbf{y_{it}}$ and also at the effects of some independent variables. Of course, Eq. (9.4) can be generalized to be vector autoregressions, but there are definite practical limits to the number of cross-serial effects that can usefully and significantly (in the statistical sense) be taken into account.

Under point (1), therefore, it is possible to use time-series methods, with readily available software, to capture the serial correlation that is present in high-frequency data. These data are becoming ever more available in this information age with less and less time delay; therefore it is possible to re-estimate forecasts at frequent intervals within a quarterly period to get improved forecasts by recalibrating models for the next few quarters.

Words from the wise to forecasters are to "forecast often." It is possible to make high-frequency forecasts of economic data every day, every week, every fortnight, every month, and so on. For my own tastes, I prefer forecasts at the end of every week, making use of the information stream that has been published that week. These high-frequency data are then related in bridge-equations to the lower frequency series, showing similar economic phenomena, on a quarterly or other basis, that make up a longer range model. The recalibrated longer range model is then used for one and two year forecasts. The high-frequency data are thus filtered regularly into rolling forecasts of quarterly, semestral or annual models (see, for example, Klein and Sojo, 1989; Klein and Park, 1993). By making use of new information as it becomes available, it is possible to improve forecast accuracy.

The third approach towards reduced variance of forecast error is to combine forecasts. Every forecast, whether model based or subjective, carries the risk of error. A way of spreading risk is to diversify among forecasts and to base decision making on a combined forecast that is an average over the possible alternatives. There are many ways of doing this, but one particular approach for aggregate economy forecasting, say for the GDP, is to forecast the magnitude from different models.

Klein and Sojo (1989) and Klein and Park (1993) describe techniques for projecting GDP and its price index by forecasting from the expenditure side of the national accounts, from the income side of the national accounts, and from regressions on principal components of many key indicators. These three methods for projecting the same magnitude often give quite different results; so an average — possibly weighted, possibly unweighted — avoids extreme forecasts and reduces variance. There are many ways of reducing risk through averaging within a "portfolio" of forecasts, but the particular averaging described here appears to be attractive and has been working well. It is all under the control of one investigator.

Construction of Regions of Uncertainty

The averaging of forecasts across models, described above, was done with point forecasts, but there is another way to allow for risk and uncertainty, namely to present forecasts in a range (single dimension) or a region (multi dimensional). The purpose of averaging across models in connection with the use of adjustments (or recalibrations) from models based on high-frequency information is to try to bring point forecasts from a lower frequency model into closer alignment with the realistic movement of the economy, as detected from the latest information available.

As the economic analyst moves out to a longer horizon of a full year and more, it is safer to present results in a range or region. This will require educating and convincing the decision-maker who is using forecast information, that one cannot, in a scientific sense, be certain about the accuracy of point forecasts. The proper way to present forecasts is:

$$P_t(y_F^l \leq y_F \leq y_F^u) = P_0$$

which reads: the probability is P_0 that a future value for y, y_F, will lie between y_F^u (upper boundary for y_F) and y_F^l (lower boundary for y_F).

The technique will be to make many replications of a forecast for y and tabulate the fraction of cases that lie between y_F^u and y_F^l.

If we make assumptions about the probability distribution of e_t in (1) and compute the variance of forecast by the formula in (3), we can construct a region:

$$\hat{y}_F \pm k S \hat{y}_F$$

where k is a constant depending on the probability of making "correct" forecast (within the region), and $S\hat{y}_F$ is the square root of the estimated variance of $\hat{y}_F$, the point forecast magnitude.

Linear approximations can be avoided and the power of the computer used to good advantage if the interval is computed by stochastic simulation.

There will have to be an assumption about the law of distribution of e_t. The usual assumption is that e_t is a normal variate, but drawings from other distributions can readily be introduced. To capture the effects of all the sources of error shown in (3), the procedure will have to be structured as follows:

1. Over the sample period, choose random drawings of (normally distributed) random variables having the same variance–covariance matrix as that estimated from the residuals for (1).
2. Simulate the model dynamically (from observed initial conditions) over the sample period using the point estimates (based on an observed sample) for parameters of the model for each drawing of random errors. The independent variables may remain fixed in these replicated simulations, or they can be computed according to same fixed stochastic model, say an autoregressive model.
3. The simulations generate values, for each sample period, of the dependent variables, y_t. These generated values, together with initial conditions and values for the independent variables constitute a sample — albeit a "pseudo" sample. With these replicated pseudo samples, we can re-estimate values for the parameters of the model. Each set of parameter values defines a new estimate of the model.
4. Given the replicated model estimates, for each case it is possible to draw fresh random disturbances, and fresh errors in a generating process for the independent

variables. The set of models can be projected over the forecast period with stochastic error inputs, initial conditions, and stochastic or fixed inputs for the independent variables. This set of projected solution paths provides a joint distribution of values for y_t that contain allowance for all the error sources.

5. A variance–covariance matrix of projections can be estimated. The point forecast for the system, plus or minus multipliers of each variable's standard deviation in the forecast period constitutes an interval that reflects the uncertainties of the situation.

For any magnitude y_{iF}, the values presented to decision-makers should not simply be $\hat{y}_{iF}$, the point projection for period F, but:

$$\hat{y}_{iF} \pm k S \hat{y}_{iF} \,.$$

A probability value will be attached, depending on the size of k.

Such intervals can be constructed, but they rarely are. This simulation approach was first developed by George Schink (1971), refined by Bianchi and Calzolari (1980), and repeated, with elaborations, by Ray Fair (1980).

The steps in stochastic simulation can be automated. They are a chore and require a great deal of attention. They are not yet standard practice. There are other, simpler, ways to allow for uncertainty. These are not in place of stochastic simulation; they are additional ways of dealing with the issues.

Some large enterprises, in deciding upon business strategies, begin the process by asking the question: What are the ingredients of the worst outcome, namely, one that would drive the firm into bankruptcy? If we denote x_F^w and x_F^b as inputs for the worst case and the best case, respectively, we then solve Eqs. (9.1), given these inputs together with the initial conditions. In this way, scenario analysis provides limits. The extreme scenarios need not be uniquely structured; other inputs can define best and worst cases besides changes in the independent variables. Entire equations can be autonomously modified; new equations can be added to the system, possibly to represent official action. Random events can still occur to disturb scenarios; therefore a combination of stochastic simulation and worst/best case scenarios would be appropriate. It is also worth while examining other scenarios that are not as extreme as the worst/best cases; these are almost always more plausible. Some investigators attach personal probabilities to the different scenarios, but that is distinctly unappealing to me.

It is not possible to anticipate all major external changes — strikes, embargoes, new legislation, natural disasters — therefore it is important to have a model on line, in computer storage, ready to be used for scenario analysis as soon as a large unexpected event occurs. If one is forecasting very frequently and always taking account of the very latest data, it is possible to react quickly (often within 24 hours), and thus reduce the amount of uncertainty for the decision-maker.

This process is expensive and not simple. It can, however, usually be directed towards improving the situation, not necessarily towards approximating the optimum but more often than not towards making improvements in the situation confronting the user of econometric information.

References

Bianchi, C. and G. Calzolari, 1980, "The one-period forecast errors in nonlinear econometric models," *International Economic Review* **21**, pp. 201–208.

Burns, Sir Terence, 1986, "The interpretation and use of economic predictions," *Proceedings of the Royal Society*, London **A407**, pp. 103–125.

Fair, R., 1980, "Estimating the predictive accuracy of econometric models," *International Economic Review*, **21**, pp. 355–378.

Feldstein, M., 1971, "The error of forecast in econometric models when the forecast-period exogenous variables are stochastic," *Econometrica* **39**, pp. 55–60.

Goldberger, A. S., A. L. Nagar, and H. S. Odeh, 1961, "The covariance matrices of reduced form coefficients and of forecasts for a structural econometric model," *Econometrica* **29**, pp. 556–573.

Klein, L. R. and E. Sojo, 1989, "Combinations of high and low frequency data in macroeconometric models," in *Economics in Theory and Practice: An Eclectic Approach*, eds. J. Marquez and L. R. Klein (Kluwer, Dordrecht), pp. 3–16.

———— and J. Y. Park, 1993, "Economic forecasting at high frequency intervals," *Journal of Forecasting* **12**, pp. 501–519.

McNees, S. K., 1988, "The accuracy keeps improving," *The New York Times*, January 10, Sec. 3, p. 2.

Schink, G., 1971, "Small sample estimates of the variance–covariance matrix of forecast errors for large econometric models: the stochastic simulation technique," PhD Thesis, University of Pennsylvania.

Editorial Note

Prefix number 9 in the equations numbering refers to Chap. 9 of the source, *Money, Inflation, and Employment, Essays in Honor of James Ball, op. cit.*

23

THE LONGEVITY OF ECONOMIC THEORY[†]

In this bicentennial year, Paul Samuelson prepared a paper for the meetings of the American Economic Association "... Vindicating Adam Smith's *Wealth of Nations*." Smith's doctrines have gone through their good and bad times over the 200 year span, often being attacked for lacking relevance to contemporary events, but we are indebted to Professor Samuelson for showing again that good arguments prevail.

So it is with modern macroeconomic theory, not of age 200, but of age 40. It has served us well through the Great Depression, World War II, and the great world wide expansion of the 50s and 60s. Now some analysts are looking at recent events, vintage 73–75, and saying that we should *go back to the drawing boards!*

I say no! Contemporary macroeconomic theory can explain the events of the past few years. The vindication of theory rests on an appropriate use of it in present circumstances. Much of the criticism is ill founded on superficial argument and inadequate analysis. The principal issues are the following:

Does the coexistence of rising prices and rising unemployment refute macroeconomic theory?

Does this unusual joint phenomenon invalidate the Phillips Curve?

I shall argue that the Phillips Curve is being misunderstood and that proper analysis of full system properties can lead to the generating of rising prices and rising unemployment in a model that is based on received doctrine, including acceptance of the hypothesis underlying the Phillips Curve.

The Meaning of the Phillips Curve

There is frequently a confusion in economic discussions between *structural* relationships and *derived* relationships, the latter being most frequently *reduced form* relationships. A *structural* relation ought to be based directly on fundamental economic behavior, according to accepted principles of economic theory or enforced by economic institutions. Structural relationships can be combined and consolidated through mathematical steps of substitution and elimination. If this is carried through to its logical conclusion, we ultimately arrive at reduced form relationships which make *dependent* (endogenous) variables functions of *predetermined* variables

[†]From *Quantitative Wirtschaftsforschung*, eds. H. Albach *et al.* (J. C. B. Mohr (Paul Siebeck), Tuebingen, 1977), pp. 411–419.

alone. The predetermined set consists of *independent* (exogenous) variables and *initial conditions* (lagged dependent and independent variables).

In the process of substitution and elimination, it is sometimes possible to obtain an intermediate, derived relationship associating two dependent variables and some predetermined variables. This is not a general result, however, and occurs only in systems with specifications that are favorable to this kind of result.

The fundamental problem is that economic observation is based on the actual working of the economy when many dependent and independent variables are moving simultaneously. We cannot, by direct observation, isolate the joint variation of just two related variables with all other effects held constant. We would need to be able to conduct a controlled experiment, and this is not generally possible. It is rare that world conditions will actually work out to give us a statistical "glimpse" of the joint variations that we are looking for. That is why we must turn to carefully constructed simulations of models in order to get the "glimpse" of joint variation that is being considered at the moment.

Added to the difficulties of isolating particular economic measurements, we must recognize that our concepts are often aggregative. There is surely an important error of aggregation because much of the underlying economic theory concerns decision making at the *micro* level while observations are at the *macro* level. Moreover, the general concepts of *inflation* and *unemployment* being considered in the present case are aggregative variables, both in theory and measurement. Consequently, aggregation error as well as behavioral error, specification error, and measurement error affect our conclusions.

Some formalities: To make the preceding discussion more definite, let us introduce some more formal expressions. A structural model of the economy can be written, quite generally as

$$f(y'_t, y'_{t-1}, \ldots, y'_{t-r}, x'_t, \theta') = e_t \qquad i = 1, 2, \ldots, n \, .$$

y_{t-j} is an n-element column vector of dependent variables at time point $t - j (j = 0, 1, 2, \ldots r)$. For $j \neq 0$, these variables are predetermined.

x_t is an m-element column vector of independent variables at time point t. In a formal sense, if there are lags in some of the elements of x_t, they can be re-classified as new independent variables at time point t.

θ is a column vector of parameters. There are several associated with each individual equation. In principle, a given parameter may occur in more than one equation of the system.

e_t is an n-element column vector of errors associated with each equation of the system, except identities. The errors are assumed to be drawings from a joint probability distribution.

The notation for the function f stands for a whole set of equations. This is to be represented by an n-element column of functional operators.

In contrast to the structural equations

$$f = e_t,$$

we could derive a reduced form, expressed as

$$y_t = g(y'_{t-1}, y'_{t-2}, \ldots, y'_{t-r}, x'_t, \theta', e'_t).$$

The functional operator g is assumed to represent an n-element column of relationships. For example, the linear structural model is

$$\sum_{i=0}^{r} A_i y_{t-i} + B x_t = e_t$$

and the corresponding reduced form is

$$y_t = -A_0^{-1} \sum_{i=1}^{r} A_i y_{t-i} - A_0^{-1} B x_t + A_0^{-1} e_t.$$

In nonlinear systems, the usual case, we do not attempt to derive a closed form expression for the reduced form, but simply work from numerical solutions (simulations). The simulations are "integrals" or "summations" of the system over successive values of t from fixed initial conditions. Again, in the linear case, a solution can be expressed in closed form but must be obtained by numerical analysis in the general nonlinear case.

The Phillips Curve: One or more of the structural equations of a typical model would represent labor demand. Demand by industry, region, occupation, or other classification would lead to a whole system of labor demand functions in a large detailed model. Let us assume the (approximate) existence of a single labor demand function in a highly aggregative context. Similarly, there will be equations of labor supply. These, too are expressed in a single relationship in a highly aggregated system.

The Phillips Curve is frequently assumed to be the structural equation for labor supply, but in my opinion, it fits best into the complete system scheme of things as a traditional market clearing relation showing how wage rates (the price of labor) adjust in response to an excess supply or demand for labor. Other variables may influence wage fluctuations besides excess supply or demand for labor. These other variables may be price fluctuations, the profit position of enterprises, the productivity situation for labor. These are the main variables to be considered; they are typical factors that influence negotiations at a bargaining table. The demographic composition of unemployment may also be a factor, as well as the situation for job vacancies. As in the case of nearly all economic relationships, there can be dynamic factors — leads and lags in the time domain.

A typical structural equation may take the form

$$\triangle \ln w_t = h(u_t, u_{t-1}, \ldots, u_{t-r}, \triangle \ln p_{t-\phi}, q_t/n_t, q_{t-1}/n_{t-1}, \ldots, q_{t-s}/n_{t-s}, z_t) + e_t$$

w_t = wage rate

u_t = unemployment rate

$p_{t-\phi}$ = price level at $t - \phi$

q_t = production

n_t = employment (q_t/n_t = productivity)

z_t = profit rate

e_t = error

It is evident that the Phillips curve does not show a relationship between inflation and unemployment. To infer such a relationship from this version of the Phillips curve, it would be necessary to show how the wage rate is related to the price level and assumptions would have to be introduced about productivity and profits.

A short cut is often introduced, namely, to assume that wage changes are proportional, or related in some simple manner, to price changes; therefore, the Phillips curve would show an inverse relationship between inflation and unemployment, for given values of other variables. But this partial and approximate relationship is not what is observed as the outcome of the economic process when one draws conclusions about the relationship between inflation and unemployment from manifest data. The data that one sees are two simultaneous solution values from the true model of the economy.

$$\triangle \ln p_t = g_p(y'_{t-1}, y'_{t-2}, \ldots, y'_{t-r}, x'_t, \theta', e'_t)$$
$$u_t = g_u(y'_{t-1}, y'_{t-2}, \ldots, y'_{t-r}, x'_t, \theta', e'_t)$$

Since both $\triangle \ln p_t$ (the inflation rate) and u_t (the unemployment rate) depend on several predetermined variables, there is, in general, no unique relationship implied between them. If each depended on the same single predetermined variable, we could eliminate that variable and obtain a relationship between $\triangle \ln p_t$ and u_t. This would be the case for simple parametric relationships of two variables.

Given that we do not have this special case, how do we obtain the relationship between $\triangle \ln p_t$ and u_t? The so-called "trade-off" relation between these two variables (inflation and unemployment) can be obtained by varying a single element (or fixed combination) of x'_t in each relationship and keeping all other elements of x'_t fixed. It is usual in such simulation studies to choose a fixed vector for random disturbances. In a deterministic sense, these are set to zero

$$e_t = 0.$$

Also, θ' is replaced by its statistical estimate

$$\text{est } \theta = \hat{\theta}.$$

In a static analysis, lags for y'_t are kept fixed. In a dynamic analysis, simulations of
the system from fixed initial conditions are computed for different assumed values
of the single element (or fixed combination) of x'_t. By varying these input values for
x'_t, we get a pair of series for $\Delta \ln p_t$ and u_t. The graph of these associated pairs
— $\Delta \ln p_t$ on one axis and u_t on the other — is the trade-off curve. This curve will
vary, depending on how x'_t is altered.

Some Empirical Estimates

The technique of changing reduced form results for two variables such as inflation
rate and unemployment rate by varying one of the common arguments of the reduced
form relationship — all in a numerical sense for nonlinear system — was first studied
for the Wharton Model by Treyz (1972). In the present case, I am extending his
methods to a different Wharton Model, the Annual and Industry Model, for medium
term simulations under alternative conditions. This model has full inter-industrial
supply content and is much better for analyzing the kinds of disturbances being
considered in the present discussion (Preston, 1975).

First, I choose a "baseline" simulation, which is a plausible, projected path for
the economy, in this case a simulation for the period 1975–1985. The baseline
simulation will be changed in three ways:

(i) An increase in real government spending at a sustained rate of $5 billion
    (1968 $) p.a.
(ii) An increase in farm prices, the index on a 1958 base increases by 20 points, on
    a sustained basis, p.a.
(iii) An increase in the price of oil imports so that the current value (for a fixed
    volume) is higher by $2.0 billion p.a. (building up from $1.5 billion in 1975 and
    $1.8 billion in 1976).

Case (i) corresponds to the standard multiplier calculation. The multiplier starts
at slightly more than 2.0, holds that value approximately for five years and gradually
drifts downward to almost 0.0 in nine years and then turns slightly negative. This is
a not uncommon pattern for the standard fiscal multiplier. For this kind of change
of simulation input values, everything else unchanged, I obtain the usual result —
lower unemployment (higher GNP) and higher prices. The higher prices are visible
either as a higher index value (level) or a higher rate of inflation (change). This
is the trade-off suggested by received doctrine. The cost of lower unemployment
(higher real performance) is the acceptance of more inflation.

Except for some end-point discrepancies, explained at the beginning by productivity changes and at the end by the declining long-term effect of the fiscal multiplier,
these figures show clearly the nature of the trade-off. This is what macroeconomic
theory teaches us to expect.

Case (ii). Consider now a situation in which farm (food) prices change domestically as a result, say, of either internal or external supply conditions. This is the

Table 1. The unemployment/inflation trade-off. Baseline case minus fiscal stimulus case (difference between baseline and case (i) simulations).

	1975	1976	1977	1978	1979	1980	1981	1982	1983	1984	1985
Difference in unemployment rate (%)	1.2	1.3	1.2	1.1	1.1	0.8	0.6	0.4	0.2	0.0	−0.2
Difference in inflation rate (%)	0.2	−0.2	−0.5	−0.3	−0.3	−0.4	−0.5	−0.6	−0.6	−0.4	−0.3
Difference in real GNP (b$ 1958)	−12.0	−12.7	−10.6	−9.6	−9.9	−9.4	−7.7	−4.1	−1.2	1.3	3.5
Difference in GNP deflator (pts.)	0.4	0.0	−0.8	−1.6	−2.2	−3.1	−4.3	−6.2	−7.8	−9.2	−10.8

Table 2. The unemployment/inflation relation for an internal price change. Baseline case minus agricultural price increase case (difference between baseline and case (ii) simulations).

	1975	1976	1977	1978	1979	1980	1981	1982	1983	1984	1985
Difference in unemployment rate (%)	−0.1	−0.2	−0.3	−0.4	−0.5	−0.6	−0.6	−0.6	−0.5	−0.6	−0.8
Difference in inflation rate (%)	−0.6	−0.1	−0.3	−0.3	−0.4	−0.4	−0.3	−0.2	−0.4	−0.5	−0.6
Difference in real GNP (b$ 1958)	1.8	2.0	3.6	5.7	7.8	10.0	11.4	12.5	15.1	19.1	23.9
Difference in GNP deflator (pts.)	−1.0	−1.3	−1.8	−2.5	−3.4	−4.3	−5.2	−6.2	−7.3	−9.0	−11.4

kind of disturbance that occurred in 1972–1975. In this case, I shall not change an ordinary fiscal stimulus/restraint variable, along text book lines. I shall instead change farm prices exogenously. This produces quite different results as far as the inflation/unemployment relation is concerned. In Table 2, there is no evidence of the usual trade-off.

The unemployment (difference) and the inflation rate (difference) rows are not of opposite sign, as in Table 1; they are of the same sign — higher unemployment and higher inflation are caused by the change introduced in Case (ii). It is possible, therefore, to simulate a model in which the usual Phillips curve hypothesis for a structural relation is embedded and not find the trade-off as in Case (i). Whether or not the trade-off case occurs depends on the type of shock administered to the economy. If the shock is from rising food prices, we should not expect to find the trade-off. We find higher prices and higher unemployment. In terms of output and price levels, we find lower real output and higher prices in the Case (ii) simulation compared with the baseline. This is just another way of looking at the same phenomenon.

Table 3. The unemployment/inflation relation for an external price change. Baseline case minus oil import price increase case (difference between baseline and case (iii) simulations).

	1975	1976	1977	1978	1979	1980	1981	1982	1983	1984	1985
Difference in unemployment rate (%)	0.1	0.0	0.0	−0.1	−0.2	−0.2	−0.3	−0.3	−0.2	−0.3	−0.4
Difference in inflation rate (%)	0.4	−0.1	−0.1	−0.1	−0.2	−0.2	−0.1	−0.1	−0.2	−0.3	−0.4
Difference in real GNP (b$ 1958)	−0.9	−0.4	0.5	1.8	2.8	3.6	4.5	5.4	6.8	8.9	10.8
Difference in GNP deflator (pts.)	0.8	0.6	0.5	0.2	−0.2	−0.6	−0.9	−1.4	−1.9	−2.6	−3.6

Case (iii). Now let us look at the case of an external fuel price increase. This simulated the kind of relationship between unemployment and price change that occurred after the oil embargo and new scheduling of OPEC prices for crude. Basically, these results show the same direction of effect as Case (ii), i.e., no trade-off exists, but the change is relatively small, in comparison with OPEC reality (four-fold increase in crude price); therefore, the effects do not show up for two to three years and the differences are small; nevertheless, they are evident. Fundamentally, the external price increase brings about more unemployment and more inflation together. The same results are found by looking at the level series for real GNP and the GNP deflator.

Explanation and Conclusions

The case of the ordinary fiscal stimulus is not difficult to comprehend. As a result of the fiscal injection to the economy, aggregate demand is stimulated; employment requirements rise; unemployment falls; and prices are bid up by virtue of the increased demand. The rising prices, together with similar pressures on money markets pushing up interest rates, tend to hold back real expansion after the passage of time. Rising prices, when divided into rising nominal income flows, produce falling real flows (i.e., those corrected for inflation). Similarly, rising interest rates eventually restrain capital formation in businesses and residential properties. These developments jointly account for falling multiplier values after about three years. That is why the figures in the rows for output and unemployment rate differences change sign at the end of the simulation period. For the bulk of the period, however, the output difference is negative and the unemployment difference is positive, and these are associated with negative differences in the inflation rate. As a result of start-up effects that give rise to higher levels of productivity right after an initial stimulus, the difference in inflation rate is positive for the first year of stimulus.

The cases of food and fuel price increases, (ii) and (iii), can be viewed as being equivalent to excise taxes. The higher agricultural price and the higher fuel price could be treated as increases in excises that are fully passed through to final purchasers. I have noted in Wharton Model simulations, for some years, that increases in excise taxes lead to reduced levels of real output and higher rates of unemployment. At the same time, the increase in excises raises price levels, contributing, in a sense, to higher rates of inflation. This has been the result in various experiments with value-added taxation suggested for the U.S. economy, from time to time. The higher food or fuel prices lead to increases in final deflators. These deflators go up faster than increases in nominal incomes that are induced by the prices. When the nominal values of income are deflated by the higher price indexes, the real values fall below baseline values. This is what gives rise to higher prices and higher unemployment simultaneously.

Both situations — case (i) or cases (ii) and (iii) — can be accommodated by simulation analysis in one system. That system contains structural relations of the Phillips curve type, but it can produce two kinds of results, one showing the usual trade-off and one not showing the trade-off. It is not necessary to reconsider basic theory; it is only necessary to use it appropriately to fit the needs of the situation.

References

Preston, R. S., 1975, "The Wharton long term model: Input–output within the context of a macro forecasting model," *International Economic Review* **16**, pp. 3–19.

Treyz, G., 1972, "An econometric procedure for export policy evaluation," *International Economic Review* **13**, pp. 212–222.

24

THE PHILLIPS CURVE IN THE U.S.

The concept of the "Phillips Curve" is much maligned and misunderstood. In the popular media the term is used in a pejorative sense in order to cast scorn on an economics argument. Broadly speaking, the Phillips Curve argument for contemporary economic issues would be that the economy should be significantly slowed down, possibly even to the point of being put through a mild recession, in order to reduce the real growth rate (raise the unemployment rate) and thereby reduce the inflation rate (rate of increase of wage rates). Many of the very people who malign the Phillips Curve concept do, indeed, want to slow the economy in order to bring down the inflation rate. It is not easily understandable how people making such an argument can object to the concept.

1. The Meaning of the "Phillips Curve"

In modeling the economy, which is my way of thinking about problems, each relationship must be identified with its place in the corpus of economic theory. In order for an equation to have proper structure it should be a behavioral, technical, legal or definitional relationship. If a relationship cannot be identified in one of these groups, it is called "ad hoc" or empirical. It would thus be without fundamental economic content.

Some economists query the lineage of the Phillips Curve, calling it "ad hoc", but I would disagree. It has, I believe, a perfectly respectable and easily understood place as a behavioral equation among the structural equations of a model. These equations consist of:

(i) decision making relationships of households,
(ii) decision making relationships of production establishments,
(iii) market clearing or bargaining relationships.

The third category suits the Phillips Curve quite well. From first principles, we are taught the law of markets, sometimes called the law of supply and demand. Demand and supply equations for goods or services are examples of (i) and (ii). But when demand exceeds supply, price rises and brings the market towards clearing. Given enough time, a dynamic market clearing process should restore balance between demand and supply. Similarly, when supply exceeds demand, price falls, and this also tends to bring about market clearing.

From *Prévision et Analyse économique* **3** (Juillet–Decembre, 1982), pp. 17–26.

The Phillips Curve is a relation between wage change and unemployment. The latter term is a measure of the difference between supply and demand in the labor market. The imbalance causes wage rates (the *price of labor*) to move in such a way as to bring the labor market towards equilibrium. It is thus a bargaining or market clearing relationship and has a time honored place among structural equations as a representation of the law of supply and demand in the labor market. It is thus perfectly sensible and not a mysterious, ad hoc relationship.

A. W. Phillips (1958) wrote a remarkable article about this relationship and gave it, unintentionally, a name. Phillips' article and analysis of the problem were very stimulating and gained immediate popularity in the economics profession. Actually, the history of this relationship, both as an empirical estimate and as a concept goes back a good deal farther. Some people have attributed its early expression to Iriving Fisher, but I first learned about it in the works of Tinbergen (1937, p. 16). In this early models, he introduced a relation between the change in wage rate, change in price, and employment. The wage variable was sometimes expressed as a level instead of rate of change, but I built on Tinbergen's concept and related wage rate change to unemployment and price change in my early attempts to model the Keynesian system [see Klein (1947, p. 116)]. I made empirical estimates of this relationship (with distributed lags) in my first models of the U.S. economy [see Klein (1950, pp. 120–121)].

Phillips investigated the relationship between wage change and unemployment on a much bolder and more sweeping basis, almost as one of the great empirical laws of economics, on a par with Engel's Law, Pareto's Law, the Quantity Equation, or the constancy of Labor's Share. He studied the relationship from longer run data and did not try to imbed it in a model of the economy as a whole.

If we look upon the Phillips curve as a global economic relationship like the Quantity Equation, then the present state of disenchantment with it is more understandable because, as a simple global relationship, it will break down when put against the complexities of real life just as the crude Quantity Equation breaks down in the face of an oil embargo, a harvest failure, or OPEC pricing strategy. But, just as a more sophisticated equation for demand for money has a sound structural slot in a complete model, so does the law of supply and demand in the labor market have a structural slot in a total model.

In order to obtain a stable demand function for money, it is necessary to introduce lag distributions, wealth variables, rates of return on various alternative financial assets, and other determinants of portfolio composition. Similarly, it will be argued in this paper that labor market dynamics and demographic structure must be introduced into a more sophisticated extension of the original Phillips hypothesis in order to obtain a stable function. Even simple functions with only overall unemployment and price change to explain wage change were perceptive in noting, as early as 1960–61, that extremely high levels of unemployment would be needed in order to bring about price stability, through its relation to wage stability. Estimates of unemployment in the United States in excess of 10 million persons

was estimated as the required amount of labor market slack for price stabilization. It is this pessimistic, but realistic, result of early Phillips Curve analysis that
turned many economists away from the original concepts of the Phillips curve, yet
they proved eventually to be quite on target [see Klein and Bodkin (1964), esp.
pp. 389–401].

R. Lipsey (1960) noted very soon after the appearance of Phillips' article that
the relationship could be improved by the inclusion of unemployment change as well
as unemployment level in the relationship. More generally, an entire lag distribution
of unemployment would seem to be an even better variable. Many other refinements
have been added or considered;

    (i) the use of vacancy statistics in addition to the unemployment rate;
   (ii) the inclusion of variables for the inflation rate, productivity gains, and the
        profit rate;
  (iii) the use of the "natural rate" in the equation;
  (iv) the introduction of the demographic composition of the labor force and
        unemployed.

Lipsey found a significant effect on the change in wage rates as a result of
"changes in unemployment." The significance of this finding is that changes in
unemployment give some added cyclical content to the relationship, and many of
the proposed amendments over the years have done just that, namely, introduced
highly cyclical sensitive variables.

The original relationship was too simple to stand up to evolving economic conditions and extrapolation, in general. It should never have been put forward in
such a strong, positive light as a simple bivariate relationship. A more proper specification, extended to include some other variables, is what is needed as *structural*
relationships. Viewed in this light, the Phillips Curve *can* stand the test of time.
The equations that I shall list and describe in the next section should be considered
from this point of view. They indicate quite clearly that the idea of a stable Phillips
Equation (not a simple curve) has an important role to play in model building.

Before we start to look at estimated Phillips Equations for the United States, it
is important to clarify another conceptual point that has led to misunderstanding.
The Phillips Curve is not a relationship between the rate of inflation and the real
rate of growth — or the rate of inflation and the rate of unemployment. Between
the rates of change of wages and prices stands the very important concept of the
rate of change of productivity. We have learned that productivity growth cannot be
taken for granted. Also, the Phillips equation does not make sense if stated purely
in terms of nominal wage rate change, with no attention paid to the role of inflation
or the real wage change.

It is better to consider the inflation–unemployment relationship as a "trade-
off" relation between two endogenous variables that are generated by a complete
system. There are many interesting diagrams that may be prepared between pairs
of generated variables. The inflation–unemployment trade-off is one of them, but

it is not a structural equation. Given a total model of the economy as a whole, we can express each endogenous variable in the system as:

$$y_1 = f_1 \text{ (initial conditions, exogenous variables)}$$
$$y_2 = f_2 \text{ (initial conditions, exogenous variables)}$$

The functions f_1 and f_2 are final solution equations of the entire system. There will be as many such equations as there are endogenous variables. We select two of these, one for general price level and one for unemployment. The first differences of the price level equation give us inflation. By changing the exogenous inputs in a systematic way, we can develop different time paths for Δp and U (inflation rate and unemployment rate, respectively). A diagrammatic plot of corresponding pairs of Δp and U values is the trade-off curve. In general, we have come to think of this curve as one that shows an inverse relationship between the two variables, but it is not unique, and it is not necessarily a falling curve, from left to right. It all depends on the type of exogenous input changes being considered. Some changes (harvest and energy price shocks in particular) may produce positively sloped curves, from left to right [see Klein (1977)]. Conventional fiscal and monetary policy changes in exogenous inputs are likely to produce negatively sloped curves, from left to right. The steepness of the trade-off curve and its position depend on the initial conditions, the types of exogenous shocks, and the general process of structural change. It is a mistake, however, to associate instability of the trade-off curve solely with instability of the Phillips Curve. The latter may be stable or unstable, but these properties must be separately investigated and not by the casual observation of simple relationships between inflation and unemployment.

The structural relationship for wage determination as a function of explanatory variables should be designed as follows: the wage bargaining process in each sector of the economy should depend on the state of the labor market in that particular sector, on the variables that each side of the bargain puts forward for its own case, and on the composition of the bargaining units. The most relevant labor market indicator is unemployment — the gap between supply and demand in the labor market — but the force of this gap may vary over the business cycle; therefore, the time shape of unemployment is also to be considered. Such indicators as vacancy statistics and capacity utilization rates can be sector specific, i.e., given by industries: therefore, they are relevant for the determination of wage change in each separate sector. Overall unemployment and sector specific conditions of the labor market are brought together in a structural relationship.

Employees come to the bargaining table arguing that their productivity gains, the sector's profitability, and cost-of-living changes justify stated wage demands. Correspondingly, employers approach the bargaining table with their own interpretation of justifiable wage gains on the basis of the same variables, to make up their wage offer. "Who" is unemployed makes a difference. Youth unemployed have less bargaining power than mature earners, with family responsibility, and with some skills. Secondary earners have less bargaining power than primary earners; or the former put their case less forcefully. In the United States some minority groups have relatively weaker bargaining power. The relationship should therefore reflect the demographic composition of those doing the bargaining and of those unemployed.

The Phillips Curve is presumably curved. It could, in principle, be a linear relationship, but from an empirical point of view there is evidence of curvature, and this makes sense. At very low levels of unemployment, below a cultural or institutional norm, wages should be bid up fast. When upward pressure makes itself felt, wages tend to move fast. Similarly, when unemployment is very high and labor markets are strongly depressed, wage rates should grow very slowly. In the present era, we rarely find falling wages; that happened on a broad scale only in a period like that of the Great Depression. But we do find marked differences in the rate of increase, depending on the state of the labor market and other relevant variables in the structural equation for wage determination.

The Phillips Curves in the extended form discussed here are structural equations that depend on several variables simultaneously. Many of these variables are contemporary or lagged endogenous variables. This is in contrast to the final equations that are used to determine the inflation–unemployment trade-off. Only fixed initial conditions or exogenous variables appear in the expressions f_1, f_2.

2. Some Estimates for the U.S.

The Wharton Quarterly Model contains estimates of Phillips Curves for wage determination by sector that demonstrate some of the features of the specifications discussed in the previous section. A uniform specification is selected for the following industry groups:

> Durable manufacturing
> Nondurable manufacturing
> Regulated industries (electricity, gas, communication, transportation, sanitation)
> Contract construction
> Wholesale and retail trade
> Finance, insurance, and real estate
> Services

Agriculture does not fit into this mold. Mining ought to be included, but did not fit this specification in a reasonable way.

For each sector, percentage change in wage rate (measured without supplements to wages and salaries) is made a distributed lag function of the ratio of the "natural" to the actual rate of unemployment and the percentage change in the price index of consumer goods (implicit deflator of consumer expenditure). The "natural" rate of unemployment is defined as a weighted average of "adjusted" unemployment rates in each demographic group based on age–sex classifications. The weights show the time-varying importance of each age–sex specific group in the whole working population. The adjusted unemployment rates by age–sex category are (in logarithm terms) estimated from:

$$\ln u_{rjt} = a_j \ln u_{pmt} + b_j \ln rp_{jt} + c_j$$

u_{rj} = unemployment rate for age–sex category j,

u_{pm} = unemployment rate for prime age males (25 to 54 years),

rp_j = percentage of labor force in category j.

The mean value of u_{pm} was inserted into each equation for u_{rjt}. These are cyclically adjusted and, with time-varying weights, give an average that is called the "natural" rate.

This specification estimates an inverse curved relationship between wage change and unemployment. The unemployment measure takes account of the age composition of the labor force and the unemployed. It also attaches special cyclical significance to the unemployment of prime working age males.

The distributed lags are estimated as Almon polynomials. In all sectors, the polynomial distribution for the coefficients of (u^*/u) (the ratio of the natural to the actual unemployment rate) are second-degree functions with restraints at $t = 0$ and $t = -6$. This means that there is only one free parameter to be estimated in the second degree case. The lag distribution is symmetrical and has the same t-statistic at each lag. In the case of the lagged price effect, the final selection varies for each sector, but all the distributions were constrained to be zero at the right end, and a search was made for different length lags distributed along a second-degree polynomial curve.

For both manufacturing sectors and the regulated sector, the sum of the price coefficients is close to unity. This means that, in the limit, nominal wage changes follow consumer price changes, as well as responding to labor market conditions. In an approximate sense, real wage rates respond inversely to labor market conditions. In the other sectors, the nominal wage adjustment to price changes falls short of complete compensation. Some of these sectors are less organized than in manufacturing or regulated sectors.

It should be noted that all equations are estimated without constant terms. Since the dependent variable is in first difference (percentage) form a nonzero constant term would estimate trend growth. These estimates limit the trend in nominal wage rates to the trend in price inflation or somewhat less, and to the trend in the "natural" rate, which has been rising in recent years as the population has changed.

The correlation coefficients are not very large, but this is typical of equations in first difference form for the dependent variable. Although the correlation is low for the estimation of $(w_t - w_{t-1})/w_{t-1}$, it is high in all cases for the estimation of w_t, given w_{t-1} and the other variables.

It is also to be noted that the coefficients of (u^*/u) are all very significant by the standards of conventional statistical testing. These are the distinctive Phillips

Curve aspects of the relationships. They do show that labor market conditions, appropriately measured and specified, have a very significant relation to wage rate. This is all that the Phillips Curve ever purported to show.

The statistical results (see Table 1) for the coefficients of u^*/u, in lag distribution form, are similar for all sectors. The six coefficients are of the same order of magnitude for each industry group, and as the denominator of u^*/u approaches zero, i.e., as unemployment gets very low, the gradient of the standard Phillips Curve becomes very steep. In some sense, it becomes vertical in the limit, but in a practical sense, u never gets really close to zero, except in an unusual situation such as wartime. The size of the slope varies, because u^* changes. It has risen over the past 25 years, but may cease to do so eventually and could even decline.

The estimated Phillips Curve, therefore, becomes vertical in the limit, but not in any practical sense, and it does not become positive in this specification. We have not, in any sense, proved that this specification is correct. We have simply shown that it is consistent with the observed data. It provides a systematic explanation of wage change, by sector, up to an unexplained random error. This is all that econometric inference can reasonably be expected to do. I would argue that no other specification is consistent with the observed data, but this specification provides good system results, in the context of the entire Wharton Quarterly Model. It shows that the Phillips Curve concept is very much alive, in tune with modern data, and capable, in this generalized form, of coping with labor market changes that have been occurring since the 1950s.

In the Wharton Annual Model, used for longer term analysis of the U.S. economy, we have estimated a slightly different form of the Phillips Curve, in which productivity figures directly as a variable. An example of this equation, for the economy as a whole, is given by the prototype estimate:

$$\triangle \ln w = 0.0097 + 0.18 \ \triangle\ln\text{PROD}_{-1} + 0.26 \ \triangle\ln\text{PROD}_{-2}$$
$$+ 0.21 \ \triangle\ln\text{PROD}_{-3} + 0.20 \ \triangle\ln p + 0.30 \ \triangle\ln p_{-1}$$
$$+ 0.30 \ \triangle\ln p_{-2} + 0.20 \ \triangle\ln p_{-3} - 0.0109 \ \ln u^+ + 0.028 \ \ln u^-$$
$$S = 0.20 \times 10^{-4} \qquad \text{DW} = 2.13$$

New variables: PROD = Productivity, measured as output per worker;

u^+ = Unemployment rate as a deviation above 6.5 percent (plus "one");

u^- = negative of unemployment rate above 4.6 percent (plus "one").

In this version, nominal wage varies inversely with unemployment but the degree of sensitivity is different for high unemployment (above 6.5 percent) and low unemployment (below 4.6 percent). The price effect is constrained so that in the steady

Table 1. Estimated Phillips curves, United States, quarterly, 1956,1–1976,4.

Sector	a_0	a_1	a_2	a_3	a_4	a_5	a_6	a_7	a_8	a_9	a_{10}	a_{11}	b_0	b_1	b_2	b_3	b_4	b_5	R^2	DW
Durable manufactures	0.33 (3.0)	0.26 (4.9)	0.19 (8.8)	0.14 (4.0)	0.092 (2.0)	0.053 (1.2)	0.023 (0.7)						0.0022 (3.7)	0.0036 (3.7)	0.0043 (3.7)	0.0043 (3.7)	0.0036 (3.7)	0.0022 (3.7)	0.52	2.08
$\Sigma_{a_i}=1.08(8.8)$ (t statistic); $\Sigma_{b_i}=0.020(3.7)$																				
Nondurable manufactures	0.39 (2.9)	0.29 (7.1)	0.19 (4.1)	0.11 (1.6)	0.047 (0.9)								0.0022 (4.0)	0.0036 (4.0)	0.0044 (4.0)	0.0044 (4.0)	0.0036 (4.0)	0.0022 (4.0)	0.52	1.46
$\Sigma_{a_i}=1.02(8.9)$; $\Sigma_{b_i}=0.020(4.0)$																				
Regulated industries	0.0081 (.085)	0.062 (1.0)	0.10 (3.1)	0.13 (6.9)	0.15 (6.3)	0.16 (4.8)	0.15 (4.0)	0.13 (3.5)	0.099 (3.2)	0.056 (3.1)			0.0032 (4.6)	0.0054 (4.6)	0.0065 (4.6)	0.0065 (4.6)	0.0054 (4.6)	0.0032 (4.6)	0.33	2.30
$\Sigma_{a_i}=1.05(6.9)$; $\Sigma_{b_i}=0.030(4.6)$																				
Contract construction	0.17 (0.4)	0.13 (0.8)	0.10 (1.1)	0.075 (0.4)	0.040 (0.3)	0.023 (0.2)							0.0046 (2.4)	0.0076 (2.4)	0.0091 (2.4)	0.0091 (2.4)	0.0076 (2.4)	0.0046 (2.4)	0.015	2.79
$\Sigma_{a_i}=0.55(1.3)$; $\Sigma_{b_i}=0.043(2.4)$																				
Wholesale and retail trade	0.29 (2.4)	0.17 (4.9)	0.081 (2.0)	0.023 (0.4)	-0.0036 (0.08)								0.0041 (8.7)	0.0068 (8.7)	0.0082 (8.7)	0.0082 (8.7)	0.0068 (8.7)	0.0041 (8.7)	0.26	1.74
$\Sigma_{a_i}=0.56(5.6)$; $\Sigma_{b_i}=0.038(8.7)$																				
Finance, insurance and real estate	—		0.050 (0.08)	0.043 (0.7)	0.072 (2.2)	0.093 (5.1)	0.10 (4.3)	0.11 (3.3)	0.10 (2.7)	0.091 (2.4)	0.069 (2.2)	0.059 (2.1)	0.0037 (5.7)	0.0061 (5.7)	0.0074 (5.7)	0.0074 (5.7)	0.0061 (5.7)	0.0037 (5.7)	0.14	2.08
$\Sigma_{a_i}=0.73(5.1)$; $\Sigma_{b_i}=0.034(5.7)$																				
Services	0.057 (0.6)	0.065 (1.1)	0.071 (2.1)	0.073 (3.7)	0.072 (3.0)	0.067 (2.1)	0.060 (1.6)	0.050 (1.4)	0.036 (1.2)	0.020 (1.1)			0.0043 (6.0)	0.0071 (6.0)	0.0085 (6.0)	0.0085 (6.0)	0.0071 (6.0)	0.0043 (6.0)	0.17	2.18
$\Sigma_{a_i}=0.57(3.7)$; $\Sigma_{b_i}=0.040(6.0)$																				

$$\frac{w_t - w_{t-1}}{w_{t-1}} = \sum_{i=\theta}^{n} a_i \frac{P_{t-1} - P_{t-1-i}}{P_{t-1-i}} + \sum_{i=0}^{m} b_i \left(\frac{u^*}{u}\right)_{t-i}$$

state wages move as prices (GNP deflator) move. Productivity change influences the wage bargain. The wage rate level is projected with small error from this equation given the lags for each time period.

The coefficients of productivity (logarithms) do not sum to unity. If they did, we would have full proportionality between the real wage and productivity in the steady state, or constancy of labor's share. This would imply an overall Cobb–Douglas production function. Instead, we have the real wage moving in percentage change by a fraction of the percentage change in productivity. This is consistent with a CES production function.

References

Klein, L. R., 1947, "Theories of effective demand and employment," *Journal of Political Economy* **55** (2), pp. 108–132.

——, 1950, *Economic Fluctuations in the United States, 1921–1941* (John Wiley and Sons, New York).

——, 1977, "The longevity of economic theory," in *Quantitative Wirtschafts-forschung*, eds. H. Albach *et al.* (J. C. B. Mohr, Tübingen), pp. 411–419.

—— and R. G. Bodkin, 1964, "Empirical aspects of the trade-offs among three goals: high employment, price stability and economic growth," in *Inflation, Growth and Unemployment, Report for the Commission on Money and Credit* (Prentice Hall, Englewood-Cliffs, New Jersey).

Lipsey, R. G., 1960, "The relation between unemployment and the rate of change of money wage rates in the United Kingdom, 1862–1957: a further analysis," *Economica* **27** (105), pp. 1–31.

Phillips, A. W., 1958, "The relation between unemployment and the rate of change of money wage rates in the United Kingdom, 1861–1957," *Economica* **25** (100), pp. 283–299.

Tinbergen, J., 1937, *An Econometric Approach to Business Cycle Problems* (Hermann & Cie, Paris).

25

PROTECTIONISM: AN ANALYSIS FROM PROJECT LINK[†]

The LINK system of world trade is used to examine present tendencies toward protectionism. In protectionist scenarios we increase the prices of manufactured imports into 13 LINK-OECD countries by 5, 10, and 20 percent, respectively, for 1978–1979. If a country's import equations do not depend significantly on relative price, we impose corresponding quantitative import restrictions of 5, 10, and 20 percent. Smaller OECD countries, developing countries, and socialist countries, are assumed to be nonprotectionist in these scenarios. The discrepancies between the values of leading variables in the protectionist scenarios and in a baseline case show the effects of the different degrees of protectionism assumed. The results describe and validate Adam Smith's principles of the gains from free trade.

Increasing talk about the use of protectionist measures to deal with contemporary economic problems in a number of countries and, indeed, increasing signs of the actual implementation of such measures leads us to look into the possible consequences of this new turn of events. The purpose of the present paper is to estimate the quantitative magnitude of today's protectionist tendencies by examining their overall impact on economic performance of individual countries as well as the world as a whole. The medium for this examination is the statistical system produced by Project LINK; therefore, we shall begin by introducing some background material on the structure of that system, emphasizing its relevance for the present problem.

1. The Nature of the LINK System

The LINK system is a world trade model based on the international linking of separate national econometric models.[1] At present, it consists of 20 models for

---

[†]From *Journal of Policy Modeling* (January, 1979), pp. 5–35; written jointly with Vincent Su.
[1]The econometric models part of Project LINK, built by a number of national and international teams, vary in size:
(a) 13 leading OECD countries:

Australia:	Reserve Bank of Australia: 226 endog., 138 exog, var.
Austria:	Institute for Advanced Studies: 159 endog., 68 exog.
Belgium:	Free University of Brussels: 111 endog., 65 exog.
Canada:	University of Toronto (Trace model): 332 endog., 386 exog.
Finland:	Bank of Finland: 178 endog., 139 exog.
West Germany:	Bonn University (Bonner model): 164 endog., 64 exog.
Italy:	University of Bologna (Prometeia model): 166 endog., 82 exog.
France:	Free University of Brussels (Pom-Pom model): 76 endog., 67 exog.
Japan:	Kyoto University: 125 endog., 150 exog.
Netherlands:	Central Planning Bureau Model: 118 endog., 62 exog.

individual countries — 13 major OECD countries and 7 CMEA countries — 4 regional models of developing areas — Africa, Latin America, Middle East, and Southeast Asia — and an aggregate residual sector consisting of some 12 developed countries whose total trade is assumed to be a stable fraction of the world total. A few other countries, notably the People's Republic of China, are also lumped in the residual category. Separate small models are being prepared for each of the 12 residual countries and also for China. Eventually, they will be separately modeled in LINK. Also, within the area models for developing countries, there is a separation between OPEC and all other trading activities. Eventually, it is hoped that major developing countries will be individually modeled, apart from the grouped regional models.

While much of the emphasis within the LINK system is on trade relationships, the major part of each model deals with internal domestic relationships. It is a function of the system to try to propagate trade effects through the domestic economy according to the multiplier/accelerator mechanism and other induced effects. Most of the OECD-type models have domestic monetary sectors, price formation, wage formation, and national income distribution by factor shares. Each model is constructed along national lines thought to be appropriate by each national model builder. Uniformity in specification is achieved in the trade accounts, where particular rules are laid down for all the model builders together.

The centerpiece of consistent world modeling in LINK is the international trade matrix, a construction, by commodity classes, that shows the flows (in U.S. dollars) from each country/region to each country/region grouping in the system (see Ball, 1973; Waelbroeck, 1976; and Klein, 1976; for complete descriptions of the systems and of typical models). A typical element of the world trade matrix is

$$a_{ij} = \frac{\mathbf{X}_{ij}}{\mathbf{M}_j},$$

the ratio of exports from i to j to the total imports of j. The corresponding matrix

---

Sweden: National Institute of Economic Research: 127 endog., 41 exog.

United Kingdom: London Business School: 359 endog., 180 exog.

United States: University of Pennsylvania (Wharton model): 514 endog., 282 exog.

(b) 7 CMEA countries:

Bulgaria: United Nations (CDPPP): 62 endog., 81 exog.

Czechoslovakia :   United Nations (CDPPP): 74 endog., 86 exog.

East Germany: United Nations (CDPPP): 60 endog., 76 exog.

Hungary: United Nations (CDPPP): 101 endog., 81 exog.

Poland: United Nations (CDPPP): 80 endog., 81 exog.

Romania: United Nations (CDPPP): 58 endog., 86 exog.

Soviet Union: WEFA and SRI (Sov-Mod 1): 275 endog., 147 exog.

(c) The models for the developing regions, built by a team of the United Nations Conference on Trade and Development (UNCTAD Models), contain 457 endog. and 168 exog. variables.

equation is

$$\mathbf{X} = A\mathbf{M},\tag{1}$$

showing the relationship between exports of each country/region ($\mathbf{X}$) and imports of each country/region ($\mathbf{M}$). Both $\mathbf{X}$ and $\mathbf{M}$ are column vectors, while A is a square matrix. If exports are evaluated from Eq. (1), then it is assured that total world exports equal total world imports. Each country's exports are evaluated by Eq. (1) as a weighted sum of partner country imports, the weights being the elements of the exporting country's row in A.

If $\mathbf{X}$ and $\mathbf{M}$ are real (deflated) values, the world trade identity is preserved in constant numéraire prices. A corresponding identity must hold in current prices, namely

$$(P\mathbf{X})'\mathbf{X} = (P\mathbf{M})'\mathbf{M}.\tag{2}$$

By substitution from Eq. (1) into Eq. (2), we obtain

$$[(P\mathbf{X})'A]\mathbf{M} = (P\mathbf{M}')\mathbf{M}.\tag{3}$$

This is an identity in $\mathbf{M}$. By term-by-term equating of left- and right-hand sides of (3) we find that import prices ($P\mathbf{M}$) are weighted averages of partner country export prices ($P\mathbf{X}$). This, too, is a consistency property of LINK. The explicit equations for export volumes and import prices are

$$X_i = \sum_{j=1}^{n} a_{ij} M_j \quad i = 1, 2, \ldots, n,\tag{4}$$

$$(PM)_j = \sum_{i=1}^{n} a_{ij} (PX)_i \quad j = 1, 2, \ldots, n.\tag{5}$$

These conversion equations using the trade matrix are worked out for the constant-dollar (real) case for A. A corresponding analysis can be worked out for the case in which A is defined in current dollars.

The LINK models are all maintained in separate research centers throughout the world and reflect distinctive characteristics of each economy or the interests of the model managers. This approach relies heavily on cooperative expertise, but it does introduce some degree of heterogeneity. To tie the system together consistently, we have imposed rules for the trade sector relations, namely, that valuations be in FOB units for both exports and imports and that each model provide results for separate SITC classes

   0, 1   food, beverages and tobacco,
   2, 4   raw materials (non fuel),
      3   fuel,
   5–9   manufactures and semi-manufactures.

Models can be based on more detailed groupings for some merchandise categories, provided that they can always be aggregated into these.

The world trade matrix must be stated in some fixed monetary unit, the "numéraire," and we have followed convention in using a U.S. dollar unit. This brings exchange rates into the system because each model is specified in local currency units. Where import and export prices are taken from the separate model solutions for use in Eqs. (1) and (3), they must be converted from local currency units to dollar units. Before computed export and import prices can be reentered into individual models in iteration stages of the LINK algorithm, it is necessary to convert back to local currency units. Eventually, exchange rates will be endogenized in the models, but presently they are exogenously assumed; nevertheless, the assumptions about exchange rates do have an effect on the solution and the workings of the system. It is possible to study the effect of changed rates without actually being able to forecast them by equations of the system.

The computer algorithm for solving the LINK system is carefully described, in broad outline, in *The Models of Project LINK* (Waelbroeck, 1976). Basically it consists of assuming exogenous values for export and import prices in each model, solving for import and export prices, substituting these (after appropriate exchange conversion) into Eqs. (1) and (3), and generating values of export and import prices to be inserted again into each model for a whole new iterative round of the same calculations. The iterations cease when the solution converges, i.e., changes by less than a pre-assigned small amount between successive iterations. The calculations are complicated and large scale, but they are straightforward. The procedure is, however, deceptively simple by virtue of our not paying attention to the time variation of the world trade matrix, A. This matrix does, in fact, vary from year to year, and it is necessary for us to account for this fact. This can be done in two ways, either by modeling the error, $\mathbf{E}_t$, in

$$\mathbf{X}_t = A_0\mathbf{M}_t + \mathbf{E}_t$$
$$A_0 = \text{base period matrix}$$

or by modeling the changes in the cell entries

$$a_{ijt} = \frac{X_{ijt}}{M_{jt}}.$$

At present, the LINK system models E_t as functions of relative trade prices and adjusts the A matrix each period by a standard arithmetic procedure, known as the RAS method, whereby all entries are specified to move according to the way corresponding row and column marginal totals move. The RAS adjusted matrices are then used to update the matrix for the price conversion calculation. The direct estimation of changing all entries is based on a method developed by Hickman and Lau (1973). It has been used experimentally in LINK simulations but is not used in the calculations for the present paper.

2. Types of LINK Models

For purposes of model building and analyzing world economic events, there are three main groupings of economic systems in the world:

(i) industrial market economies — essentially OECD countries,
(ii) socialist economies — CMEA countries, plus China, North Korea, Vietnam, and Cuba, and
(iii) developing economies.

The first group is modeled along the lines of income and employment determination, using capitalist market principles. The second group is centrally planned. Much more is known at this stage about the U.S.S.R. and other CMEA partner countries than in the past. Only first attempts are now being made to model China and other socialist countries. The modeling efforts for developing countries are being split into two subgroupings — those in OPEC and all others, but there is obviously great diversity among Asia, Africa, Latin America, and the Middle East.

Most of the models in the LINK system, particularly those for the OECD countries, are demand oriented. They have some supply-side content and can be adjusted for interpretation of supply restraints, as in the case of the oil embargo of 1973–74, but their predominant orientation is towards demand. By contrast, the models for the centrally planned economies, CMEA countries in the case of LINK, and the models for the developing countries are more supply oriented, with some demand aspects.

Imports in the OECD models are basically demand equations for imports, depending on income or activity variables and relative price variables. In other economies, imports may be treated more as supply supplements. Imports rise when supply shortfalls occur. That has been typically the case when the U.S.S.R. or China have experienced poor crop conditions. This pattern of behavior has been more in evidence for imports of basic commodities — food and industrial materials — but imports of manufactured goods also have a supply aspect. Some of these imports are being demanded now in order to raise productivity and enhance supply in later periods.

In the case of developing countries, another supply-side factor is at work, known as the principle of import substitution. To the extent that supply from domestic manufacturing can meet demand, imports are restrained. In a demand-oriented model, imports would be positively related to domestic activity, but in a supply-oriented model, the relationship is inverse. Import substitution occurs as increased domestic manufacturing activity reduces import requirements.

Whether imports come about through demand-side or supply-side influences, they dominate the LINK system. Any single country or region will respond positively to export increases and will generally have an improved trade balance, unless its marginal propensity to import is abnormally large. The latter is true for some LINK countries such as the Netherlands where the import share of GNP is about 50 percent.

While exports are a *driving* variable for the typical open economy; studied in isolation, the linked system of models responds to *imports* as a *driving* force. If exports are selectively increased, the models receiving the exogenous increases show export gains, but the world as a whole does not, except possibly by a small amount. If the total amount of world trade remains approximately unchanged, when selective increases are introduced in the exports of given models, it must follow that other model solutions show compensatory declines. This is what happens, whether the exogenous change is introduced as an increase or decrease.

On the other hand, if an exogenous shift is introduced in import equations, the model amount and the world amount will tend to change in the same direction. Higher demand for imports by a major country will provide better export markets for its partners, via Eq. (1). Those partners with the largest share coefficients corresponding to the import column where the change is introduced will get the largest share of added exports. The export multipliers in these partner countries will lead to higher activity levels for them and induce increases in their imports. These secondary effects will then increase exports of their partner countries. This is an *amplification* effect.[2] Increases (decreases) in imports will raise (lower) the total value of world trade. Some redistributions will also occur because of country differences, but imports drive the world economy as a whole, and exports react to it, via Eq. (1).

To introduce exogenous changes in either exports or imports we add (signed) adjustment terms to the equations being affected, but some imports, such as U.S. oil imports, may be wholly exogenous, in which case the variable is simply changed as an input value. An export change would be

$$X_{it} = \sum_{j=1}^{n} a_{ij} M_{jt} + \delta_{it} \tag{6}$$

where δ_{it} represents an exogenous shift.

Correspondingly, an import change would be

$$M_{it} = f_i \left(Y_{it}, \frac{p_{it}}{(PM)_{it}} \right) + \epsilon_{it}. \tag{7}$$

In this latter equation, f_i is the ith country's import equation, Y_{it} is its appropriate activity variable, and $p_{it}/(PM)_{it}$ is the relative price variable comparing the ratio of the domestic to import price for the model being used. The exogenous shift factor is ϵ_{it}.

Just as imports drive the volume or value side of world trade, depending on whether the formulation uses a nominal or real trade matrix, export prices drive the overall world inflation rate, and import prices are derived from them in Eq. (3). If export prices of some countries increase, partner countries will experience higher

---

[2]The oil embargo of 1973–74 introduced a downward amplification effect. See L. R. Klein and K. Johnson (1974).

import prices. These will increase domestic costs and result in secondary inflation effects. This is what happened when export prices for grains and then fuel went to extraordinarily high values in 1973. If import prices are selectively changed exogenously, the country experiencing the change will realize direct effects on domestic costs, but will not raise overall world prices significantly, and there will tend to be compensatory changes elsewhere in the system.

In looking at protectionist instruments as they affect imports, we should consider tariffs, relative prices, exchange rates, quotas, and some special variables for institutional arrangements. An import equation written generally as

$$M_{it} = f_i\left(Y_{it}, \frac{P_{it}}{(PM)_{it}}\right)$$

needs some explanation. The relative price variable compares domestic (P_{it}) to a weighted combination of foreign prices, $(PM)_{it}$. They must be in comparable units; therefore, each component of $(PM)_{it}$ must be converted from foreign to local currency units. This introduces exchange rates in $(PM)_{it}$. In LINK, $(PM)_{it}$ would be computed as a dollar index from a weighted average of dollar indexes making up the vector $(\mathbf{PX})_t$. $(\mathbf{PX})_t$ was converted before entering the LINK part of the algorithm from local to dollar denominations. This required the use of a whole vector of exchange rates evaluated against the dollar. For comparison with P_{it}, the dollar index must be converted to units of model i's currency. This is how exchange rates enter the calculation.

A tariff adjustment is also needed, because $(PM)_{it}$ should represent the price to the buyer in country/region i. The index $(PM)_{it}$ has to include a tariff valuation. It could be either in $(PM)_{it}$ directly or in its coefficient as

$$\alpha_i[P_{it}/(PM)_{it}].$$

If $(\mathbf{PM})_{it}$ does not include a duty adjustment, then α_i should include the factor

$$1/d_i$$

where d_i is the appropriate duty rate for imports into country/region i. These rates will vary by SITC group. Generally, governments will not levy duties on food and materials. Duties occur mainly in the case of manufactured goods.

Voluntary quotas, strict statutory quotas, special agreements must all be taken into account. The Canadian–U.S. automobile agreement is a good special case. Trade in autos and parts reacted unusually sharply to the institution of the agreement by expanding rapidly. Dummy variables or special quantitative restrictions are used directly as separate variables in the equation. Textile, steel, TV, shoe agreements are good examples of voluntary restraint factors. Dummy variables should be used for these cases.

3. A Simple Model of Protection

Whether it takes the form of voluntary quotas, reference pricing, antidumping, or outright tariffs, there is a distinct tendency in today's environment of stagflation to introduce protectionist policies. Many countries are beset by trade/payments deficits and, from a myopic view of self interest, see protectionism as a way out — after all other policies have seemingly failed.

The world trading system embodied in Project LINK will be used, in this essay, to examine various protectionist policies, in different combinations, among the trading countries of the world. Prior to the specific forms of simulated protectionism in the statistical model, let us examine some of the ideas and concepts in an extremely simplified model.

The two-country case is the simplest system that shows some interaction effect while allowing transparent derivation of closed-form results for linear relationships.[3] Let us write two definitional equations of GNP:

$$y_1 = d_1 y_1 + m_2 y_2 - m_1 y_1 + g_1 \tag{8}$$

$$y_2 = d_2 y_2 + m_1 y_1 - m_2 y_2 + g_2 \tag{9}$$

y_i = country i's GNP $(i = 1, 2)$,
$d_i y_i$ = country i's domestic expenditures (on home and foreign goods/services),
d_i = marginal propensity to spend (consume + invest),
$m_i y_i$ = country i's imports of goods/services,
m_i = marginal propensity to import,
g_i = country i's autonomous (government) expenditures.

Each equation expresses GNP as the sum of domestic expenditures on consumption and investment, plus exports minus imports, plus autonomous expenditures by public authorities. Since country 1's exports are country 2's imports in this two-country world, we can express all the trade entries from the import side. Country 1's exports, being country 2's imports, are linear in country 2's GNP level.

These are standard accounting equations that usually are written as

$$GNP = C + I + G + E - M$$
$$C + I = d_1 y_1 \;\; ; \;\; d_2 y_2$$
$$G = g_1 \;\;\;\; ; \;\;\;\; g_2$$
$$E = m_2 y_2 \; ; \;\; m_1 y_1$$
$$M = m_1 y_1 \; ; \;\; m_2 y_2 \,.$$

Naturally, all units of measurement are common. The variables are denominated in one unit of account. We shall abstract from exchange rate changes.

Let us suppose that a protectionist policy is introduced in country 1, restricting imports by the amount δ. Then exports must be reduced in country 2 by δ to

---

[3] This is essentially the model introduced by Lloyd A. Metzler (1942).

preserve the world trade identity — world exports equal world imports.

$$y_1 = \frac{m_2}{1 - d_1 + m_1} y_2 + \frac{\delta + g_1}{1 - d_1 + m_1}$$

$$y_2 = \frac{m_1}{1 - d_2 + m_2} y_1 + \frac{-\delta + g_2}{1 - d_2 + m_2}.$$

Denote, multipliers

$$M_1 = \frac{1}{1 - d_1 + m_1} \qquad ; \qquad M_2 = \frac{1}{1 - d_2 + m_2}$$

$$y_1 = m_2 M_1 y_2 + M_1(\delta + g_1)$$

$$y_2 = m_1 M_2 y_1 + M_2(-\delta + g_2).$$

Final, reduced form expressions are

$$y_1 = \frac{M_1(g_1 + m_2 M_2 g_2)}{1 - m_1 m_2 M_1 M_2} + \frac{M_1(1 - m_2 M_2)}{1 - m_1 m_2 M_1 M_2} \delta \tag{10}$$

$$y_2 = \frac{M_2(g_2 + m_1 M_1 g_1)}{1 - m_1 m_2 M_1 M_2} + \frac{M_2(m_1 M_1 - 1)}{1 - m_1 m_2 M_1 M_2} \delta. \tag{11}$$

If country 1 protects by the amount δ, the multiplier value for its GNP is, from (10)

$$\frac{M_1(1 - m_2 M_2)}{1 - m_1 m_2 M_1 M_2},$$

while the cross multiplier value for country 2 is, from (11)

$$\frac{M_2(m_1 M_1 - 1)}{1 - m_1 m_2 M_1 M_2}.$$

The sign and magnitude of the results depend on the conventional multipliers, M_1 and M_2, and the marginal propensities to import, m_1 and m_2. In general, we shall find that

$$1 - m_1 m_2 M_1 M_2 > 0.$$

Each multiplier is probably less than 2.0

$$M_1 < 2.0$$

$$M_2 < 2.0.$$

An outside figure for m_1 or m_2 is 0.5, but a more likely figure is about 0.1. If m_i is high (near 0.5) then M_i is likely to be low, because of import leakage, at about 1.0 or even smaller.

If we have

$$1 - m_i M_i > 0 \qquad i = 1, 2$$

as seems likely, then the protecting country has an income increase, while the other has a decrease. This case would be exemplified by the developed countries protecting their manufactured imports against cheap imports from developing countries. Then country 1 (developed countries) gains at the expense of economic activity in country 2 (developing countries).

A graphical analysis of the interaction of the two equations is given in Fig. 1. The plotted equations are derived from

$$y_1 = m_2 M_1 y_2 + M_1 (\delta + g_1)$$

$$y_2 = m_1 M_2 y_1 + M_2 (-\delta + g_2).$$

The second of these two equations is renormalized to make y_1 the left-hand-side variable in

$$y_1 = \frac{1}{m_1 M_2} y_2 + \frac{1}{m_1} (\delta - g_2).$$

The two solid lines in Fig. 1 are plotted for $\delta = 0$.

$$y_1 = m_2 M_1 y_2 + M_1 g_1$$

$$y_1 = \frac{1}{m_1 M_2} y_2 - \frac{1}{m_1} g_2.$$

The first intercept is positive and the second is negative. It is assumed that $1/(m_1 M_2)$ is greater than $m_2 M_1$ so that the second line cuts the first from below.

If protectionism is introduced by country 1's cutting its imports by δ, the corresponding equation shifts upward by $M_1 \delta$ and the other (also *upward*) by $1/(m_1)\delta$. Since m_1 is significantly less than unity, the shift of the second curve should be greater.

"World equilibrium" shifts from intersection point I to II. In this case, y_1 rises and y_2 falls.

World GNP is expressed as

$$y_1 + y_2 = \frac{M_1 g_1 (1 + m_1 M_2) + M_2 g_2 (1 + m_2 M_1)}{1 - m_1 m_2 M_1 M_2}$$

$$+ \delta \frac{(M_1 - M_2) + M_1 M_2 (m_1 - m_2)}{1 - m_1 m_2 M_1 M_2}. \tag{12}$$

The coefficient of δ in (12) could be positive or negative, depending on the excess of Country 1's multiplier value over that of 2 and the excess of Country 1's marginal propensity to import over that of 2. The relative sizes of the multiplier are likely to be opposite to the relative sizes of the marginal propensities. Protectionism could drive world GNP in either direction.

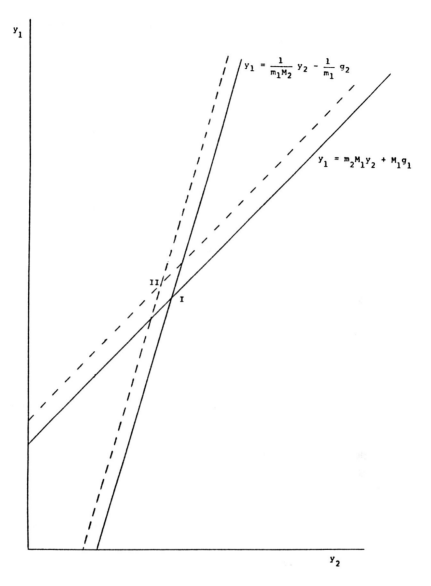

Fig. 1. GNP interaction, two-country world model.

An expression for total world trade is:

$$m_1 y_1 + m_2 y_2 - \delta = \frac{m_1 m_2 M_1 M_2 (g_1 + g_2) + m_1 M_1 g_1 + m_2 M_2 g_2}{1 - m_1 m_2 M_1 M_2}$$
$$- \delta \frac{(1 + m_2 M_2)(1 - m_1 M_1)}{1 - m_1 m_2 M_1 M_2}. \tag{13}$$

The sign of this expression will depend principally on $(1 - m_1 M_1)$. If this is positive, as is likely, world trade will vary inversely with δ.

This model can be readily extended to the case in which the second country retaliates in beggar-thy-neighbor policies. The equations would then be:

$$y_1 = m_2 M_1 y_2 + M_1(\delta - \epsilon + g_1)$$

$$y_2 = m_1 M_2 y_1 + M_2(\epsilon - \delta + g_2),$$

where ϵ is the amount by which country 2 restricts imports in a protectionist policy.

The reduced form equations then are

$$y_1 = \frac{M_1(g_1 + m_2 M_2 g_2)}{1 - m_1 m_2 M_1 M_2} + \frac{M_1(1 - m_2 M_2)}{1 - m_1 m_2 M_1 M_2}(\delta - \epsilon) \qquad (14)$$

$$y_2 = \frac{M_2(g_2 + m_1 M_1 g_1)}{1 - m_1 m_2 M_1 M_2} + \frac{M_2(m_1 M_1 - 1)}{1 - m_1 m_2 M_1 M_2}(\epsilon - \delta). \qquad (15)$$

The direction of effect is the same as before if $\delta - \epsilon$ is positive and the opposite if $\delta - \epsilon$ is negative. Since the developed countries are so much larger in the aggregate than are the developing countries, the developed countries' δ is likely to exceed the developing countries' ϵ. The effects are watered down in magnitude but unchanged in sign for this particular identification of country 1 and country 2.

The models in Eqs. (8) and (9) assume, implicitly, that there is perfect substitution between domestic and imported goods. Spending, expressed by $d_i y_i$, includes both types of goods, and the consumer or business firm is assumed to be indifferent between the two. The total depends on income available in (8) or (9) regardless whether the goods are produced at home or abroad. The spender is thus interested only in acquiring the goods and not in their origin. The concept of "import substitution" might be based on this premise; at least policies based on this concept would work most favorably for the home country if the premise is correct.

Total private spending on consumption and investment can be split into two parts, a domestic and an imported component.

$$Cd_1 + Cm_1 + Id_1 + Im_1 = d_1 y_1$$

$$Cd_2 + Cm_2 + Id_2 + Im_2 = d_2 y_2.$$

The import component of GNP is the sum of import components of consumption and investment, assuming that government spending is solely domestically based.

$$\text{Imports (1)} = Cm_1 + Im_1 = m_1 y_1$$

$$\text{Imports (2)} = Cm_2 + Im_2 = m_2 y_2.$$

Instead of including imports in domestic spending and then subtracting it, we can write

$$y_1 = dd_1 y_1 + m_2 y_2 + g_1$$

$$y_2 = dd_2 y_2 + m_1 y_1 + g_2,$$

where dd_1 and dd_2 are marginal propensities to spend on *domestic* goods and services.[4] If we assume that people do distinguish between their spending on domestic and foreign goods to the extent that they do not substitute freely between them and that dd_i are stable parameters, this is a useful model to consider. It is a variation on the previous one.

In the U.S. simulations of the oil embargo in 1973, oil imports were reduced by the amount expected to be cut off (2 million b/d in the U.S.) and domestic consumption (of both imported and home-produced oil and gasoline) was correspondingly reduced. This left no effect on the GNP, as would be the case in the above equation for y_1. In order to bring out the effect, which turned out to be not insignificant, we had to make a third entry, that was not offset. This took the form of reduced inventory change (see Klein, 1974).

Let us assume, as before, that country 1 becomes protectionist by restricting imports in the amount δ. We then have

$$y_1 = dd_1 y_1 + m_2 y_2 + g_1$$
$$y_2 = dd_2 y_2 + m_1 y_1 + g_2 - \delta .$$

Using the same steps as in the previous case; we may reduce the equations to

$$y_1 = m_2 M_1^* y_2 + M_1^* g_1$$
$$y_2 = m_1 M_2^* y_1 + M_2^* (g_2 - \delta) .$$

In this notation

$$M_i^* = \frac{1}{1 - dd_i} .$$

The expression for M_i and M_i^* may be the same, but not necessarily; accordingly, we differentiate the symbols for the traditional multiplier value in this case.

The final equations are

$$y_1 = \frac{M_1^*(g_1 + m_2 M_2^* g_2)}{1 - m_1 m_2 M_1^* M_2^*} - \frac{m_2 M_1^* M_2^*}{1 - m_1 m_2 M_1^* M_2^*} \delta \qquad (16)$$

$$y_2 = \frac{M_2^*(m_1 M_1^* g_1 + g_2)}{1 - m_1 m_2 M_1^* M_2^*} - \frac{M_2^*}{1 - m_1 m_2 M_1^* M_2^*} \delta . \qquad (17)$$

Clearly, each country's production variable is inversely related to δ_1.

If both countries protect, by δ and ϵ respectively, the model is

$$y_1 = dd_1 y_1 + m_2 y_2 + (g_1 - \epsilon)$$
$$y_2 = dd_2 y_2 + m_1 y_1 + (g_2 - \delta) ,$$

---

[4]This model is the one used by Romney Robinson (1952). His Fig. 1 is the motivation for ours.

and the final equations are

$$y_1 = \frac{m_2 M_1^* M_2^*}{1 - m_1 m_2 M_1^* M_2^*}(g_2 - \delta) + \frac{M_1^*}{1 - m_1 m_2 M_1^* M_2^*}(g_1 - \epsilon) \tag{18}$$

$$y_2 = \frac{m_1 M_1^* M_2^*}{1 - m_1 m_2 M_1^* M_2^*}(g_1 - \epsilon) + \frac{M_2^*}{1 - m_1 m_2 M_1^* M_2^*}(g_2 - \delta). \tag{19}$$

The output variables are inversely related to both δ and ϵ.

4. The Working of Protectionism (Within the LINK System)

The model of Sec. 3 has pedagogical simplicity. It can be pictured in a two-dimensional display and solved in closed-form expressions. Even within this two-country framework, it has restrictive (implicit) assumptions. There are no relative prices; exchange rates are fixed; the system is static; and the relationships are linear. The LINK system, on the other hand, is dynamic, nonlinear, strongly multilateral, and highly disaggregated. It contains exogenous, *not fixed*, exchange rates at the present time.

In simulations of the world economy, with special emphasis on trade, the LINK system has, since 1973, shown several areas of imbalance in adjusting to the large petrol surplus of some \$40 or \$50 billion per annum. It would have been large, were it not for the surplus countries' high propensity to import from the deficit countries. The distribution of the world petrol balance shows the United States with a large offsetting deficit — some \$30 billion in 1977. Large deficits have occurred for France, Italy, and the United Kingdom among major summit nations. Spain, Portugal, Denmark and, recently, Sweden are also large deficit areas. Italy and the United Kingdom show signs of turning their deficits around, by restricting imports in a deflationary domestic environment in the Italian case and by drawing on the North Sea in the British case. The non-oil-developing world is also, by and large, in a deficit position. Offsetting and contrasting with these non-OPEC deficit areas are the two large surpluses enjoyed by Germany and Japan.

Before the United Kingdom suddenly extricated itself from a deficit position by drawing on the fruits of the North Sea, its large deficit appeared to be chronic, impeding the introduction of significant reflationary measures which would have alleviated the pains of high unemployment and the accompanying slow growth. Some voices were heard to say that just about every kind of remedy had been tried for some two–three decades and that it was time to look to protectionism now. That position would argue that Britain should look after its own economic constituency first, and try to raise activity levels with a positive trade balance by restricting imports. This could be done by (1) raising tariff duties, (2) imposing quotas or ceilings, (3) enforcing antidumping legislation, and (4) requiring import deposits. These and others, too, would have the effect of holding down imports. That is the objective.

In the United States, the clamor for protection is not introduced for the sake of strengthening the overall imbalance position; it is introduced by the affected interest groups, especially steel companies, television manufacturers, textile/apparel manufacturers, and all their trade unions

If the United States or the United Kingdom were to become strongly protectionistic, it would lower imports, with the secondary effects on domestic activity, and still lower import demand. The volume of world trade and world GDP would suffer, however, even though the protectionist countries might benefit in terms of their own activity levels and trade balance. This is what is meant by "beggar-thy-neighbor" policies.

Generally speaking, on the basis of the causal structure of the LINK system, and in line with standard economic thinking, we would expect to find lower volume of world trade, lower levels of activity, more unemployment, and higher prices (more inflation) as a result of the introduction of protectionist policies. In dynamic systems with rapidly deteriorating environments, it is possible that all parties will be worse off, but a more likely outcome will be, especially in the short run, that some protectionist countries will gain at the expense of the rest of the world. The gains of the protectionist countries will not generally exceed the losses of the others.

Protectionism is practical in terms of trade in manufactures. There is some protection for agriculture in a few cases, but by and large, materials are essential to production and therefore are usually not protected. We shall concentrate our LINK calculations on trade in SITC groups 5–9. Energy conservation in the United States could be viewed as protectionism because it tries to save imports in SITC group 3, but since it is aimed at dealing with an exorbitant, non-competitive cartel price, it should not be called protectionism. It is not viewed as a means of protecting a home industry, but of developing new industries.

It seems pointless to impose protectionist policies on the imports of centrally planned or developing countries. They want imports of SITC groups 5–9 in order to enhance their growth prospects and are not likely to protect. We shall interpret protectionism narrowly as measures by OECD countries to restrain imports in favor of home production and employment.

Many LINK models estimate low or zero (statistically insignificant) price elasticities for imports. In these cases, we cannot introduce protectionism in the form of higher import prices — as through duty increases. In place of a price constraint, we introduce volume constraint, as through quota limitations. Subsidization of export prices could be another technique for gaining at the expense of others. In some instances, this may appear as "dumping."

Different levels of protection are considered in this study. The equivalent of 5% import price increases through duties is low-level protectionism. If quantity limits are used, they will be chosen so as to have about the same effect as an average of 5% price rises in other countries, or as though price elasticity were unity. A medium-sized degree of protectionism would be associated with 10% import price rises and a high degree at 20%. These increments are all estimated as changes superimposed on a baseline simulation path, without any new protectionist measures being introduced.

Protectionism will probably involve retaliation; so we are assuming that all OECD countries adopt such measures simultaneously. Exchange-rate changes, which also alter prices paid for imports and charged for exports, are differentiated. They are intended to eliminate imbalances, or move in the direction of elimination of imbalances, by having surplus countries appreciate and deficit countries depreciate their currencies; therefore the effects should compensate one another. Protectionism does not work in this way.

5. Experimental Design

As discussed above, the country models in the LINK system are grouped into four categories: 13 major OECD countries, 7 CMEA countries, 4 regions of developing areas, and a residual sector (the rest-of-world countries). The CMEA countries trade mainly with each other. It is unlikely that these countries would adopt any form of protectionist measures in order to solve their macroeconomic problems. The economic development of developing countries depends heavily on their import of finished goods and raw materials. Imports in these countries are constrained by their export capacity. As long as they can maintain a reasonable trade balance, their imports would not be restricted by regulatory measures for protectionism. The rest-of-world sector includes all countries which do not belong to the three other groups. The import value of this group accounts for 10% of total world trade. Since this group is treated as a residual in the LINK system, without structural models, protective policies are not proposed for these countries either.

In this study, the protectionist measures are applied, therefore, only to the 13 LINK OECD countries, under the assumption that the trade balance and economic growth of each country can be improved. Total trade of these 13 countries accounts for more than 60% of the world total. Because it is not practical for these countries to impose restrictions on imports of food and raw materials, the protectionist restrictions are introduced only for manufactured goods, i.e., the 5–9 SITC category in the LINK system.

Methods of introducing protectionist measures into each country model vary according to the structure of import sector. In general, there are two types of import equations used in the system. The most common import equation (7), as indicated in the previous section, is a function of the level of economic activity and relative price. The relative price is expressed by the ratio of domestic to import prices. Import prices are predetermined if the model is solved in the pre-LINK mode, i.e., the country is treated alone as a closed economy. However, when the entire system is solved in the post-LINK mode, the model import prices will be overwritten by the LINK import prices in Eq. (5), formed as a weighted average of trading partner countries' export prices in the LINK system. Equations that relate model import prices to the LINK import prices are included in the *inward linkage* which passes the influence from the world aggregates into each individual country model. However, in the *outward linkage*, which passes influence from each country to the world aggregates, the previous relationship in the inward linkage is reversed.

The models of Australia, Belgium, Canada, Finland, Germany, Japan, Netherlands, and the United States have the above type of import equations. A natural way of introducing protectionist measures into these models is to impose an import duty on manufactured goods. This can be interpreted as an increase in the import price paid for manufactured goods. In practice, it can be done by adjusting the import price of the 5–9 SITC group upward in the inward linkage. However, the same price variable would be adjusted downward back to the original level in the outward linkage. In this way, the increase in import duty influences domestic activity in the country model but does not directly affect the world prices. The latter are basically FOB export prices and, as such, should not include the duty.

Other import equations used in the LINK system do not include any price variables. The volume of imports by SITC categories is determined by the levels of economic activities, lagged imports, and other relevant variables. The models of Austria, France, Italy, Sweden, and the United Kingdom have this type of specification in the import sector. In these models, changes in import prices do not have a direct impact on import volume. Protectionist policies must, therefore, be introduced as quantitative import restrictions. The restriction is imposed directly in the import equation of manufactured goods by downward adjustment of the import volume of the appropriate category.

In the present study, the final LINK forecast, made at the end of 1977, was used as the baseline solution. This solution uses 1976 for initial conditions and generates annual forecasts of 1977, 1978, and 1979. Since the present study was done at the beginning of 1978, the simulations of different protectionist scenarios were extended to cover only 1978 and 1979.

Three simulations with different magnitudes of protectionist measures have been imposed on the baseline solution. The first scenario assumes the imposition of a 5% import tariff on the import price of manufactured goods. In those models whose import equations do not include price factors, a 5% reduction in the import volume of manufactured goods is applied. It implies that we assume the elasticity of demand for imported manufactured goods to be equal to unity. The percentages of increase in price and decrease in volume are measured in the pre-LINK calculations. In those models that have strong distributed lag effects in import equations, the reduction in import volume is carried over to later periods. In these models, special adjustments are made so that the reduction in the pre-LINK simulation is approximately 5% in each year.

Some models include only a single behavioral equation in the trade sector to explain total imports. Imports are then disaggregated into four standard SITC categories according to the distribution in the recent past. An increase of 5% in import tariff on manufactured goods in these models must first be incorporated as an increase of 5% in total import price. Total import volume, not only the import of manufactured goods, would therefore decline. In such cases, we must first ascertain the induced decline in other commodity categories when the total import price is adjusted up by 5% in a pre-LINK simulation. Then, the import volumes of other categories are adjusted up accordingly before the post-LINK simulation is run. Therefore, the 5% tariff would not directly affect the other commodity groups, and component imports still add to total imports.

The models of Australia and Canada have a built-in tariff dummy variable in their import equations. Theoretically, these tariff variables, instead of price variables, should be adjusted to reflect an increase of protectionism. The impact on import quantity, however, is relatively insignificant in a pre-LINK simulation if the tariff variable is changed by 5%. The percentage reduction of import quantity in this simulation is also substantially lower than the percentage reduction of import quantity in the pre-LINK simulation of other country models where the import prices were directly reduced by 5%. This leads us to think that the model import price, rather than the tariff variable, is the better variable to adjust in order to reflect a protectionist tariff in these two models.

The second and third simulations assume a 10 and 20% protectionist tariff on the import price or quantitative restriction of manufactured goods, respectively. The calculation procedure in these two simulations is the same as that in the 5% simulation. The results of all three simulations and the baseline solution are presented in the next section.

6. Simulation Results

Total world (export) trade value (TWX), world (export) trade price (PWX), and total world (export) trade volume (TWXR) of different simulations are compared with corresponding variables from the baseline solution in Table 1. In this table, the baseline column is reported in level form, and the other three columns are reported as deviations from the baseline. As expected from analytical considerations, when these 13 OECD countries take protectionist actions simultaneously, the total volume of world trade declines and world trade price rises. The net impact in the 10% simulation is approximately double that of the 5% simulation, and the net impact in the 20% simulation is again roughly double that in the 10% simulation. The decline in world trade volume in the second year is substantially greater than in the first. The increases in the declines in the second of these two consecutive years is about 40–50%; it indicates that there is a cumulative effect as a result of the lag structure in import behavior. There would probably be an additional decline in trade volume below the baseline if the present exercise were extended beyond 1979. The cumulative effect, however, does not occur in the world trade price index. The increase in the world price index over the baseline in the second year remains the same as in the first year. The increase in the world price index of manufactured goods over the baseline in 1979 is even slightly smaller than in 1978.

Table 1. Summary of world trade and GNP under protectionist policies.

	Baseline solution	Total trade Protectionism			Baseline solution	Manufactured goods Protectionism		
		5%	10%	20%		5%	10%	20%
1978								
TWX (bil. $)	1225.86	−22.24	−40.05	−75.06	740.12	−20.23	−36.55	−68.33
PWX	2.746	0.011	0.022	0.038	2.14	0.007	0.013	0.024
TWXR (bil. 1970 $)	495.13	−11.12	−20.35	−37.43	345.48	−10.46	−19.01	−35.26
OECD[1]								
GNP (bil. 1970 $)	2537.19	−1.81	−3.90	−6.02				
Growth (%)	4.29	−0.07	−0.16	−0.23				
Inflation (%)	6.51	0.23	0.51	0.98				
Trade (bil. $)	722.64	−17.05	−30.91	−57.41				
DEVE[2]								
GNP (bil. 1970 $)	432.4	−0.8	−1.4	−2.3				
Growth (%)t	6.4	−0.1	−0.2	−0.2				
Trade	310.18	−2.76	−4.78	−9.46				
1979								
TWX (bil. $)	1410.57	−37.43	−65.91	−138.1	850.24	−33.00	−56.90	−121.4
PWX	2.685	0.011	0.021	0.038	2.318	0.004	0.008	0.009
TWXR (bil. 1970 $)	525.31	−15.90	−28.39	−57.99	366.73	−14.72	−25.68	−53.58
OECD[1]								
GNP (bil. 1970 $)	2635.72	−4.05	−9.32	−15.99				
Growth (%)	3.83	−0.08	−0.22	−0.34				
Inflation (%)	6.35	0.02	0.09	0.11				
Trade (bil. $)	838.10	−28.07	−48.72	−99.37				
DEVE[2]								
GNP (bil. 1970 $)	457.3	−1.2	−2.1	−3.7				
Growth (%)	5.8	−0.1	−0.2	−0.3				
Trade (bil. $)	358.71	−4.99	−9.24	−18.09				

[1]13 LINK OECD countries.

[2]Developing countries.

Since the import and export price indexes used in these simulations are net of any duty charges, the higher prices shown in the protectionist cases in Table 1 reflect *reduced* changes that indicate the inflationary impact of trade restrictions. It is more expensive for trading countries to substitute for imports under the umbrella of protectionism. This is an indication of the real loss incurred by such policies.

Most of the decline in world trade is attributable to the decline in the trade of manufactured goods, on which the protectionist sanctions are applied. However, about 10% of the reduction in world trade is attributable to the decline of trade in other categories. When the level of world economic activity declines as a consequence of wide-spread protectionism, the demand for fuel and raw materials will also fall.

Table 1 indicates that total GNP of the 13 LINK OECD countries, as a whole, would also decline as a result of protectionism. Obviously, if only a single country imposes a tariff, its GNP would increase (by a multiplied amount) and its trade balance would improve in the first instance because imports would fall while exports would probably not be affected directly. However, if a number of its trading partners take protectionist actions at the same time in an attempt to improve their economic situations, then both imports and exports would decline. If it is a heavy trading country, the decline in exports may have some repercussion effects on the economy, which could lower domestic economic activity and reduce its GNP. This is an analog of the paradox of thrift.

Total real GNP of the 13 LINK OECD countries, measured in 1970 dollars, is estimated to fall by $1.81 billion in 1978 and $4.05 billion in 1979 if a 5% protectionist tariff is applied. Obviously, the effect on total GNP is also cumulative over time. Besides, the GNP of developing countries is also reduced, even though they are assumed not to impose any protectionist measures. This result agrees with the two-country world trade example given in Sec. 3. Since the major part of exports from developing regions to OECD countries is in fuel and raw materials, the decline in GNP of developing countries is mainly due to the reduction of imports of these commodities by the OECD countries as a result of the slowdown in economic activity. We have also checked the GNP of individual CMEA countries; they are the least affected.

The average rates of economic growth of 13 LINK OECD countries and of developing regions are also presented in Table 1. The growth rates of both groups seem to be equally affected under different protectionist policies. The effect in 1979 is slightly larger than that in 1978 in both groups.

The impact on the growth rate of 13 OECD countries in different protectionist scenarios is reported in Table 2. The baseline column represents the growth rate; the other three columns represent deviations from the baseline solution. Evidently, protectionism works well in Austria, France, and Sweden. These three countries would have a net gain in the two-year period in all three scenarios. In the 1975 world trade matrix, we found that more than 50% of exports of manufactured goods in Austria and Sweden and 46% of those in France were sold to the developing, CMEA, and rest-of-world groups, which do not implement any protectionist policies. It means that more than half of their exports are not affected under our hypothesis of selective international protectionism. On the other hand, Belgium and Canada lost a higher percentage of GNP than any other countries. It is because 77.2% of Belgian exports and 86.7% of Canadian exports are purchased by other OECD countries in this group. In addition, the decline of GNP in Finland, Germany, Japan, and the United Kingdom is relatively large, even though these countries trade substantially with the developing and rest-of-world countries. Among the 13 LINK countries, the

Table 2. Rate of economic growth[1] in 13 LINK OECD countries under protectionist policies.

| | Baseline solution | | Protectionism | | | | | |
| | | | 5% | | 10% | | 20% | |
	1978	1979	1978	1979	1978	1979	1978	1979
Australia	1.60	3.20	−0.10	−0.10	−0.20	−0.10	−0.40	−0.20
Austria	3.30	2.70	0.70	0.30	1.50	0.70	3.20	0.90
Belgium	3.60	1.90	−2.40	−0.70	−4.50	−0.80	−8.40	3.10
Canada	4.10	3.80	−0.60	−0.40	−1.10	−0.80	−1.90	−1.80
Finland	1.60	3.30	−0.60	−0.60	−1.00	−1.40	−2.10	−3.20
France	4.00	4.90	0.60	0.80	1.30	−0.30	2.80	3.10
Germany	4.00	0.60	−0.60	−0.20	−1.10	−0.20	−2.10	−1.40
Italy	4.00	3.90	1.00	−0.50	0.50	−0.20	1.20	−1.30
Japan	7.00	4.00	−0.40	0.10	−0.70	0.10	−1.20	0.00
Netherlands	3.20	4.40	0.30	−1.20	1.00	−2.10	1.60	−4.90
Sweden	2.90	2.60	1.20	−0.10	2.20	1.20	4.40	2.50
U.K.	1.00	1.90	−0.50	−0.30	−0.90	−0.50	−1.60	−1.20
U.S.	4.30	4.50	0.00	−0.10	0.00	−0.20	0.00	−0.40

[1]GNP or GDP at constant prices.

United States has the smallest change in the level of GNP in these protectionist simulations. It is because the United States is almost a self-sufficient country; foreign trade accounts for a rather small fraction of its GNP.

The inflation rate used in this study is calculated as the percentage change in the consumer price index. The weighted average inflation rates of the 13 OECD countries in the three simulations are also presented in Table. 1. It is obvious that protectionist policies would push up the consumer price in most of these countries. However, the impact would be strong only in the first year.

The country-by-country inflation rates are reported in Table 3. Among the 13 OECD countries, Belgium and Canada would suffer a significantly higher inflation effect than others if a protectionist tariff is implied to all 13 countries. On the other hand, the inflation rates in both Germany and Japan, two locomotive countries with large trade surpluses, are significantly reduced in these protectionist scenarios. In addition, the inflation rates in Italy are also reduced, but the reduction occurs only in 1978.

Whether a single country can improve its trade position when many partner countries implement protectionist policies depends also upon the price elasticities of its import and export goods. If the demand for exports is relatively inelastic, exports would fall less than (elastic) imports, and the trade balance would improve. If the demand for imports is relatively inelastic, the trade balance would deteriorate. The country-by-country trade balances in current U.S. dollars of the three simulations

Table 3. Rate of inflation[1] in 13 LINK OECD countries under protectionist policies.

| | Baseline | | Protectionism | | | | | |
| | | | 5% | | 10% | | 20% | |
	1978	1979	1978	1979	1978	1979	1978	1979
Australia	12.60	9.50	0.60	0.40	1.10	0.90	2.10	1.70
Austria	7.40	6.10	0.20	0.10	0.30	0.20	0.70	0.50
Belgium	4.20	6.50	1.20	−0.10	2.40	−0.10	4.80	−0.30
Canada	10.50	10.00	2.20	1.30	4.40	2.60	8.60	5.10
Finland	7.40	5.10	0.10	0.10	0.20	0.20	0.40	0.50
France	6.60	7.50	0.40	0.20	0.90	−0.10	1.80	1.20
Germany	3.00	4.30	−0.60	−0.40	−1.00	−0.50	−2.00	−1.80
Italy	8.10	6.90	−0.30	0.00	−0.20	0.00	−0.50	0.00
Japan	6.70	7.20	−0.20	−0.20	−0.30	−0.40	−0.40	−0.80
Netherlands	8.50	7.20	0.30	−0.50	0.80	−1.00	1.40	−1.70
Sweden	12.70	9.20	0.20	0.00	0.40	0.20	0.90	0.70
U.K.	12.90	10.60	0.10	0.10	0.20	1.60	0.30	−0.40
U.S.	5.60	5.30	0.30	0.00	0.60	0.00	1.10	0.10

[1]Consumer price index.

Table 4. Trade balances[1] in 13 LINK OECD countries under protectionist policies.

| | Baseline | | Protectionism | | | | | |
| | | | 5% | | 10% | | 20% | |
	1978	1979	1978	1979	1978	1979	1978	1979
Australia	1.74	1.84	−0.14	−0.16	−0.16	0.14	−0.35	−0.05
Austria	4.13	−5.67	0.24	0.42	0.52	0.88	1.09	1.71
Belgium	1.91	1.47	0.61	0.41	1.12	0.89	1.76	0.46
Canada	0.64	−2.80	0.17	−0.05	0.32	−0.13	0.51	−0.50
Finland	−0.40	−0.70	−0.09	−0.08	−0.16	−0.19	−0.32	−0.40
France	−3.14	−1.61	1.00	3.07	2.27	1.99	4.96	13.10
Germany	24.88	27.57	−1.48	−1.61	−2.63	−2.23	−5.10	−7.15
Italy	0.86	−0.19	0.77	0.10	0.56	0.23	1.21	−0.06
Japan	21.24	17.91	−1.74	−1.35	−3.18	−2.38	−5.68	−5.36
Netherlands	0.62	0.32	−0.22	1.64	−0.38	3.32	0.17	5.56
Sweden	−1.38	−1.14	0.49	0.48	0.98	2.19	2.02	4.26
U.K.	−0.93	−0.30	−0.88	−1.02	−1.61	−0.25	−3.03	−4.54
U.S.	−29.88	−25.51	1.51	0.63	3.03	1.65	5.55	1.53

[1]Current price balances.

Table 5. Percentage changes of private investments[1] in 13 LINK OECD countries under protectionist policies.

| | Baseline | | Protectionism | | | | | |
| | | | 5% | | 10% | | 20% | |
	1978	1979	1978	1979	1978	1979	1978	1979
Australia	12.70	9.70	0.50	0.20	1.10	0.50	2.20	0.90
Austria	9.10	6.30	0.60	0.60	1.30	1.60	2.70	3.00
Belgium	22.80	21.30	2.60	0.90	5.10	1.60	10.00	3.40
Canada	7.70	3.40	0.20	−0.70	0.50	−1.30	1.20	−2.80
Finland	−6.00	5.80	−0.40	−1.00	−0.70	−2.00	−1.50	−4.30
France	4.20	3.70	0.30	0.40	0.70	−0.40	1.50	1.30
Germany	8.60	2.30	−0.70	−1.60	−1.10	−2.00	−2.30	−6.20
Italy	1.40	16.50	0.80	0.50	0.40	0.50	0.60	0.40
Japan	5.80	6.30	−0.90	−0.20	−1.60	−0.40	−2.30	−1.30
Netherlands	2.20	9.70	−1.30	−6.90	−2.60	−13.30	−4.60	−23.30
Sweden	0.60	1.80	−0.10	−0.30	−0.20	−0.40	−0.40	−0.90
U.K.	20.80	12.70	0.00	−0.40	0.00	2.30	0.00	−3.00
U.S.	11.00	12.40	0.30	−0.30	0.60	−0.50	1.20	−0.90

[1]Constant prices.

are reported in Table 4. The baseline column represents the balance of merchandise trade; the other three columns represent deviations from the baseline solution.

The trade balances of Austria, France, Italy, Sweden, and the United States are improved in both years in the protectionist simulations. Canada's trade balance is improved in 1978, but not in 1979; and the Netherlands' trade balance is improved in 1979, but not in 1978. The United States and France are the two biggest gainers among all the LINK countries. On the other side, Germany and Japan are the two biggest losers.

The percentage changes in private investment of the 13 OECD countries under different protective policies are reported in Table 5. The baseline column is measured in percentage changes, and the other three columns are measured in deviations from the baseline. Private investment declines in most of the 13 countries in these three scenarios. In general, there is more decline in 1979 than in 1978. Among the 13 countries, the largest increase in private investment in the two-year period is found in Belgium and the largest decrease is found in Netherlands. In addition, large reduction in private investment is also found in Germany, Japan, and Finland.

As we move up the scale from 5 to 10 to 20 percent protectionist scenarios, some of the main changes double at each stage. Not only are the results predictable on a linear *protectionist* scale; but they are also predictable, in direction at least, on a *liberalization* scale. If we introduce trade liberalization into German and Japanese models through lowering of import prices by 10%, we find world trade rising by about \$6.0 billion in 1978, and \$14.0 billion in 1979. Liberalization in these two countries has negligible price impact. Total (LINK) OECD GDP is estimated to fall by only \$1 billion (1970 prices) in 1978, and by less than \$3.0 billion in 1979. Partner countries would have rises in GDP, but these are not enough to offset declines in Germany and Japan.

We have only scratched the surface in terms of potential for analysis of contemporary trends in commercial policy. The findings mentioned here are indicative of the type and quantitative characteristics of LINK system scenarios that can usefully be analyzed for this class of problems.

7. Conclusions

It is unfortunate that in this first year of the third century of the *Wealth of Nations*, we find major countries beset by economic difficulties that drive them towards protectionism, undoing much of the benefit of liberalization of the last 30 years, upheld by such institutions as IMF, GATT, EEC, and OECD. There are apparent gains for individual countries, but taken as a whole, the world loses, as shown in Table 1, and worst of all, the developing countries, which can least afford it, stand to lose.

Although we have not aspired to discover new findings in these quantitative exercises, our simulated scenarios serve to validate the original wisdom of Adam Smith and give it some empirical content.

References

Ball, R. J. (ed.), 1973, *International Linkage of National Economic Models* (North-Holland, Amsterdam).

Hickman, B. and L. Lau, 1973, "Elasticity of substitution and export demand in a world trade model," *European Economic Review* (December) pp. 241–250.

Klein, L. R., 1974, "Supply constraints in demand oriented systems: An interpretation of the oil crisis," *Zeitschrift für Nationalokonomie* **34**, pp. 45–56.

———, 1976, "Project LINK," *Columbia Journal of World Business* **11**, pp. 7–19.

——— and K. Johnson, 1974, "LINK simulations of international trade: An evaluation of the effects of currency realignment," *Journal of Finance* **29**, pp. 617–630.

Metzler, Lloyd A., 1942, "Underemployment equilibrium in international trade," *Econometrica* **10**, p. 97.

Robinson, Romney, 1952, "A graphical analysis of the foreign trade multiplier," *The Economic Journal* **62**, pp. 546–564.

Waelbroeck, J. (ed.), 1976, *The Models of Project LINK* (North-Holland, Amsterdam).

26

DISTURBANCES TO THE INTERNATIONAL ECONOMY[†]

1. Identification of the Disturbances

In the second full year of operation of the international trading model built under the auspices of Project LINK we encountered the first of a series of world scale shocks, NEP (President Nixon's New Economic Policy) with the closing of the gold window, surcharging of automobile imports, and a host of domestic economic restrictions. This phase, known in Japan as Nixon shocks, led to the Smithsonian agreement on exchange rates and later dollar devaluation in 1973. This was only the beginning of a tumultuous period with many other shocks of a comparable magnitude.

The specific episodes or scenarios that I shall consider in this paper are the following:

(i) Nixon shocks and the Smithsonian agreement
(ii) Soviet grain purchases, rising food prices, rising raw material prices
(iii) Oil embargo and quadrupling of OPEC prices
(iv) Protectionism
(v) Capital transfers
(vi) Wage offensive

These are actual events or hypothetical scenarios that have been simulated through the LINK system. It is worthwhile considering some cases that have not occurred but need looking into because of the threats they impose on world stability. The added shocks are

(vii) Debt default
(viii) Speculative waves in currencies and commodities
(ix) Famine as a result of large-scale crop failure.

We do not know what the next wave of shocks will be or when it will occur. Some episodes in (i)–(vi) could be repeated or some new and quite unexpected ones could occur. Some plausible cases that have been hinted at as a result of actual developments or that have been openly discussed are being considered here under (vii)–(ix).

(i) The NEP was introduced in August 15, 1971. The original edicts were temporary. The surcharge on imported cars was soon lifted and the closing of the

[†]From *After the Phillips Curve: Persistence of High Inflation and High Unemployment* (Federal Reserve Bank of Boston, Boston, 1979), pp. 94–103.

gold window was only a prelude to a more significant move, namely, the realignment of exchange rates under the terms of the Smithsonian agreement. The stated expectation of the U.S. Secretary of Treasury, John Connally, was that a prompt turn-around in the U.S. trade balance, by some $8 billion, would occur. The United States was in the middle of a strong cyclical expansion phase, while many partner countries were experiencing slowdowns. This became an ideal test situation for applications of the LINK system.

(ii) Russia experienced a significant crop failure in 1972 and began systematically and quietly buying grain in the world market for delivery mainly in 1973. The circumstances of the purchase and lax surveillance on our part made the purchase a bargain at U.S. taxpayers' expense. It also depleted our grain reserves in short order. This led to sharp increases in world and domestic food prices in 1973. The situation was made worse by the ending of phase II under NEP and the weakening of controls under the disastrous phase III. In addition there was a failure in the anchovy catch off Peru. Fish meal served as a close substitute for grain in poultry and other animal feeding.

Accompanying these shocks in early 1973 were two dollar devaluations in February and March. Later, a speculative wave took over many primary commodity markets. In this situation many monetary or fiscal authorities recommended a conscious tightening of policies in order to slow the rate of expansion.

(iii) The biggest single shock was surely the oil embargo of 1973. Given that the authorities were trying to slow down their respective countries, the oil importers as a whole were vulnerable to a large-scale synchronized shock. In place of a "soft landing," there was a significant decline. When prices were increased in 1974 and held at that level, a number of serious trade imbalances were nurtured in the OECD world.

The embargo period itself was disruptive in cutting off supplies of a necessary production ingredient. The result was a sharp fall in output, since producers did not commit their reserve stock to use during the period, not knowing how long the embargo would last or not knowing that in fact significant leakages in the embargo would occur. Although oil was not itself a large component of GNP, it was a strategic one and its shortfall in the market held back many producing processes. It also led to a reduction in many components of final demand — expenditures on gasoline and oil, household operating expenditures, purchases of automobiles, and purchases of homes.

The subsequent period of high oil prices, without the embargo, continued to be one of recession; the increase in oil prices acted like an excise tax on the economy. The general result of simulating an increased excise tax through a macro model of an industrial economy is to induce a lowering of activity and an increase of prices. When this happened, as in 1974–75, in several industrial countries simultaneously, there were international reverberation effects and the final result was worse than each individual country may have experienced had it been subjected, alone, to the price increase.

(iv) The recession of 1974–75 influenced many countries to introduce protectionist measures in order to counteract business cycle impacts. In two noteworthy cases, Germany and Japan, there were export-oriented increases to maintain domestic activity and lead the respective economies into revivals. As a consequence, both these countries realized enormous trade surpluses. When combined with the OPEC surpluses, a large burden of adjustment faced deficit countries. Deficits there would have to be, because of the world trade identity

$$\text{World exports} = \text{World imports},$$

but they were not evenly distributed throughout the world. Those countries with large deficits looked to protectionism as a way to improve their trade accounts.

Trigger prices against Japanese and European steel imported into the United States are protectionist measures that have recently been introduced. Voluntary quotas imposed on exporters of shoes, textiles, and TV sets are another version of protectionism. Enforcement of anti-dumping laws are yet another. A more straightforward form would be an increase in tariffs.

The move toward liberalization of trade on a multilateral basis has been set back in recent years and is likely to be set back further given the attitude of powerful industrialists who have been hurt by import competition, and by equally powerful trade unionists whose jobs have been displaced by imported goods. In some countries, an exceptional claim for protecting *infant* industries has been replaced by a claim for protection of *mature* industries. The end result reduces world trade and production because of widespread adoption of "beggar-thy-neighbor" protectionist policies.

(v) In North–South confrontations or dialogues there has long been a request for capital transfers from the former to the latter. The request is based on the argument that the poorer peoples of the world in the southern hemisphere, to a large extent, needed, on pure welfare or humanitarian grounds, capital in order to grow and enjoy some material economic benefits. Another argument is that the northern countries would benefit themselves by creating better markets for their products.

Some progress has been made in implementing capital transfers, but mainly on emergency conditions and not for general growth on a large enough scale to change the world pattern. OPEC nations have made some capital grants to other developing nations that do not have energy resources and find it difficult to pay the high world price for oil. IMF facilities and particularly the proceeds of gold auctions make limited funds available for capital transfer.

This is a shock or episode that has not yet taken place on a large scale, yet can be simulated through the LINK system.

(vi) Wage offensives took place in the United Kingdom, Scandinavia, and other countries where domestic prices responded to the new high oil prices after 1973. Inflation rates of 25 percent in Britain induced large wage demands of the same order of magnitude. If wage costs go up at this high rate, prices are sure to be marked up by a similar amount in the next round and we shall have a coordinated wage-push effect through the world. As in other synchronized cyclical movements the effect tends to amplify, thus increasing the inflation rate. This process can also be simulated through the LINK system. It was fairly common in 1974–75 and receded only in 1976. Wage pressures lessened a bit as the world recession wore on. It is not back to the high level of 1974–75 but it is on the rise once again. As some countries reflate, in contrast to very slow growth in the past year or two, as in the German case, trade union restiveness and assertiveness could put significant pressures on wages. If inflation rates turn up again, the rise could very well be the result of higher wage demands.

(vii) Every time a particular country gets into trouble in its debt servicing, the possibility of debt default looms. To a large extent, debt service has become a critical issue for developing countries — Peru, Zaire, Zambia are primary examples. But large amounts of outstanding debt are on the books of Mexico, Brazil, Taiwan, S. Korea, and India, all of whom are much better situated for covering service costs than are the troubled countries. For this reason, the danger of a widespread wave of international bankruptcy is far-fetched, but it is a shock scenario that is worth considering.

It is not only in the area of developing countries where debt default is a live issue but several developed countries are likely to have trouble in meeting obligations. The leading cases are Spain, Portugal, and Turkey. Some centrally planned economies have been troubled by debt burdens, but it seems unlikely that they, as a group or individually, would willingly fail to honor international obligations. They have voluntarily restrained their indebtness once it became apparent that they were overextended.

(viii) In 1973 there was substantial speculation in markets for basic materials, both agricultural and industrial. Grain market prices rose by 100 percent or more and there was much speculative activity although the primary disturbance came from the large scale Soviet purchases. Later speculative waves came in 1974 (sugar) and 1976 (coffee). As for industrial commodities, speculation in copper and other nonferrous metals was significant.

These high prices had adverse effects on the import value and external balance of several consuming countries. The United Kingdom is a case in point. This kind of disturbance led to the restrictive fiscal/monetary policies that made countries highly vulnerable to the oil shock.

Currency speculation had also been evident and caused significant international disturbances. The runs on sterling and lira in early 1976 induced domestic inflation, followed by a whole train of events that impeded the United Kingdom and Italy. In the case of sterling, there was some degree of suspicion that shifts of sterling balances by OPEC countries were responsible for much of the decline in the exchange values of sterling.

(ix) Some of the most volatile prices that have risen on a scale comparable with oil prices in 1974–75 have been food prices. They doubled, while the cartel raised oil prices by a factor of 3 or 4. The principal difference from the oil case was that supply could be quickly increased and high food prices were promptly brought down as stocks were rebuilt. Thus an agricultural harvest disturbance is likely to be shorter in duration than are others, where supply is less responsive.

Nevertheless, a large crop shortfall on a world scale could bring about significant price increases for some foods perhaps by as much as 100 percent or more. If this were to occur, suddenly, the world economy could well be faced with a new crisis with dimensions as large as or larger than those experienced earlier in this decade.

2. Outline and Use of the LINK System[1]

When modeling and studying a national economy by simulation methods, it is generally assumed that export volume and import prices are exogenous variables. Export volume depends mainly on world trade or world economic activity, or import requirements of partner countries. Either export volume itself or world (foreign) activity variables, once removed, on which exports depend, are treated as exogenous. This is not strictly correct since price competitiveness, which depends on endogenous domestic behavior, also influences exports. But as a first approximation, we shall accept the usual assumption that exports are exogenous. Similarly, import prices are determined by cost and pricing decisions of partner countries. They are, therefore, treated as exogenous, too. To the extent that a major country influences its partners' pricing decisions, for competitive reasons, import prices are not wholly exogenous, but again, as a first approximation, they are treated as exogenous variables.

Import volume and export prices are both endogenous variables. The former depend on domestic activity variables and relative prices — at home and abroad. The latter depend on domestic cost and supply conditions. To the extent that a country tries to remain competitive with its partners and prices exports accordingly, or is a price taker in a world market for basic commodity exports, it may not be appropriate to classify export prices as endogenous. But the principal practice is to put import volume and export prices in the endogenous category.

The primary purpose of the LINK model is to endogenize export volumes and import prices. For the world trade economy, as a whole, both exports and imports, export prices and import prices are endogenous. On a world basis, there are no exogenous elements in this nexus. It may also be said that the purpose of LINK is to analyze the international transmission mechanism or to form international linkages among national econometric models.

---

[1]See R. J. Ball (ed.), *International Linkage of National Economic Models* (North Holland, Amsterdam, 1973); J. Waelbroeck (ed.), *The Models of Project LINK,* (North Holland, Amsterdam, 1976). A third volume edited by John Sawyer is now in press.

The LINK system does this in a consistent way by imposing two accounting identities:

$$\sum_{i=1}^{n} X_i = \sum_{i=1}^{n} M_i \qquad \text{world export volume = world import volume}$$

$$\sum_{i=1}^{n} (PX)_i X_i = \sum_{i=1}^{n} (PM)_i M_i \qquad \text{world export value = world import value.}$$

These identities are imposed in terms of a common numeraire unit (the U.S. dollar) at FOB valuation. The identities hold for commodity classes,

SITC   0,1   food, beverages, tobacco

SITC   2,4   other raw materials

SITC   3   mineral fuels

SITC   5–9   manufactures and semimanufactures

The number of countries or areas (n) is presently 24.
There are

13 OECD Countries	(Australia, Austria, Belgium, Canada, Finland, France, West Germany, Italy, Japan, Netherlands, Sweden, United Kingdom, United States)
7 CMEA Countries	(Bulgaria, Czechoslovakia, East Germany, Hungary, Poland, Romania, U.S.S.R.)
4 Developing Regions	(Africa, Asia, Latin America, Middle East) An OPEC/non-OPEC split is also provided

A residual category (ROW) is not explicitly modeled, but assumed to have a constant share of world trade.[2]

A detailed way of insuring fulfillment of the accounting identities would be to model bilateral trade equations between countries for separate commodity groupings. An example would be

$$\text{SITC 0,1}$$
$$\ln X_{ij} = -11.327 + 1.890 \ln M_j - 1.271 \, \frac{PX_{ij}}{PC_{ij}}$$
$$\quad\quad\;\;(-6.8) \quad\;\; (12.2) \quad\quad\quad\; (-2.0)$$

$$R^2 = 0.973 \quad S.E. = 0.079 \quad D.W. = 0.989$$

i = Netherlands PX_{ij} = price index of Netherlands shipments (SITC 01) to Germany

j = West Germany PC_{ij} = price index of competing countries' shipments (SITC 01) to Germany

---

[2]This assumption is being weakened, and small models are being built for 13 separate countries (Mainland China, Denmark, Greece, Iceland, New Zealand, Norway, Portugal, South Africa, Spain, Switzerland, Turkey, Yugoslavia). For some, major models may be used.

This is just an example of many equations that have been estimated by P. Ranuzzi of the EEC, bilaterally, for commodity groups. It covers SITC (0,1) imports by Germany from the Netherlands. There is some evidence of serial correlation of residuals, which could be reduced on further research into the time shape of reaction, but most of the bilateral equations do have a more random pattern for residuals.

There are many bilateral combinations to be determined for this number of countries or areas. To simplify the work, we estimate total (not bilateral) import equations for each model, by SITC categories. Exports are (endogenously) computed from

$$X = AM$$

where A is a world trade share matrix with element

$$A_{ij} = X_{ij}/M_j$$
$$X_{ij} = \text{exports from } i \text{ to } j$$
$$M_j = \text{imports of } j.$$

X is a vector of exports (across countries/areas) and M is a vector of imports (across countries/areas). As long as the column sums of A are unity, we satisfy the world trade identity. If this identity is in volume terms (constant prices), the corresponding identity in value terms (current prices) is

$$(PX)'AM = (PM)'M$$

from which we deduce

$$(PM) = A'(PX).$$

In the LINK system, we do not assume that the elements of A are constant. They are functions of relative prices and move through time as endogenous variables of the complete system.

The system is solved by assuming export volumes and import prices for each country/area model. The individual model solutions for M and (PX) are substituted into the above matrix equations of X and (PM). The models are then solved again for M and (PX); new values for X and (PM) are computed, and the iterative process stops when the total value of world trade does not change from iteration to iteration (approximately).

This is a highly condensed description of the LINK system. How can it be used for studying world disturbances? Each of the specific disturbances (i)–(ix) described in the previous section can be examined as a scenario or structured simulation. A base simulation is first established as a dynamic projection of the system from fixed initial conditions and exogenous inputs on a "best judgment" time path that does not include the particular disturbance. Then an alternative simulation is developed with the disturbance included, everything else unchanged from the baseline path.

The difference, at each successive time point, between the scenario and baseline path provides an estimate of the effect of the disturbance.

Preliminary to the working out of scenarios, we first estimate multipliers of the system that show sensitivity to changes in exogenous variables or to exogenous shifts of entire relationships. It is instructive to examine the standard fiscal multiplier from a single country viewpoint and a world system viewpoint. To make matters simple let us use the two-country world model

$$y = ey + m^*y^* - my + g$$

$$y^* = e^*y^* + my - m^*y^* + g^* .$$

There are two countries with output levels y and y^* respectively. Output in each country is the sum of

induced spending , ey or e^*y^*, on consumption and capital goods
exports, m^*y^* or my
less imports, my or m^*y^*
exogenous government spending, g or g^*.

The relationships are assumed, for purposes of exposition only, to be linear and proportional. In this two-country world, the world trade identity is automatically satisfied because one country's imports (m^*y^*) is another country's exports. In the second country, exports (my) are the first country's imports. It is assumed that an exchange conversion makes the units comparable in the two countries.

Taking the single-country view, in isolation, we can derive the reduced form equation for the first country as

$$y = \frac{g + m^*y^*}{1 - e + m} .$$

The conventional multiplier, for a given level of exports (m^*y^*) is

$$\frac{dy}{dg} = \frac{1}{1 - e + m} .$$

The simplest multiplier formula $(1/(1-e))$ is modified by the inclusion of the import leakage factor in the denominator, thus tending to reduce the multiplier's value. Indeed, countries with very high marginal propensities to import — prototypes being the United Kingdom and the Netherlands — are known to have low multiplier values, possibly less than unity.

In the two-country case, the reduced form is

$$y = \frac{(1 - e^* + m^*)g + m^*g^*}{(1 - e + m)(1 - e^* + m^*) - mm^*}$$

and the multiplier is

$$\frac{dy}{dg} = \frac{1}{1 - e + m - \frac{mm^*}{1 - e^* + m^*}} .$$

By including the term

$$-\frac{mm^*}{1 - e^* + m^*}$$

in the denominator, we have increased the size of the multiplier. Thus the world model is more sensitive to a disturbance when intra-country trade effects are taken into account in the model. If the second country also stimulates by moving g^*, there is another effect to be added, namely

$$\frac{m^*}{(1 - e + m)(1 - e^* + m^*) - mm^*}$$

provided g^* moves *pari passu* with g. This result shows not only that international repercussion effects exist as well as direct country effects, but also that synchronized effects intensify movements in both countries simultaneously. It shows, moreover, that one country is sensitive to policy changes in another. In this example, y depends on (partial) movements in g^*. These are indirect effects.

In LINK simulations, synchronized effects and indirect policy effects have been examined across countries. Simultaneous fiscal changes; inventory drawdowns in a crisis, such as the oil embargo; simultaneous wage-push increases; simultaneous limitations on imports (protectionism) have all been studied.

Multipliers have been calculated for the LINK system without synchronization; i.e., by changes, one at a time, to fiscal variables in a given model. Both direct and indirect effects on other countries are studied in these multiplier scenarios. Although these are not simultaneously introduced, for multiplier calculations, the effects are simultaneously spread over several OECD economies at once.

Oil price increases are not synchronized except to the extent that all the countries in OPEC, plus outsiders that are large producers, will have imposed on other economies an equivalent of a world excise tax. The synchronization of this case is in the movements of the oil-importing economies.

Apart from some strictly controlled prices, like the cartel-determined oil price, domestic costs or world competition largely govern the determination of export prices. These prices are then converted into import prices (exogenous to a single country), by means of a transformation using the world trade matrix. If the world inflation rate increases, it will result from higher export prices. This is the counterpart of the strategic importance of imports in determining the volume of world trade. By using the row elements of a trade-share matrix to convert imports into each component of exports, we are doing essentially the same thing as transforming changes in export prices into changes in import prices. In this latter case, columns of trade matrix are weights in the transformation process.

An important aspect of the present stage of the LINK system has not yet been explained, namely the role of exchange rates. They are, at the present time, exogenous in the LINK system. They are not constant because frequently they are exogenously changed in the middle of a LINK simulation. Only now have we been able to turn our attention to analysis of exchange rates and endogenize them for projection and simulation analysis. Since the Smithsonian Agreement we have gained enough experience to examine the body of data available from 1971 to date in order to make first attempts at estimating equations that try to explain exchange rates — as functions of country interest rate differentials, growth rate differentials, inflation rate differentials, changes in reserves, and levels of wealth.

As import and export prices are endogenously generated by the solution of each model, they are expressed in local currency units, which are different for nearly every country.[3] In order to use these series in the LINK algorithm with dollar-denominated trade flows, we must convert import and export prices from dollar denominations into exports and import prices, also in dollar quotations. As import and export prices leave individual models, expressed in local currency units, we multiply them all by a series of exogenous exchange rates into dollar-denominated totals. The operational formulas are:

$$M(L)\text{Ex}(\$/L) = M(\$)$$

$$(PX)(L)\text{Ex}(\$/L) = PX(\$).$$

The right-hand side variables are all expressed in dollar terms. The trade matrix is based on dollar valuations; so it should be multiplied into either $M(\$)$ or $PX(\$)$, import and export prices in dollar units. These multiplications generate

$$X(\$)$$

$$PM(\$)$$

i.e., dollar valuations of exports and import prices. Before these variables can be reinserted into individual models, for the next iterative step in the system solution process, they must be converted back into local currency units appropriate to each model. This step takes the form

$$X(\$)/\text{Ex}(\$/L) = X(L)$$

$$(PM)(\$)/\text{Ex}(\$/L) = (PM)(L).$$

Exchange rates, used in this way, have significant impacts on the entire solution. So exchange rates play important roles; they are simply in need of endogenization.

By and large, when persistent deficits or surpluses appear in country accounts for simulation exercises, we find that the former lead to currency depreciation while the latter lead to currency appreciation. After exchange rates are changed, either exogenously or endogenously, on the basis of a solution, we have feedback information for altering the solution.

---

[3] Developing countries are treated by area grouping. Area models are based on dollar-denominated variables, aggregated over countries.

In SITC groups 0,1 and 2,4, the relevant prices are determined in world markets, balancing supply and demand. For the most part, primary producing countries are "price takers." In order to obtain good estimates of export prices for such countries, it is necessary to couple the LINK system with systems of simultaneous equations to explain commodity markets, either major agricultural crops and other products, or markets for industrial materials. The principal feedback on the LINK system is through determination of price for producing countries, and, consequently, export earnings in these commodity lines. Some twenty-odd commodity models have been estimated by F. G. Adams and others for combination with the LINK models.[4] They have estimated equations of the form

$$(PX01) = f(P_1, P_2, \ldots, P_n)$$

$$(PX24) = g(Q_1, Q_2, \ldots, Q_m)$$

PX01 = export price index of group SITC 0,1
PX24 = export price index of group SITC 2,4
P_i = world price of i-th food commodity
Q_i = world price of i-th industrial commodity.

These equations have been estimated for each primary producing country or area.

The commodity models are solved, for primary price determination, on the basis of input values for demand or other factors from the LINK system. The prices estimated from the commodity models are then inserted into f and g, above, to estimate new values of (PX01) and (PX24). The LINK system is resolved with these new estimates of export prices, and the commodity models are solved in another iteration. This procedure continues until convergence is attained. This extended model and program is known as COMLINK.

3. Some Empirical Results

A number of LINK studies have examined, in the past, many of the issues raised in the first section, using the procedures and systems in the second section.

Increases in basic commodity prices (hypothetically) during 1975–76, interpreted as an increase in export prices of developing countries by an extra 10 percent over a baseline case, produced the following deviations from the baseline values of GNP, GNP deflator, consumer price deflator, and trade balance.

It is evident from studying the left panel of Table 1 that higher export prices in primary producing countries in the developing world would generally increase inflation rates in the industrial (using) countries. Of the two measures of inflation presented here — GDP deflator and consumer price deflator — the latter is probably

---

[4]F. G. Adams, "Primary commodity markets in a world model system," *Stabilizing World Commodity Markets,* eds. F. G. Adams and S. A. Klein, (Lexington Books, Lexington, 1978), pp. 83–104.

more suitable, because price increase in imports can often lead to *lower* GNP prices. This is because imports enter negatively in the GNP identity. A clearer picture of domestic inflation is given by the consumer price deflator. Mainly domestic goods are being priced in this index measure. A few countries stand to make trade gains, but these are a minority, and most of the significant changes are losses, on trade account. Only the LINK OECD countries are included in Table 1. Although these are the largest countries and the ones that dominate the world economy, not all important countries are included. The results are clearest and most reliable for the major countries that are specifically modeled; those are the ones listed in Table 1.

The payment of higher prices to primary producing countries is not all negative, however. The developing countries earn some extra purchasing power since many primary products are price-inelastic. With the extra purchasing power in the hands of some developing countries, they are able to increase their imports from the industrial countries. This accounts for some of the "perverse" signs — rising GDP in the face of higher primary input prices.

The right-hand panel is possibly more interesting. It induces more pronounced changes since it is a scenario that is far from what actually happened. What if there had been no oil embargo and no forceful setting of world oil prices by OPEC? The increases in GDP rates and the fall in inflation rates are considerably bigger than those in the left panel, when prices are changed by a mere factor of 10 percent. In the case of the other simulation, oil price is, hypothetically, held constant at its 1973 value way into 1976.

Large oil-importing countries have significant declines registered in their prices as a result of having held the line on oil prices. It shows how important energy is in the pricing decision. The inflation rate is substantially down in every country except Australia and Austria. At the same time that price would have been held down in this "what if" scenario, real output rose, with the exceptions of Australia, Austria, Canada, and Finland. Canada is, of course, an energy exporter, but on a small scale. Austria is more in a swapping posture, importing and exporting energy, but Australia has real GNP gains, against the tide of most partner countries.

On balance, the trade accounts would have moved toward surplus. The right-hand side column is dotted with negative entries. Some of these are due to the fact that 1973 oil prices would allow most countries to grow. Those that do, sometimes import so much that trade becomes unsettled again.

Oil is basically a traded commodity, albeit, a highly strategic one. What would have been the disturbance to the world commodity if Saudi Arabia had not been persuaded by the U.S. authorities to use its power to freeze oil prices in 1978?

The sensitivity of the world economy to further price shocks is examined by simulating the LINK system, 1978–79, for different oil price rises — 0, $2, and $4 per barrel.[5] To carry out this calculation, the export prices for group 3 SITC was

---

[5]Dr. Vincent Su of the LINK research staff prepared these simulations of alternative oil prices, 1978–79.

Table 1. Effects of commodity price increase and constant oil price (Percentage deviation from baseline except trade balance, value of deviation, billions of U.S. dollars).

		Higher export prices Developing countries				Constant oil price (1973 value)			
		GNP	GNP deflator	Consumer price deflator	Trade balance	GNP	GNP deflator	Consumer price deflator	Trade balance
Australia	1974					−4.2	2.7	0.7	−0.35
	75	1.2	−0.7	−0.2	0.16	−3.9	4.0	1.6	0.35
	76	1.9	−1.1	−0.5	0.03	−5.5	3.4	1.5	0.74
Austria	1974					−0.9	−0.4	−1.4	0.12
	75	0.2	0.1	0.3	−0.03	0.6	−0.2	−1.3	0.24
	76	0.1	0.2	0.3	−0.04	2.2	0.7	−0.8	0.21
Belgium	1974					0.0	−3.1		−0.61
	75		0.5		0.02	2.0	−4.0		−0.78
	76	−0.1	0.6		0.01	2.9	−4.1		−1.00
Canada	1974					−3.6	−1.2	−1.3	−3.44
	75	0.9	0.5	0.6	0.85	−2.5	−3.0	−2.3	−4.14
	76	0.6	1.0	1.0	0.97	−1.8	−4.4	−3.5	−4.19
Finland	1974					−1.5	−1.5	−4.5	0.53
	75	0.5	0.3	0.8	−0.05	−1.4	−2.0	−5.4	0.90
	76	0.7	0.6	1.2	−0.09	−0.6	−3.4	−5.8	1.17
France	1974					1.3	−6.9	−6.4	0.61
	75	−0.4	1.2	1.3	−0.03	4.4	−7.0	−6.7	0.26
	76	−0.6	1.3	1.4	0.02	4.8	−7.5	−7.0	1.60
Germany	1974					0.4	−0.7	−0.7	−0.92
	75	−0.1	0.3	0.3	0.43	0.1	−0.3	−0.3	0.90
	76	0.1	0.6	0.7	1.00	0.3	0.5	0.5	3.20
Italy	1974					0.2	−3.9	−8.8	2.71
	75	0.5	−0.1	0.7	−0.43	3.9	−11.8	−16.6	1.35
	76	0.2	0.4	1.3	−1.17	5.3	−8.3	−12.7	1.52
Japan	1974					0.9	−0.3	−2.5	6.93
	75	0.0	0.0	0.6	−1.25	5.1	−5.2	−5.4	7.97
	76	−0.7	1.2	1.3	−1.29	10.1	−8.8	−7.3	8.87
Netherlands	1974					0.3	−7.0		0.68
	75	−0.1	1.4		−0.11	2.0	−9.8		0.36
	76	−0.2	2.1		0.04	3.9	−11.1		0.19
Sweden	1974					−0.5		−2.0	−0.50
	75	0.1		0.4	0.11	0.5		−2.2	−0.06
	76	0.1		0.4	0.06	1.8		−2.5	0.09
U.K.	1974					0.3	−3.8	−6.7	7.67
	75	−0.2	1.3	1.7	−1.58	1.5	−8.3	−11.3	9.85
	76	−0.3	2.1	2.6	−1.84	2.6	−10.6	−13.9	12.30
U.S.	1974					−1.0	0.3	−0.5	6.95
	75	0.3	−0.1	0.2	−1.54		−0.3	−1.1	15.01
	76	0.3	−0.1	0.3	−2.52	1.4	−1.1	−2.0	19.72

increased for the oil-exporting countries. The variable appears now as an index, and its level in 1978 was assumed to stand for $14.00 per barrel of crude oil. It was then either held constant or increased by 2/14 or 4/14 for the appropriate case being studied. The increases were implemented for the Middle East, those parts of Latin America, South and East Asia, and Africa corresponding to the inclusion of OPEC countries (Venezuela, Ecuador, Indonesia, and Nigeria), and for Canada. At the time of this calculation it was thought that the increase would come to about $1.00 per barrel, and that figure was used in the standard projections. As it turned out, the case of zero increase, which was one variant on the low side, could best have served as a baseline case. In the present circumstance, we use that as a base case to study the effect of price increases, but it probably will not be the best control position to assume now for 1979.

The clearest story is told by the global totals in Table 2. Oil priced at $2 per barrel higher in 1978 and again in 1979 is the first alternative. The increments are $4 in each year in the second alternative simulation. Each price increase lowers the estimated value of real world output and real world trade. At the same time, inflation rates go up, whether measured by the unit value of exports, the GNP deflator, or the consumer price index. The positive and negative offsets are less than perfect, but the influence of an increase in an import price is more clearly and strikingly shown in the estimates of consumer prices. Estimated inflation goes up by a full percentage point between the no-change and $2 alternative case. This is clearly a potential contribution to global inflation rates. The increase from $2 to $4 per barrel contributes less to overall inflation than does the increase from no change to $2 per barrel. It appears that the large German and Japanese external surpluses are severely reduced as the price of oil rises by an amount from $0.00 to $4.00 per barrel. The changes affect most, but not all, countries in similar ways. The results for a number of countries (LINK countries) are shown in Table 2.

The U.S. trade balance is considerably worsened, as is the real growth rate. The other locomotive countries, Germany and Japan, would be similarly affected, but large trade surpluses would not be wiped out. The U.K. deficit would improve in 1979 but deteriorate in 1978. Other oil-producing or exporting countries such as Canada and Netherlands (refined products) would benefit one way or another, the former on trade account and the latter in terms of GNP growth. But on the whole, it is good for the world economy that the line has been held on oil prices for 1978.

Simulations with the LINK system, reported in Tables 1 and 2, provide estimates of the world effect of changes in petroleum and other basic material prices. There are few, if any, systematic world-linked estimates available for verification or validation purposes, but there is a careful study of unlinked estimates of the effects on the U.S. economy alone by a staff team of the Federal Reserve Board.[6] They conclude

---

[6] R. Berner, P. Clark, J. Enzler, and B. Lowrey, "International sources of domestic inflation," *Studies in Price Stability and Economic Growth,* Joint Economic Committee, U.S. Congress (Washington, D.C. Government Printing Office, August 5, 1975), pp. 1–41.

Table 2. Effects of increasing oil prices, 1978–1979 (Percentage point deviation from no-change case, except trade balance, value of deviation, billions of U.S. dollars).

| | | \$2/Barrel increase | | | | \$4/Barrel increase | | | |
		GDP	GDP deflator	Consumer price deflator	Trade balance	GDP	GDP deflator	Consumer price deflator	Trade balance
Australia	78	−0.2	0.0	0.0	−0.25	−0.3	−0.1	0.1	−0.54
	79	−0.2	0.0	0.1	−0.64	−0.4	−0.1	0.1	−1.31
Austria	78	−0.6	−0.1	0.2	−0.29	−0.7	−0.2	0.3	−0.53
	79	−1.2	−0.2	0.2	−0.63	−2.1	−0.4	0.3	−1.04
Belgium	78	−0.9	0.4	0.7	−0.21	−2.1	1.0	1.5	−0.46
	79	−1.6	0.6	1.1	−0.67	−2.6	0.9	1.7	−1.23
Canada	78	0.0	0.5	0.3	0.15	−0.1	1.1	0.6	0.24
	79	−0.1	0.9	0.7	0.10	−0.4	1.8	1.4	0.14
Finland	78	−0.1	0.2	0.3	−0.13	−0.2	0.3	0.6	−0.25
	79	−0.3	0.3	0.5	−0.32	−0.7	0.5	0.8	−0.55
France	78	−0.6	1.6	1.9	−1.87	−1.3	2.9	3.5	−3.71
	79	−0.9	1.9	2.3	−4.31	−1.5	2.8	3.4	−7.59
Germany	78	−0.8	−0.3	—	−1.61	−1.8	−0.8	—	−3.75
	79	−1.1	−0.7	—	−4.18	−1.9	−1.2	—	−7.54
Italy	78	−0.6	−0.1	0.4	−1.18	−1.4	−0.3	0.8	−2.39
	79	−0.8	−0.1	0.6	−2.28	−1.2	0.0	1.0	−3.72
Japan	78	−2.3	1.0	6.6	−6.04	−4.9	2.0	7.6	−12.44
	79	−4.0	1.1	6.0	−13.00	−7.1	1.7	6.3	−22.27
Netherlands	78	−0.9	−1.0	0.5	−1.71	−2.4	−2.7	0.9	−2.46
	79	−0.4	−0.2	0.5	−2.86	0.0	−1.6	0.3	−4.80
Sweden	78	0.0	—	0.6	−0.66	0.0	—	1.2	−1.36
	79	−0.2	—	0.7	−1.60	−0.4	—	1.0	−2.86
U.K.	78	−0.4	0.4	0.6	−0.24	−0.8	0.8	1.2	−0.45
	79	−0.5	1.2	1.2	0.09	−0.8	2.1	2.0	0.38
U.S.	78	−0.4	0.0	0.2	−6.66	−0.7	0.1	0.4	−14.10
	79	−0.5	0.0	0.2	−15.49	−0.9	0.1	0.4	−30.68
	TWXV	78	\$10 b.			\$26 b.			
		79	\$18 b.			\$41 b.			
	PWX	78	4.36%			7.42%			
		79	2.08%			4.92%			
	TWXR	78	\$−15.0 b.			\$−25.0 b.			
		79	\$−25.0 b.			\$−43.0 b.			
	GDP(13)	78	\$−10.0 b.			\$−29.0 b.			
		79	\$−32.0 b.			\$−73.0 b.			
	PGDP(13)	78	0.25%			0.49%			
		79	0.32%			0.53%			
	PC(13)	78	1.10%			1.49%			
		79	1.08%			1.35%			

TWXV = Nominal value of world trade, billions of US\$
PWX = Unit Value of world exports, 1970: 1.0, US\$ denomination
TWXR = Real value of world trade, billions of US\$ 1970
GDP(13) = Percentage change real GDP, 13 LINK countries, billions of 1970 US\$
PGDP (13) = Percentage change GDP deflator, 13 LINK countries, 1970: 1.0
PC (13) = Percentage change consumer deflator, 13 LINK countries, 1970: 1.0.

that consumer price rises between 1971 and 1974 were strongly influenced by dollar depreciation and extraordinarily large increases in export/import prices (mainly food and fuel). About 15 percent of the consumer price rise was accounted for by decline in the dollar's exchange value and 25 percent by the price disturbance. In the simulation of Table 1, with oil prices held constant at their 1973 levels, we estimated that the overall effect on the world inflation rate was about 20 percent of the total price increase in 1974. As an order of magnitude estimate, considering that only one commodity's price rise is being held constant, that only the 1974 effect is being compared, and that the effect is world-wide, the Federal Reserve judgment and the LINK judgment are consistent with each other.

The Federal Reserve team also emphasizes that it is necessary to take into account which prices were affected and why they have risen in order to assess the effect on the domestic inflation rate. If the inflationary impulses come from external sources, stagflation, i.e., rising prices with rising unemployment, can be produced. Demand impulses, internally generated, can produce the standard trade-off relation of falling unemployment and rising prices.[7] The external shock acts like an excise tax, reducing demand, increasing unemployment, and generating inflation. This is a familiar macroeconometric result.

Among the remaining shock scenarios that have been investigated on previous occasions, let us examine capital transfers (v).[8] This case has been worked out by Carl Weinberg of the LINK staff. He assumed that $20 billion per year, 1976–78, is transferred to the developing countries of Africa, Latin America and South/East Asia. No capital transfer was (assumed to be) made to the Middle East countries. The objective was to examine the effects on growth in the recipient nations but also to estimate the feedback effect on the developed industrial countries to see how prosperity in the developing world induces imports that originate with exports of the developed world. This scenario was worked out on the assumption that the transfer did not arise as a cost item for the developed industrial country. It could presumably have been a transfer within the developing world — as if from OPEC reserves — or from the assets of world organizations such as the IMF. The other case, in which there is a genuine donor's cost, needs to be worked out. It is in process but has not been completed.

In the developing country models there is a variable representing financial inflows. The increment to these flows is distributed to the three developing

---

[7]Similar conclusions were reached with Wharton Model simulations by L. R. Klein, "The longevity of economic theory," *Quantitative Wirtschaftsforschung,* eds. Horst Albach *et al.* (J. C. B. Mohr, Tubingen, 1977), pp. 411–419. The Federal Reserve team used the Federal Reserve model.

[8]Protectionism is taken up in L. R. Klein and V. Su, "Protectionism: An analysis from Project LINK," *Journal of Policy Modeling* I (1978), pp. 1–30, and wage offensive is in L. R. Klein and K. Johnson, "Stability in the international economy: The LINK experience," *International Aspects of Stabilization Policies,* eds. A. Ando *et al.* (Federal Reserve Bank of Boston, Boston, 1975). Protectionism generally reduces world trade and growth, with more inflation. Some countries gain but losses outweigh gains. In the case of simultaneous wage pushes in many countries, together, there is noticeable amplification of the final result on price inflation but somewhat less regular than in the case of a quantity shock as occurred in the oil embargo.

regions according to their shares of capital inflows historically. It was done for a single year and for three years running. The latter case is analyzed here.

The developing nations gain most clearly and by largest amounts. Among developed nations, the Netherlands stands out. Most countries are grouped from 0.3 to 0.8 percent, as percentage deviations from the baseline case. The developed world gains from the prosperity of the developing countries, but the larger gains are with the latter.

The next world shock could come through a harvest failure.[9] This case is represented by a large price increase for agricultural exports by the big grain-exporting countries — United States, Canada, Australia, Argentina, France. We have assumed for this scenario that prices double in the first year (1978) but slacken as new acreage is brought under cultivation in a supply response.[10] The doubling in 1978 is followed by an increase of 75 percent (over the baseline PX01) in 1979 and by 25 percent in 1980.

The grain-producing countries will have higher export prices for SITC 0,1. Grain-importing countries are assumed to have demand elasticity with respect to price at the low figure of 0.25. Import values of food and imports, generally, rise greatly in the consuming countries. Inflation goes up faster, however, than nominal values; consequently, real magnitudes fall. This holds for both real trade volume and real gross domestic product. Also, the lags in import relationships as well as at other places of the macro economy, make the time pattern of reaction a bit slow. Larger effects are noted for the second year, 1979, than 1978. The effects are larger in the second year, in spite of the fact that we assumed a supply response adequate to hold PX01 to 75 percent (second year, 1979) and to 25 percent (third year, 1980) increments over the baseline.

On a global scale, PX0-9, the export unit value index for all merchandise trade goes up by at most 2.4 percent in the first year, while PX0,1, the export unit value for food, beverages, and tobacco goes up by 24.9 percent maximum — also reached in the first year.

The decline in GDP, for 13 major LINK countries in the OECD group, is held to less than 1.0 percent. In the third year, there is some slight relief in the trade surplus for Germany and Japan. In Germany the relief shows up as early as 1978, for this simulation exercise. The United States, as the world's largest grain exporter, gets enough export stimulus to make its GNP slightly larger than in the baseline solution. The U.S. trade deficit is, on balance, a gainer in this scenario. The main anomaly in Table 4 is the United Kingdom. Prices both overall and in the consumer sector are lower in the case of the harvest failure. The movement of GDP and the trade balance are as expected, but the price movement is not.

---

[9] "Scenario of a worldwide grain shortage," with Vincent Lee and Mino Polite, LINK memorandum, July, 1978.

[10] France and Australia have somewhat lower export price rises since grain exports account for only 30 and 47 percent of total agricultural exports, respectively.

Table 3. Effects of capital transfers of $20 billion on GDP.
(Percentage deviation from baseline)

	1976	1977	1978
Australia	0.5	0.7	0.4
Austria	0.6	1.1	0.5
Belgium	0.6	0.6	0.3
Canada	0.4	0.4	0.3
Finland	0.8	0.8	0.7
France	0.6	0.5	0.3
Germany	0.5	0.4	0.4
Italy	0.7	0.6	0.5
Japan	1.0	1.1	0.9
Netherlands	0.8	1.7	1.8
Sweden	0.5	0.8	0.3
U.K.	0.7	0.8	0.5
U.S.	0.3	0.4	0.2
Africa	3.1	3.4	2.8
Southeast Asia	0.7	0.9	0.8
Latin America	2.8	2.8	2.3
TWXV	2.6	2.6	2.0
PWX	−0.4	−0.2	0.3
TWXR	3.0	2.8	1.8
GDP (13)	0.5	0.6	0.4
GDP (DEVE)	1.7	1.8	1.5

Inflation goes up slightly in the harvest failure scenario. The overall index of inflation, measured by GDP prices, is about 0.2 above the baseline values in the first two years. In the individual country tabulations, we often find that consumer price inflation is more sensitive to the external price than is the overall deflator. This is perhaps one of the most dangerous and inadequately appreciated aspects of the external shock to the price system.

In the case of the oil embargo, followed by raising of oil prices, there were larger and more dramatic effects on the economy of the whole world, as well as for many national parts. Supply response to fill a gap between supply and demand was weaker in the petroleum case. Also, petroleum has a more extensive interindustry (intermediate processing) use. This makes for bottlenecks and production substitutions. Hence, the oil crisis was able to send the world economy into recession, but this particular agricultural scenario merely slows down growth by factional points. There is, of course, a great deal of difference between one year's doubling, in the case of grain price, and many years' quadrupling of price in the petroleum case. Although the assumptions may have been large in scope, the final result appears to be fairly mild. It follows a predictable path, and the main value of the LINK exercise is to put empirical magnitudes in proper perspective.

Table 4. Simulated effects of world harvest failure.

(Percentage deviation from baseline simulation
trade balance deviation billions of U.S.dollars)

		GDP	GDP deflator	Consumer price deflator	Trade balance
Australia	1978	−1.40	0.30	0.70	0.64
	79	−1.10	0.80	1.30	1.25
	80	0.30	0.90	1.20	2.47
Austria	1978	−3.80	−0.70	−0.30	−0.30
	79	−1.30	−0.70	−0.40	0.00
	80	2.80	0.00	−0.30	1.10
Belgium	1978	−1.00	0.60	0.90	−0.20
	79	−0.50	0.50	0.70	−0.10
	80	−1.50	0.10	0.30	−0.50
Canada	1978	−1.00	1.40	1.00	−1.04
	79	−0.50	1.90	1.80	−0.12
	80	−2.10	1.80	1.50	−0.43
Finland	1978	0.00	0.40	0.40	−0.60
	79	0.30	4.70	0.30	0.00
	80	4.80	−1.60	−0.60	0.60
France	1978	−1.90	1.40	−0.04	1.69
	79	−0.80	1.00	0.00	3.57
	80	−1.80	0.40	−0.20	−1.06
Germany	1978	−0.60	−0.30		−1.32
	79	−0.60	−0.50		−1.13
	80	−1.10	−0.90		−2.14
Italy	1978	5.10	−0.20	1.40	−1.30
	79	3.90	0.60	2.00	−0.06
	80	−7.30	1.20	1.40	4.12
Japan	1978	0.50	0.90	1.00	4.55
	79	0.20	1.30	1.30	4.55
	80	−1.30	0.60	0.70	−5.74
Netherlands	1978	0.20	−0.70	0.40	−1.94
	79	0.20	−0.50	0.20	0.21
	80	−4.40	1.20	0.00	−2.05
Sweden	1978	−0.20		0.20	0.60
	79	0.20		0.20	−0.10
	80	−0.40		−0.08	1.67
U.K.	1978	0.00	−1.40	−0.10	−0.52
	79	0.40	−1.10	−0.20	0.12
	80	−1.00	−0.60	−0.10	−3.03
U.S.	1978	0.20	0.00	0.07	6.37
	79	0.30	0.10	0.00	7.06
	80	0.05	0.00	0.06	0.88

(*Cont'd*)

Table 4. (*Continued*)

	Total Trade SITC 0-9	Real Trade SITC 0-9	Unit Value SITC 0-9	Unit Value SITC 0,1	LINK GDP	LINK PGDP
1978	2.00	−0.80	2.90	24.90	−0.15	0.22
79	2.00	−0.10	2.10	20.70	−0.35	0.22
80	−1.10	−2.20	1.20	9.90	−0.67	−0.17

INTERNATIONAL PRODUCTIVITY COMPARISONS (A REVIEW)[†]

Meaning of Productivity

According to the *Oxford English Dictionary* (1971), *productivity* is equated to *productiveness*,[1] which, in turn, is defined as "... fruitfulness; abundance or richness in output." Solomon Fabricant, writing in the *Encyclopedia of the Social Sciences* (Fabricant, 1968), states, "... productivity measures the fruitfulness of human labor .... In another sense, productivity measures the efficiency with which resources as a whole including capital as well as manpower are employed in production."

In these general terms, productivity carries a meaning that is fairly well known, in an intuitive sense, to most people and is, by and large, a good thing, something to be encouraged and desired. There are those, however, who fear productivity to the extent that it might lead to displacement from work. This is the case in which productivity enhancement comes about through technological progress.

Nonparametric measurement. Productivity, as I shall use the term in this essay, has a technical meaning that is obviously tied to the dictionary meaning. I shall look at productivity in two ways, nonparametrically and parametrically.

In a nonparametric sense, I shall define productivity as some simple ratio, but with common-sense meaning:

$$X/L = \text{labor productivity},$$

where X = output and L = labor input, and

$$X/TF = \text{total factor productivity},$$

where $TF = L + (r/w)K$, r = capital rental, w = wage rate, and K = capital stock.

These two key ratios for labor and for total factor productivity seem to be simple enough, but in careful measurement for quantitative economics each numerator and denominator requires precise specification.

If an economic establishment — firm, plant, enterprise — produces a single output, X is best measured as the physical number of units produced in a given

---

[†] From *Proceedings of the National Academy of Sciences*, Vol. 80 (July, 1983), pp. 4561–4568. Abbreviations: GNP, gross national product; GDP, gross domestic product; CES, constant elasticity of substitution.

[1] "To increase the productiveness of labor is really the important thing for everybody"; see Jevons, 1878.

period of time such as a week, month, quarter, semester, year, quinquennium, or decade. The usual time unit is one year, but that choice is not unique.

Most establishments produce more than one product; therefore, measurement in physical units becomes awkward. Of the many common denominators that may be used to measure X, the most natural one for an economist to use is money value, such as dollars of production in the case of the United States. This choice is not without its problems, however, because money values change rapidly, especially in an era of inflation; therefore, the money value of X must be expressed in *constant* prices. The present convention in the United States is to measure real output in terms of 1972 dollars. This means that the components of X are all valued in terms of the average price prevailing during 1972 and added to strike a total for each year, in this fixed price system.

In the case of a single establishment, it is easy enough and understandable to use gross output in obtaining the constant price value of output. This is obtained by valuing each physical unit produced in terms of the price of that unit in 1972. When we move to consideration of productivity for a larger aggregate such as all manufacturing or the entire national economy, we must face the situation that the output of one establishment (sector) is the input of another establishment (sector). To avoid multiple counting, we measure X as *value added*. This is the value of gross output *less* the value of intermediate input. The latter are materials and energy used in the production process.

From an accounting point of view, there is no problem in subtracting the value of intermediate inputs from the value of gross output. It is more of a problem to define, conceptually, real value added — i.e., constant-priced gross output less constant-priced intermediate inputs (Arrow, 1974). The prices appropriate to output and input are different; therefore, the concept of real value added may not bear a clear and simple relationship to nominal (current-priced) value added.

Economic magnitudes, in general, should satisfy the identity relationship

$$\text{price} * \text{quantity} = \text{value}.$$

If we define the price of real value added as the ratio of nominal value added to real value added, then the identity is satisfied; however, this ratio may define a peculiar or unusual price index that does not have the structure or performance of conventional price indexes.

For the economy as a whole, total value added is synonymous with the concept of gross national product (GNP), and a price index for total GNP can be constructed in terms of the prices of the end products, the final purchases of goods and services, each of which has a definite quoted or implied price. It is somewhat clearer how to define real GNP, or total value added, but it is less clear for a sector of the economy, such as a particular industry. The numerator of the productivity ratio is thus more uncertain if the value added rather than the gross output concept is used. My preference would be to use the concept of real gross output for the sector productivity ratio and the concept of value added for the economy-wide productivity ratio. At the sector level, productivity would be measured in such concepts as output of steel tonnage, grain bushels, cement tonnage, vehicles, or their real gross output value in multiproduct activities per unit of input. The choice of the numerator of the seemingly straightforward productivity ratio is thus by no means obvious; the problem of the choice of the denominator is even more complicated. Consider first, the concept of labor productivity. The consideration of this measure does not mean that labor is the only productive input; it simply means that we are trying to calculate values for a conventional nonparametric statistic, the ratio of real output to real labor input.

Two obvious choices for the (labor input) denominator are number of persons employed and number of hours worked. The latter is obtained as the product of the number of persons and the average number of hours worked per week, multiplied by 52. It seems obvious that hours worked provides a better measure of labor input than does number of employees, but the problem is that information on the working week or any other indicator of average hours worked is often lacking. This is especially true in making international comparisons. For the United States and many other industrial countries, statistics of workers employed and hours worked are generally available on a total and sectoral basis, but this is definitely not the case in many developing or centrally planned economies. If the latter areas are to be examined in the context of international comparisons, then the best *common denominator* may be number of persons working rather than number of hours worked.

Regardless of the resolution of the choice between a count of employees or hours worked, there is another problem — namely, with the implicit assumption that all workers are of the same quality. In the first place, there are distinctions between the contributions of production workers and overhead (nonproduction) workers. Similarly, there are great differences in worker skill, training, and education. Weighted averages of inputs of skill equivalents would be an appropriate denominator. To the extent that relative wage rates represent relative marginal (incremental) productivities, the weights can be readily computed from available data, as in

$$L_1 + (w_2/w_1)L_2 + (w_3/w_1)L_3 + \cdots + (w_n/w_1)L_n \,.$$

This makes the unit of measurement the productivity equivalent of labor type (i.e., 1) and weights other labor types by their wage rate relative to that of type $1(w_1)$. The choice of the *numéraire* type has no bearing on the movement of productivity but measures the level of productivity in terms of one single labor type. An average type could also be used, as in

$$(w_1/\overline{w})L_1 + (w_2/\overline{w})L_2 + \cdots + (w_n/\overline{w})L_n$$

$$\overline{w} = 1/n \sum_{i=1}^{n} w_i \,.$$

Average wage could be computed as either a weighted or an unweighted average.

All the problems in selecting an appropriate denominator for the labor productivity ratio are more serious and more complicated in choosing the denominator for the total factor productivity ratio. Total factor input for the economy as a whole is defined as a weighted combination of labor and capital inputs. This weighted sum would be appropriate for a ratio that has real value added in the numerator. For a gross output numerator, it makes more sense to include intermediate factor inputs, associated with the particular sector whose productivity is being estimated, together with the traditional value-added factors — labor and capital.

In estimating total factor inputs, there is not only the perplexing question of developing labor and capital weights but also the problem of estimating capital itself. Total factor input has been defined as

$$TF = L + (r/w)K\,.$$

This is just the same as the approach suggested for combining labor of different skill levels. The various kinds of labor were aggregated as a linear combination with weights equal to relative wage rates. Here we form a linear combination of the two factors with weights being their relative factor prices. For many years in railway engineering–economic studies, traffic units were used, as a combination of passenger miles and freight ton miles. The combination was

$$\text{ton miles} + 2.4\,(\text{passenger miles}) = \text{traffic units}\,,$$

where the coefficient is the long-run relative price of a passenger mile to a ton mile. For a railway productivity study, this could be used as a gross output measure, where the railway system provided joint (multiple) outputs.

In the productivity literature, we often find total factor input defined as

$$\frac{wL}{wL + rK}L + \frac{rK}{wL + rK}K\,.$$

The weights are factor shares in total value added. If L and K are index values on bases L_0 and K_0, and if the weights are base-period shares, then this weighting scheme, except for normalization, is equivalent to that introduced above because the ratio between the weights is r_0/w_0.

Total factor productivity could be extended to cover not only aggregate labor and capital inputs but also types of labor input, types of capital input, energy inputs, and materials inputs. This part of the problem needs explanation and research analysis but is solvable in a satisfactory way. More serious problems exist in the measurement of capital. Capital is made up of productive equipment, machinery, rolling stock, tools, buildings, right-of-way, physical facilities, and other structures. These are difficult to combine because their relative prices are not readily available or even ascertainable. Capital deteriorates, destructs, and obsolesces. The measurement of capital consumption is inherently difficult, and data are relatively sparse. Life tables for physical capital are not comprehensive, as they are for human capital.

There are measures of capital consumption, but they are known to be imperfect and are often distorted deliberately for tax purposes. Given all these thorny problems, economic statisticians try to measure capital according to the recursive formula

$$K_t = K_{t-1} + I_t - D_t,$$

where K_t = end of period stock of capital, I_t = gross real outlays on capital during t, and D_t = capital consumption during t. To work through this formula, it is necessary to have a starting value as an initial condition. A formula for computing D_t is also needed.

Even after statistical series for K_t have been prepared, after taking all the perilous steps discussed above, there is a further problem. This formula gives capital (stock) in existence but what we need to know for productivity measurement is capital in use, either as a flow of use or as the stock value that was actually used. This requires being able to distinguish between idle and active capital or to obtain statistics of capital utilization. Usually only fragmentary data are available for such concepts as (*i*) idle shipping tonnage, (*ii*) number of shifts worked, (*iii*) idle rail cars, and (*iv*) occupancy rate of buildings. These help, but are fragmentary. Labor inputs are measured by labor actually used, either as hours worked or people at work. No corresponding information about capital is available on a general basis.

Parametric measurement. The concept of a technical production function is central to economic analysis. The meaning of a production function, as this concept is used in economics, is a physical relationship between inputs and outputs of an economic process. It has clearest meaning when applied to the production process for a given establishment, but it is used on a wider scale for industries, sectors, or whole national economies.

At the specific level, it is meant to show the laws of engineering and science that serve as constraints on economic activity. It should not involve prices or market phenomena that are typical for economic analysis, but it should affect the outcome of economic analysis. The flow of gas through a pipeline is one of the clearest concepts of a production function. The gas, the pipeline capital, and the physical conditions within the pipe are the inputs. The flow of gas to users is the output. The output flow is governed by the laws of gases.

There is less specificity at a higher level of aggregation. Conceptually, there are catalogs of inputs and outputs for the whole national economy but, statistically, we proceed at a much more general level and assume that the following relationship holds:

$$X = F(K, L, E, M, t) + e,$$

where X = total production, K = total capital input, L = employment, E = energy, M = materials, t = chronological time, and e = error. Part of the error term may be associated with the use of aggregative indexes to measure the various inputs and outputs at a level beyond the individual establishment. As in the discussion of nonparametric methods, distinctions can be made among types of capital, labor, materials, and energy, not to mention the fact that there will be multiple outputs too.

Because intermediate inputs, E and M, are used on the right-hand-side to explain fluctuations in X, this output variable must also include intermediate inputs; therefore, X is truly gross output and not a value-added concept such as gross domestic product (GDP) or GNP.

The problems of capital measurement associated with distinctions between the stock of capital in existence and the flow of capital services used apply here as well as in nonparametric measurement.

The production function is written here in very general terms. In practice, some very specific forms are conventionally used. The most celebrated, following the pioneering research of Paul Douglas, is the Cobb–Douglas function, linear in the logarithms of output and inputs

$$X = AK^{\alpha}L^{\beta}E^{\gamma}M^{\delta}\exp(\rho t)e_t\,.$$

The error is made multiplicative in this expression and is additive in the logarithmic transformation. An indicator of technical progress is ρ, the instantaneous rate of improvement that comes about separately from changed inputs of *KLEM*.

A second form is called the constant elasticity of substitution specification (CES). The elasticity of substitution between input pairs is unity for the Cobb–Douglas case. It is constant but not necessarily equal to unity for the CES case. An extended CES function is

$$X = A(\delta_K K^{-\rho} + \delta_L L^{-\rho} + \delta_E E^{-\rho} + \delta_M M^{-\rho})^{-1/\rho}\exp(\rho t)e_t\,.$$

The disadvantage of this production formula is that the elasticity of substitution is exactly the same for every pair of inputs. To generalize the concepts used here, we have designed the nested CES function as

$$X = A\Big(\theta\{\eta[\delta K^{-\rho_1} + (1-\delta)E^{-\rho_1}]^{\rho_2/\rho_1}$$
$$+ (1-\eta)L^{-\rho_2}\}^{\rho_3/\rho_2} + (1-\theta)M^{-\rho_3}\Big)^{-1/\rho_3}\exp(\rho t)e_t\,.$$

In this separable specification, there is first a nested CES combination of capital (K) and energy (E). Then we obtain a relationship between a capital–energy combination and labor input. Finally we combine *KEL* (capital–energy–labor) into one single input and estimate the elasticity of substitution between a *KEL* combination and M. As in the Cobb–Douglas case, there is provision for a multiplicative error term, but in a logarithmic transformation the error term is additive as is the rate of technical improvement.

A translog production function is a logarithmic function for ln X, which is quadratic in the logarithms of the inputs. This kind of function has a great many parameters but can be transformed into simple expressions in cost shares and linear functions of input prices.

Finally, there could be general linear functions or functions that are linear with pairs in fixed proportions.

A fundamental equation for productivity analysis is

$$\frac{d\ln X}{dt} = \frac{1}{F}\left(\frac{K\partial F}{\partial K}\frac{d\ln K}{dt} + \frac{L\partial F}{\partial L}\frac{d\ln L}{dt} + \frac{E\partial F}{\partial E}\frac{d\ln E}{dt} + \frac{M\partial F}{\partial M}\frac{d\ln M}{dt} + \frac{\partial F}{\partial t}\right).$$

This expresses the rate of change (approximately the finite-step percentage change) of output as a weighted sum of the rates of change of the factor inputs $(KLEM)$ and the time rate of growth of the whole function. In the Cobb–Douglas or CES specifications with a multiplicative time factor, the rate of change of the trend term is a constant.

In a special case of the Cobb–Douglas function, a conventional workhorse for the design of productivity and other output calculations, we assume

$$\alpha + \beta + \gamma + \delta = 1,$$

which implies constant returns to scale. If all four inputs are scaled by the factor λ, then the whole function and output are also scaled by the same factor. We call this homogeneity of degree one in the input values. In this case, we can write

$$\frac{X}{L} = A\left(\frac{K}{L}\right)^{\alpha}\left(\frac{E}{L}\right)^{\gamma}\left(\frac{M}{L}\right)^{\delta}\exp(\rho t)e_t$$

$$\frac{d\ln(X/L)}{dt} = \alpha\frac{d\ln(K/L)}{dt} + \gamma\frac{d\ln(E/L)}{dt} + \delta\frac{d\ln(M/L)}{dt} + \rho + \frac{d\ln e_t}{dt}.$$

With this parametric specification, the rate of growth of labor productivity is a linear function of the growth rate of labor–factor ratios (called factor intensities) and technical progress, which measures, in a parametric sense, total factor productivity.

The parameters of the Cobb–Douglas function are the weights for combining the growth of factor intensities, and the technical progress factor is a direct estimate of total factor productivity; this is the meaning of a parametric approach.

This approach could be used with production functions in general. If they are homogeneous of degree one in the several inputs and multiplied by an exponential factor

$$\exp(\rho t),$$

then we have

$$X/L = F(K/L, E/L, M/L)\exp(\rho t)e_t$$

and

$$\frac{d\ln(X/L)}{dt} = \frac{(K/L)F_{K/L}}{F}\frac{d\ln(K/L)}{dt} + \frac{(E/L)F_{E/L}}{F}\frac{d\ln(E/L)}{dt}$$

$$+ \frac{(M/L)F_{M/L}}{F}\frac{d\ln(M/L)}{dt} + \rho + \frac{d\ln e_t}{dt}.$$

Once the parameters of F are determined, the partial derivatives

$$\frac{\partial F}{\partial K} = F_K; \qquad \frac{\partial F}{\partial E} = F_E; \qquad \frac{\partial F}{\partial M} = F_M$$

can be evaluated. They need not be constant or proportional to F, as in the Cobb–Douglas case.

If we introduce some economic theory into the specifications, we have the conditions that each productive factor is paid a unit price (cost) equal to its marginal productivity

$$\frac{\partial F}{\partial L} = \frac{w}{p}; \qquad \frac{\partial F}{\partial K} = \frac{r}{p}; \qquad \frac{\partial F}{\partial E} = \frac{g}{p}; \qquad \frac{\partial F}{\partial M} = \frac{q}{p},$$

where w = wage rate, r = capital rental, g = unit energy cost, q = unit material cost, and p = output price. In the Cobb–Douglas case, these conditions are particularly simple

$$\beta = \frac{wL}{pX}; \qquad \alpha = \frac{rK}{pX}; \qquad \gamma = \frac{gE}{pX}; \qquad \delta = \frac{qM}{pX}.$$

We can accordingly write

$$\frac{d\ln(X/L)}{dt} = \frac{rK}{pX}\frac{d\ln(K/L)}{dt} + \frac{gE}{pX}\frac{d\ln(E/L)}{dt} + \frac{qM}{pX}\frac{d\ln(M/L)}{dt} + \rho + \frac{d\ln e_t}{dt}.$$

Here we have a correspondence with the nonparametric case, where total factor productivity, with four input factors, would be calculated as

$$\frac{d\ln(X/L)}{dt} - \frac{rK}{pX}\frac{d\ln(K/L)}{dt} - \frac{gE}{pX}\frac{d\ln(E/L)}{dt} - \frac{gM}{pX}\frac{d\ln(M/L)}{dt}$$

or the rate of growth of labor productivity less the weighted sum of rates of growth of factor intensities, the weights being factor shares. This comes, in effect, to our nonparametric measures of total factor productivity, although it is often computed with only two factors, labor and capital, and value-added output.

International Measurement

The preceding two sections define the problem and approach. I now turn to some international and other practical issues. It is important to construct reliable and indicative productivity measures for the major economies to see how each one by itself performs over the course of time. There is, however, an additional dimension that is of utmost importance — namely, the intercountry comparisons of productivity. In this field, we have questions of substance. Which countries are highly competitive and efficient, from a production point of view? There is also a methodological question of how to measure productivity reliably at the international level.

First, let us consider the methodology of measurement. The first things that must be examined are the rates of exchange among currencies. In some cases, for particular industries, physical measures can be prepared. Tons of steel per worker and number of vehicles per worker are fairly good measures for cross-country comparisons. They are, however, relatively rare. For the economy as a whole and for most industrial sectors, physical measures are not applicable, and there must be resort to valuation comparisons.

To compare productivity across countries, the values of production, in own currency units, for each country, per worker hour (or per worker) must be converted to measures of production per worker hour (or per worker) in a common currency unit, the most frequently used case being U.S. dollars. For the major countries and for the economy as a whole, or broad sectors such as manufacturing, data are available on worker hours. At the industry level, across countries, or even at the aggregative level across smaller or developing countries, the number of workers rather than worker hours would have to be used.

Because productivity is meant to be a physical indicator, output per worker hour (or per worker) should be expressed in constant prices, which means that constant exchange rates as well as constant domestic prices would have to be used.

Table 1. Gross domestic product per worker: Selected industrial countries (1980).

	U.S. dollars		U.S. dollars
United States	18.0	Fed. Rep. of Germany	19.4
Canada	18.0	Italy	11.0
Japan	15.1	United Kingdom	10.3
Belgium	19.1	Denmark	17.4
France	18.4	Sweden	18.4
		Netherlands	20.6

Results are expressed in thousands of 1975 U.S. dollars, and 1975 exchange rates were used for currency conversion.

The most common procedure is to use market exchange rates bilaterally against the U.S. dollar; therefore, we would be considering output per worker hour (or per worker) in constant (base-period) prices at base-period dollar exchange rates — i.e., at constant (base-period) U.S. dollars. For an economy-wide measure, there are few reliable statistics on worker hours, so total employment is used. In Table 1, figures are given for the industrial countries in 1980. These figures show a great disparity between Italy and the United Kingdom, on the one hand, and all the others. They also show many other countries exceeding the United States in productivity level, as of 1980. Such comparison results often occur, either per worker or per inhabitant if market exchange rates are used, but the purchasing power conversion ratios developed by Kravis *et al.* (1982) show that the United States is still number one if such ratios are used in place of market rates.

If we confine our attention to rates of change of productivity or to indexes showing change over base values, then we need not convert the output measures to a common currency unit. The *changes* can be expressed in own constant-currency units; the rate of change will be insensitive to a constant factor used for currency conversion.

In a series of interesting reports, the U.S. Department of Labor has made productivity and cost comparisons across the same countries listed in Table 1, but confined to the manufacturing sector (Capdevielle *et al.*, 1982). In these reports, rates of change in productivity are measured in domestic currency units. By confining measures to the manufacturing sector and to the same major countries listed in Table 1, productivity changes are obtained based on estimates in own-currency units (Table 2).

Table 2. Changes in manufacturing productivity.

	Output per hour	
	1960–1973	1973–1981
United States	3.0	1.7
Canada	4.5	1.4
Japan	10.7	6.8
France	6.0	4.6
Fed. Rep. of Germany	5.5	4.5
Italy	6.9	3.7
United Kingdom	4.3	2.2
Belgium	7.0	6.2
Denmark	6.4	4.1
Netherlands	7.6	5.1
Sweden	6.7	2.2

Results are expressed as percent change.

The most striking thing about Table 2 is the wide pervasiveness of the world productivity slowdown. In every country examined here, the growth rate of productivity fell significantly after 1973, the time of the oil embargo. It is no surprise that the growth of Japan's manufacturing productivity was relatively high in international comparisons. But it is not so well known that Japan's growth rate slipped considerably after 1973, as did that of most other countries. The drop in the U.S. rate, however, brought this country to almost a standstill position.

Many scholars are devoting attention to explanations for the productivity slowdown. Giersch and Wolter (1982) have considered 14 different explanations of the worldwide productivity slowdown without coming to a succinct conclusion. In a parallel study, Lindbeck (1983) attributes the slowdown to structural changes in the politico–economic environment and to unusually severe disturbances of the 1970s.

International Competitiveness

A principal reason for examining productivity levels or growth rates in different countries is to assess their mutual competitive positions, particularly with respect to foreign trade. Generally speaking, those countries that have shown relatively strong productivity growth have been highly competitive and have captured markets.

Competitiveness, however, depends on more than productivity; it depends on costs, profit margins, and exchange rates. At the international level, except in carefully constructed bilateral studies, total factor productivity has not been satisfactorily measured. Most of the studies have been concerned with labor productivity. At that level of investigation, the appropriate cost item is the wage rate. Statistics of unit labor cost have been carefully prepared in tabulations by the U.S. Department of Labor. Unit labor cost is computed as the wage rate divided by productivity (or the wage bill per unit of output). The growth rates in unit labor costs, measured in U.S. dollars, are given in Table 3.

Table 3. Changes in unit labor costs in manufacturing.

	U.S. dollars	
	1960–1973	1973–1981
United States	1.9	7.7
Canada	1.9	6.5
Japan	4.9	7.2
France	2.8	9.4
Fed. Rep. of Germany	6.1	9.1
Italy	5.4	8.1
United Kingdom	2.6	15.0
Belgium	4.6	8.6
Denmark	5.0	7.7
Netherlands	6.1	8.0
Sweden	4.2	9.6

Results are expressed as percent change.

It is evident from these figures that the productivity slowdown is reflected in a unit labor cost speed-up. The high wage costs, together with poor productivity growth, contribute jointly to the poor showing by the United Kingdom.

A profit margin estimate is needed to translate these figures into final prices charged (all in U.S. dollar units) that would show the ultimate degree of competitiveness.

There are two gaps in all these tables. They do not cover many smaller countries that are important in the world trade system, particularly some fast-growing developing countries that play important roles in world export markets for manufactured goods. Second, these tabulations are mainly for large aggregates, the total GDP or output of the manufacturing sector.

Very careful data preparation must be undertaken to construct these data for developing countries. Both domestic sources and the statistical offices of the large international organizations could be used to fill the first gap. These data are available; it is only a matter of their being properly researched.

As for the specific industry analyses, a number of them have been estimated on the basis of production and employment data in some individual industries. Using Office of Economic Cooperation and Development data on indexes of production in individual industries, corresponding data on employment, and U.S. Department of Labor data on wage rates, we are able to construct series of growth rates of productivity and unit labor costs. Accompanying series for producer price indexes can also be prepared. This gives us a ready reference for looking at key industries

Table 4. Productivity, unit labor cost, and price: Iron and steel industry (1975–1980).

	Productivity	Unit labor cost		Producer price
		Local currency	U.S. dollars	
Canada	1.9	10.2	7.2	10.1
France	7.8	4.6	4.9	7.6
Fed. Rep. of Germany	4.9	2.2	8.6	1.4
Japan	8.2	−1.3	4.3	6.3
Sweden	2.1	9.3	8.9	6.9
United Kingdom	−2.2	13.6	19.8	12.9
United States	0.9	10.3	10.3	8.7

Results are expressed as percent change.

Table 5. Productivity, unit labor cost, and price: Motor vehicle industry (1975–1980).

	Productivity	Unit labor cost		Producer price
		Local currency	U.S. dollars	
Canada	−2.1	14.3	10.9	9.0
France	3.1	10.7	11.0	−
Fed. Rep. of Germany	0.1	7.8	14.5	3.7
Japan	10.5	2.2	3.3	0.3
United Kingdom	−1.3	12.7	13.7	15.7
United States	2.3	9.0	9.0	7.6

Results are expressed as percent change.

across countries during recent history. The period 1975–1980 was chosen for reasons of commonality. Tables 4–9 show these comparative statistics on competitiveness for selected countries, chosen on the basis of availability, and some key industrial sectors — areas of maturity, cyclicality, and potential growth.

In this period, the relatively strong growth performance of Japan stands out and contributes so much from the side of productivity that exchange appreciation

Table 6. Productivity, unit labor cost, and price: Electrical machinery and electronics industry (1975–1980).

| | | Unit labor cost | | |
	Productivity	Local currency	U.S. dollars	Producer price
Canada	3.3	6.8	3.8	7.2
France	5.5	9.2	9.6	–
Fed. Rep. of Germany	5.0	3.0	9.5	2.0
Japan	14.1	−6.7	−1.5	0.4
Netherlands	7.8	1.5	6.5	1.6
Sweden	0.6	11.5	11.1	8.3
United Kingdom	1.8	19.9	21.0	13.4
United States	4.0	5.0	5.0	7.5

Results are expressed as percent change.

Table 7. Productivity, unit labor cost, and price: Chemicals industry (1975–1980).

| | | Unit labor cost | | |
	Productivity	Local currency	U.S. dollars	Producer price
Canada	3.2	6.7	3.8	10.5
France	4.8	10.0	10.3	9.5
Fed. Rep. of Germany	3.5	3.3	10.4	2.9
Japan	9.7	−1.0	4.6	9.3
Netherlands	6.9	0.8	5.7	–
Sweden	0.7	11.8	11.4	11.8
Switzerland	6.9	−3.0	5.8	−0.6
United Kingdom	2.6	20.5	21.6	16.3
United States	4.4	5.3	5.3	9.4

Results are expressed as percent change.

of the yen against the dollar does not wipe out the gains when unit labor cost is computed in U.S. dollar units. Both wage and price changes were also restrained in Japan in comparison with other countries. On the negative side, the United Kingdom performed relatively poorly on both productivity and competitiveness standard. The United States is neither the worst nor the best in these sectors, but such comparisons indicate that, if a cyclical recovery in productivity growth could be attained with wage and price restraint, the United States could be fully competitive in foreign trade markets.

Some Bilateral Comparisons

A comprehensive analysis using estimates of parametric production functions has not been made for individual industries in several countries nor even for

Table 8. Productivity, unit labor cost, and price: Textile industry (1975–1980).

| | | Unit labor cost | | |
	Productivity	Local currency	U.S. dollars	Producer price
Canada	3.6	7.0	4.0	9.0
Denmark	3.4	7.3	7.7	6.8
France	3.2	10.6	10.9	3.4
Fed. Rep. of Germany	3.6	3.7	10.2	2.6
Japan	4.2	4.1	9.9	4.2
Netherlands	7.9	−0.3	4.6	3.9
Sweden	0.3	12.4	11.9	8.6
Switzerland	5.8	−0.8	6.9	0.5
United Kingdom	−0.1	15.7	16.7	12.9
United States	3.0	6.1	6.1	5.9

Results are expressed as percent change.

Table 9. Productivity, unit labor cost, and price: Paper and allied products (1975–1980).

| | | Unit labor cost | | |
	Productivity	Local currency	U.S. dollars	Producer price
Canada	3.5	7.1	4.2	9.2
France	6.1	7.7	8.1	5.8
Fed. Rep. of Germany	5.5	2.6	9.0	2.9
Japan	5.9	0.2	5.8	6.1
Netherlands	5.5	1.7	6.7	–
Sweden	3.0	9.8	9.3	7.1
United Kingdom	2.5	10.7	20.9	13.5
United States	2.6	7.4	7.4	7.9

Results are expressed as percent change.

manufacturing as a whole across a wide spectrum of countries. This could be done, and undoubtedly will, in future research, but there are some revealing studies of productivity comparisons of pairs of countries. Let us first consider Japan and the United States.

In a carefully documented study, Grossman and Sadler (1982) have estimated output per worker hour for both Japan and the United States (Table 10). They also have estimates of total factor productivity. Their findings are of particular interest because they are estimated at a detailed industry level of disaggregation. In these findings, values of output were converted to 1975 dollars by using the Kravis ratios of purchasing power parity.

Table 10. Levels of output per hour worked in the United States and in Japan (1970–1980).

Industry segment	United States				Japan			
	1970	1973	1974	1980	1970	1973	1974	1980
Private domestic business	8.27	9.06	8.28	9.27	3.59	4.64	4.73	6.01
Agriculture	6.17	6.24	6.32	7.21	1.37	2.05	2.11	2.38
Nonfarm nonmanufacturing	8.64	9.19	8.10	9.07	4.15	5.00	5.04	5.68
Mining	27.58	27.05	25.22	19.26	5.07	7.96	7.10	11.67
Construction	9.45	9.36	8.35	7.43	3.85	4.25	4.06	4.13
Transportation and communication	9.29	10.48	10.83	13.13	3.86	4.29	4.74	5.66
Electricity, gas, and water	21.98	24.40	23.32	25.38	14.01	14.09	15.05	19.74
Trade	6.88	7.70	7.55	7.92	2.88	3.90	3.98	4.53
Finance and insurance	8.21	8.32	8.45	8.20	6.69	10.32	9.03	12.03
Business services	6.79	7.10	5.04	6.70	3.39	3.60	3.60	3.60
Manufacturing	7.92	9.30	9.09	10.17	3.91	5.12	5.31	8.00
Food and tobacco	9.51	12.04	11.43	13.35	3.81	5.61	6.03	7.07
Textiles	5.11	5.60	5.33	7.10	1.58	1.82	2.47	2.93
Pulp and paper	8.28	10.75	11.02	11.16	5.11	7.13	6.83	9.20
Chemicals	10.26	13.20	12.67	14.91	6.54	10.48	10.63	17.77
Primary metals	11.51	13.47	13.52	12.01	8.61	13.20	12.12	21.43
Fabricated metals	8.53	9.27	8.60	10.05	3.32	4.85	4.16	4.75
Machinery (excluding electrical)	8.54	9.34	9.18	10.04	4.03	4.59	4.78	7.98
Electrical machinery	6.90	8.01	7.54	10.22	2.78	5.03	5.68	13.32
Transportation equipment	8.47	10.91	10.62	10.90	5.19	5.89	6.82	10.30
Other manufacturing[1]	6.56	7.47	7.45	8.23	3.83	4.26	4.16	5.13
Service producing[2]	8.16	8.80	7.75	8.98	4.20	5.16	5.26	6.03
Goods producing[3]	8.37	9.33	9.02	9.68	3.14	4.22	4.29	5.99

Results are expressed in constant 1975 U.S. dollars per hr. Japan real output in 1975 yen was converted to 1975 U.S. dollars by using the 1970 purchasing power parity (PPP) as given by Kravis (Kravis *et al.*, 1982) extrapolated to 1975; PPP in 1975 was 272.5 yen per U.S. dollar (see Summers *et al.* 1980). Source: see (Grossman and Sadler, 1982)
[1]Includes apparel; lumber; furniture; printing and publishing; petroleum; stone; clay, stone, and glass; leather; instruments; and miscellaneous manufacturing.
[2]Includes nonfarm nonmanufacturing exclusive of mining and construction.
[3]Includes manufacturing, agriculture, mining, and construction.

The results of Grossman and Sadler show an increase from $8.27 to $9.27 per hour for total private domestic business in the United States between 1970 and 1980. The corresponding gain for Japan was from $3.59 to $6.01. The United States has a much higher productivity level, but the gain over the decade was far greater in percentage terms for Japan. The same statistical pattern prevails across most industry groups, but the American agricultural performance remains impressive.

Table 11. Productivity growth in the United States and in Japan (1966–1980).

	Growth, %	
	1966–1973	1974–1980
Total factor productivity		
Japan	0.74	0.79
United States	0.35	0.18
Labor productivity		
Japan	8.90	4.69
United States	2.30	1.11

In electrical machinery and primary metals, the Japanese gains and levels by 1980 are outstanding.

From CES production functions with four factor inputs (*KLEM*), Kumasaka[2] has estimated total factor and labor productivity growth in manufacturing (Table 11). For Japan, a nested CES function was used, while, for the United States, a split level CES function with K and E at one level and L and M at another was used. Kumasaka finds that the labor productivity slowdown in Japan was associated mainly with decline in factor intensity, especially capital and materials, while the slowdown in the United States was accounted for mainly by a drop in energy and material intensity, with some overall drop in total factor productivity.

In earlier research at the University of Pennsylvania, Tange (1979) estimated generalized Cobb–Douglas functions for Japan and the United States by similar industrial classification. Her function was

$$X_{it} = A_i L_{it}^{\alpha_i} K_{it}^{\beta_i} \left(\prod_{j=1}^{n} X_{ji}^{\gamma_{ji}} \right) \exp(\lambda_{it}) e_{it} \, .$$

The γ_{ji} were estimated directly from input–output tables and include both energy and materials as intermediate inputs, and the estimation period was 1957–1974 (Table 12).

Some of the estimates do not include data for 1974, and satisfactory estimates of the production function for manufactured food products were not obtained for the United States, so this sector is not included in the comparison. The main point, however, is clear. The rate of technical progress, identified as total factor productivity, is uniformly larger in this tabulation across industrial groups for Japan. A use to which these estimates of the production functions were put was to develop indexes of relative cost efficiency, which were then correlated with relative export performance. The evidence is strongly indicative that cost efficiency promoted superior export performance.

---

[2]Kumasaka, Y., Doctoral dissertation research, Univ. of Pennsylvania, 1983.

Table 12. Estimates of total factor productivity in Japan and in the United States: Cobb–Douglas specification (1957–1974).

	Estimate, %	
	Japan	United States
Textile mill products	2.5	1.6
Paper and allied products	2.6	1.6
Chemicals and allied products	3.0	2.7
Primary metals	1.5	–
Fabricated metals	1.9	0.6
Nonelectrical machinery	3.2	1.4
Electrical machinery	5.5	2.6
Transportation equipment	5.5	1.6

International Policy Comparisons

By and large, it will be agreed among countries that productivity is a good thing, that its growth should be encouraged. It is not without its drawbacks and problems, but there are hardly any countries that will deliberately try to discourage productivity advances. Some may try to moderate its influence. But there will be wide differences among countries in the choice of policies to enhance productivity growth. At one extreme, we may find active *industrial policies* that place productivity growth at the head of the list of economic priorities. It is often felt that Japanese economic policy of the 1950s and 1960s was a case of intensive and fruitful use of industrial policy to encourage productivity growth and a high state of competitiveness (Shinohara, 1982).

In their case it was a problem of establishing a consensus, involving both the public and corporate sectors, with the cooperation of labor, to delineate the potential winning sectors, to favor them with fiscal and other incentives, and to develop them to a state at which they show the high productivity growth rates that we find in the tables presented here. It was a dedicated policy and apparently successful, as far as productivity growth is concerned.

It is sometimes felt that "le Plan" in France during the 1960s accomplished similar achievements. On the other hand, there are abundant examples of failed industrial policies in which "losers" get more support than "winners" and, as a consequence, productivity gains suffered. The United Kingdom of the 1950s, 1960s, and 1970s provides examples, as do Sweden and some other countries.

A popular view is that public authorities should simply make the overall economic environment attractive and conducive to capital formation, allowing the conventional market-oriented process to do the picking of potential winners.

Appropriate policies for establishing an environment in which productivity might thrive are plentiful support for research and development, both civilian and military, support for basic research, tax policies that favor investment incentives (accelerated depreciation, investment tax credits, research and development tax credits), easy credit policies, export financing, and similar devices.

This is the prevailing view in the United States, and some of these proposals will find expression in future policy packages. Productivity now shows some signs of reviving on its own cyclical path, and an encouraging economic environment, is likely to make U.S. productivity grow at a much better rate than in the latter part of the 1970s.

References

Arrow, K. J., 1974, in *Nations and Households in Economic Growth*, eds. P. A. David and M. W. Reder (Academic, New York), pp. 3–19.

Capdevielle, P., D. Alvarez, and B. Cooper, 1982, *Mon. Labor Rev.* **105** (12), pp. 3–14.

Fabricant, S., 1968, in *International Encyclopedia of the Social Sciences*, ed. D. L. Sills (Macmillan, New York), p. 523.

Giersch, H. and F. Wolter, 1982, in "On the recent slowdown in productivity growth in advanced economies," Kiel Working Paper No. 148, Institut für Weltwrischaft an der Universität Kiel, Kiel, Federal Republic of Germany.

Grossman, E. S. and G. S. Sadler, 1982, *Comparative Productivity Dynamics: Japan and the United States* (American Productivity Center, Houston, TX).

Jevons, W. S., 1878, *Primer of Political Economy* (Macmillan, London), p. 54.

Kravis, I. B., A. Heston, and R. Summers, 1982, *World Product and Income, International Comparisons of Real Gross Product* [Johns Hopkins Univ. Press (for the World Bank), Baltimore].

Lindbeck, A., 1983, *Econ. J.* **93**, 13–34.

Oxford English Dictionary, 1971, (Oxford Univ. Press, New York).

Shinohara, M., 1982, *Industrial Growth, Trade, and Dynamic Patterns in the Japanese Economy* (Univ. of Tokyo Press, Tokyo).

Summers, R., I. Kravis, and A. Heston, 1980, *Rev. Income Wealth* **26** (1), pp. 19–66.

Tange, T., 1979, Dissertation, Univ. of Pennsylvania.

28

**PURCHASING POWER PARITY IN
MEDIUM TERM SIMULATION OF THE WORLD ECONOMY**[†]

I. Introduction

In the 1980 Nobel Lecture[1] a possible decade-long simulation projection is described for the world economy, containing many aspects of long run equilibrium. This simulation suggested that world economic growth would enter a slower phase on an historical basis, not for all parts of the world, but definitely so, on average. The projection also estimated a gradual slowing of world inflation, a lower ratio of world trade growth to world production growth, especially among developing countries, an improved world energy balance, and some progress towards elimination of large trade imbalances, but with many persistently remaining.

Many of these features of a baseline projection can be seen in the accompanying table. By and large, this projection is the same as that presented in the Nobel Lecture, but a few revisions due to data changes or minor coding errors have been introduced; therefore, the figures in this table are not identical with those in the Lecture, but no major conclusion has been significantly changed. While the present investigation aims to study particular departures from and extensions of the analysis of the Nobel Lecture, it will do so by comparison with the base case in Table 1 which can be considered to be a revision of the projection from the Nobel Lecture.

In that first exercise with a medium term simulation of the LINK system (1980–1990) a particular simplifying assumption was made about international exchange rates, namely, that they would be treated as exogenous variables and fixed at their projected 1981 values for the remainder of the decade. This is obviously unrealistic and inappropriate for a simulation study that tried to investigate equilibrium properties of a system. Exchange rates provide a system of adjustment mechanisms that try to bring the international economy into equilibrium with repercussions on the separate national economies. In this paper we attempt to modify the baseline simulation by introducing the principle of purchasing power parity for treating exchange rates as endogenous variables.

[†]From *Scandinavian Journal of Economics* **1** (January, 1981), pp. 479–496; written jointly with Shahrokh Fardoust and Victor Filatov. The authors would like to thank Michael Papaioannou for his efforts in helping us develop exchange rate algorithms, Baudouin Velge and Said Haidar for research assistance, and Avner Aleh for computer programming assistance.
[1]"Some economic scenarios for the 1980s," *Les Prix Nobel*, © The Nobel Foundation, Stockholm, 1980.

497

Table 1. Project LINK World trade summary (billions of current U.S. dollars)[1]

Longterm baseline control solution

(A)	1980	1981	%CH	1982	%CH
13 LINK OECD COUNTRIES[2]					
Exports[3]	1036.0	1220.1	17.8	1442.1	18.2
Imports	1090.0	1258.2	15.4	1440.7	14.5
Balance	−54.0	−38.0		1.5	
U.S. and Canada					
Exports[3]	268.5	306.5	14.1	375.4	22.5
Imports	293.2	338.3	15.4	390.7	15.5
Balance	−24.7	−31.9		−15.3	
Japan and Australia					
Exports[3]	138.1	157.1	13.7	200.5	27.7
Imports	139.6	159.8	14.5	185.5	16.1
Balance	−1.5	−2.7		15.0	
Rest of OECD					
Exports[3]	629.4	756.6	20.2	866.2	14.5
Imports	657.2	760.0	15.6	864.4	13.7
Balance	−27.8	−3.5		1.8	
Developing countries					
Exports[3]	532.1	615.9	15.7	698.2	13.4
Imports	468.1	560.8	19.8	650.0	15.9
Balance	64.0	55.0		48.2	
Developing countries non-oil					
Exports[3]	224.5	260.1	15.9	289.0	11.1
Imports	296.3	340.8	15.0	382.5	12.2
Balance	−71.8	−80.7		−93.5	
Developing countries oil					
Exports[3]	307.6	355.8	15.7	409.2	15.0
Imports	171.8	220.1	28.1	267.5	21.6
Balance	135.8	135.7		141.7	
Centrally planned countries[4]					
Exports[3]	138.4	155.9	12.7	178.5	14.5
Imports	146.7	168.3	14.8	186.9	11.0
Balance	−8.3	−12.4		−8.3	
Rest of the world					
Exports[3]	163.4	198.9	21.8	189.7	−4.7
Imports	165.1	203.5	23.3	231.1	13.5
Balance	−1.7	−4.6		−41.4	
World exports	1869.9	2190.9	17.2	2508.6	14.5
World export price	3.3	3.7	14.4	4.1	8.9
World exports (real)[1]	573.2	587.0	2.4	617.0	5.1
World export price of fuel	10.9	12.8	16.9	14.4	12.6
World export of fuel (real)	40.9	39.2	−4.0	40.9	4.4

1983	%CH	1984	%CH	1985	%CH	1986	%CH
1626.9	12.8	1841.4	13.2	2077.6	12.8	2337.0	12.5
1630.3	13.2	1850.9	13.5	2080.9	12.4	2326.3	11.8
−3.3		−9.5		−3.3		10.7	
430.1	14.6	481.4	11.9	536.1	11.4	601.4	12.2
446.7	14.3	507.0	13.5	566.4	11.7	628.3	10.9
−16.7		−25.7		−30.4		−26.9	
236.1	17.7	274.9	16.5	322.0	17.1	357.3	11.0
214.7	15.7	245.1	14.2	279.3	13.9	313.2	12.1
21.4		29.8		42.7		44.1	
960.8	10.9	1085.2	12.9	1219.5	12.4	1378.2	13.0
968.9	12.1	1098.8	13.4	1235.2	12.4	1384.8	12.1
−8.1		−13.7		−15.6		−6.6	
781.5	11.9	873.0	11.7	971.2	11.2	1076.6	10.9
750.8	15.5	852.7	13.6	965.8	13.3	1085.0	12.3
30.7		20.3		5.3		−8.4	
324.6	12.3	361.9	11.5	403.1	11.4	443.0	9.9
435.3	13.8	485.9	11.6	544.9	12.1	604.0	10.8
−110.7		−124.0		−141.8		−160.9	
456.9	11.7	511.0	11.8	568.0	11.2	633.6	11.5
315.5	17.9	366.7	16.2	420.9	14.8	481.1	14.3
141.4		144.3		147.1		152.5	
203.9	14.2	234.2	14.9	267.2	14.1	304.8	14.1
208.7	11.6	237.0	13.6	268.4	13.2	306.6	14.3
−4.7		−2.8		−1.2		−1.8	
240.9	27.0	290.4	20.5	334.2	15.1	373.8	11.8
263.6	14.1	298.4	13.2	335.0	12.3	374.2	11.7
−22.6		−8.0		−0.8		−0.5	
2853.3	13.7	3239.0	13.5	3650.1	12.7	4092.2	12.1
4.4	8.2	4.7	7.3	5.1	7.2	5.4	6.4
648.6	5.1	686.2	5.8	721.6	5.2	760.3	5.4
15.9	10.4	17.5	9.9	19.2	9.7	20.9	9.3
42.6	4.0	44.3	4.1	46.0	3.7	47.8	4.1

(*Cont'd*)

Table 1. (*Cont'd*)

(B)	1986	1987	%CH	1988	%CH
13 LINK OECD countries[2]					
Exports[3]	2337.0	2608.8	11.6	2929.5	12.3
Imports	2326.3	2589.3	11.3	2894.3	11.8
Balance	10.7	19.5		35.2	
U.S. and Canada					
Exports[3]	601.4	672.1	11.8	755.5	12.4
Imports	628.3	696.3	10.8	774.2	11.2
Balance	−26.9	−24.2		−18.7	
Japan and Australia					
Exports[3]	357.3	392.0	9.7	439.2	12.0
Imports	313.2	350.1	11.8	392.3	12.1
Balance	44.1	42.0		46.9	
Rest of OECD					
Exports[3]	1378.2	1544.7	12.1	1734.8	12.3
Imports	1384.8	1543.0	11.4	1727.8	12.0
Balance	−6.6	1.7		7.0	
Developing countries					
Exports[3]	1076.6	1187.1	10.3	1308.7	10.3
Imports	1085.0	1206.2	11.2	1344.1	11.4
Balance	−8.4	−19.2		−35.3	
Developing countries non-oil					
Exports[3]	443.0	483.1	9.0	530.3	9.8
Imports	604.0	661.8	9.6	730.3	10.3
Balance	−160.9	−178.8		−200.0	
Developing countries oil					
Exports[3]	633.6	704.0	11.1	778.5	10.6
Imports	481.1	544.4	13.2	613.7	12.7
Balance	152.5	159.6		164.7	
Centrally planned countries[4]					
Exports[3]	304.8	341.1	11.9	385.6	13.1
Imports	306.6	341.7	11.4	386.5	13.1
Balance	−1.8	−0.6		−0.9	
Rest of the World					
Exports[3]	373.8	415.3	11.1	463.9	11.7
Imports	374.2	415.0	10.9	462.9	11.6
Balance	−0.5	0.3		1.0	
World exports	4092.2	4552.2	11.2	5087.7	11.8
World export price	5.4	5.7	6.3	6.1	6.1
World exports (real)[1]	760.3	795.5	4.6	838.4	5.4
World export price of fuel	20.9	23.0	9.6	25.1	9.2
World export of fuel (real)	47.8	49.2	2.9	50.9	3.4

[1] Constant dollars measures have base 1970 = 1.0.
[2] 13 LINK OECD countries are: Australia, Austria, Belgium, Canada, Finland, France, Federal Republic of Germany, Italy, Japan, Netherlands, Sweden, United Kingdom, U.S.A.
[3] Measures are for merchandise trade, f.o.b.

1989	%CH	1990	%CH	1980–1985	1985–1990	1980–1990
3282.5	12.0	3671.6	11.9	14.9%	12.1%	15.5%
3234.3	11.7	3604.2	11.4	13.8%	11.6%	12.7%
48.2		67.4		−10.5	36.2	12.8
850.2	12.5	947.7	11.5	14.8%	12.1%	13.4%
860.7	11.2	954.4	10.9	14.1%	11.0%	12.5%
−10.4		−6.6		−24.0	−17.4	−20.7
491.4	11.9	557.8	13.5	18.4%	11.6%	15.0%
442.4	12.8	498.7	12.7	14.9%	12.3%	13.6%
49.0		59.1		21.2	48.2	34.7
1940.8	11.9	2166.1	11.6	14.1%	12.2%	13.2%
1931.2	11.8	2151.1	11.4	13.5%	11.7	12.6%
9.6		15.0		−7.8	5.3	−1.2
1443.1	10.3	1589.2	10.1	12.8%	10.4%	11.6%
1496.3	11.3	1670.8	11.7	15.6%	11.6%	13.6%
−53.3		−81.6		31.9	−39.5	−3.8
582.3	9.8	639.8	9.9	12.4%	9.7%	11.0%
804.8	10.2	893.8	11.1	13.0%	10.4%	11.7%
−222.5		−254.0		−110.1	−203.3	−156.7
860.8	10.6	949.4	10.3	13.1%	10.8%	11.9%
691.5	12.7	777.0	12.4	19.6%	13.0%	16.3%
169.2		172.4		142.1	163.7	152.9
435.0	12.8	488.9	12.4	14.1%	12.8%	13.5%
436.0	12.8	488.7	12.1	12.8	12.7%	12.8%
−1.0		0.2		−5.9	−0.8	−3.4
521.9	12.5	587.5	12.6	15.4%	11.9%	13.7%
515.8	11.4	573.5	11.2	15.2%	11.4%	13.3%
6.0		14.0		−15.5	4.2	−5.7
5682.4	11.7	6337.2	11.5	14.6%	11.7%	13.0%
6.4	5.8	6.8	5.5	9.2%	6.0%	7.6%
885.0	5.6	935.6	5.7	4.7%	5.3%	5.0%
27.4	9.1	29.8	9.0	11.9%	9.2%	10.6%
52.7	3.5	54.6	3.6	2.4%	3.5%	2.9%

[4]Includes only Eastern Europe CMEA and the U.S.S.R.
[5]Period averages are calculated as the compound annual growth rate of the last over first year projection.

(*Cont'd*)

Table 1. (*Cont'd*). Project LINK. World summary. Measures of growth and inflation (annual percentage changes)[1]

Longterm baseline control solution

Country grouping	1980	1981	1982	1983	1984
Gross domestic product					
13 LINK OECD countries[2]	1.3	2.4	4.4	4.0	3.8
Level[3]	2613.5	2675.5	2792.4	2903.6	3014.3
U.S. and Canada	−0.7	2.6	4.8	4.4	3.7
Japan and Australia	4.6	3.6	4.7	4.5	4.5
Rest of OECD	3.0	1.4	3.5	3.1	3.8
Developing countries	5.0	4.8	4.9	5.2	5.2
Non-oil exporting	5.5	4.7	4.8	5.2	5.2
Oil exporting	2.2	5.3	5.3	5.3	5.3
Centrally planned countries[4]	4.2	3.4	4.2	4.4	4.6
World[5]	2.0	2.9	4.4	4.2	4.1
Private consumption deflator					
13 LINK OECD countries	11.4	8.3	6.7	6.0	5.7
(GDP deflator)	9.5	8.0	6.6	6.0	5.7
U.S. and Canada	10.4	8.3	6.5	5.6	5.5
Japan and Australia	6.9	8.3	7.1	6.2	5.7
Rest of OECD	14.6	8.3	7.0	6.7	6.0
Developing countries	33.9	28.0	21.1	18.3	15.4
Non-oil exporting	36.8	30.2	22.8	19.8	16.6
Oil exporting	13.5	12.8	9.0	8.2	7.3
World[6]	15.6	12.0	9.4	8.3	7.5

[1] Weighted averages of own country/region growth rates.
[2] 13 LINK OECD countries are: Australia, Austria, Belgium, Canada, Finland, France, Federal Republic of Germany, Italy, Japan, Netherlands, Sweden, United Kingdom, and U.S.A.
[3] Billions of 1970 U.S. $ at 1970 exchange rates.
[4] Includes only Eastern Europe CMEA and the U.S.S.R.

The LINK system emphasizes the interrelationships of trade and, at the present stage of development, gives inadequate attention to endogenous generation of capital flows. In order to explain short run, cyclical movements of exchange rates these additional factors from financial markets would need to be considered in more detail. It is, therefore, appropriate for us to focus attention on the trend aspects of exchange rate movements, where trade prices are the dominant variables.

This kind of study has at least two areas of interest: (1) It is interesting to see if purchasing power parity performs equilibrating functions; (2) apart from its equilibrating power, the doctrine of purchasing power parity is interesting in its own right as a rule of determining exchange rates in an international model. Does

1985	1986	1987	1988	1989	1990	1980–85	1985–90	1980–90
3.2	3.1	3.0	3.3	3.5	3.2	3.6	3.2	3.4
3110.8	3207.2	3302.4	3410.0	3528.0	3640.2			
2.7	2.9	2.9	3.3	3.7	3.2	3.6	3.2	3.4
4.3	3.4	3.0	3.3	3.0	3.1	4.3	3.2	3.7
3.5	3.5	3.2	3.3	3.3	3.2	3.1	3.3	3.2
5.3	5.3	5.2	5.3	5.3	5.5	5.1	5.3	5.2
5.3	5.2	5.0	5.2	5.2	5.4	5.0	5.2	5.1
5.3	6.3	6.3	6.3	6.3	6.3	5.3	6.3	5.8
4.4	4.4	4.6	4.5	4.7	4.6	4.2	4.6	4.4
3.7	3.7	3.6	3.8	4.0	3.8	3.9	3.8	3.8
5.6	5.5	5.5	5.4	5.0	4.8	6.5	5.2	5.8
5.7	5.6	5.6	5.5	4.9	4.7	6.4	5.2	5.8
5.4	5.3	5.4	5.2	4.4	4.3	6.2	4.9	5.6
5.8	5.7	5.5	5.5	5.4	5.3	6.6	5.5	6.0
5.9	5.7	5.7	5.7	5.7	5.6	6.8	5.7	6.2
12.6	10.2	10.0	9.5	9.1	8.4	19.0	9.5	14.1
13.3	10.8	10.6	10.1	9.7	9.0	20.4	10.0	15.1
7.1	6.2	6.0	5.8	5.5	5.0	8.9	5.7	7.3
6.9	6.4	6.3	6.2	5.7	5.5	8.8	6.0	7.3

[5] World = 0.6565 *OECD + 0.1494 *DEVE + 0.1851 *CMEA.
[6] World = 0.8145 *OECD + 0.1855 *DEVE.   Inflation measures for CMEA are not available.
[7] Period averages are calculated as the geometric mean of the second through last period growth rates.

the principle generate convergent solutions? Are these solutions, if obtainable, reasonable in terms of economic content or meaning? The solution to the system, with purchasing power parity imposed, will be a different solution from the baseline case, and it will be our task to study the nature of the difference.

The solutions of the various national models in the LINK system have been found to be quite sensitive to exchange rate changes; therefore, it is not at all clear that automatic adjustments of exchange rates would produce a convergent solution, when these adjustment mechanisms are superimposed on a solution that has converged, with a system of fixed rates. The exchange rate rule could potentially have a destabilizing effect, and it is worthwhile examining the stability of the system under the changed conditions to be introduced by imposition of purchasing power parity.

II. Purchasing Power Parity as a Possible Solution

The meaning of purchasing power parity may not be clear; the expression has been variously interpreted in economic literature. A convenient way of looking at the matter is to say that it means the same thing as the law of one price, namely, that an identical good (or service) would command the same price, measured in a given numeraire system, all over the trading world. This is *our* interpretation of purchasing power parity in an intuitive limiting sense. The actual mathematical rule that we use is stated below, in terms of export price and exchange rate changes. Some of the controversy centers around the issue whether *all* goods should follow the law of one price, or only *traded goods*. Should the principle be studied in level terms or in change terms? It may be asked whether exchange rates and prices actually inter-relate in such a way as to fulfill the equations suggested by the principle. This issue is treated only superficially, in this paper, for the decade of the 1970s.

We do not assert that short run variations in exchange rates be explained by purchasing power parity, but we do assert that a detailed exchange rate modeling system should satisfy purchasing power parity in the long run. This does not suggest that the rule has a causal meaning; it merely asserts that the trend equilibrium of a dynamic system should satisfy the doctrine of purchasing power parity.

This interpretation of purchasing power parity is much like our interpretation of the quantity of money. We do not look upon the quantity equation as having causal interpretation, yet it appears to hold in the long run. It has been found, for example, that long run simulations of the Wharton Model for the U.S. generate time paths for the jointly dependent (endogenous) variables M_2 and PY, money supply and nominal GNP. The two time paths have proportional movement. In this sense, the model projection satisfies the quantity theory principle. Also, we observe that global world data on money supply and GNP move, historically, in accordance with the principles of the quantity theory of money. We do not feel that this establishes a causal pattern, merely that the data follow these joint paths. The same is true of our conception of purchasing power parity for this world simulation. We say that the tendency for exchange rates and export price movements to satisfy the principles of purchasing power parity make it plausible for a rule to be imposed on the solution of the LINK system. We find that historical data for the 1970s lend support for this approach.

In the statistical equations below, we estimate the movement of exchange rates according to this principle for the past decade, a period during which rates have fluctuated somewhat freely, i.e., outside the confines of the fixed parities of the Bretton Woods System. In change form, we interpret purchasing power to mean that

$$\Delta \ln PX09_{it}(L_i) + \Delta \ln R_{it}(\$/L_i) = \Delta \ln PX09_{USt}(\$) \tag{1}$$

$PX09_{it}(L_i)$ = Export price (unit value) index of all commodities (SITC 0 through 9, denominated in local currency units), country i, time t

$R_{it}(\$/L_i)$ = The exchange rate in dollars per unit of local currency, country i, time t

$PX09_{USt}(\$)$ = U.S. export price (unit value) index of all commodities (SITC 0 through 9, denominated in dollars) at time t.

This says that export prices, stated in U.S. dollar terms, should have a common rate of change across all countries, namely, the U.S. rate of change of export prices.

If exchange rates had moved in accordance with the principle of purchasing power parity, we would find that estimates of

$$\Delta \ln R_{it}(\$/L_i) = a + b\Delta \ln PX09_{it}(L_i) + c\Delta \ln PX09_{USt} + e_{it} \qquad (2)$$

were consistent with the hypothesis

$$a = 0$$
$$b = -1.0$$
$$c = +1.0$$
$$e_{it} = \text{additive random error.}$$

Scatter diagrams of the data points are in Figs. 1 and 2. We estimated the equation with the constant term suppressed to zero and the coefficients b and c constrained to be equal in magnitude, but opposite in sign. The estimates are from a time series of cross sections; the country $(i = 1, \ldots, 12)$ observations are pooled with the annual time $(t = 1972\text{--}1980)$ observations. A more homogeneous grouping of five common market economies, now in the European Monetary System, is also used for a sub sample (pooled). A further computation with the U.K. added is also included.

$$\Delta \ln R_{it}(\$/L_i) = b(\Delta \ln PX09_{it}(L_i) - \Delta \ln PX09_{USt}(\$)) \qquad (3)$$

12 countries
108 data points
est. $b = -0.738$ (7.60) $\overline{R}^2 = 0.366$

5 countries[2]
45 data points
est. $b = -1.026$ (8.24) $\overline{R}^2 = 0.616$

6 countries[2]
54 data points
est. $b = -0.934$ (8.04) $\overline{R}^2 = 0.599$

The numbers in parentheses are t-statistics. Judging by these statistics, all the regression estimates pass significance tests. The relationship is tightest for the members of EMS and only slightly less tight when the U.K. is also included. For the common market countries, there is little doubt that $b = 1.0$ is an acceptable

---

[2]The five common market countries are Belgium, France, Germany, Italy, and Netherlands. A sixth is U.K.

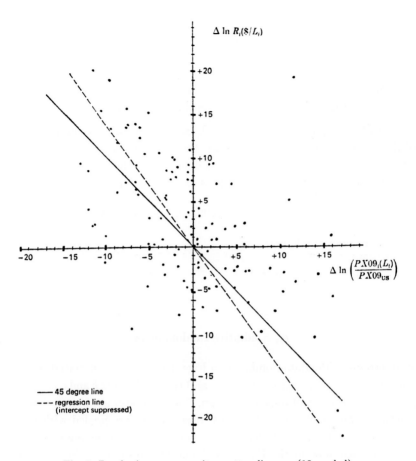

Fig. 1. Purchasing power parity scatter diagram (12-pooled).

estimate. For the larger sample, we could say that the upper end of a confidence interval just barely includes 1.0. If weighted regressions are estimated, the results conform even closer to the PPP hypothesis, including the results for all 12 countries.[3]

On this evidence, we feel justified in saying that, on average, purchasing power parity movements in exchange rates and export prices were approximately realized during the 1970s, after exchange rates were allowed to fluctuate. It is, therefore, definitely worthwhile to examine the working of this principle within the context of LINK simulations for the decade of the 1980s. We have not proved that PPP holds as a causal relationship, but that it is merely a tendency that appears to hold in terms of data for the actual economy.

---

[3]Both trade weighted regressions to account for a country's importance in OECD trade and variance adjusted regressions to account for heteroskedasticity were estimated.

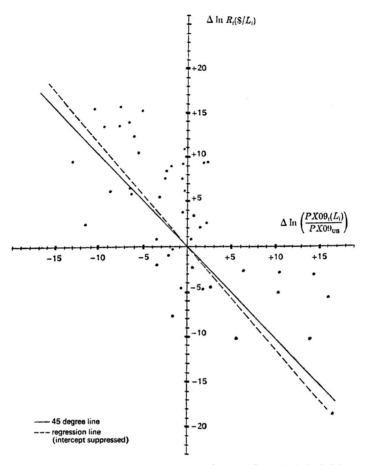

Fig. 2. Purchasing power parity scattered diagram (6-pooled). Included: Belgium, France, Germany, Italy, Netherlands, United Kingdom.

If the U.S. price is unchanging or if the principle is imposed only for the long run, in which case the U.S. price is assumed to be steady, on average, the right-hand side of Eq. (1) is a constant. If this simplified form of the rule were to hold, a country's export price movement should be inversely related to the dollar exchange rate movement.

The relation should hold only on average, not for every short run movement in exchange rates. They respond to differentials in interest rates, current account balances, capital flows, and other factors besides differential inflation rates (in total export goods). Cyclical deviations from the relationship do not dispute the existence of a trend relationship.

It is quite simple to add exchange rate equations according to the principle of PPP for each country, other than the U.S., to the LINK system in order to generate values of these rates as estimates of endogenous variables. The relationship is not an identity, but it has no unknown parameters in its pure form. It uses, besides exchange rates, only variables that are already generated within the LINK system. It could be imposed with the right-hand side equal to a constant or equal to estimated yearly values of export price inflation in the U.S. It could be imposed as an instantaneous relationship or as a lag relationship, requiring a period of adjustment or adaptation. We made the right-hand side equal to the average growth rate of 7.07 percent for U.S. export prices over the projected decade.[4]

Short run exchange rate models use variables that are entirely or mainly generated within the LINK system. These are already used for short run simulations, where it has been estimated that exchange rate changes are functions of changes in real interest rates, trade (current account) balances, and total reserve positions. Reserves, in turn, depend on capital flows. These are fundamental explanations of year-to-year (quarter-to-quarter or month-to-month) fluctuations in exchange rates, but they are not yet well established relations. It is difficult to obtain good estimates of short term capital flows. There is, in any case, a large element of uncertainty in the structure and applicability of these equations, but it does appear that exchange rate movements have a large impact on the configuration of the LINK system solution.

In the LINK system, there are two sets of trade prices (export and import prices). One set is provided from national or area model data files in own-currency units, and another set is associated with the LINK trade matrices in U.S. dollar units. In the application of the formula, figures on own currency export prices are taken from the national models. They are deflators of goods and services in the national income accounts. They are related to the deflators for the world trade matrix entries by empirical *linkage* equations, that relate one price series to another. We used the national model variables in the exchange rate equations that were used to simulate the principle of purchasing power parity.

Since Canadian prices have a special relationship to U.S. prices, we did not impose the rule for Canada, but kept its exchange rate fixed for this scenario.

It should be pointed out that in the estimated Eq. (3) the base period for the unit value indexes is 1975, a period that includes the high relative weight for energy prices. The corresponding indexes used for the LINK system are on a base of 1970, which does not reflect the high prices of energy. The individual models of LINK, which have their own international price indexes are on a variety of different base periods.

III. Some Results

How does the baseline simulation of the LINK system change, if purchasing power parity equations are added to the system for the decade of the 1980s? What happens

---

[4]We have simulated other alternatives but present the results only for the average growth rate case in this paper.

to growth, inflation, trading activity, and mutual external balance? These are the issues to be examined in this section of the paper.

First let us take a look at the workings of purchasing power parity as far as the exchange rate, itself, and also dollar export prices are concerned. The rule is imposed only on the OECD countries explicitly modeled in the LINK system. They are, in the version being used here, the following thirteen countries: Australia, Austria, Belgium, Canada, Finland, France, Germany, Italy, Japan, Netherlands, Sweden, U.K., and U.S.A.[5] The rule is imposed only for the 1982–90 period since the baseline projection kept exchange rates fixed at their projected 1981 levels.

Table 2. Exchange rates ($/$L_i$). Purchasing power parity case (percentage growth over previous year).

Country	1982	1983	1984	1985	1986	1987	1988	1989	1990
Australia	1.0	1.2	1.4	1.2	1.4	1.0	0.7	0.4	0.2
Austria	1.7	−1.2	0.3	0.9	−1.2	−2.4	−2.2	−1.5	−0.9
Belgium	1.1	0.7	0.2	−0.5	−0.9	−0.9	−1.1	−2.8	−2.4
Canada	0.0	0.0	0.0	0.0	0.0	0.0	0.0	0.0	0.0
Finland	1.3	1.2	1.0	1.2	1.2	1.1	0.9	1.0	0.8
France	−5.6	10.8	−1.3	4.7	2.9	1.4	3.9	1.8	3.8
Germany (Fed. Rep.)	1.4	1.0	1.1	1.0	1.2	1.2	1.2	1.2	1.1
Italy	−3.0	1.4	4.3	5.3	5.8	5.4	5.6	6.1	6.5
Japan	−2.6	−1.8	−0.9	−0.7	0.2	0.4	0.2	0.4	0.3
Netherlands	2.5	1.3	2.3	2.9	4.7	6.0	7.1	7.2	5.8
Sweden	−3.1	−0.8	−0.0	1.3	2.2	2.5	3.1	2.6	3.4
United Kingdom	−0.8	−3.8	−4.9	−5.5	−4.5	−2.5	−0.8	1.2	4.2
Mean[1]	−0.7	0.9	−0.0	0.6	0.8	0.9	1.4	1.3	1.8
Standard deviation	2.34	2.79	2.19	2.88	2.61	2.31	2.49	2.46	2.55
Coefficient of variation	−3.63	4.15	−64.27[2]	4.65	3.38	2.65	1.82	1.86	1.42

[1]The summary sample statistics weigh each observation by its trade share in constant dollars: $(X + M)_{it} / \sum (X + M)_{it}$), where X = exports of goods, f.o.b., and M = imports of goods, f.o.b.
[2]Since the mean is near zero for 1984, coefficient of variation is unusually large.

The projected rate of change of the dollar exchange rate is presented for individual countries in Table 2. Naturally, the U.S.A. is deleted here. The variability of exchange rate movement for individual countries does not converge to zero over the course of the decade, but they do converge to *similarity*. This can be seen from the bottom row, where the coefficient of variation across countries, year-by-year, shows a moderating tendency from relatively wide variability at the beginning of the decade to progressively smaller variability by the end of the decade.

[5]The present LINK system includes five more OECD countries in explicit models, namely, Denmark, Greece, Norway, Spain, and Switzerland.

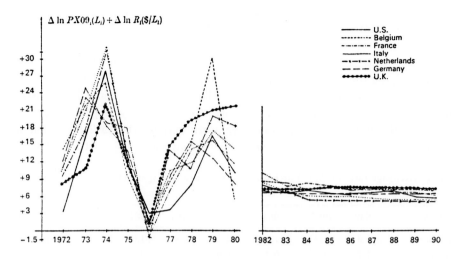

Fig. 3. Historical and projected paths of $\Delta \ln PX09_i(L_i) + \Delta \ln R_i(\$/L)$.

Table 3. Export price, SITC 0–9, in dollar unit index. Baseline case (percentage growth over previous year).

Country	1982	1983	1984	1985	1986	1987	1988	1989	1990	Mean	S.D.	C.V.
Australia	5.3	6.0	5.9	6.0	5.9	6.3	6.7	6.9	7.1	6.2	8.58	0.09
Austria	5.3	8.0	6.6	6.0	7.7	8.9	8.6	7.8	7.1	7.3	1.20	0.16
Belgium	7.0	7.3	6.8	7.0	6.7	6.3	6.2	6.4	5.8	6.6	0.48	0.07
Canada	10.0	10.0	8.7	8.7	8.0	7.4	6.8	6.4	6.0	8.4	2.26	0.27
Finland	6.7	6.7	6.7	6.8	6.8	6.8	6.9	6.9	6.9	6.8	0.08	0.01
France	8.5	8.1	7.4	7.3	6.6	6.6	6.4	6.2	5.9	7.0	0.87	0.12
Germany (Fed.Rep.)	5.1	5.4	5.1	4.9	4.4	4.0	3.6	3.0	2.5	4.2	1.03	0.24
Italy	9.0	5.8	5.0	4.9	4.7	4.8	4.5	4.0	3.7	5.2	1.55	0.30
Japan	7.1	7.7	6.9	6.6	5.7	5.3	5.6	5.6	5.7	6.3	0.85	0.14
Netherlands	5.4	6.5	5.0	4.8	4.2	3.7	3.1	3.1	3.2	4.3	1.17	0.27
Sweden	8.6	7.0	6.6	6.2	6.1	6.0	5.8	6.0	5.5	6.4	0.93	0.14
United Kingdom	7.5	7.9	7.8	7.6	6.7	6.5	6.2	5.9	5.2	6.8	0.92	0.14
United States	7.9	6.9	7.0	6.8	6.7	7.1	7.1	6.2	5.9	6.8	0.57	0.14
OECD mean[1]	7.5	7.1	6.6	6.4	5.9	5.8	5.8	5.2	4.9			
Standard deviation	2.13	1.23	1.15	1.17	1.17	1.35	1.47	1.46	1.52			
Coefficient of variation	0.28	0.17	0.17	0.18	0.20	0.23	0.26	0.28	0.31			

[1]The summary sample statistics weigh each observation by its trade share in constant dollars: $(X + M)_{it} / \sum (X + M)_{it}$, where X = exports of goods, f.o.b., and M = imports of goods, f.o.b.

Table 4. Export price, SITC 0–9, in dollar unit index. Purchasing power parity case (percentage growth over previous year).

Country	1982	1983	1984	1985	1986	1987	1988	1989	1990	Mean	S.D.	C.V.
Australia	6.2	7.1	7.1	7.1	7.1	7.2	7.3	7.2	7.4	7.1	0.34	0.05
Austria	7.0	7.0	7.0	7.0	7.0	7.0	7.0	7.0	7.0	7.0	0.01	0.00
Belgium	8.0	7.8	7.3	7.5	7.3	7.2	7.2	7.2	7.0	7.4	0.32	0.04
Canada	13.4	10.0	8.9	8.8	8.0	7.3	6.8	6.5	6.2	8.4	2.24	0.27
Finland	8.1	8.0	7.9	8.2	8.1	8.1	7.9	8.0	7.7	8.0	0.13	0.02
France	9.5	7.5	7.9	7.5	7.1	7.3	7.0	7.1	6.8	7.5	0.82	0.11
Germany (Fed. Rep.)	7.0	6.9	6.9	6.9	7.0	7.0	7.0	7.0	7.1	7.0	0.05	0.01
Italy	8.0	7.0	6.7	6.9	6.8	6.9	6.7	6.5	6.5	6.9	0.45	0.07
Japan	6.6	6.9	6.6	6.4	5.7	5.6	5.9	5.9	6.0	6.2	0.45	0.07
Netherlands	6.8	7.0	5.9	6.0	6.1	6.1	6.0	6.1	6.1	6.2	0.39	0.06
Sweden	7.7	7.5	7.4	7.4	7.4	7.5	7.5	7.6	8.6	7.6	0.38	0.05
United Kingdom	7.4	7.4	7.4	7.7	7.6	7.7	7.8	7.8	7.7	7.6	0.16	0.02
United States	7.9	6.9	7.2	6.8	6.8	6.9	7.1	6.2	6.1	6.9	0.53	0.08
OECD mean[1]	8.0	7.3	7.2	7.1	6.9	6.9	6.9	6.7	6.7			
Standard deviation	1.75	0.81	0.67	0.67	0.64	0.64	0.57	0.63	0.65			
Coefficient of variation	0.22	0.11	0.09	0.10	0.09	0.09	0.08	0.09	0.10			

[1]The summary sample statistics weigh each observation by its trade share in constant dollars: $(X + M)_{it}/\sum(X + M)_{it})$, where X = exports of goods, f.o.b., and M = imports of goods, f.o.b.

The graph in Fig. 3 shows strikingly, how the left-hand side of the basic Eq. (3)

$$\Delta \ln PX09_{it}(L_i) + \Delta \ln R_{it}(\$/L_i)$$

is stabilized during the projection period.

Another way of looking at the same results is from tabulations of estimates of

$$\Delta \ln PX09_{it}(\$) \,.$$

Generally speaking, the comparison of the results in Tables 3 and 4 shows that there is a tendency for most countries' rate of change of the dollar export price to be closer to the U.S. path for this variable in the purchasing power parity simulation. The coefficient of variation, in the bottom row for the purchasing power parity case, falls from 0.22 in 1982 and stabilizes at 0.08–0.10 in the 1983–1990 period. In the baseline case, the corresponding figure returns by 1990 to its original value in 1982. It rises from 1983 to 1990.

The comparison of coefficients of variation across time periods, country-by-country is also interesting. It shows that most of the coefficients are smaller in the PPP case than in the base case. This means that the introduction of the principle of PPP moderates the fluctuation of export prices over time. This can also be seen in Fig. 3.

These results suggest that the doctrine is working, in a plausible direction, upon implementation of purchasing power parity rules for the simulation. Thus, the doctrine is workable, as far as modeling and simulation are concerned. Now, it is time to see if it does some overall good for the world economy.

As far as trade balances, real growth rates or inflation rates are concerned, it does not appear that there is any particular pattern of systematic difference between the baseline simulation and the purchasing power parity simulation solution. Growth and inflation rates rarely differ by more than one-tenth of a percentage point. Such differences are not statistically significant. There are differences in trade balances that may be significant, but they do not seem to fall into a systematic pattern.

Although the growth rates for GDP are very close for the two quinquennia, the associated GDP aggregates are further apart. By 1990, GDP for the 13 LINK OECD countries totals 3640.2 billion ($, 1970) in the base case. It is as large as 3659.2 billion ($, 1970) in the purchasing power parity case by the same projection date. This difference of some $19 billion is not inconsequential, when measured in 1970 dollars at 1970 exchange rates. This indicates that the degree of exchange rate flexibility governed by purchasing power parity has added slightly more than 0.5% to 1990 GDP. This is why the growth rate is ever so slightly larger for 1985–90 in the purchasing power parity case. The higher growth is associated with (or even slightly caused by) the expansion of net exports for the 13 OECD countries in LINK. In Table 5, this can be seen to be associated with net exports in both quinquennia.

Table 5. Trade balances[1] (billions of current dollars, U.S.).

	Baseline		Purchasing power parity	
	1981–85	1985–90	1981–85	1985–90
13 LINK OECD countries	−10.5	36.2	−7.5	62.3
U.S. & Canada	−24.0	−17.4	−21.2	5.7
Japan & Australia	21.2	48.2	22.0	57.5
Rest of LINK OECD	−7.8	5.3	−8.2	−1.0
Developing countries (oil importers)	−110.1	−203.3	−111.9	−218.9
Developing countries (oil exporters)	142.1	163.7	141.5	161.0
Centrally planned economies	−5.9	−0.8	−5.8	1.1
Rest of world	−15.5	4.2	−16.4	−5.5
World export volume[2] (% change)	4.71%	5.33%	4.66%	5.28%

[1] Measures are for merchandise trade, F.O.B.
[2] Geometric average of period growth rates.

Table 6. Gross domestic product[1] (percent changes).

	Baseline		Purchasing power parity	
	1981–85	1985–90	1981–85	1985–90
13 LINK OECD countries	3.57	3.22	3.59	3.30
U.S. & Canada	3.64	3.20	3.65	3.28
Japan & Australia	4.31	3.17	4.50	3.56
Rest of LINK OECD	3.06	3.27	3.01	3.21
Developing countries (oil importers)	5.03	5.19	5.03	5.21
Developing countries (oil exporters)	5.30	6.30	5.30	6.30
Centrally planned economies	4.21	4.56	4.22	4.58
World	3.87	3.75	3.89	3.81

[1]Geometric average of period growth rates which are weighted averages of own country/region growth rates.

Table 7. Private consumption deflator[1] (percent changes).

	Baseline		Purchasing power parity	
	1981–85	1985–90	1981–85	1985–90
13 LINK OECD countries	6.46	5.24	6.49	5.13
U.S. & Canada	6.25	4.92	6.28	4.99
Japan & Australia	6.60	5.49	6.76	5.60
Rest of LINK OECD	6.77	5.68	6.72	5.15
Developing countries (oil importers)	20.41	10.01	20.76	11.05
Developing countries (oil importers)	9.88	5.71	10.28	7.01
World[2]	8.82	6.02	8.90	6.14

[1]Geometric average of period inflation rates which are weighted averages of own country/region inflation rates.
[2]Centrally planned economies excluded from price chart.

Purchasing power parity does not do wonders for the world economy, but it does constitute a convergent dynamic process. It is estimated to make some small contribution to holding down inflation, in the Euro-LINK OECD countries who appreciate their currency relative to the dollar. The United States depreciates, making it more competitive in world markets, keeping up its production and adding a little to its inflation. Overall, the United States and Japan gain in production, more than offsetting the output decline in Europe.

Our introduction of endogenous exchange rates in this medium term projection does not give us an accurate basis for estimating year-by-year exchange rate movements. Mainly, we have shown that PPP is a feasible process and does not upset the stability of a solution in the context of a world model. It provides a simple and readily applicable system for generating decade long endogenous exchange rate movements.

29

A MODEL OF FOREIGN EXCHANGE MARKETS:
ENDOGENISING CAPITAL FLOWS AND EXCHANGE RATES[†*]

1. Introduction

Ever since the demise of the Bretton Woods system of fixed exchange rates and the advent of a managed float in 1973 there has emerged a surge of theoretical models and empirical analyses of exchange rate determination.[1] The capital flows which played a central role in the earlier models based on fixed exchange parities are no longer in the prime focus. Instead, the main interest has shifted directly to the determination of exchange rates.[2] Nonetheless, the role of both short-term and long-term capital flows has varied substantially in the new studies. They are explicitly recognized in the "portfolio balance models" through the balance of payment equilibrium condition which is used to determine the exchange rate, but their role in the "monetary models" remains at best implicit or lies generally subsumed under the well known price parity and interest parity assumptions.[3] The purpose of this paper is to develop a simultaneous equations system of the foreign exchange market endogenising both capital flows and exchange rates. The analysis is conducted with reference to six countries, Canada plus five other countries which constitute

[†]From *Capital Flows and Exchange Rate Determination*, eds. L. R. Klein and W. E. Krelle, *Zeitschrift für Nationalökonomie*, **Supplementum 3** (Springer-Verlag, Wien, 1983), pp. 61–95; written jointly with Kanta Marwah.
[*]Prepared for the annual meetings of Project LINK, September 27–October 1, 1982, Wiesbaden, West Germany. An earlier version of this paper was presented at the United Nations meetings of Project LINK, March 3–5, 1982, New York. We are thankful to Avner Aleh for his assistance in the computer programming.
[1]Some useful reference sources are: Leamer and Stern (1970), Whitman (1975), Officer (1976), Schadler (1977), Black (1977), Kreinin and Officer (1978), Isard (1978), Helliwell (1979), Hacche and Townend (1981a), and the symposium on purchasing power parity in the *Journal of International Economics* (May 1978).
[2]There have been several studies earlier on the movements of capital flows per se. To quote a few, Branson (1968, 1970), Genberg (1976), Kouri and Porter (1974), Kouri (1975), Lybeck, Häggström and Järnhäll (1979), other references are in Bryant (1975), Magee (1976). However, these studies have mostly incorporated fixed exchange rate regimes, or have treated exchange rates as exogenously determined variables. There are some notable exceptions, especially in the context of national econometric models, e.g., Rhomberg (1964), Officer (1968). More recently, Krelle *et al.* (1979), Ball and Burns (1979), Lybeck and Järnhäll (1979), Amano *et al.* (1981).
[3]We have reviewed these models in our previous paper (1982).

the latest (1981) valuation basket of *SDR* currency. These are, France, Germany, Japan, U.K., and the U.S.

2. The Model

Assuming that the foreign exchange capital market operates efficiently without any intervention by the government and that there is no uncertainty or risk involved, a portfolio theoretic model views exchange rates as performing primarily (in the short run with a fixed stock of assets given) an equilibrating function of balancing foreign demand for domestically issued financial assets and domestic demand for foreign assets denominated in foreign currency. In a monetary model, however, the exchange rate is principally regarded as an instrument of adjustment in the domestic money market; an explicit analysis of foreign assets is assumed away by the interest parity assumption. In this model, domestic interest is exogenously fixed in parity with the foreign rate adjusted for any expected change in the exchange rate, and the actual exchange rate is determined at a point where, via associated domestic prices on par with foreign prices, it clears the domestic money market. In addition, a monetary model predicts a unitary elasticity of exchange rate with respect to money supply. It must be mentioned that these two basic models have been further extended into several variants, some include market pressures and others treat interest rate and expectations endogenously.

Our model is neither pure portfolio nor pure monetary; it is basically a balance of payment structural model which determines explicitly both capital flows and exchange rates.[4] It does not conform strictly to either purchasing power parity or interest rate parity assumptions; however, it does recognise both these elements. It is specifically relevant for a managed float system whose two adjacent polar regimes of fixed and flexible exchange rates become special cases. In developing the structure of our model an attempt is made to disaggregate total capital flows into nine categories by functional type and ownership; some risk and uncertainty factors have been duly recognized, and an official intervention function absorbing and mitigating partially the market pressures has been embedded in the adjustment process through which the exchange rate is finally determined.

We start with a standard specification of money market behavior of country i whose nominal money demand (pL) must be equal to its total money stock determined by m (multiplier) times its monetary base (H). The real money demand (L) is assumed to depend upon real income (Y) and interest rate (r). For the sake of simplicity we specify that H is fed by only two basic sources, net domestic assets

---

[4]For the detailed framework and theoretical underpinnings, we refer to our background paper (1982).

(NDA) and net foreign assets (NFA) of the central bank.[5] p is the general price level. That is,

$$m_i H_i = p_i L_i(Y_i, r_i, \ldots) \tag{1}$$

$$H_i = NDA_i + \varepsilon_{iSD} NFA_i \tag{2}$$

where ε_{iSD} is an exchange rate defined as national currency units (price) per SDR. All variables except NFA in Eqs. (1) and (2) are measured in national currency units, NFA is measured in SDRs.

Under a fully flexible exchange rate system with no intervention from the government sector, the stock of net foreign assets necessarily remains unchanged ($\Delta NFA = 0$), and thus, the national money supply stays by and large insulated from any external disturbances appearing in the balance of payment accounts. But under fixed exchange rate system or under a system of managed float with less than complete sterilization, the stock of foreign assets responds endogenously to balance of payment factors ($\Delta NFA \neq 0$), and the domestic money supply gets directly affected. The balance of payment factors and any change in net foreign assets are definitionally related as

$$\Delta NFA_i = CUB_i + CAB_i \tag{3}$$

where CUB and CAB, respectively, are balance of payment on current and capital accounts, and both are measured in SDRs. CUB is measured as a surplus on current account (exports less imports), and CAB as net inflows on capital account.

Ideally, an analysis of capital flows should be carried out in terms of portfolio shares, analogous to the trade flow analysis in terms of market share coefficients.[6] However, eschewing this approach because of the nonavailability of consistent bilateral flow data on capital accounts, we disaggregate *net* capital inflows into $k = 9$ functional and ownership categories. These are[7]

$$CAB_i = DIN_i + PIN_i + ROL_i + DBL_i + RL_i + ROS_i + DBS_i + RS_i + ERO_i \tag{4}$$

where DIN = direct investment
$\quad PIN$ = portfolio investment
$\quad ROL$ = resident official long-term capital
$\quad DBL$ = deposit money banks long-term capital
$\quad RL$ = other long-term capital (residual)
$\quad ROS$ = resident official short-term capital

---

[5]To be more precise, the money multiplier m should be treated as a variable which would normally depend upon variety of factors such as a spread between interest rate and discount rate, legally required reserve ratio, risk, and uncertainty factors, and deviations of actual rate from the target rate. It may also be noted that we assume nonunitary money multiplier ($m > 1$), but for the sake of simplicity we are assuming a unitary density of money supply (Marwah, 1979), that is the monetary institutions hold zero excess reserves. It is also worthy of note that most of the earlier studies related to foreign exchange market make the restrictive assumption that $m = 1$.

[6]A case study of bilateral flows is a subject of another paper, Marwah, Klein, and Bodkin (1983).

[7]With an exception of direct and portfolio investment these categories can be easily reclassified into short-term and long-term flows, and private and public flows.

DBS = deposit money banks short-term capital

RS = other short-term capital (residual)

ERO = errors and omissions.

A close look at the recent data for the six countries under examination confirmed our general *a priori* belief that these categories are subject to separate influences; at least, these are expected to have different degrees of elasticity and sensitivity coefficients with respect to portfolio substitution. Moreover, the resident official sectors, ROS and ROL, seem to play distinctively a balancing role in the existing managed float system. Presumably, to some extent, some of these categories are complementary and some are competitive with each other.

We specify a net capital inflow of category k in country i by a modified portfolio adjustment function derived from a stock allocation relationship. According to this function a ratio of net capital stock of category k to total capital stock (net worth, wealth) depends upon a yield differential on domestic and foreign securities, their relative risks and uncertainty factors. A linear generalization of this function for net capital inflow (change in stock) can be approximated by

$$\frac{CAB_i^k}{NFA_{i-1}} = \alpha_0 + \alpha_1 GNFA_i + \alpha_2 \frac{(\mu_{ii} - \mu_{ic})^k}{\varepsilon_{iSD}}$$

$$+ \alpha_3 \frac{\Delta(\mu_{ii} - \mu_{ic})^k}{\varepsilon_{iSD}} + \alpha_4 [\dot{\varepsilon}_{iSD} - (\dot{p}_i - \dot{p}_c)]$$

$$+ \alpha_5 \frac{CUB_i}{NFA_{i-1}} + \alpha_6 \sigma_{ic}^k + v_i^k \quad k = 1, 2, \ldots, 9 \tag{5}$$

where NFA_{i-1} = net foreign assets at the beginning of the period

$\quad GNFA_i$ = rate of change in net foreign assets

$\quad \mu_{ic}^k$ = expected competitive yield measured in i's currency on investment by country i in foreign securities denominated in foreign currency (j) defined as

$$\mu_{ic}^k = \sum_{j \neq i} w_{ij} \mu_{ij}^k \text{ and } \sum_{j \neq i} w_{ij} = 1$$

$$w_{ij} = \frac{X_{j.} + X_{.j}}{\sum_{j \neq i}(X_{j.} + X_{.j})} \text{ are relative trade weights}$$

$(X_{j.}$ = exports of j and $X_{.j}$ = imports of $j)$

$\quad \mu_{ii}$ = expected yield on domestic securities as measured by rate of interest

$$\mu_{ij}^k = \begin{bmatrix} (1 + r_j^k)\dfrac{\varepsilon_{fij}}{\varepsilon_{sij}} - 1 & \text{for } i \neq j \\ r_i^k & \text{for } i = j \end{bmatrix}$$

$\quad \varepsilon_{fij}$ = forward exchange rate, i's currency per unit of j's

$\quad \varepsilon_{sij}$ = spot exchange rate, i's currency per unit of j's

r_i^k = rate of interest on country i's security of type k

ε_{iSD} = exchange rate, i's currency per SDR

$\dot{p}_i$ = rate of change in country i's price level

$\dot{p}_c$ = rate of change in competitive price level, that is the price level of other countries transacting with country i, defined as $\sum_{j \neq i} w_{ij} \dot{p}_j$

σ_{ic} = some measure of relative risk

v_i = random error.

Net foreign assets at the beginning of the period is a normalization variable intended as a relevant proxy for foreign net worth.[8] α_1 measures approximately a scale/stock effect on capital flows of changing net worth (portfolio) size in a dynamic setting, and is generally expected to be negative, that is a rising $GNFA$ would lead to capital outflows in terms of investment in foreign securities. Alternatively, however, as we have shown in our selective survey (1982), $\alpha_1 > 0$ if the wealth effect on demand for money is stronger than on demand for foreign assets. Moreover, a growing accumulation of foreign reserves may provide a barometric measure to foreign investors of the strong economic performance of the country enticing more capital inflows. This tendency would presumably be stronger when in addition to $GNFA$ the effect of current account balance on net capital flows is also significant. The sign of α_1 would thus depend upon the relative magnitudes of opposite effects.[9]

The remaining explanatory variables in Eq. (5) are basically preference allocation variables which determine a portfolio distribution mix. An expected differential of yields between domestic and foreign securities has two built-in effects, an effect of a pure interest arbitrage transaction and a forward market speculative effect. For example,

$$\mu_{ii} - \mu_{ij} = (1 + r_i) - (1 + r_j)\frac{\varepsilon_{fij}}{\varepsilon_{sij}} = \left(r_i - r_j \frac{\varepsilon_{fij}}{\varepsilon_{sij}} \right) + \left(1 - \frac{\varepsilon_{fij}}{\varepsilon_{sij}} \right), \qquad (6)$$

where the term within the first parentheses measures a covered interest arbitrage and within the second a speculative component in terms of forward premium. Presumably an investor of country i buys security of country j at an exchange rate ε_{sij} and at the same time assumes a forward contract to reconvert the value of this security at the time of maturity back in country i's currency at exchange rate ε_{fij}. The second term, therefore, may also include some element of expectations. Alternatively, an expected yield differential may be decomposed as a sum of two interactions,

$$\mu_{ii} - \mu_{ij} = (1 + r_i)\left[1 - \frac{\varepsilon_{fij}}{\varepsilon_{sij}} \right] + (r_i - r_j)\frac{\varepsilon_{fij}}{\varepsilon_{sij}} \qquad (6a)$$

---

[8]In some experiments made in Project LINK, initial reserves have proved to provide a good normalizing base. Net foreign assets in this paper are defined broadly as total international reserves.

[9]It may be noted that in the portfolio models of capital flows, an increase in domestic wealth leads directly to capital outflows, but in the monetary models this effect is quite ambiguous. Using GNP as a proxy for wealth Lybeck *et al.* (1979) found mixed results on this count.

where the first component represents the interaction between the yield on domestic securities and forward market speculation and the second between the interest differential on domestic and foreign securities and the speculative component. As long as ε_{sij} (spot rate) is greater (less) than ε_{fij} (forward rate) the general expectation tends to be that the exchange rate in future would fall (rise) and i currency would appreciate (depreciate) and consequently an immediate capital inflow (outflow) is induced. Aggregating over all j countries the yield differential can be expressed as[10]

$$
\begin{aligned}
\mu_{ii} - \mu_{ic} &= \sum_{j \neq i} w_{ij}(\mu_{ii} - \mu_{ij}) \\
&= (1 + r_i) - \sum_{j \neq i} w_{ij}(1 - r_j)\frac{\varepsilon_{fij}}{\varepsilon_{sij}} \\
&= \left(r_i - \sum_{j \neq i} w_{ij} r_j \frac{\varepsilon_{fij}}{\varepsilon_{sij}} \right) + \left(1 - \sum_{j \neq i} w_{ij} \frac{\varepsilon_{fij}}{\varepsilon_{sij}} \right),
\end{aligned}
\tag{7}
$$

and

$$
\mu_{ii} - \mu_{ic} = (1 + r_i)\left[1 - \sum_{j \neq i} w_{ij} \frac{\varepsilon_{fij}}{\varepsilon_{sij}} \right] + \sum_{j \neq i} w_{ij}(r_i - r_j)\frac{\varepsilon_{fij}}{\varepsilon_{sij}}.
\tag{7a}
$$

By an assumption of perfect mobility of capital the forward and the spot rate would continually adjust to maintain equality of two yields, $\mu_{ii} - \mu_{ij} = 0$ ($\mu_{ii} - \mu_{ic} = 0$), which implies

$$
(1 + r_i) = (1 + r_j)\frac{\varepsilon_{fij}}{\varepsilon_{sij}}
$$

or ignoring the cross term, $r_j\left(1 - \frac{\varepsilon_{fij}}{\varepsilon_{sij}}\right)$,

$$
\frac{\varepsilon_{fij} - \varepsilon_{sij}}{\varepsilon_{sij}} \simeq (r_i - r_j)
$$

which is a well known interest parity assumption. It states that the interest differential between two countries is equal to a forward premium on the exchange rate of their currencies. A commonly used uncovered interest spread variable in the capital flow equations of various earlier studies can be justified only if the above interest

---

[10] Yet another decomposition may be viewed as

$$
(\mu_{ii} - \mu_{ij}) = (r_i - r_j) + (1 + r_j)\left[1 - \frac{\varepsilon_{fij}}{\varepsilon_{sij}} \right]
$$

and

$$
(\mu_{ii} - \mu_{ic}) = (r_i - r_c) + \left[(1 + r_c) - \sum_{j \neq i} w_{ij}(1 + r_j)\frac{\varepsilon_{fij}}{\varepsilon_{sij}} \right]
$$

where $r_c = \sum_{j \neq i} w_{ij} r_j$. After undertaking a forward contract to sell the value of foreign security denominated in foreign currency at the time of maturity at ε_{fij}, if the actual rate at that time turns out to be less than ε_{fij} the investor makes a speculative gain.

parity assumption holds. Otherwise, to be more precise, the yield differential variable as computed above or some variant of its components individually should be incorporated. The interest parity condition at the aggregate level over mutually competing all j countries may also be approximated as

$$(r_i - r_c) \simeq \sum_{j \neq i} w_{ij} \frac{\varepsilon_{fij}}{\varepsilon_{sij}} - 1 .$$

Taking an intermediate "flow-stock" view[11] that some capital inflows result from "flow" decisions and some from "stock", we attempt to include both the level as well as the change in the yield differential as explanatory variables. A pure "flow" decision would constrain $\alpha_2 > 0$ and $\alpha_3 = 0$, and a "stock" decision would imply $\alpha_2 = 0$ and $\alpha_3 > 0$. In an intermediate case α_2 must be positive but α_3 could be positive or negative depending upon the speculative and dynamic interactions between the two. A high level of domestic yield must normally induce more capital inflows, but a rising yield may also bring speculative expectations with the risk that ultimately the widening gap between domestic and foreign yield would narrow after some adjustments via the forward rate (see Eq. (8) below). Such expectations and risk would be deterrent to current capital inflows and α_3 would be negative. An additional expected risk on investment in foreign securities may be measured by a moving standard deviation of the spread between μ_{ii} and μ_{ic} variables.[12]

It must be emphasized at this point that the effect of yield differential on net capital flows as noted above by alternative decomposition is indeed governed by some interactions which may possibly work in the opposite directions. For example, denoting

$$\mu d = \mu_{ii} - \mu_{ic}$$

$$\mu d = \mu dHF + \mu dS$$

$$\mu d = \mu dHS + \mu dHFS$$

$$\mu dHF = \left(r_i - \sum_{j \neq i} w_{ij} r_j \frac{\varepsilon_{fij}}{\varepsilon_{sij}} \right)$$

$$\mu dS = \left(1 - \sum_{j \neq i} w_{ij} \frac{\varepsilon_{fij}}{\varepsilon_{sij}} \right)$$

$$\mu dHS = (1 + r_i) \left[1 - \sum_{j \neq i} w_{ij} \frac{\varepsilon_{fij}}{\varepsilon_{sij}} \right]$$

$$\mu dHFS = \sum_{j \neq i} w_{ij} (r_i - r_j) \frac{\varepsilon_{fij}}{\varepsilon_{sij}} ,$$

---

[11] See, for instance, Branson (1970).

[12] There are presumably a number of additional risks such as imposition of exchange controls, the possibility that a foreign security will have to be sold before maturity to finance a domestic transaction or for alternative investment.

μd, μdS, and μdHS are expected *a priori* to have similar effects on capital flows. However, μdHF and $\mu dHFS$ components measuring interactions between interest rates and speculation may, if strong enough, cause sufficient distortions as to bring perverse results in the final outcome. Recognising the likelihood of such distortions, we intend to produce a series of experiments with the yield variable in order to select the most significant factors.[13]

In addition to interest parity deviations, we propose to use price parity deviations of exchange rate as a measure of change in the real value of i currency. As a matter of fact, $\dot{\varepsilon}_{iSD} - (\dot{p}_i - \dot{p}_c)$ can be viewed as measuring an impact of two diverse factors, a pure demand factor and an expectational factor. The former will have a negative impact and the latter a positive. As the real value of i currency depreciates with an increase in $\dot{\varepsilon}_{iSD} - (\dot{p}_i - \dot{p}_c)$, its demand falls. However, as currency depreciates with a fall in its real value and the deviations of actual exchange rate from its price parity rate increase, people begin to form regressive expectations that the exchange rate would eventually (and soon) converge back to the inflation differential at home and abroad. This would bring speculative gains on the current capital inflows. Thus, the sign of $\dot{\varepsilon}_{iSD} - (\dot{p}_i - \dot{p}_c)$ is quite ambiguous.

And finally, current account balances are expected to have a negative impact on capital inflows. In addition to their representing the need for matching credit creation to finance trade, the standard argument is that a country would actively seek capital inflows to offset its current account deficit and would actively acquire foreign securities to spend its surplus.

Next, the formation of the forward rate can be specified in the form of a linear combination of interest parity rate and the expected spot rate.

$$\varepsilon_{fij} = \lambda \left(\frac{1+r_i}{1+r_j} \right) \varepsilon_{sij} + (1-\lambda)\varepsilon_{sij}^e \qquad j = 1, 2, \ldots, 5. \qquad (8)$$

An expected spot rate may simply be determined by some distributed lag scheme of expectation formation such as

$$\varepsilon_{sij}^e = E(\varepsilon_{sij-1}, \varepsilon_{sij-2}, \ldots, \dot{\varepsilon}_{sij} - (\dot{p}_i - \dot{p}_j)). \qquad (9)$$

As a first approximation, however, we suppress Eqs. (8) and (9) and use the forward rate as a pre-determined variable. This brings us to the determination of the actual exchange rate.

Aggregating k behavioral components of capital inflows, we obtain an estimate of CAB as specified in Eq. (4), and through the balance of payment identity in Eq. (3), we determine the change in net foreign assets, ΔNFA. CUB is assumed to be known exogenously, given by $LINK$ system solutions.

Under a fully flexible exchange rate system, ΔNFA is expected to be zero, for the foreign exchange market to be in equilibrium, and thus the balance of payment

---

[13]Our empirical analysis presented in the next section in fact shows the existence of distortion to be quite common in the yield variable.

identity, reduced to $CUB = -CAB$, determines the equilibrium exchange rate. It virtually involves inverting the capital flow equations. In other words an equilibrium exchange rate is determined at a point where foreign demand for home currency generated by balance on current account (CUB) is equal to its total supply generated by an outflow of capital ($-CAB$).

In the case of a managed float, however, the market is only partially cleared through the adjustments in the exchange rate. Part of the market pressures are absorbed by government interventions as measured by the movements of net foreign assets. By accumulating (decumulating) foreign assets, government creates forced demand (supply) for foreign currency preventing its oversupply (excess demand) in the exchange market. Thus, $\Delta NFA > 0$ implies government intervention against excessive appreciation of domestic currency and $\Delta NFA < 0$ implies deterring its depreciation. We, therefore, propose to determine actual exchange rates through a modified market clearing equation in the form of potential market pressures in which $(\dot{\varepsilon}_{iSD} - GNFA)$ appears as a dependent variable. We may call it the potential rate of change in the exchange rate variable, $\dot{\varepsilon}_{iSD}^P$; that is, the rate of change which would have taken place (and would exist) in the absence of any government intervention.[14]

We hypothesize that a potential change in the exchange rate is a joint function of interest parity and price parity variables interacting with speculative factors and a resident official sector. The resident official sector, in fact, provides a balancing force to the balance of payments accounts. The covered interest spread and the resident official sector are expected to dampen exchange market pressures and inflation spread to reinforce them. The potential exchange rate relationship may be specified as

$$(\dot{\varepsilon}_{iSD} - GNFA_i) = \beta_0 + \beta_1(\mu_{ii} - \mu_{ic}) + \beta_2(\dot{p}_i - \dot{p}_c)$$
$$+\beta_3 ROL_i + \beta_4 ROS_i + \beta_5 ERO_i + w_i \qquad (10)$$

where w_i is a random error. *A priori* $\beta_1, \beta_3, \beta_4$, and β_5 are expected to be < 0, $\beta_2 > 0$.

Equation (10) is quite general and is applicable, by and large, in all the three regimes, fixed, flexible, and managed float. Under a fixed exchange rate system where $\dot{\varepsilon}_{iSD} = 0$, $GNFA$ performs an equilibrating function determining the domestic inflation rate in the process. Alternatively, this equation may then be viewed as a truncated reduced form equation derived from the balance of payment identity. Under a flexible exchange rate system $GNFA = 0$ and $\dot{\varepsilon}_{iSD}$ performs an equilibrating function. Finally, under a system of managed float, the adjustment process is partly reflected in the net flow of international reserves and partly in the movements of exchange rate.

---

[14]This variable is quite similar but not exactly equal to the variable used by Girton and Roper (1977). Our equation, on the whole, is different. Thus, Hacche and Townend's (1981b) critique of Girton and Roper's direction is not applicable to our equation. We have, in fact, questioned the restrictiveness of some of Girton and Roper's assumptions in an early version of a related paper (1982, p. 16, fn. 16).

The model contains 16 equations (1)–(4), $k = 9$ of type (5), (8)–(10), of which 13 equations are structural and 3 are identities, and determines 16 unknowns $(r, H, \Delta NFA, CAB, CAB^k (k = 9)$, ε_{fij}, ε^e_{sij}, and $\varepsilon_{iSD})$ and thus constitutes a complete system. It must, however, be mentioned here that implicit in the system are 15 identities in the form of bridge equations linking ε_{iSD} to the cross rates ε_{sij}. For example, $\varepsilon_{sij} = \varepsilon_{iSD}/\varepsilon_{jSD}$ for $i \neq j$.

As a first approximation to the statistical estimate of the model presented in the next section we assume that the interest rate and forward rate are exogenously known, and from the remaining system, reduced to 12 equations ((3), (4), $k = 9$ of type (5) and (10); ten are structural and two are identities), determine simultaneously capital flows and the exchange rate.

3. Statistical Estimates

Our sample consists of 1972–1979 annual data pooled across six countries, five SDR countries plus Canada. The SDR countries are the five IMF member countries having the largest exports of goods and services for the period 1975–1979 and whose currencies are included in the latest SDR valuation basket beginning January 1, 1981. These five countries are France, Germany, Japan, U.K., and the U.S. Our basic data sources are the *IMF Balance of Payment Year Book* (primarily for capital flows and related items) and *International Financial Statistics*. Our balance of payment identity is maintained in such a way that each capital flow component is all inclusive of exceptional financing, and liabilities constituting foreign authorities' reserves. The definition of the variables (with *BOP* and *IFS* code wherever relevant) are listed below:

Definitions of Variables and Data

Capital Flows and Related Variables

CAB = capital account balance (9.. × 4 plus.A. × 4), millions of SDRs.

CUB = current account balance ($A..C4$), millions of SDRs.

DBL = deposit money banks long-term capital flow (5.1 × 4), millions of SDRs.

DBS = deposit money banks short-term capital flow (5.2 × 4), millions of SDRs.

DIN = direct investment (3.. × 4), millions of SDRs.

ERO = errors and omissions (in CAB) (.A. × 4), millions of SDRs.

NFA = total international reserves (gold + holding of SDRs + reserve position in the Fund + foreign exchange reserves, including counterpart items such as monetization/demonetization and valuation adjustment) (1..s), end of the period, millions of SDRs.

NFA_{-1} = total international reserves at the beginning of the period.

PIN = portfolio investment (6.1 × 4), millions of SDRs.

ROL = resident official long-term capital flow (4.1 × 4), millions of SDRs.

ROS = resident official short-term capital flow (4.2 × 4), millions of SDRs.

RL = other long-term capital flow (8.1 × 4), millions of *SDR*s.
RS = other short-term capital flow (8.2 × 4), millions of *SDR*s.
CI = counterpart items (2 ... $C4$), millions of *SDR*s.

Exchange Rate, Interest Rate, Yield, and Prices

ε_{fij} = three months forward exchange rate, units of i currency per unit of j, end of the period.

ε_{sij} = spot exchange rate, units of i currency per unit of j, end of the period.

ε_{iSD} = units of i currency per *SDR*, end of the period.

p_i = index of unit value of exports of country i in national currency, 1975 = 1.00 (# 74).

p_c = trade weighted competitive price index, $\sum_{j \neq i} w_{ij} p_j$.

r^s = short-term interest rate (60 C),% p.a., period average.

r^l = long-term interest rate (61),% p.a., period average.

μ_{ij} = % expected yield to investor of country i measured in i's currency on investment denominated in currency j, computed as

$$= \begin{cases} (100 + r_j)\varepsilon_{fij}/\varepsilon_{sij} - 100 \text{ for } i \neq j \\ r_i \text{ for } i = j \end{cases}$$

$\mu_i = \mu_{ii}$

μ_{ic} = % expected competitive yield to investor of country i measured in i currency on foreign investment, computed as $\sum_{j \neq i} w_{ij} \mu_{ij}$, w_{ij} are 1975 trade weights.

$\mu_c = \mu_{ic}$
$\mu d = \mu_{ii} - \mu_{ic}$

$$\mu dHF = \left(r_i - \sum_{j \neq i} w_{ij} r_j \frac{\varepsilon_{fij}}{\varepsilon_{sij}} \right)$$

$$\mu dS = 100 \left(1 - \sum_{j \neq i} w_{ij} \frac{\varepsilon_{fij}}{\varepsilon_{sij}} \right)$$

$$\mu dHS = (100 + r_i) \sum_{j \neq i} w_{ij} \left[1 - \frac{\varepsilon_{fij}}{\varepsilon_{sij}} \right]$$

$$\mu dHFS = \sum_{j \neq i} w_{ij} (r_i - r_j) \frac{\varepsilon_{fij}}{\varepsilon_{sij}} .$$

Note: An attached letter l denotes long term, computed by using the long-term interest rate and s denotes short term computed by using the short-term interest rate. The interest rate values are period averages because this is the way the data are most readily available. The exchange rates, on the other hand, are entered as end-of-period values, also readily available in that form.

Other Variables

D_i = dummy variable with value 1 for country i and zero for others, i = Canada (C), France (F), Germany (G), Japan (J), U.K. and U.S.

$GNFA$ = rate of change in net foreign assets (international reserves).

σ = four quarter moving standard deviation of yield spread $(\mu_{ii} - \mu_{ic})$ or associated component, (moving quarters $t - 0$ to $t - 3$).

$\cdot$ = dot above the variables is rate of change.

Δ = change from the preceding period.

The best estimates obtained by ordinary least squares and Aitken's generalized least squares are presented below. The generalized least squares estimates are obtained because the pooling of cross section and time series data may make the random error cross sectionally heteroskedastic and time-wise autoregressive. The sample size is 48, eight annual observations (1972–1979) for six countries. The numbers in parentheses below the coefficients are t-ratios.

Ordinary Least Square Estimates

Direct Investment

$$\frac{DIN}{NFA_{-1}} = \underset{(2.28)}{0.078} - \underset{(2.77)}{0.0521} - GNFA + \underset{(3.62)}{0.0563} \frac{l\mu dHS}{\varepsilon_{iSD}} - \underset{(1.12)}{0.2262} \tag{S.1}$$

$$\times [\dot{\varepsilon}_{iSD} - (\dot{p}_i - \dot{p}_c)] - \underset{(0.778)}{0.0049} \frac{\sigma l}{l\mu dHS} + \underset{(2.34)}{0.1155} D_F$$

$$+ \underset{(0.77)}{0.0373} D_G - \underset{(0.32)}{0.0153} (D_J + D_{\text{U.K.}}) - \underset{(9.62)}{0.4676} D_{\text{U.S.}} \qquad \bar{R}^2 = 0.84$$

Portfolio Investment

$$\frac{PIN}{NFA_{-1}} = \underset{(7.52)}{0.5150} + \underset{(5.44)}{0.3264} GNFA + \underset{(0.33)}{0.0190} \frac{s\mu dHS}{\varepsilon_{iSD}} \tag{S.2}$$

$$- \underset{(1.58)}{0.147} \frac{\Delta s\mu dHS}{\varepsilon_{iSD}} - \underset{(4.9)}{0.4305} \frac{CUB}{NFA_{-1}} - \underset{(2.07)}{0.1740} \sigma s$$

$$- \underset{(4.82)}{0.5085} D_F - \underset{(4.16)}{0.3719} (D_G + D_J + D_{\text{U.K.}}) \qquad \bar{R}^2 = 0.75$$

Resident Official Long-Term

$$\frac{ROL}{NFA_{-1}} = -\underset{(4.06)}{0.04796} + \underset{(2.52)}{0.03214} GNFA + \underset{(4.00)}{0.0603} \frac{\Delta l\mu dHS}{\varepsilon_{iSD}} + \underset{(2.06)}{0.0379} \sigma l \tag{S.3}$$

$$+ \underset{(3.46)}{0.1171} \frac{DIN}{NFA_{-1}} - \underset{(2.19)}{0.0442} D_J + \underset{(4.51)}{0.1129} D_{\text{U.K.}} \qquad \bar{R}^2 = 0.77$$

Deposit Money Banks Long-Term

$$\frac{DBL}{NFA_{-1}} = \underset{(0.661)}{-0.01415} + \underset{(1.33)}{0.0461} \frac{l\mu dHS}{\varepsilon_{iSD}} - \underset{(3.40)}{0.0875} \frac{\Delta l\mu dHS}{\varepsilon_{iSD}} \tag{S.4}$$

$$\underset{(1.56)}{-0.044} \frac{CUB}{NFA_{-1}} - \underset{(0.32)}{0.0092}\, \sigma l - \underset{(6.71)}{0.2257}\, D_F$$

$$\underset{(1.297)}{-0.10699}\, D_{\text{U.K.}} - \underset{(1.37)}{0.0463}\, D_{\text{U.S.}} \qquad\qquad \bar{R}^2 = 0.66$$

Other Long-Term

$$\frac{RL}{NFA_{-1}} = \underset{(0.44)}{0.00647} + \underset{(7.4)}{0.1238}\, GNFA + \underset{(6.01)}{0.12006} \frac{\Delta l\mu dHS}{\varepsilon_{iSD}} \tag{S.5}$$

$$\underset{(4.23)}{-0.0884} \frac{CUB}{NFA_{-1}} - \underset{(2.77)}{0.0663}\, \sigma l - \underset{(3.55)}{0.2941} \frac{DBL}{NFA_{-1}}$$

$$\underset{(1.14)}{-0.03117}\, D_J + \underset{(8.17)}{0.2789}\, D_{\text{U.K.}} \qquad\qquad \bar{R}^2 = 0.945$$

Resident Official Short-Term

$$\frac{ROS}{NFA_{-1}} = \underset{(0.67)}{-0.0295} + \underset{(3.79)}{0.1907}\, GNFA + \underset{(1.57)}{0.1291} \frac{s\mu dHS}{\varepsilon_{iSD}} \tag{S.6}$$

$$\underset{(2.09)}{-0.1844} \frac{\Delta s\mu dHS}{\varepsilon_{iSD}} - \underset{(4.42)}{0.3376} \frac{CUB}{NFA_{-1}} - \underset{(4.77)}{0.5083} \frac{DBS}{NFA_{-1}}$$

$$\underset{(1.76)}{+0.1483}\, D_J + \underset{(1.06)}{0.1816}\, D_{\text{U.K.}} + \underset{(1.38)}{0.1115}\, D_{\text{U.S.}} \qquad \bar{R}^2 = 0.50$$

Deposit Money Banks Short-Term

$$\frac{DBS}{NFA_{-1}} = \underset{(0.92)}{-0.0415} + \underset{(6.34)}{0.2183}\, GNFA - \underset{(5.76)}{0.4000} \frac{CUB}{NFA_{-1}} \tag{S.7}$$

$$\underset{(2.15)}{+0.1561}\, \sigma s - \underset{(5.59)}{0.7096} \frac{ROS}{NFA_{-1}} + \underset{(1.13)}{0.1007}\, D_J \qquad \bar{R}^2 = 0.72$$

Other Short-Term

$$\frac{RS}{NFA_{-1}} = \underset{(1.44)}{-0.0347} + \underset{(0.78)}{0.0272}\, \sigma s + \underset{(0.48)}{0.0198} \frac{DBS}{NFA_{-1}} \tag{S.8}$$

$$\underset{(2.63)}{+0.1055}\, D_F + \underset{(0.30)}{0.0121}\, D_G + \underset{(1.34)}{0.0558}\, D_J \qquad \bar{R}^2 = 0.18$$

Error and Omissions

$$\frac{ERO}{NFA_{-1}} = -0.4826 + 0.3865\,GNFA + 0.0994\,\frac{\Delta l\mu dHS}{\varepsilon_{iSD}} \qquad (\text{S.9})$$
$$\quad\;\;(4.54)\qquad(5.44)\qquad\qquad(1.15)$$

$$-1.536\,\frac{ROL}{NFA_{-1}} - 0.4939\,\frac{DIN}{NFA_{-1}} + 0.6674\,D_F$$
$$(1.89)\qquad\quad(1.22)\qquad\qquad(4.80)$$

$$+0.4029\,D_G + 0.2892\,D_J + 0.6174\,D_{\text{U.K.}} + 0.3419\,D_{\text{U.S.}} \qquad \overline{R}^2 = 0.765$$
$$(3.01)\qquad\quad(2.23)\qquad\quad(4.80)\qquad\qquad(1.50)$$

Capital Account Balance

$$CAB = DIN + PIN + ROL + DBL + RL + ROS + DBS + RS + ERO \quad (\text{S.10})$$

Foreign Reserves

$$\Delta NFA = CUB + CAB + CI \qquad (\text{S.11})$$

Exchange Rate/Market Adjustment

$$(\dot{\varepsilon}_{iSD} - GNFA) = -1.293 - 0.0925\,\frac{l\mu dHS}{\varepsilon_{iSD}} + 3.0535\,(\dot{p}_i - \dot{p}_c) \qquad (\text{S.12})$$
$$(1.39)\quad(1.52)\qquad\qquad(2.63)$$

$$-2.627\,\frac{ROL}{NFA_{-1}} - 1.952\,\frac{RL}{NFA_{-1}}$$
$$(2.44)\qquad\quad(3.67)$$

$$-0.6495\,\frac{ERO}{NFA_{-1}} \qquad\qquad\qquad \overline{R}^2 = 0.81$$
$$(3.54)$$

Generalized Least Squares Estimate

Direct Investment

$$\frac{DIN}{NFA_{-1}} = -0.0643 - 0.0724\,GNFA + 0.0577\,\frac{l\mu dHS}{\varepsilon_{iSD}} \qquad (\text{S.1}')$$
$$\quad\;\;(2.0)\qquad(10.2)\qquad\qquad(7.16)$$

$$-0.3718\,[\dot{\varepsilon}_{iSD} - (\dot{p}_i - \dot{p}_c)] - 0.00946\,\frac{\sigma l}{l\mu dHS}$$
$$(6.66)\qquad\qquad\qquad\quad(6.30)$$

$$+0.0915\,D_F + 0.0010\,D_G - 0.0150\,(D_J + D_{\text{U.K.}}) - 0.48121\,D_{\text{U.S.}}$$
$$(2.41)\qquad\quad(0.037)\qquad(0.40)\qquad\qquad(10.88)$$

Portfolio Investment

$$\frac{PIN}{NFA_{-1}} = 0.5478 + 0.3217\,GNFA + 0.00189\,\frac{s\mu dHS}{\varepsilon_{iSD}} \quad (S.2')$$
$$(9.78) \quad (21.02) \qquad\qquad (0.086)$$

$$- 0.1082\,\frac{\Delta s\mu dHS}{\varepsilon_{iSD}} - 0.3957\,\frac{CUB}{NFA_{-1}} - 0.2134\,\sigma s$$
$$(3.94) \qquad\qquad (13.08) \qquad\qquad (12.64)$$

$$- 0.5089\,D_F - 0.3866\,(D_G + D_J + D_{U.K.})$$
$$(8.52) \qquad\quad (6.81)$$

Resident Official Long-Term

$$\frac{ROL}{NFA_{-1}} = -0.04143 + 0.03486\,GNFA + 0.0548\,\frac{\Delta l\mu dHS}{\varepsilon_{iSD}} + 0.0354\,\sigma l \quad (S.3')$$
$$(4.97) \qquad (11.54) \qquad\qquad (13.2) \qquad\qquad (17.24)$$

$$+ 0.09784\,\frac{DIN}{NFA_{-1}} - 0.0451\,D_J + 0.08912\,D_{U.K.}$$
$$(6.23) \qquad\qquad (3.20) \qquad\quad (5.77)$$

Deposit Money Banks Long-Term

$$\frac{DBL}{NFA_{-1}} = -0.02181 + 0.04328\,\frac{l\mu dHS}{\varepsilon_{iSD}} - 0.07991\,\frac{\Delta l\mu dHS}{\varepsilon_{iSD}} \quad (S.4')$$
$$(1.98) \qquad (6.08) \qquad\qquad (16.32)$$

$$- 0.03645\,\frac{CUB}{NFA_{-1}} + 0.00721\,\sigma l - 0.20215\,D_F$$
$$(4.65) \qquad\qquad (0.936) \qquad\quad (4.38)$$

$$- 0.1088\,D_{U.K.} - 0.04665\,D_{U.S.}$$
$$(4.17) \qquad\qquad (3.06)$$

$$\frac{DBL}{NFA_{-1}} = -0.0227 + 0.0423\,\frac{l\mu dHS}{\varepsilon_{iSD}} - 0.0797\,\frac{\Delta l\mu dHS}{\varepsilon_{iSD}} \quad (S.4'a)$$
$$(2.07) \qquad (6.27) \qquad\qquad (17.00)$$

$$- 0.03994\,\frac{CUB}{NFA_{-1}} - 0.2005\,D_F - 0.1008\,D_{U.K.} - 0.04091\,D_{U.S.}$$
$$(5.76) \qquad\qquad (4.30) \qquad\quad (4.09) \qquad\qquad (2.85)$$

Other Long-Term

$$\frac{RL}{NFA_{-1}} = -0.000297 + 0.1174\,GNFA + 0.12223\,\frac{\Delta l\mu dHS}{\varepsilon_{iSD}} \quad (S.5')$$
$$(0.059) \qquad (16.33) \qquad\qquad (14.38)$$

$$- 0.095\,\frac{CUB}{NFA_{-1}} - 0.0496\,\sigma l - 0.2766\,\frac{DBL}{NFA_{-1}}$$
$$(11.42) \qquad\qquad (2.62) \qquad\quad (10.87)$$

$$- 0.03194\,D_J + 0.2604\,D_{U.K.}$$
$$(2.62) \qquad\quad (9.6)$$

Resident Official Short-Term

$$\frac{ROS}{NFA_{-1}} = \underset{(1.50)}{-0.02624} + \underset{(5.90)}{0.1477\,GNFA} + \underset{(3.99)}{0.1428}\,\frac{s\mu dHS}{\varepsilon_{iSD}} \tag{S.6'}$$

$$\underset{(4.74)}{-0.1893}\,\frac{\Delta s\mu dHS}{\varepsilon_{iSD}} - \underset{(6.22)}{0.2115}\,\frac{CUB}{NFA_{-1}} - \underset{(7.56)}{0.2991}\,\frac{DBS}{NFA_{-1}}$$

$$+\underset{(5.21)}{0.1120\,D_J} + \underset{(2.59)}{0.2318\,D_{\text{U.K.}}} + \underset{(3.82)}{0.1977\,D_{\text{U.S.}}}$$

Deposit Money Banks Short-Term

$$\frac{DBS}{NFA_{-1}} = \underset{(1.20)}{-0.02675} + \underset{(29.7)}{0.2332\,GNFA} - \underset{(14.16)}{0.4564}\,\frac{CUB}{NFA_{-1}} \tag{S.7'}$$

$$+\underset{(4.48)}{0.13513\,\sigma s} - \underset{(13.14)}{0.6824}\,\frac{ROS}{NFA_{-1}} + \underset{(2.86)}{0.10203\,D_J}$$

Other Short-Term

$$\frac{RS}{NFA_{-1}} = \underset{(3.286)}{-0.04382} + \underset{(4.8)}{0.0432\,\sigma s} + \underset{(0.81)}{0.0097}\,\frac{DBS}{NFA_{-1}} \tag{S.8'}$$

$$+\underset{(6.07)}{0.1105\,D_F} + \underset{(1.79)}{0.02498\,D_G} + \underset{(1.26)}{0.05009\,D_J}$$

$$\frac{RS}{NFA_{-1}} = \underset{(1.7)}{-0.0219} - \underset{(2.41)}{0.00376}\,\frac{DBS}{NFA_{-1}} + \underset{(5.254)}{0.1032\,D_F} \tag{S.8'a}$$

$$+\underset{(1.05)}{0.01459\,D_G} + \underset{(1.47)}{0.0569\,D_J}$$

Errors and Omissions

$$\frac{ERO}{NFA_{-1}} = \underset{(6.54)}{-0.42011} + \underset{(18.21)}{0.3178\,GNFA} + \underset{(9.83)}{0.1339}\,\frac{\Delta l\mu dHS}{\varepsilon_{iSD}} \tag{S.9'}$$

$$-\underset{(5.10)}{1.0061}\,\frac{ROL}{NFA_{-1}} - \underset{(3.90)}{0.4428}\,\frac{DIN}{NFA_{-1}} + \underset{(9.10)}{0.6186\,D_F}$$

$$+\underset{(5.64)}{0.3530\,D_G} + \underset{(4.09)}{0.2794\,D_J} + \underset{(4.97)}{0.65161\,D_{\text{U.K.}}} + \underset{(1.59)}{0.3321\,D_{\text{U.S.}}}$$

Capital Account Balance

$$CAB = DIN + PIN + ROL + DBL + RL + ROL + DBS + RS + ERO \tag{S.10}$$

Foreign Reserves

$$\Delta NFA = CUB + CAB + CI \qquad (S.11)$$

Exchange Rate/Market Adjustment

$$(\dot{\varepsilon}_{iSD} - GNFA) = -0.1626 - 0.0865 \frac{l\mu dHS}{\varepsilon_{iSD}} + 2.932 \, (\dot{p}_i - \dot{p}_c) \qquad (S.12')$$
$$\phantom{(\dot{\varepsilon}_{iSD} - GNFA) = }(2.38) \quad (1.35) \qquad\qquad\quad (3.93)$$
$$- 2.5578 \frac{ROL}{NFA_{-1}} - 2.1453 \frac{RL}{NFA_{-1}} - 0.6093 \frac{ERO}{NFA_{-1}}$$
$$ (3.52) \qquad\qquad (4.88) \qquad\qquad (4.35)$$

Before we undertake a general discussion of the statistical estimates presented above, a brief review of the experimental calculations with the yield differential variable and its related components is in proper order. The μdHS component, related respectively to long-term and short-term interest rates, as

$$l\mu dHS = (100 + r_i^l) \sum_{j \neq i} w_{ij} \left[1 - \frac{\varepsilon_{fij}}{\varepsilon_{sij}} \right]$$

and

$$s\mu dHS = (100 + r_i^s) \sum_{j \neq i} w_{ij} \left[1 - \frac{\varepsilon_{fij}}{\varepsilon_{sij}} \right]$$

appears basically in both "stock" and "flow" versions in our final results. In the six series of experimental calculations the μdHS component in fact consistently generated theoretically expected and statistically significant results across most categories of capital flows. The six experimental versions of the model used the following different forms of the yield differential as an explanatory variable.   RIGHT−¿

(1) Uncovered differential between home and competitive foreign interest rates $(r_i - r_c)$.
(2) Covered yield differential $(\mu_i - \mu_c)$ as discussed above.
(3) Unconstrained μ_i and μ_c as separate variables.
(4) μdHS and μdS components as separate variables with no equality constraints on their coefficients.
(5) μdHS and $\mu dHFS$ components as separate variables with no equality constraints on their coefficients.
(6) μdHS component only.

The ordinary least squares coefficients of the yield related variables obtained in these six experiments have been summarized in Table 1. All other variables in each equation of the model remain unchanged. It was generally noted that different versions of the yield differential variable produced significantly different coefficients; there were some minor changes in associated $\overline{R}^2$s. However, the coefficients of other variables remained practically unaffected.

Table 1. Experimental estimates based on yield variable.

Experiment / Eqs.	DIN^l 1	PIN^s 2	ROL^l 3	DBL^l 4	RL^l 5	ROS^s 6	DBS^s 7	RS^s 8	ERO^l 9	$\varepsilon_{iSD} - GNFA$ 12
Exp. #1										
$(r_i - r_c)$	−0.0259 (3.64)					−0.0272 (1.69)				0.0968 (2.82)
$\Delta(r_i - r_c)$		−0.0029 (0.106)	0.0054 (0.46)	−0.0111 (0.935)	0.03204 (1.66)	0.0059 (0.27)			−0.0111 (0.20)	
$\overline{R}^2$	0.84	0.75	0.68	0.62	0.90	0.47			0.75	0.80
Exp. #2										
$(\mu_i - \mu_c)/\varepsilon_{iSD}$	−0.0233 (2.7)	0.0662 (1.7)		−0.0301 (1.8)		−0.0682 (2.00)		−0.0142 (0.13)		0.1128 (3.2)
$\Delta(\mu_i - \mu_c)/\varepsilon_{iSD}$	−0.0099 (0.16)		0.0231 (3.16)	−0.0031 (0.19)	0.0429 (3.77)	−0.0230 (0.46)		0.0485 (2.4)	0.0032 (0.08)	
$\overline{R}^2$	0.82	0.73	0.75	0.58	0.92	0.53		0.28	0.76	0.84
Exp. #3										
μ_i	−0.0208 (2.22)	0.0481 (1.67)		−0.0132 (0.94)		−0.03226 (1.57)	−0.0216 (0.89)	−0.0092 (0.75)		0.1122 (2.56)
μ_c	−0.0154 (0.84)	−0.0855 (2.34)		0.0047 (0.23)		0.02347 (0.79)	0.020 (0.66)	0.0177 (1.16)		−0.03596 (0.47)
$\Delta\mu_i$		−0.0346 (1.13)	0.01259 (1.21)	0.0294 (1.57)	0.04565 (2.94)	0.0048 (0.19)	−0.0043 (0.16)	0.0139 (1.13)	0.00014 (0.003)	
$\Delta\mu_c$		0.02114 (0.61)	−0.0087 (0.71)	0.0153 (0.81)	−0.0216 (1.25)	0.02178 (0.43)	0.0432 (1.46)	−0.01946 (1.35)	0.01478 (0.30)	
$\overline{R}^2$	0.84	0.76	0.70	0.62	0.91	0.51	0.76	0.22	0.76	0.83
Exp. #4										
$\mu dH\, F/\varepsilon_{iSD}$	−0.00888 (0.84)	0.0886 (1.8)		−0.0090 (0.53)		−0.0819 (2.22)	−0.0947 (2.57)			0.1744 (3.18)
$\mu dS/\varepsilon_{iSD}$	0.0395 (1.31)	0.1898 (1.47)		0.0358 (0.75)		−0.0844 (0.69)	−0.1979 (2.66)			0.3174 (2.16)

Table 1. (Continued)

Experiment / Eqs.	DIN^l 1	PIN^s 2	ROL^l 3	DBL^l 4	RL^l 5	ROS^s 6	DBS^s 7	RS^s 8	ERO^l 9	$\varepsilon_{iSD} - GNFA$ 12
Exp. #4 (continued)										
$\Delta dHF/\varepsilon_{iSD}..$		-0.0217 (0.35)	-0.00743 (0.81)	-0.0136 (0.82)	-0.01131 (0.87)	-0.01956 (0.41)		-0.0483 (2.68)	-0.0404 (0.82)	
$\Delta\mu dS/\varepsilon_{iSD}..$		-0.1928 (1.73)	-0.0651 (3.75)	-0.085 (2.35)	-0.1236 (5.22)	-0.1470 (1.42)		-0.0927 (2.86)	-0.1345 (1.35)	
$\overline{R}^2$.........	0.84	0.75	0.78	0.66	0.94	0.58	0.75	0.32	0.77	0.85
Exp. #5										
$\mu dHS/\varepsilon_{iSD}..$	0.0324 (1.24)	0.1983 (1.94)				-0.0213 (0.21)	-0.1426 (1.67)	0.0201 (0.49)		0.3041 (2.21)
$\mu dHFS/\varepsilon_{iSD}$	-0.0082 (0.75)	0.0926 (1.99)		-0.00774 (0.45)		-0.0685 (1.95)	-0.0536 (1.38)	-0.00424 (0.25)		0.1759 (3.14)
$\Delta\mu HS/\varepsilon_{iSD}$		-0.2163 (1.8)	0.05965 (3.85)	-0.07671 (2.32)	0.11564 (5.51)	-0.1563 (1.61)	-0.0725 (0.70)	0.0763 (1.79)	0.1116 (1.27)	
$\Delta\mu dHFS/\varepsilon_{iSD}$		-0.0231 (0.38)	0.008 (0.89)	0.0120 (0.82)	0.01155 (0.913)	-0.0242 (0.50)	-0.0949 (1.87)	0.0564 (2.68)	-0.0366 (0.75)	
$\overline{R}^2$.........	0.84	0.76	0.78	0.66	0.94	0.58	0.76	0.37	0.77	0.84
Exp. #6										
$\mu dHS/\varepsilon_{iSD}..$	0.0563 (3.62)	0.0190 (0.33)		0.04606 (1.33)		0.1291 (1.57)				-0.0925 (1.52)
$\Delta\mu dHS/\varepsilon_{iSD}$		-0.1473 (1.58)	0.0603 (4.0)	-0.0875 (3.40)	0.12006 (6.01)	-0.1844 (2.09)			0.0994 (1.15)	
$\overline{R}^2$.........	0.84	0.75	0.77	0.66	0.94	0.50			0.76	0.81

Note: $\mu d = (\mu_i - \mu_c), \mu_i = r_i, \mu_c = \sum_{j \neq i} w_{ij}(100 + r_j)(\varepsilon_{fij}/\varepsilon_{sij}) - 100, \mu dHF = \left(r_i - \sum_{j \neq i} w_{ij} r_j\right)(\varepsilon_{fij}/\varepsilon_{sij})$

$\mu dS = 100\left(1 - \sum_{j \neq i} w_{ij}(\varepsilon_{fij}/\varepsilon_{sij})\right), \mu dHS = (100 + r_i)\sum_{j \neq i} w_{ij}\left[1 - (\varepsilon_{fij}/\varepsilon_{sij})\right], \mu dHFS = \sum_{j \neq i} w_{ij}(r_i - r_j)(\varepsilon_{fij}/\varepsilon_{sij})$

$\mu d = (\mu_i - \mu_c) = \mu dHF + \mu dS = \mu dHS + \mu dHFS$, Experiment # 6 is the same as presented in the final estimates.

By and large, experiment # 6 consisting of a μdHS component based on interactions between the yield on domestic securities and forward market speculation gives the best overall results and has been accepted in the final model. A general comparison of various experiments, specifically # 4, 5, and 6 clearly shows the presence of some distortions caused by other interactions. Uncovered interest rate differentials and covered yield differentials perform equally well in case of portfolio investment only; the latter are definitely superior in case of resident official long-term capital flows and other long-term capital flows. No form of yield variable gives fully acceptable results for deposit money banks short-term flows and other short-term flows. Experiment # 6 gives mildly acceptable results, at least in direction, of errors and omissions. Finally, in the market pressure equation determining the exchange rate, all experiments except # 6 give theoretically perverse results. Distortions are pervasive and seemingly strong.

Next, reviewing the highlights of the estimates of the whole model, we find that in the statistical equations (S.1) and (S.1′) for direct investment the signs of all the structural coefficients are as expected *a priori*. The long-term adjustment in terms of the stock allocation effect of growing foreign reserves is quite significant. Direct investment, which is presumably dominated by long-term investment, is quite sensitive to long-term yield differential component. The exchange rate deviations from the price parity rate act more like a demand variable. The risk associated with the increasing yield spread component is a deterrent (though weak) to capital inflows. Dummy variables for France and the U.S. account for important shift effects. The other dummy variables have statistically insignificant coefficients and yet make important contributions to the overall stability of the relationship.

There was some evidence that direct investment complements the resident official long-term sector, but because of the high degree of correlation between *GNFA* and *ROL* the use of both variables in Eqs. (S.1) and (S.1′) was abandoned.

Portfolio investment proved to be somewhat more sensitive to the short-term yield than to the long-term. The change in yield differential component has a somewhat more significant effect than its level. Growth of foreign assets and the payment balances on current account are the most significant structural variables and account for practically 40 percent of the total variation in portfolio investment. Growth of net foreign assets is indicative more of the state of the economy providing inducement for portfolio inflows. Current balances get significantly transformed into foreign securities. Some country differences also produce important shifts in the portfolio investment.

The resident official long-term capital flows are evidently (Eq. (S.3)) subject to the "stock" decision; the change in yield differential component measures about 26 percent of the total variation. Growing foreign assets are again indicative of a healthy economy as far as the official sector is concerned. And as has already been mentioned above, this sector strongly complements direct investment. Surprisingly, the resident official sector does not seem to be a risk averter. The coefficient of moving standard deviation of yield variable is positive and statistically significant.

Equations (S.4) and (S.4′) show that deposit money banks long-term capital inflows are affected both by "stock" and "flow" decisions; the "stock" decision is more significant. The coefficient of risk variable has mixed sign but is statistically insignificant. The current balances continue to indicate a matching credit creation in a significant way.

Equations (S.5) and (S.5′) for other long-term capital flows give the best result. The stock shift portfolio substitution effect of the yield differential component is extremely significant. The risk variable as expected *a priori* has a strong impact. The movements of other long-term capital flows seem to be inversely related to the deposit money banks flows.

To summarize, resident official long-term flows and other long-term flows are quite sensitive to changes in the yield component; the "stock" decisions are evidently more relevant. The growth of foreign assets seems to provide a measure of the strength of the economy. Risk and current balances turn out to be most significant in other capital flows. The resident official sector complements direct investment, but the other long-term flows compete with deposit money banks long-term capital.

Equations (S.6)–(S.8) and (S.6′)–(S.8′) for short-term flows are somewhat weaker than the equations for the corresponding long-term flows. Growth of net foreign assets is significant in the short-term resident official sector and deposit money banks; in both cases it has positive effect. Deposit money banks are risk takers for short-term flows as the resident official sector appears to be for long-term flows. Short-term flows, in general, seem to be more sensitive, as measured by the relative magnitude of their coefficients, to current balances than are long-term flows. The resident official sector seems to provide a balancing edge to the deposit money banks flows. There seems to be a great deal of noise and volatility in the movements of other short-term flows; Eq. (S.8) is still quite weak.

Equation (S.9) together with its counterpart (S.9′) for capital flow items listed as errors and omissions is basically an allocation equation by type of flows and by countries. In addition to the stock effect of change in yield component and growth effect of foreign assets, the resident official long-term sector (ROL) seems to account for the largest portion of error. Similarly, net capital flows of the U.K. seem to make the largest contribution towards error, followed successively by Germany and the U.S.

A brief review of our preliminary results presented above clearly proves that a disaggregation of capital flows is a promising route to follow. Substantial differences seem to exist in the sensitivity of various categories of capital flows as measured primarily by the relative magnitude of their marginal coefficients, and also by the direction of their responses.

This brings us to the final equation (S.12) which measures the adjustment behavior of foreign exchange market and determines the exchange rate. Some of its features are quite noteworthy. Nearby all its structural coefficients are statistically significant and have *a priori* consistent signs. The equation fares quite well when compared to exchange rate estimates reported in some recent studies.[15] Its two most important highlights are: First, by and large, exchange rate gyrations are basically determined by long-term flows. The resident official sector in conjunction with other long-term flows, and errors and omissions (which themselves are subject to long-term variables as is evident in Eq. (S.9)) play an important role in affecting these gyrations. Second, the coefficient of spread between domestic and foreign inflation rates is not close to unity. The equation seems to indicate that even if foreign exchange markets operated perfectly and efficiently, unencumbered by resident official flows and without any disruptions due to unaccounted errors and omissions such that $GNFA = 0$, the movements of a fully flexible exchange rate will somewhat overshoot the path of a differential in inflation rates at home and abroad. Any inherent tendency for the purchasing power parity relation to hold seems to get obstructed in the short run by the speculative activity in the forward market.[16]

Parenthetically, we may also add that although Eq. (S.12) has no seeming resemblance to the exchange rate relationship derived from the monetary model, it does implicitly incorporate an effect of any change in money supply caused by the growth of foreign reserves. The growth of foreign reserves as we have already seen in Eq. (1), unless sterilized, would affect the monetary base, money supply and finally the interest rate.

We may close the discussion of statistical estimates by saying that our equation by equation preliminary results seem to be quite promising. However, the final test would be to see how the model as a whole tracks the past data and helps in future predictions. We need to see how it functions as a simultaneous system and, eventually, how it fits into the $LINK$ model.[17]

4. A Simulation Test

The model was simulated block by block separately for each country for the 1973–1979 sample period, and post sample predictions were obtained for 1980. In solving the model, the yield variable μdHS was assumed to be exogenously known. Moreover, except for the U.K. model, total capital flows were also fixed exogenously

---

[15]See, for example, Hacche and Townend (1981a) and Klein, Fardoust, and Filatov (1981).

[16]It may be mentioned that our exchange rate equation (S.12) was reestimated without the unitary constraint on the $GNFA$ variable. A number of alternative values were selected for this coefficient from a range of values from 0.75 to 2.5 in small steps. But the $GNFA$ variable with unitary coefficient yielded the most meaningful results.

[17]It may be noted that our system may appear unstable, as the sum of the coefficients of $GNFA$ in our structural equations exceeds unity ($OLS : 1.226, GLS : 1.0998$). However, in any stability analysis one would have to include all the chain effects as well. For example, in our equation (S.3) for ROL, in addition to the positive coefficient of $GNFA$ (0.0321), we have a negative chain component, $(\partial ROL/\partial DIN)/(\partial DIN/\partial GNFA) = -0.0061$. Altogether, there are six such components in the capital flow equations. Some of these components are negative and some are positive. Adding these components to direct coefficients we get a new sum which is less than unity, $OLS : 0.954$, and $GLS : 0.921$. Calculations have been presented in the Appendix Table 4.

at their actual values, and the error and omission component was determined as a residual through the aggregate capital flow identity. Consequently, the structural equation (S.9) was suppressed in these models. For the U.K. model, however, both *ERO* and total capital flows were endogenously determined as specified in the basic model structure.

The final solution for the exchange rate ε_{iSD} for each country has been presented in Table 2. These solutions show that the performance of the system in tracking the actual exchange rate is reasonably well except in the case of U.K. for the earlier years. However, in the initial solutions the system was found to be particularly volatile for 1973 and 1975. If once it got away from the track, large errors in the predictions for subsequent years were observed. Therefore, occasionally degree of "add factoring" became necessary to prevent the occurrence of a runaway solution or to make the system converge. The primary reason behind such adjustments was that large revisions in the data had taken place since our initial estimates. These revisions were far from systematic. To accommodate these revisions in simulations, some adjustment factors (*AF*) were added to the estimated equations. These factors wherever utilized have been shown in the Appendix Table 1 which summarizes the assumptions underlying our simulations.

Furthermore, the capital flows, specifically for the U.K., were found to be extremely volatile. Large outflows in one period were followed by large inflows in the next. Not surprisingly, the model as estimated above did not always converge. Thus, we examined systematically and carefully the residuals of each equation, year by year, and found a great deal of noise. We roughly marked the dates for which the residuals were "abnormally" high and labelled them as the years of "abnormally" high or "abnormally" low level of activity. A year was identified as of "abnormally" high level of activity when we highly underestimated the capital flow component in question and of low level when we overestimated it. Thus two dummy variables, H (high) and L (low), using unitary value for years of "abnormal" activity and zero everywhere else were introduced in each equation and the whole model was reestimated. Such a procedure helped to remove a large degree of unexplained noise from the relationships. The coefficients of H and L dummies as expected turned out to be extremely significant in each equation. Similarly $\overline{R}^2$s and t-ratios were highly improved. However, the values of other structural coefficients did not change much. The reestimated system with H_i and L_i dummies has been presented in the Appendix Table 2, and H_i and L_i dates with their numerical definitions have been listed in the Appendix Table 3. The U.K. solution is based on this newly estimated system.[18]

---

[18]The solutions for other countries were also obtained on the basis of the reestimated new system. However, no systematic improvement was observed in these cases. Because of the large magnitudes of H_i and L_i coefficients we frequently ended up by overcompensating for the years of abnormal level of activity. By and large, the values of these coefficients are dominated by the level of activity in the U.K.

Table 2. Actual and estimated values of ε_{iSD}, national currency units per *SDR*.

	Canada (c$)			France (franc)			Germany (D Mark)		
	Actual	Estimated	% Error	Actual	Estimated	% Error	Actual	Estimated	% Error
1973	1.201	1.148	4.6	5.679	5.680	-0.2	3.261	3.006	8.5
1974	1.214	1.203	0.9	5.442	5.054	7.7	2.950	2.249	31.2
1975	1.190	1.223	-2.7	5.251	5.424	-3.2	3.070	2.524	21.6
1976	1.172	1.383	-15.26	5.774	5.305	8.8	2.745	2.750	-0.18
1977	1.329	1.284	3.5	5.715	5.895	-3.05	2.557	2.767	-7.6
1978	1.545	1.551	-0.4	5.446	5.227	4.2	2.381	2.745	-13.3
1979	1.540	1.576	-2.3	5.296	5.236	1.15	2.228	2.422	-8.0
1980 P	1.524	1.587	-3.8	5.760	5.826	-1.13	2.498	2.271	10.0

	Japan (Yen)			U.K. (£)			U.S. ($)		
	Actual	Estimated	% Error	Actual	Estimated	% Error	Actual	Estimated	% Error
1973	337.78	313.07	7.9	0.5193	0.5142	0.99	1.206	1.377	-12.4
1974	368.47	394.06	-6.5	0.5213	0.6933	-24.8	1.224	1.015	20.6
1975	357.23	368.51	-3.06	0.5785	0.3116	85.6	1.171	1.397	-16.2
1976	340.18	319.73	6.4	0.6285	0.5579	12.6	1.162	1.084	7.2
1977	291.53	300.61	-3.0	0.6373	1.0084	-36.8	1.215	1.219	-0.3
1978	253.52	252.09	0.56	0.6403	0.3804	68.3	1.303	1.442	-9.6
1979	315.76	297.01	6.3	0.5923	0.6297	-5.9	1.317	1.322	-0.38
1980 P	258.91	291.05	-11.0	0.5348	0.5817	-8.1	1.275	1.275	0

P: Post-sample predictions.

Based on our *a priori* judgment and empirical testing, we may conclude our analysis by saying that our experiment with the structural approach through disaggregated capital flows has been quite useful and revealing. It seems to provide a promising venue for predicting the exchange rate, especially in the short run, but we shall have to improve our ability to explain capital flows in order to determine exchange rate movements. This paper is only the start of a lengthy research process.

Appendix

Appendix Table 1. Underlying simulation assumptions.

Note: In all models except for the U.K., CAB/NFA_{-1} is assumed to be exogenous, and ERO is determined as a residual from the aggregate capital flow identity. In the U.K. model, ERO is determined from the structural equation, and CAB is obtained by summing up the components.

All assumptions with respect to capital flows are in terms of normalised flows, e. g., capital flows divided by NFA_{-1}.

Canada:

(a) ROL (1973) and PIN (1974) are fixed exogenously at actual values.
(b) Through the use of AFs from prior solution, the 1975 solution is forced close to the actual track.
(c) Revised data for CUB and CAB are used for 1978–1979. Data revision adjustments in ERO for 1976–1980 are made through $AF9$ (adjustment factor in Eq. (S.9)).
(d) $AF5$ (1980) $= 0.10$ (e.g., change in RL in 1980 over computed RL in 1979 is assumed close to the actual change in RL).

France:

(a) The 1973 solution is forced close to the actual track through AFs and thereafter up to 1979, $AF12 = 0.24$ (AF for rate of change in market pressure equation).
(b) DBL (1978) is exogenous.
(c) There is a data revision adjustment in ERO through $AF9$ for 1979–1980. Revised data for CUB and CAB for 1979.

Germany:

(a) $AF12 = 0.1347$.
(b) An additional functional factor in $\dot{\varepsilon}_{iSD}$ is based on the residuals in direct investment as $\dot{\varepsilon}_{iSD} = \cdots + 0.13476 - 1.9122(DIN - D\hat{I}N)$, where ˆ denotes estimated value.
(c) Revised CUB and CAB values are for 1978–1979.

Japan:

(a) ERO is a residual and changes in the exchange rate equation together with AF are $\hat{\varepsilon}_{iSD} = \cdots + 0.03307 + 1.6648(ERO - E\hat{R}O) + 0.1302(\hat{\dot{\varepsilon}}_{iSD} - \dot{\varepsilon}_{iSD})_{-1}$
(b) $AF12$ (1978) $= 0.22127$, (1977, 1978) $= -0.06$.

U.K.:

(a) The model structure includes high and low activity dates dummies.
(b) Revised data are used for CUB.
(c) The 1973 solution is forced close to the track.

U.S.:

(a) Revised data for CUB and CAB are for 1978 and 1979.
(b) $AF9$ (1980) $= 0.5399$ to allow for actual change in ERO over the computed 1979 value.

Appendix Table 2. Ordinary least square estimates inclusive of H_i and L_i dummies.

	DIN^l	PIN^s	ROL^l	DBL^l	RL^l	ROS^s	DBS^s	RS^s	ERO^l
Intercept	−0.07246	0.42479	−0.05557	−0.01674	−0.000019	−0.001814	−0.04904	−0.07128	−0.4954
	(3.82)	(9.59)	(8.23)	(1.65)	(0.002)	(0.07)	(1.47)	(4.14)	(7.72)
$GNFA$	−0.0535	0.3112	0.03032		0.1237	0.1697	0.21194		0.4205
	(5.39)	(8.57)	(4.22)		(13.22)	(6.21)	(9.61)		(10.12)
$\mu dHS/\varepsilon_{iSD}$	0.05777	0.2349		0.05933		0.09564			
	(6.175)	(0.68)		(3.20)		(2.13)			
$\Delta\mu dHS/\varepsilon_{iSD}$		−0.10166	0.06112	−0.10265	0.12317	−0.17312			0.02161
		(1.78)	(7.19)	(7.33)	(10.8)	(3.62)			(0.43)
$\varepsilon_{iSD} - (\dot{p}_i - \dot{p}_c)$	−0.12727								
	(1.19)								
CUB/NFA_{-1}		−0.3594			−0.09596	−0.2820	−0.35653		
		(6.55)			(8.11)	(6.56)	(7.9)		
σ	−0.00261^r	−0.1543	0.04838	−0.0645	−0.04749		0.1791	0.0392	−1.3111 ROL
	(0.76)	(3.05)	(4.83)	(4.17)	(3.49)		(3.82)	(1.7)	(2.75)
z			0.0909		−0.31344	−0.4801	−0.6966	0.00440	−0.64532 DIN
			(4.77)		(6.78)	(8.31)	(8.58)	(0.16)	(2.74)
D_F	0.1144	−0.4171		−0.2500			0.13718	0.68945	0.4144
	(4.34)	(6.39)		(13.42)			(5.05)	(8.32)	(5.18)
D_G	0.0319	−0.30584						0.0453	0.3020
	(1.226)	(5.57)						(1.67)	(3.83)
D_J	−0.01468	−0.30584	−0.04606		−0.03654	0.1093	0.0902	0.1020	0.5074
	(0.556)	(5.57)	(4.09)		(2.30)	(2.38)	(1.55)	(3.64)	(4.48)
$D_{U.K.}$	−0.4589	−0.30584	0.1100	−0.07729	0.2666	0.1543			0.2576
	(17.24)	(5.57)	(8.05)	(1.72)	(13.9)	(1.646)			(1.89)
$D_{U.S.}$				−0.06629		0.03123			
				(3.58)		(0.667)			
H_i	0.1602	0.6609	0.07307	0.1511	0.11978	0.41276	0.2666	0.2381	0.5158
	(5.09)	(7.9)	(5.96)	(6.83)	(6.17)	(5.89)	(4.95)	(6.78)	(5.06)
L_i	−0.2057	−0.2864	−0.0897	−0.13485	−0.1077	−0.38678	−0.3178	−0.1362	−0.4197
	(6.69)	(1.86)	(6.61)	(6.24)	(6.07)	(6.76)	(5.18)	(2.85)	(4.11)
$\overline{R}^2$	0.96	0.91	0.94	0.90	0.98	0.86	0.89	0.66	0.92

Note: z for ROL: DIN, for RL: DBL, for ROS: DBS, for DBS: ROS, for RS: DBS; l: using long-term interest rate, s: using short-term interest rate, r: ratio of σ to yield variable.

Appendix Table 3. Years of high and low capital flows.

Captial flows	H (high)	L (low)
(DIN/NFA_{-1}) Residuals $> |0.10|$	1972 (Canada) 1979 (U.K.) 1974 (U.S.) 1978 (U.S.)	1978 (Canada) 1976 (U.K.) 1975 (U.S.) 1979 (U.S.)
(PIN/NFA_{-1}) Residuals $> |0.30|$	1976 (Canada) 1976 (U.K.) 1972 (U.S.) 1977 (U.S.)	1978 (U.S.)
(ROL/NFA_{-1}) Residuals $> |0.05|$	1987 (Canada) 1979 (Canada) 1975 (Germany) 1976 (Germany) 1974 (U.K.) 1976 (U.S.)	1974 (Canada) 1979 (France) 1973 (U.K.) 1972 (U.S.) 1979 (U.S.)
(DBL/NFA_{-1}) Residuals $> |0.10|$	1972 (France) 1973 (France) 1979 (Germany) 1977 (Japan) 1979 (U.S.)	1975 (Canada) 1978 (France) 1975 (Germany) 1979 (Japan) 1976 (U.K.)
(RL/NFA_{-1}) Residuals $> |0.075|$	1975 (Canada) 1973 (Germany) 1976 (U.K.) 1975 (U.S.)	1977 (Canada) 1975 (France) 1979 (U.K.) 1974 (U.S.) 1976 (U.S.)
$ROS/NFA_{-1})$ Residuals $> |0.20|$	1978 (Canada) 1974 (U.S.) 1978 (U.S.)	1975 (Canada) 1977 (France) 1976 (U.K.) 1979 (U.S.)
(DBS/NFA_{-1}) Residuals $> |0.20|$	1978 (Canada) 1979 (Canada) 1978 (Germany) 1978 (Japan) 1973 (U.K.) 1973 (U.S.) 1974 (U.S.)	1974 (Canada) 1976 (Canada) 1977 (France) 1972 (Japan) 1976 (U.K.) 1975 (U.S.) 1976 (U.S.)
(RS/NFA_{-1}) Residuals $> |0.10|$	1974 (Canada) 1976 (Canada) 1979 (Canada) 1975 (U.K.)	1975 (Japan) 1976 (U.K.)
(ERO/NFA_{-1}) Residuals $> |0.30|$	1973 (Canada) 1976 (U.S.) 1978 (U.S.) 1979 (U.S.)	1976 (Canada) 1972 (U.S.) 1973 (U.S.) 1977 (U.S.)

Appendix Table 4. GNFA coefficients in capital-flow equations.

	OLS		GLS	
	Direct	Chain	Direct	Chain
DIN	−0.0521		−0.0724	
PIN	+0.3264		+0.3212	
ROL	+0.03214	+ 0.1171	+0.03486	0.09784
		(−0.0521)		(−0.0724)
DBL	0		0	
RL	+0.1238		+0.1174	
ROS	+0.1907	− 0.5083	+0.1477	− 0.2991
		(0.2183)		(0.2332)
DBS	+0.2183	− 0.7096	+0.2332	− 0.6824
		(0.1907)		(0.1477)
RS	0	+ 0.0198	0	+ 0.0097
		(0.2183)		(0.2332)
ERO	+0.3865	− 1.536	+0.3178	− 1.0061
		(0.03214)		(0.03486)
		− 0.4939		− 0.4428
		(−0.0521)		(−0.0724)
SUM	1.2257	−0.2716	1.09976	−0.1784
		0.9541		0.9214

References

Amano, A., A. Sadahiro, and T. Sasaki, 1981, "Structure and application of the EPA world economic model," discussion paper No. 22, Economic Research Institute, Economic Planning Agency, Tokyo; prepared for the Annual Meeting of Project LINK, August 31–September 4, La Hulpe, Belgium.

Ball, R. J. and T. Burns, 1979, "Long run portfolio equilibrium and balance-of-payments adjustment in econometric models," in *Modelling the International Transmission Mechanism*, ed. J. A. Sawyer (Amsterdam), pp. 311–345.

Black, S. W., 1977, *Floating Exchange Rates and National Economic Policy* (New Haven, Conn.).

Branson, W. H., 1968, *Financial Capital Flows in the U.S. Balance of Payments* (Amsterdam).

———, 1970, "Monetary policy and the new view of international capital movements," *Brooking Papers on Economic Activity*, pp. 235–270.

Bryant, R. C., 1975, "Empirical research on financial capital flows," in *International Trade and Finance*, ed. P. B. Kenen (New York), pp. 321–362.

Genberg, A. H., 1976, "Aspects of the monetary approach to balance of payments theory. An empirical study of Sweden," in *The Monetary Approach to the Balance of Payments*, eds. J. A. Frenkel and H. G. Johnson (London), pp. 298–325.

Girton, L. and D. Roper, 1977, "A monetary model of exchange market pressure applied to the postwar Canadian experience," *American Economic Review* **67**, pp. 537–548.

Hacche, G. and J. C. Townend, 1981a, "Exchange rates and monetary policy: Modelling Sterling's effective exchange rate, 1972–80," in *The Money Supply and the Exchange Rate (Oxford Economic Papers, N.S. **33**, Supplementum)*, eds. W. A. Eltis and P. J. N. Sinclair (Oxford), pp. 201–247.

——— and J. C. Townend, 1981b, "Monetary models of exchange rates and exchange market pressure: Some general limitations and an application to Sterling's effective rate," *Weltwirtschaftlichs Archiv* **117**, pp. 622–637.

Helliwell, J. F., 1979, "Policy modeling of foreign exchange rates," *Journal of Policy Modeling* **1**, pp. 425–444.

Isard, P., 1978, "Exchange rate determination; a survey of popular views and recent models," *Princeton Studies in International Finance*, No. 42 (Princeton University, Princeton, N.J.).

1978, *Journal of International Economics* **8**, May (Symposium on Purchasing Power Parity).

Klein, L. R., S. Fardoust and V. Filatov, 1981, "Purchasing power parity in medium term simulation of the world economy," *Scandinavian Journal of Economics* **83**, pp. 479–496.

Kouri, P. J. K., 1975, "The hypothesis of offsetting capital flows: A Case Study of Germany," *Journal of Monetary Economics* **1**, pp. 21–39.

——— and M. G. Porter, 1974, "International capital flows and portfolio equilibrium," *Journal of Political Economy* **82**, pp. 443–467.

Kreinin, M. and L. H. Officer, 1978, "The monetary approach to the balance of payments: A Survey," *Princeton Studies in International Finance*, No. 43 (Princeton University, Princeton, N.J.).

Krelle, W. E., K. Conrad, G. Grisse, and J. Martiensen, 1979, "The effects of foreign monetary impulses and of fiscal and monetary policy changes on the German economy: Simulation with the Bonn forecasting system," in *Modelling the International Transmission Mechanism*, ed. J. A. Sawyer (Amsterdam), pp. 347–385.

Leamer, E. E. and R. M. Stern, 1970, *Quantitative International Economics* (Boston, Mass.).

Lybeck, J. A. , J. Häggström, and B. Järnhäll, 1979, "An empirical comparison of four models of capital flows: OLS and 2 SLS estimations of the Branson, Genberg, Kouri and Lybeck models," in *Modelling the International Transmission Mechanism*, ed. J. A. Sawyer (Amsterdam), pp. 387–412.

——— and B. Järnhäll, 1979, "A simultaneous model of capital flows, exchange rates, interest rates and prices of traded goods: Theoretical considerations and estimation by alternative techniques," Paper presented at a Conference on Monetary and Financial Models, Banca d'Italia, Rome.

Magee, S. P., 1976, "The empirical evidence on the monetary approach to the balance of payments and exchange rates," *American Economic Review* **66**, *Papers and Proceedings*, pp. 163–170.

Marwah, K., 1979, "Towards money, output and prices: A capacity view of inflation (MOP-CAP)," *Empirical Economics* **3**, pp. 1–29.

―――― and L. R. Klein, 1982, "Modeling foreign exchange markets: International capital flows and exchange rates," Unpublished Mimeo, LINK Center, Philadelphia, Penn.

―――― , L. R. Klein, and R. G. Bodkin, 1983, "Bilateral capital flows and the exchange rate: The case of the U.S.A. vis-a-vis Canada, France, West Germany and the U.K.," Paper presented at the 17th Annual Meeting of the Canadian Economic Association, Vancouver, B.C., June 4. [It was published later in 1985, *European Economic Review* **29**.]

Officer, L. H., 1968, "An econometric model of Canada under the fluctuating exchange rate," *Harvard Economic Studies* **130** (Cambridge, Mass.).

―――― , 1976, "Purchasing-power-parity theory of exchange rates: A review article," *International Monetary Fund Staff Papers* **23**, pp. 1–60.

Rhomberg, R. R., 1964, "A model of the Canadian economy under fixed and fluctuating exchange rates," *Journal of Political Economy* **72**, pp. 1–31.

Schadler, S., 1977, "Sources of exchange rate variability: Theory and empirical evidence," *International Monetary Fund Staff Papers* **24**, pp. 253–296.

Whitman, M. v. N., 1975, "Global monetarism and the monetary approach to the balance of payments," *Brookings Papers on Economic Activity*, pp. 491–536.

30

GLOBAL MONETARISM[†]

The name of Colin Clark, as a pioneer in quantitative economics and econometrics, was known to me from the very first studies that I took up in economics, more than 45 years ago. But one of the most impressive comments was in a periodic survey of economic and financial literature sent out by the Federal Reserve Board, where Colin Clark was described as a statistician who did creative work where other, more cautious, professionals feared to tread. I have often thought about that comment whenever I have felt the urge to work on a problem for which there was, of necessity, a weak and obscure data base. I have always aspired to be as creative as Colin Clark in distilling scholarly truths from poor and obscure data.

For this chapter, I have undertaken a measurement task which is, I fear, worthy of Colin Clark. Does the monetarist model prevail on a world scale? The equations of the quantity theory of money have often been estimated for individual countries, covering an entire domestic economy. It is my intention to investigate whether some versions of the main equation for the world as a whole, or for very strategic groupings of countries, hold.

It is quite simplistic to think about something as complicated as the modern economy through the medium of a simple bi-variate relationship

$$M(\$) = \left(\frac{1}{v}\right) GNP(\$) e$$

where $M(\$)$ = nominal stock of cash balance (money)
v = velocity
$GNP(\$)$ = nominal value of GNP
e = error

The *crude* quantity theory is based on this equation, under the hypothesis that v is a *parameter*. It might be claimed that v follows a smooth trend and therefore departs from constancy. Try as they may, however, monetarists' theory and policies do not stand up well in the face of variable and fluctuating velocity.

[†]From *National Income and Economic Progress, Essays in Honour of Colin Clark*, eds. D. Iron-monger, J. O. N. Perkins, and Tran van Hoa (Macmillan, London, 1988), pp. 168–176.

What may have seemed to have been a steady dependable trend for velocity has suddenly fallen apart in one country after another.[1] For non-monetarists, this result is to be expected. Hardly any such simple relationships stand up well, over long stretches of time, in economics.

On a previous occasion, I examined the data series generated by the non-stochastic long-run simulation of the Wharton Model, which I know, by design, to be non-monetarist.[2] Nevertheless, I addressed the question of whether the simple quantity equation of monetarism held. The generated data indicated that the relationship did hold. But, no causal significance should be attached to this statistical relationship because it was generated by data that are known not to satisfy the postulates of monetarism.

In a similar spirit of investigation, although not with generated data — rather with actual data — I want to look at world money supply and world GNP to see if they happen to satisfy the equation in question. As in the case of the simulated data series, a relationship that does apparently seem to hold on a global basis should not by virtue of that fact alone be given a causal interpretation.

The equation in question breaks down for individual country data, but when we 'dare to tread' into the realm of shaky noisy data we may find more robustness and results that are, in fact, statistically stable when aggregated over many countries, together. There might be significant error cancellation across countries.

The specification and measurement options make some decisions necessary. Of all the possible definitions of $M_i(\$), i = 0, 1, 2, \ldots$, data are available for measuring M_1 or M_2 velocity.

$$\frac{GNP(\$)}{M_1(\$)} \quad \text{or} \quad \frac{GNP(\$)}{M_2(\$)} \quad \ldots$$

These are defined in the *International Financial Statistics* published by the International Monetary Fund as the ratio of nominal GNP in each country to the sum of currency outside banks and private demand deposits (M_1) and to the sum of M_1 and time, savings, and foreign deposits (M_2). In this terminology M_1 is *money* and M_2 is *money* plus *quasi-money*. M_2 velocity is directly available as an index number, while M_1 velocity is computed from the rate of change of GNP ($\$$) minus the rate of change of M_1 ($\$$).

Since the main issue concerning global monetarism is whether velocity is a constant or a variable, the *approach* in this chapter will be to examine the statistical significance of a particular variable concept of velocity, namely, the existence of a relationship between velocity and interest rate.

For a world interest rate, two well-known alternatives have been used, the Eurodollar rate and the U.S. treasury bill rate. The money, GNP, and velocity

---

[1] R. De Vries, "Global capital markets: Issues and implications," paper presented to the Wallenberg Forum, Washington, DC, 2 October (1986).

[2] L. R. Klein, "Money in a general equilibrium system: Empirical aspects of the quantity theory," *Economie Appliquée*, **31** (1978) pp. 5–14.

measures are all in denominations of U.S. dollars; therefore a dollar rate was used for consistency.

Both the Keynesian liquidity preference theory and Kalecki's J-curve for velocity challenge the monetarist position. They both say, in general terms, that velocity is not a parameter; it is a variable that depends on the interest rate. There may be other senses in which velocity is a variable, or not a stable parameter. Other explanatory variables besides interest rates may account for velocity fluctuations, but on a global scale data are most readily available for internationally recognised interest rates.

Four macro-correlations are reported here for industrial countries alone and for the world[3]:

Industrial Countries

$$\Delta V_2 = -0.58 \ + 0.41 \ \Delta r_E \qquad\qquad \bar{r}^2 = 0.11 \quad DW = 1.97$$
$$ (1.78) \quad (2.02)$$

$$\Delta V_2 = -0.60 \ + 0.44 \ \Delta r_T \qquad\qquad \bar{r}^2 = 0.16 \quad DW = 1.61$$
$$ (1.87) \quad (2.37)$$

$$\Delta \ln V_2 = -0.0064 + 0.044 \, \Delta \ln r_E \qquad \bar{r}^2 = 0.15 \quad DW = 1.93$$
$$ (1.97) \qquad (2.29)$$

$$\Delta \ln V_2 = -0.0062 + 0.034 \, \Delta \ln r_T \qquad \bar{r}^2 = 0.14 \quad DW = 1.47$$
$$ (1.91) \qquad (2.22)$$

World

$$\Delta V_2 = -0.82 \ + 0.39 \ \Delta r_E \qquad\qquad \bar{r}^2 = 0.12 \quad DW = 2.16$$
$$ (2.71) \quad (2.09)$$

$$\Delta V_2 = -0.83 \ + 0.41 \ \Delta r_T \qquad\qquad \bar{r}^2 = 0.16 \quad DW = 1.95$$
$$ (2.81) \quad (2.37)$$

$$\Delta \ln V_2 = -0.0085 + 0.040 \, \Delta \ln r_E \qquad \bar{r}^2 = 0.15 \quad DW = 2.11$$
$$ (2.88) \qquad (2.28)$$

$$\Delta \ln V_2 = -0.0084 + 0.032 \, \Delta \ln r_T \qquad \bar{r}^2 = 0.15 \quad DW = 1.80$$
$$ (2.85) \qquad (2.29)$$

These equations should be read in the usual way. The figures in parentheses, under the estimated coefficients, are t-ratios. The simple correlation coefficients are adjusted for degrees of freedom ($\bar{r}^2$), and DW stands for the Durbin–Watson ratio.

For V_1, an index of the level of velocity is not separately published, but data on the percentage change in M_1 are available. The approximation on the left-hand

---

[3]Industrial countries and world designations are used in the IMF sense. "Industrial countries" corresponds almost exactly to the membership of the OECD, and "world" adds the developing countries to the industrial countries. Non-members of the IMF are not included. There are also some countries from which data are not available. Annual data for the years 1960 to 1984 have been used.

side:

$$\frac{\Delta GNP}{GNP} - \frac{\Delta M_1}{M_1} \sim \Delta \ln V_1$$

is used in place of $\Delta \ln V_1$. The results are:

Industrial Countries

$$\frac{\Delta V_1}{V_1} = \underset{(3.10)}{0.0164} + \underset{(0.77)}{0.0240 \, \Delta \ln r_E} \qquad\qquad \bar{r}^2 = 0.017 \quad DW = 1.61$$

$$\frac{\Delta V_1}{V_1} = \underset{(3.14)}{0.0151} + \underset{(2.30)}{0.0532 \, \Delta \ln r_T} \qquad\qquad \bar{r}^2 = 0.15 \quad DW = 1.46$$

World

$$\frac{\Delta V_1}{V_1} = \underset{(4.61)}{0.0144} + \underset{(2.29)}{0.0425 \, \Delta \ln r_E} \qquad\qquad \bar{r}^2 = 0.15 \quad DW = 1.85$$

$$\frac{\Delta V_1}{V_1} = \underset{(4.78)}{0.0144} + \underset{(2.76)}{0.0397 \, \Delta \ln r_T} \qquad\qquad \bar{r}^2 = 0.22 \quad DW = 1.72$$

Except for the extremely low (absence of) correlation between V_1 and the Eurodollar rate in the industrial countries, these results have similar statistics and coefficients with the corresponding V_2 correlations. It should be noted, however, that the constant terms in the first-difference equations are positive for V_1 and negative for V_2, implying opposite trend effects.

The charts of changes in velocity (Figs. 1 to 4) show that, on the whole, M_1 velocity has positive percentage change, while M_2 velocity has mainly negative change over the sample period.

There is not much to choose from among these eight estimated equations for V_2; they all tell a similar story, namely that V_2 and r are correlated. The correlation is not high, but it is significant. The data enable one to make a plausible case that velocity is not a constant, but a variable that depends on interest rates. The same rate is used for the industrial country and the world regressions because either rate used is representative of charges for financial capital throughout the world.

The fact that the equations are expressed in first differences, either as arithmetic or logarithmic changes, is not of unusual significance. It merely gets us, in a simple way, towards white-noise residuals. The reason for using first differences instead of levels is purely statistical, that is, we have a transformation that, in the main, gets rid of serial correlation in the residuals. The fact that constant terms are included and that they are nearly always significant is important, for these terms indicate that (V_2) velocity follows a declining trend, as well as the fluctuations in interest rates. Correspondingly, (V_1) velocity follows a positive trend.

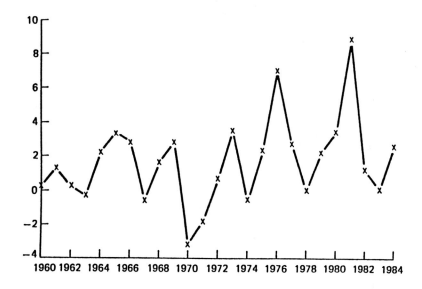

Fig. 1. Velocity of money, industrial countries.

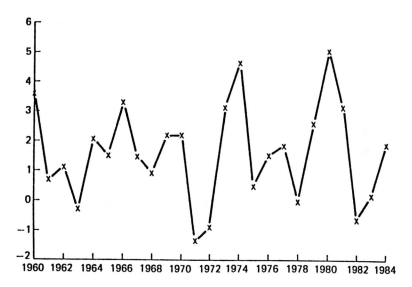

Fig. 2. Velocity of money, world.

There is not much to choose between the arithmetic and logarithmic versions. Velocity and interest rates are already scaled; they are both ratio-magnitudes; therefore the use of percentage changes in these variables instead of arithmetic changes is not of great consequence. Also there is very little difference between the estimate for industrial countries and for the whole world, except that the constant term has higher *t*-ratios in the total world case.

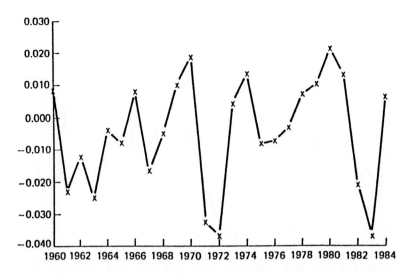

Fig. 3. Velocity of money and quasi-money, industrial countries.

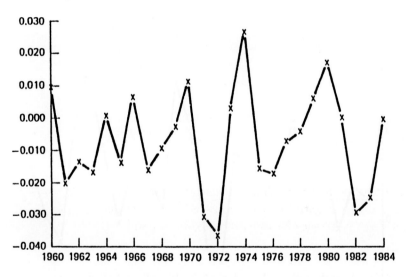

Fig. 4. Velocity of money and quasi-money, world.

A number of experimental calculations have also been made. They indicate that correlating of levels rather than changes does not tell us much. The level form equations often have insignificant negative coefficients of the interest rate term. Also the Durbin–Watson statistics suggest that there is great serial correlation in the residuals from the type of equation. The estimates of the first difference transformation are to be preferred to the others. A deeper exploration of the lag structure and consideration of wealth, debt, inflation, and other variables should be rewarding.

An examination of correlations with real, instead of nominal, interest rates does not reveal any results as good as those listed above. They have mainly insignificant coefficients and even lower values of $\bar{r}^2$. These findings are confirmed by analysis of U.S. data alone, on velocity and interest rates. The nominal rate correlates well with velocity, while the real rate does not.

Velocity measurement with M_2 is more stable than with M_1, yet M_1 is more controllable, at the hands of monetary authorities, than is M_2. This poses a dilemma for monetarists. Should they use the more stable concept (after all, they truly want a steady parameter for V) or the money concept most closely linked to central bank policy? I would argue for the more stable velocity and let money supply be endogenous. In this chapter, only M_1 and M_2 are separately considered. Benjamin Friedman has looked at a much wider U.S. spectrum for M_i and concludes that those with a higher-order subscript tend to be more closely related to GNP (in other words, provide the most stable values for V) but are harder to control through the usual channels of monetary policy.[4]

The *International Financial Statistics* data show:

Industrial Countries

$$\text{est. var.} \qquad \frac{\Delta V_1}{V_1} = 0.000609$$

$$\text{est. var.} \qquad \Delta \ln V_2 = 0.000271$$

World

$$\text{est. var.} \qquad \frac{\Delta V_1}{V_1} = 0.00026$$

$$\text{est. var.} \qquad \Delta \ln V_2 = 0.000226$$

It appears that variability of V_2 is much smaller than that of V_1 for the industrial countries and only slightly smaller for the world as a whole. In general, however, there is a slight preference for using the broader concept.

---

[4]Benjamin Friedman, "Relative stability of money and credit "velocities" in the United States: Evidence and some speculations," NBER working paper 645, 1981; also summarised in "The role of money and credit in macroeconomic analysis," in *Macroeconomics, Prices and Quantities*, ed. J. Tobin (Brookings, Washington, D.C., 1983), pp. 161–99.

31

RESTRUCTURING OF THE WORLD ECONOMY[†]

Scope and Meaning of Restructuring

There is a great deal of economic change taking place now in the world economy. New kinds of jobs are becoming available; new industries are being created; the combination of production, consumption, and trade is changing; markets are unsettled; and economic policies are shifting. There is no doubt that economic change has always occurred. It would be difficult to say that today's changes are more significant, for example, than the changes associated with the industrial revolution, the fall of the gold standard, or many other momentous economic events in history, but today's changes are here — upon us — and we must appreciate them and understand why they are occurring in order to deal with them.

In short historical perspective, it is convenient to start with the end of World War II. In the late 1940s and the 1950s, the main problem was reconstruction of the damage. There followed a period of great expansion, together with a reentry of Germany and Japan into the mainstream (eventually shared leadership) of the world economy. The United States had to play the key leadership role for several years. Now it is shared, a development that, in itself, has created imbalances requiring an adjustment process in which restructuring takes place on a large scale.

The Third World has seen enormous but very uneven development in this period. If Japan may be taken as an example of a country that moved from less to fully developed status (starting with admission to the Organization for European Cooperation and Development [OECD] membership in 1964), then we may note that other developing countries want to emulate Japan. This requires a great deal of restructuring, both in the internal economic makeup of the countries concerned and in the composition of world trade. A fundamental aspect of the immediate postreconstruction stage was the liberalization and rapid expansion of world trade volume after the 1960s.

The World Bank estimates the growth rate of trade volume (exports) in two phases, 1965–73 and 1973–85 (see Table 2-1). The very rapid pace of expansion in the late 1960s came to a slowdown phase after the change in terms of trade

[†]From *International Productivity & Competitiveness,* ed. Bert G. Hickman (Copyright ©1992 by Oxford University Press, Inc.), pp. 33–48.

for energy products. World trade expansion is still a very important basis of the world economy, but it is considerably slower in this transition period of restructuring.

Table 2-1. Annual growth rate of world exports.[1]

| 1965–73 | 10.7% |
| 1973–85 | 5.3% |

[1]Industrial market economies and developing countries (including high-income oil exporters).

There are many ways to look at restructuring, for it has many dimensions. First, consider employment opportunities. American data are readily available, and they will be used, to a great extent, as indicators of the general process, but similar developments are occurring in many countries. From 1965, employment in the United States has declined significantly in manufacturing. The share has also declined in primary sectors but grown in services. In longer perspective, covering more than a hundred years, we have had no basic trend in the manufacturing share but offsetting gains and losses in the service and primary sectors, respectively.

On a world scale, agriculture has experienced a declining share between 1965 and 1980 in developing countries, but the *level* is very high, and the decline is modest. There is a sharp fall in the agricultural share in the industrial countries and also in the socialist countries (excluding China). The industrial share (including mining, construction, and utilities) went up in both the Third World and among socialist countries. The service share rose in all areas, not always through similar declines in the other sectors, but to a certain extent from a decline in the agricultural shares (see Table 2-2).

Table 2-2. Percentage distribution of labor force.

	Agriculture		Industry		Services	
	1965	1980	1956	1980	1965	1980
Developing countries	70	62	12	16	18	22
High-income oil exporters	58	35	15	21	28	44
Industrial market economies	14	7	38	35	48	58
Socialist economies	34	22	34	39	32	39

Jobs are shifting, and it is significant that the service category is gaining generally in relative importance. It is worthwhile to probe further into the nature and composition of job gains, especially in the service sector. This route is relatively easy to pursue with U.S. data, and since job expansion has recently been unusually large in the United States, it provides a very good base for looking at some important issues. Job expansion has been much more rapid in the United States than in Japan and major European countries since the late sixties. A great deal of this employment expansion in the United States has been in "service" as opposed to "goods" production. It is hard to make a clear separation because there is much service work in the goods sectors of the economy. Some of the reverse may take place as well, but the share of employment in the goods-producing sector now is about 25 percent, whereas at the end of World War II, it was more than 40 percent. The decline over four decades has been steady, with some cyclical variation, and has not accelerated during the present expansion. In the present expansion, beginning in late 1982, the rate of growth of services-producing jobs has been about 3.7 percent per annum. The corresponding figure of goods-producing jobs is only 1.8 percent.

An important issue is whether the strong expansion of jobs in services is mainly in undesirable or relatively attractive jobs. There is a false impression that the expansion is taking place in low-quality, low-paying service jobs that offer little future potential, especially for young employees. But services comprise a mixed group of activities. Zoltan Kenessey of the Federal Reserve Board makes the interesting distinction between tertiary and quaternary sectors. The former consists of transport, wholesale trade, and retail trade. The latter consists of finance, insurance, and real estate (services per se) along with government. Finance, insurance, and real estate offer some very attractive employment opportunities — perhaps carried to excess in 1987, but nevertheless still attractive. Government service should not be looked down upon. The services per se grouping contains both low-wage, dead-end jobs and technical jobs requiring high degrees of skill and education.

Looking at the matter from the point of view of median weekly wage, one report finds that the "high-wage" ($479/week) group accounted for almost 50 percent of employment growth during the expansion of 1983–87. The "middle-wage" ($322/week) group accounted for 42 percent of job growth, while the "low-wage" ($214/week) group accounted for only 8.2 percent (Leisenring, 1988). The important high-wage group included managerial, professional, technical, and highly skilled workers.

Immediately following the stock market crash of 1987, financial service jobs and production fell, but there is evidence that there will be some recovery in this area, and other service jobs were essentially unaffected.

In an interesting comment at a meeting of Project LINK (March 1988, United Nations, New York), N. Garganas of the Bank of Greece noted that U.S. job performance had been better than Europe's because of the degree of expansion that occurred in the service sector. He conjectured that Europe would eventually follow the American path, and that this would be a sensible way to bring down the persistently high unemployment rate in most European countries.

The concept of restructuring can also be examined from the production as well as the employment side. There are some interesting trends in the American data, and they have raised important technical issues (see Figs. 2-1 and 2-2). In *real* terms, the share of U.S. GNP that originates in the manufacturing sector has been

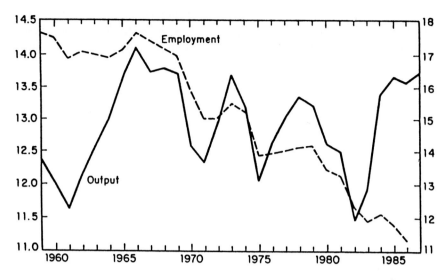

Fig. 2-1. Percent share of manufacturing durable goods in real GNP and total employment. *Source*: Bureau of Labor Statistics and Department of Commerce, Bureau of Economic Analysis.

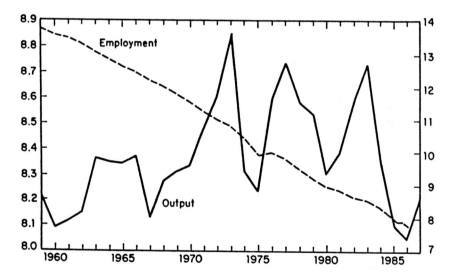

Fig. 2-2. Percent share of manufacturing nondurable goods in real GNP and total employment. *Source*: Bureau of Labor Statistics and Department of Commerce, Bureau of Economic Analysis.

remarkably steady. In 1982 prices, this share is about 20–22 percent, and it has been in this range for most of the period since the end of World War II. There is no apparent trend in the time series of official data whether for manufacturing as a whole or for durables and nondurables separately. In *current* prices, the share of total manufacturing has fallen from roughly 30 to 20 percent over four decades.

According to the data, which show approximately constant real shares, the falling employment shares imply that productivity is rising. In a sense, these data also suggest that the United States is not becoming deindustrialized; we are simply restructuring. Of course, the data can simply be interpreted as an interesting statistical constant showing a productivity gain that is not strong enough to overcome countertendencies toward lack of competitiveness. It will be noted in the next section that there is, indeed, evidence of declining competitiveness, even within the framework of these data on the constancy of the manufacturing shares.

If we enlarge the scope of the share statistics to encompass total goods production and not simply manufacturing production, we find that the real share of goods in GNP has fallen since 1950 by about 2–3 percentage points, but that the share has been very steady at about 43 percent since 1970 (Leisenring, 1988).

Value added is measured by the following formula:

$$\underset{\substack{\text{value} \\ \text{added}}}{\text{VA}} = \underset{\substack{\text{gross} \\ \text{output}}}{\text{GR}} - \underset{\substack{\text{intermediate} \\ \text{input}}}{I}$$

The controversy concerning measurement of the manufacturing share of real value added is based on several issues, the principal one being that real *intermediate* inputs that are subtracted from gross output to get value added are understated; therefore, value added is overstated (Mishel, 1988). Domestic price indexes are used to deflate I, but these make real I estimates lower than if actual price indexes reflecting foreign sourcing are used. These prices are lower and would make estimates of real I higher. Foreign sourcing grew rapidly in the period when the share statistics estimated by other methods were falling, suggesting that the official data on real shares should be lower during the past few years.

Statistics of gross output, rather than value added, and statistics of current dollar shares for value added both indicate that the manufacturing share has been falling.

The controversy has not been resolved, but there may have been a slight decline of up to 3–5 percentage points in the manufacturing share of real output. In studying productivity trends and the laws of production in general, I would argue strongly for using gross output rather than value added, together with intermediate inputs as explanatory production factors. In proceeding this way, we do find a slight decline in the manufacturing share statistics. From 1979 to 1985 the drop is estimated to be about 2 percent (from 35.6 to 33.5 percent) (Mishel, 1988, p. 13).

Even if the manufacturing share is not absolutely constant, its decline is slight and may be in the process of changing direction. A more interesting avenue of investigation is the changing composition among types of manufacturing making up the total sector share estimate (see Table 2-3). In independent compilations, the Federal Reserve Board shows changing weights between 1977 and 1984 in the makeup of the index of industrial production, using value added data. The FRB figures show large increases in shares for nonelectrical machinery (including the computer group) and electrical machinery. Rubber and plastic products and instruments are two other gaining groups. Declining in relative importance during this period were primary metals, fabricated metal products, transportation equipment, textiles, and apparel. These five declining cases are often cited in arguments that the United States is in industrial decline. Inadequate attention is paid to the impressive gains in sectors with rising shares. A comprehensive listing, using official data on shares in real value added, brings out the same kind of statistical picture.

Some high-technology sectors, but not chemicals and allied products, show gains in importance. Aerospace, included in other transportation equipment, is a gainer, whereas motor vehicles are losers. Petroleum and coal declines reflect enormous swings in the terms of trade. Many traditional sectors are losing ground, but they may revive in restructured form. Socially undesirable sectors, such as tobacco, show a decline, although their export continues on a fair scale. There are no surprises in this listing, but it does clearly show the significant restructuring that is taking place.

Table 2-3. Change in manufacturing share of GNP, 1979–86.

Industry	Percentage points
Machinery except electrical	1.44
Electric and electronic equipment	0.40
Instruments and related products	0.10
Other transportation equipment	0.14
Rubber and miscellaneous plastic products	0.07
Miscellaneous manufacturing	0.01
Paper and allied products	−0.01
Food and kindred products	−0.03
Printing and publishing	−0.04
Chemicals and allied products	−0.14
Furniture and fixtures	−0.03
Textile mill products	−0.04
Lumber and wood products	−0.08
Fabricated metal products	−0.24
Apparel and other textile products	−0.08
Stone, clay, and glass products	−0.13
Motor vehicles and equipment	−0.30
Petroleum and coal products	−0.20
Tobacco manufactures	−0.12
Primary metal products	−0.62
Leather and leather products	−0.05

Source: Paying the Bill: Manufacturing and America's Trade Deficit. Washington, D.C.: Office of Technology Assessment, 1988, p. 39.

Another way of looking at the sector distribution of growth and decline within manufacturing is in the growth of capital stock, as a main factor of production, in the individual manufacturing categories (see Table 2-4). Investment in fixed capital was not impressive during the 1980s, but some sectors exhibited notable gains. As seen in Table 2-4, we find electrical and nonelectrical machinery to be areas of strong and continuing expansion. Instruments and other transportation equipment (especially aircraft) are also expanding capital. Printing and publishing have invested in capital but do not show an increasing share of output. The same is true of tobacco. Primary metals, fabricated metals, textiles, and apparel are all seen to be retreating sectors. They may regain world competitiveness, but probably not at their earlier size and structure.

Table 2-4. Growth of real capital stock in U.S. manufacturing.

Industry	1970s	1980s
Manufacturing, total	3.3%	1.5%
Lumber and wood	4.9	−1.9
Furniture and fixtures	4.0	2.4
Stone, clay, and glass	2.7	−1.6
Primary metals	1.6	−1.6
Fabricated metals	4.0	1.4
Nonelectrical machinery	4.5	4.1
Electrical machinery	4.6	7.5
Motor vehicles and parts	2.8	0.5
Other transportation equipment	2.4	4.4
Instruments	4.4	5.3
Other	4.4	−0.2
Food	2.7	0.9
Tobacco	5.2	8.3
Textiles	1.6	−1.6
Apparel	4.3	−1.6
Paper	3.2	2.1
Printing and publishing	3.1	4.8
Chemicals	4.2	−0.3
Petroleum	3.3	1.1
Rubber	4.6	0.4
Leather	0.7	−1.3

Source: Stephen S. Roach, " Beyond restructuring: America's investment challenge," *Economic Perspectives* (Morgan Stanley, New York), July 14, 1988. (Reprinted by permission from the author.)

In the United States, some traditional sectors have trimmed facilities, laid off employees, and produced a different range or volume of output. In this process there has been a great deal of retraining, early retirement, and opening of new positions in other sectors — on balance, the service-producing sectors. There has also been a restructuring in the United Kingdom. Many workers were released, as "redundant," at British Steel, for example. The British result, however, has not been as favorable as in the United States with respect to unemployment. The rate of growth of the labor force, for one thing, slowed down much more between the 1970s and 1980s in the United States than in the United Kingdom. In both cases, though, national productivity growth responded positively in manufacturing as a result of the restructuring.

Another dimension of restructuring deals with international trade flows. In the next section I consider the market-adjustment process; in this section I focus on the changes in trade relationships. Technical change, which accounts for much of national restructuring, shows up in international trade flows. The leading industrial countries compete with one another in discovery, economic innovation, and the capturing of world markets in the new technologies, such as microelectronics, software, bioengineering, and new materials. The leaders among the newly industrialized economies (NIEs) also vie for a niche in this market as well as for growing shares of more conventional manufacturing — some of it sophisticated but not necessarily involving advanced technology. The United States maintained a trade surplus in "high-tech" manufactures until 1986, when the figure went into deficit by \$2.6 billion, and recovered to near balance by 1987. In non-high-tech manufactures, the United States has experienced a steadily worsening deficit since 1980. The main losses at the high-tech end of the scale are to Japan and East Asian NIEs.

Another force driving a restructuring of world trade has been the existence of severe debt burdens for many developing countries. The main less developed country (LDC) debtors, apart from South Korea, have been forced to restrict imports. They try to export on a scale that would enable them to service debt comfortably, but they are unable to do so because of the modest growth performance of the world economy. It was indicated previously that in the expansive period, world trade grew at a rate in excess of 10 percent. Both developing and developed economies participated in this rapid expansion, and the United States and Western Europe looked to the developing world as customers for their manufactured goods on a scale that would allow both parties to grow well. In the slowdown period after the Organization of Petroleum Exporting Countries (OPEC) forced a drastic change in terms of trade for energy products, the patterns changed, especially after the OPEC surplus had been recycled into unbearable debts for many developing countries.

In today's economy of modest growth in GDP and trade volume, there is much restructuring at the international level. Developing countries have maintained their established growth rate of exports, but much of their earnings goes to debt service. On the other hand, they have drastically reduced their import growth. With fewer capital purchases from abroad, they are forced to cut back the rate of expansion of domestic production. Industrial countries, on the other hand, have experienced a sharp drop in export growth (related to LDC import restraint) and have also reduced their import expansion. There is, however, a major exception in the industrial world, with respect to import performance. That exception is the United States, where import growth expanded as export growth fell. Herein lies much of the restructuring problem, in the international trade area, for the world economy.

The figures in Table 2-5 are striking. They present a picture of the creation of serious world imbalance that calls for restructuring guided by market adjustment. The figures indicate much of the restructuring that has already taken place. The countries that have emerged economically strong at the international level are the surplus industrial countries — Japan and West Germany — and the surplus NIEs — Taiwan and South Korea. The weakened countries are the LDC debtors and the United States. The countries with large oil export surpluses are, for the moment, living well by virtue of their past accumulation of reserves. It remains to be seen how strong they will remain.

The United States has emerged from this series of developments as the world's largest debtor, having once been the world's largest creditor. As the statistics in Table 2-5 show, the United States has not had to restrain imports as other debtors have, because people throughout the world are willing to take dollar-denominated debt instruments (securities) and supply funds to the United States in return. Other debtors cannot generally market securities in their own currencies. Obviously, this process cannot continue indefinitely; that is one reason why restructuring is taking place in the United States.

Table 2-5. Growth of merchandise trade (percent per year).

	Exports		Imports	
	1965–80	1980–85	1965–80	1980–85
Developing countries	3.1	3.9	5.3	0.4
Highly indebted countries	0.5	1.1	6.3	−8.6
Industrial market economies	7.5	3.7	6.7	3.9
United States	6.7	−2.8	6.6	8.4

Source: World Development Report, 1987. World Bank, Washington, D.C., 1987.

Both high-tech and other manufactures in trade have contributed to the large American external deficit, but agriculture remains as a major surplus area where the United States has a competitive edge. U.S. agriculture exports exceeded imports by $25 billion in 1981, making a very significant contribution toward offsetting deficits in other goods. The surplus is now between $5 billion and $10 billion, but it was as low as $3.4 billion in 1986. Improvements are occurring, but there will be declines, for example, related to drought, as in 1988, and it is unlikely that agriculture can be as important as it formerly was because other countries have become competitive in grain and food products that are crucial to the U.S. surplus. It is now considered essential that restructuring enable the United States to make significant improvements in net exports of manufactures.

Another field of trade preeminence for the United States has been in services (so-called invisibles). The main net earnings for the United States have come from investment and financial income. The shift to net debtor status has seriously impaired the ability of the United States to rely on net factor earnings abroad to offset the merchandise deficit. Formerly, this offset was possible, but interest service on the foreign debt has changed the pattern. This, indeed, is a form of (adverse) restructuring.

As far as receipts and payments of returns on existing international investment are concerned, the United States will have a long wait until it can improve the net balance by a significant amount, but it can compete with other countries now for international earnings in financial markets. The 24-hour global market is a reality, and the export or import of financial services is a growing base of international economic activity. A large pool of international financial capital has developed, and it is this pool that uses the 24-hour global market facilities.

The large financial centers (London, New York, Frankfurt, Zurich, Paris, Montreal, Sydney, Hong Kong, Tokyo, Singapore, Rome, and others) are all participating in these new activities. The source of the activity may be called *financial innovation*. This concept consists of new hardware facilities of telecommunication and computation — at amazing speed with capability of handling mass transactions — associated software, new securities instruments, and new activities, such as mergers and acquisitions. Traditional commodity markets for primary products have been made much more efficient, flexible, and available. Commodity trade has been integrated into financial markets.

At least two developing countries have been able to enter this area of international economic activity at the highest level of sophistication, Singapore and Hong Kong. Others are preparing to compete too, and the business of offshore international banking has taken hold in a few centers of the developing world. The main centers, however, are in the leading industrial countries and, in a sense, a new type of international trade has been created — trade in financial services. The major economic powers have all built up this area of activity, as a natural extension of domestic banking and finance. This area will be important for the United States and is a part of the restructuring taking place, and it is also happening in other large OECD countries in addition to Switzerland, Australia, Benelux, and Scandinavia. International finance will also prove to be more important in the future for the Soviet Union and China, as part of their restructuring. China will soon become a major player in this market through the acquisition of control over Hong Kong in 1997.

The Adjustment Process

The coexistence of unusually large international surpluses and deficits indicates that the present situation is not in equilibrium, and that change must take place on a large scale. Restructuring is a part of this change process.

There are many imbalances, but the major cases are the American current account deficit and the surpluses of Japan, Germany, Taiwan, and South Korea. Other LDC imbalances are related to hyperinflation, debt servicing, and commodity market fluctuations. These require more specialized adjustments. For the major imbalances, however, a primary adjustment process takes place through exchange-rate fluctuations. Apart from the changes that are taking place in shifting employment and output distributions, described in the previous section, there is a short-run adjustment in foreign exchange markets. Many of the structural adjustments have been taking place over decades, whereas the exchange-rate movements in one direction or another may last only a few years at a time.

There are very short-run rallies or plunges but by and large the U.S. dollar has been falling since February 1985. As a result, American goods are more price competitive on world markets, exports are enhanced, and imports are restrained. The surplus countries experience currency appreciation and the opposite effects on trade flows. After a long delay, U.S. trade figures have finally started to respond in the usual way, but the adjustment process will have to continue for several years to restore equilibrium. The German and Japanese accounts show corresponding changes, but not of a magnitude that wipes out their large surpluses. As for Taiwan and South Korea, their currencies have appreciated by smaller amounts and the resulting adjustments to trade accounts are barely visible, although they do seem to be taking place at the present time.

A useful decomposition of the factors of price competitiveness can be demonstrated by the following identity:

$$\text{Price (local foreign currency)} = \text{unit cost} \times \text{reciprocal of productivity} \\ \times \text{profit margin} \times \text{exchange rate}$$

where

$$\text{unit cost} = \text{average wage rate (\$)}$$
$$\text{productivity} = \text{output per worker-hour (labor productivity)}$$
$$\text{exchange rate} = \text{local currency units per dollar } (L/\$)$$

as first approximations, determined by data availability. The yearly tabulations of these results for manufacturing without profit margins, by the Bureau of Labor Statistics, are an invaluable reference for international comparisons. They are presented in detail by the principal investigator in Chap. 6. For purposes of this discussion, it is useful to point out that among 12 industrial countries, the United States showed the slowest rate of growth in labor productivity in 1960–73 and second slowest in 1973–79. The United Kingdom was the slowest in the latter period and second slowest in the first period. It is also important to note that all 12 major industrial countries showed very substantial slowdowns in labor productivity growth in 1973–79 compared with 1960–73. After the change in terms of trade for energy products, there was a worldwide productivity slowdown. This is more than coincidental, but it is not meant to imply that energy alone accounts for the productivity retardation.

In the most recent period, since 1979, several countries showed weaker productivity growth than the United States or United Kingdom, and Japan was usually high in the ranking. By 1986, the United States and United Kingdom ranked just below Belgium in productivity improvement. In 1987, the United Kingdom was second best (behind Norway), and the United States was in the middle of the world distribution. It appears, however, that restructuring has helped in the recuperation of efficiency in the two countries that had slipped the most.

Unit costs, measured by hourly wage rates, did not rise rapidly in the United States from 1960 to 1973. They were the slowest, and those in the United Kingdom were the second slowest. In the next phase, 1973–79, the U.S. rates rose fairly slowly, but not as slowly as those of Japan, Germany, and the Netherlands. But in 1986 and 1987, the United States held wages to a growth rate slower than that in any other major country except the Netherlands.

When the wage series are converted from local currency to U.S. dollar units, American wage rates generally rose most slowly, except for Canadian rates, up to 1979. During the period of the unusual rise in the value of the U.S. dollar, American rates rose faster than those of others in dollar units, but by 1986 and 1987 wage rates, in dollar terms, rose least in the United States, except for Canadian rates in 1986.

When productivity, wage rates, and exchange rates are combined into unit labor costs, measured in U.S. dollars, we find that the United States was cost competitive in 1960–73 and 1973–79 (only Canada was more cost effective) but was extremely noncompetitive during the period of the rising dollar, 1979–85. When the dollar fell in 1986 and 1987, U.S. costs were again rising the least (actually falling).

The Bureau of Labor Statistics recently included South Korea in the country comparisons, and this NIE was formerly cost ineffective in 1973–79 but became very effective in 1986 and 1987. South Korea remained competitive by preventing the won from appreciating very much until recent months.

These tabulations tell an interesting story, even though they do not include the fourth factor, namely, profit margin. They show how macroeconomic policy adjustments can influence exchange rates and wage rates in becoming cost competitive. They also show the fundamental contribution of technical factors, subsumed in productivity growth. In the big adjustment that is presently on-going, the United States relies heavily on exchange depreciation, almost like an "economic crutch," to promote competitiveness. There are some productivity gains, but they are not as striking in a comparative quantitative sense as the exchange-rate changes. This situation gives rise to the feeling that the United States should do more, in a technical way, to become more efficient and rely less on major swings in macroeconomic policy, because such swings have destabilizing side effects for the rest of the world, particularly for the heavily indebted developing countries. Another way of looking at the matter is to argue that restructuring can be extremely important, in a sense necessary, but that it is a long-run process. In the present phase, large-scale depreciation has not brought quick restoration of equilibrium. There are many reasons for this, one being the net debtor status, so the search for means of achieving more technical efficiency must continue.

Reliable measures of the appropriate statistics on the profit margin factor are not generally available, but the end result enabling one to compare countries for competitiveness is shown in the final price, figured in a common currency unit. Price indexes for exports and imports are reported for Japan, Germany, and a few other countries. For a limited period such indexes are available for the United States. More common statistics, which are widely available, are the estimates of *unit value*. Flawed though such measures are, they do show the most important movements. In particular, they show that the United States became seriously noncompetitive after 1980, during the periods of both dollar appreciation and dollar depreciation. The United States costs, shown by the first three factors mentioned previously, were moving in an extremely noncompetitive direction during the period of the rising dollar, 1979–85. If they have been moving in a very competitive direction since 1986, as the published data show, then changes in profit margins may have prevented our becoming competitive. General opinion prevails that some countries whose currencies have appreciated very much since 1985 have been willing to accept lower-than-usual profit margins in order to retain as much market share as possible in the U.S. economy. Profit margins are quite flexible and cyclical. Countries with appreciating currencies or rising costs due to other factors can manipulate profit margins in order to remain competitive, but such policies rarely can be maintained for long periods of time. Eventually margins must approach normal values, and the forces making for competitiveness such as exchange depreciation, restrained unit costs, and higher productivity growth will eventually prevail.

Cyclical fluctuations in profits, exchange rates, and unit costs (wage rates) will always be taking place and will affect competitiveness, sometimes benefiting one economy and sometimes another, but the underlying factors are those associated with economic efficiency — productivity in the simple formula. To improve economic efficiency, a country should look to capital formation, a stable noninflationary economic environment, attitudes supporting a strong work ethic, and vigorous scientific and technical progress.

Investment in fixed capital is very important. An economy that is able to devote abundant resources to high rates of capital formation of the most advanced vintage will realize productivity gains. The progress that people all over the world admire in Japan and other East Asian economies has been driven by strong capital formation. Macroeconomic policy should be supportive of capital formation. Such instruments as special tax concessions, favorable borrowing costs, and strong fiscal demand can all enhance the rate of capital expansion.

Favorable borrowing costs will be affected partly by public policy, partly by saving decisions. Saving at all levels — personal, business, government, and foreign — is equally important, but countries that have had great success in realizing strong capital formation have also had significant portions of personal income devoted to saving. Without going into accounting and other institutional differences, the low American rates, near 3–5 percent, are not supportive of high rates of capital formation at low rates of interest, whereas Japanese, some European, and some other Asian rates in excess of 15 percent have supported high rates of capital formation. Competitiveness has usually been effective following periods of sustained capital expansion. Achievement of a high-savings–high-investment economy is the objective. If the savings rate is high and if funds are channeled into productive investment, it is possible to limit inflation. This has been demonstrated in many of the cases cited in Japan, other East Asian economies, and some European economies. Inflation can be highly distractive and moderate interest rates can be very accommodating. Low inflation with low interest rates, both well under 5 percent, are good targets.

The analysis has been quantitative thus far, but qualitative aspects are also important. A parsimonious attitude among people helps maintain a supportive saving rate. A strong work ethic helps to promote strong productivity. Another qualitative dimension is job satisfaction, that is, interest in one's job sufficient to ensure high-quality work. Japanese and East Asian products are not competitive in price alone, but also in quality of product. Goods from this part of the world formerly were cheap and of poor quality. From the 1960s, Japan concentrated on delivering high-quality products — first in traditional lines such as textiles; then in optics, electronics, chemicals, foodstuffs; later in cars; and now in virtually any good that is significant in international trade. Some of the most recent goods are extremely sophisticated and of excellent quality. Computers, scientific instruments, and pharmaceuticals are all of world-class quality. Many NIEs have been able to follow in Japan's footsteps. They are still behind Japan at the top level but have gradually reached high quality standards in textiles, apparel, shoes, food, optics, electronics, and most recently in cars. They too will move into the latest sophisticated lines.

Scientific and technical progress are exhibited in the products now available and in their quantitative rates of increase, but the basis for strength at this level comes from the educational and scientific research establishments. While North American and Western European institutions remain preeminent, it is apparent that significant gains are being made elsewhere. Also, the established institutions educate and train scholarly workers from everywhere. In my professional lifetime, I have seen American educational and research establishments grow to staffing ratios of more than one-half foreign-born. It is evident that competition will remain keen in the production of new ideas that ultimately show up in improved economic efficiency. Every competing economy will have to give high priority to the provision of resources for teaching and research. The outcome will be important for both quantity and quality in dimensions of competitiveness.

Two other developments are taking place in the world economy that can have profound effects on competitiveness. The socialist countries, which have lagged behind, are now taking major steps to compete in the world economy, led by economic reforms in China and perestroika in the Soviet Union. These countries obviously want to deliver better living conditions to their own citizens, but they fully realize that it will be necessary for them to open their economies and participate more fully in the international trading/financing system in order to be successful.

China is much further along than is the Soviet Union in these developments. Inflation is becoming an obstacle to China's progress, but the chances of success are still overwhelmingly favorable. As for the Soviet Union, the restructuring is just beginning, and it remains to be seen how it will succeed. Both countries are competitive in some primary commodities and in selected manufactures. Both are advanced militarily and trade in weaponry. They have a long distance to travel, however, before they can become competitive in the world economy in a general sense.

The Soviet Union is involved in another major development, the possibility of large-scale disarmament. The situation has never looked better for progress along this line. If the Soviet Union is to free resources for delivering a better living standard to its citizens, it will probably be necessary to lower the priority of the military. Both the United States and the Soviet Union would stand to gain in world competitiveness if they devoted fewer resources to national defense. It is no mere coincidence that Japan and Germany are strongly competitive and bear light defense burdens.

There are technological side effects from military research and development (R&D), but this is hardly a good or efficient way to realize benefits from technical progress. It remains to be seen if large-scale mutual disarmament can be realized and how released resources from such a development might be used, but there is a sizable potential to be used for civilian economic advantage, not only for domestic production but for economic efficiency.

Policies for Achieving Competitiveness

The discussion thus far has indicated where some policy priorities might be placed, but an overall strategy for improving competitiveness in individual economies needs to be outlined. Establishment of a good balance between fiscal and monetary policy is of primary importance. All the instruments should be used together to try to achieve steadiness in exchange rates, interest rates, inflation, growth, and employment. This means that both fiscal and monetary authorities should act jointly. Through macro model simulation, rough equivalence can be established between effectiveness of the two types of policies. Within fiscal policy and within monetary policy there should also be balance. In the former case, both spending and tax changes should be used together; in the latter case, both domestic and foreign-oriented instruments should be used.

In the United States during the early part of the 1980s there was great imbalance between fiscal and monetary policies. This imbalance resulted in extremely high interest rates, which affected competitiveness in many ways. The extremely high rates that resulted from the imbalance increased unit (capital) costs, contributed to increases in the value of the dollar, and made it necessary for heavily indebted developing countries to curtail imports. These all were strongly adverse for American competitiveness. Had the same targets for the economy been reached in a balanced way, American competitiveness would not have suffered as much as it did.

International policy coordination can work in many ways to avoid extreme swings in trade and payments balances among countries participating in the coordination effort. International coordination makes use of the same instruments for fiscal and monetary policy that are used nationally; the only difference is that national choices are subordinated to the group decision about what is appropriate for each nation. Coordination does not imply complete similarity, only that policies be appropriate for world performance. Commercial policy, dealing with trade relations among countries, should be liberal, in support of free trade.

Competitiveness may be furthered by resorting to industrial policy. Such policy directions are not generally accepted by economists, but they can be important in enlarging capital facilities in promising new areas, training workers in selective skills, and supporting R&D in promising industrial sectors. Educational and research support, particularly in scientific and engineering fields, can be aligned with industrial policy.

Support for capital formation, education, and R&D can, of course, be completely general and not targeted, as with industrial policy. This kind of policy emphasis gains wider acceptance among economists. Knowledge, training, and facilities expansion generally can be supported on the assumption that the results will diffuse, undirected, through the economy in a perfectly satisfactory way. That, too, is an appropriate policy line. The movement of an economy toward a system of high savings and high investment (typical of Japan now and not typical of the United States, for example) is perfectly consistent with the general, and weaker form of policy support for capital formation, education, and R&D.

For economies that have drifted toward a series of public controls, supervision, and regulation, a policy of deregulation may be pursued in the hopes of improving economic efficiency, which is very important for competitiveness. Such policies currently are quite popular. Some gains have been realized as a result of lessening regulatory policies, but there have been many excesses. It is often claimed that a loose attitude toward regulation encouraged financial activities that pulled corporate attention from the business of achieving greater efficiency in goods production and also contributed to such disturbing excesses as the stock market crash of 1987. Since deregulation, safety factors and operational efficiency in the airline industry appear to have deteriorated. There are many overall statistics to show improvement of airline production of service since deregulation, but the quality of service has definitely deteriorated, and there are many anecdotal reports indicating the deregulated drive for profits has been detrimental to safety and to the general quality of the transport services offered. Deregulation remains a controversial policy for improving competitiveness.

In this chapter, an underlying point has been that one of the most important steps that a country can take to become or remain competitive is to achieve economic efficiency. In this respect, strong productivity growth is crucial. For simplicity, I have referred to figures of labor productivity, but the proper concept is total factor productivity. In general, policy should be directed toward achieving such overall productivity growth; to be specific, energy policy should receive a great deal of attention. In the United States, inefficient use of energy over long periods of time made the country ill prepared to deal with the oil embargo and change in terms of trade for energy products after 1973. To quantify and establish the importance of energy, it is essential to estimate production functions that determine gross output as functions of such traditional inputs as labor and capital, but also to consider intermediate inputs. In other words, the KLEM production function (or one that is more disaggregated by input category) is essential to the analysis. Value-added production functions depending on capital and labor inputs are not adequate. The importance of energy variables (including their price) in contributing to the productivity slowdown is not always appreciated.[1] From this point of view, direct interventionist energy policy is called for. The market solution has not been satisfactory. As energy prices declined, the United States retreated from conservationist tendencies, used energy wastefully, and generated significant balance-of-payments deterioration. Oil is readily available now, as it was deceptively in the 1950s and 1960s, but will the supply be as available in the 1990s and later? There is enough doubt to suggest that policies to develop synthetic substitutes, ample storage stocks, and conservation need to be reintroduced and strengthened.

References

Leisenring, C. A., 1988, "Job growth in the 1980s: McJobs and related McIssues," in *Comments on the Economy and Financial Markets* (Core States Financial Corp, Philadelphia).

Mishel, L., 1988, *Manufacturing Numbers: How Inaccurate Statistics Conceal US Industrial Decline* (Economic Policy Institute, Washington, D.C.).

Editorial Note

Prefix number 2 in the tables and figures numbering refers to chapter number 2 of the source, *International Productivity & Competitiveness, op. cit.*

---

[1] Two University of Pennsylvania dissertation studies that approach the problem both from time-series and cross-section (for different industry groups) samples are Y. Kumasaka, *A Comparison of the Slowdown in Productivity Growth After the First Oil Crisis and Productivity Experiences from the Two Oil Crises Between Japan and the USA*, 1984, and M. Prywes, *Three Essays on the Econometrics of Production, Productivity, and Capacity Utilization*, 1981. Both attribute a great deal of significance to energy changes in the productivity slowdown.

32

THE TWO-GAP PARADIGM IN THE CHINESE CASE:
A PEDAGOGICAL EXERCISE[†]

> There is no accepted paradigm for the macro model of a developing country. A two-
> gap model, which is, in fact, an open economy version of the Harrod–Domar Model,
> has been constructed for China based on recently available national accounting data.
> Some problems of growth in relation to domestic policies and the trade accounts can
> be handled for this type of system. The small two-gap model also serves as a useful
> pedagogical tool, and is very easily programmed for student use.

A useful way of looking at a macroeconomy is through the medium of a compact mathematical model, preferably one that lends itself to simple diagrams. This approach should provide insight into the overall functioning of the economy and it should be pedagogical. It is even better if it is relevant, that is, calibrated to the available macroeconomic data about the economy.

In the case of the advanced industrial economy, the paradigm for macroeconomic description and analysis is the *IS–LM* diagram, made up of two simple curves. This diagram must be generalized, and therefore loses some of its pedagogical appeal, if appropriate account is taken of inflation and international trade. Simplicity is entirely lost if we pursue realism by construction of a mainstream econometric model according to the Keynesian–neoclassical synthesis, because such a system will then consist of several hundred or even a few thousand equations. Then we are confronted with the reverse task of trying to distill the implicit "maquette" of the large system.[1]

There are thus two ways of proceeding: To build a full-scale model and reduce it to a paradigm model, or to try to build up the paradigm model directly from data. In trying to model the Chinese economy, we are confronted by the choice of these same two approaches in order to provide some pedagogical material, but we are also confronted by the choice of the paradigm. The *IS–LM* model is not relevant for an economy at China's present stage of evolution; we have, accordingly, chosen the two-gap model, as an extended variant of the Harrod–Domar growth model. It seems to us that this model is quite revealing in the China case and lends itself well to the pedagogy of easy computer programming, complete with simple diagrams.

[†]From *China Economic Review* **1** (Spring, 1989), pp. 1–8; written jointly with Y. Liang.

The Two-Gap Model

A basic accounting identity for practically any open national economic system is

$$NI = CP + CS + I + X - M \qquad (1)$$

(real) national income (NI) = private consumption (CP)
+ social consumption (CS) + Investment (I)
+ Exports (X) − Imports (M)

The terms in Eq. (1) can be rearranged to obtain

$$\underbrace{(NI - CP - CS - I)}_{S} = X - M \qquad (1)'$$

In words, Eq. (1)′ states that the domestic savings–investment gap equals the export–import gap. We define savings (S) as national income that is not spent on domestic consumption. In the first instance, we shall assume that CS and X are exogenously given. CS is determined by political authorities and X is determined by economic activity outside China. We further assume that CP varies positively with NI, I varies positively with the time change in NI, and that M varies positively with NI.

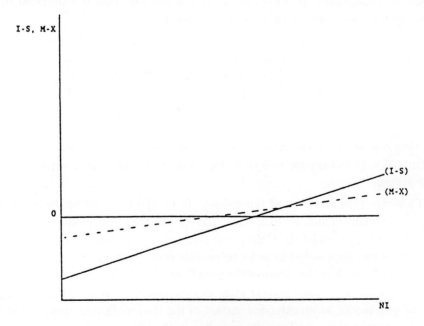

Fig. 1. The two-gap model diagram.

Given the initial condition

$$NI_{-1} = \text{known value}$$

the appropriate diagram is as shown in Fig. 1. At a given point in time, the value of *NI* and the other variables are determined by the intersection of the two curves, corresponding to the two gaps. The usefulness of the diagram can be shown by the following considerations:

(i) Suppose that there is technical progress. That will mean that more productive capital is being used in the production process; therefore the $I - S$ curve will shift downward because less investment will be needed per unit of output if the capital is superior. As the $I - S$ curve shifts downward, the intersection will move to the right, and *NI* will increase.

(ii) Suppose that people become more thrifty. Then S will rise for any given level of *NI*, and the $(I - S)$ curve will shift downward. The consequence is the same as in (i). It could also be interpreted as showing that more domestic funds are being provided for growth; that is, the domestic savings gap is being closed a bit.

(iii) Suppose that imports increase. For any level of *NI*, there will be more imports (M) and the economy will have access to more foreign capital or materials; therefore *NI* will increase as $(M - X)$ moves upward. If more imports are being obtained, the external gap is being closed. In the industrial country model, imports displace domestic activity, and *NI* tends to fall, *ceteris paribus*, but in the paradigm model for the economy in process of development, imports enable the system to reach higher levels of activity. This is a key difference.

(iv) Suppose that exports increase. In this case the $(M - X)$ curve is lowered and the intersection value of *NI* falls, because the economy is losing goods to foreign countries. In an extended model, if increases in X bring in needed foreign exchange, which is used to import capital that is technologically superior, then an increase in *NI* will eventually appear in a dynamic solution of the system. Figure 1 depicts a single period's solution of the model.

Specification and Estimation

The national income identity (1) is self-evident. The private consumption function should use after-tax income to get a better measure of purchasing power. The investment function — the well-known accelerator — is considered to be indicative of investment demand in Western industrial economies. The rate of change of *NI* is the appropriate explanatory variable to be considered, but the analysis of developing economies is usually formulated in terms of the capital–output ratio. This is a kind of production function in which capital is the limiting factor of production. The *ICOR* ratio corresponds to the capital–output ratio in development economics; therefore the accelerator equation is, for the China case, to be regarded as a primary supply-side relationship, expressed either in terms of capital and output or investment and the rate of change of output. There will be need for a simple tax equation, as long as taxes are explicitly subtracted from total national income in the consumption equation.

The estimated model, computed by the single equation ordinary least-squares (OLS) method, from annual data, 1971–1985, is listed below. Two of the equations are adjusted for first-order serial correlation of residuals — using an $AR(1)$ process.

In addition to Eq. (1), we have

$$CP = 0.726 \quad (NI - TAX) + (AR(1) = 0.352) \tag{2}$$
$$(94.73)$$
$$R^2 = 0.992 \quad SER = 54.6 \quad DW = 1.673$$

$$I = 630.4 \quad + 1.784 \ (NI - NI(-1)) \tag{3}$$
$$(9.23) \qquad (7.96)$$
$$R^2 = 0.830 \quad SER = 163.0 \quad DW = 2.248$$

$$TAX = 0.1667 \ NI + (AR(1) = 0.344) \tag{4}$$
$$(74.63)$$
$$R^2 = 0.985 \quad SER = 19.2 \quad DW = 1.851$$

$$M = -272.2 \quad + 0.156 \quad NI \tag{5}$$
$$(-8.22) \qquad (16.03)$$
$$R^2 = 0.955 \quad SER = 33.4 \quad DW = 2.012$$

To solve the numerical model for 1982, we use actual values from the data listing for $NI(-1) = 3834.84$, $X = 423.05$, and $CS = 359.88$; substitute into the equation system and find est. $NI = 4181.53$, which is 2.2% below the actual value 4276.2. In Fig. 2 (1982), we have a plot of this solution. Similarly for 1983 (Fig. 3), $NI(-1) = 4276.2$, $X = 423.07$, $CS = 389.96$. The computed value of NI from the equation system is 4795.71, which is 2.8% above the value for 1983, 4663.46.

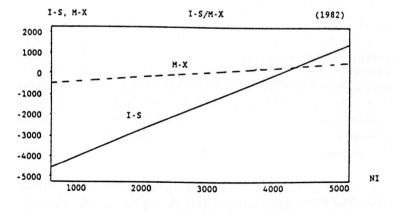

Fig. 2.

This system can be used to illustrate the appropriate quantitative nature of shifts in exogenous variables or parameters, that is, social spending (CS), exports (X), or the tax rate parameter in Eq. (4). If CS is increased by 10% from 389.96 to

428.956 in 1983, the $(I - S)$ curve shifts upward and intersects the $(M - X)$ curve at a lower level of *NI*. The reduction in real national income occurs because the increase in social spending reduces the amount available for capital spending and therefore production. Similarly, a decrease in *CS* would raise the level of *NI*. These are just opposite to what we expect to find in a model of an advanced industrial economy. The drop in computed *NI* amounts to 31.63 for this case; so the multiplier (in absolute value) is slightly less than 1.0, at a point value of 0.81.

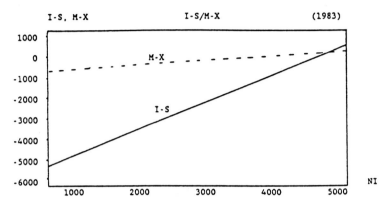

Fig. 3.

Table 1. Data listing (100 mill. Chinese *yuans*).

Year	NI	I	CP	CS	X	M	TAX	P	M1
1970	2020.73	665.50	1232.80	121.70	59.57	58.84	336.70	0.9535	129.63
1971	2191.14	742.27	1297.12	139.99	70.53	58.78	366.00	0.9215	147.77
1972	2243.04	703.74	1371.74	153.45	83.68	69.57	370.31	0.9208	164.24
1973	2454.55	802.99	1477.89	159.30	126.71	112.34	402.39	0.9228	179.94
1974	2462.81	801.34	1509.46	166.54	150.77	165.30	415.30	0.9247	190.99
1975	2688.35	911.99	1593.45	187.89	157.15	162.13	467.58	0.9101	200.68
1976	2678.67	824.88	1655.71	191.99	149.03	142.95	468.11	0.9068	224.92
1977	2816.12	907.90	1695.44	205.15	152.40	144.77	483.25	0.9164	213.27
1978	3181.14	1169.95	1800.88	231.41	180.50	201.60	573.79	0.9291	228.21
1979	3440.13	1201.37	1976.10	294.91	219.09	251.33	563.46	0.9664	277.02
1980	3677.13	1165.00	2223.20	308.00	272.22	291.30	578.53	1.0000	346.20
1981	3834.84	1086.02	2428.71	320.11	384.05	384.05	633.76	1.0184	389.18
1982	4276.20	1215.34	2642.87	359.88	423.05	364.94	696.54	1.0170	431.78
1983	4663.46	1381.89	2875.62	389.96	423.07	407.08	757.41	1.0283	515.20
1984	5222.61	1637.76	3148.47	463.69	562.41	589.74	877.74	1.0783	734.59
1985	5877.28	2108.29	3639.88	502.79	686.65	1060.34	1747.25	1.1635	849.02

A change in X will have the same multiplier effect as a change in CS, because these two variables enter the simplified system in the same way, in Eq. (1). The effect of tax **rate** changes can be illustrated by altering the tax rate coefficient in Eq. (4). For an example, we change the coefficient from 0.1667 to 0.20. The value of NI would increase by about 95.9 while tax collections would be higher by 130. There would be a decline in private consumption of 24.7 accompanied by an increase in investment of 171.0. In this model, tax increases divert funds from private consumption to investment, which paves the way for expansion of production.

This system is instructive, but it is incomplete, just as many *IS–LM* systems are incomplete, unless they are accompanied by an explanation of the price level (or inflation rate). At the same time, because we are studying an open economy, that is, one that plainly emphasizes an "open door" policy for growth, it is important to remove X from the exogenous category and try to develop equations to explain exports in terms, partly at least, of domestic variables. We have accordingly added three equations to the system — for the price level, exports, and export price. The additional equations are as follows:

$$P = \underset{(18.43)}{0.6865} + \underset{(4.49)}{1.73} \frac{M1}{NI} + \underset{(4.39)}{1.543} \left(\frac{M1}{NI}\right)_{-1} + [AR(1) = 0.766; AR(2) = -0.254]$$

$$R^2 = 0.961, \quad SER = 0.0175, \quad DW = 1.491 \tag{6}$$

$$X = \underset{(-12.52)}{-371.13} + \underset{(5.68)}{130.75} \frac{PXW}{PX/EX} + \underset{(12.74)}{0.0161} \; XW + \underset{(2.36)}{31.64} \; D_{7682} \tag{7}$$

$$R^2 = 0.992, \quad SER = 15.99, \quad DW = 1.957$$

$$PX = \underset{(7.08)}{25.94} + \underset{(16.40)}{0.727} \; PXW + \underset{(6.10)}{6.04} \; D_{7681} \tag{8}$$

$$R^2 = 0.979, \quad SER = 2.177, \quad DW = 2.302$$

where

P = National income deflator (1980: 1.0)
$M1$ = Real money supply
PXW = World export price index (1980: 100)
PX = China export price index (1980: 100)
EX = Exchange rate, ¥/$
XW = World exports (100 million *yuan*, 1980 prices)
D_{7682} = 1 in 1976, 1982; otherwise 0
D_{7681} = −1 in 1976, 1983, 1984; 1 in 1978, 1981; otherwise 0.

Equation (6) relates the price level to current and lagged velocity reciprocals. Equation (7) explains exports in terms of world trade volume and Chinese price competitiveness. There were unusual values for 1976 and 1982; other export data

Table 2. Simulation results.

Year	Actual	NI Forecast	Percent Error	Actual	I Forecast	Percent Error
1975	2688.35	2571.67	−4.3	911.99	825.61	−9.5
1976	2678.67	2701.29	0.8	890.17	862.63	4.6
1977	2816.12	2863.46	1.7	907.90	920.70	1.4
1978	3181.14	3076.70	−3.3	1169.95	1011.82	−13.5
1979	3440.13	3300.34	−4.1	1201.37	1030.39	−14.2
1980	3677.13	3567.09	−3.0	1165.00	1107.27	−5.0
1981	3834.84	3868.51	0.9	1086.02	1169.15	7.7
1982	4276.20	4219.42	−1.3	1215.34	1257.43	3.5
1983	4663.46	4723.79	1.3	1381.89	1531.19	10.8
1984	5222.61	5273.18	1.0	1637.76	1611.52	−1.6
1985	5877.28	5908.45	0.5	2108.29	2114.71	0.3

Year	Actual	CP Forecast	Percent Error	Actual	M Forecast	Percent Error
1975	1593.45	1555.80	−2.4	162.13	128.98	−20.4
1976	1655.71	1634.21	−1.3	142.95	149.20	4.4
1977	1695.44	1732.32	2.2	144.77	174.50	20.5
1978	1800.88	1861.33	3.4	201.60	207.77	3.1
1979	1976.10	1996.63	1.0	251.33	242.65	−3.5
1980	2223.20	2158.00	−2.9	291.30	284.27	−2.4
1981	2428.71	2340.35	−3.6	384.05	331.29	−13.7
1982	2642.87	2552.65	−3.4	364.94	386.03	5.9
1983	2875.62	2857.78	−0.6	407.08	464.71	14.2
1984	3148.47	3190.15	1.3	589.74	550.42	−6.7
1985	3639.88	3574.46	−1.8	1060.34	999.52	−5.7

Year	Actual	TAX Forecast	Percent Error	Actual	P Forecast	Percent Error
1975	467.58	428.70	−8.3	0.910	0.941	3.4
1976	468.11	450.30	−3.8	0.907	0.951	4.9
1977	483.25	477.34	−1.2	0.916	0.944	3.0
1978	573.79	512.89	−10.6	0.929	0.930	0.1
1979	563.46	550.17	−2.4	0.966	0.946	−2.1
1980	578.53	594.63	2.8	1.000	0.984	−1.6
1981	633.76	644.88	1.8	1.018	1.010	−1.6
1982	696.54	703.38	1.0	1.017	1.019	0.2
1983	757.41	787.46	4.0	1.028	1.033	0.5
1984	877.74	879.04	0.1	1.078	1.096	1.6
1985	1747.25	984.94	−43.6	1.164	1.150	−1.2

are not unusual. Finally, Eq. (8) demonstrates that China's export price follows movements in world export prices apart from 1976, 1978, 1981, 1983, and 1984.

These three additional equations contribute something toward an explanation of prices, competitiveness, and exports, but they require special "dummy" variables to

Table 2. (*Cont'd*)

Year	Actual	X Forecast	Percent Error	Actual	PX Forecast	Percent Error
1975	157.15	131.35	−16.4	67.46	68.25	1.2
1976	149.03	161.65	8.5	63.31	62.72	−0.9
1977	152.40	179.78	1.8	74.64	72.54	−2.8
1978	180.50	179.89	−0.3	80.57	83.24	3.3
1979	219.09	221.07	0.9	89.89	86.65	−3.6
1980	272.22	278.08	2.2	100.00	98.64	−1.4
1981	384.05	370.19	−3.6	103.40	103.96	0.5
1982	423.05	435.50	2.9	95.99	95.30	−0.7
1983	423.07	409.58	−3.2	83.97	85.54	1.9
1984	562.41	558.23	−0.7	81.86	84.09	2.7
1985	686.65	716.00	4.3	80.04	82.42	3.0

deal with unusual situations in this period of economic reform. Also they do not feed back on the core two-gap system. It will be necessary to conduct further research into the use of export earnings to purchase highly productive capital and material imports that aid in the domestic production process. Also, it will be important to show the feedback effects of inflation (or lack of it) on domestic economic activity.

Nevertheless, the added Eqs. (6)–(8) produce good dynamic simulation results for the enlarged Two-Gap Model. The results in Table 2 are multiperiod simulations, using observed values for CS and $M1$, XW, and PXW, but generated values for the endogenous variables, particularly the lagged variables. Only the initial values, prior to the start of the dynamic simulation (1975), are assumed to be given for this exercise. Many more instructive scenarios concerning export trade in the open economy can be examined with the enlarged model. Also, monetary phenomena enter the system through $M1$.

Reference

Klein, L. R., Michael D. McCarthy, and Vijaya Duggal, 1974, "The Wharton Mark III model—A modern IS–LM construct," *International Economic Review* **15**, pp. 572–594.

PART IV

POLICY FORMULATION

In his "Professional life philosophy," Lawrence Klein has told us that he does not believe "the market system, in even its purest form, provides adequate self-regulatory responses. The economy definitely needs guidance — even leadership — and it is up to professional economists to provide public policy makers with the right information to deliver such leadership." The three studies presented in Part IV on public policy formulation blend together the theory, methodology, and real-world relevance of economic policy, especially from the vantage point of experience in the United States.

"Economic policy formation: Theory and implementation," (1986) exemplifies applied econometrics of the public sector, how the invisible hand of the market can be strengthened by the visible hand of public policy. Klein provides a succinct review of major contemporary policy issues, with respect to both monetary and fiscal policies and the actors involved, from historical and doctrinaire perspectives. He also reviews the policy-making process by using the kind of models needed, such as large-scale models actually in use. Two types of policies, both macro and structural, are examined. Examples are presented of policy simulations in the context of the U.S. with Wharton Models, quarterly and annual. Simulations of these models have been used in the past for policy formation and general economic analysis.

Also, Klein briefly explains and discusses the target–instrument approach to the theory of economic policy introduced by Jan Tinbergen and the theory of optimal economic policy. He shows that there are limitations to the use of optimal control theory and that policy formation is more complex than the simplest target–instrument approach. By intertwining theory and real-world experience in the use of public policy, Klein, in this study, has described a valuable tool for teaching the theory and policy of political economy.

In this paper, Klein meets the contemporary challenges to the use of public policy from monetarists, advocates of rational expectations, and supply side economists. He criticizes public policy makers, who are always assuming or looking for precision in their choice procedures, even when the subject matter is inherently stochastic and relatively "noisy." He ends the discussion on an optimistic note. In his judgment, there is more, rather than less, need for using econometric models as guides for public policy. These models must of necessity be eclectic. Here we come full circle, back to large-scale models, containing a large number of sectors and subsectors, for policy formulation. He concludes that "macroeconometric modeling, if pursued at the appropriate level of detail, does have much to contribute." Once again he points out that "bringing into play joint Leontief–Keynes models with fully articulated input–output systems, demographic detail, resource constraints and environmental conditions are likely to be important for the development of more specific policy decisions requiring the use of more micro details from models. This is likely to be the next wave of policy applications, focusing on energy policy, environmental policy, food policy and other specific issues. It is clear that econometric methods are going to play a major role in this phase of development."

"Two decades of U.S. economic policy and present prospects," is a perceptive account of implementation of economic policy in the U.S. over the span of 1960s and 1970s. As it was written at the beginning of the Reagan Administration (1982), it also provides some perspective on U.S. economic policy that was implemented in the early 1980s. Klein divides his historical review into four periods. He starts with the Kennedy–Johnson era (1960–1968), goes over the Nixon–Ford era (1968–1976), reviews the Carter years (1976–1980) and moves into the early years of the Reagan Administration. He underscores the policy differences from administration to administration, the major issues, the policy choices, and underlying doctrinaire positions. In his usual simple and lucid style, Klein brings together for us a wealth of information on the practice of economic policy in the recent history of the U.S. Both economists and noneconomists should find it fascinating, and it should be a must-read for students of macroeconomics at the undergraduate as well as graduate levels.

Right at the beginning, the Reagan Administration put into place an extensive experiment with the so-called supply-side economics. On June 26, 1984, in a column of *The Los Angeles Times*, where, as a member of the Times Board of Economists, he was contributing regularly, Klein evaluates the success of the Reagan experiment by judging it on the criterion "how well the outcome agrees with the advanced claims." For this purpose he uses five major claims of supply-side economics.

Based on the available evidence, Klein finds that lower tax rates failed to generate tax revenue large enough to reduce the federal deficit, raise the saving rate, or induce higher productivity, and that inflation could not be stopped without a recession. Whether deregulation did indeed induce a rise in productivity is subject to a question mark. Thus he totes up the won–lost record and arrives at a cumulative score of "Won–0; Lost–4; Tied–1," a dismal score for the supply side.

Almost a decade later, Steven Greenhouse of *The New York Times* reported (See *The New York Times*, Sunday, October 31, 1993), in his column on conversations that in Paul Samuelson's view, "the American people were bamboozled by a President [Ronald Reagan] who persuaded them that tax cuts would lead to higher revenues without producing a Himalaya of debt." He quotes Samuelson, "People have the wrong idea that God will forgive Reagan. They say he didn't know what he was doing. It's true he didn't know a lot of what was going on, but he was directly responsible." The dismal score of "supply-side" still stands.

33

ECONOMIC POLICY FORMATION: THEORY AND IMPLEMENTATION (APPLIED ECONOMETRICS IN THE PUBLIC SECTOR)[†]

1. Some Contemporary Policy Issues

Mainstream economic policy, known basically as demand management, and its econometric implementation are jointly under debate now. The main criticism comes from monetarists, who focus on versions of the quantity theory of money, from advocates of the theory of rational expectations, and more recently from supply side economists. All these criticisms will be considered in this paper, as well as the criticisms of public policy makers, who are always looking for precision in their choice procedures, even when the subject matter is inherently stochastic and relatively "noisy."

Demand management is usually identified as Keynesian economic policy, i.e., as the type that is inspired by the aggregative Keynesian model of effective demand. Also, the mainstream econometric models are called Keynesian type models; so the present state of world-wide stagflation is frequently attributed to the use of Keynesian econometric models for the implementation of Keynesian policies.

These are popular and not scientific views. In this presentation the objective will be to put policy measures in a more general perspective, only some of which are purely demand management and aggregative. Also, the evolution of econometric models for policy application to many supply-side characteristics will be stressed. To a certain extent, the orientation will be towards experience derived from the application of U.S. models to U.S. economic policy, but the issue and methods to be discussed will be more general.

For purposes of exposition, two types of policy will be examined, (1) overall *macro* policies, and (2) specific *structural* policies. Macro policies refer to traditional monetary and fiscal policies, principally of central governments, but the model applications to local government policies are also relevant. As the world economy becomes more interdependent, more economies are recognizing their openness; therefore, trade/payments policies are also part of the complement known as macro policy.

[†]From *Handbook of Econometrics*, Vol. III, eds. Z. Griliches and M. D. Intriligator (1986), pp. 2057–2088, with kind permission from Elsevier Science — NL, Sara Burgerhartstraat 25, 1055 KV Amsterdam, The Netherlands.

By structural policy I mean policies that are aimed at specific segments of the economy, specific groups of people, specific production sectors, distributions of aggregative magnitudes or markets. Economists like to focus on macro policies because they have overall impacts and leave the distributive market process unaffected, able to do its seemingly efficient work. Most economists look upon the free competitive market as an ideal and do not want to make specific policies that interfere with its smooth working. They may, however, want to intervene with structural policy in order to preserve or guarantee the working of idealized market process.

Macro policies are quite familiar. Monetary policy is carried out by the central bank and sometimes with a treasury ministry. Also, the legislative branch of democratic governments influence or shape monetary policy. Central executive offices of government also participate in the formation of monetary policy. It is a many-sided policy activity. The principal policy instruments are bank reserves and discount rates. Reserves may be controlled through open market operations or the setting of reserve requirements. Policies directed at the instrument levels have as objectives specified time paths of monetary aggregates or interest rates.

At the present time, there is a great deal of interest in controlling monetary aggregates through control of reserves, but some countries continue to emphasize interest rate control through the discount window. On the whole, monetary authorities tend to emphasize one approach or the other; i.e., they try to control monetary aggregates along *monetarist* doctrinal lines or they try to control interest rates through discount policy, but in the spirit of a generalized approach to economic policy there is no reason why central monetary authorities cannot have multiple targets through the medium of multiple instruments. This approach along the lines of modern control theory will be exemplified below.

Monetary policy is of particular importance because it can be changed on short notice, with little or no legislative delay. It may be favored as a flexible policy but is often constrained, in an open economy, by the balance of payments position and the consequent stability of the exchange value of a country's currency. Therefore, we might add a third kind of financial target, namely, an exchange value target. Flexibility is thus restricted in an open economy. Monetary policies that may seem appropriate for a given domestic situation may be constrained by a prevalent international situation.

There are many monetary aggregates extending all the way from the monetary base, to checking accounts, to savings accounts, to liquid money market instruments, to more general credit instruments. The credit instruments may also be distinguished between private and public sectors of issuance. The plethora of monetary aggregates has posed problems, both for the implementation of policy and for the structure of econometric models used in that connection. The various aggregates all behave differently with respect to reserves and the monetary base. The authorities may be able to control these latter concepts quite well, but the targets of interest all react differently. Furthermore, monetary aggregates are not necessarily being targeted because of their inherent interest but because they are thought to be related to nominal income aggregates and the general price level. The more relevant the monetary aggregate for influencing income and the price level, the more difficult it is to control it through the instruments that the authorities can effect.

Benjamin Friedman has found, for the United States, that the most relevant aggregate in the sense of having a stable velocity coefficient is total credit, but this is the least controllable.[1] The most controllable aggregate, currency plus checking accounts, has the most variable velocity. Between these extremes it appears than the further is the aggregate from control, the less variable is its associated velocity. This is more a problem for the implementation of monetary policy than for the construction of models.

But a problem for both policy formation and modeling is the recent introduction of new monetary instruments and technical changes in the operation of credit markets. Electronic banking, the use of credit cards, the issuance of more sophisticated securities to the average citizen are all innovations that befuddle the monetary authorities and the econometrician. Authorities find that new instruments are practically outside their control for protracted periods of time, especially when they are first introduced. They upset traditional patterns of seasonal variation and generally enlarge the bands of uncertainty that are associated with policy measures. They are problematic for econometricians because they establish new modes of behavior and have little observational experience on which to base sample estimates.

Side by side with monetary policy goes the conduct of fiscal policy. For many years — during and after the Great Depression — fiscal policy was central as far as macro policy was concerned. It was only when interest rates got significantly above depression floor levels that monetary policy was actively used and shown to be fairly powerful.

Fiscal policy is usually, but not necessarily, less flexible than monetary policy because both the legislative and executive branches of government must approve major changes in public revenues and expenditures. In a parliamentary system, a government cannot survive unless its fiscal policy is approved by parliament, but this very process frequently delays effective policy implementation. In a legislative system of the American type, a lack of agreement may not bring down a government, but it may seriously delay the implementation of policy. On the other hand, central banking authorities can intervene in the functioning of financial markets on a moment's notice.

On the side of fiscal policy, there are two major kinds of instruments — public spending and taxing. Although taxing is less flexible than monetary management, it is considerably more flexible than are many kinds of expenditure policy. In connection with expenditures, it is useful to distinguish between purchases of goods or services and transfer payments. The latter are often as flexible as many kinds of taxation instruments.

---

[1] Benjamin Friedman, "The relative stability of money and credit 'velocities' in the United States: Evidence and some speculations," National Bureau of Economic Research, working paper No. 645, March, 1981.

It is generally safer to focus on tax instruments and pay somewhat less attention to expenditure policy. Tax changes have the flexibility of being made retroactive when desirable. This can be done with some expenditures, but not all. Tax changes can be made effective right after enactment. Expenditure changes, for goods or services, especially if they are increases, can be long in the complete making. Appropriate projects must be designed, approved, and executed. Often it is difficult to find or construct appropriate large projects.

Tax policy can be spread among several alternatives such as personal direct taxes, (either income or expenditure) business income taxes, or indirect taxes. At present, much interest attaches to indirect taxes because of their ease of collection, if increases are being contemplated; or because of their immediate effect on price indexes, if decreases are in order. Those taxes that are levied by local, as opposed to national governments, are difficult to include in national economic analysis because of their diversity of form, status, and amount.

Some tax policies are general, affecting most people or most sectors of the economy all at once. But, *specific*, in contrast to *general*, taxes are important for the implementation of structural policies. An expenditure tax focuses on stimulating personal savings. Special depreciation allowances or investment tax credits aim at stimulating private fixed capital formation. Special allowances for R&D, scientific research, or capital gains are advocated as important for helping the process of entrepreneurial innovation in high technology or venture capital lines. These structural policies are frequently cited in present discussions of industrial policy.

A favorite proposal for strictly anti-inflationary policy is the linkage of tax changes, either as rewards (cuts) or penalties (increases), to compliance by businesses and households with prescribed wage/price guidelines. Few have ever been successfully applied on a broad continuing scale, but this approach, known as incomes policies, social contracts, or TIPS (tax based incomes policies), is widely discussed in the scholarly literature.

These monetary and fiscal policies are the conventional macro instruments of overall policies. They are important and powerful; they must be included in any government's policy spectrum, but are they adequate to deal with the challenge of contemporary problems? Do they deal effectively with such problems as:

– severe unemployment among certain designated demographic groups;
– delivery of energy;
– conservation of energy;
– protection of the environment;
– public health and safety;
– provision of adequate agricultural supply;
– maintenance of healthy trade balance?

Structural policies, as distinct from macro policies, seem to be called for in order to deal effectively with these specific issues.

If these are the kinds of problems that economic policy makers face, it is worth-while considering the kinds of policy decisions with instruments that have to be used in order to address these issues appropriately, and consider the kind of economic model that would be useful in this connection.

For dealing with youth unemployment and related structural problems in labor markets, the relevant policies are minimum wage legislation, skill training grants, and provision of vocational education. These are typical things that ought to be done to reduce youth unemployment. These policy actions require legislative support with either executive or legislative initiative.

In the case of energy policy, the requisite actions are concerned with pricing of fuels, rules for fuel allocation, controls on imports, protection of the terrain against excessive exploitation. These are specific structural issues and will be scarcely touched by macro policies. These energy issues also effect the environment, but there are additional considerations that arise from non-energy sources. Tax and other punitive measures must be implemented in order to protect the environment, but, at the same time, monitor the economic costs involved. The same is true for policies to protect public health and safety. These structural policies need to be implemented but not without due regard to costs that have serious inflationary consequences. The whole area of public regulation of enterprise is under scrutiny at the present time, not only for the advantages that might be rendered, but also for the fostering of competition, raising incentives, and containing cost elements. It is not a standard procedure to consider the associated inflationary content of regulatory policy.

Ever since the large harvest failures of the first half of the 1970s (1972 and 1975, especially) economists have become aware of the fact that special attention must be paid to agriculture in order to insure a flow of supplies and moderation in world price movements. Appropriate policies involve acreage limitations (or expansions), crop subsidies, export licenses, import quotas, and similar specific measures. They all have bearing on general inflation problems through the medium of food prices, as components of consumer price indexes, and of imports on trade balances.

Overall trade policy is mainly guided by the high minded principle of fostering of conditions for the achievement of multilateral free trade. This is a macro concept, on average, and has had recent manifestation in the implementation of the "Tokyo Round" of tariff reductions, together with pleas for moderation of non-tariff barriers to trade. Nevertheless, there are many specific breaches of the principle, and specific protectionist policies are again a matter of concern. Trade policy, whether it is liberal or protectionist, will actually be implemented through a set of structural measures. It might mean aggressive marketing in search of export sales, provision of credit facilities, improved port/storage facilities, and a whole group of related policy actions that will, in the eyes of each country by itself, help to preserve or improve its net export position.

We see then that economic policy properly understood in the context of economic problems of the day goes far beyond the macro setting of tax rates, overall expenditure levels, or establishing growth rates for some monetary aggregates. It is a complex network of specific measures, decrees, regulations (or their absence), and recommendations coming from all branches of the public sector. In many cases they require government coordination. Bureaus, offices, departments, ministries, head of state, and an untold number of public bodies participate in this process. It does not look at all like the simple target-instrument approach of macroeconomics, yet macroeconometric modeling, if pursued at the appropriate level of detail, does have much to contribute. That will be the subject of sections of this paper that follow.

2. Formal Political Economy

The preceding section has just described the issues and actors in a very summary outline. Let us now examine some of the underlying doctrine. The translation of economic theory into policy is as old as our subject, but the modern formalism is conveniently dated from the *Keynesian Revolution*. Clear distinction should be made between Keynesian theory and Keynesian policy, but as far as macro policy is concerned, it derives from Keynesian theory.

The principal thrust of Keynesian theory was that savings–investment balance at full employment would be achieved through adjustment of the aggregative activity level of the economy. It was interpreted, at an early stage, in a framework of interest-inelastic investment and interest-elastic demand for cash. This particular view and setting gave a secondary role to monetary policy. Direct effects on the spending or activity stream were most readily achieved through fiscal policy, either adding or subtracting directly from the flow of activity through public spending or affecting it indirectly through changes in taxation. Thinking therefore centered around the achievement of balance in the economy, at full employment, by the appropriate choice of fiscal measures. In a formal sense, let us consider the simple *model*

$$C = f(Y - T) \qquad \text{consumption function}$$
$$T = tY \qquad \text{tax function}$$
$$I = g(\Delta Y) \qquad \text{investment function}$$
$$Y = C + I + G \qquad \text{output definition}$$

where

$$G = \text{public expenditures}$$
$$\Delta = \text{time difference operator}$$
$$Y = \text{total output (or income, or activity level)}.$$

Fiscal policy means the choice of an appropriate value of t (tax rate), or level G (expenditure), or mixture of both in order to achieve a target level of Y. This could also be a dynamic policy, by searching for achievement of a target path of Y through time. To complement dynamic policy it is important to work with a richer dynamic specification of the economic model. Lag distributions of $Y - T$ or ΔY in the C and I function would be appropriate. This kind of thinking inspired the approach to fiscal policy that began in the 1930s and still prevails today. It inspired thoughts about "fine tuning" or "steering" an economic system. It is obviously terribly simplified. It surely contains grains of truth, but what are the deficiencies?

In the first place, there is no explicit treatment of the price level or inflation rate in this system. Arguments against Keynesian policy pointed out the inflationary dangers from the outset. These dangers were minimal during the 1930s and did not become apparent on a widespread basis for about 30 years — after much successful application of fiscal policy, based on some monetary policy as time wore on. There is no doubt, however, that explicit analysis of price formation and great attention to the inflation problem must be guiding principles for policy formation from this time forward.

Another argument against literal acceptance of this version of crude Keynesianism is that it deals with unrealistic, simplistic concepts. Fiscal action is not directed towards "t" or "G." Fiscal action deals with complicated allowances, exemptions, bracket rates, capital gains taxation, value added taxation, expenditures for military hardware, agricultural subsidies, food stamps, aid to dependent children, and unemployment insurance benefits. These specific policy instruments have implications for the broad, general concepts represented by "t" and "G," but results can be quite misleading in making a translation from realistic to such macro theoretical concepts. The system used here for illustration is so simplified that there is no distinction between direct and indirect taxes or between personal and business taxes.

The Keynesian model of income determination can be extended to cover the pricing mechanism, labor input, labor supply, unemployment, wages, and monetary phenomena. There is a difference, however, between monetary analysis and monetarism. Just as the simple Keynesian model serves as the background for doctrinaire Keynesian fiscal policy, there is another polar position, namely, the monetarist model which goes beyond the thought that money matters, to the extreme that says that *only* money matters. The monetarist model has its simplest and crudest exposition in the following equation of exchange

$$Mv = Y.$$

For a steady, parametric, value of v (velocity), there is a linear proportional correspondence between M (nominal money supply) and Y (nominal value of aggregate production or income). For every different M-concept, say M_i, we would have[2]

$$M_i v_i = Y.$$

A search for a desired subscript i may attach great importance to the corresponding stability of v_i. It is my experience, for example, that in the United States, v_2 is more stable than v_1.

---

[2] See the various concepts in the contribution by Benjamin Friedman, *op. cit.*

More sophisticated concepts would be

$$Mv = \sum_{i=0}^{n} w_i Y_{-i},$$

or

$$Mv = \left(\sum_{i=0}^{n} w_i Y_{-i} \right)^{\alpha},$$

or

$$Mv = \left(\sum_{i=0}^{n} w_i X_{-i} \right)^{\alpha} \left(\sum_{i=0}^{m} q_i P_{-i} \right)^{\beta}.$$

The first says that M is proportional to long-run Y or a distributed lag in Y. The second says that M is proportional to a power of long-run Y or merely that a stable relationship exists between long-run Y and M. Finally, the third says that M is a function of long-run price as well as long-run real income (X). In these relationships no attention is paid to subscripts for M, because the theory would be similar (not identical) for any M, and proponents of monetarist policy simply argue that a stable relationship should be found for the authorities for some M_i concept, and that they should stick to it.

The distributed lag relationships in P_{-i} and X_{-i} are evidently significant generalizations of the crude quantity theory, but in a more general view, the principal thing that monetarists need for policy implementation of their theory is a *stable* demand function for money. If this stable function depends also on interest rates (in lag distributions), the theory can be only *partial*, and analysis then falls back on the kind of mainstream general macroeconometric model used in applications that are widely criticized by strict monetarists.[3]

The policy implications of the strict monetarist approach are clear and are, indeed, put forward as arguments for minimal policy intervention. The proponents are generally against activist fiscal policy except possibly for purposes of indexing when price movements get out of hand. According to the basic monetarist relationship, a rule should be established for the growth rate of M according to the growth rate of Y, preferably the long run concept of Y. A steady growth of M, according to this rule, obviates the need for frequent intervention and leaves the economy to follow natural economic forces. This is a macro rule, in the extreme, and the monetarists would generally look for the competitive market economy to make all the necessary micro adjustments without personal intervention.

The theory for the steady growth of M and Y also serves as a theory for inflation policy, for if the competitive economy maintains long-run real income ($\Sigma w_i X_{-i}$) at

---

[3] The lack of applicability of the monetarist type relationship, even generalized dynamically, to the United Kingdom is forcefully demonstrated by D. F. Hendry and N. R. Ericsson, "Assertion without empirical basis: An econometric appraisal of Friedman and Schwartz' 'Monetary trends in ... the United Kingdom,'" *Monetary Trends in the United Kingdom*, Bank of England Panel of Academic Consultants, panel paper No. 22 (October 1983), pp. 45–101.

its full capacity level — not in every period, but on average over the cycle — then steady growth of M implies a steady level for long-run price $(\Sigma q_i P_{-i})$. The monetarist rule is actually intended as a policy rule for inflation control.

There are several lines of argument against this seemingly attractive policy for minimal intervention except at the most aggregative level, letting the free play of competitive forces do the main work of guiding the economy in detail. In the first place there is a real problem in defining M_i, as discussed already in the previous section. Banking and credit technology is rapidly changing. The various M_i concepts are presently quite fluid, and there is no clear indication as to which M_i to attempt to control. To choose the most tractable concept is not necessarily going to lead to the best economic policy.

Not only are the M_i concepts under debate, but the measurement of any one of them is quite uncertain. Coverage of reporting banks, the sudden resort to new sources of funds (Euro-currency markets, e.g.), the attempts to live with inflation, and other disturbing factors have led to very significant measurement errors, indicated in part at least by wide swings in data revision of various M_i series. If the monetary authorities do not know M_i with any great precision, how can they hit target values with the precision that is assumed by monetarists? It was previously remarked that policy makers do not actually choose values for "t" and "G." Similarly, they do not choose values for "M_i." They engage in open market buying and selling of government securities; they fix reserve requirements for specific deposits or specific classes of banks; they fix the discount rate and they make a variety of micro decisions about banking practices. In a fractional reserve system, there is a money multiplier connecting the reserve base that is controlled by monetary authorities to M_i, but the multiplier concept is undergoing great structural change at the present time, and authorities do not seem to be able to hit M_i targets well.

A fundamental problem with either the Keynesian or the monetarist view of formal political economy is that they are based on simple models — models that are useful for expository analysis but inadequate to meet the tasks of economic policy. These simple models do not give a faithful representation of the economy; they do not explicitly involve the appropriate levels of action; they do not take account of enough processes in the economy. Imagine running the economy according to a strict monetarist rule or fine tuning applications of tax policy in the face of world shortages in energy markets and failing to take appropriate action simply because there are no energy parameters or energy processes in the expository system. This, in fact, is what people from the polar camps have said at various times in the past few years.

What is the appropriate model, if neither the Keynesian nor the monetarist models are appropriate? An eclectic view is at the base of this presentation. Some would argue against eclecticism on *a priori* grounds as being too diffuse, but it may be that an eclectic view is necessary in order to get an adequate model approximation to the complicated modern economy. Energy, agriculture, foreign trade, exchange rates, the spectrum of prices, the spectrum of interest rates, demography, and many other things must be taken into account simultaneously. This cannot be done except through the medium of large-scale models. These systems are far different in scope and method from either of the polar cases. They have fiscal and monetary sectors, but they have many other sectors and many other policy options too.

As a general principle, I am arguing against the formulation of economic policy through the medium of small models — anything fewer than 25 simultaneous equations. Small models are inherently unable to deal with the demands for economic policy formation. An appropriate large-scale model can, in my opinion, be used in the policy process. An adequate system is not likely to be in the neighborhood of 25 equations, however. It is likely to have more than 100 equations, and many in use today have more than 500–1000 equations. The actual size will depend on the country, its openness, its data system, its variability, and other factors. The largest systems in regular use have about 5000 equations, and there is an upper limit set by manageability.[4]

It is difficult to present such a large system in compact display, but it is revealing to lay out its sectors:

Consumer demand
Fixed capital formation
Inventory accumulation
Foreign trade
Public spending on goods and services
Production of goods and services
Labor requirements
Price formation
Wage determination
Labor supply and demography
Income formation
Money supply and credit
Interest rate determination
Tax receipts
Transfer payments
Inter industry production flows

In each of these sectors, there are several subsectors, some by type of product, some by type of end use, some by age–sex–race, some by country of origin or destination, some by credit market instrument, and some by level of government. The production sector may have a complete input–output system embedded in the model. Systems like these should not be classified as either Keynesian or monetarist. They are

---

[4]The Wharton Quarterly Model, regularly used for short-run business cycle analysis had 1000 equations in 1980, and the medium-term Wharton Annual Model had 1595 equations, exclusive of input–output relationships. The world system of Project LINK has more than 15,000 equations at the present time, and is still growing.

truly eclectic and are better viewed as approximations to the true but unknown Walrasian structure of the economy. These approximations are not unique. The whole process of model building is in a state of flux because at any time when one generational system is being used, another, better approximation to reality is being prepared. The outline of the equation structure for a system combining input–output relations with a macro model of income determination and final demand, is given in the appendix.

The next section will deal with the concrete policy making process through the medium of large scale models actually in use. They do not govern the policy process on an automatic basis, but they play a definite role. This is what this presentation is attempting to show.

There is, however, a new school of thought, arguing that economic policy will not get far in actual application because the smart population will counter public officials' policies, thus nullifying their effects. On occasion, this school of thought, called the *rational expectations* school, indicate that they think that the use of macroeconometric models to guide policy is vacuous, but on closer examination their argument is seen to be directed at any activist policy, whether through the model medium or not.

The argument, briefly put, of the rational expectations school is that economic agents (household, firms, and institutions) have the same information about economic performance as the public authorities and any action by the latter, on the basis of their information has already been anticipated and will simply lead to reaction by economic agents that will nullify the policy initiatives of the authorities. On occasion, it has been assumed that the hypothetical parameters of economic models are functions of policy variables and will change in a particular way when policy variables are changed.[5]

Referring to a linear expression of the consumption function in the simple Keynesian model, they would assume

$$C = \alpha + \beta(Y - T)$$
$$\beta = \beta(T, G).$$

This argument seems to me to be highly contrived. It is true that a generalization of the typical model from fixed to variable parameters appears to be very promising, but there is little evidence that the generalization should make the coefficients depend in such a special way on exogenous instrument variables.

The thought that economic models should be written in terms of the agent's perceptions of variables on the basis of their interpretation of history is sound. The earliest model building attempts proceeded from this premise and introduced lag distributions and various proxies to relate strategic parameter values, to information at the disposal of both economic agents and public authorities, but they did not make the blind intellectual jump to the conclusion that perceptions of the public at

---

[5]R. Lucas, "Econometric policy evaluation: A critique," *The Phillips Curve and Labor Markets*, eds., K. Brunner and A. H. Meltzer (North-Holland, Amsterdam, 1976), pp. 19–46.

large and authorities are the same. It is well known that the public, at any time, holds widely dispersed views about anticipations for the economy. Many do not have sophisticated perceptions and do not share the perceptions of public authorities. Many do not have the qualifications or facilities to make detailed analysis of latest information or history of the economy.

Econometric models are based on theories and estimates of the way people *do* behave, not on the way they *ought* to behave under the conditions of some hypothesized decision-making rules. In this respect, many models currently in use, contain data and variables on expressed expectations, i.e., those expected values that can be ascertained from sample surveys. In an interesting paper dealing with business price expectations, de Leeuw and McKelvey find that statistical evidence on expected prices contradict the hypothesis of rationality, as one might expect.[6]

The rise of the rational expectations school is associated with an assertion that the mainstream model, probably meaning the Keynesian model, has failed during the 1970s. It principally failed because of its inability to cope with a situation in which there are rising rates of inflation and rising rates of unemployment. In standard analysis the two ought to be inversely related, but recently they have been positively related. Charging that macroeconomic models have failed in this situation, Lucas and Sargent, exponents of the school of rational expectations, seek an equilibrium business cycle model consisting of optimizing behavior by economic agents and the clearing of markets.[7] Many, if not most, macroeconometric models are constructed piece-by-piece along these lines and have been for the past 30 or more years. Rather than reject a whole body of analysis or demand wholly new modeling approaches, it may be more fruitful to look more carefully at the eclectic model that has, in fact, been in use for some time. If such models have appropriate allowance for supply side disturbances, they can do quite well in interpreting the events of the 1970s and even anticipated them in many instances.[8]

3. Some Policy Projections

Rather than move in the direction of the school of rational expectations, I suggest that we turn from the oversimplified model and the highly aggregative policy in-

---

[6]F. de Leeuw and M. McKelvey, "Price expectations by business firms," *Brookings Papers on Economic Activity* (1981), pp. 299–314. The findings in this article have been extended, and they now report that there is evidence in support of long-run lack of bias in price expectations, a necessary but not sufficient condition for *rationality* of price expectations. See "Price expectations of business firms: Bias in the short and long run," *American Economic Review* **74** (March, 1984), pp. 99–110.

[7]Robert S. Lucas and Thomas J. Sargent, "After Keynesian macroeconomics," *After the Phillips Curve: Persistence of High Inflation and High Unemployment* (Federal Reserve Bank of Boston, Boston, 1978), pp. 49–72.

[8]L. R. Klein, "The longevity of economic theory," *Quantitative Wirtschaftsforschung*, eds. H. Albach *et al.* (J. C. B. Mohr (Paul Siebeck), Tübingen, 1977), pp. 411–419; "Supply side constraints in demand oriented systems: An interpretation of the oil crisis," *Zeitschrift für Nationalökonomie* **34** (1974), pp. 45–56; "Five-year experience of linking national econometric models of forecasting international trade," *Quantitative Studies of International Economic Relations*, ed. H. Glejser (North-Holland, Amsterdam, 1976), pp. 1–24.

struments to the eclectic system that has large supply side content, together with conventional demand side analysis and examine structural as well as macro policies.

In the 1960s, aggregative policies of Keynesian demand management worked very well. The 1964 tax cut in the United States was a textbook example and refutes the claim of the rational expectations school that parametric shifts will nullify policy action. It also refutes the idea that we know so little about the response pattern of the economy that we should refrain from activist policies.

Both the Wharton and Brookings Models were used for simulations of the 1964 tax cut.[9] A typical policy simulation with the Wharton Model is shown in the accompanying table.

Table 1. Comparative simulations of the tax cut of 1964 (The Wharton Model).

	Real GNP (bill 1958 $)			Personal tax and nontax payments (bill of curr. $)		
	Actual	Tax cut simulation	No tax cut simulation	Actual	Tax cut simulation	No tax cut simulation
1964.1	569.7	567.0	563.1	60.7	61.3	64.0
1964.2	578.1	575.8	565.4	56.9	57.9	64.5
1964.3	585.0	581.0	569.6	59.1	59.0	65.6
1964.4	587.2	585.0	574.7	60.9	59.9	66.7

This is a typical policy simulation with an econometric model, solving the system dynamically, with and without a policy implementation. The results in the above table estimate that the policy added about $10 billion (1958 $) to real GNP and sacrificed about $7 billion in tax revenues. Actually, by 1965, the expansion of the (income) tax base brought revenues back to their pre-tax cut position.

The Full Employment Act of 1946 in the United States was the legislation giving rise to the establishment of the Council of Economic Advisers. Similar commitments of other governments in the era following World War II and reconstruction led to the formulation of aggregative policies of demand management on a broad international scale. New legislation in the United States, under the name of the Humphrey–Hawkins Bill, established ambitious targets for unemployment and inflation during the early part of the 1980s. The bill, however, states frankly that aggregative policy alone will not be able to accomplish the objectives. Structural policies will be needed, and to formulate those, with meaning, it will be necessary to draw upon the theory of a more extensive model, namely, the Keynes–Leontief model.

The Wharton Annual Model is of the Keynes–Leontief type. It combines a model of income generation and final demand determination with a complete input–output system of 65 sectors and a great deal of demographic detail. It is described

---

[9]L. R. Klein, "Econometric analysis of the tax cut of 1964," *The Brookings Model: Some Further Results*, eds. J. Duesenberry *et al.* (North-Holland, Amsterdam, 1969).

in general terms in the preceding section and laid out in equation form in the appendix. To show how some structural policies for medium-term analysis work out in this system, I have prepared a table with a baseline projection for the 1980s, together with an alternative simulation in which the investment tax credit has been increased (doubled to 1982 and raised by one-third thereafter), in order to stimulate capital formation, general personal income taxes have been reduced by about 6% and a tax has been placed on gasoline (50¢ per gallon).[10] To offset the gasoline tax on consumers, sales taxes have been cut back, with some grants in aid to state and local governments increased to offset the revenue loss of the sales taxes.

These policies mix aggregative fiscal measures with some structural measures to get at the Nation's energy problem. Also, tax changes have been directed specifically at investment in order to improve the growth of productivity and hold down inflation for the medium term. It is an interesting policy scenario because it simultaneously includes both stimulative and restrictive measures. Also, it aims to steer the economy in a particular direction towards energy conservation and inducement of productivity.

Table 2. Estimated policy projections of the Wharton Annual Model 1980–89.
(Deviation of policy simulation from baseline)
Selected economic indicators

	1980	1981	1982	1983	1984	1985	1986	1987	1988	1989
GNP (bills $ 1972)	−1	14	35	44	50	51	131	48	48	46
GNP deflator (index points)	−0.4	−0.7	−1.4	−1.7	−2.1	−2.4	−3.0	−3.6	−4.6	−5.7
Unemployment rate (percentage points)	0.0	−0.5	−1.2	−1.6	−1.8	−1.9	−1.7	−1.5	−1.3	−1.1
Productivity change (percentage points)	−0.1	0.6	0.5	0.0	0.0	−0.1	0.0	0.1	0.1	0.0
Net exports (bill $)	0.8	6.8	4.7	10.5	6.2	2.2	0.8	0.9	−0.5	−1.6
Federal surplus (bill $)	−2.7	1.1	−0.2	−1.0	4.5	0.1	−2.5	−0.6	−9.2	−2.7
Energy ratio (thou BTU/Real GNP)	−0.9	−0.8	−0.6	−0.5	−0.3	−0.3	−0.2	−0.3	−0.2	−0.2
Nonresidential investment (bill $ 1972)	0.9	4.1	8.4	11.3	13.8	14.8	16.0	16.7	17.2	17.2

As the figures in Table 2 show, the policy simulation produces results that induce more real output, at a lower price level. Lower unemployment accompanies the higher output, and the improvement in productivity contributes to the lower

---

[10]The investment tax credit provides tax relief to business, figured as a percentage of an equipment purchase, if capital formation is undertaken. The percentage has varied, but is now about 10 percent.

price index. The lowering of indirect taxes offsets the inflationary impact of higher gasoline taxes.

A cutback in energy use, as a result of the higher gasoline tax, results in a lower BTU/GNP ratio. This holds back energy imports and makes the trade balance slightly better in the policy alternative case.

A contributing factor to the productivity increase is the higher rate of capital formation in the policy alternative. There are no surprises in this example. The results come out as one would guess on the basis of *a priori* analysis, but the main contribution of the econometric approach is to try to *quantify* the outcome and provide a basis for *net* assessment of both the positive and negative sides of the policy. Also, the differences from the baseline case are not very large. Econometric models generally project moderate gains. To some extent, they *underestimate* change in a systematic way, but they also suggest that the present inflationary situation is deep seated and will not be markedly cured all at once by the range of policies that is being considered.

4. The Theory of Economic Policy

The framework introduced by Tinbergen is the most fruitful starting point.[11] He proposed the designation of two kinds of variables, *targets* and *instruments*. A target is an endogenous (dependent) variable in a multivariate–multiequation representation of the economy. An instrument is an exogenous (independent) variable that is controlled or influenced by policy-making authorities in order to lead the economy to targets. Not all endogenous variables are targets; not all exogenous variables are instruments.

In the large eclectic model, with more than 500 endogenous variables, policy makers cannot possibly comprehend the fine movements in all such magnitudes. Some systems in use have thousands of endogenous variables. At the national economy level, top policy makers may want to focus on the following: GDP growth rate, overall inflation rate, trade balance, exchange rate, unemployment rate, interest rate. There may be intermediate or intervening targets, too, as in our energy policy today — to reduce the volume of oil imports. This is partly a goal on its own, but partly a means of improving the exchange value of the dollar, the trade balance, and the inflation rate. There may be layers of targets in recursive fashion, and in this way policy makers can extend the scope of variables considered as targets, but it is not practical to extend the scope much beyond 10 targets or so. This refers to policy makers at the top. Elsewhere in the economy, different ministers or executives are looking at a number of more specialized targets — traffic safety, agricultural yield, size of welfare rolls, number of housing completions, etc.

The large-scale eclectic model has many hundreds or thousands of equations with an equal number of endogenous variables, but there will also be many exogenous variables. A crude rule of thumb might be that there are about as many

---

[11] J. Tinbergen, *On The Theory of Economic Policy* (North Holland, Amsterdam, 1952).

exogenous as endogenous variables in an econometric model.[12] Perhaps we are too lax in theory building and resign ourselves to accept too many variables in the exogenous category because we have not undertaken the task of explaining them. All government spending variables and all demographic variables, for example, are not exogenous, yet they are often not explicitly modeled, but are left to be explained by the political scientist and sociologist. This practice is rapidly changing. Many variables that were formerly accepted as exogenous are now being given explicit and careful endogenous explanation in carefully designed additional equations; nevertheless, there remains a large number of exogenous variables in the eclectic, large-scale model. There are, at least, hundreds.

Only a few of the many exogenous variables are suitable for consideration as instruments. In the first place, public authorities cannot effectively control very many at once. Just as coordinated thought processes can comprehend only a few targets at a time, so can they comprehend only a few instruments at a time. Moreover, some exogenous variables cannot, in principle, be controlled effectively. The many dimensions of weather and climate that are so important for determining agricultural output are the clearest examples of non-controllable exogenous variables — with or without cloud seeding.

The econometric model within which these concepts are being considered will be written as

$$F\left(y', y'_{-1} \ldots y'_{-p}, x', x'_{-1} \ldots x'_{-q}, w', w'_{-1} \ldots w'_{-r}, z', z'_{-1}, z'_{-s}, \Theta'\right) = e \quad (1)$$

F = column vector of functions:

$$f_1, f_2, \ldots f_n \, .$$

y = column vector of target (endogenous) variables:

$$y_1, y_2, \ldots, y_{n_1} \, .$$

x = column vector of non-target (endogenous) variables:

$$x_1, x_2, \ldots, x_{n_2}$$
$$n_1 + n_2 = n \, .$$

w = column vector of instrument (exogenous) variables:

$$w_1, w_2, \ldots, w_{m_1} \, .$$

z = column vector of non-instrument (exogenous) variables:

$$z_1, z_2, \ldots, z_{m_2}$$
$$m_1 + m_2 = m \, .$$

---

[12] The Wharton Quarterly Model (1980) has 432 stochastic equations, 568 identities, and 401 exogenous variables. The Wharton Annual Model (1980) had 647 stochastic equations, 948 identities, and 626 exogenous variables. Exclusive of identities (and input–output relations), these each have approximate balance between endogenous and exogenous variables.

Θ = column vectors of parameters
e = column vector of errors:

$$e_1, e_2, \ldots, e_n.$$

In this system, there are n stochastic equations, with unknown coefficients, in n endogenous variables and m exogenous variables. A subset of the endogenous variables will be targets $(n_1 \leq n)$, and a subset of the exogenous variables will be instruments $(m_1 \leq m)$.

The parameters are unknown, but estimated by the statistician from observable data or *a priori* information. The estimated values will be denoted by $\hat{\Theta}$. Also, for any application situation, values must be assigned to the random variables e. Either the assumed mean $(E(e) = 0)$ will be assigned, or values of e will be generated by some random drawings, or fixed at some *a priori* non-zero values. But, given values for e and $\hat{\Theta}$, together with initial conditions, econometricians can generally "solve" this equation system. Such solutions or integrals will be used in the policy formation process in a key way.

First, let us consider Tinbergen's special case of equality between the number of instruments and targets, $n_1 = m_1$. Look first at the simplest possible case with one instrument, one target, and one estimated parameter. If the f-function expresses a single-valued relationship between y and w, we can invert it to give

$$w = g(y, \hat{\Theta}).$$

For a particular target value of $y(y^*)$, we can find the appropriate instrument value $w = w^*$ from the solution of

$$w^* = g(y^*, \hat{\Theta}).$$

If the f-function were simple proportional, we can write the answer in closed form as

$$y = \hat{\Theta} w$$

$$w^* = \frac{1}{\hat{\Theta}} y^*.$$

For any desired value of y we can thus find the appropriate action that the authorities must take by making $w = w^*$. This will enable us to hit the target exactly. The only exception to this remark would be that a legitimate target y^* required an unattainable or inadmissable w^*. Apart from such inadmissible solutions, we say that for this case the straightforward rule is to interchange the roles of exogenous and endogenous variable and resolve the system, that is to say, treat the $n_1 = m_1$ instruments as though they were unknown endogenous variables and the $n_1 = m_1$ targets as though they were known exogenous variables. Then solve the system for all the endogenous as functions of the exogenous variables so classified.

It is obvious and easy to interchange the roles of endogenous and exogenous variables by inverting the single equation and solving for the latter, given the target value of the former. In a large complicated system linear or not, it is easy to indicate how this may be done or even to write closed form linear expressions for doing it in linear systems, but it is not easy to implement in most large-scale models.

For the linear static case, $n_1 = m_1$, we can write

$$\begin{pmatrix} A_{11} & A_{12} \\ A_{21} & A_{22} \end{pmatrix} \begin{pmatrix} y \\ x \end{pmatrix} + \begin{pmatrix} B_{11} & B_{12} \\ B_{21} & B_{22} \end{pmatrix} \begin{pmatrix} w \\ z \end{pmatrix} = e$$

A_{11} is $n_1 \times n_1$; A_{12} is $n_1 \times n_2$; A_{21} is $n_2 \times n_1$; A_{22} is $n_2 \times n_2$

B_{11} is $n_1 \times m_1$; B_{12} is $n_1 \times m_2$; B_{21} is $n_2 \times m_1$; B_{22} is $n_2 \times m_2$.

The solution for the desired instruments w^* in terms of the targets y^* and of z is

$$\begin{pmatrix} B_{11} & A_{12} \\ B_{21} & A_{22} \end{pmatrix} \begin{pmatrix} w^* \\ x \end{pmatrix} + \begin{pmatrix} A_{11} & B_{12} \\ A_{21} & B_{22} \end{pmatrix} \begin{pmatrix} y^* \\ z \end{pmatrix} = e$$

$$\begin{pmatrix} w^* \\ x \end{pmatrix} = - \begin{pmatrix} B_{11} & A_{12} \\ B_{21} & A_{22} \end{pmatrix}^{-1} \begin{pmatrix} A_{11} & B_{12} \\ A_{21} & B_{22} \end{pmatrix} \begin{pmatrix} y^* \\ z \end{pmatrix} + \begin{pmatrix} B_{11} & A_{12} \\ B_{12} & A_{22} \end{pmatrix}^{-1} e.$$

The relevant values come from the first n_1 rows of this solution.

This solution is not always easy to evaluate in practice. Whether the system is linear or nonlinear, the usual technique employed in most econometric centers is to solve the equations by iterative steps in what is known as the Gauss–Seidel algorithm. An efficient working of this algorithm in large dynamic systems designed for standard calculations of simulation, forecasting, multiplier analysis, and similar operations requires definite rules of ordering, normalizing, and choosing step sizes.[13] It is awkward and tedious to re-do that whole procedure for a transformed system in which some variables have been interchanged, unless they are standardized.

It is simpler and more direct to solve the problem by searching (systematically) for instruments that bring the n_1 values of y as "close" as possible to their targets y^*. There are many ways of doing this, but one would be to find the minimum value of

$$L = \sum_{i=1}^{n_1} u_i (y_i - y_i^*)^2$$

subject to $\hat{F} = \hat{e}$

where $\hat{F}$ = estimated value of F for $\Theta = \hat{\Theta}$

$\hat{e}$ = assigned values to error vector

In the theory of *optimal* economic policy, L is called a loss function and is arbitrarily made a quadratic in this example. Other loss functions could equally well be chosen. The u_i are weights in the loss function and should be positive.

---

[13]L. R. Klein, *A Textbook of Econometrics* (Prentice-Hall, New York, 1974), p. 239.

If there is an admissible solution and if $n_1 = m_1$, the optimal values of the loss function should become zero.

A more interesting optimization problem arises if $n_1 \geq m_1$; i.e., if there are more targets than instruments. In this case, the optimization procedure will not, in general, bring one all the way to target values, but only to a "minimum distance" from the target. If $m_1 > n_1$, it would be possible, in principle, to assign arbitrary values to $m_1 - n_1$ (superfluous) instruments and solve for the remaining n_1 instruments as functions of the n_1 target values of y. Thus, the problem of excess instruments can be reduced to the special problem of equal numbers of instruments and targets.

It should be noted that the structural model is a *dynamic* system, and it is un-likely that a static loss function would be appropriate. In general, economic policy makers have targeted paths for y. A whole stream of y-values are generally to be targeted over a policy planning horizon. In addition, the loss function could be generalized in other dimensions, too. There will usually be a loss associated with instrumentation. Policy makers find it painful to make activist decisions about run-ning the economy, especially in the industrial democracies; therefore, L should be made to depend on $w - w^*$ as well as on $y - y^*$. In the quadratic case, covaria-tion between $y_i - y_i^*$ might also be considered, but this may well be beyond the comprehension of the typical policy maker.

A better statement of the optimal policy problem will then be

$$L = \sum_{t=1}^{h} \left\{ \sum_{i=1}^{n_1} u_i (y_{it} - y_{it}^*)^2 + \sum_{i=1}^{m_1} v_i (w_{it} - w_{it}^*)^2 \right\} = \min .$$

w.r.t. w_{it} subject to $\hat{f} = \hat{e}_t$
$$t = 1, 2, \ldots, h .$$

The v_i are weights associated with instrumentation losses. If future values are to be discounted it may be desirable to vary u_i and v_i with t. A simple way would be to write

$$u_i/(1+\rho)^t; \ v_i/(1+\rho)^t ,$$

where ρ is the rate of discount.

A particular problem in the application of the dynamic formulation is known as the end-point problem. Decisions made at time point h (end of the horizon) may imply awkward paths for the system beyond h because it is a dynamic system whose near term movements $(h+1, h+2, \ldots)$ will depend on the (initial) conditions of the system up to time h. It may be advisable to carry the optimization exercise beyond h, even though policy focuses on the behavior of the system only through period h.

Many examples have been worked out for application of this approach to policy making — few in prospect (as genuine extrapolations into the future) but many in retrospect, assessing what policy should have been.[14] A noteworthy series of experimental policies dealt with attempts to have alleviated the stagflation of the late 1960s and the 1970s in the United States; in other words, could a combination of fiscal and monetary policies have been chosen that would have led to full (or fuller) employment without (so much) inflation over the period 1967–75?

The answers, from optimal control theory applications among many models, suggest that better levels of employment and production could have been achieved with very little additional inflationary pressures but that it would not have been feasible to bring down inflation significantly at the same time. Some degree of stagflation appears to have been inevitable, given the prevailing exogenous framework.

Such retrospective applications are interesting and useful, but they leave one a great distance from the application of such sophisticated measures to the positive formulation of economic policy. There are differences between the actual and optimal paths, but if tolerance intervals of error for econometric forecasts were properly evaluated, it is not likely that the two solutions would be significantly apart for the whole simulation path. If the two solutions are actually far apart, it is often required to use extremely wide ranges of policy choice, wider and more frequently changing than would be politically acceptable.

Two types of errors must be considered for evaluation of tolerance intervals,

$$\text{var}(\hat{\Theta})$$

$$\text{var}(e) \, .$$

The correct parameter values are not known, they must be estimated from small statistical samples and have fairly sizable errors. Also, there is behavioral error, arising from the fact that models cannot completely describe the economy. Appropriate valuation of such errors does not invalidate the use of models for some kinds of applications, but the errors do preclude "fine tuning."

A more serious problem is that the optimum problem is evaluated for a fixed system of constraints; i.e., subject to

$$\hat{F} = \hat{e} \, .$$

The problem of optimal policy may, in fact, be one of varying constraints, respecifying F.

It has been found that the problem of coping with stagflation is intractable in the sense that macro policies cannot bring both unemployment and inflation close

---

[14] A. Hirsch, S. Hymans, and H. Shapiro, "Econometric review of alternative fiscal and monetary policy, 1971–75," *Review of Economics and Statistics* **LX** (August, 1978), pp. 334–345.

L. R. Klein and V. Su, "Recent economic fluctuations and stabilization policies: An optimal control approach," *Quantitative Economics and Development*, eds. L. R. Klein, M. Nerlove, and S. C. Tsiang (Academic Press, New York, 1980).

M. B. Zarrop, S. Holly, B. Rutem, J. H. Westcott, and M. O'Connell, "Control of the LBS econometric model via a control model," *Optimal Control for Econometric Models*, eds. S. Holly *et al.* (Macmillan, London, 1979), pp. 23–64.

to desired targets simultaneously. On the other hand, there may exist policies that do so if the constraint system is modified. By introducing a special TIPS policy that ties both wage rates and profit rates to productivity

$$X/hL = \text{real output per worker-hour}$$

it has been found that highly favorable simulations can be constructed that simultaneously come close to full employment and low inflation targets. These simulation solutions were found with the same (Wharton) model that resisted full target approach using the methods of optimal control. The wage and profits (price) equations of the model had to be re-specified to admit

$$\Delta \ln w = \Delta \ln(X/hL)$$
$$\Delta \ln(PR/K) = \Delta \ln(X/hL)$$
$$PR = \text{corporate profits}$$
$$K = \text{stock of corporate capital.}$$

Equations for wages and prices, estimated over the sample period had to be removed, in favor of the insertion of these.[15]

A creative policy search with simulation exercises was able to get the economy to performance points that could not be reached with feasible applications of optimal control methods. This will not always be the case, but will frequently be so. Most contemporary problems cannot be fully solved by simple manipulation of a few macro instruments, and the formalism of optimal control theory has very limited use in practice. Simulation search for "good" policies, realistically formulated in terms of parameter values that policy makers actually influence is likely to remain as the dominant way that econometric models are used in the policy process.

That is not to say that optimal control theory is useless. It shows a great deal about model structure and instrument efficiency. By varying weights in the loss function and then minimizing, this method can show how sensitive the uses of policy instruments are. Also, some general propositions can be developed. The more uncertainty is attached to model specification and estimation, the less should be the amplitude of variation of instrument settings. Thus, William Brainard has shown, in purely theoretical analysis of the optimum problem, that policy makers ought to hold instruments cautiously to a narrow range (intervene less) if there is great uncertainty.[16] This is valuable advice developed from the analysis of optimal policy.

---

[15] L. R. Klein and V. Duggal, "Guidelines in economic stabilization: A new consideration," *Wharton Quarterly* **VI** (Summer, 1971), pp. 20–24.

[16] W. Brainard, "Uncertainty and the effectiveness of policy," *American Economic Review* **LVIII** May, 1967), pp. 411–425. See also L. Johansen, "Targets and instruments under uncertainty," Institute of Economics, Oslo, 1972. Brainard's results do not, in all theoretical cases, lead to the conclusion that instrument variability be reduced as uncertainty is increased, but that is the result for the usual case.

A particular case of uncertainty concerns the business cycle. The baseline solution for y_t should reflect whatever cyclical variation is present in the actual economy if predictions of y_t are at all accurate. For example, the existence of a cycle in the United States has been well documented by the National Bureau of Economic Research and has been shown to be evident in the solutions of macro econometric models.[17]

Although the baseline solution of a macro economy extending over 5 to 10 years should reflect a normal cyclical pattern unless some specific inputs are included that wipe out the cycle, that is not the usual practice in public policy planning. Policy makers are reluctant to forecast a downturn in their own planning horizon. The accompanying table illustrates this point in connection with U.S. budget planning in early 1984. The official baseline path assumes steady growth of the economy, contrary to historical evidence about the existence and persistence of a 4-year American cycle. An argument in support of this practice has been that the exact timing of the cyclical turning points is in doubt. If they are not known with great precision, it is argued that it is better not to introduce them at all. An appropriate standard error of estimate is probably no larger than ± 1.0 year; therefore, they ought to be introduced with an estimated degree of certainty.

Table 3. Growth assumptions and budget deficit fiscal policy planning, USA February 1984.[1]

	1984	1985	1986	1987	1988	1989
Real GNP estimates or assumptions(%)						
administration	5.3	4.1	4.0	4.0	4.0	4.0
Congressional Budget Office						
Baseline	5.4	4.1	3.5	3.5	3.5	3.5
Low alternative	4.9	3.6	−0.9	2.1	3.8	3.1
			Fiscal Years			
Estimated deficit ($ billion)						
administration	186	192	211	233	241	248
Congressional Budget Office						
Baseline	189	197	217	245	272	308
Low alternative	196	209	267	329	357	390

[1] *Source*: Baseline Budget Projections for Fiscal Years 1985–1989, Congressional Budget Office, Washington, D.C., February, 1984, Testimony of Rudolph G. Penner, Committee on Appropriations, U.S. Senate, February 22, 1984.

The Congressional Budget Office in the United States has a fairly steady expansion path for its baseline case, but introduces a cycle downturn for 1986, in a low growth alternative case, between 4 and 5 years after the last downturn. It would

---

[17]See I. and F. Adelman, "The dynamic properties of the Klein–Goldberger model," *Econometrica* **27** (October, 1959), pp. 596–625. See also, *Econometric Models of Cyclical Behavior*, ed. B. G. Hickman (Columbia University Press, New York, 1972).

seem more appropriate to consider this as a baseline case, with the steady growth projection an upper limit for a more favorable budget projection.

A series of randomly disturbed simulations of an estimated model

$$F = e_t^{(i)} \qquad t = 1, 2, \ldots H \qquad i = 1, 2, \ldots R,$$

with R replications of random error disturbances, generates solutions of the estimated equation system F. Each replication produces

$$\begin{pmatrix} y_1^{(i)} \\ y_2^{(i)} \\ \vdots \\ y_H^{(i)} \end{pmatrix} \quad \text{given} \quad \begin{pmatrix} z_1 \\ z_2 \\ \vdots \\ z_H \end{pmatrix} \quad \text{and initial conditions.}$$

The R stochastic projections will, on average, have cycles with random timing and amplitude. They will produce R budget deficit estimates. The mean and variance of these estimates can be used to construct an interval that includes a given fraction of cases, which can be used to generate a high, low, and average case for budget deficit values. The stochastic replications need not allow only for drawings of $e_t^{(i)}$; they can also be used to estimate distributions of parameter estimates for F.[18] This is an expensive and time-consuming way to generate policy intervals, but it is a sound way to proceed in the face of uncertainty for momentous macro problems.

It is evident from the table that provision for a business cycle, no matter how uncertain its timing may be, is quite important. The higher and steadier growth assumptions of the American administration produces, by far, the lowest fiscal deficits in budgetary planning. A slight lowering of the steady path (by only 0.5 percentage points, 1986–89) produces much larger deficits, and if a business cycle correction is built into the calculations, the rise in the deficit is very big. In the cyclical case, we have practically a doubling of the deficit in five years, while in the cycle-free case the rise is no more than about 50 percent in the same time period.

Also, optimal control theory can be used to good advantage in the choice of exogenous inputs for long-range simulations. Suppose that values for

$$w_t, z_t$$

are needed for $t = T+1, T+2, T+3, \ldots, T+30$ where $T+30$ is 30 years from now (in the 21st century). We have little concrete basis for choice of

$$w_{T+30}, z_{T+30}.$$

By optimizing about a *balanced growth path* for the endogenous variables, with respect to choice of key exogenous variables, we may be able to indicate sensible

---

[18]The technique employed in G. Schink, "Estimation of forecast error in a dynamic and/or non-linear econometric model," Ph.D. dissertation, University of Pennsylvania, 1971, can be used for joint variation of parameters and disturbances.

choices of these latter variables for a *baseline* path, about which to examine alternatives. These and other analytical uses will draw heavily on optimal control theory, but it is unlikely that such theory will figure importantly in the positive setting of economic policy.

The role of the baseline (balanced growth) solution for policy making in the medium or long term is to establish a reference point about which policy induced deviations can be estimated. The baseline solution is not, strictly speaking, a forecast, but it is policy reference set of points. Many policy problems are long term. Energy availability, other natural resource supplies, social insurance reform, and international debt settlement are typical long-term problems that use econometric policy analysis at the present time.

At the present time, the theory of economic policy serves as a background for development of policy but not for its actual implementation. There is too much uncertainty about the choice of loss function and about the constraint system to rely on this approach to policy formation in any mechanistic way.[19] Instead, economic policy is likely to be formulated, in part at least, through comparison of alternative simulations of econometric models.

In the typical formulation of policy, the following steps are taken:

(i) definition of a problem, usually to determine the effects of external events and of policy actions;

(ii) carry out model simulations in the form of historical and future projections that take account of the problem through changes in exogenous variables, parameter values, or system specification;

(iii) estimation of quantitative effects of policies as differences between simulations with and without the indicated changes;

(iv) presentation of results to policy decision makers for consideration in competition with estimates from many different sources.

Policy is rarely based on econometric information alone, but it is nearly always based on perusal of relevant econometric estimates together with other assessments of quantitative policy effects. Among econometric models, several will often be used as checking devices for confirmation or questioning of policy decisions.

It is important in policy formulation to have a baseline projection. For the short run, this will be a forecast of up to three years' horizon. For the longer run, it will be a model projection that is based on plausible assumptions about inputs of exogenous variables and policy-related parameters. For the longer-run projections, the inputs will usually be smooth, but for short-run forecasts the inputs will usually move with perceptions of monthly, quarterly, or annual information sources in a more irregular or cyclical pattern.

---

[19] See, in this respect, the conclusions of the Royal Commission (headed by R. J. Ball) Committee on Policy Optimisation, *Report* (HMSO, London, 1978).

The model forecast or baseline projection serves not only as a reference point from which to judge policy effects. It also serves as a standard of credibility. That is to say, past performance of forecast accuracy is important in establishing the credibility of any model.

Judgmental information, quantitative reduced form extrapolations (without benefit of a formal model) and estimated models will all be put together for joint information and discussion. Models are significant parts of this information source but by no means the whole. In many respects, model results will be used for confirmation or substantiation of decisions based on more general sources of information.

Models are most useful when they present alternative simulations of familiar types of changes that have been considered on repetitive occasions in the past, so that there is an historical data base on which to build simulation analyses. A new tax, a new expenditure program, the use of a new monetary instrument, or, in general, the implementation of a new policy that calls on uses of models that have not been examined in the past are the most questionable. There may be no historical data base in such situations from which to judge model performance.

In new situations, external *a priori* information for parameter values or for respecification with new (numerical) parameter values is needed. These new estimates of parameters should be supplied by engineers or scientists for technical relations, by legal experts for new tax relationships, or by whatever expertise can be found for other relationships. The resulting simulations with non-sample-based parameter estimates are simply explorations of alternatives and not forecasts or projections.

Much attention has been paid, in the United States, recently to changes in laws for taxing capital gains. There is no suitable sample that is readily available with many observations at different levels of capital gains taxation. Instead, one would be well advised to look at other countries' experience in order to estimate marginal consequences of changing the tax laws for treatment of capital gains. In addition, one could investigate state-to-state cross section estimates to see how capital gains taxes might influence spending behavior. Similar analyses across countries may also be of some help. Finally, we might try to insert questions into a field survey on people's attitudes towards the use of capital gains. These are all basic approaches and should be investigated simultaneously. There is nothing straightforward to do in a new situation, but some usable pieces of econometric information may be obtained and it might help in policy formation. Recently, claims were made about the great benefits to be derived from the liberalization of capital gains rates in the United States, but these claims were not backed by econometric research that could be professionally defended. For the ingenious econometric researcher, there is much to gain on a tentative basis, but care and patience are necessary.

In all this analysis, the pure forecast and forecasting ability of models play key roles. Forecasts are worthwhile in their own right, but they are especially valuable when examined from the viewpoint of accuracy because users of model results are going to look at forecast accuracy as means of validating models. It is extremely important to gain the confidence of model users, and this is most likely to be done through the establishment of credibility. This comes about through relative accuracy of the forecast. Can forecasts from models be made at least as accurately as by other methods and are the forecasts superior at critical points, such as business cycle turning points?

These questions are partly answered by the accuracy researches of Stephen Mc-Nees and others.[20] The answer is that models do no worse than other methods and tend to do better at cyclical turning points and over larger stretches of time horizon. The acceptability of model results by those who pay for them in the commercial market lends greater support to their usefulness and credibility. This supports their use in the policy process through the familiar technique of alternative/comparative simulation.

International policy uses provide a new dimension for applications of econometric models. Comprehensive models of the world economy are relatively new; so it is meaningful to examine their use in the policy process. The world model that is implemented through Project LINK has been used in a number of international policy studies, and an interpretation of some leading cases may be helpful.

Some of the problems for which the LINK model has been used are: exchange rate policy, agricultural policy associated with grain failures, oil pricing policy, coordinated fiscal policies, coordinated monetary policies.

When the LINK system was first constructed, the Bretton Woods system of fixed exchange rates was still in force. It was appropriate to make exchange rates exogenous in such an environment. At the present time exchange rate equations have been added in order to estimate currency rates endogenously. An interesting application of optimal control theory can be used for exchange rate estimation and especially for developing the concept of *equilibrium* exchange rates. Such equilibrium rates give meaning to the concept of the degree of *over- or under-evaluation* of rates, which may be significant for the determining of fiscal intervention in the foreign exchange market.

In a system of multiple models, for given exchange rates there is a solution, model by model, for

$$(PX)_i * X_i - (PM)_i * M_i = \text{trade balance for } i\text{th country}$$
$$(PX)_i = \text{export price}$$
$$X_i = \text{export volume (goods/services)}$$
$$(PM)_i = \text{import price}$$
$$M_i = \text{import volume (goods/services).}$$

These are all endogenous variables in a multi-model world system. The equilibrium exchange rate problem is to set targets for each trade balance at levels

---

[20] Stephen McNees, "The forecasting record for the 1970s," *New England Economic Review* (September/October, 1979), pp. 33–53.

Vincent Su, "An error analysis of econometric and noneconometric forecasts," *American Economic Review* **68** (May, 1978), pp. 360–372.

that countries could tolerate at either positive or negative values for protracted periods of time — or zero balance could also be imposed. The problem is then transformed according to Tinbergen's approach, and assumed values are given to the trade balance, as though they are exogenous, while solutions are obtained for

$$(EXR)_i = \text{exchange rate of the } i\text{th country.}$$

The exchange rates are usually denominated in terms of local currency units per U.S. dollar. For the United States, the trade balance is determined as a residual by virtue of the accounting restraints.

$$\sum_i (PX)_i * X_i = \sum_i (PM)_i * M_i$$

and the exchange rate in terms of U.S. dollars is, by definition, 1.0.

As noted earlier, this problem, although straightforward from a conceptual point of view, is difficult to carry out in practice, especially for a system as large and complicated as LINK; therefore, it has to be solved empirically from the criterion

$$\sum_i \left\{ [(PX)_i * X_i - (PM)_i * M_i] - [(PX)_i * X_i - (PM)_i * M_i]^* \right\}^2 = \min = 0,$$

with the entire LINK system functioning as a set of constraints. The minimization is done with respect to the values of the exchange rates (instruments). With modern computer technology, hardware, and software, this is a feasible problem. Its importance for policy is to give some operational content to the concept of equilibrium exchange rate values.

Optimal control algorithms built for Project LINK to handle the multi-model optimization problem have been successfully implemented to calculate Ronald McKinnon's proposals for exchange rate stabilization through monetary policy.[21]

As a result of attempts by major countries to stop inflation, stringent monetary measures were introduced during October, 1979, and again during March, 1980. American interest rates ascended rapidly reaching a rate of some 20% for short-term money. One country after another quickly followed suit, primarily to protect foreign capital holdings and to prevent capital from flowing out in search of high yields. An internationally coordinated policy to reduce rates was considered in LINK simulations. Such international coordination would diminish the possibility of the existence of destabilizing capital flows across borders. Policy variables (or near substitutes) were introduced in each of the major country models. The resulting simulations were compared with a baseline case. Some world results are shown, in the aggregate, in Table 4.

---

[21] Ronald I. McKinnon, *An International Standard for Monetary Stabilization* (Institute for International Economics, Washington, D.C., March, 1984).
Peter Pauly and Christian E. Petersen, "An empirical evaluation of the McKinnon proposal," *Issues in International Monetary Policy, Project LINK Conference Proceedings* (Federal Reserve Bank, San Francisco, 1985).

The results in Table 4 are purely aggregative. There is no implication that all participants in a coordinated policy program benefit. The net beneficial results are obtained by summing gains and losses. Some countries might not gain, individually, in a coordinated framework, but on balance they would probably gain if coordination were frequently used for a variety of policies and if the whole world economy were stabilized as a result of coordinated implementation of policy.

Table 4. Effects of coordinated monetary policy, LINK system world aggregates.
(Deviation of policy simulation from baseline)

	1979	1980	1981	1982	1983	1984
Value of world trade (bill $)	15	53	85	106	125	149
Volume of world trade (bill $, 1970)	4.7	14.4	20.2	22.8	24.7	26.9
OECD (13 LINK countries)						
GDP growth rate (%)	1.9	1.9	1.0	−0.2	−0.5	−0.4
Consumer price inflation rate (%)	−0.2	−0.5	−0.4	0.1	0.3	0.3

Coordinated policy changes of easier credit conditions helps growth in the industrial countries. It helps inflation in the short run by lowering interest cost, directly. Higher inflation rates caused by enhanced levels of activity are restrained by the overall improvement in productivity. This latter development comes about because easier credit terms stimulate capital formation. This, in turn, helps productivity growth measured as changes in output per worker. A pro-inflationary influence enters through the attainment of higher levels of capacity utilization, but it is the function of the models to balance out the pro and counter inflationary effects.

Policy is not determined at the international level, yet national forums consult simulations such as this coordinated lowering of interest rates and the frequent repetition of such econometric calculations can ultimately stimulate policy thinking along these lines in several major countries. A number of fiscal and exchange rate simulations along coordinated international lines have been made over the past few years.[22,23]

---

[22] L. R. Klein, P. Beaumont, and V. Su, "Coordination of international fiscal policies and exchange rate revaluations," *Modeling the International Transmission Mechanism*, ed. J. Sawyer (North-Holland, Amsterdam, 1979), pp. 143–159.
H. Georgiadis, L. R. Klein, and V. Su, "International coordination of economic policies," *Greek Economic Review* **I** (August, 1979), pp. 27–47.
L. R. Klein, R. Simes, and P. Voisin, "Coordinated monetary policy and the world economy," *Prévision et Analyse économique* **2** (October 1981), pp. 75–104.
[23] A new and promising approach is to make international policy coordination a dynamic game. See Gilles Oudiz and Jeffrey Sachs, "Macroeconomic policy coordination among the industrial countries," *Brookings Papers on Economic Activity* **1** (1984), pp. 1–64.

5. Prospects

Economic policy guidance through the use of econometric models is clearly practiced on a large scale, over a wide range of countries. Fine tuning through the use of overall macro policies having to do with fiscal, monetary, and trade matters has been carried quite far, possibly as far as it can in terms of methodological development. There will always be new cases to consider, but the techniques are not likely to be significantly improved upon. To some extent, formal methods of optimal control can be further developed towards applicability. But significant new directions can be taken through the development of more supply side content in models to deal with the plethora of structural policy issues that now confront economies of the world. This situation is likely to develop further along supply side lines. The bringing into play of joint Leontief–Keynes models with fully articulated input–output systems, demographic detail, resource constraints, and environmental conditions are likely to be important for the development of more specific policy decisions requiring the use of more micro details from models. This is likely to be the next wave of policy applications, focusing on energy policy, environmental policy, food policy, and other specific issues. It is clear that econometric methods are going to play a major role in this phase of development.

Appendix: An Outline of a Combined (Keynes–Leontief) Input–Output/Macro Model

The first five sectors listed on p. 590 are the components of *final demand* as they are laid out in the simple versions of the Keynesian macro model, extending the cases cited earlier by the explicit introduction of inventory investment and foreign trade. When the Keynesian system is extended to cover price and wage formation, then the production function, labor requirements, labor supply and income determination must also be included. These, together, make up the main components of national income. Interest income and monetary relationships to generate interest rates must also be included. This outlines, in brief form, the standard macro components of the mainstream econometric model. The interindustry relationships making up the input–output system round out the total model.

The flow of goods, in a numeraire unit, from sector i to sector j is denoted as

$$X_{ij} \, .$$

Correspondingly, the total gross output of j is X_j. The technical coefficients of input–output analysis are defined as

$$a_{ij} = X_{ij}/X_j$$

and the basic identity of input–output analysis becomes

$$X_i = \sum_{j=1}^{n} X_{ij} + F_i = \sum_{j=1}^{n} a_{ij} X_j + F_i \, ,$$

where F_i is final demand, and the total number of sectors is n. In matrix notation this becomes

$$(I - A)X = F.$$

X is a column vector of gross outputs, and F is a column vector of final demand. F can be decomposed into

$$F_C + F_I + F_G + F_E - F_M = F$$

where F_C is total consumer demand, F_I is total investment demand (including inventory investment), F_G is public spending, F_E is export demand, and F_M is import demand. The detail of decomposition of F used here is only illustrative. Many subcategories are used in a large system in applied econometrics.

The elements of F sum to GNP. If we denote each row of F as

$$F_i = F_{iC} + F_{iI} + F_{iG} + F_{iE} - F_{iM}$$

and divide each component by its column total, we get

$$a_{iC} = \frac{F_{iC}}{F_C}; \quad a_{iI} = \frac{F_{iI}}{F_I}; \quad a_{iG} = \frac{F_{iG}}{F_G}; \quad a_{iE} = \frac{F_{iE}}{F_E}; \quad a_{iM} = \frac{F_{iM}}{F_M}.$$

The array of elements of these final demand coefficients make up a rectangular matrix, called C. If we denote the column

$$\mathcal{G} = \begin{pmatrix} F_C \\ F_I \\ F_G \\ F_E \\ -F_M \end{pmatrix}$$

by $\mathcal{G}$ (standing for GNP), we can write

$$F = C\mathcal{G}$$

or

$$(I - A)X = C\mathcal{G}$$
$$X = (I - A)^{-1}C\mathcal{G}.$$

This gives a (row) transformation expressing each sector's gross output as a weighted sum of the components of GNP. It shows how a model of $\mathcal{G}$ (GNP) values can be transformed into individual sector outputs if we make use of the matrix of input–output and final demand coefficients.

This transformation is extended from gross output values to *values-added* by sector. The transformation is

$$X = BY$$

where

$$B = \begin{pmatrix} \dfrac{1}{1-\sum_{i=1}^{n} a_{i1}} & & 0 \\ & \ddots & \\ 0 & & \dfrac{1}{1-\sum_{i=1}^{n} a_{in}} \end{pmatrix} .$$

We observe also that the sum of Y_i gives the GNP total, too.

$$Y = B^{-1}(I - A)^{-1}C\mathcal{G} .$$

This gives the (row) transformation between elements of $\mathcal{G}$ and elements of Y, where both column vectors are different decompositions of the GNP, one on the side of spending and the other on the side of production.

If we construct synthetic price deflators for values added P_y and for final demand P_g, we find the relationship

$$P_y'Y = P_g'\mathcal{G} .$$

This can be transformed into

$$P_y'B^{-1}(I - A)^{-1}C\mathcal{G} = P_g'\mathcal{G} .$$

By equating corresponding terms in the elements of $\mathcal{G}$ we have the (column) transformations

$$P_{gi} = \sum_{j=1}^{n} h_{ji}p_{yj} \qquad i = C, I, G, X, M .$$

A typical element of $B^{-1}(I - A)^{-1}C$ is denoted as h_{ji}.

Industry outputs are weighted sums of final expenditures, and expenditure deflators are weighted sums of sector output prices. Prices, in this model, are determined by mark-up relations, over costs, at the industry sector level and transformed into expenditure deflators. Demand is determined at the final expenditure level and transformed into output levels.

The relation

$$X = BY$$

provides a set of simple transformations to convert from sector gross output values to sector values added. There is a corresponding price transformation

$$(I - A')P_x = B^{-1}P_y$$
$$P_y = B(I - A')P_x .$$

This is derived as follows:

$$P_{xj}X_j = P_{yj}Y_j + \sum_{i=1}^{n} P_{xi}X_{ij}$$

$$P_{xj}X_j = P_{yj}Y_j + \sum_{i=1}^{n} P_{xi}a_{ij}X_j$$

$$P_{xj} = P_{yj}\frac{Y_j}{X_j} + \sum_{i=1}^{n} P_{xi}a_{ij}\,.$$

The ratio Y_j/X_j (value added to gross output of sector j) can be written as

$$\frac{Y_j}{X_j} = 1 - \sum_{i=1}^{n} a_{ij}\,;$$

they are the reciprocals of the diagonal elements of B. In matrix notation we have

$$P_x = B^{-1}P_y + A'P_x$$

or more compactly

$$P_y = B(I - A')P_x\,.$$

This system of equations provides transformation from gross output prices to value added prices, or vice-versa. In the model's behavioral equations, there is first determination of P_x; then the above transformation derives P_y, and from these, we estimate P_g.

The integration of input–output analysis with macro models of final demand, income generation, and monetary relationships is seemingly straightforward and non-stochastic, to a large extent. This is, however, deceptive because the a_{ij} from the inter-industry flow matrix, and the expenditure shares in the final demand coefficient matrix are not time-invariant parameters; they are ratios of variables. This model has been generalized so that production functions are written as

$$X_j = F_j(X_{1j}, \ldots, X_{nj}, L_j, K_j, t)$$

and the input–output coefficients

$$\frac{X_{ij}}{X_j}$$

must be generated from a set of relationships describing behavior of the producing units of the economy. Similarly, the final demand ratios should be generated by behavioral relationships in consuming and market trading sectors of the economy. The main point is that these coefficients should all depend on *relative* prices.

The Wharton Model has been estimated for the case in which the functions F_j are generalized CES functions for the intermediate output flows, while the original factors L_j and K_j are related to value added production in a Cobb–Douglas relationship.[24]

$$X_j = \left(\sum_{i=1}^{n} \delta_{ij} X_{ij}^{-\rho_j} \right)^{-\frac{1}{\rho_j}} + A_j L_j^{\alpha_j} K_j^{\beta_j} e^{\gamma_j}$$

$$\sigma_j = \frac{1}{1 + \rho_j}$$

σ_j = elasticity of substitution.

The associated optimization equations for producer behavior are

$$\frac{X_{ij}}{X_{kj}} = \left(\frac{\delta_{ij}}{\delta_{kj}} \right)^{+\sigma_j} \left(\frac{p_j}{p_k} \right)^{-\sigma_j}$$

$$\frac{L_j}{K_j} = \frac{\alpha_j}{\beta_j} \left(\frac{w_j}{r_j} \right)^{-1}.$$

This system has an implicit restriction that the elasticity of substitution between pairs of intermediate inputs is invariant for each sector, across input pairs. This assumption is presently being generalized as indicated in the preceding footnote. In other models, besides the Wharton Model, different production function specifications are being used for this kind of work, e.g., translog specifications.

The demand side coefficients of final expenditure have not yet been estimated in terms of complete systems, but they could be determined as specifications of complete expenditure system.[25]

$$P_{xi} F_{ic} = \varepsilon_i P_{xi} + \eta_i \left(F_c - \sum_{j=1}^{n} P_{xj} \varepsilon_j \right).$$

All these equations are stochastic and dynamic, often with adaptive adjustment relations.

[24]R. S. Preston, "The Wharton long term model: Input–output within the context of a macro forecasting model," *Econometric Model Performance*, eds. L. R. Klein and E. Burmeister (University of Pennsylvania Press, Philadelphia, 1976), pp. 271–287. In a new generation of this system, the sector production functions are nested CES functions, with separate treatment for energy and non-energy components of X_{ij}.

[25]See Theodore Gamaletsos, *Forecasting Sectoral Final Demand by a Dynamic Expenditure System* (Center of Planning and Economic Research, Athens, 1980), for a generalization of this expenditure system.

34

TWO DECADES OF U.S. ECONOMIC POLICY AND PRESENT PROSPECTS: A VIEW FROM THE OUTSIDE[†]

The Kennedy–Johnson Era

The well documented history of U.S. business cycles compiled by the National Bureau of Economic Research puts the average period for peace-time experience at about four years. In an unusual expansion lasting nine years, the economy grew during the 1960s (1960–1969, peak-to-peak) without having a genuine cyclical interruption. There was an abortive recession in 1966, but it did not fully qualify as a downturn. On the basis of this excellent record alone, it must be presumed that the two administrations did a number of things right, as far as economic policy is concerned.

First, I shall emphasize what must have been done right, but any full account must also recognize the planting of seeds that led to grave inflationary problems of the 1970s. Nevertheless, there were significant successes, and these must surely be related to the active and vigorous tax policies that were pursued:

(i) investment tax credit,
(ii) accelerated depreciation,
(iii) 1964 personal tax cut.

Economists' views on policy are never wholly in agreement, but most general impressions would converge to the view that the investment tax credit and accelerated depreciation contributed significantly to the expansion of private fixed capital formation. An entire conference (1967) on this subject came to this conclusion but Robert Eisner dissented, at least to the extent of discounting the size of the gains that were produced by these policies.[1] In more recent studies, Eisner argues the same point, but his views are challenged by many others.[2] From the point of view of economic analysis there are two important aspects of the investment tax incentives that are extremely relevant for today's fiscal debate.

During the 1960s the investment incentives, particularly the tax credit, were regarded as counter cyclical devices. During the Johnson Administration, they were turned off and on, in dealing with the 1966–1967 mini recession. To me, this

---

[†] From *The Political Economy of The United States*, ed. C. Stoffaes (North-Holland, Amsterdam, 1982), pp. 111–124.
[1] Fromm (1971).
[2] See the contributions by Dale Jorgenson and myself in *Technology in Society* (1981).

seems to be wholly inappropriate. Capital plans are often long range and require many years for completion; therefore, these incentives ought to be long-run policies and not for short-run cyclical adjustments. From another point of view, economic policy should be as steady as possible and not varied unnecessarily in the short run. The credit or depreciation program should be set in accordance with long-range investment targets for the economy as a whole, and left in that position unless intolerable conditions develop. This is not the way these innovative policies were handled during the Kennedy–Johnson era.

At the present time, thinking has turned again to investment incentives, principally in order to regain the growth rate of productivity that was so favorable in the Kennedy years. The recovery of productivity will take time. It is not something that can be changed in a fundamental way overnight, especially if it is achieved through the medium of fixed capital formation. This concern suggests that investment incentives be kept in place for long-term trend gains and not varied in counter cyclical fashion.

A second aspect of the investment incentives is that they are *directed* policies. Instead of seeking more capital formation through a general lowering of business taxes, as with reductions of the corporate income tax or the general rate of personal income tax for unincorporated business, the tax concession is tied to the act of investment. The economic policy makers of the 1960s were not hesitant about making specific, as well as overall macro policy. Much of the criticism today of directed policies, particularly the investment tax credit, is that it interferes with the strict market allocation process; therefore, some economists criticize it or eschew its use. The implementation went even further during the 1960s for the investment tax credit was varied, by type of investor. The rate was lower for utilities. In view of our energy needs, which should have been accommodated at even earlier periods than the 1970s, this was a wrong headed differentiation. I would argue for differential credits, with favoritism for energy and other critical or "winner" sectors where investment is especially needed.

One reason why the era of the 1960s proved to be an exceptional period in business cycle chronology is that the escalation of the Vietnam War created an expansionary environment for the second quinquennium. It was not entirely favorable, but it did keep the level of output from falling into a recessionary pattern.

When the war was being pursued in its early stages, economists failed to perceive the inflationary consequences. The extent of the rise in defense spending was not foreseen, even at the highest policy levels, and its effect on the economy was underestimated. In 1965, after the success of the 1964 tax cut, which proved to be a textbook example of the way demand management ought to work, the view prevailed that another round of tax cutting was needed. I remember vividly a particular social party in Washington at which the thought of inflationary pressure in 1965 was not considered serious and recall the extent to which various government economists had conflicting information on the defense build-up. The end result was that a further stimulus, in the form of an excise tax cut, was introduced in

1965, when thoughts should have been turned towards dealing with inflation. By 1966, however, the President's advisers had fully appreciated the need to have tax increases for War finance, but that policy was not to be implemented until 1968.

Precious time was lost, and this is where three interrelated developments took place that were to be troublesome for future administrations:

The Vietnam War was costly from both a human and economic point of view. In terms of War outlay it was very expensive and required large expenditures by the United States for offshore purchases to support an overseas operation of very large magnitude. Defense spending, which had settled down to a plateau of about $50 billion annually, spurted to more than $75 billion per year.

The trading world accumulated a large surplus of dollars, and our currency became highly over valued. At the same time, the economic recoveries of Germany and Japan produced unsustainable external surpluses. The nice equilibrium of the world monetary system, overseen by the IMF according to Bretton Woods principles, was upset and could not persist in its then present state, with the key currency over valued and large imbalances building up. By the end of the decade, the system gave way to the managed float of the 1970s.

War spending, whether it is domestic or foreign is never productive in a conventional economic sense. The large-scale military build up produced a great deal of hardware — tanks, planes, missiles, electronic gear, weapons — but little of it had a useful economic life. Our energies were dissipated in non-productive, even anti-productive, directions and a consequence was, understandably, a decline in productivity growth. Had the same amount of money been devoted to productive investment, we as a nation would have had long lasting capital to produce goods with the same labor force all during the latter part of the 1960s, the whole of the 1970s, and beyond. This would surely have generated a more favorable pattern of productivity, even though other forces, notably the energy crises of the period after 1973, made independent inroads on the growth of productivity.

It is often wisely said that inflation was long in building up over the years and will correspondingly take a long time in winding down to a more acceptable rate for the future. The starting point for the inflationary episode of our times is conventionally put at the beginning of the escalation of the War in Vietnam — at 1965. Had War finance been appropriately turned to higher taxation at an early stage, the build-up of inflationary pressure may not have been so great. Once President Johnson's economic advisers recognized the inflationary implications of the War, they recommended, in 1966, higher taxation, but it was not until 1968 that a tax bill was enacted, and appeared to be relatively weak in stopping inflation. Unfortunately, President Johnson's "Great Society" concept was promoted when it was least affordable, confronting a veritable "guns or butter" trade. Also, unfortunately, for the academic and research community, President Johnson's fiscal package for 1968 carried in addition to a tax surcharge, an expenditure control feature that cut into research support, among other cuts. Not only was this period significant in laying the foundations for inflation and slow productivity growth, but also in generating

for academic institutions, who were suddenly faced with large reductions in research support. From 1968 onwards, scientific research received a setback in the United States, measured either in real terms or as a percentage of GNP. This was also an additional contributor to the productivity slow down. From 1969 to 1977, Federal research obligations to universities and colleges fell short of doubling but nominal GNP more than doubled.[3] In real terms, using the GNP deflator, research expenditures of the Federal government fell after 1969, recovered from a trough during the 1970s, and reached its previous high by about 1977. Gains have been modest and irregular since then.

Before I leave the period of the 1960s, there is one specific economic issue that is worth pointing out, for it has significant implications for later policies put in place, and possibly for some yet to come. This issue is that of wage–price guidelines. For some time, at the beginning of the Kennedy Administration, a framework for tying wage increases to productivity growth was developed as a means for holding down inflation. Emphasis was placed heavily on wage control by itself, and this ultimately turned labor against incomes policies, in general. The guidelines had a measure of success for a while, but ultimately broke down in 1966, with the outbreak of the airline mechanics strike. We were not to see anything revived along these lines until the surprising adoption of the New Economic Policy (NEP) by President Nixon in August, 1971. That was not a guideline policy but a strict freeze, followed by phases of wage and price control. The Nixon policy ultimately went out of existence in 1974 in combination with large price increases. For a long time, incomes policy in the United States has had to bear the stigma of two unsuccessful and, I may say, inept implementations of schemes that spoiled the possibility of doing anything constructive since that time. Recently, there have been only proposals and discussion, without concrete actions.

The Nixon–Ford Era

Although the United States economy is predominantly inward looking, with a large domestic market and often treated as closed, international developments played a large role in shaping economic evolution during the 1970s. This is not to deny the importance of the recession of 1969, the build-up of stagflation, the problems of absorption of a large increase in the work force, and the continuing worsening of productivity trends, but we started out the decade with a continuing shift in the trade/payments balance that made dollar devaluation inevitable. It may be noted as a successful policy of the Nixon Administration that they undertook dollar devaluation, beginning with the Smithsonian Agreement of 1971, from which the present floating rate system eventually emerged. There will not be broad agreement on the preference for variable vs. fixed rates of exchange, but there can be little doubt that dollar devaluation and later depreciation were needed. The Nixon Administration

---

[3]National Science Foundation (1979).

cannot be congratulated for good forecasting ability in recognizing the problems of timing or magnitude, but eventually they realized the right direction of effect.

President Kennedy tried to lure Japanese investors to the United States, but it was not until they had exploited more of their own growth potential and achieved a better exchange rate that they turned significantly to investment in the United States. This was the sequence for Europe, too, but our economic relations with Japan have consistently been narrow minded, focusing unduly on strict bilateral mercantilist goals. This perspective may have originated in the Kennedy–Johnson years, but gained fervor during the Nixon–Ford years.

Along another dimension, there was a significant expansion of trade with the centrally planned economies, stimulated especially by President Nixon's approaches toward the U.S.S.R. and China. Trade with those two socialist giants grew from virtually nothing before 1965 to figures as high as $ 3,500 million (U.S.S.R.) and $1,500 million (PRC) in 1979. Diplomatic and cultural exchanges promoted by President Nixon were largely responsible for getting these trade movements started.

President Nixon started his Administration on an unfortunate step, for the policy of gradualism became too difficult to manage with enough finesse to avoid a recession, and the great expansionary period that began in 1961 came to an end at the upper turning point of October, 1969. It was a brief and shallow recession, yet unemployment reached 6 percent in its aftermath, and the economy had deteriorated so much by summer, 1971, that an emergency plan (NEP) had to be implemented. To a large extent, pressure against the dollar and highly unfavorable trade accounts precipitated the crisis measures.

Another new phenomenon that had already appeared on the postwar economic scene in 1966 gained strength during these early years of the Nixon Administration, namely the "credit crunch" — extremely tight credit conditions, high (for the times) interest rates, and resort to new loopholes or money market instruments by financial institutions. In this case, use of the Eurodollar market on a large scale became more or less routine, but the Federal Reserve did institute reserve restrictions for use of this new instrument.

These are facts, but at the same time there was an ideological shift, towards *monetarism* as a theory of economic behavior and policy. Econometric estimates of money equations, often resulting in some variant of the quantity theory of money with citations of impressive correlations were introduced, even to the point of construction of complete, but small, macro models built on this base. There was great faith in the reliability of these money equations until the impressive correlations were confronted by the General Motors strike of 1970 and the various edicts of the NEP, not to mention the shocks that lay ahead — Watergate, commodity price speculation, and the oil embargo.

The NEP represented a complete shift of philosophy, away from the comfortable ideas of *gradualism*, monetary growth rules, and free market operation of the economy, towards wage freezes, price freezes, closing of the gold window, taxation of imports, and assorted Keynesian-type fiscal actions to stimulate the economy. There was a take-off to a strong growth performance through the various NEP phases, culminating in the devastating Soviet grain purchases, run-up of non-ferrous and other commodity prices, and finally the oil embargo. This set the stage for another recession, the upper turning point being November, 1973.

Between the two recessions 1969 and 1973, the Vietnam War was finally concluded, in an official sense. There was no renewed downturn generated, such as occurred after the Korean War. The winding down of Vietnam was stretched out so long that it had no immediate impact, but it did have severe effects on the deep seated inflation, productivity decline, adverse balance of payments trends, weak dollar, and general economic pessimism of the population at large.

The NEP could not be judged, in historical perspective, as a successful program. It was not carefully planned, I recall vividly, how eager civil servants were to receive Wharton forecasts that were put through last-minute revisions just prior to August 17th, 1971, in a search for some basis for interpreting what was happening. For a time inflation was held in check, but the follow-through was half-hearted, and the piecemeal dismantling of NEP gradually undid what good had come of its earlier phases.

As NEP was fading, a stupendous new event was brewing in the energy field. Precipitated by the Israeli–Egyptian–Syrian War of October, 1973, OPEC followed the Arab embargo with enormous price jumps. This constituted the "oil crisis." This was a shock to the oil importing world as a whole, and it could not be said that any one country could have done anything to avoid some serious repercussions. It is not surprising that the United States joined other industrial democracies in a synchronized recession, with some spread to other parts of the world, too, especially the oil importing developing countries.

The United States, possibly even more so than other countries, were not fuel-efficient in the use of energy to power the economy, and it may be said that the industrial nations on the whole started, reluctantly, a process of adaptation of economic life to the changed relative price structure in the world economy. The policy response could have mitigated the ensuing stagflation, but could not have avoided it. Tight money to fight oil price increases and general fiscal austerity do not seem to be the appropriate responses, yet these were the policies followed by the Nixon Administration and later the Ford Administration. A strict and vigorous energy policy would have been more appropriate, but that did not come for some years.

The longer-term results of the "energy crisis" that started in autumn 1973 were that the poor productivity performance was exacerbated, as industry started the long process of introducing more fuel efficient capital, that the economy was shifted towards acceptance of a higher rate of inflation, a higher rate of unemployment, and a lower rate of real growth.

The long-run presence of an expensive fuel import component in the trade accounts meant that there would be significant pressure for some time to come on the balance of payments. All these problems could be overcome; some would have cyclical gains and losses; and some would depend more on trend correction.

The Ford Administration found difficulty at its onset in sorting out the relative strength of inflationary and deflationary factors, but after a shaky start, settled into an economic policy pattern of seeking simultaneous cuts in public expenditures and taxes. This was, indeed, a forerunner of present policies but was put forward on a much smaller scale than President Reagan's plans. Both the expenditure reductions and tax cuts contemplated by President Ford were far less sweeping in terms of magnitude than those of the present Administration, but the philosophy of the approach was the same. Both run counter to the so-called "balanced budget theorem" of macroeconomics by appeal to supply-side gains, which have yet to be demonstrated statistically or in actual test cases of policy formation.

Increasing attention was placed during both the Nixon and Ford Administrations on the unfavorable bilateral balance of trade between Japan and the United States. Pressures were put on Japan to limit exports to the United States. Later this policy extended to other Pacific Basin countries but originated in the Japan–U.S. case. Eventually, this built up, in the Carter Administration, to the point of trigger-pricing for steel, continuing earlier voluntary quotas for sensitive items (shoes, textiles, TV sets), and ultimately, in the Reagan Administration, to cars. Try as they could, economists could not convince generations of American politicians about the virtues of free trade. Politicians succumbed to industry arguments about the virtues of "fair trade." The political excuse for concentrating attention on the bilateral balance with Japan was, consistently, that it was so large, as a component of the total U.S. deficit, that the only way to swing the deficit to surplus would be to work through the medium of this one bilateral balance.

The Carter Years

It is generally felt that the Carter performance in the economic area was poor and a major cause of electoral defeat in 1980 because of an inability to deal with inflation. During 1980, there was recession, a high rate of inflation, and a large federal deficit. All these contributed to a picture of overall economic failure.

There were, however, some successful ventures in economic policy under President Carter. The trend toward deregulation got a good start in his Administration. The most notable case was the deregulation of airline traffic by the Civil Aeronautics Board. During the various phases of anti-inflation policy, President Carter's economists cited the inflationary implications of the regulatory process as an area of policy implementation. The monitoring of the inflation content of regulation began on a systematic scale, initiated by the "Cotton Dust Case," which was eventually set back by the courts. The trend towards deregulation that was started during the Carter Administration is being pushed even more forcefully by President Reagan.

At an early stage of his Presidency, Carter laid great emphasis on an energy policy that stressed conservation. His policy proved to be unacceptable to Congress and eventually, under great strain turned into a policy of phased deregulation of energy prices, together with public sector support for synthetic fuel production or interfuel substitution. Also, a policy for stocking a strategic reserve got started. The achievement of the Carter Administration was to get an energy policy in place. It is still being executed, but for the first time since 1973, the country had a realistic energy policy and it showed up in two important respects: (1) Energy/GNP ratios fell significantly, and (2) oil imports were cut back. These developments are still taking place and have a considerable distance to go, but they had a start during the Carter period.

For three of the four years, unemployment was reduced by larger amounts than was thought possible by most observers and the budget was brought towards balance. From a starting deficit of about $60 billion, the balance was reduced to about $20 billion, but the recession of 1980, which was never appropriately allowed for in Administration planning, devastated their program. The deficit climbed rapidly during the recession of 1980, and unemployment rose. The deliberate creation of a recession by a Democratic government had been thought to be implausible, but it turned out to be the Carter Administration policy of 1980.

Most economists considered the dollar to be overvalued in 1976, and the policy of letting the dollar depreciate, or even encouraging it to do so, turned out to be a wise decision. It was not done with the greatest of finesse, but it did contribute greatly towards the turning around of the U.S. current account deficit into a surplus. There was great apprehension and cynicism during the early and unfavorable experience of the J-curve effect, but eventually the laws of economics prevailed, and the trade position responded nicely to the better competitive position of the U.S. after the dollar fell a great deal.

While the exchange rate policy was sound, the performance in commercial policy was mixed. As was noted already, protectionist inroads were made through quotas and the trigger price for steel, but other trade policies were liberal, especially the support for the Tokyo Round.

In substance, Carter economics was criticized for not achieving its goals and for losing the battle against inflation, but from a stylistic point of view, it was criticized for being unsteady, shifting ground often between expansion and contraction. The same charges were levied against Presidents Nixon and Ford. President Carter was tutored on the importance of being consistent and steady, but he got off to a very poor start by proposing a tax rebate in January, 1977 and rescinding it a couple of months later. Throughout the Administration, there were charges of shifting ground often and by sizable amounts.

From a slightly different perspective, Carter economic policy may be called short sighted and opportunistic. Rather than focusing on what was best for the American people, attention was paid to policies that would bring quick results and also conform to a pattern of showing economic improvement during 1980. Longer-run policies aimed at stimulating business capital formation were put aside until it was too late (summer, 1980) to take advantage of them. There was also a tendency to be very even-handed. This prevented the Carter Administration from tilting the tax system in favor of business rather than personal tax cuts. This distributional view prevails in the Reagan Administration, too, but for different reasons, on the supply side.

During the last year of the Carter Administration, there was a drastic shift in the operating rules for conducting monetary policy, with a return towards monetarism once more. In early October, 1979, the Federal Reserve adopted a new set of operating rules whereby they would focus on controlling the monetary aggregates $(M_{1A}, M_{1B}, \ldots M_7$, total credit). The success of this new policy approach has yet to be determined, but its philosophy is clear. Strict adherence to monetarist views means that attention is paid only to the aggregates and interest rates are allowed to fall where they will. This apparently is — all over the map. There have been unusual swings in interest rates since 1979, and at present they are being squeezed towards record high values. This is causing economic damage at home and abroad, yet monetarist principles outweighed friendly advice, and urging for policy shifts, at the Ottawa Summit, Summer, 1981.

The Reagan Administration

A bold experiment is being conducted, and its success or failure is not yet determined. The policy has just been put into place, in its first phase, but a year or more of observation of the economy will be required before we can begin to see its consequences, and it may require a longer historical perspective — perhaps a decade — in order to make a more definitive judgment.

Of all the policies of the present Administration, there is one in particular where results have already become apparent, namely, the decision to decontrol crude oil prices in January, 1981. This is seemingly small in scope because it merely accelerated, by some nine months, a policy process that was already put in place by President Carter. Nevertheless, speedier decontrol, which fitted neatly into President Reagan's overall goal of more deregulation of U.S. economic activity, appears to have encouraged additional conservation of energy and gave further incentive for domestic exploration. It also caused a sudden jump in some energy prices, but these were absorbed rapidly, and further rises were restrained, in part by oversupply in the world oil market. At any rate, U.S. imports of crude oil have fallen markedly this year, and the energy/GNP ratio continues to move in a favorable direction; therefore, it is hard to find fault with this particular economic policy decision by President Reagan.

As it was remarked earlier, simultaneous public expenditure and tax cuts were proposed by President Ford; deregulation was encouraged by President Carter; a balanced federal budget was a powerful goal for President Carter; monetarist policies were started by President Nixon and put into practice by the Federal Reserve System in October, 1979. Thus many of the aims and policies of the present Administration build on themes that were already present in American economic policy. It is the boldness, suddenness, and size of the policies by President Reagan that deserve special consideration.

The budgeting and monetary policies are already in position, if not yet fully implemented, but they are surely just the initial policy thrusts. There may be more of the same kinds of policies in months to come; that is to say, if the present fiscal policies, just adopted, prove to be leading towards larger deficits of the federal government, which is a prevalent external forecast, then the Administration will have to make additional budget cuts or consider some new tax levies, or change course on monetary policy if the balanced budget goal is to be met. There may be other options, too, but open discussion of further budget cuts has already taken place.

There could well be U.S. initiatives towards increase in other kinds of taxation — value-added taxes, expenditure taxes, excise taxes. These considerations would seem to contradict the policy objectives of reducing taxation, but compromise of principles may be necessary in order to resolve inner contradictions of the present program, especially in connection with attainment of budget balance.

Other policy areas under discussion at present, but by no means, part of the Reagan program are:

(1) industrial policy,
(2) incomes policy,
(3) use of supply side policies.

The decline in productivity growth, the weakness of the dollar some years ago, the persistence of a merchandise trade deficit, and the general erosion of U.S. economic power in the world have given rise to the thought that we may have lost our competitive edge. To some extent, this view represents a hasty interpretation of the facts. Our total trade position has been reversed during the last couple of years, and the dollar became strong again. Moreover, the United States have become extremely attractive as an investment haven in unsteady world. It is much too early to conclude that we have lost our competitive edge, and the cyclical aspects of our troubles must be separated from the secular aspects; nevertheless, it is meaningful to examine tenets of industrial policy for re-establishing U.S. pre-eminence in some lines (steel, motors, machinery) and to ensure our position in new emerging fields (micro-processes, bio-engineering, information, agriculture). To the extent that industrial policy is *activist* and a displacement of traditional market forces, it is likely to get little encouragement from the present government but it will remain on the debate platform.

In the same sense that the present Administration would oppose an activist industrial policy, it would be extremely cool towards an income policy. The Carter White House had some sympathy and interest, but it was not strong enough for the Administration to promote the concept in congressional circles. It received the most modest encouragement. If the present government does not succeed, in its own way, in dealing with inflation, it is quite possible that a future administration would try income policy concepts for the future.

The large scale and prolonged tax cuts of the Reagan Administration apparently means supply side economic policy to the adherents, but it is my view that supply side considerations go far beyond savings and work incentives, which are thought by the econometric community to be relatively small. A broader concept of supply side economics covers the encouragement of agricultural supplies, many of which are destined for export. It also means the confrontation of problems in dealing with the demographic composition of the work force, with limited supplies of basic materials, including oil and gas, the harnessing of the energy in coal. Food, fuel, environment, demography are presently all issues on the supply side of the economy; these are well known and popular. New crises will reveal new supply side sources. In this way we shall move gradually away from preoccupation with aggregative demand management. That policy served well in its time, in the United States and elsewhere. It is an essential component of a rounded policy, but macro demand management cannot meet many of the policy problems in the economy of today; that is why we should be looking for a shift toward more supply side involvement.

Summary and Conclusions

This historical review, brief as it is, looks at the differences from administration to administration over a span of two decades, yet commonality rather than difference is the main purpose of this review. There is something typically *American* about a common thread that runs through this review. The present range of policies that seem to be so different, on the surface, all have well established roots in earlier stages. In a democratic society like that of the United States, policy makers come and go, but economic policies follow an established path.

Monetarist views have appeared in cyclical swings; emphasis on tax cuts or tax increases has long standing popularity; trade policy has been largely liberal, with occasional lapses into protectionism. These are typical American policies and will be pursued further in this and future administrations along established lines, shifting to more micro or structural policies where needed, under changing circumstances.

Perhaps, it is irrelevant, at this point, to close with some observations on the distinction between American optimism and Euro-pessimism. American economists remain optimistic that policy can eventually succeed in breaking through stagflation. We see flexibility and adaptibility of the U.S. economy, where Europeans see the obstacles of inflexible institutions, lack of mobility, and prolonged stagnation, particularly in private capital formation. Some European economists are pessimistic about the potential success of industrial policy, especially in stimulating productivity growth, because they see insurmountable obstacles in achieving cooperation of trade unions. The American labor scene does not appear to be so rigid or unified in objection to unusual technical progress. It will not be easy to make progress in transforming the industrial structure of the United States, but we do remain optimistic that reasonable policy will eventually prevail.

References

Fromm, G., 1971, *Tax Incentives and Capital Spending* (Brookings, Washington, DC, 1971).

Jorgenson, Dale and Lawrence R. Klein, 1981, in *Technology in Society 1 and 2*, eds. Ralph Landau and N. Bruce Hannay, (Pergamon Press, New York, 1981).

National Science Foundation, 1979, *Federal Funds for Research and Development, NSF 79–310* **XXVII**, June (Washington, DC, 1979), p. 17.

35

SUPPLY SIDE: 0 WINS, 4 LOSSES, 1 TIE[†]

Economics, like other social sciences, does not usually permit experimental investigation, especially controlled experimentation. Typically, we rely on observation of real-world outcomes of the economic process for drawing conclusions about the validity of propositions on behavior of people.

Following these procedures, it is difficult to be convincing and definitive. Each protagonist in an economic debate will cite "third factors" to justify a position if events do not reveal confirmation of a theory about economic behavior.

The American people have been put through an extensive experiment with supply-side economics since 1981, and it is useful to see how well the outcome agrees with the advance claims. It was not a controlled experiment, so there were some "third factors." Still, it is useful to sift the evidence and see where the weight of professional opinion lies. I am going to try to tote up a won–lost record on the claims of supply-side economics to see if a score can be tabulated.

During the previous presidential election campaign, Vice President George Bush called the ideas of supply-side economics "voodoo economics." The claims that generated such an epithet were:

• That inflation could be stopped (or significantly reduced) without a recession, by applying the principles of supply side.

• That by cutting tax rates, tax revenues would be increased and the federal deficit would fall from its level of $60 billion.

• That lower tax rates would induce a higher tendency to save.

• That lower tax rates would induce a rise in productivity.

• That deregulation of industry would induce a rise in productivity.

Let's see how these claims have worked:

• Avoiding a recession: The application of the principles of supply side definitely did not enable us to avoid a recession. Inflation was, in fact, brought down, but at the expense of the cruelest recession since the end of World War II. The unemployment rate hit more than 10% and production fell.

Score for supply-side economics: Won — 0; Lost — 1.

• Increasing tax revenues: A remarkable feature of the tax cut of 1964 was that by 1965 tax revenues had significantly increased. The tax cuts of 1981–1982 and 1983 slowed the growth in tax revenue which, together with expenditure increases,

[†]From *Los Angeles Times* (Tuesday, June 26, 1984).

propelled the federal budget into the biggest deficit in our peacetime history. Far from moving toward balance from the initial deficit point of $60 billion, we moved toward the outlandish figure of $100 billion, followed by almost $200 billion, bringing the whole world's financial market into near-panic by the summer of 1982. The starting-point deficit of $60 billion became an ever-distant point that looked better and better in retrospect.

Cumulative score for supply side: Won — 0; Lost — 2.

• Savings: A principal behavioral argument by the proponents of supply-side economics was that a large and repetitive cut in tax rates would mean that people would be able to retain larger and larger portions of every extra dollar saved, and that this would promote savings to such an extent that investment expansion could take place without causing upward pressure on market rates of interest. This did not happen at all. Savings fell drastically. The rate of personal savings dipped to a low point of about 4% and interest rates soared to unprecedented levels. After the damage was done, both at home and abroad, the Federal Reserve managed to bring down interest rates and bring about a weak upward tendency in the savings ratio, but personal thriftiness is still far below long-run values and is far from providing capital-market relief for the large claims that are being imposed by the federal deficit.

Cumulative score for supply side: Won — 0; Lost — 3.

• Productivity: Related to the savings arguments of the proponents of supply-side economics, there was a claim that if workers were able to retain a larger fraction (after taxes) of every extra dollar earned, they would be induced to work harder and thus raise productivity. Productivity did pick up from its stagnant or falling values of recent years, but it remains below par. What we have seen is the usual business-cycle recovery of productivity, not a supply side-inspired increase.

Cumulative score for supply side: Won — 0; Lost — 4.

• Deregulation: By deregulation of industry (and finance and commerce), it was expected that there would be more competition and that this, too, would promote economic efficiency, thus giving rise to higher productivity. Total deregulation of oil prices in January, 1981, did promote better supply conditions and help bring down oil prices through economic efficiency. This was a mere acceleration of a process that was already under way. Deregulation of banks, other financial institutions and airlines was also under way before supply side was practiced. And we have been treated to the deregulation of the communications system through the breakup of AT&T, a move that started much earlier but was made final during the great experiment with.

The outcome is mixed. Energy decontrol has been beneficial for economic efficiency and many, if not most, economists look with favor on airline and financial deregulation. But there are strong indications that monetary authorities have, temporarily, at least, lost control over the money supply as a result of deregulation. As for the breakup of AT&T and the attempted infusion of competition in communications, there are mixed feelings. One of the best systems functioning anywhere in the world may have been sacrificed to satisfy some over-enthusiastic faiths in the market mechanism.

Cumulative score for supply side: Won — 0; Lost — 4; Tied — 1.

With this 0–4–1 record, it hardly looks like a validation of supply-side economics. The economic outcome is as unkind to the supply-side theoreticians as they have been to us by forcing the economy needlessly through a wringer while they toyed irresponsibly with the economy in an experimental model.

What about the "third factors?" What will the supply-side proponents cite in trying to justify their intellectual positions?

In the first place, they say that the Federal Reserve was so restrictive in supplying money to the economy that we were thrown into a recession. That is why, they say, interest rates became so punitive and the budget deficit so large.

I would make two arguments against this appeal to "third factors." The very deregulation of the financial system, part of the approach of supply-side economics, made it increasingly difficult, perhaps even impossible for the Federal Reserve to control money supply with any reasonable degree of accuracy. The colleagues of supply-side proponents in the Administration declared over and over again that they were all working in harmony — monetarists and supply-side adherents together. It is hard to know which statements or claims to believe.

The second argument, with more scientific support, is that statistical estimates of crucial reaction coefficients have never, on the basis of careful professional analysis, shown large enough or speedy enough effects to accomplish the policy objectives of supply-side economists in this great experiment.

Supply-side economics is a misnomer. In practice, the term has been used to describe and justify policies of massive tax cuts and deregulation. These are very limited manifestations of the supply side. Measures to improve productivity growth more directly — to deal with training for unemployed youths, to help bring more resources to market, to lay the base for new thrusts in research and development, and a host of other measures to improve the physical base for operation of the economy — these are straightforward and do not rest on grand promises.

In their modest way, they will all contribute to the better functioning of the economy, provided that a balanced and prudent program of demand management from both the fiscal and monetary side accompany them.

PART V
CLOSING REFLECTIONS

36

PROBLEMS WITH MODERN ECONOMICS[†]

Modern macroeconomics has become vague, subjective, uncertain, and unhelpful in policy formation, revealing too much faith in automatic corrections of markets. Criticisms can be made, in particular, about the use of rational expectations, principal agent analysis, and monetarism. Modern econometrics can be criticized for diversion of attention away from the central role of statistical specification of the probability distribution of error together with economic specification of structural relationships towards preoccupation with the statistical properties of individual or small subgroups of economic variables, which are the very objects of the whole econometric investigation. The unquestioning reliance on cointegration and lead–lag studies of causations in simple, bivariate relationships have taken attention away from the role of economics in specifying multivariate nonlinear systems. Some comments are made on the use of high-frequency data for improving econometric forecasting. (JEL EO)

I am going to discuss my problems with modern economics. That means modern economics in the last two or three decades, and its contrast with economics of a somewhat earlier era. I want to focus mainly on macroeconomic theory and econometrics, but I will sometimes drift off into consideration of some more general aspects of economics. When I took my first post-doctoral position, I was confronted by Jacob Viner. I was a member of the Cowles Commission, the University of Chicago, and he was in the economics department there at that time. He said, "You people in the Cowles Commission are entirely on the wrong track. You are just imitating the physicists with your use of mathematical or quantitative methods. It will not work." Then I felt very much in the position of being a protestor, an advocate of a new approach. By and large, I think we won that battle. In those days, mathematical economics and econometrics were in the underground of the subject and hardly taught in the universities across the country or around the world. But now they are fully entrenched.

Now my problem with modern tendencies in economics is that they have become much too subjective. We in the forties, fifties, and sixties were trying to be as objective and quantitative as possible. I find the subjectivity very bothersome because people cannot come to decisions. A wide spectrum of possibilities can take place. This is mainly so in theoretical economics journals and in teaching. It is not true so much in applied economics or in economic policy formation. There, decisions are made and they are made quite objectively, maybe not always on the

---

[†]From *Atlantic Economic Journal* **22** (March, 1994), pp. 34–38.

soundest information or analysis, but there is much more convergence. But, in modern economic theory, I find that too many options are being considered, and no concrete decision making occurs. There is one exception; the modern generation of economists are totally ready to fall back on the magic of the market, as the one machine that works. Of course, it is an important machine, but it is obviously overworked and often used in what I consider to be a "cop-out," by not being able to get better solutions. The problem with this approach to economics, is that I find it not to be constructive. It is highly uncertain, and does not give any guidance. Let us consider the situation of macroeconomics. I have three difficulties or three bêtes-noires in this area. One is the treatment of expectations, especially rational expectations. Second is principal agent analysis and third is monetarism.

First, on expectations, there is not any doubt at all that expectations are important. But the theory of rational expectations, I believe, is simply a contrived concept for two reasons. It is contrived either to make the calculations straightforward and simple or it provided an endogenous way of generating expectations. I find it wholly unrealistic, but it works on paper, from the point of view of having a closed system. Secondly, it is not realistic in the sense that people do not really make decisions in that way, and the distribution of expectations has a very big variance. The people who advocate rational expectations have no track record. That is to say, I sit in meetings all over the country, all over the world, trying to come to decisions about economic policy or economic change, and I keep asking myself, is there a single situation in the last 20 years when rational expectations gave guidance to providing an answer. I cannot find a single situation. Nor can I find a single projection or decision that was based on rational expectations that proved to be very insightful or superior. Yet, it is very popular and is attractive not only because it is self-contained or endogenous, but mainly because people want a simple approach to the problem, and this is a very simple approach.

Now consider principal agent analysis. I think principal agent analysis or the representative firm or the representative consumer is useful as a very first step in macroeconomics. But there is no attention paid to the bridging of macro decision making and individualistic decision making. That bridge is index number theory, aggregation theory, or distribution theory, in which we aggregate the individual agents' decisions into final macroeconomic relationships. Of course, the obvious one, and one that has the longest history of consideration, is something like the aggregate propensity to consume. Very soon after that concept was formulated in macroeconomics by Keynes, the first people to test the theory went to family budget studies and looked at Gini coefficients and variances of income distributions, or other higher moments, in order to take account of distributional factors in relating aggregate consumption to aggregate income. Of course, this has relevance not only for a simple relation, but for many more complicated relations in macroeconomics. Principal agent analysis is totally devoid of distributional phenomena. In the very short run, some distributional phenomena may not look very important, but if you study the statistics of income distribution in the U.S. for at least 20 years, you will find that there has been a systematic tendency toward more and more inequality; this is surely of great importance. There are many more instances in which distributional phenomena are important. This will introduce new magnitudes, new branches of analysis, and make the theory more complicated. There is a tendency in modern macroeconomics to look for very simple rules of thumb for guidance or, as we used to call them in England, ready reckoners. People should carry ready reckoners in their hip pocket for quick reference, but they just do not work.

The third problem is monetarism, which I think has done a great deal of damage to the world. On the occasion of the ninetieth anniversary, two years ago, of the awarding of the Nobel Prizes, the Swedish authorities had a jubilee ceremony in which all living Nobel Prize winners were invited to the annual award ceremonies and asked to give seminars around the country. I got an invitation from a provincial Swedish University to give a lecture on the monetarist revolution. I said I would give that lecture, but I would not be in support of the monetarist revolution. I entitled my paper, "Has There Been a Monetarist Revolution?" Also, in the Far Eastern meetings of the Econometrics Society, which took place in June, 1992, I gave a follow-up paper, ending with another question mark, "Is Monetary Policy Alone Capable of Stabilizing the Modern Economy?" The general conclusion that I came to is that two principal parameters of monetarism, parameters that make the theory very simple, have really fallen apart and have given no guidance. In some cases, they have given very perverse guidance. One parameter is the money multiplier in the fractional reserve system. This has given serious trouble in the U.S. in the last two or three years. The other parameter is velocity M_0, velocity M_1, velocity M_2, velocity M_3, as you like. The problem with velocity is a problem that has been recognized for a long time but came into very sharp focus when we had financial innovation.

Money markets transcended national borders. Money markets, or financial markets in general, introduced dozens of new instruments into the spectrum of people's holdings. To a large extent, the average citizen, through pension funds or individual investments, became involved with a much larger spectrum of financial asset holdings. Telecommunication played an important role. Reports are available, in real time, all day long for those who want to look at them. The concept of monetarism paid no attention to this technological revolution in banking, the conduct of financial market affairs, or internationalization of such markets. Not long after I gave the paper at the Econometric Society meetings in the Far East last summer, the Federal Reserve announced that M_2 was being dropped as a reliable indicator for the U.S. economy, and in a somewhat earlier era M_1 had already been dropped. We all recognized the problems that the money multiplier was giving in the last year because the authorities, not only in the U.S. but also in Japan and Germany, were completely dissatisfied with their ability to control or have an effect on M_3 in Germany, M_2 plus CDs in Japan, or M_2 in the U.S. Monetarism is very simple and gives quick answers like the principal agent theory, or like rational expectations, but they do not give the right answers. That is the only problem.

I want to say just a few words on tendencies in econometrics. These are more technical, but I think they are very important. First, the kind of econometrics that I think is very constructive and useful is econometrics in which the whole system is driven by the probability distribution of the errors. The errors are, of course, the non-economic random impulses that are constantly hitting a system. Especially in macroeconomics, they are of great importance. Econometrics should specify the properties of the probability distribution of error, and then study those properties to make sure that when numerical work is done, the error terms satisfy tests for the kind of distributions we have assumed. The tendency of modern econometrics is to look not at the error structure, not at the residual variation for estimated equations, but to look at the economic data themselves and impose restrictions on them that the investigators believe to be good properties. They start with fixed ideas about the very things that are to be explained by the analysis. One property that I think is probably very misleading is stationarity. Stationarity means that in a time distribution of data, one would get the same moments of the distribution no matter where you took that block of time. It is a mathematical property of a time series or other kind of collection of sample data. I do not think economic data are necessarily stationary or that economic processes are stationary. The technique of co-integration, to keep differencing data until stationarity is obtained and than relate the stationary series, I think can do damage. It does damage in this sense that it is almost always done on a bi-variate basis or maybe tri-variate basis. That keeps the analysis simple, and simplicity is wanted. But the world is not simple.

Second, the youngest of the young generation of econometricians simply do it mechanically, without thinking about what are they doing, and do not understand their original data series as well as they should. Also, there is an extremely interesting classical paper of the 1930s by Frisch and Waugh, in which it was established as an identity, although people had not thought about it, that if one has data with simultaneous linear trends, you get precisely (to the limits of arithmetic accuracy) the same numbers whether you make a regression between the two variables including the trend variable or form deviations from the trend (in effect to make variables stationary in a somewhat different way from the process used in co-integration) and then form the regression without a trend variable. Therefore, I would conclude that one should accept the fact that the economic data are not stationary, relate the non-stationary data, but include the explicit trends and think about what could cause the trends in the relationship. One then uses that more complicated relationship with trend variables. Successive differencing, as it is done in co-integration techniques, may introduce new relationships, some of which we do not want to have in our analysis.

The second questionable tendency occurs in testing for causation. I believe in large-scale modeling, because the world is complicated, and we can harness the power of the computer to deal with large-scale models. In that context, causation cannot be studied by looking at pairs of variables. Does money cause GDP or does GDP cause money? I think that is a completely trivial question and a completely wrong-headed way to approach the matter of causation. A much more intricate and complicated test is needed to handle that problem. To study, as is done in modern econometrics, various lead–lag combinations between money and GDP or between any pair of variables is an indication of the tendency to want to look at the world in very simplified terms, even terribly over-simplified, and come to some specific conclusion. I think that those conclusions are wrong, and have been misleading. I am not happy about what I see going on. Certainly in econometrics, there should have been serious investigations of parameter change. When we study money market or financial market relationships, using advanced telecommunications, and computer facilities in the modern age, we can see right before our eyes, various tendencies of these data to show the effect of the new era in which parameters have changed. Parameter drift or variability should be introduced into economic relationships. That provides a very fruitful line of research. It is not totally neglected, but it is not the focus of attention now. The focus of attention now is on co-integration, simplistic causation testing, unit root extraction, and other things that I think are not giving us any useful information that we do not already have.

An important problem which is very much related to parameter change is non-linearity. In inflationary situations, we see a change in character at certain points of macroeconomic processes. Prices or other kinds of processes take off. I think non-linearity is the rule rather than the exception. Most statistical studies make linear approximations, which are all right for limited change, but not all right for studying systems in the large. This is a third area of concern to me in econometrics.

A fourth thing, and one on which I am working at the moment, is to deal with high-frequency information. High-frequency information would be daily, weekly, monthly kinds of information. We get it quite regularly, of course, in financial markets, but it is coming through from other sources too. Eventually, economic information will become much more available in real time. That gets us almost to continuous processes. To be very practical, I have constructed a system, that I keep operating, from which we make weekly projections for the U.S. economy. Every Monday morning we come up with a fresh projection on the basis of all the information that we could assemble in the proceeding week and then make a rolling forward projection from a dynamic system. This stands by itself, but it can also be used to provide information to lower-frequency systems of quarterly and annual data.

I think that high-frequency analysis is relevant for extending modern economics, in this case, econometrics. It relies on new developments in both the availability of information, and on the techniques of delivering it. We are bombarded with information all day, and the question is, can we filter that in a systematic way to get some signal about what today's overall tendencies are? I think there are many useful things that the young group of economists and econometricians could have been doing, but I think that they really have been diverted into less fruitful activities. Now this, of course, is not true of everything, but I have told you about some of the more fruitless activities that I perceive at the moment.

INDEX